HISTORICAL DICTIONARY

The historical dictionaries present essential information on a broad range of subjects, including American and world history, art, business, cities, countries, cultures, customs, film, global conflicts, international relations, literature, music, philosophy, religion, sports, and theater. Written by experts, all contain highly informative introductory essays of the topic and detailed chronologies that, in some cases, cover vast historical time periods but still manage to heavily feature more recent events.

Brief A–Z entries describe the main people, events, politics, social issues, institutions, and policies that make the topic unique, and entries are cross-referenced for ease of browsing. Extensive bibliographies are divided into several general subject areas, providing excellent access points for students, researchers, and anyone wanting to know more. Additionally, maps, photographs, and appendixes of supplemental information aid high school and college students doing term papers or introductory research projects. In short, the historical dictionaries are the perfect starting point for anyone looking to research in these fields.

HISTORICAL DICTIONARIES OF SPORTS

Jon Woronoff, Series Editor

Historical Dictionary of Ice Hockey

Laurel Zeisler

The Scarecrow Press, Inc.
Lanham • Toronto • Plymouth, UK
2013

Published by Scarecrow Press, Inc.
A wholly owned subsidiary of The Rowman & Littlefield Publishing Group, Inc.
4501 Forbes Boulevard, Suite 200, Lanham, Maryland 20706
http://www.scarecrowpress.com

10 Thornbury Road, Plymouth PL6 7PP, United Kingdom

British Library Cataloguing in Publication Information Available

Library of Congress Cataloging-in-Publication Data

Zeisler, Laurel.
Historical dictionary of ice hockey / Laurel Zeisler.
p. cm. -- (Historical dictionaries of sports)
Includes bibliographical references.
ISBN 978-0-8108-7862-4 (cloth : alk. paper) -- ISBN 978-0-8108-7863-1 (ebook) 1. Hockey--
History--Dictionaries. I. Title.
GV847.Z45 2013
796.96203--dc23
2012033380

 The paper used in this publication meets the minimum requirements of American
National Standard for Information Sciences Permanence of Paper for Printed Library
Materials, ANSI/NISO Z39.48-1992.

Printed in the United States of America

Contents

Editor's Foreword

Brains and brawn are important in any contact sport, but rarely are they as significant and crucial as in ice hockey. The brawn is immediately noticeable in the sheer bulk of the players, to which is added their padding and equipment, and this brawn is used against one another repeatedly, and sometimes to great effect, as the teams chase the puck about. On occasion—and this aspect is certainly regrettable to some at least—they plow into one another in play in a friendly or less friendly brawl that can result in severe injuries. But the brain is always there as well, since players must direct the puck to places where they think teammates and opponents will be in another few seconds and finally get it into the goal, and all this at speeds of 100 miles per hour or so. All of this makes ice hockey an exciting game for the players, and also a wonderful spectator sport, and it draws large crowds. While this book deals mainly with professional hockey, it does not forget amateur hockey or games played in other forms, or even on a nearby pond, and it also gives women their due.

Historical Dictionary of Ice Hockey follows the standard format of the increasing number of other volumes on sports by starting out with a list of plentiful acronyms that help readers navigate not only this historical dictionary, but other material on hockey. The introduction provides an overview of the game and how it is played and organized. The biggest and most important part for most, in particular, fans, is the dictionary section, which includes numerous entries on the various teams, associations, and players, as well as what the Hockey Hall of Fame regards as builders. Numerous appendixes provide a detailed listing of the main franchises, Hall of Fame inductees, and champions. For those who want further information, the best place to look for sources is the copious bibliography.

This book was written by an ice hockey fan, this being a first for the series, but a successful first. After all, fans follow the game more intensively than others, and some of them also develop a considerable knowledge of the sport's rules and regulations, teams and associations, as well as prominent players. What may be lacking is the historical background, which can be gleaned from the literature and also contributes to the compilation of a useful bibliography. Certainly, in this case, Dr. Laurel Zeisler has done an excellent job of gathering the essential information, presenting it in a manner that is factual, without becoming dull or pedantic. Otherwise, in real life, Dr. Zeisler is a speech language pathologist, and also a member of the Society for

International Hockey Research. This being said, I am certain other fans of ice hockey, and even those closer to the game, will appreciate her effort and keep this book handy.

Jon Woronoff
Series Editor

Reader's Note

Team statistics are reported in the order of wins, losses, ties, overtime losses, and total points (1,342-1,448-391-81) (3,156 points). To facilitate the rapid and efficient location of information and make this book as useful a reference tool as possible, extensive cross-references have been provided in the dictionary section. Within individual entries, terms that have their own entries appear in **boldface type** the first time they appear. Related terms that do not appear in the text are indicated in the *See also. See* refers to other entries that deal with this topic.

Preface

This book is written specifically about ice hockey, although the term *hockey* is mainly used to discuss the sport. While the majority of the references relate to men's ice hockey, there are several instances explaining women's ice hockey, and entries are included for the more well-known female athletes.

Each player or builder in this dictionary deserves their own book written just about them, and many biographies and autobiographies have been written (see the bibliography). These entries are meant to give readers a brief glimpse into the fascinating lives of people throughout the history of hockey. Due to space limitations, your favorite player may have been omitted. For that, I apologize; however, you may find a new favorite after reading some of these sketches. Statistics, quotes, and anecdotal details have been blended to help readers become more familiar with these amazing individuals. For further information on any of the individuals detailed in this book, your local library or bookstore surely has additional reading on these people. In fact, many of the books I accumulated for the bibliography came from used bookstores in upstate New York, as well as through the interlibrary loan service provided by my neighborhood library.

I would like to thank the Four County Library System serving Broome, Chenango, Delaware, and Otsego counties, and specifically the Huntington Memorial Library in Oneonta, New York. Many thanks go to my father, John Grasso, who got me involved in this project, not knowing how much I would enjoy this research adventure. He and my mother, Dorothy Grasso, were helpful and supportive, as they have been my entire life. The members of the Society for International Hockey Research and the International Society of Olympic Historians were cooperative with their facts. I'd like to thank Craig Campbell, manager at the Resource Centre and Archives at the Hockey Hall of Fame. I'd also like to thank Jon Woronoff, series editor, for trusting that I would complete this book to his standards; April Snider, acquisitions editor; and the staff at Scarecrow Press. They helped turn my rough manuscript into a well-assembled book.

Thanks also go to my children, James, Lindsey, and Dorothy, who are each very talented. I am so proud of you three! This book is dedicated to my husband, Rob Zeisler, for being everything I am not.

Acronyms and Abbreviations

ORGANIZATIONS

AHA	Amateur Hockey Association
AHAC	Amateur Hockey Association of Canada
AHL	American Hockey League
CAHA	Canadian Amateur Hockey Association
CAHL	Canadian Amateur Hockey League
CBC	Canadian Broadcasting Corporation
CHA	Canadian Hockey Association
CHL	Canadian Hockey League, Central Hockey League
COHA	Central Ontario Hockey Association
COHL	Central Ontario Hockey League
CPHL	Central Professional Hockey League, Canadian Professional Hockey League
EAL	Eastern Amateur League
ECAHA	Eastern Canada Amateur Hockey Association
ECHA	Eastern Canada Hockey Association
ECL	Eastern Canada League
ECHL	East Coast Hockey League
EHL	Eastern Hockey League
EPHL	Eastern Professional Hockey League
FAHL	Federal Amateur Hockey League
IHHF	International Hockey Hall of Fame
IHL	International Hockey League
IIHF	International Ice Hockey Federation
IOC	International Olympic Committee
JAHA	Junior Amateur Hockey Association
JOA	Jamaican Olympic Association
JOIHT	Jamaican Olympic Ice Hockey Team
KHL	Kontinental Hockey League

LIHG	Ligue Internationale de Hockey Sur Glace
NCAA	National Collegiate Athletic Association
NHA	National Hockey Association
NHL	National Hockey League
NHLPA	National Hockey League Players' Association
NOHA	Northern Ontario Hockey Association
NWHL	National Women's Hockey League
OHA	Ontario Hockey Association
OHL	Ontario Hockey League
OWHA	Ontario Women's Hockey Association
PCHA	Pacific Coast Hockey Association
PCHL	Pacific Coast Hockey League
PCL	Pacific Coast League
QAHA	Quebec Amateur Hockey Association
QHL	Quebec Hockey League
QSHL	Quebec Senior Hockey League
SIHR	Society for International Hockey Research
USHL	United States Hockey League
WCHL	Western Canada Hockey League
WHA	World Hockey Association
WHL	Western Hockey League, World Hockey League

OTHER

A	assists
C	center
D	defense
G	goals, goaltender
GA	goals against (team)
GAA	goals against average (goalie)
GP	games played
GW	game-winning goals
L	loss
LW	left wing

MVP	Most Valuable Player
OT	overtime
OTL	overtime losses
OTW	overtime wins
PCT	shooting percentage
PIM	penalties in minutes
POS	position played
PP	power play goals
PTS	total points
RW	right wing
S	saves
SA	shots against
SH	short-handed goals
SO	shutouts
SOG	shots on goal
SV PCT	save percentage
T	tie
W	win

COUNTRIES

CAN	Canada
CZE	Czech Republic
DEN	Denmark
FIN	Finland
CBR	Great Britain
GER	Germany
JAM	Jamaica
NOR	Norway
RUS	Russia
SLO	Slovenia
SUI	Switzerland
SVK	Slovakia
SWE	Sweden
USA	United States of America
YUG	Yugoslavia

Chronology

17th century Holland: A game on ice, similar to hockey, is played. It is known as "kolven" and eventually becomes popular in England.

1797 London, 1 September: The earliest known engraving or painting depicting an activity similar to ice hockey on skates with the inscription "London Published by J Le Petit 22 Suffolk Street, Middlesex Hospital 1st Sep 1797" is made by Joseph Le Petit Jr. (London c. 1770–1858).

1875 Montreal, 3 March: The first organized hockey game takes place at the Victoria Rink in Montreal. Students from McGill University play against one another, with nine players per side. The team captained by James Creighton wins, 2–1.

1876 Montreal, 7 February: The first recorded use of the word *puck* is published by the *Montreal Gazette*.

1877 Montreal, 27 February: The first-known playing rules for the game of hockey are published by the *Montreal Gazette*.

1892 Frederick Arthur, Lord Stanley of Preston and governor general of Canada, donates a trophy to be called the Dominion Hockey Challenge Cup. It is a simple silver-plated nickel cup that cost $48.67. The trophy becomes more commonly known as the Stanley Cup.

1893 Montreal, 22 March: The first official Stanley Cup match is played between the Montreal Hockey Club (Montreal Amateur Athletic Association) and Ottawa Capitals. Montreal wins, 3–1, in front of 5,000 fans.

1894 Baltimore, December: The first indoor arena in North America with artificial ice is opened in Baltimore. This rink is used by students from John Hopkins University.

1895 Women's hockey gains popularity at universities, mainly at the University of Toronto and Queen's University in Kingston, Ontario.

1899 Montreal: The first printed Canadian book of hockey, *Hockey: Canada's Royal Winter Game*, is written by Arthur Farrell and published by C. R. Corneil.

1900 A fishing net is first used as a goal net to catch the puck and try to stop the arguments regarding whether a goal had been scored.

1901 Montreal, 31 January: Dan Bain makes history when he scores the first Stanley Cup-winning goal scored in overtime. His Winnipeg Victorias defeat the Montreal Shamrocks, 2–1.

1905 Ottawa, 16 January: Frank McGee sets a Stanley Cup Playoff record for goals in a single game (14), in a 23–2 victory over the Dawson City Nuggets. The Nuggets are exhausted from their month-long journey from the Yukon Territory. **Ontario, 24 February:** Allan Loney clubs Alcide Laurin to death during a hockey game. He becomes the first hockey player to be charged with murder for the death of another player. Loney claims self-defense. The charges are reduced to manslaughter, and he is found not guilty.

1908 Montreal, 2 January: The Montreal Wanderers and a team of All-Star players from the teams in the Eastern Canada Amateur Hockey Association hold a benefit game in memory of Montreal Wanderers player Hod Stuart, who had drowned three months after the Wanderers won the Stanley Cup in 1907. The proceeds of that game go to Stuart's family. **Paris, 15 May:** The International Ice Hockey Federation (IIHF) is founded at 34 Rue de Provence in Paris, France, as Ligue International de Hockey sur Glace. The founders of the federation are representatives from Belgium, France, Great Britain, Switzerland, and Bohemia (now the Czech Republic).

1911 British Columbia December: Lester and Frank Patrick found the Pacific Coast Hockey Association and require players to wear numbers on their uniforms.

1913 Quebec, 8 March: Joe Malone sets a record by scoring nine goals in Game One of the 1913 Stanley Cup Finals, with his Quebec Bulldogs winning, 14–3.

1917 26 November: The National Hockey League (NHL) is founded with five teams: the Montreal Canadiens, Montreal Wanderers, Ottawa Senators, Quebec Bulldogs, and Toronto Arenas. Frank Calder becomes the NHL's first president. **Montreal, 15 December:** The NHL holds its first exhibition hockey game between the Montreal Canadiens and Montreal Wanderers. **Montreal, 19 December:** The NHL holds its first game. Six players from each team compete at a time. The first NHL goal ever scored is recorded. This goal is credited to Montreal Wanderers' defenseman Dave Ritchie in the 10–9 victory over the Toronto Arenas. The five NHL teams go on to play a 22-game schedule during the season.

1918 Toronto, 2 January: The Montreal Arena burns down, and the Montreal Wanderers franchise disbands shortly afterward. **Toronto, 18 February:** Montreal Canadiens' goaltender Georges Vezina records the first shutout in a NHL game against the Toronto Arenas (9–0). **Toronto, 20 March:**

The first professional Stanley Cup match is played between the NHL champion, the Toronto Arenas, and the Pacific Coast League (PCL) champion, the Vancouver Millionaires. Toronto wins, 3–2.

1919 Seattle, 1 April: The Stanley Cup series between the Montreal Canadiens and Seattle Metropolitans is cancelled due to the outbreak of the Spanish influenza. **Seattle, 5 April:** Montreal Canadiens player Joe Hall dies from complications of the Spanish influenza.

1920 Quebec, 31 January: Joe Malone, "The Phantom," of the Quebec Bulldogs, makes history when he scores seven goals in one game, helping his team defeat the Toronto St. Patricks, 10–6. **Antwerp, Belgium, 23 April–29 April:** An ice hockey tournament is played at the Summer Olympics. Canada wins the gold medal. Years later it was declared the first World Ice Hockey Championships.

1921 Vancouver, 12 December: Tommy Dunderdale of the Victoria Cougars scores the first penalty-shot goal in history. Taken from one of three dots painted on the ice 35 feet (11 meters) from the goal, the shot is against Hugh Lehman of the Vancouver Millionaires.

1922 Toronto, 28 March: The Toronto St. Patricks defeat the Vancouver Millionaires, 5–1, in the last professional hockey game having seven players on each side.

1923 Toronto, 16 February: Foster Hewitt gives the first radio broadcast of a hockey match, a contest featuring the Toronto Argonauts and Kitchener Greenshirts. Hewitt yells later becomes his trademark goal-scoring call when he says, "He shoots! He scores!" **Toronto, 15 March:** L. D. "Pete" Parker gives an early radio broadcast of a Western Canada Hockey League match featuring the Edmonton Eskimos and Regina Capitals; however, most history books overlook this fact.

1924 Chamonix, France, 28 January–3 February: Ice hockey debuts at the Winter Olympics, with Canada winning the gold medal. **Montreal, 29 November:** The Montreal Forum opens, and fans watch the Montreal Maroons defeat the Toronto St. Patricks, 7–1.

1925 Bobbie Rosenfeld and Myrtle Cook, former track stars and hockey players in their own rights, become Canada's first female sports reporters, specializing in hockey during the winter. **New York, 15 December:** The New York Americans and Montreal Canadiens are the first teams to play hockey at Madison Square Garden. Shorty Green of the Americans scores the first goal. The Canadiens win, 3–1.

1927 Kingston: Queen's University goalie Elizabeth Graham starts wearing a wire fencing mask to protect her face from the speeding puck. This is the first evidence of a face mask worn during a hockey game.

1929 New York to Toronto, 13 December: The New York Rangers are the first hockey team to fly. They hire the Curtiss-Wright Corporation to fly them to Toronto for a game against the Maple Leafs. The Rangers lose, 7–6. Teams previously traveled by train.

1930s The, Preston Rivulettes, a women's ice hockey team, rule the ice with Hilda Ranscombe. The team has an impressive 348-2 win-loss career record.

1930 New York, 20 February: Clint Benedict of the Montreal Maroons becomes the first male goaltender to wear a face mask during a 3–3 game against the New York Americans. He wears the homemade apparatus to protect his previously injured nose. Unfortunately, the mask keeps coming loose, and the nosepiece blocks his vision. As a result, the habit of wearing a face mask does not catch on quickly by other goaltenders at this point in time.

1931 Toronto, November: *Hockey Night in Canada* makes its radio debut. **Toronto, 12 November:** Maple Leaf Gardens opens with a crowd of 13,000 fans, who watch the Toronto Maple Leafs and Chicago Black Hawks compete. Maple Leafs' owner Conn Smythe enforces a dress code, and many men wear tuxedos to watch the game. **New York, 3 December:** Playing against the New York Americans, the Boston Bruins set a record by icing the puck 87 times in one game, resulting in a scoreless draw and many disappointed fans.

1934 St. Louis, 13 November: Ralph Bowman of the St. Louis Eagles scores the first NHL penalty-shot goal.

1936 Germany, 16 February: Great Britain wins the Olympic gold medal, marking Canada's first significant loss in international ice hockey. **Montreal, 24 March:** The longest Stanley Cup Playoff game takes place, with Mud Bruneteau of the Detroit Red Wings scoring the winning goal (1–0) against the Montreal Maroons at 16:30 in the sixth overtime period. With the 116:30 of overtime, the game almost equals three full hockey games in a row.

1937 Montreal, 28 January: Howie Morenz of the Montreal Canadiens is checked by Earl Seibert, of the Chicago Black Hawks. Morenz is carried off the ice on a stretcher with a shattered leg. **Montreal, 8 March:** Morenz passes away as the result of complications from his injury. **Toronto, 24**

September: The NHL introduces the first rule to address icing. **Montreal, 3 November:** The Howie Morenz Memorial Game between two teams of All-Stars is held to benefit Morenz's family.

1939 Montreal, 29 October: A benefit is held for the family of Babe Siebert, a player with the Montreal Canadiens who had drowned. The Canadiens play against a team of "NHL All-Stars." Although the Canadiens lose 5–2, a large sum of money is raised.

1942 The war halts any development of women's ice hockey, which does not revive until the early 1970s. **Boston, 17 March:** The Brooklyn Americans play their last game before withdrawing from the NHL. For the next 25 years, the league will be comprised of the Montreal Canadiens, Toronto Maple Leafs, Detroit Red Wings, Boston Bruins, New York Rangers, and Chicago Black Hawks, known as the "Original Six." **Detroit and Toronto, 4 April–18 April:** The greatest comeback in NHL history occurs in the Stanley Cup Finals between the Toronto Maple Leafs and Detroit Red Wings. In the best-of-seven series, the Red Wings are ahead 3–0 going into the fourth game. After losing the first three games, the Maple Leafs win the next four to win the series, 4–3, giving them their fourth Stanley Cup. It is the first Stanley Cup Finals in history to go the full seven games.

1943 Chicago, 11 November: Clint Smith scores the first empty net goal in history in Chicago's 6–4 win over the Boston Bruins.

1945 Canada, 30 April: The first nine hockey players are inducted into the Hockey Hall of Fame. They include Hobey Baker, Charlie Gardiner, Eddie Gerard, Frank McGee, Howie Morenz, Tommy Phillips, Harvey Pulford, Hod Stuart, and Georges Vezina.

1946 30 January: Babe Pratt becomes the first NHL player to be suspended for betting on games. **April:** Bill Chadwick is the first referee to begin using hand signals to indicate penalties and other rulings. He does this during the Stanley Cup Finals to communicate his calls to the fans.

1947 Montreal, 13 November: Billy Reay of the Montreal Canadiens becomes the first NHL player to raise his arms and stick in celebration after scoring a goal.

1947–1948 Emile Francis is the first goaltender to wear a glove. The 22-year-old goalie finds that the glove, which is similar to a baseball mitt, makes it easier to catch the puck. The NHL approves the new piece of equipment, and its use by other goaltenders catches on quickly.

1949 The center red line first appears on the ice for NHL games. **California:** Frank Zamboni invents a four-wheel-drive vehicle to scrape, clean, and flood the surface of a hockey rink. His rough prototype is used for amateur matches.

1951 Toronto, 21 April: Bill Barilko of the Toronto Maple Leafs scores a goal in overtime of the fifth game to win the Stanley Cup series against the Montreal Canadiens. It becomes his final goal ever scored. **26 August:** Barilko's plane does not return from a weekend fishing trip to Seal River, Quebec.

1952 *Hockey Night in Canada* makes its television debut.

1955 NHL officials wear striped sweaters for the first time. **Montreal, 10 March:** During a Montreal Canadiens' game, a professionally designed Zamboni makes its NHL debut to maintain the ice between periods. **Montreal, 17 March:** Maurice Richard is suspended for the remainder of the season and the playoffs after punching a linesman during a fight. The suspension sparks the "Richard Riot" in Montreal. **Montreal, 5 November:** Jean Béliveau scores three goals in 44 seconds, all on the same power play, in a 4–2 victory over the Boston Bruins.

1956 23 January: Jean Béliveau is the first hockey player to appear on the cover of *Sports Illustrated*. The NHL makes a rule to limit power play goals. Abby Hoffman challenges hockey's gender barrier by playing in a boys' league disguised as a male. **Italy 4 February:** The Union of Soviet Socialist Republics (U.S.S.R.) enters Olympic ice hockey for the first time and wins the gold medal.

1957 The first National Hockey League Players' Association (NHLPA) is formed, with Detroit's Ted Lindsay as president. The owners soon crush the organization, and the Red Wings trade Lindsay to the last-place Chicago Black Hawks. CBS is the first U.S. television network to carry NHL games.

1958 Montreal, 18 January: Willie O'Ree of the Boston Bruins becomes the first black athlete to play in a NHL game. Boston defeats the Montreal Canadiens, 3–0.

1959 1 November: The first goaltender to wear a face mask on a continuous basis is Jacques Plante of the Montreal Canadiens. Plante suffers a cut that requires seven stitches when he is struck in the face during the first period by a hard shot by Andy Bathgate of the New York Rangers. Plante, who had previously suffered from broken noses and more than 200 stitches in his face during his career, had a fiberglass mask made before the game. He refuses to return to the ice unless he is allowed to wear face protection. He makes 27 saves, and his team wins the game, 3–1. When the other goaltenders see that the face mask does not interfere with Plante seeing the puck, the use of masks by goalies becomes more common.

1961 Toronto: The Hockey Hall of Fame, in Toronto, Canada, opens to the public.

1962 Chicago, 22 April: The Toronto Maple Leafs break the "Barilko Curse" by beating the Chicago Black Hawks (4–2) to win the Stanley Cup for the first time since his disappearance. **6 June:** Eleven years after its crash, the wreckage from Bill Barilko's plane is discovered by a helicopter pilot in Cochrane, Ontario, about 35 miles off the original course.

1963 Montreal, 5 June: The first NHL Amateur Draft is held in Montreal, and 21 players are selected. **Toronto, 8 November:** Separate penalty box doors are installed at Maple Leaf Gardens with the labels "Les Canadiens - Good Guys," and "Visiteurs - Bad Guys."

1964 Montreal, 26 March: The playoff game between the Montreal Canadiens the Toronto Maple Leafs sets a record for the most penalties in a single playoff game (31) and the most penalties in a single period (16). The Montreal Canadiens win, 2–0.

1965 New York, 27 January: Ulf Sterner plays the first of four games with the New York Rangers, becoming the first Swedish-born player in the NHL.

1965–1966 The two goaltender rule is introduced, whereby an injured or ill goaltender can be replaced as long as there is no delay of game. Prior to this rule, teams would only have one goaltender, and, when he got injured, the game would be delayed until he was able was resume playing.

1967 Toronto, 2 May: George Armstrong of the Toronto Maple Leafs scores the final goal of the "Original Six" Era in a 3–1 Toronto victory over the Montreal Canadiens.

1967–1968 The NHL doubles in size, adding six franchises. These new teams (California Seals, Los Angeles Kings, Minnesota North Stars, Philadelphia Flyers, Pittsburgh Penguins, and St. Louis Blues) play in the West Division. The East Division is composed of the previously existing six teams.

1968 Minnesota, 13 January: In a game between the Minnesota North Stars and California Seals, forward Bill Masterton is body checked, hits the ice, and suffers a severe head injury. It is the first fatality in the history of the NHL.

1970 The Buffalo Sabres and Vancouver Canucks join the NHL. During this decade, Shirley Cameron becomes the first female ice hockey star of the modern era.

1971 April: Johnny Bucyk sets a record for being the oldest player to reach his first 50-goal season. He reached his first 50-goal season in his 16th season, at the age of 35 years and 10 months, while with the Boston Bruins.

1972 The World Hockey Association (WHA) begins play, outbidding NHL teams for several star players. Bobby Hull becomes hockey's first million-dollar man, when he leaves the Chicago Black Hawks and signs a 10-year, $2.75 million contract with the WHA's Winnipeg Jets. The Atlanta Flames and New York Islanders join the NHL. **Canada and the Soviet Union, 2–28 September:** The Summit Series matches the best Canadian professionals against the best players from the Soviet Union for the first time. Canadian players who have jumped from the NHL to the WHA are not invited to play. Canada wins the last three games to finish with four wins, three losses, and a tie, clinching the series on a dramatic goal by Paul Henderson in the final game.

1973 Minnesota, 21 June: The U.S. Hockey Hall of Fame, located in Eveleth, Minnesota, is established.

1974 Soviet Union, 6 January: The Soviet Union men's ice hockey team wins the first World Junior Hockey Championship. The Kansas City Scouts and Washington Capitals join the NHL. **7 April:** Andy Brown of the Pittsburgh Penguins is the last NHL goaltender to play without a face mask. His team loses to the Atlanta Flames, 6–3. **Canada and the Soviet Union, 7 September–6 October:** A second Canada–Soviet exhibition series takes place, featuring Canadians from the WHA against the Soviet nationals. The Soviet team wins the last four games to finish with five wins, two losses, and a tie.

1974 Buffalo: Taro Tsujimoto becomes the first fictional hockey player to be legally drafted. He joins the Buffalo Sabres in the 11th round of the 1974 NHL Entry Draft.

1975 28 December–11 January 1976: Soviet teams play in North America for the first time, when the Central Red Army and Soviet Wings play a series of exhibition games against NHL teams.

1976 Two franchises move, with the California Seals becoming the Cleveland Barons and the Kansas City Scouts becoming the Colorado Rockies. **Sweden, 21–28 February:** The first Winter Paralympic Games are held in

Örnsköldsvik, Sweden, with sledge hockey as one sport. **Montreal, 15 September:** Canada defeats Czechoslovakia in the final to win the first Canada Cup tournament.

1978 14 June: The Cleveland Barons merge with the Minnesota North Stars.

1979 The WHA folds, with the Edmonton Oilers, Quebec Nordiques, Hartford Whalers, and Winnipeg Jets joining the NHL. **Philadelphia, 11 March:** Randy Holt of the Los Angeles Kings sets a record for the most penalty minutes in a single game, with 67 in a match against the Philadelphia Flyers. **Los Angeles, 10 November:** The Los Angeles Kings and Minnesota Stars play an entire NHL game without the puck leaving the ice surface, allowing that single disk to be used throughout the entire game.

1980 The Atlanta Flames move to Calgary. **Lake Placid, 22 February:** The most memorable game in Olympic hockey history is played between the U.S. Men's Olympic Ice Hockey Team and the Soviet Union Men's Olympic Ice Hockey Team. The U.S. team is the underdog, and they upset the Russian team in the semifinals by a score of 4–3. The "Miracle on Ice" is later enshrined as one of the greatest moments in the history of American sports. The United States goes on to defeat Finland in the final to win the Olympic gold medal.

1982 The Colorado Rockies move to New Jersey and become the Devils. **Vancouver, 28 November:** Philadelphia Flyers' rookie Ron Sutter plays his first NHL game. It is the first time in history that five brothers played in the NHL.

1983 The NHL introduces a five-minute sudden-death overtime period at the end of tie games in the regular season. **New York, 12 June:** Dave Semenko fights boxing legend Muhammad Ali in an exhibition match.

1987 Toronto, 21–26 April: The first-ever Women's World Ice Hockey Championships takes place in Canada; however, it is not recognized as an official tournament by the IIHF.

1988 31 December: Mario Lemieux of the Pittsburgh Penguins becomes the only player in history to score a goal in all five possible game situations in the same game (even strength, shorthanded, penalty shot, power play, and empty net).

1989 Alan Eagleson, a longtime executive director of the NHLPA, becomes the first member to resign from a North American sports hall of fame. Inducted to the Hockey Hall of Fame as a builder in 1980, he resigns after pleading guilty to mail fraud and embezzling hundreds of thousands of dollars from the NHLPA pension funds. **Calgary, 31 March:** Sergei Priakin plays for the Calgary Flames, becoming the first Soviet player permitted to join a NHL club.

1990 Ottawa, 19–25 March: The first IIHF-sanctioned Women's World Ice Hockey Championships is held, with Canada as the winner. This is the only major international tournament in women's hockey to allow bodychecking. After the tournament, the IIHF disallows bodychecking in women's ice hockey.

1991 The San Jose Sharks join the NHL. The NHL introduces video review. **St. Louis, 9 March:** Theo Fleury becomes the only player to score three short-handed goals in NHL play. This unique hat trick occurs in an 8–4 Calgary win over the St. Louis Blues. Fleury finishes the game with three goals and one assist. **Las Vegas, 27 September:** The first outdoor game between two NHL teams is held in an official preseason matchup, featuring the Los Angeles Kings and New York Rangers. The game-time temperature reaches 80 °F (27 °C). During the match, grasshoppers jump onto the ice and freeze, and, by the end of the second period, the ice is littered with bugs. Nearly 14,000 fans watch the Kings defeat the Rangers, 5–2.

1992 The Ottawa Senators and Tampa Bay Lightning join the NHL.

1993 The Florida Panthers and Mighty Ducks of Anaheim begin play. The Minnesota North Stars move to Dallas and become the Stars.

1994 New York, 14 June: The New York Rangers end their long losing streak by winning the Stanley Cup for the first time since 1940. Rangers' defenseman Brian Leetch is the first American-born player to win the Conn Smythe Trophy as playoff Most Valuable Player (MVP). **1 October–19 January 1995:** In the league's first major labor dispute, NHL players are locked out for 103 days at the beginning of the 1994–1995 season. The regular season, which begins 20 January 1995, is the shortest in 53 years. This cancellation of 468 games results in a drastically reduced 48-game season for the NHL.

1995 The Quebec Nordiques move to Denver and become the Colorado Avalanche. **Pittsburgh, 28 May:** Jaromír Jágr becomes the first European to lead the NHL in scoring.

1996 The Winnipeg Jets move to Phoenix, where they are renamed the Coyotes. **Montreal, 11 March:** The last goal is scored at the historic Montreal Forum by right wing Andrei Kovalenko of the Montreal Canadiens in a 4–1 win against the Dallas Stars.

1997 The Hartford Whalers become the Carolina Hurricanes. **St. Louis, 27 April:** Craig MacTavish, the last remaining helmetless player in the NHL, retires. **Detroit, 3 October:** At the age of 70, Gordie Howe signs a one-game contract with the Detroit Vipers and plays a single shift to become hockey's first six-decade player.

1998 The NHL begins using two referees in each game. **Nagano, February:** NHL players compete at the Olympics for the first time, with the Czech Republic winning the gold medal. Women's ice hockey becomes a full medal sport at the Olympic Winter Games for the first time. Six teams compete, and the United States defeats Canada to win the first Olympic gold medal in women's ice hockey. The host country's team, Japan, finishes in last place. **Nashville, 10 October:** As the newest member of the NHL, the Nashville Predators play their first game against the Florida Panthers but lose, 1–0.

1999 Finland, 8 March: The women's division at the World Ice Hockey Championships expands to two pools, A and B. **Atlanta, 2 October:** As the newest member of the NHL, the Atlanta Thrashers play their first game against the New Jersey Devils but lose, 4–1.

2000 23 June: The Columbus Blue Jackets and Minnesota Wild join the NHL, bringing the total number of teams to 30.

2002 Utah, 21 February: Canada defeats the United States to win the second Olympic gold medal in women's hockey. **Utah, 24 February:** NHL players return to the Winter Olympics, with Canada winning the gold medal. The victory comes 50 years to the day after the last Canadian gold medal in men's ice hockey. **Detroit, 13 June:** The Detroit Red Wings win the Stanley Cup, with Swedish-born defenseman Nicklas Lidström claiming the Conn Smythe Trophy as playoff MVP. Lidström is the first European to win the award.

2004 Finland, 5 January: The United States wins its first-ever World Junior Hockey Championships. **Florida, 6 June:** The Stanley Cup arrives in Tampa Bay, as the Tampa Bay Lightning win the NHL championship in their 12th season. **Toronto, 14 September:** Canada wins the second World Cup of Hockey, defeating Finland, 3–2, in the championship game and finishing the tournament undefeated. Vincent Lecavalier is named tournament MVP. **15 September:** The owners lock out the players, putting the 2004–2005 NHL season on hold pending a new collective bargaining agreement.

2005 16 February: The NHL season is officially cancelled because of the failure to reach a new collective bargaining agreement. **Edmonton, 21 February:** After playing for 240 straight hours, a record is set for the longest hockey game ever played. Organized by Dr. Brent Saik, 40 players helped raise $250,000 for cancer research. **9 April:** The U.S. women's ice hockey team ends Canada's streak of eight straight (nine unofficial) world titles in a shootout. **13 July:** On the 301st day of the lockout, the NHL and NHLPA announce a tentative agreement, allowing the league to resume play in October. **5 October:** The NHL introduces a series of rules changes for the 2005–2006 season, including shootouts to end tied games.

2006 Italy, 20 February: The Swedish women's ice hockey team becomes the first non-North American team to earn silver at the Winter Olympic Games, beating the United States in the semifinals.

2007 Atlanta, 16 January: Goaltender Yutaka Fukufuji makes history as the first player born in Japan to start in a NHL game, as he begins the game for the Los Angeles Kings against the Atlanta Thrashers. **Anaheim, 6 June:** The Anaheim Ducks become the first California-based team to win the Stanley Cup. **7 June:** Sidney Crosby of the Pittsburgh Penguins finishes the season with 120 points, making him the youngest scoring champion in NHL history, at 19 years, 244 days of age.

2010 Ottawa, 30 January: CBC broadcasters Charlie Panigoniak and Annie Ford make history as they call the first NHL game in Inuktitut, the most commonly spoken language in Nunavut; however, broadcasting problems leave many fans watching the game on mute and listening to their radios. The Ottawa Senators beat the Montreal Canadiens, 3–2, in overtime. **Vancouver, 25 February:** The Canadian women's ice hockey team wins its third straight Olympic gold medal, defeating the rival Americans in a hard-fought 2–0 final. **Toronto, 8 November:** Cammi Granato and Angela James become the first women inducted into the Hockey Hall of Fame.

2011 Pittsburgh, 1 January: The fourth edition of the annual outdoor ice hockey game, known as the NHL Winter Classic, is held. The Pittsburgh Penguins are defeated by the Washington Capitals by a score of 3–1. **Vancouver, 15 June:** The Boston Bruins end a 39-year Stanley Cup drought with a 4–0 win over the Vancouver Canucks in the seventh game of the Stanley Cup Finals.

2012 Switzerland, 18 May: Jamaica and Qatar join the IIHF, bringing the total number of participating countries to 72. **Los Angeles, 11 June:** The Los Angeles Kings win their first Stanley Cup in franchise history, by defeating the New Jersey Devils in six games. The Kings are only the second California-based NHL team to win the Stanley Cup following the Anaheim Ducks in 2007.

Introduction

The *Webster's Sports Dictionary* defines ice hockey as,

> A game played on an enclosed rink between two teams of six players wearing ice skates and using a thin-bladed stick to propel a hard rubber puck up and down the ice with the object to drive the puck past the opposing goalkeeper into the goal for a score and to prevent the other team from scoring.

While this definition seems straightforward and simple, ice hockey is much more complicated and colorful. The game has evolved from one played by young college students to one played by fighting athletes to one played by people of all ages. The rise of good sportsmanship has allowed fans to appreciate the true athleticism of these individuals. The sport of hockey has also been highly successful internationally, and it has even branched out to women's ice hockey, to say nothing of amateur or friendly matches in ice-bound countries.

THE BEGINNINGS OF HOCKEY

Ice hockey evolved from the game of field hockey, which was played in Northern Europe for hundreds of years. A similar game called "knattleikr" had been played for 1,000 years by the Vikings of Ireland, as documented in the Icelandic Sagas; however, most historians credit the beginnings of ice hockey to 17th-century Holland. This is mainly based on its similarities to modern hockey. Known as "kolven," a version of it was being played in England in the 1820s. The game called "bandy" was played on frozen ponds, with players hitting a cork or wooden ball with sticks made from branches. The name of the sport came from the French word *hoquet*, meaning "bent stick." The playing area for ice hockey was used in the game of curling in Scotland during the 18th century. Initially, there were as many as 30 players for each side, and the goals were two frozen stones on one end of the ice. On 3 March 1875, the first organized hockey game took place at the Victoria Rink in Montreal. Students from McGill University played against one another, with nine players per side. The team captained by James Creighton won (2–1).

The modern version of ice hockey finds its origins in the rules outlined by Creighton, which were published on 27 February 1877, in the *Montreal Gazette*. The teams that once had nine men per side were now reduced to seven. In the late 1880s, a hockey club showed two men short at the Montreal Winter Carnival. Their opponents also agreed to play with seven men. The athletes preferred the smaller squad, consisting of one goaltender, three forwards, two defensemen, and one rover. The seven-man game remained until 1922, when the rover position was eliminated.

By 1893, the sport of ice hockey made its way to the United States, and, a year later, the first indoor rink in North America, with artificial ice, opened in Baltimore. This rink was used by students attending John Hopkins University. By 1895, women's hockey had gained popularity at Canadian universities. Female students at the University of Toronto and Queen's University in Kingston, Ontario, played ice hockey while wearing long skirts. In 1899, the first printed Canadian book of hockey, *Hockey: Canada's Royal Winter Game*, was written by Arthur Farrell and published by C. R. Corneil. By the early 1900s, hockey became prevalent in parts of Europe, including the United Kingdom.

THE STANLEY CUP

In 1893, Frederick Arthur, Lord Stanley of Preston and governor general of Canada, donated a trophy to be called the Dominion Hockey Challenge Cup. It was a plain silver-plated nickel cup roughly seven inches high and 11 inches wide. The cup cost the equivalent of $48.67. The trophy became commonly known as the Stanley Cup, and is the oldest trophy competed for by North American professional athletes. On 22 March 1893, the first official Stanley Cup match was played between the Montreal Amateur Athletic Association and Ottawa Capitals. Montreal won, 3–1, with 5,000 hockey fans in attendance. The National Hockey Association (NHA) took possession of the Stanley Cup in 1910. In 1912, the tournament was opened to professional teams, and the Quebec Bulldogs won. In 1917, the cup went international, and the Seattle Metropolitans were the first non-Canadians to win the trophy. In 1926, the National Hockey League (NHL) and its 10 members became the only ones eligible to compete for it. Today, this is also true; however, the NHL has grown to 30 teams. The Montreal Canadiens have won the trophy a record 24 times.

The Stanley Cup is the only professional sports trophy on which the name of each member of the winning team is inscribed, including players, coaches, management, and club staff. Henri Richard of the Canadiens had his name engraved the most, 11 times. Of the 12 women who have had their names engraved on the cup, Marguerite Norris was the first, as the president of the winning Detroit Red Wings in 1954 and 1955. Tiered rings were originally added to the bottom of the bowl when more room was needed. This was followed by long narrow bands in 1927, which were later replaced by uneven bands in 1947. Metal bands are often retired to make room for new champions. Retired bands, along with the original Stanley Cup bowl, are proudly displayed in Lord Stanley's Vault at the Hockey Hall of Fame in Toronto. The current Stanley Cup has a bowl, three tiered bands, a collar, and five uniform bands. The entire trophy stands close to three feet tall and weighs 34 ½ pounds.

There have only been four official engravers of the Stanley Cup. The first engravers were comprised of two generations of the Peterson family, with assistance from Fred Light. Sr. Doug Boffey, owner of Boffey Silversmiths of Montreal, followed them. The current engraver is Louise St. Jacques, who took over Boffey's engraving business and left the legacy of the shop's name in place. First, the cup is disassembled from the top down, and then the band being engraved is clamped onto a homemade circular jig that creates a steel background for stamping. Special hammers of various weights are used to strike against a letter punch to sink each letter into the silver.

In 1955, Larry Hillman of the Red Wings became the youngest player to win the Stanley Cup, at 18 years, two months, and nine days of age. Johnny Bower was the oldest player to win the Stanley Cup. He was 42 years and nine months of age, and he won while playing with the Toronto Maple Leafs in 1967. After winning the trophy, players traditionally skate around the rink holding the trophy above their heads. This tradition began in 1950, when Ted Lindsay holsted it above his head to give fans a better look at it. The winning team's captain is typically the first person to hold the Stanley Cup; however, three exceptions stand out. In 1993, after the Montreal Canadiens defeated the Los Angeles Kings, Guy Carbonneau handed the cup to Denis Savard, as Savard had been the player that many fans had urged the Canadiens to draft back in 1980; in 1998, after the Detroit Red Wings had defeated the Washington Capitals, Steve Yzerman immediately passed the cup to Vladimir Konstantinov, whose career with the Red Wings ended due to serious injuries in an accident the previous year, and he had to be wheeled onto the ice; in 2001, the Colorado Avalanche won the Stanley Cup, and when captain Joe Sakic received the trophy, he immediately handed it to Ray Bourque. The deciding game of the finals was the last of Bourque's 22-year NHL career, and he had never been on a Stanley Cup–winning team until then. Each year after the trophy is presented to the championship team, a summer celebration begins. Each member of the winning team gets to enjoy 24 hours with the trophy.

During its long existence, the Stanley Cup has traveled around the world, including visits to Russia, Japan, and Switzerland, as well as inside igloos in Canada's newest territory, Nunavut. The Hockey Hall of Fame website has a Stanley Cup journal so fans can see where it has traveled. Many books have been written about hockey's most famous trophy, including the quest for it and the adventures the cup has been on once acquired. One book by Kevin Allen (2001) is entitled, *Why Is the Stanley Cup in Mario Lemieux's Swimming Pool?* It is no surprise that a chaperone has since been appointed to protect the historic Stanley Cup during its travels.

EARLY LEAGUES

The early leagues of hockey were mostly short-lived. Before the NHA was established in 1909, there were several other clubs in existence. The Amateur Hockey Association (AHA) lasted from 1893 to 1898. The AHA was the first league to play for the Stanley Cup, which was awarded to the best amateur teams at the time on a challenge basis. Any amateur team could challenge the current champion for the cup. The teams in the league included the Montreal Amateur Athletic Association, Montreal Crystals, Montreal Shamrocks, Montreal Victorias, Ottawa Capitals, Ottawa Hockey Club, Quebec Hockey Club, and Winnipeg Victorias. The Montreal AAA were the first league champions. In 1899, the AHA changed its name to the Canadian Amateur Hockey League (CAHL), which lasted until 1905. In 1903, the Ottawa Hockey Club became known as the "Silver Seven," after winning the Stanley Cup championship. The Federal Amateur Hockey League (FAHL) existed from 1904 to 1906, and they then changed their name to the Eastern Canada Amateur Hockey Association (ECAHA). The ECAHA had six clubs, including four from the CAHL and two from the FAHL. The ECAHA league changed its name to the Canadian Hockey Association, but it folded after only a few games into the 1909–1910 season. Then the NHA was created. It lasted from 1909 to 1917, when it was dissolved, and the NHL was formed.

FOR THE LOVE OF THE GAME

The Dawson City Nuggets, also known as the Klondikes, were a hockey team from Dawson City, Yukon Territory, Canada. They challenged the reigning Stanley Cup champions, the Ottawa "Silver Seven." Dawson City's challenge was accepted in the summer of 1904 by the Stanley Cup trustees, and the match was scheduled for Friday, 13 January 1905. The date of the challenge meant that Weldy Young had to travel later, because he had to work in a federal election that December. In December 1904, for the purpose of playing hockey, the Dawson City Nuggets traveled 4,000 miles (6,400 kilometers) from the Yukon to Ottawa for a best-of-three Stanley Cup challenge series. On 18 December 1904, several players set out by dog sled, and the rest left the next day by bicycle for a 330-mile trek to Whitehorse. At first the team made good progress, but the weather turned warm enough to thaw the roads, meaning that the players had to walk several hundred miles. The team spent the nights in police sheds along the road. At Whitehorse, the weather was bad, so much so that it prevented the trains from running for three days. As a result, the Nuggets missed their steamer in Skagway. The next one could not dock for three days due to the ice buildup. The club found the sea journey treacherous, causing seasickness amongst the team. When the steamer reached Vancouver, the area was too fogged in to dock, so the steamer docked in Seattle. From there the hockey players caught a train to Vancouver, and the team finally left Vancouver on 6 January 1905. They finally arrived in Ottawa on 11 January 1905. Despite the difficult journey, the Ottawa team refused to change the date of the first game, which was only two days away.

After the brutal trip, the players were exhausted and covered with bruises from the dog sled ride. In addition, the team's strongest player, former Ottawa star Weldy Young, was unable to make it to Ottawa in time. The first game started off well for Dawson, and they were only down 3–1 at the half, but things soon turned ugly. Norman Watt of Dawson tripped Ottawa's Art Moore, who retaliated with a stick to the mouth of Watt, who then knocked Moore out by hitting him on the head with his stick. The game ended with a 9–2 victory for Ottawa. Before the second game, Watt made the mistake of saying that Frank McGee wasn't that good, because he had only scored one goal in the first game. McGee proved him wrong when he scored four goals in the first half of the second match and 10 in the second half, leading Ottawa to a 23–2 win. McGee's record of 14 goals in one game has never been broken. Despite the high score, the newspapers claimed that Albert Forrest, the Dawson City goalie, had played a "really fine game," otherwise the score "might have been doubled." Ottawa celebrated by hosting the Dawson players at a banquet, and afterward the players took the Stanley Cup and tried to drop-kick it over the Rideau Canal. The stunt was unsuccessful, and the cup landed on the frozen ice. The hockey players continued celebrating and retrieved the trophy the next day. The Nuggets played a series of exhibition hockey games in the east before returning home to the Yukon.

THE NATIONAL HOCKEY ASSOCIATION

The National Hockey Association (NHA) was formed in 1909. Frank Calder was the league's first secretary. Early teams included the Cobalt Silver Kings, Haileybury Comets, Montreal Canadiens, Montreal Shamrocks, Montreal Wanderers, Ottawa Senators, and Renfrew Creamery Kings. The Montreal Wanderers won the 1910 Stanley Cup. The Quebec Bulldogs and Toronto Blueshirts also later joined the NHA.

In 1911, brothers Frank and Lester Patrick organized the Pacific Coast Hockey Association (PCHA). The league competed with the NHA for the country's best players. The PCHA began with the New Westminster Royals, Victoria Senators, and Vancouver Millionaires. The Millionaires played in the first professional Stanley Cup championship. The Patrick brothers were responsible for building Canada's first artificial ice rink in Victoria. After building another rink in Vancouver, they added the western teams of the Portland Rosebuds, Seattle Metropolitans, Vancouver Maroons, and Victoria Aristocrats. They were the first Canadian league to expand into the United States. By 1914, an East Coast–West Coast challenge had begun for the Stanley Cup. In 1924, the PCHA suspended their operations when Lester Patrick realized that they could not match the salaries that the NHL businessmen were offering to their players.

The NHA was responsible for several innovations to the sport of hockey. The league changed the sport from seven-man teams to six-man teams by eliminating the rover position. In 1912, the NHA put jersey numbers on their players. The goaltender was number 1, defensemen 2 and 3, and center 4, and the wings were 5 and 6. Replacement players were assigned 7, 8, and 9. This made it easier for the referees to identify players when calling fouls. The NHA also instituted match penalties and allowed quick line changes. World War I disrupted the entire hockey establishment, and the NHA folded in 1917. It was the precursor to the current NHL.

THE IMPACT OF WORLD WAR I

The start of World War I meant that players started enlisting in the military to fight overseas. By 1915, World War I and the PCHA raiding left the NHA without enough quality players. The two leagues tried to work out an agreement, but disputes with the PCHA and within the NHA led to the end of the NHA. Toronto Shamrocks' team owner Eddie Livingstone had caused many of the problems. The league demanded that he sell the Toronto franchise, but instead he threatened to sue the NHA. The owners of the Canadiens, Wanderers, Senators, and Bulldogs wanted to get rid of Livingstone, and they found a creative way to accomplish that. In November 1917, they voted to suspend the NHA's operations, and they formed the NHL so that they could continue without Livingstone. He still had his NHA team, but he did not have any teams to compete against. The NHA's rules and trophies were carried over into the NHL. When the Quebec Bulldogs could not afford to finance a team, the NHL granted a temporary franchise to the Toronto Blueshirts. This team evolved into the Toronto Maple Leafs of today. Due to legal proceedings, the NHA organization was not formally dissolved for several years, and Frank Calder was the president of both leagues.

THE NATIONAL HOCKEY LEAGUE

Founding Era (1917–1942)

The National Hockey League (NHL) can be divided into different eras: Founding Era (1917–1942), "Original Six" Era (1942–1967), Expansion Era (1967 1992), and Modern Era (1992–present). Throughout the history of hockey, several teams dominated the game at different times. The Hockey Hall of Fame classifies these powerhouses as hockey dynasties. During the years of the Founding Era, the Ottawa Senators were the most successful team. Ottawa's star players during this time included Jack Adams, Clint Benedict, Frank Boucher, George Boucher, Harry Broadbent, King Clancy, Sprague Cleghorn, Alex Connell, Jack Darragh, Cy Denneny, Eddie Gerard, Tommy Gorman, Frank Nighbor, and Hooley Smith.

The Impact of World War II

The NHL was negatively impacted during World War II. Many players interrupted their careers for military service. Several team owners were said to have intervened, ensuring that their athletes received noncombat assignments. The depletion of NHL wartime rosters created opportunities for athletes who might otherwise have never played an NHL game. To make the sport more enjoyable for the fans, rule changes were made to encourage a more fast-paced game. Until 1943, a player was not allowed to make a forward pass across his own blue line. That changed in the 1943 1944 season, when the NHL ruled that players could pass from their defensive zone up to the middle of the rink, which would be marked by a new red line at center ice.

The war also shifted the power balance in the league. While other NHL teams watched their players depart for military camps, the Montreal Canadiens took advantage of the war years to get a head start on a new dynasty. By finding jobs for players in essential industries like munitions and shipbuilding, the Canadiens helped keep their talent home, building the foundation for several Stanley Cup championships.

After the war, some British World War II veterans wanted to continue to enjoy the sport of hockey but were limited by their injuries. In 1948, they started the Paralympic Games, an international sporting event in which athletes with a physical disability compete. Just like the seasonal Olympic Games, there are Winter Paralympic Games and Summer Paralympic Games. The first Winter Paralympic Games were held in 1976, in Örnsköldsvik, Sweden. A form of hockey incorporating sleds instead of skates and called ice sledge hockey became one of the five events of the 1994 Winter Paralympic Games. The Winter Paralympic Games were held every four years with the summer ones, just as the Olympics were. This tradition was practiced until the 1992 Paralympic Games in Albertville, France. Then, beginning with the 1994 Games, the Winter Paralympics and Winter Olympics have been held in even-numbered years separate from the Summer Games. During the 2010 games, in Vancouver, Canada, women were allowed to be part of the men's teams for the first time at the Paralympics. Eleven countries participated in the 2010 ice sledge hockey event. Since 1994, Canada, Japan, Norway, Sweden, and the United States have all won medals.

"Original Six" Era (1942–1967)

The "Original Six" Era refers to a time when only six NHL teams competed against one another. These six teams were the Boston Bruins, Chicago Black Hawks, Detroit Red Wings, Montreal Canadiens, New York Rangers, and Toronto Maple Leafs. All six franchises continue to play in the NHL today. The six original NHL arenas included Boston Garden (1928–1995), Chicago Stadium (1929–1994), the Detroit Olympia (1927–1979), Madison Square Garden (1925–1968), Maple Leaf Gardens (1931–1999), and the Montreal Forum (1924–1996). During this hockey era, the dominant teams were the Toronto Maple Leafs (1946–1947 to 1950–1951), the Detroit Red Wings (1949–1950 to 1954–1955), the Montreal Canadiens (1955–1956 to 1959–1960), the Maple Leafs again (1961–1962 to 1966–1967), and the Canadiens again (1964–1965 to 1968–1969). Toronto players during this time period included Hockey Hall of Famers Syl Apps, George Armstrong, Max Bentley, Turk Broda, Clarence Day, Fernie Flaman, Tim Horton, Ted Kennedy, Frank Mathers, Bud Poile, Joe Primeau, Conn Smythe, and Harry Watson. In addition to the legendary Gordie Howe, the Detroit Red Wings also had such strong players as Red Kelly, Ted Lindsay, and Marcel Pronovost. The most well-known player for the Canadiens during their Stanley Cup reign was Maurice Richard. His brother, Henri Richard, and teammates Jean Béliveau, Bernie Geoffrion, Doug Harvey, Tom Johnson, Dickie Moore, and Jacques Plante all contributed to Montreal's solid franchise.

Expansion Era (1967–1992)

During the Expansion Era, the NHL doubled in size by adding six franchises. This marked the first change in the composition of the league since 1942, when the Brooklyn Americans folded. This expansion ended the era of the "Original Six." The new teams the California Seals, Los Angeles Kings, Minnesota North Stars, Philadelphia Flyers, Pittsburgh Penguins, and St. Louis Blues played in the West Division. The East Division was composed of the previously existing six teams. Of the six added franchises, four still play in their original cities (Los Angeles Kings in Los Angeles, California; Philadelphia Flyers in Philadelphia, Pennsylvania; Pittsburgh Penguins in Pittsburgh, Pennsylvania; St. Louis Blues in St. Louis, Missouri). The one team that relocated was the Minnesota North Stars in Bloomington, Minnesota. In 1978, they merged with the Cleveland Barons and later relocated to Dallas, Texas, as the Dallas Stars in 1993. The expansion franchise that ceased operations was the California Seals in Oakland, California. They were renamed the Oakland Seals and then became the California Golden Seals. The franchise later relocated to Cleveland, Ohio, as the Cleveland Barons in 1976. In 1978, they ceased operations with the merger into the Minnesota North Stars.

While these new teams were working to put together strong franchises, the Montreal Canadiens continued to dominate the NHL. From 1975–1976 to 1978–1979, the Canadiens were the team to beat. No one was surprised that they became the team to win the Stanley Cup more than 20 times. But by the early 1980s, they began to experience competition from the younger franchises. The New York Islanders had talented players like Mike Bossy, Clark Gillies, Bob Nystrom, Stefan Persson, Denis Potvin, Billy Smith, and Bryan Trottier. The Islanders' dynasty (1979–1980 to 1982–1983) was only interrupted by the success of the Edmonton Oilers. After the World Hockey Association (WHA) disbanded, the Oilers merged with the NHL, keeping the same name. At the time, young Wayne Gretzky was beginning to capture the attention of fans across Canada and the United States. Other strong Edmonton players at the time were Glenn Anderson, Grant Fuhr, Jari Kurri, and Mark Messier. The Oilers won five Stanley Cups from 1983–1984 to 1989–1990. When Wayne Gretzky was traded to the Los Angeles Kings, the hockey world was stunned, but, as an ambassador of the sport, he popularized hockey in California. Many movie stars began following the games, which also added to the sport's success and spread across the United States.

Also in the late 1980s, the best Russian players started filtering into the NHL. Alexander Mogilny led the way for other players when he defected and joined the Buffalo Sabres two decades ago. Peter Stastny and his brother left Czechoslovakia for Canada due to the opportunities that the NHL could provide for them. Coach Scotty Bowman made headlines in the mid-1990s, in Detroit, when he announced the "Russian Five," consisting of forwards Sergei Fedorov, Slava Kozlov, and Igor Larionov, and defensemen Viacheslav Fetisov and Vladimir Konstantinov. These were just the first of the changes that were come to the sport of ice hockey.

Modern Era (1992–present)

The Modern Era of hockey can be described as explosive. In addition to Gretzky, many other young superstars have burst onto the scene and shattered NHL records. Players from Europe have also joined the NHL, which has made for exciting matches. Stars during this time include Pavel Bure, Chris Chelios, Sidney Crosby, Dominik Hašek, Mario Lemieux, Nicklas Lidström, Eric Lindros, Teemu Selänne, and Steve Yzerman. The era of 21 teams ended in 1990, when the league made major expansions. The first three new teams were the San Jose Sharks, Ottawa Senators, and Tampa Bay Lightning. A year later, the Mighty Ducks of Anaheim and Florida Panthers began playing. The NHL's expansion to the south continued in 1993, when the Minnesota North Stars moved to Dallas, Texas, and became the Dallas Stars. Other changes included the Quebec Nordiques moving to Denver and becoming the Colorado Avalanche, the Winnipeg Jets relocating to Arizona and becoming the Phoenix Coyotes, and the Hartford Whalers becoming the Carolina Hurricanes in 1997. Franchise expansion continued in the United States with the addition of the Nashville Predators, Atlanta Thrashers, Minnesota Wild, and Columbus Blue Jackets in Columbus, Ohio. The "Original Six" hockey teams of the NHL have now become the expanded 30 teams.

This hockey era was also marked by the greed of both players and management. In 1994, the players were locked out by the owners because of these financial disagreements. The 1994–1995 NHL lockout lasted 104 days and resulted in the season being shortened from 84 games to only 48. This was just one example of how the sport of hockey has been turned into a business throughout the years and tarnished by the greed of the team owners, players, television networks, and advertisers. Based on the success of their movie, the Walt Disney Company even created a new NHL team in 1993, the Mighty Ducks of Anaheim. Appendix C shows the current teams, and many of the arenas are named after the owners, which are large corporations like Pepsi, Prudential, and Staples. Old-time ice hockey consisted of amateur players, some of whom even refused to become professionals, for example, Harry E. Watson. Many of the early professional players needed to hold full-time jobs in the off-season, because hockey salaries were not extravagant, as they are today. For example, in the 1950s, star player Jean Béliveau was only earning $20,000 a year. By contrast, in the 1970s, 18-year-old rookie Mark Howe was offered a four-year contract worth $500,000, with a signing bonus of $125,000, by the Houston Aeros of the WHA. His father, the legendary Gordie Howe said that, "That's $25,000 more than I ever made in a year."

When teams sign players with such large contracts, they need to raise money. Several ways they accomplish this is by increasing ticket prices, selling rights to television stations, and advertising along the boards and throughout the arenas. Many other sports have also become just as commercialized. For example, if Babe Ruth were alive today, fans would not know if he were pointing to right field or to a billboard advertising soda. Despite the business side of hockey, it continues to remain an exciting spectator sport.

BLACK PLAYERS

During the 2011–2012 playoffs, right wing Joel Ward of the Washington Capitals scored the winning goal in the seventh playoff game against the reigning Stanley Cup holders, the Boston Bruins. As a black hockey player, Ward has opportunities today that players before him did not have. The small African American population in Canada, combined with racial biases throughout history, have made hockey a sport predominantly played by white people. At the end of the 19th century, Hippo Galloway was the first black player in the Central Ontario Hockey League. Charley Lightfoot played for the Central Ontario Hockey Association until he gave up hockey to pursue a baseball career. From 1900 to the 1920s, the Colored Hockey League often drew large crowds. The teams in this league were the Africville Seasides, Dartmouth Jubilees, Halifax Eurekas, Truro Victorias, and Amherst Royals. Bud Kelly, an outstanding player in the 1910s, almost had the opportunity to play in the NHL with the Toronto St. Patricks. Unfortunately, he played poorly in the one game that the scouts attended and missed his chance at breaking the color barrier.

In the late 1930s, Herb Carnegie often practiced at Maple Leaf Gardens as a member of the Young Rangers Junior A club in Toronto. After watching him on the ice, Toronto Maple Leafs' boss Conn Smythe allegedly said that, "I will gladly give $10,000 to anyone who can turn Herb Carnegie white." Herb became the first African-Canadian player to be offered an opportunity to play in the NHL. A year after Jackie Robinson broke Major League Baseball's color barrier, New York Rangers' coach Frank Boucher offered Carnegie a contract in 1948, but Boucher wanted him to play for the minor-league team first. At the time, Herb was part of what is believed to be the first all-black line in hockey. Known as "The Black Aces," Herb played center, with his brother Ossie as right wing and Manny McIntyre as left wing. Carnegie refused the contract offer, insisting that he was good enough to play in the NHL and refusing to play in the minor leagues. He also did not want to move his family or take a cut in pay. Carnegie was a member of the Quebec Aces (1949–1953) with teammate Jean Béliveau and coach Punch Imlach. He earned the nickname "Swivel Hips" because of his elusive dekes on the ice. Unfortunately, racism blocked his way into the NHL.

On 18 January 1958, Willie O'Ree became the first black player to play in the NHL, when he played right wing for the Boston Bruins at the Montreal Forum in a 3–0 win over the Montreal Canadiens. He only played two games that season before returning to the minor league. The Bruins gave him another chance during the 1960–1961 season, and fast-skating O'Ree played in 43 more games. He had four goals, 10 assists, and 26 penalty minutes. He faced a lot of discrimination, and players taunted him, but since O'Ree did not back down, he spent time in the penalty box for fighting. After breaking the color barrier, he was often referred to as the "Jackie Robinson of Hockey." After O'Ree, there were no other black players in the NHL until 1974, when Canadian player Mike Marson was drafted by the Washington Capitals. Marson was also responsible for making the team change their uniform from white pants to blue because he did not wear underwear while he played and the sweat made his pants transparent. From 1975–1979, in 139 games, Marson's teammate, Bill Riley, scored 31 goals and 30 assists. While he was in the minor leagues, due to the racial taunting he was subjected to, Riley had more than 100 fights.

Goaltender Grant Fuhr was a hockey star in the 1980s. He helped the Edmonton Oilers win five Stanley Cups. Fuhr won 403 games during his 19 seasons in the NHL. During the 1989–1990 season, Dirk Graham was the first player of African American descent to become an NHL team captain. He led his Chicago Blackhawks all the way to the Stanley Cup Finals in 1991–1992, where they lost to the Pittsburgh Penguins. He retired after the 1990s lockout. In 2003, Jarome Iginla became the team captain for the Calgary Flames and only the second black captain in NHL history. Tony McKegney was a top NHL scorer who scored 40 goals during the 1987–1988 season with the St. Louis Blues. In 1991, he finished his NHL career with 320 goals in 912 games. Left wing Donald Brashear was a tough hockey player who led the league in penalty minutes, with 372, during the 1997–1998 season with the Vancouver Canucks. In 2000, Brashear was severely injured after Marty McSorley of the Boston Bruins hit him on the head with his hockey stick. Herb Carnegie and Willie O'Ree opened the hockey doors for these black athletes, as well as others, including Anson Carter, Mike Grier, Kevin Weekes, and Peter Wornell.

WOMEN'S HOCKEY

During the 1890s, women's hockey became popular at universities, specifically at the University of Toronto and Queen's University in Kingston, Ontario. In the 1920s, Bobbie Rosenfeld and Myrtle Cook, former track stars and hockey players, became Canada's first female sports reporters, and they specialized in hockey during the winter. Elizabeth Graham was a goaltender in Kingston, Ontario, for the Queen's University women's hockey team. In 1927, she appeared in a game wearing a fencing mask. She may have been the first goalie to ever wear a face mask in an organized hockey game. The Preston Rivulettes, with star player Hilda Ranscombe, dominated women's ice hockey during the 1930s. World War II in the 1940s halted the development of women's ice hockey, but then, in 1956, Abby Hoffman challenged hockey's gender barrier by disguising herself as a male and playing in a boys' league. Women's ice hockey eventually made a strong comeback in the early 1970s, with Shirley Cameron as the first star of the modern era.

In 1987, the first Women's World Ice Hockey Championships took place in Toronto; however, it was not recognized as an official tournament by the International Ice Hockey Federation (IIHF). In 1990, the first official and IIHF-sanctioned Women's World Ice Hockey Championships were held in Ottawa. Women's hockey became a full medal sport at the 1998 Olympic Winter Games for the first time. Due to the international growth of the sport, the women's division at the World Championships expanded to two pools, A and B, in 1999. Finally, in 2005, the United States ended Canada's streak of eight straight (nine unofficial) world titles in a shootout. Sweden became the first non-North American team to earn a silver medal at the 2006 Winter Olympic Games, after beating the United States in the semifinals. In 2010, Canada won its third straight Olympic gold medal by defeating the rival Americans in a tough 2–0 final. Cammi Granato and Angela James became the first women inducted into the Hockey Hall of Fame.

Several of the best Canadian players include Jennifer Botterill, Cassie Campbell, Danielle Goyette, Geraldine Heaney, Jayna Hefford, Angelea James, Caroline Ouellette, Cherie Piper, Manon Rhéaume, and Hayley Wickenheiser. Star American players include Karyn Bye, Julie Chu, Natalie Darwitz, Cammi Granato, Katie King, Jenny Potter, Angela Ruggiero, and Krissy Wendell. Riikka Nieminen played for Finland, and Maria Rooth played for Sweden.

INTERNATIONALIZATION OF HOCKEY

In 1908, the International Ice Hockey Federation (IIHF [Ligue Internationale de Hockey Sur Glace]) was established to govern, develop, and organize hockey throughout the world. The five founders of the federation were representatives from Belgium, France, Great Britain, Switzerland, and Bohemia (now the Czech Republic). The IIHF was composed entirely of European teams until 1920, when Canada and the United States joined. It is based in Zurich, Switzerland, and currently has 72 countries as members, with Jamaica and Qatar becoming recent members. The IIHF is responsible for the management of international ice hockey tournaments, and the federation maintains the IIHF World Ranking. Eight nations that have achieved a top-10 ranking each year from 2003–2011 are Canada, Sweden, Russia, Czech Republic, Finland, the United States, Slovakia, and Switzerland. An additional four nations, Latvia, Germany, Belarus, and Norway, have been in the top 10 at least once. The IIHF Hall of Fame was created in 1997, with 30 individuals being honored. This museum is located in Toronto, Ontario, in the same building as the Hockey Hall of Fame.

With similarities to the Olympic Games, the IIHF focuses on athletes meeting and competing from all across the world; however, world leaders have managed to interfere politically with sporting events. International hockey tournaments have reflected conflict in the real world. The most obvious example is the Cold War era. From the 1960s through the 1980s, sporting events between Western nations and the Soviet Bloc reflected the international standoff. One of the most memorable "political" games in hockey history took place at the 1969 World Ice Hockey Championships, a few months after a Soviet invasion of Czechoslovakia. The Czechs defeated the Soviets twice during the tournament, which was played in Sweden. Thousands of people poured into the streets of Prague in celebration. A memorable sign in the crowd told the Soviets that, "This time you can't count on your tanks." In 1972 and 1974, the Soviet Union team and the Canadian team met in an eight-game series known as the Summit Series. In each tournament, the locations of the matches were split between the two countries. At the conclusion of the two tournaments, each team had won a championship. Tensions remained between the countries into the 1980s. Their rivalry culminated in what has come to be known as the "Miracle on Ice" at the 1980 Olympics. The dramatic on-ice upset fueled an even stronger competition.

In addition to hockey at the Winter Olympics, countries were able to match their skills at the short-lived World Cup of Hockey, as well as the currently held World Ice Hockey Championships. When the competitions are over and the athletes have an opportunity to socialize with one another, artificial nationalistic barriers can be broken down. One result of this is the influx of European players to the NHL. Athletes are often unable to have opportunities to play ice hockey in their own countries, and, like the Stastny brothers of Czechoslovakia, they defect to Canada or the United States.

OLYMPIC GAMES

The sport of men's ice hockey made its debut at the 1920 Summer Olympics in Belgium. Four years later, it became a permanent sport at the 1924 Winter Olympics in France. Between 1920 and 1968, the Olympic hockey tournament also counted as the World Ice Hockey Championships for that year. The Olympics were originally intended for amateur athletes only, but, after other countries sent professionals to compete, the United States did the same, starting in 1998. Canada was the most successful team of the first three decades and won six of seven gold medals. Czechoslovakia, Sweden, and the United States were also competitive during this period and won several medals. When the Soviet Union Men's Olympic Ice Hockey Team first participated in 1956, they replaced Canada as the dominant international team, winning seven of the nine tournaments in which they participated. The United States won gold medals in 1960 and 1980, which included their "Miracle on Ice" upset of the Soviet Union. Canada went 50 years without another gold medal, until 2002 and 2010.

Erich Kühnhackl was part of the West German bronze-medal winning team in 1976. It was one of only two Olympic ice hockey medals for Germany. At the 1992 Olympics, Armenia, Belarus, Kazakhstan, Russia, Ukraine, and Uzbekistan competed as one entity, known as the Unified Team. In the final, the Unified Team defeated Canada to win gold, while Czechoslovakia won the bronze. Other nations to win gold medals include Great Britain in 1936, the Unified Team in 1992, Sweden in 1994 and 2006, and the Czech Republic in 1998. Other medal-winning nations include Switzerland, Finland, and Russia. The sport of women's ice hockey made its debut at the 1998 Winter Olympics in Nagano, Japan. Six countries competed for the gold medal. The U.S. Women's Olympic Ice Hockey Team won gold, the Canadian Women's Olympic Ice Hockey Team won silver, and the Finnish Women's Olympic Ice Hockey Team won bronze. China, Sweden, and Japan also participated. The U.S. women's team won silver medals during the 2002 and 2010 Olympics, as well as a bronze medal during the 2006 competition.

MODERN RULES OF HOCKEY

The NHL outlines all of the rules of ice hockey in their annual publication, *NHL Official Rules*. These rules address the equipment allowed, rink dimensions, various penalties, and any new rules. It also includes a list of current on-ice officials and the season's team schedules. Since the start of the NHL in 1917, the rules have evolved as the game has changed.

A professional hockey game consists of individuals with heavy padding skating on a rink of ice for three periods of 20 minutes each. The two teams switch ends for the second period; again for the third period; and at the start of each overtime period, when needed. Each team has one goaltender, who tries to prevent the other team from shooting a black rubber puck into his team's net. The three offensive players form a line, and their positions are called the left wing, center, and right wing. These skaters try to pass the puck to one another and down the length of the ice with their hockey sticks. Two defensemen on each team try to help their goalie block the net. Players are permitted to check one another, which means that they can slam into each other if the puck is involved. The rink is surrounded by boards, and hockey players hit each other into them as they attempt to retrieve the puck. Ice hockey is a physical contact sport, but it requires much more than muscle. Most players are good skaters with stick handling skills. In the early days of hockey, there was a seventh person on the team who was called a rover and who would play both offense and defense. Current hockey teams have six players on the ice at a time, and the team is penalized if an extra player steps on the ice. Because of the physical nature of the sport, the players skate in shifts, and are constantly leaving and returning to the ice.

A referee and two linesmen are the individuals who officiate the hockey games. When the referee blows his whistle, the clock stops. The main reasons that play is stopped are because of a penalty call, a call for offsides, a call for icing, or the puck is out of play. When opponents become too aggressive, a penalty is called, and one or both of the players must sit in a time-out called the penalty box. Examples of penalties are tripping, hooking, and high-sticking. Offsides is called when a skater is past one of the lines before his opponents. Icing is a stall tactic of hitting the puck the length of the ice, but it is only allowed when a team is short-handed. If one team has a player sitting in the penalty box, they must skate without him. Sometimes the puck will go out of play if it is hit over the Plexiglas surrounding the rink. The rule to stop the clock came about when players deliberately hit the puck over the glass to take a rest.

To resume play after the clock has been stopped, two opponents meet for a face-off. The referee drops the puck, and each skater tries to gain control of it. Hockey games are won by hitting the puck past the other team's goalie and into the net. This is called scoring a goal. Hockey matches are not known for having high-scoring games; however, a final score of 2–1 does not necessarily mean that it was an uneventful game. A strong team may face an excellent goaltender, and although they may have shot the puck 14 times, only one slipped past him. Goaltenders have a statistic called shots on goal, which shows how effective they are at defending the net.

In addition to the physical aspect of hockey, it is also a mental sport. Wayne Gretzky excelled at knowing the angles of where his shots would land and anticipating where he should skate to receive a teammate's pass. In addition, players often try to unnerve their opponents by provoking or instigating a fight. Players cannot score from the penalty box, so an agitator who can disrupt the other team's flow is often an asset to a team. Unfortunately, other hockey players just enjoy fighting, and they negatively impact the fans' appreciation of the athletes' talents.

A

ABEL, SIDNEY GERALD "SID," "OLD BOOTNOSE". B. 22 February 1918, Melville, Saskatchewan. D. 7 February 2000, Farmington Hills, Michigan. Sid Abel's **ice** hockey career included playing, **coaching**, scouting, and managing teams. Abel started as a **center** and **left wing** for the **Detroit Red Wings** (1938–1943, 1946–1952) in the **National Hockey League (NHL)**. He was away from hockey for almost three years while he was in the Royal Canadian Air Force. Abel was a member of two famous **lines**: the "Liniment Line," with Eddie Wares and Don "The Count" Grosso, and the "Production Line," with **Ted Lindsay** and **Gordie Howe**. With the amazing teamwork of Lindsay and Howe, Abel was among the top five NHL players in **points** in 1948–1949 (54), 1949–1950 (69), and 1950–1951 (61). Detroit also won their first **Prince of Wales Trophy** in 1949, with six consecutive ones following. Individually, Abel won the **Hart Memorial Trophy** once (1949). As a team player with the Red Wings, he won three **Stanley Cups** (1943, 1950, 1952).

Abel earned the **nickname** "Old Bootnose" after a **fight** with **Maurice Richard**. Gordie Howe punched Richard and knocked him to the ice. Then Abel said, "How do you like that, you Frenchman?" At that point, Richard jumped up and punched Abel, breaking his nose in two places. On 22 July 1952, Abel was traded to the **Chicago Black Hawks**, where he had a dual role as a player and coach. He then returned to Detroit and coached the Red Wings (1957–1968, 1969–1970). He was also their general manager from 1962–1971. Although he knew all sides of the sport, Abel's love of the game truly came out when he said, "We played hockey for money, but we would play the **Toronto Maple Leafs** for nothing." Abel was inducted as a player into the **Hockey Hall of Fame** in 1969. During his career 612 games played, he amassed 472 points, 189 **goals**, and 283 **assists**. After retirement, Abel became a radio and television color commentator for Detroit. His hockey talents were passed on to his grandson, Brent Johnson, who is a current **goaltender** for the **Pittsburgh Penguins**.

ADAMS, JOHN JAMES "JACK," "JOLLY JACK," "TRADER JACK". B. 14 June 1895, Fort William, Ontario. D. 1 May 1968, Detroit, Michigan. Jack Adams played **center** in the **National Hockey League (NHL)** and the **Pacific Coast Hockey Association** for the Toronto Arenas (1917–1919), **Vancouver Millionaires** (1919–1922), Toronto St. Patricks (1922–1926), and **Ottawa Senators** (1926–1927). He led the NHL in **penalty minutes**, with 64, in 1922–1923. His NHL career included 83 **goals** and 32 **assists** in 173 games played. Hockey fans also remember Adams as the **Detroit Red Wings' coach** and general manager for 36 years. Adams and Red Wings' owner James Norris Sr. were a strong and successful team. They were responsible for assembling a strong Detroit team, with such players as **Sid Abel, Alex Delvecchio, Gordie Howe, Red Kelly, Ted Lindsay,** and **Terry Sawchuk**. The Lindsay, Abel, Howe **line** became known as the "Production Line." It was this solid group of players who led the Red Wings to seven straight first-place season finishes from 1948–1955 and four **Stanley Cups**.

Adams holds the distinction as the only person to have his name engraved on the Stanley Cup as a player (1918, 1927), coach (1936–1937, 1943), and general manager (1936–1937, 1943, 1950, 1952, 1954–1955). He earned the **nickname** "Jolly Jack" as a player who was happy-go-lucky, but his nickname changed to "Trader Jack" because he was known for shaking things up to keep his Detroit team strong. Adams was inducted into the **Hockey Hall of Fame** in 1959 as a player. In 1963, he became president of the Central Professional Hockey League. The Adams Cup, named for him, is currently awarded annually to the regular-season champions of the Central Hockey League. In 1966, Adams was the first recipient of the **Lester Patrick Trophy** for his contribution to **ice** hockey in the **United States**. In 1974, the Jack Adams Award was created to recognize the coach of the year. The award is presented annually by the NHL Broadcasters Association.

AGITATION. Agitation is a tactic used by hockey players to interfere with their opponents' focus and rhythm on the **ice**. While **intimidators** frighten their opponents, agitators bother them with endless talking and taunting. Some well-known players with this skill include **Bobby Clarke,** Ulf Samuelsson, **Esa Tikkanen,** and **Dave "Tiger" Williams. Right wing Claude Lemieux** was so good at being an agitator that he earned the **nickname** "Superpest." *See also* PENALTY; PENALTY BOX "SIN BIN"; PENALTY KILLER; PENALTY MINUTES.

ALLAN CUP. In 1908, Montreal businessman and sportsman Sir H. Montague Allan donated a trophy to recognize amateur hockey in **Canada**. Although the **Stanley Cup** began as an amateur trophy, it was changed to honor professional teams. The Ottawa Cliffsides were the first recipients of the Allan Cup in 1908–1909, but they were then defeated by a challenge from the Queen's University team. In 1928, the Canadian Amateur Hockey Association accepted the Allan Cup as the symbol for the senior amateur hockey championship of Canada. The South East Prairie Thunder won the trophy in 2011–2012. They were presented with a copy of the trophy, because the original Allan Cup is on display at the **Hockey Hall of Fame**.

ALL-STAR TEAM. Midway through the regular season, the **National Hockey League (NHL)** holds an exhibition **match** to benefit the players' pension fund. The best players, or "All-Stars," from each position are assembled to form two teams. Hockey fans get the chance to see many of the top players at once. It has been played almost every year since the first official NHL All-Star Game occurred in **Maple Leaf Gardens** on 13 October 1947. Throughout the years, other benefit games have been played to raise money for specific causes. On 2 January 1908, the **Montreal Wanderers** and a team of All-Star players from the teams of the Eastern Canada Amateur Hockey Association had a game to raise money for the family of Wanderers' player **Hod Stuart**, who had drowned three months after the Wanderers won the **Stanley Cup** in 1907. On 14 February 1934, at Maple Leaf Gardens, the Toronto Maple Leafs played against an All-Star team made up of players from the other seven teams. This benefit was for **Ace Bailey** and his family following his **career-ending injury** from **Eddie Shore**. On 3 November 1937, a **Howie Morenz** Memorial Game was held to benefit his family after he passed away from complications of a broken leg received during a game. Another benefit was held for the family of **Babe Siebert**, a player with the **Montreal Canadiens** who had drowned. The Canadiens and **Montreal Maroons** organized a game on 29 October 1939, at the **Montreal Forum**, between the Canadiens and the "NHL All-Stars." Although the Canadiens lost, 5–2, a large sum of money was raised.

AMERICAN HOCKEY LEAGUE (AHL). The American Hockey League (AHL) is the **minor-league** division below the **National Hockey League (NHL)**. Each AHL team is connected to a NHL team. Many players drafted by a NHL team will hone their skills while playing for the AHL "farm team" and waiting for their chance to be called up to play in a NHL game. The current AHL evolved from the 1926–1927 Canadian Professional League, the International League, and the Canadian-American League. By 1936–1937, the International League had overtaken the other two and went from being called the International-American League to the current American Hockey League. Dave Andrews is the current president and chief executive officer of the AHL. He began that role in 1994, taking over from longtime president Jack Butterfield. Andrews was instrumental in increasing annual AHL attendance and operating the league with an all-time high of 30 teams for the 2010–2011 season. As a result, he was awarded the **Lester Patrick Trophy** in 2010.

ANAHEIM DUCKS. The Anaheim Ducks are a professional **ice** hockey team in the **Pacific Division** of the **National Hockey League (NHL) Western Conference**. Originally known as the Mighty Ducks of Anaheim, the club was founded in 1993 by The Walt Disney Company. They based the name based on the 1992 **movie** *The Mighty Ducks*. After the 2004–2005 **lockout**, Disney sold the franchise. The team name was changed to the Anaheim Ducks for the 2006–2007 season. In its NHL history, the team has made the **Stanley Cup** Finals twice. As the Mighty Ducks, they lost to the **New Jersey Devils** in 2003 (4–3). Anaheim's **goaltender**, John-Sebastien Giguere, faced **Martin Brodeur** of the Devils. Giguere won the **Conn Smythe Trophy** for his talent shown in the **Stanley Cup Playoffs**. He became only the fifth player in NHL history to win the trophy as a member of the losing team. Anaheim forward Rob Niedermayer played against his brother, **Scott Niedermayer**, who later joined the Ducks as a **defenseman**. During their first year with the new name, the Ducks went to the finals and beat the **Ottawa Senators** (4–1) to win their first and only Stanley Cup. Other notable players for the Ducks include Ryan Getzlaf; Paul Kariya; Scott Niedermayer; **Teemu Selänne**; and one **Hockey Hall of Famer, Jari Kurri**. There have been eight head **coaches** for the team. The franchise's first head coach was Ron Wilson, who coached them from 1993–1997. Randy Carlyle coached the team the longest (2005–2011). Former NHL player Bruce "Gabby" Boudreau joined the Ducks as coach in 2011–2012. The Anaheim Ducks won the **Clarence S. Campbell Bowl** twice (2002–2003, 2006–2007). In 18 seasons in the NHL, from 1993–1994 to 2011–2012, the Ducks have compiled a record of 638-605-107-94 (1,477 **points**) and made eight playoff appearances.

ANDERSON, GLENN CHRISTOPHER "ANDY". B. 2 October 1960, Vancouver, British Columbia. As a child, Glenn Anderson was not a hockey lover. He disliked the early morning practices and said, "The first **goal** I ever **scored** was in my own net." But he did want to play in the Winter Olympics, and he found his way there in 1980 as part of Team **Canada**. He was selected by the **Edmonton Oilers** in the 1979 **National Hockey League (NHL)** draft. Anderson was a left-handed **right wing** for 10 full seasons with the Oilers (1980–1991). He helped them win five **Stanley Cups**, in 1984, 1985, 1987, 1988, and 1990. After being crushed by the Oilers, 11–2, **Chicago Blackhawks' goaltender** Murray Bannerman said, "It seemed like Glenn Anderson scored while they were playing the national anthem." Anderson was known for being an abrasive but consistent player. He had 22 **points** in 22 **Stanley Cup Playoff** games when the Oilers won the Stanley Cup in 1990.

In 1992, he and goalie **Grant Fuhr** were traded to the **Toronto Maple Leafs**. Anderson became one of their top scorers and a playoff leader again as Toronto made it to within one game of the Stanley Cup Finals in 1993. In the middle of the 1993–1994 season, NHL commissioner **Gary Bettman** refused to allow Anderson to play in the 1994 Lillehammer **Olympic Games**. Before the 1994 playoffs, Anderson was traded to the **New York Rangers** for **Mike Gartner**. During those playoffs, he scored three goals, two of which were game winners. At the time, only **Maurice Richard** had more **overtime** playoff goals, and only **Mark Messier**, **Wayne Gretzky,** and **Jari Kurri** had more playoff points. With Anderson's help, the Rangers beat the **Vancouver Canucks** for their first Stanley Cup in 54 years, and his sixth. He briefly played with the **St. Louis Blues** and then back with the Oilers. Internationally, he played in the 1984 and 1987 **Canada Cup**, the 1989 and 1992 **World Ice Hockey Championships**, and the European professional hockey leagues in **Germany**, **Finland**, Italy, and **Switzerland**, before retiring in 1997. During his NHL career, Anderson played 1,129 games, scoring 498 goals, 601 **assists**, and 1,099 total points. After clearing up a long legal battle involving child support, Anderson was finally recognized for his hockey legacy in 2008, when he was inducted into the **Hockey Hall of Fame**.

APPS, JOSEPH SYLVANUS "SYL". B. 18 January 1915, Paris, Ontario. D. 24 December 1998, Kingston, Ontario. Syl Apps had many talents. He was the valedictorian of his high school, and he played football and hockey at McMaster University. Apps was also a pole vaulting champion, and he won a gold medal while representing **Canada** at the 1934 British Empire Games in London. At the 1936 Summer **Olympics** in **Germany**, he came in sixth place. Then he began his professional hockey career in the **National Hockey League (NHL)** as a star **center** for the **Toronto Maple Leafs** (1936–1943, 1945–1948). In 1937, Apps won the **Calder Trophy** for his **rookie** year. After replacing **Busher Jackson**, Toronto's **coach**, **Dick Irvin**, formed the D-A-D **line**, with **Gordie Drillon**, Apps, and Bob Davidson. With passes from Apps, Drillon led the NHL in scoring during the 1937–1938 season, with 26 **goals** and 26 **assists**, for 52 **points**. Apps finished in second place, with 21 goals and 29 assists, for 50 points. He played the entire 1941–1942 season without receiving a single **penalty**. As a gentleman on and off the **ice**, Apps was awarded the **Lady Byng Memorial Trophy** in 1942. **Conn Smythe** tried to inspire Apps to **fight** on the ice but was unsuccessful.

From 1943–1945, Apps left hockey to join the Canadian Army. After returning from service, he was the captain of the Maple Leafs during the NHL **All-Star** Game on 13 October 1947, at **Maple Leaf Gardens**. In 1948, he led the Leafs to first place and another **Stanley Cup,** his third. That same year, Apps retired from hockey and became a successful Canadian politician. From 1963–1980, he was a member of the Ontario Parliament. He was often called "the **Bobby Orr** of the pre–World War II era." Apps was inducted into the **Hockey Hall of Fame** in 1961. In 1975, he was elected to **Canada's Sports Hall of Fame.** His athletic talents were passed on to family members. His son, Syl Apps Jr., was also a center in the NHL and played a total of 10 seasons (1970–1980) with the **New York Rangers, Pittsburgh Penguins,** and **Los Angeles Kings.** His grandson, Darren Barber, won a gold medal at the 1992 Barcelona Olympics in a rowing event. His granddaughter, Gillian Apps, was a member of the **women's ice hockey** team of Canada and won gold medals at the 2006 and 2010 Winter Olympics.

ARBOUR, ALGER JOSEPH "RADAR," "AL". B. 1 November 1932, Sudbury, Ontario. Al Arbour was a **defenseman** in the **National Hockey League (NHL)** from 1953–1971 with the **Detroit Red Wings, Chicago Black Hawks, Toronto Maple Leafs,** and **St. Louis Blues.** Arbour helped each team, except the Blues, win the **Stanley Cup.** He is one of only 10 players in history to win the Stanley Cup with three different teams. The **nickname** "Radar" came from his appearance. He was one of the few professional athletes to wear glasses during **matches** and the last NHL player to wear them on the **ice.** Although Arbour was a good player, he was an even better **coach.** In 1970, Arbour became the coach of the St. Louis Blues, and he then joined the **New York Islanders** in June 1973. By making strong draft picks, Arbour drastically improved the team. In the 1975 **Stanley Cup Playoffs,** his team beat their rivals, the **New York Rangers.** They went on to defeat the **Pittsburgh Penguins,** but they lost in the semifinals to the Philadelphia Flyers in seven games. The Islanders made it to the semifinals for the following two years, only to be defeated by the **Montreal Canadiens.** Arbour also coached them to number one during the 1978–1979 NHL season. He became a four-time Stanley Cup–winning coach (1980–1983). Arbour retired from coaching following the 1985–1986 season but returned in 1988. He retired for a second time after the 1993–1994 season, with 739 games won as an Islander coach. On 3 November 2007, at the request of Islanders' coach Ted Nolan, 75-year-old Arbour returned to coach his 1,500th game for the Islanders, which made him the oldest man ever to coach a NHL game. The Islanders beat the Penguins 3–2, giving Arbour his 740th win. After **Scotty Bowman,** Arbour is second in NHL wins and games coached. He received both the **Jack Adams Award** (1979) and **Lester Patrick Trophy** (1992). In 1996, Arbour was inducted into the **Hockey Hall of Fame** as a **builder.**

ARMSTRONG, GEORGE EDWARD "CHIEF". B. 6 July 1930, Skead, Ontario. **Conn Smythe**, owner of the **Toronto Maple Leafs**, thought that George Armstrong would be a suitable replacement for **Syl Apps** when he retired. Armstrong had a two-game trial with the Leafs in 1949–1950, and he then played 20 games with them during the 1951–1952 season. Although he was not the best skater, he was a solid **right wing**, with a good two-way game and leadership skills. After teammate **Ted Kennedy** retired, Armstrong became Toronto's captain, and **Punch Imlach** became their **coach**. During this time, the Toronto Maple Leafs were at the top of their game, and the team won the **Stanley Cup** four times (1962–1964, 1967). On 2 May 1967, Armstrong **scored** the final **goal** of the **"Original Six"** Era in a Toronto 3–1 victory over the **Montreal Canadiens**. He retired after the 1969–1970 season but returned the following year. After 19 full seasons, he permanently retired with a career record of 1,187 games, 296 goals, 417 **assists**, and 713 total **points**. Armstrong was inducted into the **Hockey Hall of Fame** in 1975. After his playing days, he became a scout for the **Quebec Nordiques** (1978–1987) and coached the Maple Leafs for one season (1988–1989). The **nickname** "Chief" came from his Native American heritage. When asked if the **Chicago Black Hawks'** logo offended him he once replied, "When I was playing, it wasn't the Black Hawk crest that bothered me. It was **Bobby Hull's slapshot**."

ARMSTRONG, NEIL "IRONMAN". B. 29 December 1932, Plympton, Ontario. Neil Armstrong played hockey as a youth, but when he was offered a chance to officiate a game, he accepted, and he earned his certification. He had a long career as a **linesman** and **referee** in the **National Hockey League (NHL)** from 1957–1978. He was the **on-ice official** for 1,744 regular-season games and 208 **Stanley Cup Playoff** games, including 48 in the finals. Armstrong earned the **nickname** "Ironman" because he didn't miss a single assignment in 16 years. One of his more memorable games includes one when he was only 24 years old. On 17 November 1957, the **Boson Bruins** and **Toronto Maple Leafs** got into a fight near the end of the third period. Armstrong had broken it up, and then Boston's **Fernie Flaman** dangled his arm and screamed, "You broke my arm!" Armstrong was scared and didn't move, but Flaman soon started laughing and moving his arm normally. On 16 October 1973, Armstrong was honored for officiating his 1,314th game and breaking the previous record set by George Hayes. Throughout his career, he only had one serious **injury**. In 1971, Gary Dornhoefer fell along the **boards** near Armstrong, and his **hockey stick** cut Armstrong's hand and broke a bone. Armstrong was forced to wear a cast for three months, but he still didn't miss any games. He retired in 1978 and then worked as a scout for the **Montreal Canadiens**. During his hockey career, Armstrong also worked as a golf pro at the Sarnia Golf and Curling Club in the summer for two decades. He was elected to the **Hockey Hall of Fame** in 1991. His son, Doug Armstrong, was the general manager of the **Dallas Stars** and is a current executive with the **St. Louis Blues**.

ARTHUR, FREDERICK. *See* LORD STANLEY OF PRESTON, FREDERICK ARTHUR.

ART ROSS TROPHY. The Art Ross Trophy was donated by the general manager of the **Boston Bruins, Art Ross**, during the 1947–1948 season. It is awarded to the **National Hockey League**'s **(NHL)** leading **scorer** during the regular season. If two players finish the season with the same number of **points**, the trophy is awarded to the player with most **goals**, the player with fewer games played, or the player **scoring** first goal of the season, whichever comes first. In 1948, **Elmer Lach** was the first recipient, and **Wayne Gretzky** has won the trophy the most times (10). In 2011, Daniel Sedin of the **Vancouver Canucks** won the trophy after finishing the season with 104 points (41 goals, 63 **assists**). His twin **brother**, Henrik Sedin, also of the Canucks, won the award in 2009–2010, making it the first time in NHL history that brothers have won scoring titles in consecutive seasons. **Evgeni Malkin** of the **Pittsburgh Penguins** received the award in 2012.

ASSIST. An assist is credited to a player who passes or deflects the **puck** toward the **scoring** teammate or who touches it in any way that enables a **goal**. There can be a maximum of two assists per goal. **Wayne Gretzky** holds the record for the most assists in a **National Hockey League (NHL)** single season. In the 1985–1986 season, Gretzky had 163 assists. Only 13 times in the history of the NHL has a player ever had more than 100 assists in a season; Gretzky did it 11 times, and **Mario Lemieux** and **Bobby Orr** each did it once. Gretzky also set the record for the most career assists, with 1,963. It is rare to have 1,000 career assists, and, so far, in addition to Gretzky, it has only been accomplished by following other **Canadian**-born players: **Ray Bourque, Paul Coffey, Marcel Dionne, Ron Francis, Gordie Howe, Mark Messier, Adam Oates**, Joe Sakic, and **Steve Yzerman**. **Jaromír Jágr**, of the **Czech Republic**, is an active player for the **Philadelphia Flyers** who is close to reaching the 1,000 career assist milestone.

ATLANTA FLAMES. See CALGARY FLAMES.

ATLANTA THRASHERS. The Atlanta Thrashers (1999–2011) were a professional **ice** hockey team in the **National Hockey League (NHL)** based in Atlanta, Georgia. They started playing during the 1999–2000 NHL season as part of the **Southeast Division** of the **Eastern Conference**. They qualified for the **Stanley Cup Playoffs** only once (2006–2007) and were swept in the first round by the **New York Rangers**. The franchise was sold in May 2011, and the Atlanta Thrashers moved to Winnipeg, Manitoba. This marked the second life for the **Winnipeg Jets**. Atlanta became the first city in the NHL's modern era to lose two hockey teams. The city's previous NHL team, the Atlanta Flames, moved to Calgary, Alberta, in 1980, to become the **Calgary Flames**. In total, the Thrashers had a record of 342-437-45-78 (807 **points**). To date, no member of the Thrashers has been inducted into the **Hockey Hall of Fame**.

ATLANTIC DIVISION. In 1993, the **National Hockey League (NHL)** renamed the conferences and divisions to reflect their geographic locations. The Atlantic Division is one of the three sections of the **Eastern Conference** in the NHL. The **Northeast Division** and **Southeast Division** are the other two.

AVERY, SEAN CHRISTOPHER. B. 10 April 1980, North York, Ontario. In 2001–2002, Sean Avery played 36 games in the **National Hockey League (NHL)** as a **left wing** for the **Detroit Red Wings**. Detroit went on to win the **Stanley Cup** that season, but since he did not play in the **Stanley Cup Playoffs** or play the required 40 games, his name wasn't engraved on the cup. During the 2002–2003 season, Avery was traded to the **Los Angeles Kings**. In 2003–2004, he played 76 games for the Kings, scoring nine **goals** and 19 **assists**. He made a name for himself as an **agitator** who led the NHL in **penalty minutes**, with 261 that season. His confrontational personality played a role in his bouncing from the Los Angeles Kings (2003–2007), to the **New York Rangers** (2007–2008), to the **Dallas Stars** (2008), and back to the New York Rangers (2009–2012).

Avery often caused controversy with his public statements, which have resulted in fines and suspensions. He wanted to be noticed for both his hockey and his interest in fashion, for agitating in his sport and away from it. In 2008, he spent his NHL off-season as an intern at *Vogue*. The media made comparisons between him and Dennis Rodman. He was even a guest judge on *Project Runway All Stars*. On 14 March 2012, Avery announced that he was giving up hockey at the age of 31 to start a new career with an advertising agency. He left the NHL with an outrageous 1,512 penalty minutes, 87 goals, and 244 **points** in 565 career games. He set a record for the fastest goal **scored** by a Ranger on home **ice**, when he scored only 10 seconds into a game against the **Buffalo Sabres** on 16 February 2008. He will mainly be remembered for the NHL rule named for him. During a 13 April 2008 first-round playoff game against the **New Jersey Devils**, Avery faced **goaltender Martin Brodeur** during a two-man advantage on the **power play** and turned his back on the **puck**. He also waved his hands and **hockey stick** in front of Brodeur to distract him and block his view. The puck was cleared out of the Devils' zone, but on the Rangers' second offensive attack, Avery scored the power-play goal. The following day, the NHL issued an interpretation of the league's unsportsmanlike conduct rule to cover such actions. The Sean Avery rule would now result in a minor **penalty**.

B

BACKHAND. A backhand is a shot or pass made with the back side of the **hockey stick** blade. Although it is typically less accurate and less powerful than a **forehand** shot, it is more confusing to **goaltenders**. The backhand is often used on **breakaways** and **penalty** shots and in shootouts, and it is used for **dekeing**. **Left wing Busher Jackson** was known for his lethal backhand.

BAILEY, IRVINE WALLACE "ACE". B. 3 July 1903, Bracebridge, Ontario. D. 7 April 1992, Toronto, Ontario. Not to be confused with Garnet "Ace" Bailey (1948–2001), this Ace Bailey was a **right wing** for the **Toronto Maple Leafs** from 1926–1934. He was the **National Hockey League's (NHL)** leading **scorer** in 1928–1929, with 22 **goals** and 10 **assists** in 44 games. Bailey scored the **Stanley Cup** game-winning goal in Toronto's 6–4 victory over the **New York Rangers** on 9 April 1932, but his career was cut short when he suffered a **head injury** after **Boston Bruins defenseman Eddie Shore's tripping** on 12 December 1933. His condition was so severe that he received last rites from a priest, and his death notice was printed in a Boston newspaper. Bailey never held a grudge against Shore, saying, "It was just one of those things that happens." At the start of the 14 February 1934 **All-Star** benefit game for his family, Bailey showed his good sportsmanship by shaking hands with Shore at center **ice** in front of hockey fans. He became a **coach** at the University of Toronto (1935–1940, 1945–1949) and was a timekeeper at **Maple Leaf Gardens** for more than 40 years (1938–1984). When Bailey was about 70 years old, he asked the Leafs to allow Ron Ellis to wear his retired **jersey number** (6), because he respected the way he played the game. After Ellis retired in 1981, the number six was again retired by Toronto. Bailey was inducted into the **Hockey Hall of Fame** in 1975.

BAIN, DONALD HENDERSON "DAN". B. 14 February 1874, Belleville, Ontario. D. 15 August 1962, Winnipeg, Manitoba. Dan Bain was a **center** for the Winnipeg Victorias from 1895–1902. With his talent and leadership skills, he helped his team win the **Stanley Cup** in 1896 and 1901. Bain made history on 31 January 1901, when he **scored** the first Stanley Cup-winning

goal scored in **overtime** during a **match** with the Montreal Shamrocks (2–1). That same year, he also caused a stir by wearing a basic wooden **face mask** to protect his broken nose. The media labeled him the "Masked Man" for many years after his pioneering use of the **equipment**. Not only a strong hockey player, Bain was an all-around athlete, and he won numerous championships during a span of more than 35 years. He won the Manitoba three-mile roller skating title, he was a champion gymnast of Winnipeg, and he was the one-mile bicycle racing champion for three years in a row (1894–1896). He won the **Canadian** trap-shooting title in Toronto. He also won championships in speed skating, figure skating, snowshoeing, **lacrosse**, and golf. Bain was inducted into the **Hockey Hall of Fame** in 1945, as one of the 12 original inductees.

BAKER, HOBART AMERY HARE "HOBEY". B. 15 January 1892, Wissahickon, Pennsylvania. D. 21 December 1918, Toul, France. Hobey Baker was a **rover** for St. Paul's School (1906–1910), Princeton University (1910–1914), and New York St. Nicholas (1914–1916). He was such a dominant player that the teams he was on were often referred to as "Baker and six other players." In addition to being skilled in **ice** hockey, Baker also excelled in football, golf, track, swimming, and gymnastics. He joined the Lafayette Esquadrille flying unit during World War I. He survived the war, but shortly afterward he was involved in a fatal crash while testing a new plane. Since 1950, Princeton University has awarded the Hobey Baker Trophy to the "freshman hockey player who, among his classmates, in play, sportsmanship, and influence, has contributed most to the sport." The Hobey Baker Award was established in 1981, and it is awarded annually to the best **college hockey** player in the **National College Athletic Association**. Baker was elected to the **Hockey Hall of Fame** in 1945, as one of the 12 original inductees. He was one of the original inductees of the **U.S. Hockey Hall of Fame** in 1973. In 1975, he was inducted into the College Football Hall of Fame, and he is the only person to be in both the Hockey Hall of Fame and College Football Hall of Fame as a player. In 1987, Baker was awarded the **Lester Patrick Trophy**.

BANANA BLADE. *See* HOCKEY STICK.

BANTAMS. *See* YOUNG PLAYERS.

BARBER, WILLIAM CHARLES "BILL," "THE SWAN". B. 11 July 1952, Callander, Ontario. As a child, Bill Barber and his four **brothers** played hockey on the backyard **rink** that their father built. Barber credits the arm strength he brought to his professional career from all the snow shoveling he did on that rink. He was a **left wing** in the **National Hockey League (NHL)** for 12 seasons with the **Philadelphia Flyers** (1972–1984). Barber was part of the famous LCB **line**, along with Reggie Leach and **Bobby Clarke**. While Leach was famous for his quick shots, earning him the **nickname** "Rifle," Barber was a fast all-around player who was essential to their **scoring** success. Together, they helped the Flyers become the first expansion team to win the **Stanley Cup**, in 1974 and 1975. Barber was nicknamed "The Swan," because he could draw **penalties** from minor incidents by diving on the **ice** in an exaggerated manner.

Internationally, Barber played for **Canada** in the 1976 **Canada Cup**. In 1982, at the **World Ice Hockey Championships**, he was a leading **scorer**, with eight **goals**, and he helped Canada win a bronze medal. Away from hockey, he enjoyed the speed of motorcycles and stock car racing. During the regular seasons of his NHL playing career, he played in 903 games and had 420 goals and 463 **assists** for a total of 883 points. That included five seasons in which he scored 40 or more goals. During a 1982 game in Pittsburgh, Barber crashed into the **boards** while back **checking** an opponent, and his left knee was never the same again. After the 1983–1984 season, he applied his talents to **coaching** and scouting for **American Hockey League** teams in Philadelphia. He also had a management role with the **Tampa Bay Lightning** franchise from 2002–2008, before returning to Philadelphia as a scouting consultant. Barber was inducted into the **Hockey Hall of Fame** in 1990 as a player. As head coach, he led the Philadelphia Phantoms to the franchise's first **Calder Cup** Championship in 1998 and won the **Jack Adams Award** for 2000–2001.

BARILKO, WILLIAM "BILL," "BASHIN BILL". B. 25 March 1927, Timmins, Ontario. D. 26 August 1951, Cochrane, Ontario. Bill Barilko was a **defenseman** of Ukrainian heritage who played for the **National Hockey League (NHL)** with the **Toronto Maple Leafs** (1946–1951). **Conn Smythe** overlooked Barilko's youth because of his toughness and aggressive style of play. Smythe said that, "We want a hard, aggressive team with no **Lady Byngers**. I'm not interested in players who don't play to win." It was his aggressiveness on the **ice** that earned him the **nickname** of "Bashin Bill." He was famous for his snake-hip body checks. During his five NHL seasons, Barilko and the Maple Leafs won the **Stanley Cup** four times (1947–1949, 1951). His last **goal** came in the fifth game of the Stanley Cup Finals, on 21 April 1951, as he **scored** on a **backhander** in **overtime** to win the series against the strong **Montreal Canadiens**. Four months later, on 26 August 1951, Barilko and his dentist, Henry Hudson, never returned from a weekend fishing trip to Seal River, Quebec.

The mysterious disappearance of the single-engine plane led to rumors that the passengers had survived. On 6 June 1962, a helicopter pilot discovered the wreckage of the plane in Cochrane, Ontario, about 35 miles off their original course. Pilot inexperience, poor weather, and overloaded cargo were found to be the causes of the accident. The "Barilko Curse" was used to explain why the Maple Leafs never won a Stanley Cup during the 11 years that he was missing. In 1992, the Tragically Hip's song "Fifty Mission Cap" featured Barilko's story and the lack of another Leafs championship with the lyrics, "Bill Barilko disappeared, that summer, he was on a fishing trip. The last goal he ever scored, won the Leafs the cup. They didn't win another, 'til 1962, the year he was discovered."

BARRY, MARTIN "MARTY," "GOAL-A-GAME BARRY". B. 8 December 1905, Quebec City, Quebec. D. 20 August 1969, Halifax, Nova Scotia. Marty Barry was a **center** for the **New York Americans** (1927–1928), **Boston Bruins** (1929–1935), **Detroit Red Wings** (1935–1939), and **Montreal Canadiens** (1939–1940). The **nickname** "Goal-a-Game Barry" came from his consistent **scoring**. In fact, Barry often finished the season as one of the top five **National Hockey League (NHL)** players for **goals, assists,** and **points**. With the Bruins, he tallied five consecutive 20-goal seasons, from 1930–1935. He also only missed two **matches** during his first 10 seasons. On 30 June 1935, Barry was involved in a trade that sent him to Detroit, while former Bruin **Cooney Weiland** returned to Boston. As a member of the Red Wings, a strong forward **line** was formed with teammates **Herbie Lewis** and Larry Aurie. They helped Detroit win the **Stanley Cup** in 1936, and again in 1937. Not only did Barry lead the NHL **Stanley Cup Playoffs** in goals (4), assists (7), and points (11) in 1936–1937, he also **scored** the Stanley Cup-winning goal in Detroit's 3–0 victory over the **New York Rangers** on 15 April 1937. That same year, he was awarded the **Lady Byng Trophy**. After he retired, Barry became a **coach** for the Halifax St. Mary's **junior** team. He was inducted into the **Hockey Hall of Fame** in 1965.

BATHGATE, ANDREW JAMES "ANDY". B. 28 August 1932, Winnipeg, Manitoba. Andy Bathgate was a **right wing** with the **New York Rangers** (1952–1964), **Toronto Maple Leafs** (1963–1965), **Detroit Red Wings** (1965–1967), and **Pittsburgh Penguins** (1967–1968, 1970–1971) of the **National Hockey League (NHL)**. He also played one season for the Vancouver Blazers of the **World Hockey Association** (1974–1975). In his **rookie** year, he **scored** zero **goals** in 18 games with the Rangers, but he then won the Hart Trophy for being the Most Valuable Player during the 1958–1959 season. Bathgate was a clean player known for his **penalty-killing** abilities. He was also one of the players to use a curved **hockey stick** known as a "banana blade." Bathgate scared **goaltenders** with his **slapshot** and scored 349 goals during his career. On 1 November 1959, Bathgate's hard shot struck goaltender **Jacques Plante** in the face. After that incident, Plante became the first goalie to regularly wear a **face mask**. Bathgate was traded to the Maple Leafs in February 1964, and he scored the **Stanley Cup**-winning goal in Toronto's 4–0 win over the **Detroit Red Wings** on 25 April 1964. After a disagreement with **coach Punch Imlach**, he was traded to Detroit. He had a total of 973 **points** in his 1,069 regular-season games. He played hockey briefly in **Switzerland**, before returning to **coach** the Vancouver Blazers. Bathgate was inducted into the **Hockey Hall of Fame** in 1978.

BAUER, DAVID WILLIAM. B. 2 November 1924, Kitchener, Ontario. D. 9 November 1988, Goderich, Ontario. David Bauer was the younger **brother** of the **Boston Bruins' Bobby Bauer**. Although he played hockey himself, he made greater contributions to the sport as a **coach**. After his ordination as a priest in 1953, Bauer became a teacher and hockey coach for the St. Michael's College **junior** team, and then later at St. Mark's College. Father Bauer was also a coach and general manager for **Canada** in the 1968 Winter **Olympics**, and general manager in the 1965, 1966, 1967, and 1969 **World Ice Hockey Championships**. He managed the 1980 Canadian Olympic team as well. Father Bauer was inducted into the **Hockey Hall of Fame** in 1989 and the **International Ice Hockey Federation Hall of Fame** in 1997.

BAUER, ROBERT THEODORE "BOBBY". B. 16 February 1915, Waterloo, Ontario. D. 16 September 1964, Kitchener, Ontario. Bobby Bauer was the older **brother** of Father **David Bauer**, who also played hockey. Bobby was a **right wing** for nine seasons in the **National Hockey League (NHL)**, all with the **Boston Bruins** (1936–1942, 1945–1947, 1951–1952). Bauer was part of the famous **line** known as the "(Sauer) kraut Line," along with **Woody Dumart** and **Milt Schmidt**. Dumart gave Bobby the credit for being the brains of the line and making great plays. They helped the Bruins win the **Stanley Cup** in 1939 and 1941. On 12 April 1941, Bauer **scored** the Stanley Cup-winning **goal** against the Detroit Red Wings to sweep the series, 4–0. He was a recipient of the **Lady Byng Trophy** in 1940, 1941, and 1947. On 18 March 1952, Bauer came out of retirement for one game on the Bruins' "Kraut Line" and assisted on Schmidt's 200th career goal. After 327 NHL regular-season games and 260 **points**, Bauer retired for good. In 1952, he began **coaching** the Kitchener–Waterloo Dutchmen. As their coach, Bauer won a bronze medal at the 1956 Winter **Olympics** and a silver medal at the 1960 Olympic Games. He passed his coaching secrets on to his brother David, who became successful at St. Michael's College. For his great **ice** hockey playing, Bauer was inducted into the **Hockey Hall of Fame** in 1996.

BELFOUR, EDWARD JOHN "ED," "EDDIE THE EAGLE". B. 21 April 1965, Carman, Manitoba. On a hockey scholarship at the University of North Dakota, Ed Belfour was the winning **goaltender** for 29 out of 34 games. In 1988, he played in the **National Hockey League (NHL)** with the **Chicago Blackhawks**. His first few years were not his best, but, during the 1991–1992 season, he played 74 games and won 43 of them, with a 2.47 **goals** against average (GAA), 4 **shutouts**, and a .910 **save** percentage. That season, Chicago made it to the **Stanley Cup** Finals, but the team lost to the **Pittsburgh Penguins** in four straight games. **Coach** Mike Keenan and Belfour often clashed, and fans watched as Keenan routinely pulled Belfour from the **net**. For the 1996–1997 season, Belfour played for the **San Jose Sharks**, before joining the **Dallas Stars** (1997–2002). With Belfour at the net, the Dallas Stars won their first Stanley Cup after beating the **Buffalo Sabres**, 4–2, in 1999. In 2002, Belfour was a member of **Canada**'s gold medal-winning team at the Salt Lake City **Olympics**. That same year, he joined the **Toronto Maple Leafs**, and, in 2005, Belfour passed **Terry Sawchuk** for second place in all-time wins by a goalie. He finished his playing career with the **Florida Panthers** (2006–2007) and then joined a team in **Sweden** for a year.

Belfour's NHL career included 963 regular-season games. He won 484, lost 320, tied 125, and had 14 **overtime** losses. He had 76 shutouts and finished with a GAA of 2.50 and a save percentage of .906. In recognition of his talent, he won the **Vezina Trophy** twice and the **William M. Jennings Trophy** four times. During his career, when it was available, Belfour wore **jersey number** 20 to honor his childhood hero, **Vladislav Tretiak**. Belfour also had an eagle painted on the side of his **face mask** to represent his **nickname**, "Eddie the Eagle." No one was ever allowed to touch his **equipment**, due to his **superstition**. Belfour was inducted into the **Hockey Hall of Fame** in 2011.

BÉLIVEAU, JEAN ARTHUR "LE GROS BILL". B. 31 August 1931, Trois Rivieres, Quebec. Jean Béliveau was the oldest of eight children, and his family had a backyard **rink**, where he played **pond hockey** with the **young players** in the neighborhood. Béliveau was known for his stickhandling expertise, and he showed his talent at a young age. His family turned down an offer of a **minor league** pro contract for him at the age of 15. Béliveau happily played for the Quebec Aces in the Quebec Senior Hockey League (QSHL) alongside **Herb Carnegie**. The Aces were part of the amateur league, which was very strong in **Canada**, and they paid their players well. Béliveau was earning $20,000 a year and had no desire to leave. **Montreal Canadiens**' general manager Frank Selke really wanted Béliveau to play for them, so he had the franchise owners purchase the entire QSHL. This forced Béliveau to play for the Canadiens in the 1953–1954 **National**

Hockey League (NHL) season. He remained with them for eighteen seasons, until he retired after the 1970–1971 Stanley Cup-winning season. As a player, Béliveau won the Stanley Cup 10 times, and, as an executive, he was part of another seven championship teams, the most Stanley Cup victories by an individual in NHL history.

Béliveau was 6 feet, 3 inches tall and weighed 210 pounds and nicknamed after a hero from Québécois folklore, "Le Gros Bill." In 1955, he was the first hockey player to be featured on the cover of *Sports Illustrated*. He won both the Art Ross Trophy and the Hart Trophy in 1956, also the same year he won his first Stanley Cup. In 1957, Béliveau appeared in full uniform on the American game show *To Tell the Truth*. In 1964, he won the Hart Memorial Trophy, and he was then the first recipient of the Conn Smythe Trophy the following year. Béliveau was a powerful skater and a great passer and playmaker, but he also had a quiet confidence that made him well-liked by fans, teammates, and even his opponents.

When Béliveau retired, he was the Montreal's all-time leader in points and second all-time in goals and the NHL's all-time leading playoff scorer. He scored 507 goals and had 712 assists for 1,219 points in 1,125 NHL regular-season games, plus 79 goals and 97 assists for 176 points in 162 playoff games. His jersey number (4) was retired by the Canadiens. After retiring, he remained with the Canadiens as an executive and goodwill ambassador. Béliveau's name appears on the Stanley Cup a record 17 times. He was inducted into the Hockey Hall of Fame in 1972 as a player. Along with Wayne Gretzky and Mario Lemieux, he was one of the best centers in NHL history.

BENEDICT, CLINTON STEVENSON "CLINT," "PRAYING BENNIE". B. 26 September 1892, Ottawa, Ontario. D. 12 November 1976, Ottawa, Ontario. Clint Benedict was a goaltender in the National Hockey League (NHL) with the Ottawa Senators (1912–1924) and Montreal Maroons (1924–1930). He led the NHL in wins numerous times, with 12 in 1917–1918, 19 in 1919–1920, 14 in 1920–1921, 14 in 1921–1922, 14 in 1922–1923, and 15 in 1923–1924. Prior to 19 January 1918, when the NHL made a rule to allow goalies to fall to their knees to make a save, Benedict would pretend to lose his balance and fall on the puck or act like he was praying, preventing the goal and avoiding the penalty and fine. That is how he earned his nickname, "Praying Bennie." Once when Benedict was assessed a penalty, defenseman Sprague Cleghorn briefly minded the net in a 4–3 win against the Toronto Maple Leafs. Benedict was the first goaltender to win the Stanley Cup with two different teams, Ottawa (1920–1921, 1922–1923) and Montreal (1925–1926).

During the 1923–1924 season, Benedict developed a drinking problem, which the Senators kept hidden from the public. When management kept part of his salary, Benedict sued them, and the media learned of the secret. On 20 October 1924, he was traded to the Maroons. Benedict then set NHL records for **shutouts**, with four during the 1926 **Stanley Cup Playoffs**, including three consecutive ones. He was also credited as the first goaltender in the NHL to wear a **face mask**. On 20 February 1930, while playing for the Montreal Maroons he wore a crudely made leather mask to protect his broken cheekbone. Unfortunately, it kept coming loose, and the large nosepiece obstructed his vision, so he stopped wearing it. When a shot by **Howie Morenz injured** Benedict later that season, he retired. In recognition of his hockey contributions, Benedict was finally inducted into the **Hockey Hall of Fame** in 1965.

BENTLEY, DOUGLAS WAGNER "DOUG". B. 3 September 1916, Delisle, Saskatchewan. D. 24 November 1972, Saskatoon, Saskatchewan. Doug Bentley played **left wing** and **center** in the **National Hockey League (NHL)** with the **Chicago Black Hawks** (1939–1944, 1945–1952) and **New York Rangers** (1953–1954). During the 1942–1943 season, Doug and his **brothers**, Max and Reggie, were the NHL's first all-brother **line**. On 28 January 1943, Max **scored** four **goals** in one period in a game against the Rangers, with Doug **assisting** on all four. From 1945–1948, Chicago had the "Pony Line," made up of Doug, **Max Bentley**, and **Bill Mosienko**. They were small but fast, and exciting to watch. Doug led Chicago in **points**, with 57, during the 1947–1948 season. After Max went to the **Toronto Maple Leafs**, Doug wanted to quit the sport, but he stayed on for four more NHL seasons. Unfortunately, he never played on a **Stanley Cup** championship team. He finished his career with 543 points, one less than Max. He became a **coach** for the Saskatoon Quakers but came out of retirement during the 1953–1954 season to help Max and the Rangers drive toward a spot in the **Stanley Cup playoffs**. In his first game, Doug scored a goal and had three assists, and the Rangers won, 8–3, but they didn't make the playoffs. Doug was inducted into the **Hockey Hall of Fame** in 1964.

BENTLEY, MAXWELL HERBERT LLOYD "MAX," "PINOCCHIO," "DIPSY DOODLE DANDY FROM DELISLE". B. 1 March 1920, Delisle, Saskatchewan. D. 19 January 1984, Saskatoon, Saskatchewan. Max Bentley had several **nicknames**. He was called "Pinocchio," because of his large nose, and the "Dipsy Doodle Dandy from Delisle." That one referred to his fast **skating**, great stickhandling, and the name of his hometown. **Doug Bentley** was a **center** in the **National Hockey League (NHL)** with the **Chicago Black Hawks** (1939–1944, 1945–1952) and **New York Rangers**

(1953–1954). During the 1942–1943 season, Max and his **brothers**, Doug and Reggie, were the NHL's first all-brother **line**. On 28 January 1943, Max **scored** four **goals** in one period in a game against the Rangers, with Doug **assisting** on all four. This tied the record set by **Busher Jackson** on 20 November 1934. Max also won the **Lady Byng Trophy** that year. From 1945–1948, Chicago had the "Pony Line," consisting of Max, Doug Bentley, and **Bill Mosienko**. Max was the Black Hawks' first Hart Trophy winner as the NHL's Most Valuable Player in 1945–1946. He also won the **Art Ross Trophy** as the top scorer that year and again in 1946–1947. Max won three **Stanley Cups** (1948, 1949, and 1951). He spent his final NHL season playing for the Rangers with Doug in 1953–1954, and he then retired. Max finished his career with 544 **points**, one more than Doug. In 1966, Max was inducted into the **Hockey Hall of Fame**.

BERENSON, GORDON ARTHUR "RED" "THE RED BARON". B. 8 December 1939, Regina, Saskatchewan. Red Berenson, **nicknamed** "Red" for his hair color, played **college hockey** at the University of Michigan while he earned his undergraduate degree. Then he was a **center** for a total of 17 seasons in the **National Hockey League (NHL)** with the **Montreal Canadiens** (1961–1966), **New York Rangers** (1966–1967), **St. Louis Blues** (1967–1971, 1974–1978), and **Detroit Red Wings** (1971–1974). Berenson continued to study in the off-season and earned a master's degree in business administration. The Rangers' **coach, Emile Francis**, once said that, "If I ever see him read a book on the bus again, I'm going to throw him off." He helped his team win the **Stanley Cup** in 1965 and 1966. On 7 November 1968, Berenson **scored** six **goals** in an 8–0 victory against the **Philadelphia Flyers**. He became the first player to score that many goals in a road game. Altogether, in 17 NHL seasons, Berenson recorded 261 goals and 397 assists in 987 games.

In the off-season, Berenson was involved in two dangerous boating incidents. He was lost in the fog once and almost drifted over a waterfall on another occasion. After he retired from playing, Berenson became a coach for the St. Louis Blues (1979–1982) and won the **Jack Adams Award** in 1981. In 1984, he became the men's hockey coach at the University of Michigan, and he is still coaching the Wolverines 28 years later. Berenson has led the Wolverines to 11 Frozen Four appearances and **National Collegiate Athletic Association (NCAA)** championships in 1996 and 1998. His squads have qualified for the NCAA Tournament in each of the last 21 seasons, the longest streak ever in college hockey history. His all-time record as Michigan's head coach is 749-350-77, a record that currently places him fifth in NCAA history for career victories. For his hockey contributions, Berenson received the **Lester Patrick Trophy** in 2006.

BETTMAN, GARY BRUCE. B. 2 June 1952, Queens, New York. Gary Bettman graduated from Cornell University and New York University School of Law. He served as a senior vice president and general counsel to the National Basketball Association. On 1 February 1993, Bettman became the first **National Hockey League (NHL)** commissioner, replacing Gil Stein, who served as the NHL's final president. In 1999, prior to **Wayne Gretzky**'s retirement, Bettman announced that because the **jersey number 99** had become so associated with Gretzky, it would be retired by the entire NHL. In 2001, he received the **Lester Patrick Trophy** for his contributions to the sport; however, Bettman has often been criticized for attempting to "Americanize" the game and expanding the league into nontraditional hockey markets at the expense of the more traditional markets in **Canada** and the Northern **United States**. Under his direction, the **Nashville Predators** (1998), **Atlanta Thrashers** (1999), **Minnesota Wild** (2000), and **Columbus Blue Jackets** (2000) franchises were added, bringing the NHL to 30 teams. In addition, during the 1990s, he relocated four teams: the Minnesota North Stars to Dallas (1993), the **Quebec Nordiques** to Denver (1995), the **Winnipeg Jets** to Phoenix (1996), and the Hartford Whalers to North Carolina (1997). He was also a main figure in the 1994–1995 and 2004–2005 NHL **lockouts**, which upset many hockey fans. For the 2008–2009 season, Bettman was paid $7.23 million by the NHL, of which $5,529,490 was his base salary.

BILL MASTERTON MEMORIAL TROPHY. While playing for the Minnesota North Stars, **Bill Masterton** was body **checked** and fell unconscious after hitting his head on the **ice**. He died two days later, on 15 January 1968. Masterton was the first fatality in the history of the **National Hockey League (NHL)**. In his honor, at the end of the 1967–1968 season, the NHL introduced the Bill Masterton Memorial Trophy. It is awarded to the player who best exhibits the perseverance, dedication, and sportsmanship Masterton embodied. The first recipient was Claude Provost, and there have not been any multiple winners. **Defenseman** Bryan Berard won this award in 2004, because he persevered after a potentially **career-ending injury** to his eye in 2000. Jose Theodore of the **Washington Capitals** (2010), Ian Laperriere of the **Philadelphia Flyers** (2011), and Max Pacioretty of the **Montreal Canadiens** (2012) are the most recent recipients of this trophy.

BISCUIT. *See* PUCK.

BLAKE, HECTOR "TOE," "OLD LAMPLIGHTER". B. 21 August 1912, Victoria Mines, Ontario. D. 17 May 1995, Montreal, Quebec. "Toe" Blake earned his **nickname** as a child, when his younger sister pronounced his name, "Hec-toe." He was later called "Old Lamplighter," because he often activated the **goal light** by frequently **scoring goals**. Blake was a **left wing** with the **Hamilton Tigers** (1932–1934), **Montreal Maroons** (1934–1935), and **Montreal Canadiens** (1935–1948). In 1939, he was the leading **scorer** in the **National Hockey League (NHL)**, and he also won the Hart Trophy. He helped the Maroons win the **Stanley Cup** in 1935. He was also a member of the famous Canadiens' **line**, the Punch Line, with **Maurice Richard** and **Elmer Lach**. For his last eight seasons with the Canadiens, Blake was the team captain, and he led them to Stanley Cups in 1944 and 1946. In 1946, he received the **Lady Byng Trophy** for his sportsmanship. After his playing career ended, Blake had a successful **coaching** career. In 1955, he replaced **Dick Irvin** as head coach of the Montreal Canadiens. Blake was the coach who told **Jacques Plante** that he wasn't allowed to wear a **face mask** because it would block his vision. Plante insisted and changed the sport of hockey. Blake coached the Canadiens for 13 years and helped them win eight Stanley Cups. His record was broken by **Scotty Bowman**, who coached his teams to a total of nine cups. In 1966, Blake was inducted to the **Hockey Hall of Fame** as a player.

BLUE LINE. The blue line in **ice** hockey has existed since 1918. The blue line runs across the width of the **rink**, on each side of the **red line**. The distance from each **goal** line and their width has changed throughout history. Currently, the blue lines are 12 inches wide and 60 feet from each goal line. For the team defending the goal, the area between the goal line and the blue line is the **defensive** zone, and for the opponents it is the attacking zone. The area between the blue lines is the neutral zone.

See also OFFSIDES.

BOARDING. When a player is thrown violently into the **boards** of the **rink** by an opponent who takes more than one stride to reach and **check** his man, it is called boarding. The **on-ice official** pounds a closed fist of one hand into the open palm of the other hand to signal this foul. It is often a major **penalty** due to the likelihood of **injury** sustained by the player who was boarded. The **referee** uses his discretion as to whether to call a game misconduct on the offending player. In the **National Hockey League (NHL)**, if no injury is sustained, then a minor penalty will be called. In **college hockey**, the player does not need to be injured for it to be considered a major penalty. Any player in the NHL who incurs a total of two game misconducts for boarding in the regular season or in the **Stanley Cup Playoffs** is suspended for the next game.

BOARDS. The wooden wall that encloses the inside of an **ice** hockey **rink** is known as the boards. It is between three and four feet high, and a protective screen or unbreakable glass runs along the top to protect the fans from a stray **puck**. Prior to the protective glass rule in 1966–1967, fans would often interfere with the players along the boards.

See also BOARDING.

BODY CHECKING. *See* CHECKING.

BOON, RICHARD ROBINSON "DICKIE". B. 10 January 1878, Belleville, Ontario. D. 3 May 1961, Montreal, Quebec. Dickie Boon was a proficient speed **skater**, and he won the 1892 Junior Amateur Championship. He also participated in other sports, including rowing and canoeing. As a **young player**, Boon played hockey with **Mike Grant** in Montreal. He was a **defenseman** for the Montreal Amateur Athletic Association team. When they defeated the Winnipeg Victorias in a thrilling three-game series to win the **Stanley Cup**, they earned the **nickname** "Little Men of Iron," because they hung on for a 2–1 victory in the final game. He was recruited by the **Montreal Wanderers** of the Federal Amateur Hockey League when they were formed in 1903. During his playing career, from 1899–1905, Boon was known as the first player to use the poke **check**, which he used successfully in stopping opposing forwards. He was a player and manager of the Wanderers from 1903–1905, before focusing on just managing them from 1905–1916. He led them to four Stanley Cups (1906, 1907, 1908, 1910). In 1910, Boon and **Jimmy Gardner** were instrumental in setting up the **National Hockey Association**. After his hockey retirement, Boon became a cofounder of a coal business. He also played golf and participated in curling, and the Outremont Curling Club's Boon Trophy was named for him. His niece, Lucille Wheeler-Vaughan, became a world skiing champion. Boon was inducted into the **Hockey Hall of Fame** in 1952 as a player.

BOSSY, MICHAEL DEAN "MIKE". B. 22 January 1957, Montreal, Quebec. Mike Bossy played **right wing** in the **National Hockey League (NHL)** with the **New York Islanders** from 1977–1987. He was rarely **penalized**, because early in his career he made the decision not to retaliate. He once said that, "Each time you knock me down, I'll get up and **score** more **goals**." That is exactly what he did by scoring 573 goals in only 10 seasons. Bossy became the first **rookie** to score 50 goals in the regular season (1977–1978), and he won the **Calder Memorial Trophy**. He scored 50 or more goals in nine consecutive seasons. He scored 60 or more goals five times. Both records have since been matched by **Wayne Gretzky**. On 24 January 1981, Bossy tied **Maurice Richard**'s record of 50 goals in 50 games. During the

1981–1982 season, he set a record for a right wing, with 83 **assists**. That same season, he also set a record for the most **power play** goals (nine) during the **Stanley Cup Playoffs**, which **Cam Neely** has since tied. Bossy was known for his "faster than a speeding bullet" shot that scared **goaltenders**. In 1982, he won the **Conn Smythe Trophy**. For his sportsmanship, he won the **Lady Byng Memorial Trophy** in 1983, 1984, and 1986. He and **center Bryan Trottier** helped their team win the **Stanley Cup** in 1980, 1981, 1982, and 1983. Bossy scored the Stanley Cup–winning goals in 1982 against the **Vancouver Canucks**, and in 1983 against the **Edmonton Oilers**. He played on the **Canadian** team in the 1981 and 1984 **Canada Cups**. Chronic back pain caused him to retire in 1987. Bossy was inducted into the **Hockey Hall of Fame** in 1991.

BOSTON BRUINS. The Boston Bruins are a professional **ice** hockey team in the **Northeast Division** of the **National Hockey League (NHL) Eastern Conference**. The franchise began in 1924, and it is the oldest team based in the **United States**. From 1928–1995, the Bruins played at **Boston Garden**. Their current home arena is TD Garden, also in Boston. The Bruins were one of the **"Original Six"** teams, a term used to describe the teams that made up the NHL from 1942 until the 1967 expansion. In 1924, businessman Charles Adams convinced the NHL to expand to the United States and grant him a franchise in Boston. **Art Ross** became the team's general manager, and sometimes **coach**, for the next 30 years. On 1 December 1924, the Boston Bruins played their first NHL match against the **Montreal Maroons** at Boston Arena and won, 2–1. In 1929, the Bruins defeated the **New York Rangers** to win their first **Stanley Cup**. Star players from that team included **Dit Clapper**, Dutch Gainor, **Harry Oliver**, **Eddie Shore**, and goaltender **Tiny Thompson**. In the 1930s, goaltender **Frank Brimsek**, Mel Hill, **Babe Siebert**, and **Cooney Weiland** also played for the team. The Bruins also had the high-scoring **line** known as the "Kraut Line," with **center Milt Schmidt**, **right wing Bobby Bauer**, and **left wing Woody Dumart**.

In 1954, the Bruins became one of the first teams to order an ice resurfacer from **Frank Zamboni**. The Bruins' Zamboni Model E, factory serial number 21, which was used up until the 1980s as a backup, can now be seen at the **Hockey Hall of Fame**. On 18 January 1958, **Willie O'Ree** made history as the first black player in the NHL, when he played for the Bruins. The Bruins hold the record for the most consecutive **Stanley Cup Playoff** appearances. They made the playoffs every season from 1968–1996, for a total of 29 straight years. Other great Boston players include **Ray Bourque**, Johnny Bucyk, **Zdeno Chára**, goalie **Gerry Cheevers**, **Phil Esposito**, **Cam Neely**, **Bobby Orr**, and Tim Thompson. The Bruins won six Stanley Cup championships sporadically (1929, 1939, 1941, 1970, 1972, 2011).

Their most recent win was in 2011, when they defeated the **Vancouver Canucks** in seven games. Boston became the first team in NHL history to win the seventh game three times in the same playoffs. Hockey Hall of Famer Cam Neely was the president of the franchise, and it was their first Stanley Cup championship since 1972. Ray Bourque played 20 seasons with the Bruins (1979–1999), until he was traded to the **Colorado Avalanche** franchise at his request so he could have a chance of winning the Stanley Cup before retiring. Colorado won the cup in 2001, and then Bourque retired. Sportscaster Dan Kelly called the Bruins' most famous **goal** in hockey history. It was Bobby Orr's Stanley Cup–winning **overtime** goal in 1970. Kelly yelled, "Bobby Orr . . . behind the **net** to Sanderson to OOOORR! BOBBY OOOORR! . . . **scores** and the Boston Bruins have won the Stanley Cup!" In 1990, the team won the **Presidents' Trophy**. In 87 seasons in the NHL (1924–1925 to 2011–2012), the Boston Bruins have compiled a record of 2,856-2,207-791-106 (6,609 **points**) and made 67 playoff appearances.

BOSTON GARDEN. Boston Garden was one of the six original **National Hockey League (NHL)** arenas. It was located in Boston, Massachusetts, and was home to the **Boston Bruins** from 1928–1995. The first NHL regular-season game was held on 20 November 1928, between the Bruins and the **Montreal Canadiens**, and it was won by the Canadiens, 1–0. The **match** was attended by 17,000 fans, with 2,000 over capacity. Fans without tickets stormed their way in, and windows and doors were broken during the chaos. Because the arena was built prior to the 1929–1930 NHL season, the **rink** was grandfathered into the rules. The rink at Boston Garden was 191 feet by 88 feet, instead of the 200-foot by 85-foot regulation-size one. Boston Garden was the first arena to host the **Stanley Cup** Finals and National Basketball Association Finals at the same time in 1957, and again in 1958 and 1974. The Bruins' Stanley Cup Finals appearances in 1988 and 1990 were both disrupted by power outages. On 24 May 1988, a power transformer blew up during Game 4 of the finals between the Bruins and the **Edmonton Oilers**, and the match was ruled a 3–3 tie. Two years later, on 15 May 1990, the lights went out during an **overtime** finals game between the same two teams. After the lights were turned back on, the Oilers won, 3–2, in triple overtime. The last official game played at Boston Garden was on 14 May 1995. It was Game 5 of a NHL **Eastern Conference** quarterfinal series between the Boston Bruins and **New Jersey Devils**. The Devils beat the Bruins, 3–2, winning the series four games to one. The last event ever held at the facility was a preseason game between the Boston Bruins and Montreal Canadiens, on 28 September 1995.

See also ORIGINAL ARENAS.

BOUCHARD, EMILE JOSEPH "BUTCH". B. 4 September 1919, Montreal, Quebec. Before playing professional hockey, Butch Bouchard was an entrepreneur in high school. He purchased a bee ranch and made it so successful that he was able to purchase his parents a house. He used his business skills to negotiate a larger contract than fellow Canadiens **Elmer Lach** and **Kenny Reardon**. Bouchard was a **defenseman** who played 15 seasons in the **National Hockey League (NHL)** with the **Montreal Canadiens** (1941–1956). He served as the team captain from 1948–1956. Bouchard was known for his large size, physical play, and defensive plays. He lifted weights to improve his upper arm strength. Bouchard was good at body **checking**, but he played cleanly. Bouchard and **Doug Harvey** worked together as a stong backline pair. Bouchard won the **Stanley Cup** in 1944, 1946, 1953, and 1956. He recorded 49 **goals**, 144 **assists**, 193 **points**, and 863 **penalty minutes** in 785 NHL regular-season games, plus he recorded 11 goals, 21 assists, 32 points, and 0 penalty minutes in 113 **Stanley Cup Playoff** games. The **nickname** "Butch" came from a teammate in the **juniors** who said his last name was similar to the word "butcher." Interestingly, when Bouchard retired from hockey, he bought a beet farm and opened a restaurant in Montreal named Chez Butch. Bouchard was inducted into the **Hockey Hall of Fame** in 1996.

BOUCHER, FRANÇOIS-XAVIER "FRANK," "RAFFLES". B. 7 October 1901, Ottawa, Ontario. D. 12 December 1977, Ottawa, Ontario. Frank Boucher was the youngest son in a family of six sons and two daughters. He was one of four brothers who played in the **National Hockey League (NHL)**. His brother, **George Boucher**, played for the **Ottawa Senators** during the 1920s and won four **Stanley Cups**. Brothers Bobby and Billy also played in the NHL. Frank's nephew, Sgt. Frank Boucher, George's son, was the head **coach** of **Canada**'s 1948 **Olympic** gold medal-winning **ice** hockey team. Frank inherited some of his athletic ability from his father Tom, who played rugby for the Ottawa Rough Riders, winning Canadian championships in 1894, 1896, 1897, and 1901. Tom played on a team with Tom "King" Clancy, whose son was hockey player **King Clancy**.

Frank played 18 professional hockey seasons as a **center** for the **Ottawa Senators** (1921–1922) and **New York Rangers** (1926 1944) of the NHL. He also played for the Vancouver Maroons (1922–1926), originally part of the **Pacific Coast Hockey Association**. Frank played on the Rangers' **line** known as the "Bread Line," with brothers Bill Cook and **Bun Cook**. Together, they won the Stanley Cup in 1928 and 1933. Frank even **scored** the Stanley Cup–winning **goal** in the 2–1 victory over the **Montreal Maroons** on 14 April 1928. The **nickname** "Raffles" came from a literary character who was a gentlemanly thief. Frank had the ability to poke **check** and steal the **puck**, all while playing a clean game. In fact, he won the **Lady Byng**

Trophy seven times in eight seasons from 1928–1935, with **Joe Primeau** winning in 1932. As a result, Frank was given the original trophy to keep. He also coached the Rangers (1939–1949, 1953–1954) and was the first NHL coach to pull his goalie in favor of an extra forward with two minutes to go in a 1939–1940 regular-season game. Frank was inducted into the **Hockey Hall of Fame** in 1958. In 1973, he wrote *When the Rangers Were Young*, a book about his hockey experiences. In 1993, he was awarded the **Lester Patrick Trophy** posthumously.

BOUCHER, JOHN GEORGE "BUCK". B. 19 August 1896, Ottawa, Ontario. D. 17 October 1960, Ottawa, Ontario. George Boucher was a solid football player before he switched to **ice** hockey. He was the older **brother** of **Frank Boucher**, who also had a long career in the **National Hockey League (NHL)**. Their other brother, Billy Boucher, played with the **Montreal Canadiens** and **New York Americans** (1921–1928), and Bobby Boucher played one season with the Canadiens (1923–1924). George was a professional hockey player in the NHL for 17 seasons with the **Ottawa Senators** (1915–1929), **Montreal Maroons** (1928–1931), and **Chicago Black Hawks** (1931–1932). George began as a forward, but he then switched to **defenseman** in his third season. He was partnered with **King Clancy**, and together they formed one of the toughest and most effective duos in the league. George was a leader in **assists** (10) in 1923–1924 and **penalty minutes** (95) in 1924–1925. He was known for his excellent stickhandling skills, and he helped his team win the **Stanley Cup** in 1920, 1921, 1923, and 1927. During his career of 486 regular-season games, he recorded 136 **goals**, 93 assists, 229 **points**, and had 927 penalty minutes. George also had a long **coaching** career with the Maroons (1930–1931), Senators (1933–1934), **St. Louis Eagles** (1934–1935), and **Boston Bruins** (1949–1950). George's son, Sgt. Frank Boucher, was the head **coach** of **Canada**'s 1948 **Olympic** gold medalwinning ice hockey team. In 1960, George was inducted into the **Hockey Hall of Fame** while he was battling throat cancer. He was presented his Hall of Fame insignia at his hospital bed. After a courageous six-year battle, George passed away three weeks later.

BOURQUE, RAYMOND JEAN "RAY". B. 28 December 1960, Montreal, Quebec. Ray Bourque was a **d efenseman** in the **National Hockey League (NHL)** for 20 seasons with the **Boston Bruins** (1979–1999). In March 2000, he was traded to the **Colorado Avalanche** franchise at his request so he could have a chance of winning the **Stanley Cup** before retiring. After falling in the **Western Conference** Finals in 2000, Bourque signed with Colorado for a second season. In a feat called "Mission 16W," the Avalanche defeated the **New Jersey Devils** in seven games to win the Stanley Cup in

June 2001. Bourque finally had the championship he had been chasing for 22 seasons, and he then retired. He holds the NHL record for most career shots-on-goal, with 6,206. During his career, he played in 1,612 regular-season games and recorded 410 **goals**, 1,169 **assists**, 1,579 **points**, and 1,141 **penalty minutes**. Bourque always used several pairs of **gloves** during **matches** due to heavy sweating. He had a **superstition** about changing his **skate** laces during each intermission and throwing them all out at the end of each game. Also, in the 1980s, he wished his **goaltender** "good luck" by tapping him four times on his pads. The Bruins won that game, and Bourque added that ritual to his others. Internationally, Bourque played for **Canada** in the 1981, 1984, and 1987 **Canada Cups**. He was also a member of the 1998 **Canadian Men's Olympic Ice Hockey Team**, which won a silver medal. His other awards include the **Calder Memorial Trophy** (1980), **James Norris Memorial Trophy** (1987, 1988, 1990, 1991, 1994), **King Clancy Memorial Trophy** (1992), and **Lester Patrick Trophy** (2003). Bourque was inducted into both the **Hockey Hall of Fame** (2004) and **Canada's Sports Hall of Fame** (2011).

BOWER, JOHN WILLIAM "JOHNNY," "THE CHINA WALL". B. 8 November 1924, Prince Albert, Saskatchewan. Johnny Bower's name at birth was John Kiszkan, but he changed it legally as a young adult. Bower played in the **minor leagues** before becoming a **goaltender** in the **National Hockey League (NHL)** with the **New York Rangers** (1953 1955, 1956 1957) and **Toronto Maple Leafs** (1958–1970). He got the **nickname** "The China Wall" because it was hard to get a **puck** past him. He won the **Stanley Cup** in 1962, 1963, 1964, and 1967. Bower won his first **Vezina Trophy** in 1961. Then, at the age of 41, he shared the Vezina Trophy with **Terry Sawchuk** in 1965. Bower set a record for being the oldest player to win the Stanley Cup, at 42 years and nine months of age, when he was with the Toronto Maple Leafs in 1967. He won 250 games and had 37 **shutouts** during his NHL career. Saving the **hockey stick** he used during a shutout was one of his many **superstitions**. He had to be the first player out of the dressing room for every game, and he had to sit next to teammate **Marcel Pronovost** when the team traveled by plane or bus.

When asked why he decided to become a goaltender, Bower said that, "I just made up my mind I was going to lose teeth and have my face cut to pieces. It was easy." Bower also recorded "Honky, the Christmas Goose," with Little John and the Rinky-Dinks. Little John was his son, and the Rinky-Dinks were a few Toronto neighborhood kids who helped on the 1965 recording of what would become the highest-selling Canadian-produced recording to date. The flipside of the 45 rpm recording was "Banjo the Mule." After retiring from playing, Bower became a scout for the Maple Leafs. In 1976, he was inducted into the **Hockey Hall of Fame**.

BOWIE, RUSSELL G. "RUSS," "DUBBIE". B. 24 August 1880, Montreal, Quebec. D. 8 April 1959, Montreal, Quebec. Russ Bowie was a **Canadian ice** hockey player generally regarded as one of the best players of the pre-**National Hockey League (NHL)** era. He played 10 seasons for the Montreal Victorias from 1898–1910. Bowie accumulated 234 **goals** in 80 games, for an average of almost three goals per game, a record that has only been matched by **Frank McGee**. Bowie **scored** seven goals in a game twice and had six goals in a game five times. He credited his great stickhandling skills to the short **hockey stick** he used. In his **rookie** season, he helped Montreal defend a mid-season challenge by the Winnipeg Victorias to win the **Stanley Cup** in 1899. Despite being offered large sums of money, he remained an amateur throughout his career. The **Montreal Wanderers** even offered him a grand piano, which the music-loving Bowie refused. Bowie once said that, "I am an amateur, was an amateur, and will die an amateur. I played for fun." Unfortunately, his career was cut short when he broke his collarbone in 1910. After retiring from playing, he became a **referee** in the **National Hockey Association**. Bowie was inducted into the **Hockey Hall of Fame** in 1947, as one of the original 12 inductees. *See also* CAREER-ENDING INJURIES.

BOWMAN, WILLIAM SCOTT "SCOTTY". B. 18 September 1933, Verdun, Quebec. Scotty Bowman played **minor-league** hockey until a fractured skull resulting from a slash by Jean-Guy Talbot ended his playing career. As a result, he began his long **coaching** career. Bowman is the **National Hockey League's (NHL)** winningest coach, with 1,244 victories. He coached the **St. Louis Blues, Montreal Canadiens, Buffalo Sabres, Pittsburgh Penguins**, and **Detroit Red Wings**. He also won a record nine **Stanley Cups**, breaking **Toe Blake**'s record of eight. Bowman won with Montreal (1973, 1976, 1977, 1978, 1979), Pittsburgh (1992), and Detroit (1997, 1998, 2002). He retired at the end of the 2001–2002, after his Red Wings won the Stanley Cup by defeating the **Carolina Hurricanes**, 4–1. In 1991, Bowman was inducted into the **Hockey Hall of Fame** as a **builder**. In 2001, he received the **Lester Patrick Trophy**. *See also* INJURIES.

BREAKAWAY. A breakaway is when a player **skates** to face the **goaltender** with no **defensive** players to stop him. It is a potential **scoring** situation, because there are no defenders between the **puck** carrier and the goaltender. The term *breakaway pass* is when one player passes the puck to a teammate who is already skating forward for a breakaway. **Pavel Bure** of the **Vancouver Canucks**, **Patrick Kane** of the **Chicago Blackhawks**, and **Alexander Ovechkin** of the **Washington Capitals** are a few players known for their breakaway talents.

BRIMSEK, FRANCIS CHARLES "FRANK," "MR. ZERO". B. 26 September 1915, Eveleth, Minnesota. D. 11 November 1998, Virginia, Minnesota. Frank Brimsek was a **goaltender** for 10 seasons in the **National Hockey League (NHL)** with the **Boston Bruins** (1938–1943, 1945–1949) and **Chicago Black Hawks** (1949–1950). He played hockey for the U.S. Coast Guard Cutters during World War II. When he joined the Bruins, he replaced goalie **Tiny Thompson**, and he even wore the same **jersey number** (1). Boston fans were not happy with the **rookie**, until he proved himself. Brimsek earned the **nickname** "Mr. Zero" after recording six **shutouts** in his first seven NHL games. He liked that name better than the others he was called, which included "The Minnesota Icicle" and "Frigid Frankie." Brimsek was known for using his **hockey stick** to knock players off their feet if they **skated** too close to his **crease**. He was also quick to catch the **puck** with his **glove**, and **Art Ross** said that, "The kid had the fastest hands I ever saw, like lightning." Brimsek helped the Bruins win the **Stanley Cup** in 1939 and 1941. In 1939, he became the first goalie to win both the Calder Trophy and **Vezina Trophy** in the same season. When he retired in 1950, his regular-season 514-game record was 252 wins, 182 losses, 80 ties, and 40 shutouts. Brimsek was the first American-born player to be inducted into the **Hockey Hall of Fame** (1966). He was also inducted into the **U.S. Hockey Hall of Fame** (1973).

BROADBENT, HARRY L. "PUNCH," "OLD ELBOWS". B. 13 July 1892, Ottawa, Ontario. D. 5 March 1971, Ottawa, Ontario. Harry Broadbent earned the **nickname** "Punch" for his **fighting** skills, as well as for his knockout **scoring** talent. He was also called "Old Elbows," because he used his elbows to **intimidate** his opponents. Punch played **right wing** in the **National Hockey League (NHL)** with the **Ottawa Senators** (1912–1915, 1918–24, 1927–1928), **Montreal Maroons** (1924–1927), and **New York Americans** (1928–1929). He left his hockey career to serve three years overseas in World War I. Broadbent returned with a **Canadian** military medal for his heroic combat service. In 1922, he was the NHL scoring leader, with 32 **goals** and 46 **points** in 24 games. He also holds the long-standing NHL record of scoring at least one goal in 16 consecutive games, which he established from 21 December 1921 to 15 February 1922. He had a talent of **skating** around or over his opponents, and he was considered one of the earliest power forwards of the sport. Broadbent helped his team win the **Stanley Cup** in 1920, 1921, 1923, and 1926. He even **scored** the Stanley Cup–winning goal on 23 March 1923, in Ottawa's 1–0 victory over the Edmonton Eskimos. In 14 NHL seasons, he played 360 regular-season games and recorded 171 goals, 61 **assists**, 232 points, and 755 **penalty minutes**. In 1962, Broadbent was inducted into the **Hockey Hall of Fame**. At a hockey reunion of old-timers, **Aurèle Joliat** threw punches at his former rival Broadbent. A full fight ensued, and NHL president **Clarence Campbell** had to intervene and make the two senior citizens call a truce.

BRODA, WALTER EDWARD "TURK". B. 15 May 1914, Brandon, Manitoba. D. 17 October 1972, Toronto, Ontario. Turk Broda was a **goaltender** in the **National Hockey League (NHL)** for 14 seasons with the **Toronto Maple Leafs** (1936–1943, 1945–1952). There are two stories about how he got his **nickname**. Some said that his neck would get dark red like a turkey when he got angry, while others said his freckles resembled the surface of a turkey egg. He led the NHL in wins in 1940–1941 (28) and 1947–1948 (32). Broda also led the NHL in **shutouts** in 1940–1941 (6) and 1949–1950 (9). He was known for his ability to play his best during the **Stanley Cup Playoffs**. On 27 March 1952, Broda became the first NHL goaltender to play 100 playoff games. He holds the Toronto team record for career playoff games (101), playoff wins (60), and playoff shutouts (13). Broda was known as an unflappable goalie, and **Jack Adams** said that, "He could play in a tornado and never blink an eye." Before the 1949 season, Maple Leafs' owner **Conn Smythe** gave him an ultimatum to lose seven pounds in a week or face the consequences. The press called it "The Battle of the Bulge," and Broda lost the weight by dieting on grapefruit and soft-boiled eggs. Smythe was happy, and Broda celebrated by eating a steak. Broda helped Toronto win the **Stanley Cup** in 1942, 1947, 1948, 1949, and 1951. He had a 1.98 goals against average in the Stanley Cup playoffs. Broda won the **Vezina Trophy** in 1941 and 1948. During his hockey career, he played 629 regular-season games and had 302 wins, 224 losses, 101 ties, and 62 shutouts. Broda was inducted into the **Hockey Hall of Fame** in 1967.

BRODEUR, MARTIN PIERRE "MARTY". B. 6 May 1972, Montreal, Quebec. Martin Brodeur's father, Denis Brodeur, won a bronze medal at the 1956 **Olympic Games** while playing hockey for the **Canadian** team. He went on to have a long career as the photographer for the **Montreal Canadiens**, and he brought Martin along to many of the practices and games. As a **young player**, Martin idolized Montreal's **goaltender**, **Patrick Roy**. Martin began his professional hockey career as a goalie in the **National Hockey League (NHL)** for the **New Jersey Devils** during the 1991–1992 season. Although Brodeur won his NHL debut against the **Boston Bruins** (4–2), he spent most of the season and the following season with the Utica Devils of the **American Hockey League**. During the 1993–1994 season, Martin led the Devils to the second-best record in the league and the **Eastern Conference** Finals in the **Stanley Cup Playoffs**. As a result, he won the **Calder Memorial Trophy** (1994). Since then, Brodeur has remained in the NHL and is a current player for New Jersey. An impressive game was played on 27 April 1994. **Dominik Hašek** made 70 **saves** in a four-**overtime shutout** against the **rookie** Brodeur, who made 49 saves before being beaten by Dave Hannan. The **Buffalo Sabres** beat the Devils, 1–0. Brodeur won the **William M. Jennings Trophy** in 1996–1997 (with Mike Dunham), 1997–1998, 2002–2003 (tied with Roman Cehmanek and Robert Esche), and 2003–2004. He also won the **Vezina Trophy** four times (2003, 2004, 2007, 2008). He won the **Stanley Cup** three times (1995, 2000, 2003). Brodeur even **scored** a **goal** by firing the **puck** down the **ice** into the empty **net** during the 1997 Stanley Cup Playoffs against the Montreal Canadiens.

Brodeur combines the stand-up style with the butterfly style of goaltending to form his own effective way of protecting the goal. He also has fast reflexes and catches the puck often with his **glove**. Like most goaltenders, Brodeur has a few quirks. His **superstition** includes writing his children's initials on the back of his **mask**. He also uses a new **hockey stick** for every game and writes their names on it for luck. During a 13 April 2008 first-round playoff game, **Sean Avery** of the **New York Rangers** faced Brodeur during a two-man advantage on the **power play** and turned his back on the puck. He also waved his hands and hockey stick in front of Brodeur to distract him and block his view. After losing the series, Brodeur refused to shake Avery's hand. Shortly thereafter, the NHL revised its unsportsmanlike conduct rule, outlawing those antics and naming it the Sean Avery Rule.

Brodeur also played for **Canada** in the 1996 and 2004 **World Cup of Hockey**, winning silver and gold medals, respectively. He also won two Olympic gold medals (2002, 2010), two **World Ice Hockey Championships** silver medals (1996, 2005), and one World Cup of Hockey gold medal (2004). Brodeur is the youngest goaltender in NHL history to reach the 300, 400, and 500 regular-season win milestones and the only goaltender to reach 600 regular-season wins. In 2009, he broke **Terry Sawchuk**'s record of 103 regular-season career shutouts. In his NHL career to date, Brodeur has played 1,191 regular-season games, with 656 wins, 371 losses, and 119 shutouts. He also played in 205 playoff games, with 113 wins, 91 losses, and 24 shutouts. He recently helped his team rally against the **Los Angeles Kings** in the 2012 Stanley Cup Finals. Although the Devils lost (4–2), Brodeur made many saves against the impressive shooting skills of the opponents. As one of the best goalies in history, he will surely be inducted into the **Hockey Hall of Fame**.

BROOKLYN AMERICANS. *See* NEW YORK AMERICANS.

BROOKS, HERBERT PAUL, JR. "HERB". B. 5 August 1937, St. Paul, Minnesota. D. 11 August 2003, Forest Lake, Minnesota. Herb Brooks was a member of the high school team that won the state hockey championship in 1955. The next year, he joined the **college hockey** team at the University of Minnesota. He also tried out for the **U.S. Olympic Men's Ice Hockey Team** but was cut in the final round. The 1960 U.S. team went on to win their first gold medal in hockey. He did make the 1964 and 1968 U.S. Olympic hockey teams, but those teams did not win any medals. Brooks then became a hockey **coach** for the University of Minnesota (1972–1979) and St. Cloud State University (1986–1987). He was best-known for being the coach of the U.S. Olympic Men's Ice Hockey Team that defeated the **Soviet Union Olympic Men's Hockey Team** at the 1980 Winter **Olympics** at **Lake Placid**, New York. Even nonhockey fans are familiar with that famous **"Miracle on Ice"** game. After the Olympics, Brooks coached the **New York Rangers**, Minnesota North Stars, **New Jersey Devils**, and **Pittsburgh Penguins** of the **National Hockey League (NHL)**. His NHL career coaching record was 219 wins, 222 losses, and 66 ties in 507 regular-season games.

In 1990, Brooks was inducted into the **U.S. Hockey Hall of Fame**. He also coached the French team in the 1998 Olympics. In 1999, he was inducted into the **International Ice Hockey Federation Hall of Fame**. Brooks then led the U.S. men's team to the silver medal in 2002, which included a 3–2 win over **Russia** in the semifinals. That **match** was 22 years to the day after the "Miracle on Ice" game. In 2002, he received the **Lester Patrick Trophy**. Brooks died in a car crash near Forest Lake, Minnesota, on 11 August 2003, at the age of 66. In 2005, the Olympic Center **ice** arena in Lake Placid was renamed in his honor. In 2006, Brooks was inducted posthumously into the **Hockey Hall of Fame** as a **builder**.

BROTHERS. Throughout history, the sport of hockey has been enjoyed by multiple sets of brothers. **Wayne Gretzky**'s younger brother, Brent Gretzky, also played professional hockey. **Hockey Hall of Famers** and brothers Alf Smith and Tommy Smith were forwards who played elite amateur and professional hockey in the early 1900s. In 1911, hockey **builders** and brothers Frank Patrick and **Lester Patrick** inaugurated their own professional **ice** hockey league on the West Coast, the **Pacific Coast Hockey Association**, creating three teams, the Victoria Aristocrats, New Westminster Royals, and the **Vancouver Millionaires**. **Defensemen** George McNamara and Howard McNamara were called "The Dynamite Twins," even though there was a three-year age difference between the two. A third brother, Harold McNamara, was also often teamed with them. The Boucher brothers, Billy, Frank, George, and Rob, all played in the 1920s. **George Boucher** and **Frank Boucher** were the first set of brothers to face each other in a **Stanley Cup** Final (along with Corb Denneny and **Cy Denneny**), when George's **Ottawa**

Senators beat Frank's Vancouver Maroons in 1923. The Denneny brothers had the highest combined **goals** of brothers prior to World War II (475). **Lionel Conacher** and his younger brothers, **Charlie Conacher** and **Roy Conacher**, all played in the **National Hockey League (NHL)**. **Doug Bentley** and **Max Bentley** played together in the 1940s. **Maurice Richard** and younger brother **Henri Richard**, nicknamed "Rocket" and "Pocket Rocket," respectively, overlapped their careers from the 1940s through the 1970s. Several sets of brothers played in the NHL during the 1970s, including **Phil Esposito** and **Tony Esposito**, Dave Dryden and **Ken Dryden**, Brian Hextall Jr. and Dennis Hextall, Marty Howe and **Mark Howe**, and Dennis Hull and **Bobby Hull**. The Stastny brothers from Czechoslovakia played together on a **line** with the **Quebec Nordiques** in the 1980s. **Peter Stastny** was the **center**, with Anton and Marian as his wings.

The six Sutter brothers, Brent, Brian, Darryl, Duane, Rich and Ron, all played in the NHL in the 1970s and 1980s. In their combined total, the Sutter brothers played more than 5000 games and won six Stanley Cups. Darryl Sutter won the 2012 Stanley Cup as the **coach** of the **Los Angeles Kings**. During the 2009–2010 and 2010–2011 seasons, **Vancouver Canucks'** players Henrik Sedin and his twin brother, Daniel, each won the **Art Ross Trophy**, making it the first time in NHL history that brothers won **scoring** titles in consecutive seasons. The fictitious **Hanson Brothers** in the 1977 movie *Slap Shot* were based on the real hockey players Jack, Steve, and Jeff Carlson. A recent NHL family includes the Staal brothers, Eric, Jordan, and Marc, and their younger brother, Jared, plays center for the Ontario Hockey League's Sudbury Wolves. *See also* CHERRY, DONALD STEWART "DON," "GRAPES"; FAMILIES.

BUFFALO SABRES. The Buffalo Sabres are a professional ice hockey team in the **Northeast Division** of the **National Hockey League (NHL) Eastern Conference**. The Sabres joined the league in the 1970–1971 season as an expansion team, along with the **Vancouver Canucks**. With his brother, Northrup, Seymour Knox III brought the NHL to Buffalo, New York. Under their guidance, the Buffalo Sabres became a model of how to integrate a sports franchise into the community. Unfortunately, the team has never won the **Stanley Cup**. The Sabres were defeated in the 1974–1975 Stanley Cup Finals by the **Philadelphia Flyers**, four games to two. That series included the legendary Fog Game. Due to unusual heat in Buffalo in May 1975, and the lack of air conditioning in the Buffalo Memorial Auditorium, parts of the game were played in heavy fog. Players, officials, and the **puck** were invisible to many spectators. During a **face-off** and through the fog, Buffalo's **center**, Jim Lorentz, killed a flying bat with his **hockey stick**. The Sabres won that game with René Robert's **goal** in **overtime**. In the 1998–1999 Stanley Cup Finals, they lost to the **Dallas Stars**, also 4 games to 2. From

1992–2001, **Dominik Hašek** was their **goaltender**. Some of the best players for the Sabres included **Hockey Hall of Famers Dick Duff, Grant Fuhr, Clark Gillies, Doug Gilmour, Dale Hawerchuk, Tim Horton, Pat LaFontaine**, and **Gilbert Perreault**. Six of the 14 head **coaches** previously played for the Sabres. The first head coach, Hall of Famer **Punch Imlach**, had the lowest winning percentage of any Sabres coach (.370) during his 120-game tenure. The current head coach, Lindy Ruff, joined the team in 1997. Buffalo won the **Presidents' Trophy** (2006–2007) and **Prince of Wales Trophy** (1974–1975, 1979–1980, 1998–1999). In 41 seasons in the NHL (1970–1912), the Sabres have compiled a record of 1,569-1,219-409-83 (3,630 **points**) and made 29 **Stanley Cup Playoff** appearances.

BUILDER. The builder category was created by the **Hockey Hall of Fame** to recognize influential individuals who have made significant contributions to the sport of hockey in a nonplaying capacity. In 1945, the first two individuals inducted were H. Montague Allen and **Lord Stanley of Preston**, who were responsible for donating the **Allan Cup** and **Stanley Cup**. Father and son team Charles Adams and Weston Adams were both inducted as builders. **Foster Hewitt** is the only media member fully inducted as a builder. In 1989, Alan Eagleson, a longtime executive director of the National Hockey League Players' Association (NHLPA), was inducted as a builder, but he resigned nine years later after pleading guilty to mail fraud and embezzling hundreds of thousands of dollars from the NHLPA pension funds. His resignation came just before he was going to be expelled from the Hall of Fame. Other notable builders include **Al Arbour, Scotty Bowman, Herb Brooks, Frank Calder, Clarence Campbell, Craig Patrick, Glen Sather, James Sutherland**, and **Arthur Wirtz**. Recently inducted builders include Jim Devellano and Daryl "Doc" Seaman. *See also* APPENDIX E for a list of Hall of Fame inductees.

BURCH, HARRY WILLIAM "BILLY". B. 20 November 1900, Yonkers, New York. D. 30 November 1950, Toronto, Ontario. Billy Burch was on a winning canoeing team and played both football and **lacrosse** before focusing on a career in **ice** hockey. He played both **center** and **left wing** in the **National Hockey League (NHL)** with the **Hamilton Tigers** (1922–1925), **New York Americans** (1925–1932), and **Boston Bruins** and **Chicago Black Hawks** (1932–1933). He was one of the players on the Hamilton Tigers team that refused to play in the 1925 playoffs without extra pay. That incident was considered the earliest NHL strike. On 2 December 1925, Burch **scored** the first **goal** in the history of the New York Americans franchise in a 2–1 win over the **Pittsburgh Pirates**. He was the first hockey player born in the **United States** to become a star. To increase attendance at games, the

Americans promoted him as the "Babe Ruth of hockey." He won the Hart Trophy (1925) and **Lady Byng Trophy** (1927). He recorded 137 goals, 61 **assists**, 198 **points**, and 255 **penalty minutes** in 390 NHL regular-season games. Unfortunately, he was never on a team that won the **Stanley Cup**. Burch was inducted into the **Hockey Hall of Fame** in 1974.

BURE, PAVEL VLADIMIROVICH "THE RUSSIAN ROCKET". B. 31 March 1971, Moscow, Russia. By 11 years of age, Pavel Bure was named the best forward in his league. As a **young player** in July 1982, he had the opportunity to practice with **Wayne Gretzky** and Soviet national **goaltender Vladislav Tretiak**. Bure was a left-handed **right wing** in the **National Hockey League (NHL)** for 13 seasons. He played for the **Vancouver Canucks** (1991–1998), **Florida Panthers** (1999–2002), and **New York Rangers** (2002–2003). He earned the **nickname** "The Russian Rocket" due to his speed on the **ice**. At the start of the 1995–1996 season, Bure changed his **jersey number** from 10 to 96. The switch marked the day that he came to North America from Moscow, on 6 September 1991 (ninth month, sixth day). In his first three seasons, Bure **scored** more **goals** than any other player, except **Mike Bossy** and Wayne Gretzky. Bure scored 437 goals in only 702 games. Only Mike Bossy and **Mario Lemieux** had better scoring rates. Bure scored 50 goals or more five times, including four seasons of 58 or more; furthermore, he scored 50 goals or more in each season in which he played more than 68 games. He scored 70 **points** in 64 **Stanley Cup Playoff** games and won the **Calder Memorial Trophy** as **Rookie** of the Year by defeating **Nicklas Lidström**.

Bure played in three World Junior Championships (scoring 39 points in 21 games), two Winter Olympics (scoring 11 goals in 12 games), and two **World Ice Hockey Championships**. His teams earned medals at every event in which he played (2 gold, 3 silver, 2 bronze). Bure scored five goals in a 7–4 win for **Russia** over **Finland** in the semifinals of the 1998 **Olympics** in Nagano. Playing the **Czech Republic** in the final, however, Bure and the Russians were shut out by goaltender **Dominik Hašek** and lost the gold medal by a 1–0 score. Bure finished with a tournament-high nine goals and was named the top forward.

During the Canucks' famous 1994 **Stanley Cup** run, Bure led his team in scoring and finished second overall to **Brian Leetch**. After having several knee surgeries, he retired in 2003. Bure comes from an athletic family. Both of his parents were Russian swimmers. Bure's father competed in the 1968, 1972, and 1976 Olympic Games and won a bronze medal in 1976. Bure's paternal grandfather, Valeri Bure, also competed for the Soviet Union in the Olympics as a goalie for the national water polo team. Pavel's younger **brother**, also named Valeri Bure, was a hockey player in the NHL for 10 years. They played together as members of the Florida Panthers, and also on the Russian national team. In 2012, Pavel was inducted into the **International Ice Hockey Federation Hall of Fame**. He was also inducted into the **Hockey Hall of Fame** in 2012.

BUZINSKI, STEVEN RUDOLPH "THE PUCK GOESINSKY". B. 15 October 1917, Dunblane, Saskatchewan. D. February 1992. When many hockey players left the game to join the action in World War II, **National Hockey League (NHL)** teams filled their vacancies with players from the **minor leagues**. Steve Buzinski was a **goaltender** with the Swift Current Indians who made the jump to the NHL in 1942. During his nine-game NHL career with the **New York Rangers**, Buzinski gave up almost six **goals** per **match**, which is how he earned the **nickname** "The Puck Goesinsky." In one memorable match, he managed to catch the **puck** in his **glove**, only to accidentally toss it into his own **net**. His second and last win, a 5–3 victory over the **Chicago Black Hawks** on 10 November 1942, was noteworthy because it was the last regular-season **overtime** game played for more than 40 years. Eleven days later, NHL president **Frank Calder** eliminated them as part of wartime cutbacks, and they weren't restored until 1983. Buzinsky's short NHL record was 2-6-1, with 5.89 goals against average. He briefly tried **coaching** and then was a plant breeder for Agro **Canada** for more than 40 years.

C

CALDER CUP. The Calder Cup is the **American Hockey League** award given annually to the league's playoff champion. It should not be confused with the **Calder Memorial Trophy**, which is awarded annually to the **Rookie** of the Year in the **National Hockey League (NHL)**. Both awards were named after the first president of the NHL, **Frank Calder**. After the **Stanley Cup**, the Calder Cup is the oldest continuous professional **ice** hockey award, having first been awarded in 1937 to the Syracuse Stars. The Cleveland Barons won it nine times, and the Hershey Bears won it 11 times. The Binghamton Senators won the Calder Cup in 2010 2011, and the Norfolk Admirals won the cup in 2011–2012.

CALDER, FRANK. B. 17 November 1877, Bristol, England. D. 4 February 1943, Montreal, Quebec. Frank Calder was an **ice** hockey executive, a journalist, and an athlete. He is most notable for serving as the first president of the **National Hockey League (NHL)** from 1917 until his death in 1943. During his first season, Calder earned $800, a vast difference from **Gary Bettman's** current salary. Calder was the last president of the NHL's predecessor league, the **National Hockey Association (NHA)**. He was instrumental in the transition from the NHA to the NHL. He presided over the expansion of the NHL from **Canada** into the **United States**, while at the same time fending off of rivals to the NHL's status as the premier ice hockey league. When players from the **Hamilton Tigers** went on strike over a financial dispute with owner Percy Thompson, Calder suspended the players and fined them. Although he was not a hockey player, his calm demeanor made him successful as a hockey leader. Two trophies are named in his honor. The first is the **Calder Cup**, the **American Hockey League** award given annually to the league's **playoff** champion. The second is the Calder Trophy. From 1937 until his death in 1943, Calder bought a trophy each year to be permanently given to the NHL's outstanding **rookie**. After his death, the NHL changed the name of the Calder Trophy to the **Calder Memorial Trophy**.

CALDER MEMORIAL TROPHY. In 1933, the **National Hockey League (NHL)** announced the "**Rookie** of the Year," and Carl Voss of the **Detroit Red Wings** was honored but did not receive a trophy. From 1937 until his death in 1943, **Frank Calder**, NHL president, bought a trophy each year to be permanently given to the outstanding rookie. After Calder's death, the NHL changed the name of the Calder Trophy to the Calder Memorial Trophy in his memory. The first trophy recipient was **Syl Apps**. By definition, the award cannot be won more than once; however, it has been won the most times by rookies from the **Toronto Maple Leafs** (9). In 1990, Sergei Makarov of the **Calgary Flames** became the oldest player to receive the trophy, at the age of 31. Recent recipients include **Patrick Kane** of the **Chicago Blackhawks** (2008), Steve Mason of the **Columbus Blue Jackets** (2009), Tyler Myers of the **Buffalo Sabres** (2010), Jeff Skinner of the **Carolina Hurricanes** (2011), and Gabriel Landeskog of the **Colorado Avalanche** (2012).

CALDER TROPHY. *See* CALDER MEMORIAL TROPHY.

CALGARY FLAMES. The Calgary Flames are a professional **ice** hockey team in the **Northwest Division** of the **National Hockey League (NHL) Western Conference**. The team was previously the Atlanta Flames, who moved to Calgary, Alberta, in 1980 to become the Calgary Flames. Founding Calgary Flames owner Daryl "Doc" Seaman was inducted into the **Hockey Hall of Fame** in 2010 as a **builder**. In its NHL history, the team has only made the **Stanley Cup** Finals twice. They defeated the **Montreal Canadiens**, 4–2, in 1989, for their only Stanley Cup win. The Flames lost to the **Tampa Bay Lightning** in seven games in 2004. During the 2004 **Stanley Cup Playoffs,** a new Calgary Flames' tradition began as the "C of Red" spilled out onto 17th Avenue and fans wearing red came out of the bars that lined the street and together became the "Red Mile." Fans flooded the area, and the police were there to provide safety if things got out of control, but they never did, even when the Flames lost the seventh game. The Calgary Flames won the **Presidents' Trophy** in 1988 and 1989. Some of the best players for Calgary include **Theo Fleury**; Hall of Famers **Grant Fuhr, Doug Gilmour**, Al MacInnis, **Lanny McDonald, Joe Nieuwendyk**; and current captain **Jarome Iginla**. Several notable **coaches** for the Flames include **Bernie Geoffrion** (1972–1975), **Bob Johnson** (1982–1987), and Brian Sutter (1997–2000, 2009–2012). In 39 seasons in the NHL, from 1972–1973 to 2011–2012, the Flames have compiled a record of 1,437-1,214-379-94 (3,347 **points**) and made 26 playoff appearances. In May 2012, former **Colorado Avalanche** coach Bob Hartley replaced Brent Sutter as the head coach of the Flames.

CALIFORNIA GOLDEN SEALS. *See* MINNESOTA WILD.

CAMERON, HAROLD HUGH "HARRY". B. 6 February 1890, Pembroke, Ontario. D. 20 October 1953, Pembroke, Ontario. Harry Cameron was known for being one of the earliest offensive **defenseman** who made end-to-end rushes. He played in the **National Hockey Association** for the Toronto Blueshirts (1912–1917) and **Montreal Wanderers** (1916–1917). During Cameron's **National Hockey League (NHL)** career, he played for the Toronto Arenas (1917 1919), **Ottawa Senators** (1918–1919), **Montreal Canadiens** (1919–1920), and Toronto St. Patricks (1919–1923). Cameron was the first hockey player to develop a curved shot with a straight blade. As one of the team's top **point scorers**, management often tolerated his temper. He was the first player to record a **goal**, an **assist**, and a **fight** in one game, on 22 December 1920, in a 6–3 loss against the Ottawa Senators. This has since been called a "**Gordie Howe hat trick**." Cameron became the first NHL defenseman to score four goals in a single game twice, once on 26 December 1917, and once on 3 March 1920. During 1917–1918, he led the NHL in **assists** (10), which he did again in 1921–1922 (17). He won the **Stanley Cup** in 1914, 1918, and 1922. **Eddie Gerard** replaced the injured Cameron in one **Stanley Cup Playoff** game for the Toronto St. Patricks in 1922. Cameron was inducted into the **Hockey Hall of Fame** in 1962.

CAMPBELL, CASSIE. B. 22 November 1973, Richmond Hill, Ontario. Cassie Campbell was a **Canadian** female **ice** hockey player. She captained the **Canadian Women's Olympic Ice Hockey Team** during the 2002 Winter Olympics and led the team to a gold medal. Playing **left wing**, Campbell became team captain again at the 2006 Winter Olympics in Turin, Italy, and she successfully led her team to another gold medal with a 4–1 win over **Sweden**. As a national team member from 1994–2006, Campbell was a pioneer in the growth and development of **women's ice hockey**. She retired from competitive hockey on 30 August 2006, and then became the first female color commentator on a *Hockey Night in Canada* broadcast. In 2007, Campbell became the first women's ice hockey player inducted into **Canada's Sports Hall of Fame**. On 22 November 2009, she ran a leg in the Vancouver 2010 **Olympic** Torch relay, through the town of Cavendish, Prince Edward Island. Campbell and her husband, Brad Pascall, have one daughter, Brooke Violet.

CAMPBELL, CLARENCE SOUTHERLAND. B. 9 July 1905, Fleming, Saskatchewan. D. 24 June 1984, Montreal, Quebec. Clarence Campbell graduated from the University of Alberta with a law degree in 1924, and he was a Rhodes Scholar at Oxford University, where he also played hockey. Campbell was a **National Hockey League (NHL) referee** from 1933–1939. He was an **on-ice official** at the 28 January 1937 match during which **Howie Morenz** suffered a **career-ending injury**. But Campbell was mainly known for being the longtime NHL president (1946–1977). While Campbell was in the **Canadian** Army during World War II, **Frank Calder** died and **Red Dutton** assumed the NHL presidency. In 1946, Campbell returned to Canada and accepted the presidency after Dutton resigned. He increased the number of NHL regular-season games from 50 to 70 and started the NHL **All-Star** Game. More importantly, he initiated the breakthrough NHL Pension Plan, with contributions from the players and the league. But Campbell is perhaps best remembered for suspending **Montreal Canadiens'** superstar **Maurice Richard** for the remaining three games of the 1955 regular season and the entirety of the **Stanley Cup Playoffs**. His action came as a result of Richard punching **linesman** Cliff Thompson during the 13 March game against the **Boston Bruins**. He also oversaw the NHL's expansion. Between 1967–1975, the league tripled in size and was very popular across North America. The Clarence S. Campbell Conference and **Clarence S. Campbell Bowl** were named in his honor. Campbell was inducted into the **Hockey Hall of Fame** in 1966 in the **builder** category. In 1972, he received the **Lester Patrick Trophy** for his contributions to the sport. In 1976, Campbell was charged and convicted of bribing Senator Louis Giguère. The NHL paid his fine, and he didn't serve any time due to his age. When he retired as NHL president in 1977, he was sick with respiratory ailments. **John A. Ziegler Jr.** replaced him.

CANADA. Lacrosse was the national sport of Canada until 1994. **Ice** hockey has always been extremely popular, but there were objections to changing it to the new national sport. As a result, since 1994, Canada's winter sport is hockey, and the summer sport is lacrosse, even though it is played in the spring. The **Hockey Hall of Fame**, a museum dedicated to the history of ice hockey, is located in Toronto, Ontario. In 1920, Canada became a member of the **International Ice Hockey Federation (IIHF)**. They competed in their first **Olympic Games** in 1920. In their 20 appearances, the **Canadian Men's Olympic Ice Hockey Team** has won eight gold medals, four silver medals, and two bronze medals. Their most recent gold medal was at the 2010 Winter Olympics, when **Sidney Crosby scored** the winning **overtime goal** against the **United States**. From 1920–1963, Canada's international representation was by senior amateur club teams. Canada's national men's team was founded in 1963 by Father **David Bauer**. Also in 1920, the team competed in their first **World Ice Hockey Championships**. They have amassed 24 gold medals in 67 tournaments. Canada also created the **Canada Cup,** which was an international competition that included amateurs and professionals.

The **nickname** "Team Canada" was coined for the 1972 **Summit Series**, and it has been used to refer to the Canadian national team ever since. Canada has been one of the leading national ice hockey teams in international play, winning the 1972 Summit Series against the **Soviet Union** and four of the five Canada Cups. Canada is also a member of the "Big Six," which is a term for the six strongest men's ice hockey nations. The other five teams are **Russia**, **Sweden**, the **United States**, the **Czech Republic**, and **Finland**. The **Canadian Women's Olympic Ice Hockey Team** has represented Canada in the Olympic Games since 1998, where they have been dominate, winning won one silver medal and three gold medals. The men's team currently has a fourth-place ranking by the IIHF, and the women's team has a second-place ranking.

See also CANADA'S SPORTS HALL OF FAME; HOCKEY HALL OF FAME; *HOCKEY NIGHT IN CANADA*; MONTREAL CANADIENS; TORONTO MAPLE LEAFS.

CANADA CUP. The Canada Cup was an international **ice** hockey competition held five times (1976, 1981, 1984, 1987, 1991). It was created to allow the best international players to compete regardless of their amateur or professional status. It was sanctioned by the **International Ice Hockey Federation (IIHF)**, Hockey Canada, and the **National Hockey League (NHL)**. The Canada Cup trophy was shaped like half of a maple leaf and made of solid nickel, and it weighed close to 140 pounds. **Canada** won the first Canada Cup in 1976, by defeating the 1976 **World Ice Hockey Championships** gold medalists, Czechoslovakia, 5–4, in the final. **Darryl Sittler** scored the game-winning **goal** in **overtime**. In 1981, the **Soviet Union** team won their first and only Canada Cup with an 8–1 win over Canada in the final. In 1984, **Mike Bossy** of Canada scored an overtime game winner to defeat the Soviets in the semifinals. Canada won their second Canada Cup after defeating the team from **Sweden** in the final. The 1987 Canada Cup was noteworthy, because star players **Wayne Gretzky** and **Mario Lemieux** joined together on a **line** for the Canadian team to capture the country's third championship. All three games in the final between Canada and the Soviets ended in 6–5 scores, with two games going to overtime. In the final minutes of the deciding game, Lemieux scored the championship-winning goal on a pass from Gretzky. The last Canada Cup was held in 1991, with Canada defeating the **United States** for their third-straight championship and fourth overall. The Canada Cup tournament was replaced by the **World Cup of Hockey** in 1996.

CANADA'S SPORTS HALL OF FAME. In 1955, Canada's Sports Hall of Fame was established to "preserve the record of **Canadian** sports achievements and to promote a greater awareness of Canada's heritage of sport." It once shared a building with the **Hockey Hall of Fame**, but it is now located in Canada Olympic Park in Calgary, Alberta. Unlike the Canadian Hockey Hall of Fame, this group honors athletes from 60 different sports. Of the 540 athletes, some of the **ice** hockey players inducted include **Syl Apps**, **Mike Bossy**, **Ray Bourque**, **Cassie Campbell**, **Wayne Gretzky**, **Angela James**, **Aurèle Joliat**, **Patrick Roy**, and **Steve Yzerman**. *See also* U.S. HOCKEY HALL OF FAME.

CANADA–U.S.S.R. SERIES. *See* SUMMIT SERIES.

CANADIAN HOCKEY HALL OF FAME. *See* HOCKEY HALL OF FAME

CANADIAN MEN'S OLYMPIC ICE HOCKEY TEAM. Canada is a country known for its talented hockey players. The Canadian Men's Olympic Ice Hockey Team has represented Canada in the Winter Olympics since 1920. They defeated the **United States** in the finals six times (1920, 1924, 1932, 1952, 2002, 2010). In total, the Canadian team has won six gold medals. Former amateur player and **Hockey Hall of Famer** Fred "Steamer" Maxwell **coached** the gold medal team at the 1920 **Olympics**. At the 1924 Olympics, another member of the Hall of Fame, Harry E. Watson, led his team in **goals** (36) and **points** (50) to help Canada win the gold. That team was coached by former player Frank Rankin, who was inducted into the Hall of Fame in 1961. In **Germany**, in 1936, **Great Britain** won the gold; Canada won silver; and the United States won bronze. The **U.S. Men's Olympic Ice Hockey Team** defeated the Canadian and **Soviet** teams to win its first gold medal in the 1960 Olympics. In 2002, Canada's 5–2 win over the U.S. team broke the team's 50-year goldless drought. In 2010, after the U.S. team beat **Finland**, 6–1, Canada faced the United States in the finals again. This gold-medal **match** between Canada and the United States became the most watched hockey game in the United States, with an estimated 27.6 million U.S. households watching Canada win in **overtime**, 3–2.

CANADIAN WOMEN'S OLYMPIC ICE HOCKEY TEAM. The Canadian Women's Olympic Ice Hockey Team has represented **Canada** in the Winter Olympics since 1998, and they have dominated. Women's hockey was played in the **Olympics** for the first time ever in Nagano, Japan, from 7–22 February 1998. The **United States** won the gold, Canada won silver, and **Finland** won bronze. China, **Sweden**, and Japan were the other three participating countries. The Canadian women's team won gold medals during the 2002, 2006, and 2010 Olympics. The team's coaches have included Melody Davidson, Shannon Miller, and Danièle Sauvageau. Notable Olympic team players include Jennifer Botterill, **Cassie Campbell**, Danielle Goyette, Jayna Hefford, Becky Kellar, **Manon Rhéaume**, and **Hayley Wickenheiser**.

CAREER-ENDING INJURIES. Several hockey players have had their careers end abruptly due to **injuries** received on the **ice**. **Shorty Green** of the **New York Americans** retired after a kidney injury on 27 February 1927. On 12 December 1933, **Eddie Shore** of the **Boston Bruins tripped** the **Toronto Maple Leafs' Ace Bailey**. Bailey's **head injury** was so severe that he was not expected to live. He survived, but his playing career was over. Lou Fontinato of the **Montreal Canadiens** broke his neck after crashing into the **boards** on 9 March 1963. The Montreal Canadiens' **Jacques Laperriere** suffered a career-ending injury to his knee in a game against the Boston Bruins on 19 January 1974. The **Philadelphia Flyers' goaltender**, **Bernie Parent**, suffered a career-ending injury when he was hit in the eye in a game against **New York Rangers** on 17 February 1979. **Walt Tkaczuk** of the New York Rangers retired at the age of 33 following a severe eye injury from a deflected **puck** shot by Larry Murphy in a game against the **Los Angeles Kings** on 2 February 1981. On 20 October 1995, only 11 seconds into his first shift for Boston University's **college hockey** team, 20-year-old Travis Roy slid headfirst into the boards after University of North Dakota player Mitch Vig avoided Roy's **check**. The awkward impact with the boards left him paralyzed. On 8 March 2004, Steve Moore of the **Colorado Avalanche** had his **National Hockey League** career cut short because of a punch to the head by Todd Bertuzzi of the **Vancouver Canucks**. Moore suffered a broken neck and a concussion. As a result of the brutality, Bertuzzi was suspended for the rest of the season. *See also* CHADWICK, WILLIAM LEROY "BILL," "THE BIG WHISTLE"; MASTERTON, WILLIAM J. "BILL".

CARNEGIE, HERBERT H. "HERB," "SWIVEL HIPS". B. 8 November 1919, Toronto, Ontario. D. 9 March 2012, Toronto, Ontario. Born to Jamaican parents, Herb Carnegie was a former **Canadian ice** hockey player. He was the first African-Canadian player to be offered an opportunity to play in the **National Hockey League (NHL)**. In 1948, the **New York Rangers'** **coach, Frank Boucher**, offered Carnegie a contract, but Boucher wanted him to play for the **minor-league** team first. At the time, Carnegie was part of what is believed to be the first all-black **line** in hockey. Known as "The Black Aces," Herb played **center**, with his brother Ossie as **right wing** and Manny McIntyre as **left wing**. Carnegie refused the contract offer, insisting he was good enough to play in the NHL and refusing to play in the minor leagues. He also did not want to move his family or take a cut in pay. Carnegie was a member of the Quebec Aces (1949–1953), along with teammate **Jean Béliveau** and coach **Punch Imlach**. He earned the **nickname** "Swivel Hips" because of his elusive **dekes** on the ice. Unfortunately, racism blocked his way into the NHL. The **Toronto Maple Leafs**' boss, **Conn Smythe**, allegedly said that, "I will gladly give $10,000 to anyone who can turn Herb Carnegie white." After retiring from the game of hockey in 1953, Carnegie started the Future Aces Hockey School, one of the first hockey schools in Canada. In 1954, he wrote the "Future Aces Creed" in an attempt to foster respect, tolerance, diversity, and sportsmanship among **young players**. Carnegie continued his athletic career as a golfer, winning the Canadian Seniors Golf Championship in 1977 and 1978. In 1996, he published his autobiography, *A Fly in a Pail of Milk: The Herb Carnegie Story*, before going legally blind. He recently passed away at the age of 92. *See also* FUHR, GRANT SCOTT; IGINLA, JAROME ARTHUR LEIGH ADEKUNLE TIG JUNIOR ELVIS "IGGY"; O'REE, WILLIAM ELDON "WILLIE".

CAROLINA HURRICANES. The Carolina Hurricanes are a professional **ice** hockey team in the **Southeast Division** of the **National Hockey League (NHL) Eastern Conference**. They were originally part of the New England Whalers. New England played in the **World Hockey Association (WHA)** from 1972–1979. Then they played in the NHL from 1979–1997, as the renamed Hartford Whalers. **Hockey Hall of Famer Gordie Howe** played **left wing** for the New England Whalers and Hartford Whalers from 1976–1980. In 1994, computer executive Peter Karmanos Jr. purchased the team, but he was unable to significantly increase attendance. Disappointing loyal Connecticut hockey fans, the franchise was relocated to Raleigh, North Carolina, and renamed the Colorado Hurricanes in 1997. In its NHL history, the team has made the **Stanley Cup** Finals twice and won once. They lost to the **Detroit Red Wings** in 2002 (4–1). Game 3 was especially memorable, as it featured a triple-**overtime match**. Detroit's **Igor Larionov scored** the winning **goal**, making him the oldest player (41 years, seven months) to score a last-round goal. In 2006, the team defeated the **Edmonton Oilers** in a seven-game series. Notable players for the Hurricanes include **Paul Coffey**, **Ron Francis**, **Mark Howe**, and Keith Primeau.

Since 1972, the Whalers have had 19 head **coaches**. Hall of Famer John "Jack" Kelly coached his team to become the first WHA champions in 1973. For the Hurricanes franchise, the first head coach was Paul Maurice, who coached them for six seasons. Maurice leads the team for the most regular-season games coached and game wins, as well as **Stanley Cup Playoff** games coached and playoff game wins. Their second coach, Peter Laviolette, was the coach that helped them win the Stanley Cup. On 28 November 2011, Kirk Muller became the third coach for the Hurricanes. The team won the **Prince of Wales Trophy** twice (2001–2002, 2005–2006). In 32 seasons in the NHL, from 1979–1980 to 2011–2012, the Hurricanes have compiled a record of 1,040-1,163-263-83 (2,426 **points**) and made 13 playoff appearances.

CENTER. The term *center* is used to describe a player who plays the position between the **left wing** and **right wing**. They **skate** down the center and pass the **puck** side to side attempting to move the puck down the ice and **score** a goal. Centers, along with the wings, are also known as forwards. Defensively, they try to prevent the other team's wings and centers from moving forward and scoring. The three positions of left wing, center, and right wing are also collectively known as a **line**.

CENTER LINE. *See* RED LINE.

CENTRAL DIVISION. In 1993, the **National Hockey League (NHL)** renamed the conferences and divisions to reflect their geographic locations. The Central Division is one of the three sections of the **Western Conference** In the NHL. The **Northwest Division** and **Pacific Division** are the other two.

CENTRE. *See* CENTER.

CHADWICK, WILLIAM LEROY "BILL," "THE BIG WHISTLE". B. 10 October 1915, Manhattan, New York. D. 24 October 2009, Cutchogue, New York. Bill Chadwick began his hockey career as a **center** in the 1930s as an amateur player in the Metropolitan Junior Hockey League before earning a spot on the New York Rovers, which was the **New York Rangers**-sponsored club of the Eastern Amateur League. After an **injury** blinded his right eye, Chadwick switched to officiating and joined the **National Hockey League (NHL)** as a **linesman** for the 1939–1940 season. When fans or players complained that he was blind, Chadwick humorously told them that they were "only 50 percent right." Just before he turned 25, he was promoted to NHL **referee**, and he worked in that position from 1940–1955. He was the referee when **Bill Barilko scored** the 1951 **Stanley Cup**–winning **goal**, which was also his last. During his career, Chadwick became the first referee to use hand signals so that fans in the stands would know what type of **penalty** was being called. During his 15 seasons as a referee, he worked more than 900 regular-season **matches** and a record 42 Stanley Cup Finals. He was **nicknamed** "The Big Whistle" by Rangers' statistician Arthur Friedman.

Rangers' **coach** and general manager **Emile Francis** convinced Chadwick to pursue a second hockey career in broadcasting. Rangers' fans remember Chadwick for the 14 seasons he spent as a radio and television color commentator. He was outspoken and had a distinct New York accent. From 1967–1972, he worked on the radio with Marv Albert. From 1973–1981, he was paired with Jim Gordon. Chadwick and Gordon called more than 650 regular-season and **Stanley Cup Playoff** games, and the pair was there when the Rangers went all the way to the 1979 Stanley Cup Finals. Gordon often had to keep the opinionated Chadwick in check, and their banter became entertainment for fans watching the Rangers on television. Chadwick was not a fan of the current two-man referee system. In 2002, he told a reporter: "Look at the game today, it's too damned crowded out there. You got two linesmen, you got two referees. And they're not getting any better officiating." In 1964, Bill Chadwick was inducted into the **Hockey Hall of Fame** in the **on-ice official** category. He was inducted into the **U.S. Hockey Hall of Fame** in 1974, and is the only referee inducted to date. He wrote his autobiography, *The Big Whistle*, with Hal Brock, in 1974. In 1975, Chadwick received the **Lester Patrick Trophy**.

CHÁRA, ZDENO. B. 18 March 1977, Trencin, Czechoslovakia. Zdeno Chára is a current **defenseman** in the **National Hockey League (NHL)**. His playing career includes the **New York Islanders** (1997–2001), **Ottawa Senators** (2001–2004, 2005–2006), and **Boston Bruins** (2006–). During the 2004–2005 NHL **lockout**, he played hockey for a team in **Sweden**. In 2009, he won the **James Norris Memorial Trophy**. He is known for being a good **penalty killer** and for having a fast shot. During the 2012 NHL **All-Star** Skills Competition, Chára set the record for the hardest shot, at 108.8 miles per hour, breaking his 2011 record of 105.9 miles per hour. During a game on 8 March 2011, Chára hit **Montreal Canadiens'** forward Max Pacioretty, which resulted in Pacioretty colliding with the end of the bench. His **injury** included a concussion and fractured back. Chára received a five-minute major **penalty** and a game misconduct. After a NHL tape review and a criminal investigation, the play was not considered malicious, and no charges were filed against Chára. Pacioretty made a full recovery and won the **Bill Masterton Memorial Trophy** in 2012. In 2011, with the Bruins, Chára became only the second European-born and trained captain to win the **Stanley Cup** and the first from **Slovakia** to do so. In his NHL playing career to date, Chára has played in 1,007 regular-season games, with 137 **goals**, 322 **assists**, 459 **points**, and 1,471 **penalty minutes**. Internationally, Chára represented Slovakia in the 1999, 2000, 2001, 2004, 2005, 2007, and 2012 **World Ice Hockey Championships**, winning silver medals in 2000 and 2012. His father, Zdenek, was a prominent Greco-Roman wrestler who competed for Czechoslovakia in the 1976 Summer Olympics. Zdeno had the opportunity to play in the 2006 and 2010 Winter Olympics, missing a medal by finishing fourth in 2010. At six feet, 9 inches tall, he is the tallest player in the history of the NHL. His **coaches** in Slovakia told him he should play basketball instead of hockey.

CHECKING. Using one's body to knock an opponent into the **boards** or to the **ice** is called checking. The purpose of checking is to gain possession of the **puck** or disrupt the opposition's play. It is encouraged in ice hockey but is against the rules in **roller hockey**. Overly aggressive defensive play is against the rules, and the player gets a **penalty**. The most common type of checking is when a player puts his shoulder into his opponent to push the opponent out of position. His elbow must be tucked in or he risks getting a penalty for elbowing. A hip check at or below the knees is called clipping and is not allowed. A poke check is when the player uses his **hockey stick** to poke the puck away from his opponent. Body checking is only allowed against an opponent who is in possession of the puck. Checking is what makes hockey a full–contact, physical team sport, like football. Players specifically known for their checking abilities include **Bill Barilko**, Leo Boivin, **Harry Broadbent**, Johnny Bucyk, **Tim Horton**, Gilles Marotte, and **Jack Stewart**. **Frank Nighbor** popularized the poke check, and Ernie Johnson, **Marcel Pronovost**, and **Bill Quackenbush** were also known for that skill.

CHEEVERS, GERALD MICHAEL "GERRY," "CHEESIE". B. 7 December 1940, St. Catharines, Ontario. Gerry Cheevers was a **goaltender** who played a total of 17 seasons in the **National Hockey League (NHL)** and **World Hockey Association (WHA)**. Cheevers played for the **Toronto Maple Leafs** (1961–1962), **Boston Bruins** (1965–1972, 1975–1980), and WHA Cleveland Crusaders (1972–1976). In 1965, he totaled 48 victories and led the Rochester Americans to their first **Calder Cup** championship. That same year, he won the **Hap Holmes** Memorial Award for the best goaltender of the season in the **American Hockey League (AHL)**. He finished second in NHL wins, with 23 (1967–1968) and 28 (1968–1969). Cheevers helped the Bruins win the **Stanley Cup** in 1970 and 1972. During the 1971–1972 regular season, he set the record for the longest winning streak by a goaltender (32 games). He led the WHA in **shutouts**, with 5 (1972–1973), 4 (1973–1974), and 4 (1974–1975). In 1974, he played for **Canada** as part of the WHA **All-Star Team** against the Union of Soviet Socialist Republics and in the 1976 **Canada Cup**. Cheevers played when NHL goalies were transitioning into wearing **face masks**. He had a habit of decorating his mask with stitches drawn in the spots where the **puck** had hit it. He stopped when the mask was covered with stitches, but it illustrated how much protection masks provide. He was not a stand-up goalie, and he preferred to use a flopping style. Cheevers would also stray from his **crease** to help his **defensemen**. When the opponents got too close to the crease, he would hit them with his **hockey stick**. He had a NHL career record of 230 wins, 102 losses, 74 ties, 26 shutouts, and a 2.89 **goals** against average. After he retired from playing, Cheevers **coached** the Bruins from 1980–1985, and he had a record of 204 wins, 126 losses, and 46 ties. Cheevers was inducted into the **Hockey Hall of Fame** in 1985. He served as a color commentator for the Hartford Whalers (1986–1995) and Boston Bruins (1999–2002). From 1995–2006, he was a scout for the Bruins. In addition to hockey, Cheevers enjoyed thoroughbred horse racing.

CHELIOS, CHRISTOS KOSTAS TSELIOS "CHRIS," "CHELI". B. 25 January 1962, Chicago, Illinois. Chris Chelios played **college hockey** and won a **National Collegiate Athletic Association** championship with the University of Wisconsin in 1983. He went on to become a **defenseman** for 26 seasons in the **National Hockey League (NHL)**. He played with the **Montreal Canadiens** (1983–1990), **Chicago Blackhawks** (1990–1999), and **Detroit Red Wings** (1998–1909). He is the all-time leader in games played by a defenseman in NHL history, with 1,651. He won three **Stanley Cups** (1986, 2002, 2008). Chelios also won the **James Norris Memorial Trophy** three times (1989, 1993, 1996). He had a **superstition** about having to be the last player to be fully dressed before going out on the **ice**. Known for his love of the game, Chelios would often drive around with his **equipment** in the trunk of his car looking for a pick-up game of hockey. Former Chicago defenseman Troy Murray said that, "He would just go out there and **skate** with the guys. Half the time he didn't even know the people. He'd go any-where. He was a **rink** rat. He would just stop in and play. That's just the way he was. He loved being on the ice." He also played goalie while his sons and **Nicklas Lidström**'s sons practiced on the ice. During the 2004–2005 **lock-out**, Chelios played with the Motor City Mechanics.

Chelios was also known for playing strong hockey internationally for more than three decades. He is one of only two male players to represent the **United States** at four **Olympic Games** (1984, 1998, 2002, 2006), and he also captained his final three Olympic squads. He won a gold medal at the 1996 **World Cup of Hockey** and a silver medal at the 2002 Winter Olym-pics. In addition, he played for the United States at the 1984, 1987, and 1991 **Canada Cups**. During his NHL career, he played in 1,651 regular-season games and had 185 **goals**, 763 **assists**, 948 **points**, and 2,891 **penalty min-utes**. Chelios was inducted into the **U.S. Hockey Hall of Fame** in 2011, and he will surely be inducted into the **Hockey Hall of Fame**. He enjoys playing other sports and trained with the U.S. bobsled team, hoping to form the first Greek bobsled team at the 2006 Winter Olympics. Chelios also enjoys stand-up paddle surfing, which he credits with keeping him in shape during his hockey career. His sons Jake and Dean both play college hockey at Michigan

State University, and his daughter Caley is a **lacrosse** player at Northwestern University. Chelios's friend, John C. McGinley, often wore a Red Wings **jersey** with Chelios's name and **jersey number** (24) on the television show *Scrubs*.

CHERRY, DONALD STEWART "DON," "GRAPES". B. 5 February 1934, Kingston, Ontario. Don Cherry was a hockey **defenseman** who signed with the Hershey Bears of the **American Hockey League (AHL)** in 1954. He played **minor-league** hockey for 18 years. In March 1955, Cherry played in his first and last game in the **National Hockey League (NHL)** when the **Boston Bruins** called him up during the **Stanley Cup Playoffs** against the **Montreal Canadiens**. He once said that, "When I was a kid, I prayed for enough talent to be a pro hockey player, but I forgot to say NHL, because they only gave me enough to make the minors." His younger **brother**, Dick Cherry, played two seasons in the NHL with the Bruins and **Philadelphia Flyers**. Don won the **Calder Cup** championship (AHL) four times (1960, 1965, 1966, 1968). He went on to become a successful **coach** for the Bruins (1974–1979) and led them to two **Stanley Cup** Semifinals and two Stanley Cup Finals, but in the seventh game of the 1979 semifinals, with a **score** of 4–3, Cherry sent too many men on the **ice** and, as a result, the Montreal Canadiens scored the tying **goal** and then won in **overtime**. He was then fired.

Cherry made a name for himself as a flamboyant, outspoken coach who consulted his bull terrier "Blue" on hockey decisions and encouraged his players to **fight**. He also coached the **Colorado Rockies** from 1979–1980. To encourage fan attendance, the slogan "Come to the fights and watch a Rockies game break out!" was posted on billboards all across Denver. Cherry's hiring as head coach rejuvenated the ailing franchise. He is also well-known as an author, a syndicated radio commentator for The Fan Radio Network, and the creator of the *Rock'em Sock'em Hockey* video series. Cherry is easily recognized by his brightly colored sports jackets, and he currently cohosts the "Coach's Corner" segment with Ron MacLean on the long-running **Canadian** sports program *Hockey Night in Canada*. Cherry has mentioned that his all-time favorite player was **Bobby Orr**, who he said was the greatest player of all time. Cherry also expressed fondness for **Doug Gilmour**, Vincent Lecavalier, and **Cam Neely**. On the other hand, he criticized Ulf Samuelsson and Matt Cooke for being dirty players responsible for many **injuries**. Cherry has been known for creating controversy in both hockey and politics.

CHICAGO BLACK HAWKS. This **National Hockey League (NHL)** team used two words, Black Hawks, as their name from 1926 until the official spelling changed to one word, Blackhawks, in 1985.

See also CHICAGO BLACKHAWKS.

CHICAGO BLACKHAWKS. The Chicago Blackhawks are a professional **ice** hockey team in the **Central Division** of the **National Hockey League (NHL) Western Conference**. The team used two words, Black Hawks, as their name from 1926 until the official spelling changed to one word, Blackhawks, in 1985. The **Chicago Stadium** was one of the six original NHL arenas and was home to the **Chicago Black Hawks** from 1929–1994. Their first game at the Chicago Stadium was on 15 December 1929, when they defeated the **Pittsburgh Pirates** (3–1) before 14,212 fans. The Chicago franchise was one of the **"Original Six"** teams, a term used to describe the teams that made up the NHL from 1942 until the 1967 expansion.

In 1927, the Black Hawks allegedly had a **curse**, the "Curse of Muldoon," placed on them by head **coach Pete Muldoon** when he was fired. According to the curse, they would never again finish in first place. In 1943, Toronto sportswriter Jim Coleman printed it. Chicago did not finish in first place in their division (1928–1937) or in the single-division NHL (after 1938) until 1967, the final season of the "Original Six" Era, despite winning the **Stanley Cup** three times since Muldoon supposedly cursed the team. In 1967, the last season of the six-team NHL, Chicago finished in first place, finally breaking the curse; however, they lost in the Stanley Cup Semifinals to the **Toronto Maple Leafs**.

Future **Hockey Hall of Famer** Dick Irvin was Chicago's first captain (1926–1929). The team played in the Stanley Cup Finals six times (1962, 1965, 1971, 1973, 1992, 2010), but they did not win the Stanley Cup from 1961 until 2010, when they defeated the **Philadelphia Flyers** (4–2), the longest drought of any current NHL team. Until the 2009 **Stanley Cup Playoffs**, they had not advanced beyond the first round since 1996, when they defeated the **Calgary Flames** in the opening round and the **Vancouver Canucks** in the conference semifinals, before falling to the **Detroit Red Wings** in the conference finals. Players who have played for Chicago include **goaltenders Tony Esposito** and **Glenn Hall**; forwards **Bobby Hull**, **Stan Mikita**, and **Denis Savard**; and **defensemen** Keith Magnuson and **Pierre Pilote**. **Patrick Kane** is a current player, and Joel Quenneville is the team's coach. In 85 seasons in the NHL (1926–1927 to 2011–2012), the Blackhawks have compiled a record of 2,460-2,528-814-92 (5,826 **points**) and made 57 playoff appearances.

CHICAGO STADIUM. The Chicago Stadium was one of the six original **National Hockey League (NHL)** arenas. It was located in Chicago, Illinois, and was home to the **Chicago Black Hawks** from 1929–1994. The Chicago Stadium opened on 28 March 1929, with a boxing match between world light heavyweight Tommy Loughran and world middleweight champion Mickey Walker. The Black Hawks played their first game at the facility nine months later. On 15 December 1929, Chicago defeated the **Pittsburgh Pirates**, 3–1, before 14,212 fans, which was 6,000 more people than the largest crowd ever assembled at the Black Hawks' previous arena, the Chicago Coliseum. Because the arena was built during the 1929–1930 NHL season, the **rink** was grandfathered into the rules. The rink at Chicago Stadium was 188 feet by 85 feet, instead of the regulation-size 200 feet by 85 feet.

The Chicago Stadium was the largest sports arena in the world when it was built, with a seating capacity of 25,000 people. The building had a reputation as the loudest rink in the world, and a large pipe organ was played during hockey games. As a result, the arena was **nicknamed** the "Madhouse on Madison." The stadium also had stairs that led down to the dressing rooms. Players had to walk down the stairs in their **skates**. Before each game, **Stan Mikita** always smoked one cigarette as he walked up the stairs to the **ice**, and he would toss the butt over his left shoulder. During the 1970s, Elvis Presley performed there to sold-out crowds. The Chicago Bulls basketball team played their home games there from 1967–1994. On 14 April 1994, the **Chicago Blackhawks** played their final regular-season game there. In the audience were four of the **Hockey Hall of Famers** whose **jersey numbers** had been retired: **Tony Esposito**, **Glenn Hall**, **Bobby Hull**, and Stan Mikita. The Blackhawks lost to the **Toronto Maple Leafs**, 6–4, but they advanced to the **Stanley Cup Playoffs**. The last hockey game ever played at the Chicago Stadium was on 28 April 1994, when the Leafs won, 1–0

See also ORIGINAL ARENAS.

CLANCY, FRANCIS MICHAEL "KING". B. 25 February 1903, Ottawa, Ontario. D. 8 November 1986, Toronto, Ontario. King Clancy was a **defenseman** in the **National Hockey League (NHL)** for the **Ottawa Senators** (1921–1930) and **Toronto Maple Leafs** (1930–1937). On 21 March 1923, he played all six positions for Ottawa in a 1–0 win over the **Montreal Canadiens**. On 31 March, he repeated the feat to help Ottawa win the 1923 **Stanley Cup** by defeating the Edmonton Eskimos, 1–0. He also won the Stanley Cup in 1927 and 1932. Clancy began his hockey career in 1921, with the Senators, playing for $400 a year, with a $100 signing bonus. By 1930, the Maple Leafs' owner, **Conn Smythe**, used his racetrack winnings to acquire Clancy and two other players for the Toronto team for $35,000. Clancy was **nicknamed** after his father, who was a king on the Ottawa football field.

The defenseman was known for his trash-talking and aggressiveness on the ice. He once challenged a heckling fan in Boston to a **fight**, only to realize that the fan was Jack Sharkey, the heavyweight boxing champion.

Clancy was involved in the **Eddie Shore** and **Ace Bailey** incident on 12 December 1933, which almost ended Bailey's life. Toronto's Clancy tripped Boston's Shore, who mistakenly retaliated against Bailey with a **check** from behind. On 14 November 1936, he became the first defenseman in NHL history to **score** on a **penalty** shot during a 6–2 victory over the **Chicago Black Hawks**. During 16 NHL seasons, Clancy played in 592 regular-season games and recorded 136 **goals**, 147 **assists**, 283 **points**, and 914 **penalty minutes**. When Clancy retired from playing, he remained active in hockey by **coaching** the **Montreal Maroons** (1937–1938), Cincinnati Mohawks (1949–1951), Pittsburgh Hornets (1951–1953), and Toronto Maple Leafs (1953–1956). He filled in as Toronto's coach in 1967 for **Punch Imlach** and in 1972 for John McLellan. Clancy was also an **on-ice official** for NHL and **American Hockey League** games (1938–1949), and he became a spokesman for a **skating** company. He was inducted into the **Hockey Hall of Fame** in 1958 as a player. In 1975, he was inducted into **Canada's Sports Hall of Fame**. Clancy remained with the Toronto organization as an executive until his death in 1986. In 1988, the **King Clancy Memorial Trophy** was created by the NHL Board of Governors in his honor. It is awarded annually to the NHL player who demonstrates leadership qualities on and off the ice.

CLAPPER, AUBREY VICTOR "DIT". B. 9 February 1907, Newmarket, Ontario. D. 21 January 1978, Newmarket, Ontario. As a boy, Dit Clapper was known by his middle name, Victor, but because his younger brother pronounced Victor as "Ditter," he picked up the **nickname** "Dit." He was the first **National Hockey League (NHL)** player to play 20 seasons, and one of only two, besides **Red Kelly**, to play on an **All-Star Team** at two different positions, as he played both **right wing** and defense. Clapper spent his entire NHL career with the **Boston Bruins**. He was a member of the famous Boston **line** known as the "Dynamite Line," with **Cooney Weiland** and Dutch Gainor. Together they helped Boston win the **Stanley Cup** in 1929. With Clapper's help, the Bruins lost only five games during the 1930–1931 season, but they were defeated in the playoffs by the **Montreal Canadiens**. During the 1937 playoffs, Clapper got into a **fight** with Dave Trottier of the **Montreal Maroons**. At the time, **Clarence Campbell** was the **referee**. As Campbell tried to separate the two, Clapper turned around and hit Campbell, which resulted in a $100 fine.

Clapper was well-liked by his teammates and the fans because he played a tough game on the **ice** and carried himself with dignity off the ice. He was the Bruins' captain from 1932–1938 and 1939–1946. In 1939, after 10 years as a powerful forward, he became a **defenseman**. Paired with **Eddie Shore**, the two men helped Boston win the Stanley Cup in 1939 and 1941. In 833 NHL regular-season games, Clapper recorded 228 **goals**, 246 **assists**, 474 **points**, and 462 **penalty minutes**. Immediately after retiring from playing, he was inducted into the **Hockey Hall of Fame** in 1947. He also **coached** the Boston Bruins (1945–1949) and Buffalo Bisons (1959–1960). Clapper's grandson, Greg Theberge, also played in the NHL with the **Washington Capitals** (1979–1984).

CLARENCE S. CAMPBELL BOWL. The Clarence S. Campbell Bowl is one of only four team awards given out by the **National Hockey League (NHL)**. The other three include the most famous one, the **Stanley Cup**, as well as the **Presidents' Trophy** and **Prince of Wales Trophy**. The Clarence S. Campbell Bowl was introduced in 1968, as recognition of the services of the NHL's president (1946–1977). The prize was originally awarded to the regular-season champions of the Western Division. Then, in 1975, it was given to the regular-season champion of the Campbell Conference. From 1982–1993, the bowl was awarded to the Campbell Conference playoff champion. Since the 1993–1994 season, the trophy has been given to the playoff champion of the **Western Conference**. The **Philadelphia Flyers** were the first winner. The **Edmonton Oilers** and Philadelphia Flyers have each won this trophy the most often (6). The **Vancouver Canucks** (2011) and Los Angeles Kings (2012) won the trophy most recently.

CLARKE, ROBERT EARLE "BOBBY". B. 13 August 1949, Flin Flon, Manitoba. As a **young player**, Bobby Clarke was a star, but teams in the **National Hockey League (NHL)** were hesitant to sign him due to his diabetic condition. The **Philadelphia Flyers** took a chance on him, and he was their **center** from 1969–1984. After Clarke had two serious diabetic seizures during training camp, **coach** Frank Lewis designed a dietary plan, which Bobby strictly followed from then onward. Before a game, Clarke would drink a bottle of Coca-Cola with three spoonfuls of dissolved sugar. Between periods, he would drink half a glass of orange juice with sugar added, and after the game a whole glass. Lewis always kept several chocolate bars and a tube of 100% glucose in his bag, just in case. The diet worked well, and, by his third season, Clarke recorded the highest number of **points** in the club's history (81). At the end of the 1971–1972 season, he was awarded the **Bill Masterton Memorial Trophy** for his perseverance and dedication to hockey.

After his first season with the Flyers, Clarke wore the **jersey number** 16, except during a road trip in the mid-1970s when his **jersey** was stolen, and then he wore 36 for one game. As one of the best **checkers** at the time, he helped the Flyers win the **Stanley Cup** in 1974 and 1975. Individually,

Clarke won the **Hart Memorial Trophy** (1973, 1975, 1976), Lester B. Pearson Award (1974), **Lester Patrick Trophy** (1980), and **Frank J. Selke Trophy** (1983). He was also the captain of the Flyers from 1982–1984. He and **Boston Bruins'** center **Phil Esposito** were rivals. Clarke's goofy, toothless grin was deceptive because he resorted to dirty play at times. **Montreal Canadiens' coach Scotty Bowman** said, "I think the guy is a mean hockey player." **Fred Shero** replied, "What Bowman was trying to say was that Bobby's the ultimate competitor."

Clarke played for **Canada** in the 1972 **Summit Series**, and he slashed **Valeri Kharlamov's** ankle in the sixth game. Clarke won the 1976 **Canada Cup** and won a bronze medal at the 1982 **World Ice Hockey Championships**. He retired with 358 **goals**, 852 **assists**, 1,210 points, and 1,453 **penalty minutes** during 1,144 regular-season games. After his playing career ended, he became the general manager of the Flyers (1984–1990, 1994–2007), Minnesota North Stars (1990–1992), and **Florida Panthers** (1993–1994). In the 1990s, he and **Eric Lindros** had several serious disputes, and Lindros eventually left the Flyers. They both played for the Philadelphia Flyers Alumni during the 2012 **Winter Classic** Alumni Game on 31 December 2011, against the **New York Rangers** Alumni. Both Clarke and Lindros acknowledged that it was their opportunity to mend fences. Clarke was inducted into the **Hockey Hall of Fame** in 1987.

CLEARY, WILLIAM JOHN, JR. "BILL". B. 19 August 1934, Cambridge, Massachusetts. Bill Cleary is a former American **ice** hockey player, **coach**, and administrator. He was an All-American college player at Harvard University, where he still holds several records, including most **points** in a single season (89). After turning down a professional offer from the **National Hockey League's (NHL) Montreal Canadiens**, Cleary won a silver medal as a member of the **U.S. Men's Olympic Ice Hockey Team** at the 1956 Winter Olympics. At the 1959 **World Ice Hockey Championships**, he won an award as the best forward. At the 1960 Winter Olympics, in Squaw Valley, California, he won a gold medal with the U.S. team that defeated the heavily favored **Soviet Union Men's Olympic Ice Hockey Team**. Cleary also **coached college hockey** at Harvard for more than 20 years, leading them to the 1989 **National Collegiate Athletic Association** National Championship. He compiled a career 324-201-22 record, for a .612 winning percentage. After leaving coaching in 1990, Cleary became the athletic director at Harvard, where he supervised a program of more than 40 varsity sports teams until retiring in 2000. In 1997, he received the **Lester Patrick Trophy** for his many contributions to hockey. That same year, Cleary was inducted into the **International Ice Hockey Federation Hall of Fame**.

CLEGHORN, HENRY WILLIAM SPRAGUE "PEG". B. 11 March 1890, Montreal, Quebec. D. 12 July 1956, Montreal, Quebec. Sprague Cleghorn was an aggressive hockey player who played in the **National Hockey Association** and **National Hockey League (NHL)**. He was **defenseman** for the **Montreal Wanderers** (1911–1917), **Ottawa Senators** (1918–1920), Toronto St. Patricks (1920–1921), **Montreal Canadiens** (1921–1925), and **Boston Bruins** (1925–1928). His missed the 1917–1918 season due to a broken leg. On 22 December 1912, **Newsy Lalonde** pounded Cleghorn's **brother**, Odie, into the **boards**. Cleghorn retaliated by smashing Lalonde over the head with his **hockey stick**. The **injury** required 12 stitches, and Cleghorn was suspended for four weeks. In 1922, he injured three Ottawa players (**Cy Denneny**, **Eddie Gerard**, and **Frank Nighbor**) in a brawl, leading Ottawa police to offer to arrest him. Many people only remember his **fighting** and forget that he was actually a talented player. He helped his teams win the **Stanley Cup** in 1920, 1921, and 1924. He even played the position of **goaltender** twice. On 18 February 1919, Cleghorn replaced penalized **Clint Benedict** for a 4–3 Ottawa win over the Toronto St. Pats. Then, on 1 February 1922, Cleghorn replaced penalized Canadiens' goalie **Georges Vezina** in a 4–2 loss to Ottawa.

During 489 regular-season games, Cleghorn recorded 84 **goals**, 123 **points**, and 489 **penalty minutes**. He ranked among the league leaders in penalty minutes for nine of the first 10 seasons of the NHL's history. Cleghorn was hit by a car in early June 1956, and he died of his injuries in July. His younger brother, Odie, died from heart failure on the day of Sprague's funeral, 14 July 1956. Sprague was inducted into the **Hockey Hall of Fame** in 1958.

CLEVELAND BARONS. *See* MINNESOTA WILD.

COACH. The hockey coach is the person who leads the team, directs the practices, and develops a team strategy. The head coach often has assistant coaches to help him manage the players. Retired **National Hockey League (NHL)** players often remain active in the league by using their knowledge to coach other players. **Toe Blake** holds the record as the coach who won the **Stanley Cup** the most times (8). **Scotty Bowman** holds the record for the most games coached (2,141), as well as the most games won (1,244). Other notable NHL coaches include **Sid Abel, Al Arbour, Herb Brooks, Don Cherry, Punch Imlach, Bob Johnson, Pete Muldoon,** and **Fred Shero**. *See also* COOK, FREDERICK JOSEPH "BUN"; LALONDE, EDOUARD CHARLES "NEWSY"; ROSS, ARTHUR HOWEY "ART"; SHORE, EDWARD WILLIAM "EDDIE," "THE EDMONTON EXPRESS".

COFFEY, PAUL DOUGLAS. B. 1 June 1961, Weston, Ontario. Paul Coffey was a **defenseman** for 21 seasons in the **National Hockey League (NHL)**. He was known for his speed and **skating** skills, as well as his **scoring** talents. He played for the **Edmonton Oilers** (1980–1987), **Pittsburgh Penguins** (1987–1992), **Los Angeles Kings** (1991–1993), **Detroit Red Wings** (1992–1996), Hartford Whalers (1996–1997), **Philadelphia Flyers** (1996–1998), **Chicago Blackhawks** (1998–1999), **Carolina Hurricanes** (1998–2000), and **Boston Bruins** (2000–2001). Although he was a defenseman, Coffey **scored** two **goals** and six **assists** for eight **points** during a game against the **Detroit Red Wings** on 14 March 1986. On 22 December 1990, Coffey became the second defenseman ever to record 1,000 points, which he did in only 770 games. During his NHL career, he played in 1,409 regular-season games, with 396 goals, 1,135 assists, 1,531 points, and 1,802 **penalty minutes**. Coffey ranks second, behind **Ray Bourque**, in all-time career goals, assists, and points by an NHL defenseman. He won the **Stanley Cup** four times (1984, 1985, 1987, 1991) and the **James Norris Memorial Trophy** three times. Coffey holds the NHL record for goals in a single season (48), set in 1985–1986. He also holds the NHL career record for **Stanley Cup Playoff** goals (59) and career playoff points by a defenseman (196). Internationally, Coffey played for **Canada** and won three gold medals in the 1984, 1987, and 1991 **Canada Cups**. He also played in the 1990 **World Ice Hockey Championships** and won a silver medal in the 1996 **World Cup of Hockey**. Coffey was inducted into the **Hockey Hall of Fame** in 2004.

COLLEGE HOCKEY. Many universities in the **United States** have Division I **ice** hockey teams. They are regulated by the **National Collegiate Athletic Association (NCAA)**. Solid college programs can be found at Boston College, Boston University, Bowling Green State University, Colorado College, Cornell University, Harvard University, Lake Superior State University, Michigan State University, Michigan Tech, Northern Michigan University, Rensselaer Polytechnic Institute, University of Denver, University of Maine, University of Michigan, University of Minnesota, University of Minnesota Duluth, University of North Dakota, and University of Wisconsin. Since 1981, the **Hobey Baker** Award has been presented to the year's most outstanding player in the NCAA. Jerry York is the men's head **coach** at Boston College. York is currently the winningest active coach in NCAA hockey and second on the all-time list, with 899 wins, behind retired Michigan State University coach Ron Mason (924 wins). Murray Murdoch, former **left wing** for the **New York Rangers**, coached at Yale University from 1938–1965. He was awarded the **Lester Patrick Trophy**. Other coaches who have also received the trophy for their contributions to hockey include **Herb Brooks, Bob Johnson**, John MacInnes, Jack Parker, and Jerry York.

COLORADO AVALANCHE. The Colorado Avalanche are a professional **ice** hockey team in the **Northwest Division** of the **National Hockey League (NHL) Western Conference**. They were originally part of the **Quebec Nordiques**. The Quebec Nordiques played in the **World Hockey Association** (1972–1979) and **National Hockey League (NHL)** (1979–1995). In 1991, **Eric Lindros** was drafted by Quebec, but he refused to play for the last-place team. He was then auctioned off to the **Philadelphia Flyers**. The Nordiques gained several key players for him, including **Peter Forsberg**, and they became a strong team. In 1995, the franchise was relocated to Denver, Colorado, and renamed the Colorado Avalanche. Since the Lindros trade, the franchise has won eight division titles and two **Stanley Cup** championships. They had a famous rivalry with the **Detroit Red Wings** as a result of meeting each other five times in seven years in the Western Conference **Stanley Cup Playoffs** between 1996–2002. Colorado had a great season in 2000–2001, with the all-time leading **scorer** in Avalanche history, **center** Joe Sakic. Sakic finished the regular season with 118 **points** (54 **goals** and 64 **assists**), only three behind **Jaromír Jágr**'s 121 points.

In its NHL history, the team has made the Stanley Cup Finals twice and won both times. They defeated the **Florida Panthers** in 1996 (4–0) and the **New Jersey Devils** in 2001 (4–3). Other strong players for the Avalanche have included **Hockey Hall of Famers Ray Bourque**, **Patrick Roy**, and **Jari Kurri**. **Bryan Trottier**, who was an assistant **coach** when the Avalanche won their second Stanley Cup in 2001, was inducted to the Hockey Hall of Fame as a player in 1997. As the Avalanche franchise, there have been 6 head coaches. The first head coach was Marc Crawford, who coached the team for three seasons. Bob Hartley coached the most games for the Avalanche, with 359 games. The Colorado team won the **Presidents' Trophy** in 1996–1997 and 2000–2001. In 32 seasons in the NHL, from 1979–1980 to 2011–2012, the Avalanche have compiled a record of 1,166-1,053-261-70 (2,663 points) and made 21 playoff appearances.

COLORADO ROCKIES. The Colorado Rockies were a professional **ice** hockey team in the **National Hockey League (NHL)** that played in Denver, Colorado, from 1976–1982. In six seasons in Denver, the Rockies made the **Stanley Cup Playoffs** only once, during the 1977–1978 season. Even then, they finished with the sixth-worst record in the league. One of their star players was **right wing Lanny McDonald**. A highlight of the Rockies' history was during the 1979–1980 season, when **Don Cherry** was named head **coach** after being fired by the **Boston Bruins**. With Cherry, the Rockies adopted the motto, "Come to the fights and watch a Rockies game break out!" This could be seen on billboards all across Denver during the 1979–1980 season, and it no doubt helped the ailing club. But even with seven coaches in four years, the team couldn't turn things around. The franchise moved to East Rutherford, New Jersey, in 1982, and it was renamed the **New Jersey Devils**. The NHL did not return to Denver until the **Quebec Nordiques** moved there to become the **Colorado Avalanche** following the 1994–1995 season.

COLUMBUS BLUE JACKETS. The Columbus Blue Jackets are a professional **ice** hockey team in the **Central Division** of the **National Hockey League (NHL) Western Conference**, based in Columbus, Ohio. The Blue Jackets joined the league in the 2000–2001 season. In its NHL history, the team has made the **Stanley Cup Playoffs** only once (2008–2009), and the Blue Jackets in the quarterfinals. Typically, the Columbus team ends the season in fourth or fifth place of their division. To date, no players from the team have been inducted into the **Hockey Hall of Fame**. Steve Mason and Rick Nash are among the team's best players. There have been eight head **coaches** for the team, including Dave King, who coached them for three seasons. Todd Richards is their current coach. In 11 seasons in the NHL (2000–2001 to 2011–2012), the Blue Jackets have compiled a record of 340-440-33-86 (799 **points**).

COLVILLE, NEIL MCNEIL. B. 4 August 1914, Edmonton, Alberta. D. 26 December 1987, Richmond, British Columbia. Neil Colville played **ice** hockey for 12 seasons in the **National Hockey League (NHL)** as both a forward and **defenseman** with the **New York Rangers** (1935–1942, 1944–1949). The Rangers had a **line** known as the "Bread Line," because **scorers** Mac Colville, Neil Colville, and Alex Shibicky were the bread and butter of the team. They helped their team defeat the **Toronto Maple Leafs** in six games to win the **Stanley Cup** in 1940. Neil was a stronger player than his younger brother Mac. After returning from the **Canadian** Armed Forces, Mac played 14 games and then retired. Neil only scored four **goals** in 60 games, but he then successfully switched positions, to defenseman. He remained a player until 1949, and he was then the Rangers' **coach** (195–1952) until his retirement. In 1967, Colville was inducted into the **Hockey Hall of Fame**.

CONACHER, CHARLES WILLIAM "CHARLIE," "THE BOMBER". B. 20 December 1909, Toronto, Ontario. D. 30 December 1967, Toronto, Ontario. Charlie Conacher played **right wing** in the **National Hockey League (NHL)** with the **Toronto Maple Leafs** (1929–1938), **Detroit Red Wings** (1938–1939), and **New York Americans** (1939–1941). He was also a substitute **goaltender**, three times for Toronto and once for Detroit. Conacher played a total of 10 minutes as goalie and did not give up a single **goal**. **Busher Jackson, Joe Primeau**, and Conacher were a young forward **line** of the Maple Leafs **nicknamed** the "Kid Line." Conacher earned his **nickname**

from his explosive shot. Commenting on Conacher's **slapshot, King Clancy** once said, "It felt like somebody had turned a blowtorch on me. I couldn't sit down for a week." Conacher led the NHL in goals **scored** five times between 1931–1936. On 19 January 1932, he became the first Maple Leafs' player to score five goals in one game in an 11–3 victory over the Americans. Conacher holds the league record for the fastest game-winning goal (6 seconds) in Toronto's 6–0 win over the Boston Bruins on 6 February 1932. He helped Toronto defeat the **New York Rangers** to win the **Stanley Cup** in 1932.

During his hockey career, Conacher missed several games due to his numerous injuries, which included a broken hand, broken wrist, broken collarbone, and dislocated shoulder. Conacher played in 459 NHL regular-season games and recorded 225 goals, 173 **assists**, 398 **points**, and 523 **penalty minutes**. After retiring from playing, Conacher **coached** the **Chicago Black Hawks** from 1947–1950. He had nine siblings, including **Hockey Hall of Famers Lionel Conacher** and **Roy Conacher**. He was also the father of retired NHL forward Pete Conacher. Charlie was inducted into the Hockey Hall of Fame in 1961 and **Canada's Sports Hall of Fame** in 1975. In 1967, he passed away from throat cancer. The Charlie Conacher Humanitarian Award was named after him. Although it was not an NHL award, it was presented to the NHL player who best exhibited outstanding humanitarian and public services contributions (1968–1984). **George Armstrong, Jean Béliveau, Bobby Orr**, and **Börje Salming** are a few of the past recipients. The current NHL equivalent is the **King Clancy Memorial Trophy**.

CONACHER, LIONEL PRETORIA "BIG TRAIN". B. 24 May 1901, Toronto, Ontario. D. 26 May 1954, Ottawa, Ontario. Lionel Conacher was an all-around sportsman. He was a member of a winning Toronto Canoe Club. In 1921, he won a championship as a member of the Toronto Argonauts, a **Canadian** football team. That same year, Conacher also won an amateur lightweight boxing championship in Canada. He even fought heavyweight champion Jack Dempsey in an exhibition match but was knocked out. He went on to play 12 seasons in the **National Hockey League (NHL)** as a **defenseman** with the **Pittsburgh Pirates** (1925–1927), **New York Americans** (1926–1930), **Montreal Maroons** (1930–1933, 1934–1937), and **Chicago Black Hawks** (1933–1934). Conacher earned the **nickname** "Big Train" because he had endless energy and great stamina. During the 1929–1930 season, he was both a player and **coach** for the Americans. Conacher won the **Stanley Cup** in 1934 and 1935, with the Maroons. During the 1930s, he also played professional **lacrosse** and football. In 1937, he retired from hockey and was elected to the Ontario legislature that same year. He was also elected to the Canadian House of Commons in 1949, where he remained active until his death in 1954. In 1950, he was named Canada's Athlete of the Half-Century. Conacher played in 498 regular-season NHL games and recorded 80 **goals**, 105 **assists**, 185 **points**, and 882 **penalty minutes**. He was elected to **Canada's Sports Hall of Fame** (1955), the Canadian Football Hall of Fame (1963), and the Canadian Lacrosse Hall of Fame (1966). In 1994, he was inducted into the **Hockey Hall of Fame**. His younger **brothers, Charlie Conacher** and **Roy Conacher**, also played in the NHL and are Hockey Hall of Fame members.

CONACHER, ROY GORDON. B. 5 October 1916, Toronto, Ontario. D. 29 December 1984, Victoria, British Columbia. Roy Conacher was part of a famous hockey **family**. His older **brothers, Lionel Conacher** and **Charlie Conacher**, also played in the **National Hockey League (NHL)**. Roy was a **left wing** in the NHL and played for **Boston Bruins** (1938–1942, 1945–1946), **Detroit Red Wings** (1946–1947), and **Chicago Black Hawks** (1947–1952). He was the first **rookie** in NHL history to lead the league in **goals** when he **scored** 26 (1938–1939). Four times he finished second in NHL goals, with 24 (1940–1941), 24 (1941–1942), 30 (1946–1947), and 26 (1948–1949). During World War II, he played hockey as a member of the Royal **Canadian** Air Force. Conacher helped the Bruins win the **Stanley Cup** in 1939 and 1941. He even scored the Stanley Cup–winning goal in Boston's 3–1 win over the **Toronto Maple Leafs** on 16 April 1939. He won the **Art Ross Trophy** in 1949 as the NHL's leading scorer, with 68 **points**. During his 11 NHL seasons, Conacher played in 490 regular-season games and recorded 226 goals, 200 **assists**, and 426 points. In 1998, he was inducted into the **Hockey Hall of Fame** posthumously.

CONN SMYTHE TROPHY. The Conn Smythe Trophy is the **National Hockey League (NHL)** award given annually to the Most Valuable Player to his team during the **Stanley Cup Playoffs**. It is named for the former **coach**, general manager, and owner of the **Toronto Maple Leafs, Conn Smythe**. Smythe was inducted into the **Hockey Hall of Fame** in 1958 as a **builder**. The first recipient was **Jean Béliveau** of the **Montreal Canadiens**, in 1965. **Patrick Roy** has won this trophy the most times, with three wins. His is also the only player to win for different teams, as he won it with the Montreal Canadiens twice, and in 2001 with the **Colorado Avalanche**. The **St. Louis Blues** are the only team without a Stanley Cup to have a Conn Smythe Trophy winner. Their **goaltender, Glenn Hall**, won it in 2001. The winners of this trophy have all been **Canadian**, except for five. The non-Canadian winners include Americans **Brian Leetch** of the **New York Rangers** (1994) and Tim Thomas of the **Boston Bruins** (2011), **Russian** player **Evgeni Malkin** of the **Pittsburgh Penguins** (2009, 2012), and **Swedish** players **Nicklas Lidström** (2002) and Henrik Zetterberg (2008) of the **Detroit Red Wings**.

CONNELL, ALEX "THE OTTAWA FIREMAN". B. 8 February 1902, Ottawa, Ontario. D. 10 May 1958, Ottawa, Ontario. Alex Connell was a professional **ice** hockey **goaltender** in the **National Hockey League (NHL)** with the **Ottawa Senators** (1924–1931, 1932–1933), Detroit Falcons (1931–1932), **New York Americans** (1933–1934), and **Montreal Maroons** (1934–1935, 1936–1937). The **nickname** "The Ottawa Fireman" was given to him because Connell was the secretary of the Ottawa Fire Department in the off-season. On 27 December 1927, **defenseman King Clancy** replaced the penalized Connell. Clancy did not allow a Toronto **goal** during his two minutes at the **net**. Connell led the NHL in games won, with 24 (1925–1926) and 30 (1926–1927). During his time with the Falcons, he was almost killed. In a **match** against the Americans, Connell had an argument with the **goal judge** and tried to hit him with his **hockey stick**; however, the judge was a hit man for bootlegger and team owner **Bill Dwyer** and was ordered to Connell him after the game. Luckily, the police protected Connell. When **Roy Worters** was **injured**, Connell played one game for the New York Americans as his replacement. It was 15 March 1934, and he helped the Americans defeat his own Senators by a **score** of 3–2. Connell has the distinction of being the only NHL goalie to record 15 or more **shutouts** in the regular season twice (1926–1927 and 192–1928), and he totaled 81 in his career. He also won the **Stanley Cup** with Ottawa (1927) and Montreal (1935). Connell tied **George Hainsworth**'s career record goals against average of 1.91. Connell was elected into the **Hockey Hall of Fame** in 1958, but he died before the induction ceremony.

COOK, FREDERICK JOSEPH "BUN". B. 18 September 1903, Kingston, Ontario. D. 19 March 1988, Kingston, Ontario. Frederick Cook was **nicknamed** "Bun" after a journalist saw his fast **skating** and said he was "as quick as a bunny." He was a **left wing** for the Saskatoon Crescents (1924–1926) and helped them win the **Allan Cup** in 1924. He then joined the **National Hockey League (NHL)** and played for the **New York Rangers** (1926–1936) for most of his career. On 16 November 1926, Cook **assisted** on the first **goal** in Rangers' franchise history in a 1–0 win over the **Montreal Maroons**. He was on a **line** known as the "Bread Line," with his **brother**, Bill Cook, and **Frank Boucher**. Together, the three men **scored** every goal for the Rangers in the **Stanley Cup** Finals against the Maroons in 1928. In 1933, Cook helped the Rangers defeat the **Toronto Maple Leafs** in four games to win a second Stanley Cup. Cook was one of the first players to use the drop pass and the **slapshot**. He was traded and played one season with the **Boston Bruins** (1936–1937). After he retired from playing, Cook became a **coach** for the Providence Reds (1937–1943) and Cleveland Barons (1943–1954). As a hockey coach, he won the **American Hockey League** championship trophy and the **Calder Cup** seven times (1938, 1940, 1945,

1948, 1951, 1953, 1954). During his playing career, Cook was in 531 regular-season games and recorded 183 goals, 152 assists, 335 **points**, and 510 **penalty minutes**. In 1959, he was inducted into the **Hockey Hall of Fame** as a player.

CORBEAU, BERTRAM ORIAN "BERT," "OLD PIG IRON". B. 9 February 1894, Penetanguishene, Ontario. D. 21 September 1942, Georgian Bay, Ontario. Bert Corbeau was a professional **ice** hockey **defenseman** who played 10 seasons in the **National Hockey League (NHL)** for the **Montreal Canadiens** (1914–1922), **Hamilton Tigers** (1922–1923), Toronto St. Patricks (1923), and the **Toronto Maple Leafs** (1923–1927). He was a member of the first **Stanley Cup**–winning squad of the Montreal Canadiens in 1916. He and **Newsy Lalonde** formed a powerful defensive duo. Corbeau was the first player to play for both the Canadiens and Maple Leafs. He became the first player to record 100 minutes in **penalties** in one season (1926–1927). Only 10 of Corbeau's 1923 V 145-1 hockey cards are known to exist, and they are valued at more than $20,000 each. After retiring from playing, Corbeau was an NHL **referee**. His **brother**, Con Corbeau, was also a NHL defenseman and was on the 1914 Stanley Cup–winning Toronto Blueshirts. Bert died tragically in a boating accident. When the boat hit a sand bar, water entered the vessel, sinking it quickly. Twenty-five of the 42 people onboard died.

COULTER, ARTHUR EDMUND "ART," "TRAPPER". B. 31 May 1909, Winnipeg, Manitoba. D. 14 October 2000, Mobile, Alabama. Art Coulter was a **defenseman** in the **National Hockey League (NHL)** with the **Chicago Black Hawks** (1931–1936) and **New York Rangers** (1936–1942). He earned the **nickname** "Trapper" because he loved to talk about fishing and hunting with his teammates. On 15 January 1936, Chicago traded him to New York in exchange for **Earl Seibert**. Coulter was a great **penalty killer**. He and Muzz Patrick made a strong defensive team for the Rangers. Coulter led the NHL in **penalty minutes** in 1937–1938, with 90, and he finished in second in 1939–1940, with 68. He won the **Stanley Cup** in 1934 and 1940. Once, while trying to get at an **on-ice official**, **Toronto Maple Leafs'** owner **Conn Smythe** accidentally struck Coulter. During World War II, he played with the U.S. Coast Guard Clippers hockey team. During a career of 465 regular-season NHL matches, he recorded 30 **goals**, 82 **assists**, 112 **points**, and 543 penalty minutes. After retiring from hockey, Coulter ran a hardware store in Miami, Florida. He was inducted into the **Hockey Hall of Fame** in 1974. His **brother**, Tom Coulter, also played in the NHL with the Chicago Black Hawks for one season (1933–1934).

COURNOYER, YVAN SERGE "ROADRUNNER". B. 22 November 1943, Drummondville, Quebec. As a **young player**, Yvan Cournoyer practiced hitting steel **pucks** against the carpet-padded walls of his basement. He credited that activity with strengthening his wrists for his future hockey career. Cournoyer spent 16 seasons in the **National Hockey League (NHL)** as a **right wing** with the **Montreal Canadiens** (1963–1979), and he earned the **nickname** "Roadrunner" because of his fast **skating**. As a top **scorer**, he led the NHL in game-winning **goals**, with 7 (1966–1967) and 12 (1975–1976). He also led the NHL in **power play** goals, with 20 (1966–1967). Cournoyer helped his team win the **Stanley Cup** 10 times from 1965–1979. On 10 May 1973, Cournoyer scored the Stanley Cup–winning goal in Montreal's 6–4 win over the **Chicago Black Hawks**. That same year, he was also awarded the **Conn Smythe Trophy**. From 1975–1979, Cournoyer was the captain of the Canadiens. During his NHL career, he played in 968 regular-season **matches** and recorded 428 goals, 435 **assists**, 863 **points**, and 255 **penalty minutes**. In 1982, Cournoyer was inducted into the **Hockey Hall of Fame**. The Montreal Roadrunners of the **Roller Hockey** International League were named after him, and he served as their **coach** for one season (1994–1995). He then acted as an assistant coach for the Canadiens (1996–1997).

COWLEY, WILLIAM MAILES "BILL," "COWBOY". B. 12 June 1912, Bristol, Quebec. D. 31 December 1993, Ottawa, Ontario, Bill Cowley was a hockey player in the **National Hockey League (NHL)** who played for the **St. Louis Eagles** (1934–1935) and **Boston Bruins** (1935–1947). As a **center**, he was a strong playmaker, but his efforts tended to be overshadowed by teammate **Milt Schmidt**. Cowley won the Hart Trophy in 1941 and 1943. During the 1940–1941 season, with 62 **points**, he was the NHL's leading **scorer.** He recorded more **assists** (45) than the next leading scorer had in total points. The only other player in history to do so is **Wayne Gretzky.** Cowley helped Boston win the **Stanley Cup** in 1939 and 1941. He led the **Stanley Cup Playoffs** in points, with 14 (1938–39). He also set the record for regular-season career points, with 548. **Elmer Lach** broke his record in 1953. The formation of the **Art Ross Trophy** in 1947 was likely inspired by Cowley's accomplishments. During his NHL career, Cowley played in 549 regular-season games and recorded 195 **goals**, 353 assists, 548 points, and 143 **penalty minutes**. After retiring from playing, he became a **coach** for the Ottawa Army (1947–1948) and **Vancouver Canucks** (1948–1949). In 1968, Cowley was inducted into the **Hockey Hall of Fame**. He holds the distinction of being the only member to have started his NHL career with the St. Louis Eagles.

CRAIG, JAMES "JIM". B. 31 May 1957, North Easton, Massachusetts. **Goaltender** Jim Craig burst onto the hockey scene when he joined the U.S. National Team following his **college hockey** career at Boston University. He is best-known for helping the **U.S. Men's Olympic Ice Hockey Team** win an upset gold medal at the 1980 **Olympic Games.** Craig had 39 **saves** versus the **Soviet Union Men's Olympic Ice Hockey Team** and a 6-0-1 record in the tournament. Craig was vital to the **"Miracle on Ice,"** which was when the underdog U.S. team defeated the Soviet team. Immediately following the Olympics, Craig joined the **National Hockey League (NHL)** with the Atlanta Flames. He was victorious in his NHL debut but didn't add another win to his record until the last three games he played at the end of the 1979–1980 season. Craig was then traded to the **Boston Bruins.** With the Bruins, he played 23 games and had a 9-7-6 record. The next season, Craig went to the **minor league.** He joined the U.S. National Team again and played in the 1983 **World Ice Hockey Championships.** When former "Miracle on Ice" player Neal Broten offered Craig a contract with the Minnesota North Stars, he played three games for them (1983–1984) before retiring from hockey. Craig used his college degree to become a marketing service consultant and motivational speaker. He was inducted into the **International Ice Hockey Federation Hall of Fame** in 1999. In 2003, he was inducted into the **U.S. Hockey Hall of Fame.** His son and daughter both play hockey, but not as goaltenders.

CRAWFORD, SAMUEL RUSSELL, "RUSTY". B. 7 November 1885, Cardinal, Ontario. D. 19 December 1971, Prince Albert, Saskatchewan. Rusty Crawford played **left wing** for 16 professional and elite amateur hockey seasons. He played for the **Quebec Bulldogs** (1912–1917) of the **National Hockey Association.** He helped them defend their **Stanley Cup** title during his **rookie** season (1912–1913). Crawford also played for the Toronto Arenas of the **National Hockey League** from 1917–1919. In 1918, in a best-of-five series against the Seattle Metropolitans, Crawford again won the Stanley Cup. He was known for his **skating** speed, back-checking skills, and longevity. He played competitive hockey until he was 45 years old. Crawford was inducted into the **Hockey Hall of Fame** in 1962.

CREASE. The term *crease* was originally used in the sport of cricket to describe the furrowed playing area in front of the wickets. In **ice** hockey, the crease describes the area in front of the **goal** marked off by a thin **red line.** Over time, the size and method of marking the crease has varied, but the crease has always been a protected area for the **goaltender.** An attacking player who does not have possession of the **puck** cannot enter the crease. Prior to the 1999–2000 **National Hockey League (NHL)** season, if a player

scored a goal while his teammate was in the crease, the goal was ruled out by the **referee**. The rule preventing goals while an attacking player is in the crease was eliminated from the NHL and other North American professional leagues beginning in the 1999–2000 season. Goaltender **Frank Brimsek** of the **Boston Bruins** was known for using his **hockey stick** to knock players off their feet if they **skated** too close to his crease.

CROSBY, SIDNEY PATRICK "SID THE KID". B. 7 August 19 1987, Halifax, Nova Scotia. Sidney Crosby is a current **center** in the **National Hockey League (NHL)** and captain of the **Pittsburgh Penguins**. He wears the **jersey number** 87 for the year he was born. Crosby was the first draft pick in 2005 by the failing Pittsburgh Penguins franchise. The signing of Crosby sparked excitement in the Pittsburgh fans who were ready to give up on the last-place team. Ticket sales soared. **Wayne Gretzky** recognized Crosby's talent. When he was asked if there was one player who might one day break his records, Gretzky said, "Yes, Sidney Crosby. He's the best player I've seen since Mario." In 2007, at the age of 19, Crosby became the youngest player ever to win the **Hart Memorial Trophy** as the NHL's Most Valuable Player. On 2 March 2007, he also became the youngest NHL player to reach 200 career **points**. Previously, the only teenager to reach 200 points was Gretzky during the 1980–1981 season.

Internationally, Crosby played for **Canada** in the 2006 **World Ice Hockey Championships**, where he won both the leading point **scorer** award and the best forward award. In 2007, he won the **Art Ross Trophy** and Lester B. Pearson Award. Crosby recorded a **Gordie Howe hat trick** on 20 December 2007, in a game against the **Boston Bruins**. On 18 October 2008, he scored one **goal** and three **assists** to surpass benchmarks of 100 goals, 200 assists, and 300 points for his career. On his goal, his teammate, **Evgeni Malkin**, assisted to record his own 200th point. Crosby had a team trainer cut the **puck** in half so each player could have a souvenir to mark the achievement. After defeating the **Detroit Red Wings** in the 2009 **Stanley Cup** Finals, Crosby won his first Stanley Cup with the Penguins in seven games. At 21 years, 10 months, and 5 days of age, he became the youngest NHL captain to hold the Stanley Cup. Whether he was caught up in the excitement or deliberately being rude, Crosby was publicly criticized for neglecting to shake hands with Detroit's captain, **Nicklas Lidström**.

Crosby also has many **superstitions**, including walking the same path to the dressing room, not talking to his mother on game days, having to sit between Maxime Talbot and Pascal Dupuis when he eats, and refusing to let anyone touch his **hockey sticks**. In 2010, after recording 51 goals, Crosby received the **Maurice "Rocket" Richard Trophy**. From 5 November 2010 to 28 December 2010, he had a 25-game point streak that consisted of 27 goals, 24 assists, and 51 points. During the course of his career, Crosby has been plagued by numerous **injuries**. He missed the second half of the 2010–2011 season and most of 2011–2012 because of a concussion and neck injury. He played the final 14 games of the last regular season, recording six goals and 19 assists. In six **Stanley Cup Playoff** games, he had three goals and five assists. He won a gold medal at the 2010 **Olympic Games** in Vancouver. In his seven NHL seasons to date, Crosby has played in 434 regular-season games and recorded 223 goals, 386 assists, 609 points, and 401 **penalty minutes**. If he can overcome his injuries, this young star will have a long hockey career and surely be inducted into the **Hockey Hall of Fame** when he becomes eligible.

CURSES. Many hockey players are **superstitious,** and the **National Hockey League (NHL)** also has several famous curses. The refusal of **Madison Square Garden**'s management to allow the resurrection of the **New York Americans** after World War II was one of the popular theories underlying the Curse of 1940, which supposedly prevented the **New York Rangers** from winning the **Stanley Cup** again until 1994. The curse was finally broken when the Rangers defeated the **Vancouver Canucks**, 4–3, in 1994. A second curse is the Curse of Marty McSorley. In the 1993 Stanley Cup Finals, the **Los Angeles Kings** led, 2–1, when the **Montreal Canadiens** suspected that Kings' player Marty McSorley's **hockey stick** was too curved. After the stick was examined, McSorley was sent to the **penalty box** for playing with illegal **equipment**. Montreal then tied the game on the **power play**. Inspired by the curse-establishing **goal**, Montreal won the 1993 Stanley Cup. No **Canadian** hockey team has won the Stanley Cup since. Four Canadian teams have made the finals, only to lose to an American team. Strangely, the **Quebec Nordiques**, who moved from Canada to the **United States**, immediately won the Stanley Cup in 1996, and again in 2001, as the **Colorado Avalanche**.

A third curse is the Curse of Muldoon. It was allegedly placed on the **Chicago Black Hawks** in 1927 by head **coach Pete Muldoon** when he was fired. He stated that they would never again finish in first place. In 1943, Toronto sportswriter Jim Coleman printed it. Chicago did not finish in first place in their division (1928–1937) or in the single-division NHL (after 1938) until 1967, the final season of the **"Original Six"** Era, despite winning the Stanley Cup three times since Muldoon supposedly cursed the team.

Another curse involved Toronto's **Bill Barilko**. He **scored** the winning goal in the fifth game of the Stanley Cup Finals on 21 April 1951, in **overtime**, to win the series against the **Montreal Canadiens**. Four months later, he disappeared during a plane trip. The Barilko Curse was used to explain why the **Toronto Maple Leafs** didn't win a Stanley Cup during the 11 years that he was missing. Coincidentally, in 1962, when the plane wreckage and Barilko's body were found, the Leafs won the Stanley Cup again.

CZECH REPUBLIC. In 1908, in Paris, France, the federation known as the Ligue Internationale de Hockey sur Glace was created with representatives from Belgium, France, **Great Britain**, **Switzerland**, and Bohemia (now the Czech Republic). After being one of the founding members of the organization also known as the **International Ice Hockey Federation (IIHF)**, the Bohemian men's **ice** hockey team became a successful team in the early 20th century. The country of Czechoslovakia split into the Czech Republic and **Slovakia**. After 1992, the team disbanded and was replaced with the Czech and Slovak national men's hockey teams. The IIHF recognized the Czech national men's hockey team as the successor of the Czechoslovakian national ice hockey team. The Czech Republic is a member of the "Big Six," which is a term for the six strongest men's ice hockey nations. The other five teams are **Russia**, **Sweden**, the **United States**, **Finland**, and **Canada**. The Czechs won the gold medal at the 1998 **Olympic Games**. At the 2006 Winter Olympics, the Czechs won a bronze medal by defeating **Russia**, 3–0, in the third-place game. They also won three straight gold medals at the **World Ice Hockey Championships** from 1999–2001. The Czechs also won gold at the 2005 tournament, which was the only World Ice Hockey Championships where all **National Hockey League** players were available to participate because of the 2004–2005 **lockout**. At the 2006 World Ice Hockey Championships, the Czechs won silver, falling to Sweden in the final; however, the Czech Republic won the 2010 World Ice Hockey Championships in Germany. The men's team currently has a fifth-place ranking by the IIHF, and the women's team has a 14th-place ranking. Well-known hockey players born in the Czech Republic include **Jaroslav Drobný**, Patrik Eliáš, **goaltender Dominik Hašek**, Milan Hejduk, **Jaromír Jágr**, Petr Klíma, and **Petr Nedvěd**.

CZECHOSLOVAKIA. *See* CZECH REPUBLIC.

D

DALLAS STARS. The Dallas Stars are a professional **ice** hockey team in the **Pacific Division** of the **National Hockey League (NHL) Western Conference**. Previously known as the Minnesota North Stars, they were one of the six NHL expansion teams that joined the league in 1967. In 1978, the Cleveland Barons merged with the North Stars, and, in 1993, they relocated to Dallas, Texas, and became the Dallas Stars. As the North Stars, they advanced to the **Stanley Cup** Finals twice. In 1981, the **New York Islanders** defeated them, 4 games to 1, in the finals. Ten years later, in the finals, the **Pittsburgh Penguins** defeated them, 4 games to 2. In 1999, with Ken Hitchcock as their **coach**, the Dallas Stars won their first and only Stanley Cup by defeating the **Buffalo Sabres** in six games. The following year, the **New Jersey Devils** defeated them, 4 games to 2, in the finals. Among their best players were **Hockey Hall of Famers** Leo Boivin, Dino Ciccarelli, **Mike Gartner, Larry Murphy,** and **Gump Worsley** of the North Stars, and **Ed Belfour, Brett Hull,** and **Joe Nieuwendyk** of the Stars. There have been five head coaches for the Stars team. The team's first head coach was **Bob Gainey,** who coached for four seasons. Ken Hitchcock was the team's all-time leader for the most regular-season games coached (503), the most regular-season game wins (277), the most regular-season **points** (626), the most **Stanley Cup Playoff** games coached (80), and the most playoff game wins (47). Marc Crawford is the current head coach of the Stars. The Dallas Stars have won the **Presidents' Trophy** (1997–1998, 1998–1999) and the **Clarence S. Campbell Bowl** (1998–1999, 1999–2000). In their combined 44 seasons (1967–1968 to 2011–2012), the Minnesota North Stars/Dallas Stars have a record of 1,510-1,457-459-80 (3,559 points) and have appeared in 29 playoffs.

DARRAGH, JOHN PROCTOR "JACK". B. 4 December 1890, Ottawa, Ontario. D. 25 June 1924, Ottawa, Ontario. Jack Darragh was a professional hockey player who played **right wing** for the **Ottawa Senators** in the **National Hockey League (NHL)** and its predecessor, the **National Hockey Association**. Darragh was known for his **backhand** shot, fast **skating**, and good stickhandling skills. He was a large part of the team's success, and the Senators won four **Stanley Cups** while he was with them (1911, 1920, 1921, 1923). He led the league in **assists** (15) during the 1920–1921 season. He **scored** the Stanley Cup-winning **goal** in Ottawa's victory over the Seattle Metropolitans on 1 April 1920. In the 1921 final against the **Vancouver Millionaires,** Darragh scored both goals in a 2–1 deciding game victory. He and **Mike Bossy** of the **New York Islanders** are the only two players in NHL history to score Stanley Cup-winning goals in back-to-back seasons. Darragh retired after that season, but he returned to play for the Stanley Cup-winning team of 1922–1923, the third in four seasons. He retired after the 1923–1924 season and died a few months later from a ruptured appendix. In 1962, he was inducted posthumously into the **Hockey Hall of Fame.**

DATSYUK, PAVEL VALERIEVICH. B. 20 July 1978, Sverdlovsk, **Russia,** USSR. Pavel Datsyuk was a star soccer player in his youth. Today he is a current hockey player in the **National Hockey League (NHL).** He has played **center** for the **Detroit Red Wings** since 2001. Early in his career, he was mentored by Russian stars **Igor Larionov** and Sergei Fedorov, as well as Detroit's captain, **Steve Yzerman.** Datsyuk is known for his stickhandling expertise and for mastering the fancy version of **dekeing** known as dangling the **puck.** He helped Detroit win the **Stanley Cup** in 2002 and 2008. Datsyuk played on a **line** with **Brett Hull** and Henrik Zetterberg that was nicknamed the "Two Kids and an Old Goat Line." During the 2002–2003 season, he played only 64 **matches** because of a knee **injury,** but he still recorded 51 **points.** Datsyuk won four consecutive **Lady Byng Memorial Trophies** from 2006–2009 for his **ice** performance and good sportsmanship. He also won the **Frank J. Selke Trophy** three times (2008, 2009, 2010). He became the first NHL player in more than 70 years to win the Lady Byng Memorial Trophy three consecutive times. **Frank Boucher** of the **New York Rangers** was the last player to do so (1933–1935). Datsyuk and **Ron Francis** are the only players to have been awarded both the Selke and Lady Byng trophies during their careers.

Internationally, Datsyuk played for Russia in the **World Ice Hockey Championships** and won a bronze (2005), a silver (2010), and a gold medal (2012). He also competed in the 2002 Winter Olympics and won a bronze medal. In his 10 NHL seasons to date, Datsyuk has played in 732 regular-season games and recorded 240 **goals,** 478 **assists,** 718 points, and only 186 **penalty minutes.** He has also played in 126 **Stanley Cup Playoff** games and recorded 33 goals, 61 assists, 94 points, and 45 penalty minutes. Datsyuk will surely be inducted into the **Hockey Hall of Fame.**

DAVIDSON, ALLAN MCLEAN "SCOTTY". B. 6 March 1892, Kingston, Ontario. D. 16 June 1915, Belgium. Scotty Davidson was a **right wing** who was **coached** in his hometown by **James Sutherland**, "The Father of Hockey." Davidson led his Kingston **junior** team to two Ontario Hockey Association championships in 1910 and 1911. He then moved to Calgary for the 1911–1912 season and led the Calgary Athletics senior team to the Alberta provincial championship. In 1912, Davidson turned professional with the Toronto Blueshirts of the **National Hockey Association (NHA)**. He was known for his great **skating** talent, and it was said that he could skate faster backward than most players could forward. He was among the NHA's leading **scorers** the following two seasons, and he also led the NHA playoffs in **penalty minutes**, with 11 (1913–1914). Davidson was the captain of the Blueshirts when they defeated the **Montreal Canadiens** (6–2) in a two-game, total-**goal** series for the **Stanley Cup** championship in 1914. It was the first time a team from Toronto had won the Stanley Cup. At the outbreak of World War I in 1914, Davidson was the first professional hockey player to enlist with the **Canadian** Army. Tragically, he was killed in action while fighting in Belgium in 1915. Davidson's peers said he died in heroic efforts. He was commemorated on the Canadian National Vimy Memorial in France. In 1950, he was posthumously inducted into the **Hockey Hall of Fame**.

DAVIDSON, JOHN "J. D". B. 27 February 1953, Ottawa, Ontario. John Davidson was a **goaltender** in the **National Hockey League (NHL)** with the St. Louis Blues (1973–1975) and **New York Rangers** (1975–1983). The Rangers brought him in to replace the aging and **injured Eddie Giacomin**. Davidson wore the **jersey number** 00 for one season in the 1970s. He was also the inspiration for the title song of the 1978 hit album *Double Vision*. Members of the rock group Foreigner were watching a **Stanley Cup Playoff** game between the Rangers and **Buffalo Sabres**. During the game, Davidson was shaken up after a player on the Sabres took a hard shot that hit his goalie mask. As he was recovering, the announcers said that he was suffering from "double vision." He was also known for leading the Rangers to the 1979 **Stanley Cup** Finals on an injured left knee. Davidson was a good sport. Teammate **Nick Fotiu** loved to play jokes on his teammates, and he once filled Davidson's car with garbage. After retiring from playing, Davidson began a new career as a longtime hockey broadcaster (1984–1906). In 2004, he received the **Lester Patrick Trophy** for his contributions to hockey. In 2009, Davidson also received the Foster Hewitt Memorial Award for his contributions to broadcasting through the **Hockey Hall of Fame**. He is currently the president of hockey operations for the St. Louis Blues franchise.

DAY, CLARENCE HENRY "HAPPY," "HAP". B. 14 June 1901, Owen Sound, Ontario. D. 17 February 1990, Toronto, Ontario. Because of his upbeat personality, Clarence Day was **nicknamed** "Happy Day," which was later shortened to "Hap." He graduated with a degree in pharmacy from the University of Toronto while playing **college hockey**. Then the owner of the Toronto St. Patricks convinced Day to join them. He played **left wing** in his **rookie** season and then became a **defenseman**. In 1927, the St. Pats were purchased by **Conn Smythe** and renamed the **Toronto Maple Leafs**. Smythe kept Day as the team captain and also made him a partner in his sand and gravel business. After Smythe acquired defenseman **King Clancy** from the **Ottawa Senators** in 1931, Day and Clancy became a strong presence on the **ice** together. The team won the **Stanley Cup** in 1932. On 15 April 1932, Day **scored** the first Stanley Cup Finals **goal** in the history of the Toronto Maple Leafs. While still playing for the Leafs, Day became **coach** of the West Toronto Nationals **junior** team and led them to a Memorial Cup victory in 1936. On 23 September 1937, Day was traded to the **New York Americans** and spent one season there before retiring as a player in 1938. His 11-year career as captain of the St. Pats and Maple Leafs is second only to **George Armstrong**. During his playing days, he also owned a drugstore located inside **Maple Leaf Gardens**. Day worked as a **referee** for the next two years before returning to coach the Leafs. He guided the team through the 1940s, winning the Stanley Cup five times in 10 seasons and making him the winningest coach in Maple Leafs' history (until **Punch Imlach** passed him). Known as a teetotaler, Day was so excited when his Toronto Maple Leafs rallied from a 3–2 deficit to defeat the **Detroit Red Wings** for the 1942 Stanley Cup that he surprised everyone when he dipped his fingers in the celebratory champagne and licked them. He was inducted into the **Hockey Hall of Fame** in 1961 as a player.

DEFENSEMAN. A defenseman is a player who tries to keep the opposing players from getting into **scoring** position. They line up on the **blue line** as the game starts and try to stop the opposing forwards from carrying the **puck** into the defensive zone. The defenseman blocks shots and clears pucks and opponents from in front of and around the **net**. This player also carries the puck up the **ice** for his team and passes it to his forwards and then follows the play into the attacking zone to help his team keep control of the puck.

DEKE. Deke is short for "decoy," and it is a move by a player with the **puck** to fake out the opponent or get the **goaltender** out of position. To deke, you move your body or the puck to one side and then move in the opposite direction. A fancier version of dekeing is known as dangling the puck, and **Pavel Datsyuk**, **Patrick Kane**, and Mike Legg are several of the current players known for this skill.

DELVECCHIO, ALEXANDER PETER "ALEX," "FATS". B. 4 December 1932, Fort William, Ontario. Alex Delvecchio was a forward for 24 seasons in the **National Hockey League (NHL)**, from 1950–1974. Delvecchio played the 1950–1951 season for the Oshawa Generals of the Ontario Hockey Association, and he then went on to help the **Detroit Red Wings** win the 1952 **Stanley Cup**. He played both **center** and **left wing** for 22 full seasons and parts of two others. He won the Stanley Cup in 1952, 1954, and 1955. During the first 32 games of the 1969–1970 season, he couldn't **score a goal**, but when Miss America mailed him a small jeweled pin for good luck, he pinned it to his suspenders and scored his first goal of the season on 31 December 1969. Three nights later, while wearing the lucky pin, Delvecchio scored a **hat trick** against the **Philadelphia Flyers**. He was affectionately **nicknamed** "Fats" because of his round face. Delvecchio was known for covering for his **injured** teammates on the **ice**, so management wouldn't replace them. He also won the **Lady Byng Memorial Trophy** in 1959, 1966, and 1969 for his classy conduct. In 1974, he received the **Lester Patrick Trophy**. On 30 October 1970, he stole the **puck** from **Bobby Orr** of the **Boston Bruins** to score his 400th goal. Later in the same game, **Gordie Howe** registered his 1,000th **assist** on Delvecchio's second goal of the night. Delvecchio is one of only four NHL players to play at least 20 seasons with only one organization. **Stan Mikita, Mike Modano,** and **Steve Yzerman** are the other three players. No player in NHL history, except **Nicklas Lidström**, has played more games with just a single team.

Delvecchio recorded 456 goals, 825 assists, and only 383 **penalty minutes** during his NHL career, and he retired when he was 41 years old. By comparison, **Dave Schultz** recorded 472 penalty minutes in just one season (1974–1975). Delvecchio played on a **line** with Gordie Howe and **Ted Lindsay**. They were known as Detroit's "Production Line" due to their high scoring abilities. Delvecchio set up Howe's 700th goal, and another Howe goal marked Delvecchio's 1,000th NHL **point**. When he retired from playing in 1973, Delvecchio served as Detroit's **coach** and general manager (1973–1977). At the time of his retirement, he ranked second in nearly every significant offensive category in the Red Wings' history behind only Gordie Howe. He has since been passed in most of those categories by Steve Yzerman, but he still ranks second all-time in games played as a Red Wing. Delvecchio was inducted into the **Hockey Hall of Fame** in 1977. After his hockey career, he became a successful businessman.

DENMARK. In 1946, Denmark became a member of the **International Ice Hockey Federation (IIHF)**. In 1949, the Danish men's national **ice** hockey team held the record for the largest loss when they were crushed by **Canada**, 47–0. In 1987, this record was broken by New Zealand, when they were defeated by Australia, 58–0. While the Denmark team is not one of the top 10 hockey teams and they have never qualified for the **Olympic Games**, they have had some notable upsets. After not qualifying for a **World Ice Hockey Championships** since 1949, the country surprised many in 2003 by finishing in 11th place, including a tie game against that year's champions, Canada. In 2003, Denmark returned to the elite pool of the World Ice Hockey Championships after 54 years. The team **scored** two historic, unexpected upsets in Tampere, **Finland**, defeating the **United States**, 5–2, on 26 April 2003, and tying Canada, 2–2, six days later, on 2 May 2003. Since then, Denmark has remained in the top division. At the 2010 World Ice Hockey Championships, the country finished in eighth place, their best placing to date. The men's team currently has a 13th-place ranking by the IIHF, and the women's team has a 21st-place ranking. There have been seven **National Hockey League** players born in Denmark. Recent players include Mikkel Boedker, Lars Eller, Jannik Hansen, Philip Larsen, Frans Nielsen, and Peter Regin.

DENNENY, CYRIL JOSEPH "CY," "THE CORNWALL COLT". B. 23 December 1891, Farrow's Point, Ontario. D. 9 September 1970, Ottawa, Ontario. Cy Denneny played 15 professional hockey seasons for the **National Hockey Association** and **National Hockey League (NHL)**. He played the positions of **rover** and **left wing**. Denneny played for the Toronto Blueshirts (1915–1916), **Ottawa Senators** (1916–1928), and **Boston Bruins** (1928–1929). On 7 March 1921, he **scored** six **goals** in a single game in the Ottawa Senators' 12–5 win over the **Hamilton Tigers**. In 1924, Denneny was the NHL scoring leader, with 24 **points**. As one of the earliest players to modify his **hockey stick**, he used hot water to shape and bend the blade. Denneny's **nickname**, "The Cornwall Colt," came from his fast **skating** and feisty attitude. He and teammate **Harry Broadbent** often paired up as strong **enforcers** against Ottawa's opponents. Denneny helped his teams win the **Stanley Cup** in 1920, 1921, 1923, 1927, and 1929. He scored the 1927 Stanley Cup-winning goal in Ottawa's victory over Boston. Then, in 1929, in addition to playing, he **coached** the Bruins to their first Stanley Cup. He held the NHL record for career goals (248) and career points (333). Both records were later broken by **Howie Morenz**. His **brother**, Corbett Denneny, also played in the NHL. On 22 December 1917, the two men became the first brothers to face each other in NHL regular-season play. Together they had the highest combined goals of brothers prior to World War II (475). After retiring from playing, Cy served as an **on-ice official** (1929–1931) and coach. In 1959, he was inducted into the **Hockey Hall of Fame**.

DETROIT OLYMPIA. *See* OLYMPIA STADIUM.

DETROIT RED WINGS. The Detroit Red Wings are a professional **ice** hockey team in the **Central Division** of the **National Hockey League (NHL) Western Conference**. In the 1926–1927 season, the Detroit Cougars became part of the NHL. They were first renamed the Detroit Falcons (1930–1931) and then became the Detroit Red Wings (1932–1933). **Olympia Stadium** was one of the six original NHL arenas. It was **nicknamed** "The Old Red Barn" and sometimes called the Detroit Olympia. It was located in Detroit, Michigan, and was home to the Red Wings from 1927–1979. The dynasty years of the Red Wings were from 1949–1950 to 1954–1955. **Gordie Howe, Red Kelly, Ted Lindsay,** and **Marcel Pronovost** were on all four of the Stanley Cup-winning teams. During the 1952 series, **goaltender Terry Sawchuk** made his debut and recorded two **shutouts** in the Stanley Cup Finals against the **Montreal Canadiens**. In 1954, the team's president, Marguerite Norris, became the first woman to have her name engraved on the Stanley Cup.

The Red Wings were one of the **"Original Six"** teams, a term used to describe the teams that made up the NHL from 1942 until the 1967 expansion. In 1952, Detroit fans began the tradition of throwing an **octopus** on the ice for good luck. Since then, several other NHL teams have created similar traditions. As of 2012, the Red Wings have won the most **Stanley Cup** championships of any NHL franchise based in the United States, with 11, and they are third overall in total NHL championships, behind the Montreal Canadiens (24) and **Toronto Maple Leafs** (13). Their most recent Stanley Cup was in 2008, when they defeated the **Pittsburgh Penguins** (4–2). The Red Wings have also won the **Prince of Wales Trophy** 11 times, the **Clarence S. Campbell Bowl** six times, and the **Presidents' Trophy** six times. **Coaches** for the Detroit franchise have included **Jack Adams** (1927–1947), Tommy Ivan (1947–1954), **Sid Abel** (1957–1968), Jacques Demers (1986–1990), **Scotty Bowman** (1999–2002), and Mike Babcock (2005–2012). In 85 seasons in the NHL (1926–1927 to 2011–2012), the Red Wings have compiled a record of 2,711 2,284-815-84 (6,321 **points**). They have made 60 **Stanley Cup Playoff** appearances, including in 26 of the last 28 seasons, and 21 in a row (1991–2012). Current players include Todd Bertuzzi, **Pavel Datsyuk, Jan Muršak,** goalie Jimmy Howard, and Henrik Zetterberg. At the end of the 2011–2012 season, team captain **Nicklas Lidström** announced his retirement after playing 20 consecutive seasons with the Red Wings.

DIONNE, MARCEL ELPHEGE "LITTLE BEAVER". B. 3 August 1951, Drummondville, Quebec. Marcel Dionne was a **center** for 18 seasons in the **National Hockey League (NHL)**. He played with the **Detroit Red Wings** (1971–1975), **Los Angeles Kings** (1975–1986), and **New York Rangers** (1986–1989). Dionne was an excellent playmaker who had the misfortune of playing for teams that didn't do well in the postseason. During his **rookie** season, he **scored** 77 **points**. His best season was 1979–1980, when he had 137 points. That season, he was tied for the league lead in points with **Wayne Gretzky**. Dionne's eight 100-plus point seasons is the third highest in NHL history. Only Gretzky's 14 100-plus point seasons and **Mario Lemieux's** 10 100-plus point seasons were higher. He was a member of the Los Angeles **line** known as the "Triple Crown Line," with Dave Taylor and Charlie Simmer. Together, they scored 161 **goals** during the 1979–1980 season. Dionne's awards include the **Lady Byng Memorial Trophy** (1975, 1977), Lester B. Pearson Award (1979, 1980), **Art Ross Trophy** (1980), and **Lester Patrick Trophy** (2006).

Dionne currently ranks fourth among all-time goal scorers, with 731. He is ranked fifth in points, with 1,771, and ninth in career **assists**, with 1,040. When he retired in 1989, Dionne's career assists, goals, and points were all ranked third only to Wayne Gretzky and **Gordie Howe**. While playing for the Kings, Dionne once said, "I think I've been able to maintain my scoring pace while guys like **Guy Lafleur** have tailed off. I always get an extra two months of rest because we never make the playoffs." He was never on a **Stanley Cup** championship team. Internationally, Dionne played for **Canada** in the 1976 and 1981 **Canada Cups,** and he won gold in 1976 and silver in 1981. He also won three bronze medals at the 1978, 1983, and 1986 **World Ice Hockey Championships**. Dionne was inducted into the **Hockey Hall of Fame** in 1992. His younger **brother**, Gilbert Dionne, also played in the NHL (1991–1996) and won the 1993 Stanley Cup with the **Montreal Canadiens**.

DIVISIONS. During the 2011–2012 season, the **National Hockey League (NHL)** was equally divided with six balanced divisions of five teams each; however, since the **Winnipeg Jets** inherited the **Atlanta Thrashers'** position in the **Southeast Division** for the 2011–2012 season, the NHL has planned a realignment that corrects the fact that Winnipeg (in the Central Time Zone) is in the **Eastern Conference**, while two teams in the Eastern Time Zone (the **Detroit Red Wings** and **Columbus Blue Jackets**) are in the **Western Conference**. The current plans would reduce the number of divisions from six balanced divisions of five teams to four unbalanced divisions with either seven or eight teams.

DOMI, TAHIR "TIE". B. 1 November 1969, Windsor, Ontario. Tie Domi played **right wing** in the **National Hockey League (NHL)** from 1989–2006. As an **enforcer**, Domi holds the record for third-highest **penalties** in minutes, at 3,515, after **Dave Williams** and Dale Hunter. Domi played with the **Toronto Maple Leafs** (1989–1990, 1994–1906), **New York Rangers** (1990–1993), and **Winnipeg Jets** (1992–1995). He was part of the Rangers in 1992 when they won the **Presidents' Trophy**, but he was never on a **Stanley Cup** championship team. In 1995, Domi received an eight-game suspension and a fine for punching Rangers' **defenseman** Ulf Samuelsson and knocking him unconscious. On 3 May 2001, in the final seconds of the fourth game of the **Stanley Cup Playoffs**, Domi threw an elbow at the head of **New Jersey Devils'** defenseman **Scott Niedermayer**, knocking him unconscious. Domi received a five-minute penalty and was later suspended by the NHL for the remainder of the playoffs. His best year came during in the 2003–2004 NHL season, when he recorded 15 **goals** and 29 **points**. In his last season (2005–2006), Domi **scored** his 100th NHL goal. During his NHL career, he played in 1,020 regular-season games, with 104 goals, 141 **assists**, 245 points, and 3,515 **penalty minutes**.

DRILLON, GORDON ARTHUR "GORDIE". B. 23 October 1913, Moncton, New Brunswick. D. 23 September 1985, Saint John, New Brunswick. Gordie Drillon played **right wing** in the **National Hockey League (NHL)** for a total of seven seasons, with the **Toronto Maple Leafs** (1936–1942) and **Montreal Canadiens** (1942–1943) In his **rookie** year (1936–1937), Drillon **scored** 16 **goals** and 17 **assists** for 33 **points** in 41 games. With 52 points the next season (1937–1938), he was the leading scorer in the NHL, and he also won the **Lady Byng Trophy** that year. Drillon was part of the D-A-D **line**, with **Syl Apps** and Bob Davidson. He won the **Stanley Cup** with the Maple Leafs in 1942. Drillon's scoring strategy was to plant himself in front of the **net** and let the passes ricochet off his **hockey stick** into the goal before the goalie could react. Some people said he was just lucky and scored "garbage goals." **Red Dutton, coach** of the **New York Americans**, told his players to study Drillon instead of mock him. One night he still managed to score two goals for the Maple Leafs, which made the Americans lose the game and Dutton lose the hat he threw onto the **ice** in disgust. Later players Dino Ciccarelli and **Phil Esposito** imitated his strategy. During his 311 NHL regular-season games, he recorded 155 goals, 139 assists, 294 points, and only 56 **penalty minutes**. After retiring from hockey, he joined the Royal **Canadian** Air Force. After World War II, Drillon was a hockey coach before working a civil service job in New Brunswick. In 1985, he became the first New Brunswick native to be inducted into the **Hockey Hall of Fame**. In 1989, Drillon was inducted into **Canada's Sports Hall of Fame**.

DRINKWATER, CHARLES GRAHAM. B. 22 February 1875, Montreal, Quebec. D. 26 September 1946, Montreal, Quebec. Graham Drinkwater played both football and hockey while at McGill University. After graduating in 1895, he played the position of **rover** for the Montreal Victorias in the Amateur Hockey Association of Canada from 1892–1899, in the era before professional hockey. Drinkwater was known for his combination of excellent **skating** and smart thinking on the **ice**. He was a **defenseman** with offensive talents as well. This versatility made Drinkwater one of the best players in the early years of hockey. He **scored** 10 **goals** during the 1897–1898 season for a career high. He and teammate **Mike Grant** helped the Victorias win the **Stanley Cup** five times (1895, 1896–1899). A memorable **match** in 1899 against the Winnipeg Victorias included controversy during the game. A dispute over a **penalty** call caused **referee** J. A. Findlay to leave the arena, but when he returned, the Winnipeg players refused to take to the ice. The game was awarded to Montreal, who was leading, 3–2, at the point of the dispute, and they retained the Stanley Cup. Drinkwater served as an original trustee for the amateur trophy, the **Allan Cup**. After retiring from hockey, he became a stockbroker and was a partner in two firms, Oswald and Drinkwater, and then Drinkwater Weir and Company. He and his wife were strong supporters of the Montreal Symphony Orchestra, and he even held the position of vice president until 1941. For his hockey contributions, Drinkwater was inducted to the **Hockey Hall of Fame** in 1950.

DROBNÝ, JAROSLAV. B 12 October 1921, Prague, Czechoslovakia. D. 13 September 2001, London, England. Jaroslav Drobný was both an **ice** hockey player and tennis player. He entered his first Wimbledon tournament in 1938. In 1946, he was a finalist at the French national championships, losing to Marcel Bernard after winning the first two sets. Drobný played **center** in the Czechoslovakian ice hockey league from 1938–1949, and also in the 1947 **World Ice Hockey Championships** for the winning Czechoslovakian team. In the 1948 **Olympic Games**, he also won a silver medal with them. In 1949, the **Boston Bruins** of the **National Hockey League** offered Drobný $20,000 to play for them, but he did not want to forfeit his amateur standing and chance to play tennis. Although a hockey **injury** affected his eyesight, he wore prescription sunglasses while playing tennis and was able to play well. In 1954, he was ranked the number one singles tennis player in the world. He had a long tennis career, beginning at Wimbledon in 1938, and concluding at Roland Garros in 1965. Drobný was inducted into both the International Tennis Hall of Fame (1983) and **International Ice Hockey Federation Hall of Fame** (1997).

DROP THE GLOVES. *See* FIGHTING, "DROP THE GLOVES".

DRYDEN, KENNETH WAYNE "KEN". B. 8 August 1947, Hamilton, Ontario. Ken Dryden played **college hockey** at Cornell University (1966–1969). He went on to become a professional **goaltender** in the **National Hockey League (NHL)**. Dryden played eight seasons with the **Montreal Canadiens** (1970–1972, 1973–1979). He helped Montreal win the **Stanley Cup** in 1971, 1973, 1976, 1977, 1978, and 1979. His career **Stanley Cup Playoff** record was 80 wins and 32 losses. Individually, Dryden was the only player to win the **Conn Smythe Trophy** (1971) before winning the **Calder Memorial Trophy** (1972). He also won the **Vezina Trophy** five times (1973, 1976, and shared with Michel Larocque in 1977, 1978, and 1979). Dryden was 6 feet, 4 inches tall, and he was often seen resting with his blocker propped up by his goalie stick, angled to its maximum possible height during play stoppages. On 20 March 1971, Ken and his **brother**, Dave Dryden, played goalie against one another in a **match** between Montreal and the **Buffalo Sabres**. Ken never lost more than 10 games in a season, and during his NHL career he won 258 games, lost 57, and tied 74, and he had a career 2.24 **goals** against average.

Internationally, Dryden played for **Canada** in the 1969 **World Ice Hockey Championships** and the 1972 **Summit Series**. Due to a contract dispute, he sat out during the 1973–1974 season. Dryden spent that time working at a Toronto law firm and completing his McGill University law degree. Although he was smart, he was also **superstitious**, like most other goalies. He had to hit the **puck** a certain way during the warm-up period, make one final save before leaving the **ice**, and speak to a certain usher at home games during his winning streak. During his playing days, he wrote the book *Face Off at the Summit* (1973), about his experiences at the famous Summit Series. After retiring, Dryden wrote *The Game* in 1983, which remains a hockey classic. He was inducted into the **Hockey Hall of Fame** in 1983. He was a Liberal member of parliament from 2004–2011.

DUFF, TERRANCE RICHARD "DICK". B. 18 February 1936, Kirkland Lake, Ontario. Dick Duff was a **left wing** in the **National Hockey League (NHL)** for a total of 18 seasons, with the **Toronto Maple Leafs** (1954–1964), **New York Rangers** (1963–1965), **Montreal Canadiens** (1964–1970), **Los Angeles Kings** (1969–1971), and **Buffalo Sabres** (1970–1972). Duff won the **Stanley Cup** six times, two with Toronto (1962, 1963) and four with Montreal (1965, 1966, 1968, 1969). He is one of only six players to win two or more Stanley Cups with two or more teams. Duff even **scored** the winning **goal** in Toronto's 2–1 victory over the **Chicago Black Hawks** on 22 April 1962. On 9 April 1963, he set the record for scoring the fastest two goals (1:08) from the start of a **Stanley Cup Playoff** game in Toronto's 4–2 victory over the **Detroit Red Wings**. During his 1,030 NHL regular-season games, Duff recorded 283 goals, 289 **assists**, 572 **points**, and

743 **penalty minutes**. After retiring from playing, he joined the Maple Leafs' coaching team (1979–1981). In 2006, Duff was inducted into the **Hockey Hall of Fame** as a player.

DUMART, WOODROW WILSON CLARENCE "PORKY," "WOODY". B. 23 December 1916, Kitchener, Ontario. D. 20 October 2001, Needham, Massachusetts. Woody Dumart was a **left wing** for 16 seasons in the **National Hockey League (NHL)** with the **Boston Bruins** (1935–1942, 1945–1954). He was part of the famous **line** known as the "Kraut Line," with **Bobby Bauer** and **Milt Schmidt**. Dumart helped his team win the **Stanley Cup** in 1939 and 1941. During the 1939–1940 season, he finished second in NHL **goals** (22). He left hockey to join the service but returned after World War II ended. Dumart was known for his **checking** and defensive skills. During the 1953 semifinals against the **Detroit Red Wings**, he shadowed top **scorer Gordie Howe** so well that Howe only scored two goals. Boston won the series but then lost to the **Montreal Canadiens** in the Stanley Cup Finals. During his career, Dumart played 772 regular-season games and had 211 goals, 218 **assists**, 429 **points**, and only 99 **penalty minutes**. In 1992, he was inducted into the **Hockey Hall of Fame**.

DUNDERDALE, THOMAS "TOMMY". B. 6 May 1887, Benella, Australia. D. 15 December 1960, Winnipeg, Manitoba. Tommy Dunderdale was born in Australia, but he moved to **Canada** with his family when he was 17 years old. He learned to love hockey as a **young player**. He was a **center** and a **rover** in the **Pacific Coast Hockey Association (PCHA)** with the Victoria Aristocrats, Portland Rosebuds, and Victoria Cougars. He led the league in **goals** three times, in 1912–1913 (24), 1913–1914 (24), and 1919–1920 (26). During the 1913–1914 season, Dunderdale **scored** goals in 15 straight **matches** and tied **Cyclone Taylor** for the league lead. He was known for being an excellent stickhandler and a fast **skater**. Dunderdale is also credited with scoring the first **penalty** shot goal in history. The first goal was scored on 12 December 1921, on Hugh Lehman. The shot was taken from one of three dots painted on the **ice** 35 feet from the goal. Dunderdale retired at the end of the 1923–1924 season as the PCHA's leading goal scorer, with 194 goals. After retiring from playing, he **coached** and managed teams in Edmonton, Los Angeles, and Winnipeg. In 1974, Dunderdale became the first Australian-born player to be inducted into the **Hockey Hall of Fame**.

DURBANO, HARRY STEVEN "STEVE," "DEMOLITION DURBY". B. 12 December 1951, Toronto, Ontario. D. 16 November 2002, Yellowknife, Northwest Territories. Steve Durbano was a **defenseman** in the **National Hockey League (NHL)**. Although he was drafted by the **New York**

Rangers in 1971, they traded him before he played a single game. He made his NHL debut with the **St. Louis Blues** during the 1972–1973 season. He also played with the **Pittsburgh Penguins** before returning to St. Louis in 1978 for his last season. In his hockey career, Durbano **scored** 13 **goals** and 73 **points** in 220 NHL games. He sat out with 1,127 **penalty minutes** in his 220 NHL games, an average of more than five minutes a game. His 5.1 **penalties** in minutes per game is the highest mark for anyone with more than 1,000 minutes. Even when the **Philadelphia Flyers'** Broad Street Bullies were brawling their way through the 1970s, Durbano led the league in penalty minutes, with 370 (1975–1976). He was known for both his bad behavior on the **ice** and his questionable activities off it. In addition to being **nicknamed** "Demolition Durby," some writers referred to him as "Mental Case." Many of his **fights** did not happen on the ice. As an alcoholic, Durbano was often in bar room brawls. In 1983, he was convicted for drug trafficking and sentenced to seven years in prison. Then, in 1998, Durbano was found guilty of running a prostitution ring. In 2002, he died from liver cancer.

DURNAN, WILLIAM RONALD "BILL". B. 22 January 1916, Toronto, Ontario. D. 31 October 1972, Toronto, Ontario. Bill Durnan was a top fast-pitch softball pitcher who once struck out 24 batters in a row. He was also a **goaltender** for seven seasons in the **National Hockey League (NHL)** with the **Montreal Canadiens** (1943–1950). He has the distinction of being the only ambidextrous goalie in NHL history. Durnan was also the first **rookie** in history to win the **Vezina Trophy** (1944). He went on to win it five more times. He helped the Canadiens win the **Stanley Cup** in 1944 and 1946. Durnan twice led the league in **shutouts**, with four (1945–1946) and 10 (1948–1949). In the 1948–1949 season, Durnan recorded four consecutive shutouts. This record stood until Brian Boucher of the **Phoenix Coyotes** surpassed it with five shutouts (2003–2004). During the 1947–1948 season, Durnan served as the Canadiens' captain, but when he left the **crease** to argue calls, other teams claimed he was giving the Canadiens unscheduled timeouts. After the season, the NHL passed a rule barring goaltenders from performing the duties of captain, known as the "Durnan Rule." This rule stood until 2008, when goaltender Roberto Luongo of the **Vancouver Canucks** was allowed to serve as team captain. During his career, Durnan won 208 games, lost 112, and tied 62, with a 2.36 career **goals** against average. In 1964, he was inducted into the **Hockey Hall of Fame**.

DUTTON, NORMAN ALEXANDER "MERVYN," "RED". B. 23 July 1897, Russell, Manitoba. D. 15 March 1987, Calgary, Alberta. Red Dutton, **nicknamed** for his hair color, was a **defenseman** for the Calgary Tigers (1921–1926), and he then played in the **National Hockey League (NHL)**

with the **Montreal Maroons** (1926–1930) and **New York Americans** (1930–1936). Dutton led the NHL in **penalty minutes** in 1928–1929 (139) and 1931–1932 (107). He retired from playing due to a back injury but remained active in hockey. He **coached** and managed the New York Americans from 1936–1942. In 1938, he published the book *Hockey: Fastest Game on Earth*. After **Frank Calder** died, Dutton reluctantly served as NHL president (1943–1946), until **Clarence Campbell** returned from World War II and replaced him. In 1958, Dutton was inducted into the **Hockey Hall of Fame** as a player. In 1993, he was awarded the **Lester Patrick Trophy** posthumously. Dutton's multimillionaire father provided money to keep the New York Americans franchise going after owner **Bill Dwyer** could no longer do so. But by spring of 1942, major financial difficulties forced the renamed Brooklyn Americans franchise to fold.

DWYER, WILLIAM VINCENT "BILL," "BIG BILL". B. 1883. D. 23 December 1946, Queens, New York. In the 1920s, Bill Dwyer was a gangster and successful bootlegger during Prohibition. With his profits, he purchased sports teams, including the **New York Americans** and **Pittsburgh Pirates** of the **National Hockey League (NHL)**, as well as the Brooklyn Dodgers of the National Football League. He owned the New York Americans from 1925–1937. During this time, Dwyer spent 13 months in the Atlanta Federal Penitentiary. In a **match** between the **Ottawa Senators** and New York Americans, **goaltender Alex Connell** had an argument with the **goal judge** and tried to hit him with his **hockey stick**; however, the judge was a hit man for Bill Dwyer and was ordered to kill Connell after the game. Luckily, the police protected Connell. By the end of Prohibition in 1932, Dwyer had retired from bootlegging and lived with his wife and five children in Queens, New York. In 1936, the U.S. government won a big large lawsuit against Dwyer, leaving him broke except for his ownership of the Americans. After the 1936–1937 season, claiming that the financial status of the team was critical, the NHL took control of the Americans. In 1946, at the age of 63, Dwyer had a fatal heart attack.

DYE, CECIL HENRY "BABE". B. 13 May 1898, Hamilton, Ontario. D. 3 January 1962, Chicago, Illinois. Cecil Dye played football with the Toronto Argonauts. He earned the **nickname** "Babe" because he was also a professional baseball player, beginning his career with the International League in 1920. During his hockey career, he was a **right wing** in the **National Hockey League (NHL)** with the Toronto St. Patricks (1919–1926), **Chicago Black Hawks** (1926–1928), **New York Americans** (1928–1929), and **Toronto Maple Leafs** (1930–1931). In 1920, Dye was loaned to the **Hamilton Tigers** for their first game, and he **scored** two **goals** before returning to the Toronto team. He helped them win the **Stanley Cup** in 1922. Dye was the NHL's leading scorer in 1923 and 1925. His 38 goals in the 30-game 1924–1925 season set a St. Patricks/Maple Leafs franchise record that stood for 35 years, until **Frank Mahovlich** broke it in the 70-game 1960–1961 season. During his first six seasons in the NHL, Dye scored 176 goals in 170 games. When he was with Chicago, he played on a **line** with **Dick Irvin**. After an **injury** during training camp, he was scoreless during the 1927–1928 season. After retiring in 1931, Dye coached the St. Louis Flyers (1930–1931) and Chicago Shamrocks (1931–1932). In 1970, he was inducted posthumously into the **Hockey Hall of Fame**.

E

EAST COAST HOCKEY LEAGUE (ECHL). The East Coast Hockey League (ECHL) is a professional **ice** hockey organization one step below the **American Hockey League (AHL)**, which is one step below the **National Hockey League (NHL)**. While part of the ECHL, players try to improve their skills and move up to the next league. The ECHL was formed in 1988, and it is based in Princeton, New Jersey, with teams scattered across the **United States** and **Canada**. Players signed to an entry-level NHL contract and designated for assignment report to a club either in the AHL or the ECHL. Twenty-six of the 30 NHL teams have affiliations with the ECHL. The Kelly Cup is awarded yearly to the winning ECHL team in a best-of-seven series. In 2012–2013, two new teams are scheduled to begin: the Orlando Solar Bears and San Francisco Bulls.

EASTERN CONFERENCE. In 1993, the **National Hockey League (NHL)** renamed the conferences and divisions to reflect their geographic locations. The Eastern Conference is one of two conferences in the NHL used to divide the teams. Its counterpart is the **Western Conference**. The Eastern Conference is currently comprised of 15 teams in three divisions: **Atlantic, Northeast,** and **Southeast**.

EDMONTON OILERS. The Edmonton Oilers are a professional **ice** hockey team in the **Northwest Division** of the **National Hockey League (NHL) Western Conference**. They played their first season in 1972, as one of 12 founding franchises of the **World Hockey Association (WHA)**. In 1979, the Oilers were one of the four franchises added to the NHL through the WHA merger. The Edmonton Oilers won the **Stanley Cup** five times during their 1980s dynasty (1984, 1985, 1987, 1988, 1990). In both 1986 and 1989, the **Calgary Flames** and **Montreal Canadiens** met in the Stanley Cup Finals. During this time, the star player for the Oilers was the legendary **Wayne Gretzky**. In 1988, Gretzky was traded to the **Los Angeles Kings**, and the Oilers' Stanley Cup wins came to an end shortly thereafter. Some of the best

Edmonton players have included **Hockey Hall of Famers Glenn Anderson, Paul Coffey, Grant Fuhr**, Wayne Gretzky, **Jari Kurri, Mark Messier, Jacques Plante**, and **Norm Ullman**.

The Oilers won the **Presidents' Trophy** twice (1986, 1987) and the **Clarence S. Campbell Bowl** seven times (1983, 1984, 1985, 1987, 1988, 1990, 2006). Edmonton **coaches** have included **Glen Sather** (1977–1980, 1980–1989, 1993–1994), John Muckler (1989–1991), Craig MacTavish (2000–2009), and Tom Renney (2010–2012). In 2006, the Oilers had a strong season and made it to the Stanley Cup Finals, but they lost to the **Carolina Hurricanes** in the seven games. In 32 seasons in the NHL (1979–1980 to 2011–2012), the Edmonton Oilers have compiled a record of 1,176-1,036-262-94 (2,708 **points**) and made 20 **Stanley Cup Playoff** appearances.

EMRICK, MICHAEL "MIKE," "DOC". B. 1 August 1946, La Fontaine, Indiana. Mike Emrick received a Ph.D. in communications from Bowling Green State University in 1976, where he got the **nickname** "Doc." He has been the voice of some of the most memorable **matches** in modern hockey history. In almost 40 years as a play-by-play announcer, Emrick has called 14 **Stanley Cup** Finals as the lead national announcer on NBC, Versus, FOX, and ESPN, and also 24 game sevens in **National Hockey League (NHL) Stanley Cup Playoffs**. He was also the broadcaster for the 2010 **Olympic Games** gold medal men's hockey match between **Canada** and the **United States**. It was the most watched hockey game in the United States in 30 years. Emrick has called NHL games for all major networks, while also serving as the voice of the **New Jersey Devils** from 1993–2012. His numerous awards include seven local Emmy Awards and a national one for "Outstanding Sports Personality, Play-by-Play" in 2011. In 2004, he received the NHL's **Lester Patrick Trophy** for his media work. In 2008, he received the Foster Hewitt Memorial Award from the **Hockey Hall of Fame**. Emrick was also the first member of the media to be inducted into the **U.S. Hockey Hall of Fame** (2011). He is a founding member and the current president of the NHL Pronunciation Guide, which is used by NHL broadcasters for hockey's difficult names. He is also the vice president of the NHL Broadcaster's Association. On 2 January 2012, Emrick was the announcer for the **Winter Classic** between the **New York Rangers** and **Philadelphia Flyers**.

ENFORCER. A hockey player whose main purpose is to **fight** the opponents who **check** his team's players is called an **enforcer**. They are sometimes called goons, implying that their only talent is fighting. Some enforcers use their strength and presence to play a good game, while others just play dirty. Notable enforcers in the **National Hockey League** include **Sprague Cleghorn**, Billy Coutu, Dennis Hextall, John Ferguson, **Marty McSorley, Dave Schultz, Dave Semenko**, and **Dave Williams**.

See also AGITATION; INTIMIDATION.

EQUIPMENT. In the early days of hockey, players' equipment included **skates, gloves**, woolen sweaters, **hockey sticks, pucks**, and some padding. Throughout the years, more protective gear has been added to increase the safety of the players. **Face masks**, visors, neck guards, mouth guards, **helmets**, gloves, and overall padding protects current players, but it also weighs them down. **Goaltenders** also wear chest protectors and sometimes add cage to their helmets. In the early days of the **National Hockey League (NHL)**, players would try to get a rest by having the **referee** stop the game while they fixed their equipment. The NHL subsequently made a rule that play would not be stopped to make adjustments to equipment. Today, players will continue skating after they've dropped or broken a stick.

ERUZIONE, MICHAEL "MIKE," "RITZ," "RIZZO". B. 25 October 1954, Winthrop, Massachusetts. Mike Eruzione was a star **college hockey** player at Boston University. As a forward, he averaged more than 20 **goals** a season for four years. He also played for the **United States** at the 1975 and 1976 **World Ice Hockey Championships**. Eruzione won the **Rookie** of the Year award in 1978, as a member of the Toledo Goaldiggers of the **International Hockey League**, but his claim to hockey fame came after he was named captain of the 1980 **U.S. Men's Olympic Ice Hockey Team**. With the **score** tied, 3–3, Eruzione netted the winning goal against the **Soviet Union Men's Olympic Ice Hockey Team**. As the clock was winding down, with a score of 4–3, sportscaster **Al Michaels** yelled that it was a miracle, and the **"Miracle on Ice"** went down in history. Eruzione's winning goal against the Soviet Union has become one of the most-played highlights in American sports, and a **movie** by the same name has been made. Shortly afterward, Eruzione helped the Americans win the gold medal by defeating **Finland**, which was only the second gold medal won by the United States at the **Olympic Games** in hockey, with the first being captured in 1960. Eruzione decided not to follow his Olympic teammates to the **National Hockey League (NHL)**, saying, "I didn't play in the NHL, because I wanted to walk away a winner." He became a popular public speaker and commentator for televised Olympic hockey games. He later returned to Boston University, where he **coached** and was athletic director of development. In 2003, Eruzione was inducted into the **U.S. Hockey Hall of Fame** as a member of the 1980 Olympic Team.

ESPOSITO, ANTHONY JAMES "TONY O". B. 23 April 1943, Sault Ste. Marie, Ontario. After playing **college hockey** at Michigan Tech, Tony Esposito joined the **Vancouver Canucks** in the Western Hockey League (1967–1968). He then played with the Houston Apollos in the Central Hockey League (1968–1969), before joining the **National Hockey League (NHL)**. He was a NHL goalie with the **Montreal Canadiens** (1968–1969), before joining the **Chicago Black Hawks** (1969–1984). He was the first goalie to wear the **jersey number** 35. Esposito had a **superstition** about his **hockey sticks**, and he had to line them up in a certain way. Crossed sticks upset him. Esposito popularized the butterfly style of **goaltending**. The **nickname** "Tony O" was due to his **shutout** talent. During his 16-season NHL career, he had 76 shutouts and led the league with 15 (1969–1970), 9 (1971–1972), and 6 (1979–1980). His **brother, Phil Esposito**, was a **center** for 18 seasons in the NHL, from 1963–1981. On one memorable occasion when that they faced one another, Phil **scored** two **goals** for the **Boston Bruins**, and the game ended in a 2–2 tie. Tony won the **Stanley Cup** in 1969, by defeating the **St. Louis Blues**, 4–0. He won the **Calder Memorial Trophy** (1970) and **Vezina Trophy** (1970; 1972, with Gary Smith; 1974, tied with Bernie Parent). He was one of just eight goalies to win the Vezina catching the **puck** right-handed. Others who did the same included **Charlie Gardiner, Bill Durnan, Gilles Villemure**, and **Grant Fuhr**. Tony led the NHL in wins, with 38 (1969–1970) and 35 (1970–1971). He played in 886 regular-season games and had 423 wins, 306 losses, and 151 ties. He played hockey for **Canada** in the 1972 **Summit Series**, sharing duties with **Ken Dryden**, and in the 1977 **World Ice Hockey Championships**. After becoming a U.S. citizen, he played for the **United States** in the 1981 **Canada Cup**. Esposito was inducted into the **Hockey Hall of Fame** in 1988.

ESPOSITO, PHILIP ANTHONY "PHIL," "ESPO". B. 20 February 1942, Sault Ste. Marie, Ontario. Phil Esposito was a **center** for 18 seasons in the **National Hockey League (NHL)**. He played for the **Chicago Black Hawks** (1963–1967), **Boston Bruins** (1967–1976), and **New York Rangers** (1976–1981). His **brother, Tony Esposito**, was a **goaltender** in the NHL from 1968–1984. Phil won the **Stanley Cup** in 1970 and 1972 with the Bruins. He was the first player in history to **score** 100 **points** in a single season. In 1968–1969, Phil scored a total of 126 points in 74 games. He holds the record for most shots on **goal** in one season, at 550 (1970–1971). From 1970–1975, he had at least 55 goals and 127 points in each season. His 1970–1971 records of 76 goals and 152 points in one season stood for a decade, until **Wayne Gretzky** broke them. Esposito was known for parking himself in front of the opposition **net** to score. He once said, "Scoring is easy. You simply stand in the **slot,** take your beating, and shoot the **puck** into the net." Boston fans held signs that said, "Jesus Saves . . . but Espo scores on the rebound." He won the **Hart Memorial Trophy** in 1969 and 1974, and the Lester B. Pearson Award in 1971 and 1974. Esposito won the **Art Ross Trophy** five times from 1969–1974. In 1978, he received the **Lester Patrick Trophy**. Esposito had many hockey **superstitions**. He drove the same route to **Boston Garden**, kept good-luck charms in his locker, and believed that crossed **hockey sticks** meant that someone would get **injured** on the **ice**. He always wore a black turtleneck backward under his **equipment**. Teammate **Nick Fotiu** loved to play jokes on his teammates, and he once hid cockroaches in the uniform of the bug-fearing Esposito. Internationally, Esposito played for **Canada** in the 1972 **Summit Series**, the 1976 **Canada Cup**, and the 1977 **World Ice Hockey Championships**. During his NHL career, he played in 1,282 regular-season games and had 717 goals, 873 **assists**, 1,590 points, and 910 **penalty minutes**. In 1984, Esposito was inducted into the **Hockey Hall of Fame**.

F

FACE MASK. The face mask is a piece of **ice** hockey **equipment** that the **goaltender** wears for protection against **hockey sticks** and flying **pucks**. While the **National Hockey League (NHL)** currently requires players to wear **helmets** for safety, the league has never implemented a rule requiring goaltenders to wear face masks; however, since 1974, all goalies have worn masks for their own protection. **Clint Benedict** was the first goalie to ever wear a face mask. On 20 February 1930, while playing for the **Montreal Maroons**, he wore a crudely made leather mask to protect his **injured** cheekbone. Unfortunately, it kept coming loose and the large nosepiece blocked his vision, so he stopped wearing it. In 1959, **Jacques Plante** of the **Montreal Canadiens** invented a plain version of the type of goalie mask that is still worn today. Plante once said, "I already had four broken noses, a broken jaw, two broken cheekbones, and almost 200 stitches in my head. I didn't care how the mask looked." The last goaltender to play without a mask was Andy Brown, who played his last NHL game in 1974. The last **Hockey Hall of Famer** to play without a mask was **Gump Worsley**, who said, "My face is my mask."

In the 1970s, a helmet/cage combination mask was popularized by **Vladislav Tretiak**, the noted **Russian** goaltender. **Dominik Hašek**, used this type of mask in the late 1990s until he retired from the NHL in 2008. Current **New York Rangers'** goalie **Henrik Lundqvist** uses this same style of mask. Goalies sometimes decorate their masks. **Gerry Cheevers** of the **Boston Bruins** drew stitches in the spots where the puck hit his mask. His mask was practically covered with stitches illustrating how much it protected his face. Felix Potvin had masks with a cat theme, and **Ed Belfour** had masks decorated with eagles. Peter Budaj, a current goalie for the Canadiens, adds characters to his masks, including many from *The Simpsons*.

FACE-OFF. Before instituting the face-off, **referees** would place the **puck** between the two opposing **centers** and get all bruised while they wildly swung their **hockey sticks**. **On-ice official Fred Waghorne** decided to drop the puck and jump out of the way, which is how current face-offs take place.

They are used to start or resume a game. There are currently a total of five face-off circles on the **ice**. The center face-off circle is in the middle of the **red line**. Play starts at the center face-off circle at the beginning of each period and after a **goal** has been **scored**. In the 1930s, there were face-off circles in front of each goal. They were removed, and today there are circles in each corner of the **rink**. They are 15 feet in diameter to prevent interference from other players. On 26 March 1964, in the **Stanley Cup Playoff** game with the most **penalties** ever recorded, referee Frank Udvari penalized the **Montreal Canadiens'** Claude Provost for face-off interference in the third period. The **Toronto Maple Leafs** failed to capitalize on the **power play** and lost, 2–0.

FAMILIES. Hockey is very much a family sport. Notable hockey families include the **Bentleys, Conachers, Espositos, Granatos, Howes, Hulls, Hextalls,** Plagers, **Richards, Smiths,** and Sutters. Since the **National Hockey League (NHL)** was formed in 1917, family members have been involved in all areas of the sport. While most of the connections are among players, there have also been family members involved in **coaching** and managing. Five members of the **Patrick** family have won the **Stanley Cup.** Craig Patrick won most recently (1991, 1992) as general manager of the **Pittsburgh Penguins.** Other Stanley Cup winners in his family include Lester Patrick (Craig's grandfather), Frank Patrick (Craig's great uncle), Lynn Patrick (Craig's father), and Murray Patrick (Craig's uncle).

Forty-seven pairs of **brothers** have played together on the same team, and 10 pairs have won the Stanley Cup together. Brothers have also played against one another five times in the Stanley Cup Finals, most recently in 2003. Twenty-six sons have followed in their father's footsteps and played for the same team. The only time in history that a father played with his sons was when Gordie Howe played with his sons, Mark and Marty, with the Hartford Whalers (1979–1980). The **Chicago Blackhawks** have had the most familial connections, with 35, including 22 brother pairs, eight father-and-son combinations, two uncle-nephew combinations, and two sets of cousins. Bobby Hull and Brett Hull are the only father-and-son combination to each win the **Hart Memorial Trophy** and **Lady Byng Memorial Trophy.** When Blake Geoffrion made his NHL debut with the **Nashville Predators** in 2011, he became the NHL's first fourth-generation player. His great-grandfather (paternal grandmother's father) was **Hockey Hall of Famer Howie Morenz;** his paternal grandfather, **Bernie Geoffrion,** was also a Hall of Famer; and his father, Dan Geoffrion, played three seasons with the **Montreal Canadiens** and **Winnipeg Jets.**

FARM TEAM. *See* AMERICAN HOCKEY LEAGUE (AHL).

FATHER OF HOCKEY. *See* SUTHERLAND, JAMES THOMAS "FATHER OF HOCKEY".

FEDERKO, BERNARD ALLAN "BERNIE," "THE MAGICIAN". B. 12 May 1956, Foam Lake, Saskatchewan. Bernie Federko was a **center** in the **National Hockey League (NHL)** for 14 seasons. He played the majority of his career with the **St. Louis Blues** (1976–1989). He then spent one season with the **Detroit Red Wings** (1989–1990). Bernie earned the **nickname** "The Magician" due to his wizardry behind the **net**. He would pass the **puck** to his teammates, who would then **score goals**. Federko was the first player in NHL history to record at least 50 **assists** in 10 consecutive seasons. During the 1985–1986 **Stanley Cup Playoffs**, he led the league in **points**, with 21. On 18 March 1988, he scored his 1,000th career NHL point in a game that the Hartford Whalers won, 5–3. Unfortunately, Federko was never on a **Stanley Cup**–winning team. In 1990, he retired after playing 1,000 NHL regular-season games, with 369 goals, 761 assists, 1,130 points, and 487 **penalty minutes**. In 1993 and 1994, Federko was the **coach** and general manager of the St. Louis Vipers **roller hockey** team. In 2002, he was inducted into the **Hockey Hall of Fame**.

FEMALE PLAYERS. Women have played hockey since the 1890s, but the sport's popularity has gone through several phases. **Women's ice hockey** was popular in the 1930s, due to the success of the all-female team, the **Preston Rivulettes**. Fans enjoyed watching the skills of **Hilda Ranscombe**. After World War II, women's **ice** hockey stayed in the shadows of the men's sport. Its popularity returned in the 1970s, with Shirley Cameron's talents, but it wasn't until the 1990s that female players started to gain the deserved recognition. In 1987, the first Women's **World Ice Hockey Championships** took place in Toronto, but it was not recognized as an official tournament by the **International Ice Hockey Federation (IIHF)**. In 1990, the first official and IIHF-sanctioned Women's World Ice Hockey Championships were held in Ottawa. Women's hockey became a full medal sport for the first time at the 1998 **Winter Olympics**. Both **Canada** and the **United States** have strong female teams. Due to the international growth of the sport, the women's division at the World Ice Hockey Championships expanded to two pools in 1999. In 2010, the **Hockey Hall of Fame** established a category for female players. **Cammi Granato** and **Angela James** became the first women inducted into the Hall of Fame. Some other notable female hockey players include Lisa Brown Miller, Karyn Bye, **Cassie Campbell**, Shannon Miller, **Manon Rhéaume**, **Angela Ruggiero**, **Hayley Wickenheiser**, and Stacy Wilson.

FETISOV, VIACHESLAV ALEXANDROVICH "SLAVA". B. 20 April 1958, Moscow, Union of Soviet Socialist Republics. Viacheslav Fetisov was a **Russian ice** hockey player, who, along with **Igor Larionov**, was a pioneer in breaking the barrier that kept Soviet players from joining the **National Hockey League (NHL)**. Fetisov was part of the unit known as "The Russian Five," which consisted of him and fellow **defenseman Vladimir Konstantinov**, and forwards Igor Larionov, Sergei Fedorov, and Vyacheslav Kozlov. Fetisov played a total of nine seasons in the NHL with the **New Jersey Devils** (1989–1995) and **Detroit Red Wings** (1994–1998). Internationally, he represented his country in the 1980, 1984, and 1988 Winter Olympics; the 1978, 1981, 1982, 1983, 1985, 1986, 1987, 1989, 1990, and 1991 **World Ice Hockey Championships**; the 1981 and 1987 **Canada Cups**; and the 1996 **World Cup of Hockey**. Fetisov won two **Olympic** gold medals (1984, 1988) and then a silver medal (1980) following the upset by the **United States** in the **"Miracle on Ice."** He also won seven gold medals, one silver medal, and two bronze medals at the World Ice Hockey Championships. Fetisov also won the **Stanley Cup** in 1997 and 1998 as a player, and in 2000 as the Devils' assistant **coach**. He held that coaching position from 1999–2002. He coached the bronze medal-winning Russian team at the 2002 Winter Olympics in Salt Lake City.

In June 1985, Fetisov was involved in a car accident that killed his younger **brother**, Anatoly, who was 18 years old at the time. Then, on 13 June 1997, Fetisov, his teammate, Vladimir Konstantinov, and the team masseur, Sergei Mnatsakanov, hired a limousine to drive them home after celebrating Detroit's Stanley Cup win. The driver was drunk and crashed into a tree. Konstantinov and Mnatsakanov both suffered severe **head injuries**. Fetisov only had minor **injuries** and was able to play the following season. During his NHL career, he played in 546 regular-season games and recorded 36 **goals**, 192 **assists**, 228 **points**, and 656 **penalty minutes**. Fetisov was inducted into both the **Hockey Hall of Fame** (2001) and **International Ice Hockey Federation Hall of Fame** (2005). He is one of only 25 players in the **Triple Gold Club**. He became the oldest player to join the Triple Gold Club when he won the Stanley Cup at 39 years and 48 days of age. On 11 December 2009, the 51-year-old Fetisov came out of retirement after 11 years to play one game for CSKA Moscow.

FIELD HOCKEY. Field hockey is a form of hockey played on a rectangular field 90 to 100 yards long and 50 to 60 yards wide. Two teams of 11 players each use curved **hockey sticks** to try to move a ball down the field past the goalkeeper to **score** a **goal**. The sport was popular in British schools and universities in the early 19th century. Other than the ball and stick, mouth guards and shin pads are the main pieces of **equipment** for players other than the goalkeepers (who are fully protected). It is not a contact sport, and such

penalties as hitting, **hooking**, and **tripping** are punished by free hits or corner kicks by the nonoffending team. Similar to **ice** hockey, play is started at the beginning of each period and after each goal with a **face-off**, known as a bully. Field hockey is played internationally by both men and women. At the 1908 **Olympic Games** in London, men's field hockey made its debut. It has been an official Olympic sport since 1928. Women's field hockey was demonstrated at the 1976 Montreal Olympics on artificial turf, and it became an official sport in 1980. The **International Ice Hockey Federation** is the global governing body, and it organizes both the Hockey World Cup and Women's Hockey World Cup. Indoor field hockey is a variation of the sport.

FIGHTING, "DROP THE GLOVES". Unlike **college hockey** and international hockey organizations, professional leagues in North America have always tolerated fighting. It is considered to be a natural part of the fast and furious sport. Historically, entire benches have been cleared while numerous players have punched one another on the **ice**. Throughout the years, the **National Hockey League (NHL)** has added specific rules about fighting in an effort to reduce the severity of the **injuries**. For the players' safety, **hockey sticks** must be dropped and not used as weapons, and players are to remove their **gloves** and fight bare-knuckled. An **on-ice official** will often allow the fighting to continue until one or both players end up on the ice. Players must stop immediately if the **referee** warns them to stop. Refusal to do so will result in a fine or suspension. The **Philadelphia Flyers** of the 1970s were **nicknamed** the "Broad Street Bullies" because they liked to fight. Teams often have specific players, known as **enforcers**, who handle most of the fighting. **Coach Don Cherry** once said that, "The fans love fighting. The players don't mind. The coaches like the fights. What's the big deal?" In 1905, Alcide Laurin died after being hit by a hockey stick wielded by Allan Loney. Loney was charged with murder but was acquitted. In 2000, **Marty McSorley** hit Donald Brashear in the head with his stick. The only professional hockey player to go to jail for a stick assault was Dino Ciccarelli, who spent a few hours in jail in 1988.

FINLAND. In 1928, Finland became a member of the **International Ice Hockey Federation (IIHF)**. At the 2011 IIHF **World Ice Hockey Championships,** Finland won their second gold medal by beating **Sweden** in the final by a **score** of 6–1. They competed at that tournament 51 times, with their first appearance coming in 1939. They won their first gold medal at the 1995 championships. Finland also participated in 14 **Olympic Games**, with their first appearance being in 1952. Their highest finish was second place in 1988 and 2006. They lost to Sweden in 2006, 3–2. The Finnish team also won three bronze medals in the Olympics (1994, 1998, 2010). At the 1980

Olympics, the **United States** beat them in the final to win the gold medal. Due to the Olympic scoring system, Finland finished in fourth place. Finland is a member of the "Big Six," which is a term for the six strongest men's **ice** hockey nations. The other five teams are **Russia**, Sweden, the United States, the **Czech Republic**, and **Canada**. The men's team currently has a second-place ranking by the IIHF, and the **women's ice hockey** team has a third-place ranking. Some players in the **National Hockey League** of Finnish descent include Pekka Rinne of the **Nashville Predators, Teemu Selänne** of the **Anaheim Ducks,** and Kimmo Timonen of the **Philadelphia Flyers.** Other well-known Finnish hockey players include female goalie Anna-Kaisa Piiroinen; **Hockey Hall of Famer Jari Kurri**; Timo Nummelin, who was the athlete of the year in Finland both in soccer and hockey; and **Esa Tikkanen.** *See also* APPENDIX F for a list of IIHF Hall of Fame inductees.

FISCHLER, STANLEY "STAN," "THE HOCKEY MAVEN". B. 31 March 1932, Brooklyn, New York. Stan Fischler has a master's degree in education from Long Island University and is a prolific hockey writer. His interest in **ice** hockey began in 1939, when his father took him to see his first game at **Madison Square Garden**. During the last four decades, he has written for the *New York Times*, *Sports Illustrated*, *Sport Magazine*, *Newsweek*, and *Hockey Digest*. In 2007, he received the **Lester Patrick Trophy** for his journalistic contributions to the sport. With the help of his wife, Shirley, he has authored or coauthored more than 90 books. In addition to hockey, Fischler is also an expert on the New York City subway system.

FLAMAN, FERDINAND CHARLES "FERNIE," "THE BULL". B. 25 January 1927, Dysart, Saskatchewan. Fernie Flaman was a hockey player in the **National Hockey League (NHL)** with the **Boston Bruins** (1944–1951, 1954–1961) and **Toronto Maple Leafs** (1950–1954). During his 17 NHL seasons, Flaman played in 910 games, with 34 **goals** and 174 **assists** for a total of 208 **points**. He also accumulated 1,370 career **penalty minutes** and led the NHL with 150 penalty minutes during the 1954–1955 season. He was known for being a tough **defenseman** with good body checking and shot blocking skills. Those talents earned him the **nickname** "The Bull." He once badly **injured** the **Montreal Canadiens'** **Henri Richard** during a game at **Boston Garden**. During his first year with Toronto, Flaman won the 1951 **Stanley Cup**. In 1958, he was one of the founders of the first National Hockey League Players' Association. After retiring from playing, Flaman became a hockey **coach**. He was elected into the **Hockey Hall of Fame** in 1990.

FLEURY, THEOREN WALLACE "THEO". B. 29 June 1968, Oxbow, Saskatchewan. In 1986, Theo Fleury was invited to the training camp for the team that would represent **Canada** at the World Junior Championships in Czechoslovakia. Scouts thought that Fleury, who stood at only 5 feet, 6 inches tall, would be too small to play in the **National Hockey League (NHL)**. This made Fleury determined to prove himself as a member of Team Canada. Unfortunately, Fleury's aggressiveness led to the "Punch-up in Piešťany" that cost Canada a chance at the gold medal. On 4 January 1987, after scoring the first **goal** and celebrating, Fleury aimed his **hockey stick** at the Soviet team like a machine gun. Then, in the second period, with Canada leading, 4–2, Pavel Kostichkin slashed Fleury, leading to a **fight** between the two. It quickly escalated into a line brawl involving all **skaters** on the **ice**, after which the Soviet players left their bench, followed closely by the Canadians. Both teams were disqualified from the tournament, and the **International Ice Hockey Federation** suspended each player involved for six months from participating in international tournaments.

The **Calgary Flames** signed Fleury to play **center** and **right wing**. He used his feisty style of play to help the Flames capture the **Stanley Cup** in 1989, and, in his first full season, he **scored** 31 goals. Fleury is the only player to ever score three shorthanded goals in one NHL game. This unique **hat trick** occurred in an 8–4 Calgary win over the **St. Louis Blues** on 9 March 1991. Fleury finished the game with 3 goals and one **assist**. In 1990–1991, he netted 51 goals and 104 **points** and then went on to score 30 goals in each of his next three seasons. Although outspoken and often brash, aggravating opponents, with time Fleury matured and became team captain in 1995. Later that year, he was diagnosed with Crohn's disease. On 29 November 1997, Fleury scored his 315th career goal, passing **Joe Nieuwendyk** for first place on the Flames' all-time list. On 19 February 1999, he surpassed Al MacInnis as the franchise's scoring leader with his 823rd career point. Fleury held the record for 10 years, until it was surpassed by **Jarome Iginla** in 2009. Fleury also played for the **Colorado Avalanche** (1998–1999), **New York Rangers** (1999–2002), and **Chicago Blackhawks** (2002–2003). He also earned a spot on the 2002 Canadian **Olympic** team and recorded two assists in six games as the **Canadian Men's Olympic Ice Hockey Team** won its first Olympic gold medal in 50 years. Fleury's battle with alcohol addiction led to NHL suspensions in 2002 and 2003. He attempted a comeback in 2009 and played four exhibition games, scoring four points for the Calgary Flames. The same that year, he officially retired and published his autobiography, *Playing with Fire: The Theo Fleury Story*.

FLORIDA PANTHERS. The Florida Panthers are a professional **ice** hockey team in the **Southeast Division** of the **National Hockey League (NHL) Eastern Conference**. President "Bowtie" Bill Torrey's Panthers started out well in 1993–1994, by winning 33 **matches** and accumulating 83 **points**, both NHL records for first-year clubs. Two years later, the Panthers reached the **Stanley Cup** Finals, the fastest trip ever by an expansion club; however, they lost to the **Colorado Avalanche** in four games. In 1998–1999, they acquired the "Russian Rocket," **Pavel Bure**, in a trade with the **Vancouver Canucks**. They reached the **Stanley Cup Playoffs** in 1999–2000, but the team lost in the first round to the **New Jersey Devils**, the eventual Stanley Cup winners. Florida's other great players have included **Hockey Hall of Famers Ed Belfour**, Dino Ciccarelli, **Igor Larionov**, and **Joe Nieuwendyk**. The Panthers won the **Prince of Wales Trophy** in 1996. In 18 seasons in the NHL (1993–1994 to 2011–2012), the Florida Panthers have compiled a record of 573-605-142-124 (1,412 points) and made only 4 playoff appearances. In 2012, they advanced to the playoffs for the first time in 12 years, but they were eliminated by the New Jersey Devils in the Eastern Conference Quarterfinals, 4–3, in double **overtime**.

FOREHAND. A forehand is a shot or pass made from the player's dominant side with the blade of the **hockey stick** and **puck** facing forward from the player's body. It is more accurate and more powerful than a **backhand** shot.

FORSBERG, PETER MATTIAS "FOPPA". B. 20 July 1973, Örnsködsvik, **Sweden**. Peter Forsberg was a Swedish **ice** hockey player who played a total of 13 seasons in the **National Hockey League (NHL)** as a forward. When **Eric Lindros** was auctioned off by the last-place **Quebec Nordiques** to the **Philadelphia Flyers**, Quebec gained several key players for Lindros, including Forsberg. Since then, the team renamed the **Colorado Avalanche** has won eight division titles and two **Stanley Cup** championships. In 1996, the Stanley Cup visited a European player's home for the first time when Forsberg brought it to his hometown of Ornskoldsvik, Sweden. Forsberg's NHL career included playing **center** for Quebec and Colorado (1994–2004, 2007–2008, 2010–2011), the Flyers (2005–2007), and the **Nashville Predators** (2006–2007). In 1995, Forsberg won the **Calder Memorial Trophy**. Then, in 2003, he won both the **Art Ross Trophy** and the **Hart Memorial Trophy**. Forsberg **scored** the famous gold medal-winning **goal** against **Canada** in the penalty shootout at the 1994 **Olympic Games** in Lillehammer. He became the fourth Swedish player to score more than 100 points (116) in a NHL season (1995–1996). Forsberg was only one of eight Swedish players that have scored three goals in a Stanley Cup game. Representing Sweden in international play, he competed in three Winter Olympics and five **World Ice Hockey Championships**, as well as two World Junior Championships and one European Junior Championship. He won four gold medals in his career, winning titles at the 1992 and 1998 World Ice Hockey

Championships and the 1994 and 2006 Winter Olympics. Forsberg also won a bronze medal at the **World Cup of Hockey** in 1996. He is one of only 25 players in the **Triple Gold Club** and only the third player in history to have enough titles to be a member of the Triple Gold Club twice (the others are **Viacheslav Fetisov** and **Igor Larionov**). Forsberg will likely be inducted into the **Hockey Hall of Fame** when he becomes eligible.

FORWARD. *See* CENTER; LEFT WING; RIGHT WING.

FOTIU, NICHOLAS EVLAMPIOS "NICK," "NICKY BOY". B. 25 May 1952, Staten Island, New York. Nick Fotiu was the son of a Greek father and Italian mother who was very tough during his **National Hockey League (NHL)** games, but he was soft with the fans, and after pregame warm-ups he would throw **pucks** into the highest seats at **Madison Square Garden**. Fotiu was a Golden Gloves boxer and could have had a professional boxing career. As a tough forward, not many players wanted to **fight** him. He once said, "I'm no goon. I play hockey, I **check** If anybody wants to fight, I'll fight." **Dave Schultz** wrote in his book that Fotiu was the only man he was afraid to fight in his NHL career. But Fotiu was also a big practical joker. One time he put Vaseline in the folds of the dressing room towels, and **Lanny McDonald** got it smeared into his bushy mustache. He also played tricks other teammates, including **John Davidson** and **Phil Esposito**. For the 1974–1975 season, Fotiu was a **left wing** with the **World Hockey Association (WHA)** team the New England Whalers. Two years later, he joined his hometown **New York Rangers** and made his mark as an **enforcer**. The majority of his career was spent with the Rangers, but he was also a member of the **Calgary Flames** (1985–1987), **Philadelphia Flyers** (1987–1988), and **Edmonton Oilers** (1988–1989). Fotiu played in 646 NHL games and recorded 60 **goals**, 137 **points**, and 1,362 **penalty minutes**. He also played 110 games in the WHA, scoring five goals and nine points, with 238 penalty minutes. After he retired in 1980, Fotiu **coached minor-league** hockey.

FRANCIS, EMILE PERCY "CAT". B. 13 September 1926, North Battleford, Saskatchewan. Emile Francis was a **National Hockey League (NHL) goaltender** for the **Chicago Black Hawks** (1946–1948) and **New York Rangers** (1948–1952). He was **nicknamed** "Cat" because of his slight frame and quick reflexes between the pipes. Francis was the first NHL goalie to use a first baseman's **glove** with a cuff added to protect his hand and wrist. He used this glove to catch the **puck**. During his playing days, Francis had numerous **injuries**, including losing 18 teeth, breaking his nose five times, and receiving 250 stitches. He also tore ligaments in both knees, had ankle surgery, and suffered a separated shoulder. After retiring as a player, Francis became a **coach** for the New York Rangers (1965–1975) and **St. Louis Blues** (1976–1977, 1981–1982). He was also the general manager of the Rangers (1964–1976), Blues (1976–1983), and Hartford Whalers (1983–1989). Francis became the winningest coach in Rangers' history (654-342-209-103) but never won the **Stanley Cup**. In 1982, he received the **Lester Patrick Trophy**. Francis was inducted into the **Hockey Hall of Fam**e in 1982 as a **builder**. His son, Bobby Francis, was the head coach of the **Phoenix Coyotes** and received the **Jack Adams Award** (2002).

FRANCIS, RONALD MICHAEL, JR. "RON," "RONNIE FRANCHISE". B. 1 March 1963, Sault Ste. Marie, Ontario. Ron Francis was a **center** in the **National Hockey League (NHL)** and one of the few players in NHL history to have 500 **goals** and 1,000 **assists**. He played for the Hartford Whalers (1981–1991), **Pittsburgh Penguins** (1991–1998), **Carolina Hurricanes** (1998–2004), and **Toronto Maple Leafs** (2003–2004). He helped the Penguins win the **Stanley Cup** in 1991 and 1992. In fact, Francis **scored** the Stanley Cup–winning goal against the **Chicago Blackhawks** on 1 June 1992. His best season was 1995–1996, when he had 119 **points** and led the league in assists, with 92. The previous season, he not only led the league in assists, with 48, over the strike-shortened season, but he also became the first player to win both the **Frank J. Selke Trophy** and **Lady Byng Memorial Trophy** in the same season. **Pavel Datsyuk** is the only other player to win both trophies. Francis won the Lady Byng Memorial Trophy for sportmanship again in 1998 and 2002. Also in 2002, he won the **King Clancy Memorial Trophy**. Internationally, Francis played for **Canada** in the 1985 **World Ice Hockey Championships** and the 1996 **World Cup of Hockey**. During 25 NHL seasons and 1,731 regular-season games, he had 549 goals, 1,249 assists, 1,798 points, and 979 **penalty minutes**. Francis was inducted into the **Hockey Hall of Fame** in 2007.

FRANK J. SELKE TROPHY. The Frank J. Selke Trophy is the **National Hockey League (NHL)** award given annually to the best defensive forward in the league. It is named for Frank Selke, an executive for the **Toronto Maple Leafs** and **Montreal Canadiens** who helped build up **Maple Leaf Gardens**. The first recipient was **Bob Gainey**, in 1977. Gainey also won the trophy the most times, with four wins. Guy Carbonneau, Jere Lehtinen, and **Pavel Datsyuk** have each won it three times. Ryan Kesler of the **Vancouver Canucks** won the trophy in 2011, and Patrice Bergeron of the **Boston Bruins** won it in 2012.

FREDRICKSON, FRANK. B. 11 June 1895, Winnipeg, Manitoba. D. 28 May 1979, Vancouver, British Columbia. Frank Fredrickson played amateur hockey with the Winnipeg Falcons (1913–1916, 1919–1920). He was of Icelandic descent and studied law at the University of Manitoba before enlisting in the armed forces. He was a hero in World War I, where he served as a pilot. Fredrickson was the captain of the Winnipeg hockey team when they won the **Allan Cup** in 1920. He also helped them win a gold medal at the 1920 **Olympic Games** in Antwerp, which were later given **World Ice Hockey Championships** status by the **International Ice Hockey Federation.** Fredrickson then went on to became a professional **ice** hockey player. He played for the Victoria Cougars (1920–1926) of the **Pacific Coast Hockey Association (PCHA),** the Western Canada Hockey League, and the Western Hockey League. With the **National Hockey League (NHL),** he played for the Detroit Cougars (1926–1927), **Boston Bruins** (1926–1929), **Pittsburgh Pirates** (1928–1930), and the Detroit Falcons (1930–1931). As a **center,** Fredrickson was known as a **scoring** ace. He led the PCHA in **goals** (39), **assists** (16), and **points** (55) in 1922–1923. In Boston, Fredrickson played on a **line** with **Harry Oliver** and Perk Galbraith. He won the **Stanley Cup** in 1925. When the Bruins won the Stanley Cup in 1929, his name was engraved on the trophy, even though he was a member of the Pirates when they won. After retiring in 1931 due to a knee **injury,** he coached hockey and **lacrosse.** In 1958, Frederickson was inducted into the **Hockey Hall of Fame.**

FUHR, GRANT SCOTT. B. 28 September 1962, Spruce Grove, Alberta. As a **young player** at hockey school, Grant Fuhr ignored the wisdom of legendary **goaltender Glenn Hall,** who said, "Don't be a goalie. Goalies are insane." Fuhr became a goaltender in the **National Hockey League (NHL).** He played a total of 19 seasons with the **Edmonton Oilers** (1981–1991), **Toronto Maple Leafs** (1991–1993), **Buffalo Sabres** (1992–1995), **Los Angeles Kings** (1994–1995), **St. Louis Blues** (1995–1999), and **Calgary Flames** (1999–2000). Fuhr is one of the few black players in NHL history He helped his teams win the **Stanley Cup** in 1984, 1985, 1987, 1988, and 1990. Fuhr won the **Vezina Trophy** in 1988. He set an NHL record for goalies by playing in 79 games during the 1995–1996 season with St. Louis. Fuhr was one of just eight goalies to win the Vezina catching the **puck** right-handed. Some others include **Charlie Gardiner,** Davey Kerr, **Tony Esposito,** and José Théodore. In 1994, Fuhr won the **William M. Jennings Trophy** (with **Dominik Hašek**).

Fuhr suffered from shoulder **injuries** and battled substance abuse problems and was suspended by the NHL for 59 games of the 1990–1991 season. Internationally, he played for **Canada** in the 1984 and 1987 **Canada Cups** and won gold medals. During the 1987 tournament, Fuhr earned a reputation as one of the best goaltenders in the game. Playing against a tough Soviet team, he deflected shot after shot during the three-game final. After retiring from playing, Fuhr became a goaltending consultant with the Flames. **Wayne Gretzky** has said several times that he believes Fuhr was the greatest goaltender in NHL history. Fuhr was inducted into the **Hockey Hall of Fame** in 2003. *See also* CARNEGIE, HERBERT H. "HERB," "SWIVEL HIPS"; O'REE, WILLIAM ELDON "WILLIE".

G

GÁBORÍK, MARIÁN. B. 14 February 1982, Trenčín, Czechoslovakia. Marián Gáborík is a professional **ice** hockey forward from **Slovakia**. He currently plays for the **New York Rangers** of the **National Hockey League (NHL)**. He began his NHL career in 2000, with the **Minnesota Wild**. During his **rookie** season, he **scored** 18 **goals** and 36 **points**. In 2001–2002, he had his first 30-goal season and recorded 67 points. He also had his first NHL **hat trick** on 13 November 2001. In 2002–2003, Gáborík was named to his first NHL **All-Star** Game and won the fastest **skater** competition, lapping the **rink** in 13.71 seconds. He also helped lead the Wild to their first **Stanley Cup Playoff** appearance. On 20 December 2007, Gáborík recorded a six-point game against the New York Rangers with five goals and an assist, making him the first player in Wild history to score five goals in one game. He spent eight seasons in Minnesota and was the Wild's all-time leading scorer in goals (219) and points (437). With the Rangers in 2009–2010, Gáborík scored 10 goals in the first 12 games. Even with **injuries**, he played in 76 games, matching his career high with 42 goals, and set a new career high in points, with 86. Internationally, Gáborík is a two-time **Olympian** with Slovakia, and he won a bronze medal at the 1999 World Junior Championships. He has used his success to help **young players** learn how to play hockey. In 2005, he opened his own ice rink, Arena Mariána Gáboríka, in his native city of Trenčín, and, in 2009, Gáborík's ice rink began a hockey school program.

GADSBY, WILLIAM ALEXANDER "BILL". B. 8 August 1927, Calgary, Alberta. Bill Gadsby was a **defenseman** for 20 seasons in the **National Hockey League (NHL)**, from 1946–1966. He played for the **Chicago Black Hawks** (1946–1954), **New York Rangers** (1954–1961), and **Detroit Red Wings** (1961–1966). In his first game as a Ranger, he dove in front of a **Boston Bruins'** shot and prevented a **goal**, but he also broke several of bones. That act symbolized Gadsby's gutsy style of playing hockey. Gadsby once said that, "You're not really a hockey player until you've lost a few teeth." After he retired from playing, Gadsby **coached** the Red Wings for two seasons (1968–1970). He is one of the few players inducted into the **Hockey Hall of Fame** who was never on a **Stanley Cup**–winning team. Gadsby's solid playing during a span of 20 years earned him that honor in 1970.

GAINEY, ROBERT MICHAEL "BOB," "LE CAPITAINE". B. 13 December 1953, Peterborough, Ontario. Bob Gainey was a **left wing** for 16 seasons in the **National Hockey League (NHL)** with the **Montreal Canadiens** (1973–1989). He won the **Conn Smythe Trophy** in 1979. Gainey was the captain of the Canadiens from 1981–1989, and he was known as a great **penalty killer**. He won the **Frank J. Selke Trophy** four consecutive times as the NHL's best defensive forward (1978–1981). He also helped Montreal win the **Stanley Cup** five times (1976, 1977, 1978, 1979, 1986). In his NHL career, Gainey played in 1,160 regular-season games, **scored** 239 **goals**, recorded 263 **assists**, and had 585 **penalty minutes**. He had a **superstition** where he would mix water and soda and drink it between periods. Gainey also played for **Canada** and won two bronze medals in the 1982 and 1983 **World Ice Hockey Championships**. He competed in the 1976 and 1981 **Canada Cups**, winning in 1976. After retiring from playing, Gainey **coached** the Epinal Squirrels in France (1989–1990), the Minnesota North Stars (1990–1993), the **Dallas Stars** (1993–1996), and the Montreal Canadiens (2005–2006, 2008–2009). He was also the general manager of the Minnesota North Stars (1992–1993), Dallas Stars (1993–2002), and Montreal Canadiens (2003–2010). He won a Stanley Cup as an executive with the Dallas Stars in 1999. Gainey was inducted into the **Hockey Hall of Fame** in 1992 as a player.

GAME. *See* MATCH.

GARDINER, CHARLES ROBERT "CHARLIE," "CHUCK". B. 31 December 1904, Edinburgh, Scotland. D. 13 June 1934, Winnipeg, Manitoba. Because he moved to **Canada** when he was a child, Charlie Gardiner was not part of **Great Britain's** successful **Olympic ice** hockey team, but he was mutlitalented. In addition to his hockey skills, Gardiner was a baseball player, trapshooter, and vocalist who gave recitals on the radio. He was a **goaltender** in the **National Hockey League (NHL)** for the **Chicago Black Hawks** from 1927–1934. He led the NHL in **shutouts** in 1930–1931 (12) and 1933–1934 (10). Gardiner was the first goalie to win the **Vczina Trophy**, which he did in 1932 and 1934. In 1933, he was named captain of the Black Hawks, and he is the only NHL goaltender to captain his team to a **Stanley Cup** victory. In 1934, the team won their first Stanley Cup in the franchise's history when they defeated the **Detroit Red Wings**, three games to one.

Gardiner had been ill from a tonsil infection, but he was motivated to win the Stanley Cup. Chicago won the first two games of the series, but Detroit came back to win the third. By the fourth game, Gardiner was weak and in pain but determined. He lasted through a full game and two sudden-death **overtime** periods until "Mush" March shot the winning **goal**. Sadly, two months later, at the age of 29, Gardiner died of a brain hemorrhage brought on by the infection. For his contributions to hockey, he was inducted into the **Hockey Hall of Fame** in 1945, as one of the 12 original inductees.

GARDINER, HERBERT MARTIN "HERB". B. 8 May 1891, Winnipeg, Manitoba. D. 11 January 1972, Philadelphia, Pennsylvania. Herb Gardiner was a **defenseman** in the **National Hockey League (NHL)** for the **Montreal Canadiens** (1926–1928, 1928–1929) and **Chicago Black Hawks** (1928–1929). He was also the head **coach** of the Black Hawks for part of the 1928–1929 NHL season. In 1927, Gardiner won the Hart Trophy as the NHL's Most Valuable Player after playing every minute of every game for the Canadiens. Gardiner was the second-oldest player to ever win the award, after **Eddie Shore**. Gardiner also appeared in all 44 games the Canadiens played in 1927–1928, but he was loaned to the Chicago Black Hawks at the beginning of the 1928–1929 season. After retiring as a player, he became a coach for several **minor-league** teams in Philadelphia. Gardiner was inducted into the **Hockey Hall of Fame** in 1958 as a player.

GARDNER, JAMES HENRY "JIMMY". B. 21 May 1881, Montreal, Quebec. D. 6 November 1940, Montreal, Quebec. As a **young player**, Jimmy Gardner played hockey in Montreal with **Dickie Boon**. He then went on to play 15 elite amateur and professional seasons as a **left wing** from 1900–1915. He had a dual role as player and **coach** with the **Montreal Canadiens** for two seasons (1913–1915). Gardner won the **Stanley Cup** twice with the Montreal AAA (1902, 1903) and once with the **Montreal Wanderers** (1910). The 1902 team was known as the "Little Men of Iron" due to their perseverance. After his playing career, Gardner was an **on-ice official** from 1923–1924, and he then became a **minor-league** coach. To recognize his hockey contributions, Gardner was posthumously inducted into the **Hockey Hall of Fame** in 1962.

GARTNER, MICHAEL ALFRED "MIKE". B. 29 October 1959, Ottawa, Ontario. Mike Gartner was a speedy hockey player who played **right wing** for both the **World Hockey Association** and the **National Hockey League (NHL)**. He played a total of 20 seasons with the Cincinnati Stingers (1978–1979), **Washington Capitals** (1979–1989), Minnesota North Stars (1988–1990), **New York Rangers** (1989–1994), **Toronto Maple Leafs**

(1993–1996), and **Phoenix Coyotes** (1996–1998). Gartner holds the NHL record for most seasons with at least 30 **goals** (17). He also shares the NHL record with **Jaromír Jágr** for the most consecutive seasons with at least 30 goals (15). Gartner is the only player in NHL history to record his 500th goal, 500th **assist**, and 1,000th **point** and play in his 1,000th game in the same season (1991–1992). He was never a member of a team that won the **Stanley Cup**, but he did win several "Fastest Man in Hockey" **skating** competitions. During the 1994 SuperSkills Competition, he set the modern record for the fastest skater event with a time of 13.38. He was also known for his ability to beat defenders down the **ice**. Gartner played for **Canada** at the 1984 and 1987 **Canada Cup**. He was also part of the Canadian teams that won bronze medals at the **World Ice Hockey Championships** in 1982 and 1983. He topped the 40-goal mark in a season seven times and **scored** a total of 708 goals during his regular-season NHL career. In 2001, Gartner was inducted into the **Hockey Hall of Fame** as a player. His son, Josh Gartner, played **college hockey** at Yale University. Gartner and his former teammate, Wes Jarvis, are business partners and own skating **rinks** in the Toronto area. Gartner also keeps busy instructing **young players** in Ontario.

GEOFFRION, JOSEPH ANDRÉ BERNARD "BERNIE," "BOOM BOOM," "BOOMER". B. 16 February 1931, Montreal, Quebec. D. 11 March 2006, Atlanta, Georgia. Bernie Geoffrion was a **right wing** in the **National Hockey League (NHL)** with the **Montreal Canadiens** (1951–1964) and **New York Rangers** (1966–1968). In his first NHL game, Geoffrion was **checked** into a goalpost, and he broke his nose and lost several teeth. On 28 January 1958, he suffered a ruptured intestine when he collided with his teammate, Andre Provost, during a practice session. Geoffrion was even given last rites, but he went on to make a full recovery. He popularized the **slapshot**, which led to his **nickname**, "Boom Boom," because of the sound that his **hockey stick** made when it struck the **puck**, and when the puck hit the **boards**. Geoffrion won the **Stanley Cup** six times, including five consecutive championships (1953–1954, 1956–1960). He also received the **Calder Memorial Trophy** (1952), **Art Ross Trophy** (1955, 1961), and **Hart Memorial Trophy** (1961). During the 1960–1961 season, he became the second player in NHL history to **score** 50 **goals** in the regular season; **Maurice Richard** was the first (1944–1945). Geoffrion took a break from playing from 1964–1966 to **coach** the Quebec Aces. During his NHL career, he played in 883 regular-season games, scored 393 goals, recorded 429 **assists**, and had 689 **penalty minutes**. After retiring from playing, he also coached the Rangers (1968–1969), Atlanta Flames (1972–1975), and Canadiens (1979–1980). His father-in-law was NHL star **Howie Morenz**. Geoffrion was inducted into the **Hockey Hall of Fame** in 1972. His son, Dan Geoffrion, played three NHL seasons with the Montreal Canadiens and **Win-**

nipeg Jets. His grandson, Blake Geoffrion, became the NHL's first fourth-generation player when he made his debut with the **Nashville Predators** on 26 February 2011.

GERARD, EDWARD GEORGE "EDDIE". B. 22 February 1890, Ottawa, Ontario. D. 7 August 1937, Ottawa, Ontario. Eddie Gerard played 10 professional hockey seasons (1913–1923) as both a forward and **defenseman**. He played almost entirely for the **Ottawa Senators**. Gerard replaced **injured** defenseman **Harry Cameron** in one **Stanley Cup Playoff** game for the Toronto St. Patricks in 1922. That same year, he suffered a **head injury** when **Sprague Cleghorn** attacked him, **Cy Denneny**, and **Frank Nighbor**. The Ottawa police then arrested Cleghorn. As a player, Gerard won the **Stanley Cup** in 1920, 1921, 1922, and 1923. He also **coached** the Ottawa Senators (1917–1918), **Montreal Canadiens** (1923–1924), **Montreal Maroons** (1924–1929, 1932–1934), **New York Americans** (1930–1932), and **St. Louis Eagles** (1934–1935). He won another Stanley Cup in 1926, his first as a coach. Gerard was also an all-around athlete and a halfback for the Ottawa Rough Riders football club (1909–1913). In 1937, he passed away from a growth in his throat that stopped his breathing. Gerard was elected to the **Hockey Hall of Fame** in 1945, as one of the 12 original inductees.

GERMANY. In 1909, Germany became a member of the **International Ice Hockey Federation (IIHF)**. At the 1930 IIHF **World Ice Hockey Championships**, Germany won a silver medal during their first appearance. In 1934, they won a bronze medal, and, in 1953, they won their second silver medal. They competed in that tournament 56 times but have never won gold. Germany also participated in 12 **Olympic Games**, with their first appearance in 1928. Their highest finish was third place in 1932 and 1976. Rudi Ball was the sole Jewish athlete to represent Germany in the 1936 Winter Olympics. At the time, there was much controversy surrounding his inclusion on the 1936 German Men's Olympic Ice Hockey Team by the Nazi government. Ball was inducted into the **International Ice Hockey Federation Hall of Fame** in 2004. Walt Tkaczuk joined the **New York Rangers** in 1968 as a **center**, making him the first German-born player to play in a **National Hockey League (NHL)** game. Other well-known German hockey players include Dieter Hegen, Hans Rampf, and Alois Schloder. Although neither is of German descent, both **Pavel Bure** and **Jaromír Jágr** played hockey for Germany during the 1994–1995 **lockout**. Current NHL players of German descent include forwards Marco Sturm and Jochen Hecht, **defensemen** Christian Ehrhoff and Dennis Seidenberg, and **goaltender** Thomas Greiss.

The men's team of Germany currently has an eighth-place ranking by the IIHF, and the **women's ice hockey** team has a tenth-place ranking. *See also* APPENDIX F for a list of IIHF Hall of Fame inductees.

GIACOMIN, EDWARD "EDDIE," "FAST EDDIE". B. 6 June 1939, Sudbury, Ontario. Eddie Giacomin suffered serious burns as a teenager, but he recovered and became a successful hockey player. He credited his **coach** with the Providence Reds, **defenseman Fernie Flaman**, with nurturing his stickhandling and **puck**-handling abilities. Giacomin was a **goaltender** for 13 seasons in the **National Hockey League (NHL)**. He played with the **New York Rangers** (1965–1976) and **Detroit Red Wings** (1975–1978). When asked about going gray at the age of 19, Giacomin said, "My decision to make goaltending a career must have had something to do with it." He earned the **nickname** "Fast Eddie" because he liked to leave the **net** and beat the forwards to the puck. Giacomin was the Rangers' starting goalie for nine seasons, leading the league in games played four straight years from 1967–1971, and in **shutouts** in 1967, 1968, and 1971. During the 1970–1971 season, he became one of the last goalies to wear a **face mask** because he thought it would interfere with his vision. In 1971, Giacomin shared the **Vezina Trophy** with teammate **Gilles Villemure**. Giacomin showed his courage when **Bobby Hull skated** over the back of his hand during a game in the 1971–1972 **Stanley Cup Playoffs** against the **Chicago Black Hawks**. Giacomin remained in the game and helped the Rangers win. They were defeated by the **Boston Bruins** in the **Stanley Cup** Finals in six games. During the 1972–1973 season, Giacomin recorded his 41st career shutout with the Rangers, breaking **Chuck Rayner**'s previous record. Due to his aging and **injuries**, the Rangers traded him to the Red Wings and replaced him with **John Davidson**. One memorable moment in hockey history was on 31 October 1975, when Detroit played in New York. When Giacomin made his debut for the Red Wings, New York fans honored their hero by giving him a prolonged standing ovation and cheering for him throughout the **match**. Rangers' fans booed their own team and chanted "Ed-die! Ed-die!" during the game. Giacomin won that game for the Red Wings. He retired on 17 January 1978, with a career record of 289-208-97 and a 2.82 **goals** against average. Giacomin was inducted into the **Hockey Hall of Fame** in 1987. From 1986–1989, he served as the goaltending coach for the Rangers.

GILBERT, RODRIGUE GABRIEL "ROD". B. 1 July 1941, Montreal, Quebec. During his 1959–1960 season in the **juniors**, Rod Gilbert slipped on the **ice** and fell back into the **boards**. He broke the fifth vertebra in his back and had complications from blood clots. He played a total of four years with the Guelph Biltmores of the Ontario Hockey Association, and, in his final season, he **scored** 54 **goals** and 103 **points** in just 47 games. The **New York Rangers** of the **National Hockey League (NHL)** liked what they saw in Gilbert. He played **right wing** for them for 18 seasons (1960–1978). He missed most of the 1965–1966 season due to back surgery and recovery. He then came back to have a strong season in 1966–1967. On 24 February 1968, Gilbert scored four goals in a game against the **Montreal Canadiens**. Gilbert was part of the GAG (goal-a-game) **line**, with Vic Hadfield and **Jean Ratelle**. In 1972, the strong unit combined for 138 goals. Gilbert and Ratelle grew up playing **pond hockey** together. Internationally, Gilbert played for **Canada** in the 1972 **Summit Series** and 1977 **World Ice Hockey Championships**. He and Montreal's John Ferguson had an on-ice feud. Gilbert retired shortly after Ferguson became the general manager of the Rangers. Gilbert played in 1,065 regular-season NHL games and had 406 goals, 615 **assists**, 1,021 points, and 508 **penalty minutes**. On 14 October 1979, he became the first player for the Rangers to have his **jersey number** (7) retired. Although he never won the **Stanley Cup**, Gilbert once said, "I was a very lucky guy considering my dream of making the NHL and being able to do what I did with all those back problems." He won the **Bill Masterton Memorial Trophy** in 1976 for his perseverance despite his back pain. Gilbert was inducted into the **Hockey Hall of Fame** in 1982. In 1991, he received the **Lester Patrick Trophy**. He continues to work on the management team for the New York Rangers.

GILLIES, CLARK "JETHRO". B. 7 April 1954, Moose Jaw, Saskatchewan. Prior to playing professional hockey, Clark Gillies played three seasons of Minor League Baseball as a first baseman and outfielder for the Houston Astros (1970–1972). He then became a **left wing** in the **National Hockey League (NHL)** with the **New York Islanders** (1974–1986) and **Buffalo Sabres** (1986–1988). During the **Stanley Cup Playoffs** of his **rookie** year, Gillies stood up to **Dave Schultz**, an **enforcer** with the **Philadelphia Flyers**. It was one of the few **fights** that Schultz lost. With the Islanders, Gillies played on a **line** with Billy Harris and **Bryan Trottier**. They helped the Islanders win the **Stanley Cup** four years straight (1980–1983). After losing in the finals to the **Edmonton Oilers** in 1984, Gillies said, "It really took a lot of the heart and soul out of me. It took me awhile to even want to play the game again." His teammates **nicknamed** him "Jethro" because he resembled the character of the same name on the *Beverly Hillbillies*. Gillies also played for **Canada** in the 1981 **Canada Cup**. During his NHL career, He **scored** 44 game-winning **goals** and 93 **power play** goals. He was inducted into the **Hockey Hall of Fame** in 2002. His nephew, Colton Gillies, was drafted by the **Minnesota Wild** in 2007.

GILMOUR, DOUGLAS ROBERT "DOUG," "DOUGIE," "KILLER".
B. 25 June 1965, Kingston, Ontario. Doug Gilmour was a forward in the
National Hockey League (NHL) for 20 seasons. He played for many different teams, including the **St. Louis Blues** (1983–1988), **Calgary Flames**
(1988–1992), **Toronto Maple Leafs** (1991–1997), **New Jersey Devils**
(1996–1998), **Chicago Blackhawks** (1998–2000), **Buffalo Sabres**
(1999–2001), and **Montreal Canadiens** (2001–2003). Despite his small size,
Gilmour was a tough player and earned the **nickname** "Killer." His teammate Brian Sutter also said Gilmour resembled serial killer Charles Manson.
In 1989, Gilmour won the **Stanley Cup** with the Calgary Flames. For good
luck, he shook hands with *Hockey Night in Canada* commentator **Don
Cherry** before Game 6. Gilmour then **scored** two **goals**, including the Stan-
ley Cup–winning goal against **Patrick Roy** of the **Montreal Canadiens**.
During the 1993 Campbell Conference final, Toronto's Gilmour faced
Wayne Gretzky of the **Los Angeles Kings**. In **overtime** of the sixth game,
Gretzky high-sticked Gilmour, but **referee** Kerry Fraser did not see it or call
a **penalty**. Gretzky then scored the winning goal. Gilmour finished the post-
season with 35 **points**, second to Gretzky, and won the **Frank J. Selke
Trophy**. Internationally, he played for **Canada** in the 1987 **Canada Cup**
and the 1990 **World Ice Hockey Championships**. During his NHL career,
he played 1,474 regular-season games, with 450 goals, 964 **assists**, 1,414
points, and 1,301 **penalty minutes**. Gilmour was inducted into the **Hockey
Hall of Fame** in 2011. He is currently the general manager of the Kingston
Frontenacs of the Ontario Hockey League.

GILMOUR, HAMILTON LIVINGSTONE "BILLY". B. 21 March 1885,
Ottawa, Ontario. D. 13 March 1959, Montreal, Quebec. Billy Gilmour came
from a prominent family, and his **brothers**, Dave and Suddy Gilmour, also
played for the Ottawa Silver Seven. Billy was a **right wing** for the Ottawa
Silver Seven (1902–1907), Montreal Victorias (1907–1908), and **Ottawa
Senators** (1908–1909, 1911–1912). He was known for his stickhandling
skills. While he played hockey, he also studied engineering at McGill University. He won the **Stanley Cup** in 1903, 1904, 1905, and 1909. During the
1908–1909 season, he tallied 74 **penalty minutes**. On 15 January 1916,
Gilmour **scored** the final **goal** of his career against **goaltender Georges
Vezina** in Ottawa's 5–2 win over the **Montreal Canadiens**. In 1916, Gilmour enlisted in the **Canadian** Army for service in World War I. In 1962, he
was posthumously inducted into the **Hockey Hall of Fame**.

GLOVES. There are three styles of gloves worn by **ice** hockey players.
Players wear matching gloves as hand protection from **pucks, hockey sticks,**
and **skates**. A skater may use his glove to bat down an airborne puck, but a

minor **penalty** is called if he catches the puck. When **fighting**, skaters drop the gloves to the ice and fight with bare fists. **Goaltenders** wear a different type of glove on each hand. They offer protection but are also designed to help the goalie catch and block the puck. On his stick hand, the goaltender wears a blocker with a large pad across the back of the forearm, usually extending just beyond the wrist. **National Hockey League (NHL)** rules mandate that the blocking glove, used for deflecting shots, may be no wider than eight inches and no longer than 15 inches. On the other hand, the glove worn is a trapper, similar to a baseball glove. Goalies use it to catch shots and toss the pucks to their teammates. The NHL rules limit the perimeter of the catching glove to 45 inches, and the widest part of the glove may not exceed 18 inches.

GOAL. When the hockey **puck** crosses the goal **line**, the last person on the **scoring** team who touched the puck is credited with the goal. One or two players who make passes that directly lead to the goal are credited with an **assist**. Statisticians keep track of the different types of goals **scored**. An even-strength goal is a goal scored when both teams have the same number of players on the **ice**. A **power play** goal is a goal scored by a team on a power play, which is a numerical advantage in players due to a **penalty** being served by one or more of the other team's players. A shorthanded goal is a goal scored by a team that is on the **penalty kill**, which is a numerical disadvantage due to a penalty being served by one or more of its players. An empty **net** goal is a goal scored when there is no **goaltender** guarding the net because he has been pulled for an extra attacker. A penalty shot goal is a goal scored on a penalty shot, that is, a one-on-one confrontation between a single offensive player and the goalie as a result of a penalty. An own goal is when a player puts the puck into their own net, scoring for the other team. An **overtime** goal is a goal scored in sudden-death overtime. Examples of famous **Stanley Cup**–winning goals include **Bill Barilko**'s of the **Toronto Maple Leafs** (1951), Bobby Baun's of the Maple Leafs (1964), and **Bobby Orr**'s of the **Boston Bruins** (1970). Some other well-known goals include **Mike Eruzione's** Team USA goal against the **Soviet Union Men's Olympic Ice Hockey Team** in the 1980 **Olympic Games**; **Wayne Gretzky**'s 77th goal on 24 February 1982, which beat **Phil Esposito**'s single-season record for goals; and **Sidney Crosby**'s "golden goal" in overtime of the 2010 Vancouver Winter Olympics. *See also* GOAL JUDGE; GOAL LIGHT.

GOAL JUDGE. The goal judge is the official who sits behind the **goal** and signals when the **puck** has entered the **net**. One goal judge is positioned outside the **rink**, directly behind each goal net. In many arenas, the goal judge turns on a red **goal light** behind the goal to signal a **score**. When the red light is on, the game clock stops. The **referee** has the ability to overrule the goal judge. In the early days of hockey, fans would act as goal judges; however, they were not always impartial. If their calls were disputed, they would be replaced by other fans. Those goal judges stood on the **ice** behind the net unprotected, leaving them exposed to angry players and fans, as well as dangerous pucks. During the 1922 **Stanley Cup** Finals, **Cecil Dye** of the Toronto St. Patricks scored a goal against goalie **Hugh Lehman** of the **Vancouver Millionaires**, giving the St. Pats a 2–0 lead. The Vancouver team disputed the goal and argued with goal judge Frank Warren so much that the referee agreed to replace him. During the 1960s, goal judges were finally given a protected area to sit in. Prior to the 1991–1992 season, a video replay rule was introduced in the **National Hockey League**. When a goal is disputed, play is stopped until the video goal judge reviews it.

GOAL LIGHT. The goal light is a red light behind each **goal** that is lit by the **goal judge** to indicate that a goal has been **scored**. In addition to **ice** hockey, the goal light is used in box **lacrosse**. The term *light the lamp* refers to the goal light.

GOALIE. *See* GOALTENDER.

GOALKEEPER. *See* GOALTENDER.

GOALTENDER. The player in the position of goaltender has the main job of keeping the **puck** out of the **net** with his body and/or **hockey stick**. The goaltender is also known as the goalie, goalkeeper, or netminder. Historically, teams only had one goaltender, and most of them stayed in the game even after getting **injured**. Although teams today have more than one goalie, it is rare to substitute a goalie during a game. Gilles Gilbert of the **Boston Bruins** holds the **National Hockey League (NHL)** record for most consecutive wins by a goaltender, with 17, which he accomplished during the 1975–1976 NHL season. Some notable goalies include **Martin Brodeur**, **Ken Dryden**, **Glenn Hall**, **Patrick Roy**, **Terry Sawchuk**, and **Georges Vezina**. The **Vezina Trophy** is awarded annually in recognition of the accomplishments of hockey players in this position.

GOHEEN, FRANCIS XAVIER "MOOSE". B. 8 February 1894, White Bear Lake, Minnesota. D. 13 November 1979, Maplewood, Minnesota. Moose Goheen was a **defenseman** who played 16 elite amateur and professional hockey seasons (1914–1932). He mainly played for the St. Paul Athletic Club and St. Paul Saints. Goheen was given the **nickname** "Moose" by a teammate who thought he had a large chest and huge legs. He captained the

U.S. Men's Olympic Ice Hockey Team at the 1920 Winter Olympics. Goheen **scored** seven **goals** in four games to help his team win the silver medal. Goheen also played in the 1920 **World Ice Hockey Championships**. He turned down an offer to play for the **Boston Bruins** to keep his off-season job in Minnesota. Goheen was inducted into the **Hockey Hall of Fame** in 1952, as the second American-born and trained player. In 1945, inductee **Hobey Baker** was the first. In 1973, Goheen was also inducted into the **U.S. Hockey Hall of Fame**.

GOODFELLOW, EBERNEZER RALSTON "EBBIE". B. 9 April 1906, Ottawa, Ontario. D. 10 September 1985, Sarasota, Florida. Ebbie Goodfellow played in the **National Hockey League (NHL)** for 14 seasons. He was both a **center** and **defenseman** with the Detroit Cougars (1929–1930), Detroit Falcons (1930–1932), and **Detroit Red Wings** (1932–1943). As a **rookie**, he held the Detroit franchise record for **points** (34). Goodfellow won the **Stanley Cup** in 1936, 1937, and 1943. On 30 March 1934, he **scored** the series-winning **goal** in Detroit's 1–0 win over the **Toronto Maple Leafs** in the fifth and deciding game of the semifinals. Goodfellow was the captain of the Red Wings in 1934–1935 and from 1938–1941, and he served as Detroit's assistant **coach** during the 1941–1942 season when **Jack Adams** was suspended after an outburst. In 1940, he won the Hart Trophy. After retiring from playing, he coached the **Chicago Black Hawks** (1950–1952) but had a losing record of 30-91-19. Goodfellow was inducted into the **Hockey Hall of Fame** in 1963.

GOULET, MICHEL. B. 21 April 1960, Peribonka, Quebec. Before joining the **National Hockey League (NHL)**, Michel Goulet was a high-scoring **junior** hockey player. In his first full season with the Quebec Remparts, he led his team with 73 **goals** and 135 **points** in 72 games. In 1978, Goulet and five other teenagers played for the Birmingham Bulls in the **World Hockey Association** and were **nicknamed** the "Baby Bulls." In 1979, Goulet became the first-ever draft pick for the new NHL **Quebec Nordiques** franchise. He played **left wing** for them from 1979–1990, and for the **Chicago Blackhawks** from 1989–1994. From 1983–1986, Goulet **scored** 50 goals for four consecutive seasons. He played with Dale Hunter and **Peter Stastny**. Goulet was known for scoring both shorthand and **power play** goals. During his NHL career, he scored 548 goals in regular-season games.

Internationally, Goulet played for **Canada** at the 1983 **World Ice Hockey Championships** in West Germany, and he scored nine points in 10 games. He also played in the 1984 and 1987 **Canada Cups**. The 1987 Team Canada included the **line** of Goulet, **Wayne Gretzky**, and **Mario Lemieux**. On 16 March 1994, Goulet suffered a severe **injury** when he slid into the **boards** headfirst after losing his footing. As a result, he had a severe concussion and head trauma and never returned to the **ice**. Goulet was inducted into the **Hockey Hall of Fame** in 1998. He never won a **Stanley Cup** as a player, but he did win it twice with the **Colorado Avalanche** in 1996 and 2001 as an executive. Goulet is currently a scout for the **Calgary Flames**.

GRANATO, CATHERINE "CAMMI". B. 25 March 1971, Downers Grove, Illinois. Cammi Granato's name is synonymous with **women's ice hockey**. Ever since her parents spent their first date at a **Chicago Black Hawks** game, hockey has been a way of life for the Granato **family**. Granato's oldest **brother**, Tony, played **right wing** in the **National Hockey League (NHL)** from 1989–2001. Donny **coached** hockey, and Robby played professional **roller hockey**. Cammi once said that, "My brothers used to beat me up and throw me in the **goal**, but they made me an athlete." Cammi played organized hockey with boys starting at the age of five. She once commented that, "I always liked hockey too much to stop playing, so I worked harder and pushed myself to be better. If I was average, people wouldn't accept me. If I was better, they'd respect me." As a forward, she played **college hockey** at Providence College and was named the Eastern College Athletic Conference Player of the Year in 1991, 1992, and 1993. She set every school **scoring** record and led the Lady Friars to back-to-back conference titles in 1991–1992 and 1992–1993.

Just like male hockey players, Granato had **superstitions**. She always tapped the goal posts and the crossbar for good luck and traveled with her lucky beanbag frog named "Floppy." Granato was named the U.S. Women's Player of the Year in 1996, and she became the first U.S. women's captain. On the **ice**, her competitive play and scoring talent made her an exciting player to watch. Granato has attracted worldwide attention as a five-time member of Team USA. Internationally, she played for the **United States** in the 1990, 1992, 1994, 1997, 1999, 2000, and 2001 **World Ice Hockey Championships**. She led her country to the silver medal in the last three World Ice Hockey Championships.

Women's ice hockey debuted as a medal sport at the **Olympic Games** in Nagano, Japan, in 1998. For the first time in history, the best female players from around the world got to compete for gold. As team captain, Granato carried the flag for the U.S. team in the closing ceremonies and successfully led her team to the first-ever gold medal in women's hockey. After the Olympics, Cammi was hired by the **Los Angeles Kings** as a radio color commentator, making her the only current female broadcaster in the NHL and only the second in league history. Cammi has been listed as one of the top-10 dominant women in world hockey. She rejoined Team USA for the 2002 Olympics in Salt Lake City. In the gold medal game, the United States finished second to **Canada**. In May 2002, Granato signed with the Vancouver Griffins of Canada's National Women's Hockey League. In 2007, she became the first individual female recipient of the **Lester Patrick Trophy**. In 2008, Granato, Geraldine Heaney, and **Angela James** were the first women inducted into the **International Ice Hockey Federation Hall of Fame**. In 2010, Granato and James became the first women inducted into the **Hockey Hall of Fame**.

GRANT, MICHAEL "MIKE". B. 27 November 1873, Montreal, Quebec. D. 20 August 1955, St. Lambert, Quebec. Mike Grant was only 11 years old when he won three speed **skating** titles in the under-12, under-14, and under-16 age groups in Montreal. He was one of the original rushing **defensemen** in the sport of **ice** hockey. In addition to hockey and skating, Grant also played amateur **lacrosse**. He was a member of the **junior** champion Crystal Junior Hockey Club in 1890–1891 and went on to win Intermediate championships with the Crystal Intermediates in the 1891–1892 and 1892–1893 seasons. Grant gained the most fame as a member and captain of the Montreal Victorias. He and teammate **Graham Drinkwater** helped the Victorias win the **Stanley Cup five times** (1895, 1896–1899). At 21 years and 2 months of age, Grant was the youngest player ever to captain a team to the Stanley Cup. He then joined the Montreal Shamrocks as an emergency replacement and played against the Winnipeg Victorias in a Stanley Cup challenge series in January 1901. Grant retired after the 1901–1902 season but returned to the game as a **referee** in the March 1905 Stanley Cup challenge between Ottawa and the Rat Portage Thistles, wearing a stylish derby hat during one of the games. He was also one of **Canada**'s first ambassadors of hockey to the **United States**, demonstrating and organizing exhibition games. In addition, his father's trade as a blacksmith allowed him to associate with horseracing in both Montreal and Ottawa, and later in his life he was a familiar figure at the track as a paddock judge for more than 40 years. For his contributions to hockey, Grant was inducted into the **Hockey Hall of Fame** in 1950.

GREAT BRITAIN. In 1908, in Paris, France, the federation known as the Ligue Internationale de Hockey sur Glace was created with representatives from Belgium, France, Great Britain, **Switzerland**, and Bohemia (now the **Czech Republic**). After being one of the founding members of the organization also known as the **International Ice Hockey Federation (IIHF)**, the British men's **ice** hockey team was a successful team in the early 20th century. They were the bronze medalists at the 1924 **Olympic Games** in Chamonix, France, and won their first and only gold medal in 1936 in **Germany**. Great Britain also won a bronze medal (1935) and two silver medals (1937, 1938) at the **World Ice Hockey Championships**. Unfortunately, Great Britain has not been a strong team since then. The British **women's ice hockey** team has not qualified for an Olympic tournament to date. The men's team currently has a 21st-place ranking by the IIHF, and the women's team has an 18th-place ranking.

GREEN, WILFRED THOMAS "SHORTY". B. 17 July 1986, Sudbury, Ontario. D. 19 April 1960, Sudbury, Ontario. In 1923, Shorty Green played **right wing** on a **line** with his **brother**, "Red" Green, and **Billy Burch** for the last-place **Hamilton Tigers**. Green was team captain during the 1924–1925 season. That year, the Tigers played so well that they qualified for the **Stanley Cup Playoffs** for the first time, but the team never got a chance to play for the **Stanley Cup**, because Green and his teammates went on strike over money issues. As a member of the **New York Americans**, he **scored** the first-ever **goal** at **Madison Square Garden**, on 15 December 1925, against the **Montreal Canadiens**. On 27 February 1928, Green suffered a **career-ending injury** to his kidney after being body checked by **New York Rangers' defenseman** Taffy Abel. After recovering from the **injury**, he returned to Ontario. Green founded and ran the Sudbury Golf Club with two partners until his death in 1960. In 1962, he was inducted into the **Hockey Hall of Fame** posthumously.

GRETZKY, WAYNE DOUGLAS "THE GREAT ONE". B. 26 January 1961, Brantford, Ontario. Even nonhockey fans have heard of Wayne Gretzky because of his impressive contributions to the sport. Gretzky holds or shares 61 **National Hockey League (NHL)** records, with 40 for the regular season, 15 for the **Stanley Cup Playoffs**, and six as part of the **All-Star Team**. As a child, Gretzky loved hockey, and all of his **skating** before school, after school, and after dinner helped improve his skills. In his early days, his teammates **nicknamed** him "Ink" because his name was in the newspaper so often. The other **young players** were jealous of his talent and the large amounts of playing time the **coaches** gave him. Gretzky had 137 **points** and 86 **assists** with the **Edmonton Oilers** (1979–1980), but he was not considered a **rookie** because he had previously played eight games for the Indianapolis Racers and a season with Edmonton in the **World Hockey Association**. His playing career lasted 21 seasons, and he played for the Oilers until 1988. He also played for the **Los Angeles Kings** (1988–1996), **St. Louis Blues** (1995–1996), and **New York Rangers** (1996–1999). As a leader and clean player, Gretzky was the captain of the Edmonton Oilers (1983–1988) and Los Angeles Kings (1989–1996). He won the **Lady Byng Memorial Trophy** five times.

Gretzky holds the distinction of **scoring** more **goals** than any other player in NHL history (894). At the time, **Gordie Howe** of the **Detroit Red Wings** held the record, with 801. **Marcel Dionne** summed it up when he said, "There's a record book for Wayne and one for everybody else in the league." The legendary Howe once said, "There's only one way to stop Wayne Gretzky, and that's to lock him in the dressing room." He was known for his amazing passing skills and his anticipation of where the **puck** would go. In addition to his natural talent, Gretzky was a hard worker who would study the game and repeat drills so he could improve his skills. He won the **Hart Memorial Trophy** as Most Valuable Player (MVP) a record nine times, with eight consecutive wins. Gretzky has been named MVP more times than any other player in the history of the other three North American major professional leagues (baseball, basketball, and football). Gretzky had the longest consecutive point-scoring streak of 51 games, with 61 goals and 92 assists, totaling 153 points (5 October 1983 to 28 January 1984). Gretzky also won the **Art Ross Trophy** 10 times, the Lester B. Pearson Award five times, the **Conn Smythe Trophy** twice, and the **Lester Patrick Trophy** once (1994).

Known as "The Great One," Gretzky wore the number 99 on his **jersey**. When he retired from playing on 18 April 1999, following a game between the Rangers and **Pittsburgh Penguins**, the NHL retired his number. Individual teams often retire **jersey numbers**, but his was the only one to be retired by the entire league. He had 1,963 assists in 1,487 regular-season games, more than any other player's point total. Gretzky won four **Stanley Cups** (1984, 1985, 1978, 1988) and had an amazing 2,857 points, 970 more than the second-place record holder, **Mark Messier**. Hundreds of books have been written about Gretzky, and all of his specific records can be located in them.

Gretzky played for **Canada** in the 1982 **World Ice Hockey Championships**; the 1981, 1984, 1987, and 1991 **Canada Cups**; the 1996 **World Cup of Hockey**; and the 1998 **Olympic Games**. He also became the general manager of the 2002 gold medal-winning **Canadian Men's Olympic Ice hockey Team**. Gretzky believed that the "**lucky loonie**" had something to do with Canada winning their first Olympic gold medal in 50 years. He had several **superstitions** that he followed during his career. These included putting his equipment on in a certain order from left to right; always firing the first puck wide and to the right of the goal during the warm-up; and drinking a Diet Coke, **ice** water, Gatorade, and another Diet Coke before each game. Once when he got a haircut during a road trip, the team lost the game. From that point onward, he refused to cut his hair on the road. Gretzky was inducted into the **Hockey Hall of Fame** (1999) without a waiting period, and he was also inducted into the **International Ice Hockey Federation Hall of Fame** (2000). He was well-liked and respected by his teammates and even became the godfather to former teammate **Jari Kurri**'s children. Gretzky married actress Janet Jones, and she encouraged him to do a sketch on *Saturday Night Live* on 13 May 1989. The six-minute spoof is entitled **"Wai-kiki Hockey."**

GRIFFIS, SILAS SETH "SOX," "SI". B. 22 September 1883, Onaga, Kansas. D. 9 July 1950, Vancouver, British Columbia. Si Griffis was born in Kansas, but he grew up in Rat Portage, Ontario. As a **young player**, he played hockey with Tom Hooper, Billy McGimsie, and **Tommy Phillips**. In addition to hockey, he excelled in rowing, golf, and bowling. He was known for his fast **skating** and for being one of the larger players of his era. Griffis was a **rover** and **defenseman** for the **Kenora Thistles** (1905–1907) and **Vancouver Millionaires** (1911–1919). In 1907, he won the **Stanley Cup** and retired shortly thereafter. When the **Patrick family** started the **Pacific Coast Hockey Association**, Griffis returned to captain the Millionaires. He **scored** three **goals** and two **assists** in his first game out of retirement. He captained the Millionaires in their 1915 Stanley Cup–winning victory over the **Ottawa Senators**. Due to a broken leg, he did not play in that series. In 1918, Griffis once again retired and became a competitive bowler and golfer. He was inducted into the **Hockey Hall of Fame** in 1950.

GUOTH, STANISLAV. *See* MIKITA, STANISLAV "STAN," "MOUSE".

H

HABS. The **Montreal Canadiens** are **nicknamed** "Habs," based on the shortened form of "les Habitants." The French term was originally used to describe the settlers of New France, which is now Quebec. At the time the team was formed, the name Canadiens was commonly used to describe the local working people of Montreal. *See also* CANADA.

HAINSWORTH, GEORGE. B. 26 June 1895, Toronto, Ontario. D. 9 October 1950, Gravenhurst, Ontario. George Hainsworth was a **goaltender** in the **National Hockey League (NHL)** with the **Montreal Canadiens** (1926–1933, 1936–1937) and **Toronto Maple Leafs** (1933–1936). At five feet, five inches tall, he was one of the shortest goalies in NHL history. During the 1928–1929 season, he only allowed 43 **goals** in 44 games, for a low goals against average (GAA) of 0.92. With **Cecil Hart** as their **coach**, Hainsworth and his teammates won the **Stanley Cup** in 1930 and 1931. Hainsworth also won the **Vezina Trophy** three years in a row (1927–1929). He holds the record for the most **shutouts** in one season, with 22 (1928–1929), and ranks third in career shutouts, with 94. He set the NHL record of six shutouts in a single calendar month in February 1929. **Dominik Hašek** tied it in December 1997. After receiving a **penalty**, Hainsworth was replaced in the **net** by Albert Leduc on 2 December 1931. On 16 March 1935, Toronto's **right wing**, **Charlie Conacher**, replaced an **injured** Hainsworth to defeat the Canadiens, 5–3. In 1937, Hainsworth retired with a career-record GAA of 1.91, which was later matched by **Alex Connell**. After he retired, Hainsworth was elected alderman in Kitchener, Ontario. He died in an automobile accident in October 1950. Hainsworth was inducted into the **Hockey Hall of Fame** posthumously in 1961.

HALL, GLENN HENRY "MR. GOALIE". B. 3 October 1931, Humboldt, Saskatchewan. Glenn Hall was a **goaltender** for the **Detroit Red Wings** (1952–1957), **Chicago Black Hawks** (1957–1967), and **St. Louis Blues** (1967–1971). He spent his first few years with Detroit in the **minor league**. In the 1952 **Stanley Cup Playoffs**, Hall was called up to be the backup goalie in the finals but did not play. Hall made the Detroit Red Wings' lineup as their starting goalie in the 1955–1956 season, when **Terry Sawchuk** was traded to the **Boston Bruins**. He played in every game and recorded 12 **shutouts** to win the **Calder Memorial Trophy**. The **nickname** "Mr. Goalie" began as a play on **Gordie Howe**'s "Mr. Hockey," but Hall is regarded by many as one of the best goalies. He was one of the first players to use the butterfly style of goaltending. As a player who seldom missed a game, Hall holds the **National Hockey League (NHL)** record as the only goalie to play 502 consecutive complete games. His streak was broken due to a back **injury**. Even though he loved hockey, his nerves led him to a ritual of throwing up before every game. When asked about how it was to play all those years without a **face mask**, Hall replied, "Our first priority was staying alive. Our second was stopping the **puck**." He led the NHL in wins in 1956–1957 (38), 1962–1963 (30), 1963–1964 (34), and 1965–1966 (34). Hall won the **Vezina Trophy** three times (1963, 1967, and 1969). His name is on the **Stanley Cup** three times, in 1952 as part of Detroit, in 1961 as goalie for Chicago, and in 1989 as goaltender **coach** for the **Calgary Flames**. Hall once told **young player Grant Fuhr**, "Don't be a goalie. Goalies are insane," but luckily Fuhr ignored him. Hall was inducted into the **Hockey Hall of Fame** in 1975.

HALL, JOSEPH HENRY "JOE," "BAD JOE," "THE BAD MAN". B. 3 May 1882, Staffordshire, England. D. 5 April 1919, Seattle, Washington. Joe Hall began his career as a forward but then became a star **defenseman** known for his bad temper. He was a member of the **Stanley Cup**–winning **Kenora Thistles** in 1906–1907, but did not play. He played for the **Quebec Bulldogs** (1910–1917) and won the Stanley Cup twice (1911–1912, 1912–1913). In 1917, he joined the **Montreal Canadiens** and helped them win the **National Hockey League** championship in 1918–1919. That year, the Stanley Cup Finals were cancelled due to the outbreak of the Spanish influenza. Unfortunately, Hall died from complications of the disease on 5 April 1919. He was posthumously inducted into the **Hockey Hall of Fame** in 1961.

HAMILTON TIGERS. In 1920, the struggling **Quebec Bulldogs**, a National Hockey Association team, moved and was renamed the **Hamilton Tigers** (1920–1925). **Toe Blake, Billy Burch, Shorty Green**, and **Joe Malone** played for the Tigers. **Art Ross coached** them for one season (1922–1923). During the 1924–1925 season, the Tigers made it to the **Stanley Cup Playoffs**, but the players went on strike over money disputes and lost their chance at the **Stanley Cup**. In 1925, **Bill Dwyer** bought the Tigers and renamed them the **New York Americans**.

HANSON BROTHERS. The Hanson Brothers were fictional characters in the 1977 **movie** *Slap Shot*, with Paul Newman. They were known for starting **fights**, interrupting the **coach** during pregame speeches with overzealous shouting, wearing thick glasses, and playing with toy cars in their hotel room. The characters were based on the Carlson Brothers, who were actual hockey players. Two of them starred in the film. **Left wing** Jack Hanson was portrayed by David Hanson. **Center** Steve Hanson was portrayed by Steve Carlson, and **right wing** Jeff Hanson was portrayed by Jeff Carlson. Jack Carlson was unable to act in the film, as the **Edmonton Oilers** called him up for the **World Hockey Association (WHA)** playoffs. Steve Carlson played in 225 games in both the **National Hockey League (NHL)** and the WHA. Dave Hanson played in 136 games in the NHL and WHA. Jeff Carlson played in seven games in the WHA. Like their characters, both Dave Hanson and Jeff Carlson were known for a willingness to "drop the gloves." Steve Carlson was more of a finesse player. Dave Hanson's son, Christian Hanson, currently plays for the **Washington Capitals**. Jeff Carlson, Steve Carlson, and Dave Hanson continue to make personal appearances as the Hanson Brothers, typically at **minor-league** hockey games.

HART, CECIL "CECE". B. 28 November 1883, Bedford, Quebec. D. July 1940. In 1923, Cecil's father, Dr. David Hart, donated the Hart Trophy to recognize the Most Valuable Player of the regular hockey season. Cecil Hart played, **coached**, organized, and managed amateur baseball and hockey teams in Montreal from 1900–1922; however, he was best-known for coaching the **Montreal Canadiens** between 1926–1927 and 1938–1939, and for winning back-to-back **Stanley Cup** championships in 1930 and 1931. But after an argument with the team's owner, Leo Dandurand, he was fired. The Canadiens played poorly without Hart, and he was rehired in 1937. Hart insisted that **center Howie Morenz** also return to the team. Morenz came back, and, even though he died during the season, Hart was able to lead the Canadiens to first place. Then, as some key players aged, the team once again declined. Hart resigned as coach and manager in 1939. He passed away after a lengthy illness in July 1940.

HART MEMORIAL TROPHY. The Hart Memorial Trophy is the **National Hockey League (NHL)** award given annually to the Most Valuable Player to his team during the regular season. It was donated in 1923, by Dr. David Hart, the father of **Montreal Canadiens coach Cecil Hart**. The original Hart Trophy was retired in the **Hockey Hall of Fame** in 1960, and the NHL began presenting the new Hart Memorial Trophy in its place. The first recipient was **Frank Nighbor** of the **Ottawa Senators**. **Wayne Gretzky** has won this trophy the most, at nine times, with eight consecutive wins. He and his

Edmonton Oilers teammate **Mark Messier** are the only players to win the Hart Memorial Trophy with more than one team. Only five **goaltenders** have received this trophy, including **Roy Worters** (1929), **Chuck Rayner** (1950), Al Rollins (1954), **Jacques Plante** (1962), and **Dominik Hašek** (1997, 1998). Recent Hart recipients include **Sidney Crosby, Alexander Ovechkin**, Henrik Sedin, and Corey Perry.

HART TROPHY. *See* HART MEMORIAL TROPHY.

HARTFORD WHALERS. *See* CAROLINA HURRICANES.

HARVEY, DOUGLAS NORMAN "DOUG". B. 19 December 1924, Montreal, Quebec. D. 26 December 1989, Montreal, Quebec. Doug Harvey was a heavyweight boxing champion in the **Canadian** Navy in the late 1940s. He was offered professional baseball and football contracts before choosing to play hockey in the **National Hockey League (NHL)**. Harvey was a **defenseman** for 19 seasons with the **Montreal Canadiens** (1947–1961), **New York Rangers** (1961–1964), **Detroit Red Wings** (1966–1967), and **St. Louis Blues** (1968–1969). He had a **superstition** about shaving before every game, which he felt made him play better. He won the **Stanley Cup** six times (1953, 1956, 1957, 1958, 1959, 1960). Unfortunately, Harvey **scored** the 1954 Stanley Cup-losing **goal** when he tipped the **puck** with his **glove** past Montreal's **goaltender**, Gerry McNeil. He helped **Ted Lindsay** organize the first players' union. As one of the league's best defensemen, Harvey received the **James Norris Memorial Trophy** seven times from 1955–1962. He was known for his talent at stealing the puck. Harvey also originated the spin-o-rama move to avoid being **checked**. It was later popularized by **Serge Savard**. On 4 April 1959, **Red Storey** was officiating the sixth game of the **Stanley Cup Playoffs** between the Montreal Canadiens and the **Chicago Black Hawks**. Late in the third period, with a 4–4 tie, a **penalty** was not called on Montreal, which allowed the Canadiens to score the series-winning goal. The fans went wild. When one dumped a beer on Storey's head, Harvey punched the fan. He continued to protect Storey as they made their way off the **ice**. Harvey played his final season at the age of 44. During his NHL career, he played in 1,113 regular-season games and recorded 88 goals, 452 **assists**, 540 **points**, and 1,216 **penalty minutes**. After retiring from playing, Harvey **coached** the Kansas City Blues (1967–1968), Laval Saints (1969–1970), and Houston Aeros (1973–1975). Harvey was inducted into the **Hockey Hall of Fame** in 1973, but he did not attend the ceremony. He was disappointed that he was not inducted his first eligible year, believing that he was passed over because of his alcohol problem.

HAŠEK, DOMINIK, "THE DOMINATOR". B. 29 January 1965, Pardu- bice, Czechoslovakia. Dominik Hašek was **goaltender** in the **National Hockey League (NHL)** for the **Chicago Blackhawks** (1990–1992), **Buffalo Sabres** (1992–2001), **Detroit Red Wings** (2001–2004, 2006–2008), and **Ottawa Senators** (2005–2006). His playing style was unique, and he has been described as a "flopper." He would often drop his **hockey stick** and drop down to grab the **puck** with his blocker hand. When interviewed by the *Sporting News* in 2006, Hašek said, "They say I am unorthodox, I flop around the **ice** like some kind of fish. I say, who cares as long as I stop the puck?" One of the most impressive single game performances by any player in NHL history came on 27 April 1994. Hašek made 70 **saves** in a four- **overtime shutout**. The opposing goalie was **rookie Martin Brodeur**, who made 49 saves before being beaten by Dave Hannan. The Sabres beat the **New Jersey Devils**, 1–0. Hašek's 70 saves set a record for the most saves without allowing a **goal** that still stands today. In 1997, he became the first goalie since **Jacques Plante**, in 1962, to win the **Hart Memorial Trophy** as the league's Most Valuable Player. When Hašek won it again the following year, he set a record for being the only goalie to win the award twice. In addition, he earned three **William M. Jennings Trophies** and six **Vezina Trophies**. Another one of his most memorable performances came in the 1998 **Olympic Games**, when Hašek led Czechoslovakia's national team to the gold medal. He allowed six goals in total, with only two of them coming in the medal round. Against Team **Canada** in the semifinals, Hašek stopped **Theoren Fleury, Ray Bourque, Joe Nieuwendyk, Eric Lindros**, and Bren- dan Shanahan in a dramatic shootout win. He then went on to shut out the **Russian** team, 1–0, in the final game by stopping 20 shots. At the time of his retirement in 2008, Hašek was the oldest active goalie in the NHL, at the age of 43, and he had a career save percentage of .922. Hašek will likely be inducted into the **Hockey Hall of Fame** when he becomes eligible.

HAT TRICK. The term *hat trick* is used to describe three **goals scored** by a single player in a single game. It was first used in 1858 to describe a cricket **match**. As a hockey term, it became popular in the 1940s, and there are a couple of stories as to how this began. In the 1940s, a haberdasher used to give **Toronto Maple Leaf** players free hats when they scored three goals in a game; however, the **Hockey Hall of Fame** credits the hat trick's origin to Alex Kaleta of the **Chicago Black Hawks**, on 26 January 1946. When Kale- ta entered Sammy Taft's shop to purchase a new hat he couldn't afford, Taft promised him a free hat if Kaleta scored three goals as he played the Toronto Maple Leafs that night. Kaleta then scored four goals against the Maple Leafs, and Taft made good on his offer. Also in the 1950s, the Guelph Biltmore Mad Hatters of the Ontario Hockey Association and a farm team of the **National Hockey League's (NHL) New York Rangers** were sponsored by Guelph-based Biltmore Hats, a leading manufacturer of hats with North American dominance. The sponsor would award any Mad Hatters player who scored three goals in a game with a new fedora. Now when a player scores a hat trick, fans throw hats onto the **ice** from the stands. The NHL record for the fastest natural hat trick is 21 seconds, set by **Bill Mosienko** in 1952 for the Chicago Black Hawks. **Wayne Gretzky** holds the NHL record for most natural hat tricks in a career, with 50. Two players from each team scored hat tricks in one game during the 1983 **Stanley Cup Playoff** Semifinals. They were **Mark Messier** of the **Edmonton Oilers** and Paul Reinhart of the **Calgary Flames**. More recently, **Alexander Ovechkin** of the **Washington Capitals** and **Sidney Crosby** of the **Pittsburgh Penguins** each scored hat tricks in the 2009 playoff semifinals.

Sportswriters created the term *Gordie Howe hat trick* to describe a player having a goal, an **assist**, and a **fight** in one game. Howe is credited with two of these during his career. Two players in hockey history have scored reverse hat tricks, with three goals in their own net. The **New York Americans'** Pat Egan scored three against his own **goaltender, Roy Worters**, in a 1941 game. **Defenseman Marcel Pronovost** had a reverse hat trick against his own goalie, **Terry Sawchuk**. In 1995, the **Florida Panthers'** goalie, John Vanbiesbrouck, coined the term *rat trick*, when his teammate, Scott Mellanby, slapped a rat with his **hockey stick** in the locker room before a game and then went on to score two goals in a 4–3 win over the **Calgary Flames**. In later games, Panther fans threw rubber rats onto the ice, but this delayed the start of the game and throwing anything on the ice was banned.

HAWERCHUK, DALE "DUCKY". B. 4 April 1963, Toronto, Ontario. Dale Hawerchuk was a **center** in the **National Hockey League (NHL)** for a total of 16 seasons, with the **Winnipeg Jets** (1981–1990), **Buffalo Sabres** (1990–1995), **St. Louis Blues** (1995–1996), and **Philadelphia Flyers** (1996–1997). He set a record for being the youngest 100-**point** player, finishing with 103 during the 1981–1982 season and winning the **Calder Memorial Trophy** as the NHL's **Rookie** of the Year. Hawerchuk reached that milestone at 18 years and 11 months of age. His record was broken by **Sidney Crosby** of the **Pittsburgh Penguins** in 2006. Hawerchuk recorded 91 points in his second season and then hit the 100-plus point plateau for the next five consecutive years, including a career-high 53 **goals** and 130 points in 1984–1985. He was the captain of the Jets from 1984–1989. Internationally, he played for **Canada** in the 1982, 1986, and 1989 **World Ice Hockey Championships** and won two bronze medals and one silver. Hawerchuk also competed in the 1987 and 1991 **Canada Cups** and won a gold medal in 1991. He had a chance to win the **Stanley Cup** during the 1996–1997 season with the Flyers, but they lost to the **Detroit Red Wings** in four games. Hawerchuk retired after playing in 1,188 regular-season games and recording

518 goals, 891 **assists**, and a total of 1,409 points. A rock band in Quebec is called Les Dales Hawerchuk in his honor. In 2005, they released an album by the same name, with the image of Hawerchuk on the cover in a retro Winnipeg Jets **jersey**. Hawerchuk was inducted into the **Hockey Hall of Fame** in 2001. In 2010, he became the head **coach** for the Barrie Colts of the Ontario Hockey League.

HEAD INJURIES. As a full-contact sport, head injuries are the most common **injury** in hockey. Prior to the introduction of **helmets**, several players had **career-ending injuries**, including **Ace Bailey**, Donald Brashear, and **Pat LaFontaine**. In 1968, while playing for the Minnesota North Stars, forward **Bill Masterton** suffered a fatal head injury after being body **checked** and hitting his head on the **ice**. Checking from behind and checking to the head are the main causes of head injuries today. Due to the seriousness, the **National Hockey League (NHL)** has made **penalty** rules to enforce this major and gross misconduct. Players also can hit the **boards** on their own due to their **skating** speed. On 16 March 1994, the **Chicago Blackhawks'** **Michel Goulet** slid into the boards headfirst after losing his footing. He suffered a severe concussion and head trauma and never returned to the ice. Concussions are one reason players miss games, and repeated concussions cause players to retire early. **Eric Lindros**, his **brother**, Brett Lindros, and the **Philadelphia Flyers'** Keith Primeau are a few players who have gotten multiple concussions resulting from aggressive hockey play.

HEBENTON, ANDREW ALEXANDER "ANDY," "IRON MAN," "SPUDS". B. 3 October 1929, Winnipeg, Manitoba. Andy Hebenton was a **right wing** in the **National Hockey League (NHL)**. He held the record for the longest streak without missing a game in the history of professional **ice** hockey. He played nine consecutive seasons of 70 games each for a total of 630 **matches** straight. His record was later broken by **Garry Unger** (914), and it is currently held by **Doug Jarvis** (964). Hebenton made his professional debut in 1949, for the Cincinnati Mohawks of the **American Hockey League**. The next season, he moved on to the Victoria Cougars of the Pacific Coast Hockey League (PCHL). Hebenton starred with Victoria for five seasons and had his best year in 1955, when he **scored** 46 goals. The following season, he joined the **New York Rangers** of the NHL and played eight seasons with them before joining the **Boston Bruins** (1963–1964). He scored 20 goals or more during five of the seasons with the Rangers. His best season was 1958–1959, when he scored 33 goals and had 29 **assists**. Hebenton earned the **nickname** "Spuds" because of his love for potatoes, and "Iron Man" due to his consecutive playing. He played a clean game and averaged only nine **penalty minutes** per season. As a result, he won the **Lady Byng**

Memorial Trophy in 1957. He also became one of the all-time leading scorers in the World Hockey League (WHL) and never missed a game. In his 630 NHL games, Hebenton recorded 189 goals and 202 assists for 391 **points**. He also played in 1,056 PCHL/WHL games, scoring 425 goals and completing 532 assists for 957 points. His son, Clay Hebenton, was a professional hockey **goaltender** (1973–1980). It was only the second time a father and son were active in professional ice hockey at the same time. **Gordie Howe** and his sons **Mark Howe** and Marty Howe were the first in 1974. Hebenton retired from hockey in 1975 and worked in the cement business in Portland.

HELMET. When hockey was first played in the late 1800s, **ice skates**, a **puck**, and a **hockey stick** were the main pieces of **equipment** used. Throughout the years, protective gear, including padding and hard plastic guards, were added. In 1928, George Owen, a **center** for the **Boston Bruins**, wore his leather football helmet from Harvard during ice hockey games. He became the first player to regularly wear a helmet for protection. At the time, most professional players were hesitant to use helmets and **face masks**, believing that they would cause interference and show signs of weakness, but after **Ace Bailey**'s **career-ending injury** caused by **Eddie Shore** on 12 December 1933, several Boston players, including Shore, started wearing helmets in fear of retaliation by other NHL players. Helmet use was rare for the next 30 years, but the players who regularly wore helmets included Shore, Des Smith, **Bill Mosienko**, **Dit Clapper**, and Don Gallinger. **Maurice Richard** and **Elmer Lach** briefly wore helmets. Jack Crawford wore a helmet to cover baldness, and Charlie Burns and Ted Green wore them to protect the metal plates in their heads. After **Bill Masterton**'s fatal **head injury** in 1968, more players, the likes of **Pierre Pilote**, **Stan Mikita**, Ken Wharram, and Doug Mohns, started wearing helmets, but, throughout the 1970s, the majority of **National Hockey League (NHL)** players went helmetless. In August 1979, the NHL made a rule mandating that players must wear helmets for their safety. Veterans who signed contracts prior to 1 June 1979 were able to choose whether they wanted to wear helmets. The last player to play without a helmet was Craig MacTavish, who last played during the 1996–1997 season for the **St. Louis Blues**. Although not mandatory, plastic visors and shields can be attached to the front of a helmet for added protection. Their popularity increased after NHL defenseman Bryan Berard suffered a potentially career-ending eye injury in 2000. **Goaltenders** are not required to wear face masks, but every current NHL goalie wears one for protection.

HERN, WILLIAM MILTON "RILEY". B. 5 December 1880, St. Mary's, Ontario. D. 24 June 1929, Montreal, Quebec. Riley Hern was an **ice** hockey **goaltender** signed by the **Montreal Wanderers** in 1906–1907. He earned the **nickname** "Riley" because he often "riled" the opposition with his constant chattering. Riley used primitive goalie equipment, such as cricket pads. It was also the era of standing goalies, not like the goaltenders of today who are allowed to sprawl on the ice. Those are reasons why his 4.68 career **goals** against average seems high by today's standards. Hern posted a 10–0 regular-season record in his first season with the Wanderers. Montreal won the **Stanley Cup** four times, in three straight seasons, from 1906–1908, and in 1910. They also successfully defended the Stanley Cup in six out of seven challenges in that time span. The only challenge they lost was against the **Kenora Thistles** in January 1907, but the Wanderers reclaimed the cup in their own successful challenge two months later. Hern is often credited for their wins. Although he retired from playing in 1911, Hern remained active in hockey as a **goal judge** and **referee**. In 1962, Hern's hockey contributions were fully recognized when he was inducted into the **Hockey Hall of Fame** posthumously.

HEWITT, FOSTER WILLIAM. B. 21 November 1902, Toronto, Ontario. D. 21 April 1985, Scarborough, Ontario. Foster Hewitt's father, W. A. Hewitt, was the sports editor of the Toronto *Daily Star.* Although Foster was a champion boxer in the 112-pound weight class at the University of Toronto, he became well-known for his connection to **ice** hockey. On 16 February 1923, radio editor Basil Lake assigned Hewitt to broadcast a Senior League hockey **match** between Toronto's Argonauts and Kitchener's Greenshirts. After that, Hewitt's play-by-play hockey broadcasts became famous. His knowledgable and enthusiastic style made him the voice of hockey. On 24 May 1925, Foster and his father made one of the world's first broadcasts of a horse race. In 1927, Foster was invited as guest announcer to broadcast the first game from the new **Detroit Olympia**. In 1927, he became the radio announcer for the **Toronto Maple Leafs**. Hewitt later served as the master of ceremonies when **Maple Leaf Gardens** opened on 12 November 1931.

On 1 November 1952, Hewitt broadcast the first televised hockey game in **Canada**, between the **Montreal Canadiens** and the Maple Leafs. He signed on at the beginning of each broadcast with, "Hello, Canada, and hockey fans in the **United States** and Newfoundland." Hewitt's most popular phrase became, "He shoots! He **scores!**" Five years later, he turned the microphone of *Hockey Night in Canada* over to his son, Bill, while he handled the postgame wrap up. Hewitt retired in 1963 to devote all of his time to his radio station. In 1965, he became the only media member fully inducted into the **Hockey Hall of Fame** as a **builder**. In 1972, he came out of retirement to broadcast the historic **Summit Series** between Canada and the Union of

Soviet Socialist Republics. His description of the winning **goal** by Paul Henderson also became legendary. Hewitt was elected to **Canada's Sports Hall of Fame** in 1975. The Foster Hewitt Memorial Award for broadcasters from the Hockey Hall of Fame is named in his honor.

HEXTALL, BRYAN ALDWYN. B. 31 July 1913, Grenfell, Saskatchewan. D. 25 July 1984, Portage La Prairie, Manitoba. Bryan Hextall was a **right wing** in the **National Hockey League (NHL)** for 11 seasons with the **New York Rangers** (1936–1944, 1945–1948). He was known for his **skating** speed, great stickhandling, and toughness on the **ice**. Not only did he win the **Stanley Cup** in 1940, but he was one of the top players for the Rangers against the **Toronto Maple Leafs**. Hextall **scored** a **hat trick** against the Leafs and added an **assist** to help his team come from behind to win Game 2 two of the series. On 13 April 1940, he scored the **overtime** winning **goal** in the sixth game that clinched the Stanley Cup championship. Unfortunately, the Rangers did not win another Stanley Cup for 54 years. Then, in 1944, **Canadian** war authorities refused to let Hextall cross into the **United States**. After World War II ended, he resumed playing hockey with the Rangers, but he was hospitalized shortly thereafter due to a liver condition. During his NHL career, he played in 449 regular-season games and recorded 187 goals, 175 assists, and 362 **points**. Hextall was inducted into the **Hockey Hall of Fame** in 1969. His son, Bryan Hextall Jr., was a **center** in the NHL (1963–1976). His other son, Dennis Hextall, was a **left wing** in the NHL (1969–1980). Hextall's grandson, **Ron Hextall**, was an NHL **goaltender** (1986–1999).

HEXTALL, RONALD JEFFREY "RON". B. 3 May 1964, Brandon, Manitoba. Ron Hextall was a **goaltender** in the **National Hockey League (NHL)** with the **Philadelphia Flyers** (1986–1992, 1994–1999), **Quebec Nordiques** (1992–1993), and **New York Islanders** (1993–1994). He was known for being one of the NHL's most aggressive goalies. Hextall was suspended for six or more games on three different occasions and had more than 100 **penalty minutes** in each of his first three seasons. During the 1987–1988 season with the Flyers, Hexall set a single-season record for penalty minutes by a goaltender, with 113. During his career, he amassed a goaltender record of 714 penalty minutes. He was the first goalie to keep a water bottle on top of the **goal**. He also had several **superstitions**, including driving the same route at the same speed to the arena each day. During games he had a "herky-jerky" style, and during game stoppages Hextall would go through a certain routine of hitting the goalposts with his **hockey stick**. In 1987, he won the **Vezina Trophy** and **Conn Smythe Trophy**. On 8 December 1987, against the **Boston Bruins**, he became the first NHL goaltender to score a goal by shooting the **puck** into the opponent's empty **net**. Then, on 11 April 1989, he became the first goalie to score in the **Stanley Cup Playoffs** by shooting the puck into the **Washington Capitals'** empty net. Hextall won 296 of the 608 regular-season games that he played during his career. Internationally, Hextall played for **Canada** in the 1987 **Canada Cup** and 1992 **World Ice Hockey Championships**. He is currently vice president and assistant general manager of the **Los Angeles Kings**. His father, Bryan Hextall Jr., and his uncle, Dennis Hextall, both played in the NHL. Ron's grandfather was **Hockey Hall of Famer Bryan Hextall**. His son, Brett Hextall, signed a contract with the **Phoenix Coyotes** in 2011.

HIGH-STICKING. When a player carries a **hockey stick** above the shoulders to use it against an opponent, a high-sticking **penalty** is called. Any contact by a high-stick causing **injury** is a major penalty. During the 1992–1993 season, the *NHL Official Rules* redefined high-sticking to include any use of the stick above the waist. *See also* HOOKING; SLASHING; TRIPPING.

HOCKEY. *See* COLLEGE HOCKEY; FIELD HOCKEY; POND HOCKEY; ROLLER HOCKEY; VARIATIONS.

HOCKEY HALL OF FAME. The Hockey Hall of Fame is a hall of fame and museum dedicated to the history of **ice** hockey. It was established in 1943, and is located in Toronto, Ontario, Canada. There were originally two categories for induction, players and **builders**, but, in 1961, a third category for **on-ice officials** was introduced. In 2010, a subcategory was established for **female players**, and **Cammi Granato** and **Angela James** were inducted. **Gordie Howe** and **Mark Howe** joined **Bobby Hull** and **Brett Hull** and **Craig Patrick**, **Lester Patrick**, and **Lynn Patrick** as the only father-and-son teams in the Hockey Hall of Fame. To be inducted, players must have been retired for a minimum of three years and be nominated by a selection committee. The waiting period was waived for 10 exceptional players, including **Dit Clapper** (1947), **Maurice Richard** (1961), **Ted Lindsay** (1966), **Red Kelly** (1969), **Terry Sawchuk** (1971), **Jean Béliveau** (1972), **Gordie Howe** (1972), **Bobby Orr** (1979), **Mario Lemieux** (1997), and **Wayne Gretzky** (1999).

As of 2010, up to four players can be inducted per year, but 27 players were inducted in 1962. The majority of inducted players were born in Canada, and only 10 were born in Europe. The most recent inductees were **Pavel Bure**, **Adam Oates**, Joe Sakic, and Mats Sundin. Hall of Famers who were never part of a **Stanley Cup**–winning team include Leo Boivin, **Marcel Dionne, Mike Gartner, Harry Howell, Brad Park, Gilbert Perreault,**

Jean Ratelle, **Darryl Sittler**, and **Norm Ullman**. If you are unable to travel to Toronto, you can learn more about the history of hockey from your home. The Hockey Hall of Fame and Seneca College's faculty of continuing education have created an online course that takes a serious look at the history and evolution of the game. Each week's topics examine the cultural, social, and economic impact hockey has had on Canada. *See also* APPENDIX D for a list of Hockey Hall of Fame player inductees.

HOCKEY NIGHT IN CANADA. One of the most popular and longest-running television programs in **Canada** is a weekly game featuring **National Hockey League (NHL)** teams on Saturday nights. **Mario Lemieux** and his older **brothers**, Alain and Richard, loved the program so much that when their babysitter changed the channel, the three brothers locked her in the bathroom so they could watch **ice** hockey. On 12 November 1931, *Hockey Night in Canada* began as a radio broadcast called the *General Motors Hockey Broadcast*. **Foster Hewitt** was a broadcaster for the program. His famous catch phrase was, "He shoots! He **scores!**" On 1 January 1937, the Canadian Broadcasting Corporation (CBC) was launched as a public network, and it carried the program, which was renamed *Hockey Night in Canada*. On 1 November 1952, Hewitt broadcast the first televised ice hockey game in Canada, between the **Montreal Canadiens** and **Toronto Maple Leafs**. Hewitt's son, Bill, then handled the television broadcast, while Foster returned to the radio broadcasts. Other broadcasters throughout the years for *Hockey Night in Canada* include former **coach Don Cherry**, Bob Cole, Dick Irvin Jr., Ron MacLean, and Harry Neale. From 1968–2008, the **music** for the show was "The Hockey Theme," which some people have called the second national anthem of Canada. In 2008, the CBC lost their rights to the song, and it was replaced by the contest-winning "Canadian Gold."

HOCKEY STICK. The hockey stick is a piece of **equipment** in **ice** hockey that many players have **superstitions** about. Rules regarding the stick have also been created throughout the years to standardize the sport. Ernie Johnson of the **Montreal Wanderers** was known for his long reach and 75-inch hockey stick, which he often threw at opposing players' feet to trip them. At the start of the 1927–1928 season, the **National Hockey League (NHL)** made a rule that no stick could be longer than 53 inches in length. In the 1940s, the **Montreal Canadiens' center**, Billy Reay, was the first player to raise his stick to celebrate a **goal**. From 1985–1997, NHL **left wing** Petr Klima broke his hockey stick after each goal he **scored** (312). The curve of the blade was another rule that needed to be addressed. The "banana blade" was a highly curved stick blade made popular in the late 1950s and early 1960s by **Andy Bathgate**, **Stan Mikita**, and **Bobby Hull**. It added more speed, height, and spin to the **puck**; however, the NHL outlawed it. The regulation curve allowed went from one inch (1967–1968) to no more than half an inch (1970–1971), which is the current rule. A famous hockey stick incident happened during the second game of the 1993 **Stanley Cup** Finals. **Referee** Kerry Fraser was asked to measure the stick of **Los Angeles Kings'** defenseman **Marty McSorley**, and Fraser determined that it was illegal. While McSorley was in the **penalty box**, the Montreal Canadiens tied the game and won in **overtime**. The Canadiens went on to win the Stanley Cup in five games. This stick incident has been referred to as a **curse**. In addition to being terrific **skaters**, hockey players are also known for their stick skills. **Hockey Hall of Famer** George Hay of the **Chicago Black Hawks** and **Detroit Red Wings** was **nicknamed** "The Western Wizard" for his stickhandling expertise. Some other players also known for this talent include **Jean Béliveau**, **Herb Carnegie**, **Pavel Datsyuk**, **Jaromír Jágr**, **Joe Malone**, **Alexander Ovechkin**, and **Denis Savard**. *See also* HIGH-STICKING; HOOKING; SLASHING; TRIPPING.

HOLMES, HARRY GEORGE "HAPPY," "HAP". B. 21 February 1888, Aurora, Ontario. D. 27 June 1941, Fort Lauderdale, Florida. Hap Holmes played hockey for 16 professional seasons, from 1912 1928. He has the distinction of being the only **goaltender** to play for the **Stanley Cup** championship as part of four different teams, including the 1914 Toronto Blueshirts, 1917 Seattle Metropolitans, 1918 Toronto Arenas, and 1925 Victoria Cougars (the last non-**National Hockey League (NHL)** club to win the Stanley Cup). Holmes made an impact in the **National Hockey Association, Pacific Coast Hockey Association, Western Canada Hockey League,** Western Hockey League, and NHL. He backstopped two Stanley Cup wins in Toronto and one each in Seattle and Victoria. He outperformed other legendary goalies the likes of **Georges Vezina** and **Clint Benedict**. Holmes was even successful when he was loaned to the Toronto Arenas in January 1918, and he helped them win the Stanley Cup in the inaugural NHL season. Holmes then returned to Seattle for the 1918–1919 season, and he stayed there for more than five years. He was playing during the tragic final series against the **Montreal Canadiens** that was called off due to the influenza epidemic and claimed the life of **Joe Hall**. The fourth game of the series was one of Holmes's career highlights. His excellent goaltending resulted in a scoreless 60 minutes of regulation time and 20 minutes of **overtime**, after which the **referee** declared the game a draw. Holmes used a stand-up style of goaltending and wore a cap to shield himself from angry fans who would throw things or spit tobacco juice at his bald head. He recorded 17 NHL **shutouts** during his two seasons with the Cougars.

After his playing career ended, Holmes coached several **minor-league** teams, including the Toronto Millionaires of the Canadian Professional Hockey League and the Cleveland Indians of the International Hockey League. The Hap Holmes Memorial Award for the best goaltender of the season in the **American Hockey League** was named after him. In 1972, Holmes was inducted into the **Hockey Hall of Fame** posthumously.

HOOKING. When a player uses a **hockey stick** to tug or pull on any part of an opponent's body, a hooking **penalty** is called. The player then sits out of the game in the **penalty box** for two minutes.

See also HIGH-STICKING; SLASHING; TRIPPING.

HORNER, GEORGE REGINALD "RED". B. 28 May 1909, Lynden, Ontario. D. 27 April 2005, Toronto, Ontario. Red Horner was a **defenseman** in the **National Hockey League (NHL)** with the **Toronto Maple Leafs** from 1928–1940. He was the team captain from 1938–1940. On 15 March 1932, Horner replaced penalized **goaltender** Lorne Chabot at the **net**. Horner allowed one **goal** in the one minute he was the goalie. In 1932, the Maple Leafs defeated the **New York Rangers**, 3–0, in a five-game series to win the **Stanley Cup**. Horner was an **enforcer** known for his body **checking** skills, and he retired with 42 goals, 110 **assists**, and 1,264 **penalty minutes** in 490 regular-season games. On 12 December 1933, after **Eddie Shore** of the **Boston Bruins** almost killed **Ace Bailey**, Horner was infuriated and punched Shore in the jaw. Horner led the NHL in penalty minutes for eight consecutive seasons (1933–1940). He retired as the league's all-time penalty minute leader, a record he held until **Ted Lindsay** passed him. After retiring as a player, Horner became a **linesman** for a few seasons. In 1965, his induction into the **Hockey Hall of Fame** was controversial. His critics considered him a goon, but his supporters recognized his team contributions. Horner was last surviving member of Toronto's 1932 Stanley Cup team. At the time of his death in 2005, he was the oldest living NHL player and Hall of Famer.

HORTON, MILES GILBERT "TIM," "SUPERMAN". B. 12 January 1930, Cochrane, Ontario. D. 21 February 1974, St. Catherines, Ontario. Tim Horton played hockey for St. Michael's College **junior** team. He was then a **defenseman** in the **National Hockey League (NHL)** for 22 seasons, until his untimely death in a car accident. He played for the **Toronto Maple Leafs** (1951–1970), **New York Rangers** (1970–1971), **Pittsburgh Penguins** (1971–1972), and **Buffalo Sabres** (1972–1974). On 12 March 1955, after being body **checked** by **Bill Gadsby** of the Rangers, Horton suffered a broken leg and jaw and missed most of the following season. Horton won four **Stanley Cups** with Toronto (1962, 1963, 1964, 1967). **Goaltenders** at the time, including **Jacques Plante**, said that Tim had the hardest **slapshot** in the league. According to **enforcer** John Ferguson, Horton was extremely powerful when he checked his opponents, but he also "didn't have a mean bone in his body," according to **coach Punch Imlach**. Instead of **fighting**, he would give his opponents a strong "Tim Horton Bear Hug," earning him the **nickname** "Superman." He also had poor eyesight and was called "Mister Magoo." During the 1963–1964 season, Horton led the NHL in game-winning **goals** by a defenseman (7). In 1964–1965, he played **right wing** for the Leafs.

To make a living in the off-season, Horton started a coffee and donut business in 1964, in Hamilton, Ontario. In 1967, he became partners with former police officer Ron Joyce. Unfortunately, he did not live to see the success of the franchise. He was traveling back to Buffalo from a game at **Maple Leaf Gardens** when he was killed in an automobile accident on 21 February 1974. At the time of Horton's death, there were 40 Tim Hortons restaurants. His partner, Joyce, bought out Mrs. Horton's shares. Today, there are franchises all across **Canada** and the **United States**. Horton's widow sued Joyce, believing that he had taken advantage of her, but she lost her court case; however, one of Tim's daughters married Joyce's son, effectively returning the company to the Horton family. Tim was posthumously inducted into the **Hockey Hall of Fame** in 1977. During his NHL career, he played in 1,446 regular-season games and recorded 115 goals, 403 **assists**, 518 **points**, and 1,611 **penalty minutes**.

HOUSLEY, PHILLIP FRANCIS "PHIL". B. 9 March 1964, South St. Paul, Minnesota. Phil Housley was an American **ice** hockey **defenseman** who played for the **Buffalo Sabres, Winnipeg Jets, St. Louis Blues, Calgary Flames, New Jersey Devils, Washington Capitals, Chicago Blackhawks,** and **Toronto Maple Leafs**. He is the second leading **scorer** of players born in the **United States**, with 1,232 **points** (338 **goals** and 894 **assists**). Housley held the record for most points by a **National Hockey League (NHL)** player born in the United States, until **Mike Modano** surpassed it on 7 November 2007. Housley never won the **Stanley Cup**, but he came close in 1998, with the Capitals, but they lost in the finals to the **Detroit Red Wings**. Housley has the unfortunate distinction of playing more NHL games without winning the Stanley Cup than any other player in NHL history. Housley played in 1,495 NHL games. For almost seven years, he held the record for most games played by an American-born player, until **Chris Chelios** broke it on 24 November 2006. In 2002, Housley was a member of the silver medal-winning **U.S. Men's Olympic Ice Hockey Team**. He was inducted into the **U.S. Hockey Hall of Fame** in 2004. For his contributions to hockey, he received the **Lester Patrick Trophy** in 2008. Housley currently **coaches** high school hockey in Minnesota.

HOWE, GORDON "GORDIE," "MR. HOCKEY". B. 31 March 1928, Floral, Saskatchewan. Gordie Howe is commonly known as one of the best **ice** hockey players of all time. He is most famous for his **scoring** prowess, physical strength, and career longevity. He is the only player to have competed in the **National Hockey League (NHL)** in six different decades (1940s through 1990s). Howe played **right wing** for the **Detroit Red Wings** and Hartford Whalers of the NHL, and the Houston Aeros and New England Whalers of the **World Hockey Association (WHA)**. Early in his career, Howe became known as a great **goal scorer** and talented playmaker who liked to **fight**. During his **rookie** season, **coach Jack Adams** told him that, "I know you can fight. Now, can you show me you can play hockey?" When a player scores a goal and an **assist** and has a fight in one game, it is called a "Gordie Howe **hat trick**." Howe was part of Detroit's famous **line**, the "Production Line," with **Ted Lindsay** and **Sid Abel**. He won the **Stanley Cup** four times with the Red Wings (1950, 1952, 1954, 1955). Howe also won the **Art Ross Trophy** and **Hart Memorial Trophy** six times each.

Howe's **nickname**, "Mr. Hockey" and his wife's, "Mrs. Hockey," are both registered trademarks. During his career, he was also called "Mr. Everything," "Mr. All-Star," "The Most," "The Great Gordie," "The King of Hockey," "The Legend," "The Man," "No. 9," and "Mr. Elbows." The last name came about because Howe was a physical player who liked to elbow his opponents. He received the **Lester Patrick Trophy** in 1967. Howe retired for the first time in 1971, and he was inducted into the **Hockey Hall of Fame** in 1972. When he returned to play for the Houston Aeros in the WHA with his sons, **Mark Howe** and Marty Howe, Gordie joined **Guy Lafleur** and **Mario Lemieux** as the only three Hall of Fame members to return to the ice. Gordie played on a line with both of his sons in Hartford's 4–4 tie with the Red Wings on 12 March 1980. On 3 October 1997, Gordie signed a one-game contract with the Detroit Vipers and played a single shift to become hockey's first six-decade player. Howe holds the record for the most seasons played, with 26, and also for the most games played, with 1,767, from 1946–1980. He held the record for the most NHL career goals, with 801, until **Wayne Gretzky** surpassed it. Howe continues to hold NHL career records for NHL right wings in the categories of goals (801), assists (1,049), and **points** (1,850). Gordie's **brother**, Vic Howe, briefly played with the **New York Rangers** (1952–1954).

HOWE, MARK STEVEN. B. 28 May 1955, Detroit, Michigan. Mark Howe is the son of legendary **Gordie Howe** and the younger **brother** of Marty Howe. As a **young player**, Mark practiced with **Terry Sawchuk**'s **goaltender** pads and **Bobby Hull**'s used **hockey sticks**. When he visited his father at work, **Eddie Shack** used to sing the chorus to the song "Gordie Howe Is the Greatest of Them All" when young Mark entered the opponents' dressing room. At 18 years of age, Mark was offered a four-year contract worth $500,000, with a signing bonus worth $125,000, by the Houston Aeros of the **World Hockey Association**. Mark said, "Dad just pulled me aside one day and said 'That's $25,000 more than I ever made in a year. If I have to, I'll break your arm and sign it for you.'" Mark accepted the deal and became a **left wing** for Houston (1973–1977). He also played for the **New England Whalers** in the WHA (1977–1979). Mark then played in the **National Hockey League (NHL)** with the Hartford Whalers (1979–1982), **Philadelphia Flyers** (1982–1992), and **Detroit Red Wings** (1992–1995). Colleen Howe suggested that Gordie play with both his sons, Mark and Marty, which he did from 1973–1980. On 12 March 1980, the whole **family** played on a **line** in a **match** against the Detroit Red Wings, which ended in a 4–4 tie. Later that year, on 27 December, Mark suffered a major leg **injury** when he was impaled on the goalpost. During the 1979–1980 NHL season, Mark switched his position to **defenseman**.

Internationally, Mark won a silver medal for the **United States** at the 1972 **Olympic Games**, and, at 16 years of age, he was the youngest ice hockey player to ever win an Olympic medal. Howe played for **Canada** against the Soviet Union with the 1974 WHA **All-Star Team**. Knee and back injuries influenced his retirement decision. Howe played for the United States in the 1981 **Canada Cup**. He had 197 **goals** and 545 **assists** in 929 career NHL games. Howe was inducted into both the **U.S. Hockey Hall of Fame** (2003) and **Hockey Hall of Fame** (2011). He is currently the director of scouting for the Detroit Red Wings.

HOWE, SYDNEY HARRIS "SYD". B. 28 September 1911, Ottawa, Ontario. D. 20 May 1976, Ottawa, Ontario. Syd Howe was a **center** and **left wing** for 17 seasons in the **National Hockey League (NHL)**. He played for the **Ottawa Senators** (1929–1930, 1932–1934), **Philadelphia Quakers** (1930–1931), **Toronto Maple Leafs** (1931–1932), **St. Louis Eagles** (1934–1935), and **Detroit Red Wings** (1934–1946). He won the **Stanley Cup** three times with Detroit (1936, 1937, 1943). Howe finished second in NHL **points**, with 47 (1934–1935) and 44 (1940–1941). On 19 March 1940, he **scored** the fastest **overtime goal** in the **Stanley Cup Playoffs** (25 seconds) against the **New York Americans**. This record was surpassed by Ted Irvine, on 2 April 1969, with a 19-second goal. Howe scored a **hat trick** during Detroit's 15–0 victory over the **New York Rangers** on 23 January 1944. On 3 February 1944, in Detroit's 12–2 win over the Rangers, he became only the sixth player in NHL history to score six goals in a single game. He played a total of 698 NHL regular-season games and had 237 goals, 291 **assists**, 528 points, and 212 **penalty minutes**. In 1965, Howe became the only player inducted to the **Hockey Hall of Fame** who also played for the Quakers. Coincidentally, Syd Howe and **Gordie Howe** were both stars with the Detroit Red Wings, but the two men were not related.

HOWELL, HENRY VERNON "HORSE," "HARRY". B. 28 December 1932, Hamilton, Ontario. Harry Howell was a **defenseman** in the **National Hockey League (NHL)** for 21 seasons with the **New York Rangers** (1952–1969), Oakland Seals (1969–1970), California Golden Seals (1970–1971), and **Los Angeles Kings** (1970–1973). He holds the Rangers' record for most career games played (1,160). The **nickname** "Horse" came from his hard work ethic and only missing 20 games during his first 16 NHL seasons. He was also known for his passing and poke **checking** skills. In 1967, Howell won the **James Norris Memorial Trophy** as the game's best defenseman. In his acceptance speech, Howell humbly said, "I'm glad I won this award this year, because I have a feeling that **Bobby Orr** will win it next year and every year until he retires." Howell's prediction was accurate, and Orr won the trophy for the next eight seasons. After retiring from playing, Howell stayed involved with hockey as a **coach**. In 1979, he was inducted into the **Hockey Hall of Fame**. Although he was on seven **All-Star Teams**, Howell never won the **Stanley Cup** as a player. In 1990, he finally won the Stanley Cup as a member of the **Edmonton Oilers** while he was serving as a scout. His brother, Ron Howell, also played for the Rangers (1954–1956).

HULL, BRETT ANDREW "THE GOLDEN BRETT". B. 9 August 1964, Belleville, Ontario. Brett Hull is the son of **Hockey Hall of Famer Bobby Hull**. His mother was a professional figure **skater,** and she taught Brett how to skate when he was five years old. Hull played two years of **college hockey** for the University of Minnesota Duluth. Although he was born in **Canada,** he held dual citizenship because his mother was an American citizen. Hull made his international debut representing the **United States** at the 1986 **World Ice Hockey Championships** in Moscow, and he was his team's leading **scorer.** He then played 20 seasons as a **right wing** in the **National Hockey League (NHL)** with the **Calgary Flames** (1985–1988), **St. Louis Blues** (1988–1998), **Dallas Stars** (1998–2001), **Detroit Red Wings** (2001–2004), and **Phoenix Coyotes** (2005–2006). Hull's **nickname,** "The Golden Brett," referred to his blonde hair, and it was also a play on his father's nickname, "The Golden Jet." On 25 January 1991, Brett joined the company of **Maurice Richard, Mike Bossy, Wayne Gretzky,** and **Mario Lemieux** when he scored 50 **goals** in 50 or fewer games. Hull won the **Lady Byng Memorial Trophy** for his sportsmanship (1990). In 1991, he also won the **Hart Memorial Trophy** and Lester B. Pearson Award. Hull scored the winning **overtime** goal for the Dallas Stars in the 1999 **Stanley Cup** Finals against the **Buffalo Sabres**. He also won the Stanley Cup in 2002 with the Red Wings. Hull played on a Detroit **line** with **Pavel Datsyuk** and Henrik Zetterberg, nicknamed the "Two Kids and an Old Goat Line."

Brett's shooting style was similar to his father's. They could both release the **puck** quickly, while still keeping the shot hard and accurate. Brett holds the NHL record for career **Stanley Cup Playoff power play** goals (38). He shares the NHL record with Wayne Gretzky for career playoff game-winning goals (24). During his career, Hull played in 1,269 regular-season NHL games and recorded 741 goals, 650 **assists**, 1,391 **points**, and 458 **penalty minutes**. He also played for the United States in the 1991 **Canada Cup** and 1996 **World Cup of Hockey**, winning silver and gold medals, respectively. Hull played in the 1998 **Olympic Games** and won a silver medal at the 2002 Olympics in Salt Lake City. In 2009, he was inducted into the Hockey Hall of Fame.

HULL, ROBERT MARVIN "BOBBY," "THE GOLDEN JET". B. 3 January 1939, Point Anne, Ontario. Bobby Hull was **nicknamed** "The Golden Jet" for his speed on the **ice**, as well as for his blonde, curly hair. His blazing **slapshot** was estimated to have traveled at approximately 120 miles per hour. Hull was a **left wing** in the **National Hockey League (NHL)** with the **Chicago Black Hawks** (1957–1972). During the 1960s, he played on the "MPH line," with **Stan Mikita** and Jim Pappin. The name came from the initials of their last names, as well as for their speed. With Mikita, Hull developed the curved **hockey stick**, known as the "banana blade." It caused the **puck** to curve, and **goaltenders** had trouble anticipating the shots. Sharply curved hockey sticks were later banned by the NHL. Hull helped his team defeat the **Detroit Red Wings** (4–2) to win the 1961 **Stanley Cup**. He also received several awards for his individual contributions, including the **Art Ross Trophy** (1960, 1962, 1966), **Hart Memorial Trophy** (1965, 1966), **Lady Byng Memorial Trophy** (1965), and **Lester Patrick Trophy** (1969).

On 12 March 1966, Hull became the first player in NHL history to record more than 50 **goals** in a season. In 1971–1972, Hull hit the 50-goal mark for the fifth time in his career. Then the **Winnipeg Jets** of the **World Hockey Association (WHA)** drafted him. Hull made headlines as he signed the first $1 million contract in the history of hockey. He remained with the Jets for 18 games during the 1979–1980 season, after they merged with the NHL. He spent his final season with the **Hartford Whalers** (1979–80), playing alongside **Gordie Howe**. During his years with the WHA, Hull developed ulcers from the stress of playing several games on consecutive nights with conditions that were quite poor compared to those in the NHL. He retired after playing in 1,063 regular-season NHL games and recording 610 goals, 560 assists, 1,170 **points**, and 640 **penalty minutes**. He also played in 411 regular-season WHA games and recorded 303 goals, 335 assists, and 638 points, adding 43 goals and 37 assists in 60 playoff games.

During his career, Hull led the NHL in goals seven times, and he led the WHA in goals during the 1974–1975 season, with 77. He also led the NHL **Stanley Cup Playoffs** in goals, with eight (1961–1962), eight (1962–1963), and 10 (1964–1965). Hull once had his jaw broken by **Montreal Canadiens'** tough guy John Ferguson, and, in a WHA game **fight**, **defenseman** Dave Hanson accidentally pulled off Hull's toupee. Internationally, Hull played for **Canada** in the 1974 **Summit Series** and was the top-scoring Canadian forward in the 1976 **Canada Cup**. After retiring from hockey, he worked in the cattle ranching business. Hull was inducted into the **Hockey Hall of Fame** in 1983, and he is the only member that played in all seven seasons of the WHA's existence. Bobby's son, **Brett Hull**, is also a Hall of Famer. Bobby and Brett are the only father and son to both achieve more than 50 goals in a season and 600 NHL goals.

HYLAND, HAROLD MACARIUS "HARRY". B. 2 January 1889, Montreal, Quebec. D. 8 August 1969, Montreal, Quebec. Harry Hyland was a **right wing** for the **Montreal Wanderers** of the **National Hockey Association (NHA)**. He was known for his fast **skating** and high **scoring**. On 2 January 1909, Hyland **scored** two **goals** in Montreal's 9–8 victory over the **Quebec Bulldogs**. During the 1909–1910 season, he led the Wanderers in goals, with 24. He helped Montreal win the **Stanley Cup** in 1910. In 1912, Hyland won a national **lacrosse** championship with the New Westminster Salmonbellies. On 25 January 1913, Hyland scored eight goals in a 10–6 Wanderers victory over the Bulldogs. When the Wanderers joined the **National Hockey League (NHL)**, Hyland scored five goals in their NHL debut against the Toronto Arenas on 19 December 1917. He also played one season for the **Ottawa Senators** (1917–1918), before retiring. In 1962, Hyland was inducted into the **Hockey Hall of Fame**.

I

ICE. The playing surface for the game of ice hockey or curling is a **rink** made of ice. There are two types of ice rinks mainly used today. Natural ones are when the freezing occurs from cold temperatures, such as in **pond hockey** and the **Winter Classic**. Artificial or mechanically frozen ones are when a coolant produces cold temperatures in the surface below the water, causing the water to freeze. The machine used to resurface the ice between periods of a game is called a **Zamboni**.

ICE HOCKEY. The official term for the sport of hockey is **ice** hockey. While the game is often referred to simply as hockey, the two-word name is used at the **Olympic Games** and other international events. *See also* POND HOCKEY.

ICING. Icing is a **line** violation called when the **puck** is shot from a player's own side of center **ice** and goes past the **red line** of the other team uninterrupted. The result is a **face-off** back at the shooting team's end of the **rink**. Icing is currently only allowed during a **power play**. Before the icing rule, teams with an early lead would hit the puck down the ice to use up the clock and protect their lead. Two notable games in which this occurred were between the **New York Americans** and the **Boston Bruins**. On 8 November 1931, the Americans had a 3–2 lead when they sent the puck down the length of the rink 50 times. The Boston crowd was upset with the boring game. Then the Bruins' president, Charles Adams, told his players to imitate New York's style. On 3 December 1931, in New York, the Boston Bruins set a record by icing the puck 87 times in one game. It resulted in a scoreless tie and many disappointed fans. On 24 September 1937, the icing rule was passed by the **National Hockey League**.

IGINLA, JAROME ARTHUR LEIGH ADEKUNLE TIG JUNIOR ELVIS "IGGY". B. 1 July 1977, Edmonton, Alberta. Jarome Iginla was a baseball catcher on the **Canadian** national team when he was younger. Then he was a hockey **goaltender** for two years in the **juniors**, because he admired

Grant Fuhr. As one of the few black hockey players in the **National Hockey League (NHL)**, Fuhr became Iginla's role model. Since 1996, Iginla has played **right wing** for the **Calgary Flames**. From 2001–2007, he averaged more than 40 **goals** per season. In 2002, he won the Lester B. Pearson Award, **Art Ross Trophy**, and the **Maurice "Rocket" Richard Trophy**. In 2003, he became the team captain of the Flames and only the second black captain in NHL history. In 1989–1990, Dirk Graham was the first player of African American descent to become an NHL team captain. He led his **Chicago Blackhawks** all the way to the **Stanley Cup** Finals in 1991–1992, where they lost to the **Pittsburgh Penguins**. Iginla also led his team to the Stanley Cup Finals (2004), but they lost to the **Tampa Bay Lightning**.

Iginla recently reached two major milestones. He **scored** his 1,000th career **point**, with a goal against the **St. Louis Blues** on 1 April 2011. Then he scored his 500th career goal on 7 January 2012, against the **Minnesota Wild**. He scored the goal against goaltender Niklas Bäckström during Calgary's 3–1 victory. In a game against the **San Jose Sharks** on 13 March 2012, he scored his 30th goal of the 2011–2012 season, making him only the seventh player in NHL history to score at least 30 goals in 11 consecutive seasons. To date, Iginla has played in 1,188 regular-season NHL games and recorded 516 goals, 557 **assists**, 1,073 points, and 809 **penalty minutes**. He holds the record as the all-time scoring leader for the Calgary Flames, breaking **Theoren Fleury**'s record. Internationally, Iginla played for Canada in the 1997 **World Ice Hockey Championships**. He also helped Team Canada win gold medals at both the 2002 and 2010 **Olympic Games**. Iginla and his teammates also won the **World Cup of Hockey** in 2004. Iginla is known for being a strong team leader and a charitable person off the **ice**. He will surely be inducted into the **Hockey Hall of Fame** when he becomes eligible. *See also* CARNEGIE, HERBERT H. "HERB," "SWIVEL HIPS"; O'REE, WILLIAM ELDON "WILLIE".

IMLACH, GEORGE "PUNCH". B. 15 March 1918, Toronto, Ontario. D. 1 December 1987, Toronto, Ontario. As a player, George Imlach earned the **nickname** "Punch" after being knocked out during a game. Still dazed in the dressing room, he mistakenly punched the trainer, thinking that he was involved in the **fight**. Imlach was a **center** with the Toronto Goodyears (1938–1940), Toronto Marlboros (1940–1941), and Quebec Aces (1945–1949), but he is better known for his **coaching** career. He coached the Quebec Aces (1949–1950), **Toronto Maple Leafs** (1958–1969, 1979–1980), and **Buffalo Sabres** (1970–1972). As coach of the Maple Leafs, Imlach won four **Stanley Cups** (1962, 1963, 1964, 1967). He had a reputation for being tough on his players, but there was mutual respect. Imlach once said, "I even like the guys I don't like. They're a terrific buncha bums." When he was the general manager of the Sabres (1970–1978), he convinced former Leafs' player **Tim Horton** to come out of retirement and join his team. During the 1974 NHL Draft, Imlach became annoyed with the slow telephone drafting process, which was intended to keep draft picks secret from the rival **World Hockey Association**. Imlach planned a prank at the expense of the league and president of 28 years, **Clarence Campbell**, and found a common Japanese name in a Buffalo phone book. Then **Taro Tsujimoto**, a fictional hockey player, was legally drafted by the Buffalo Sabres 183rd overall in the 11th round of the draft. Imlach later admitted to the fake draft pick, but Campbell was not amused. His coaching career came to an end due to his heart attacks. During his career, Imlach amassed a coaching record of 423 wins, 373 losses, and 163 ties. He holds the record for most wins in the history of the Toronto Maple Leafs' franchise, with 365. In 1984, Imlach was inducted into the **Hockey Hall of Fame** as a **builder**.

INJURIES. Ice hockey is a full-contact sport with strong athletes, sharp **skate** blades, long **hockey sticks**, and hard **pucks** flying at speeds up to 100 miles per hour. It is no wonder that injuries are prevalent. **Marcel Pronovost** of the **Detroit Red Wings** and **Toronto Maple Leafs** was known as the most injured hockey player in **National Hockey League (NHL)** history. The NHL has tried to reduce the number of injuries by encouraging the use of protective **equipment**. Although **fights** are common in the sport, **penalty** rules have been instituted to enforce major and gross misconduct, but sometimes accidental injuries occur. **Goaltender** Clint Malarchuk of the **Buffalo Sabres** suffered one of the worst injuries in hockey history on 22 March 1989, when he collided with Steve Tuttle of the **St. Louis Blues** and got his carotid artery severed by Tuttle's skate. He nearly bled to death on the ice while waiting for medical assistance. Remarkably, he was back in the **goal** less than two weeks later. As a result of that incident, goalies began wearing protective collars. *See also* BILL MASTERTON MEMORIAL TROPHY; CAREER-ENDING INJURIES; SAWCHUK, TERRANCE GORDON "TERRY," "UKEY".

INTERNATIONAL HOCKEY LEAGUE (IHL). The International Hockey League (IHL) was a professional **ice** hockey **minor league** in the **United States** and **Canada** (1945–2001). The IHL served as the **National Hockey League**'s alternate farm team system to the **American Hockey League (AHL)**. After 56 years of operation, it was dissolved due to financial difficulties. The six surviving teams that merged into the AHL in 2001 included the Chicago Wolves, Grand Rapids Griffins, Houston Aeros, Manitoba Moose, Milwaukee Admirals, and Utah Grizzlies.

INTERNATIONAL ICE HOCKEY FEDERATION (IIHF). The International Ice Hockey Federation (IIHF, Ligue Internationale de Hockey sur Glace) is the worldwide governing body for **ice** hockey and inline hockey. Established in 1908, it is based in Zurich, **Switzerland**, and has 72 current members. The federation is responsible for the management of international ice hockey tournaments, and it also maintains the IIHF World Ranking. Eight nations that have achieved a top 10 ranking each year from 2003–2011 include **Canada, Sweden, Russia**, the **Czech Republic, Finland**, the **United States, Slovakia**, and **Switzerland**. An additional four nations, Latvia, **Germany**, Belarus, and **Norway** have been in the top 10 at least once. From 1966–1969, American William Thayer Tutt was president of the IIHF. Since 1994, former Swiss player and **referee** René Fasel has been the president. The IIHF's museum is located in Toronto, Ontario, in the same building as the **Hockey Hall of Fame**.

INTERNATIONAL ICE HOCKEY FEDERATION HALL OF FAME. The International Ice Hockey Federation Hall of Fame is a hall of fame established by the **International Ice Hockey Federation (IIHF)** in 1997, when 30 individuals were inducted at the **World Ice Hockey Championships** in Helsinki. The IIHF Hall of Fame is intended to honor individuals who have made valuable contributions both in their home countries and internationally. Members are inducted annually in three separate categories: player, **referee**, and **builder** (an individual who manages or grows the sport). Father **David Bauer**, from **Canada**, is one notable builder inducted into the hall. Several player inductees include **Wayne Gretzky**, Geraldine Heaney, and **Mario Lemieux** from Canada; **Vladislav Tretiak** and **Pavel Bure** from **Russia**; **Jaroslav Drobný** from the **Czech Republic**; **Jari Kurri** from **Finland**; and **Cammi Granato, Mark Johnson**, and **Lou Nanne** from the **United States**. Inducted referees include Quido Adamec from the Czech Republic, Ove Dahlberg from **Sweden**, Yuri Karandin from Russia, Josef Kompalla from **Germany**, Laszlo Schell from Hungary, and Unto Wiitala from Finland. The IIHF Hall of Fame is located in the same building as the **Hockey Hall of Fame**, in Toronto, Ontario. *See also* APPENDIX F for a list of IIHF Hall of Fame inductees.

INTIMIDATION. Intimidation is a tactic used by hockey players to interfere with their opponents' focus and rhythm on the **ice**. By using their **hockey sticks**, elbows, speed, or sheer large presence, players who rattle the opposition are powerful intimidators. Five well-known players with this talent were **Gordie Howe, Eric Lindros, Ted Lindsay, Mark Messier**, and **Eddie Shore**.

See also AGITATION; PENALTY; PENALTY BOX "SIN BIN"; PENALTY KILLER; PENALTY MINUTES.

IRVIN, JAMES DICKINSON "DICK". B. 19 July 1892, Hamilton, Ontario. D. 16 May 1957, Montreal, Quebec. Dick Irvin was a professional hockey **center** for the Winnipeg Monarchs (1911–1916), Portland Rosebuds (1916–1917), Regina Capitals (1921–1925), Portland Capitals (1925–1926), and **Chicago Black Hawks** (1926–1929). Irvin was Chicago's first captain. During the 1926–1927 season, he lead the **National Hockey League (NHL)** in **assists**, with 18. After his playing career, Irvin turned to **coaching**. He coached the Chicago Black Hawks (1928–1929, 1930–1931, 1955–1956), **Toronto Maple Leafs** (1931–1940), and **Montreal Canadiens** (1940–1955). In 1932, Irvin led Toronto to the **Stanley Cup** against the **New York Rangers**. He was responsible for creating the D-A-D **line**, with **Gordie Drillon**, **Syl Apps**, and Bob Davidson. He also helped Montreal win the Stanley Cup three times (1944, 1946, 1953). Irvin was inducted into the **Hockey Hall of Fame** in 1958 as a player. His son, Dick Irvin Jr, was a **Canadian** sports broadcaster and author who was inducted into the Hockey Hall of Fame in 1988, in the broadcaster category.

J

JACK ADAMS AWARD. The Jack Adams Award is the **National Hockey League (NHL)** award given annually to the best **coach** of the year. In 1974, the award was created in honor of **Jack Adams**. Although Adams was inducted into the **Hockey Hall of Fame** in 1959 as a player, he was also known as the coach of the **Detroit Red Wings** in the 1940s and 1950s. **Fred Shero** of the **Philadelphia Flyers** was the first recipient of the award. Jacques Demers of the Detroit Red Wings is the only coach who has won the award in consecutive seasons (1986–1987, 1987–1988). **Jacques Lemaire, Pat Quinn**, and **Scotty Bowman** have each won the award with two different teams. Lemaire won as coach of the **New Jersey Devils** and **Minnesota Wild**. Quinn won as coach of the Philadelphia Flyers and **Vancouver Canucks**. Bowman won as coach of the **Montreal Canadiens** and Detroit Red Wings. Pat Burns won the award three times with three different teams. Burns was voted as the coach who contributed the most to his team's success with the Montreal Canadiens, **Toronto Maple Leafs**, and **Boston Bruins**. In 2011, Dan Bylsma of the **Pittsburgh Penguins** received the Jack Adams Award for his coaching, and Ken Hitchcock of the **St. Louis Blues** received it in 2012.

JACKSON, HARVEY "BUSHER". B. 19 January 1911, Toronto, Ontario. D. 25 June 1966, Toronto, Ontario. Busher Jackson was a **l eft wing** in the **National Hockey League (NHL)** with the **Toronto Maple Leafs** (1929–1939), **New York Americans** (1939–1941), and **Boston Bruins** (1941–1944). He was only 18 years old when he joined Toronto. **Charlie Conacher, Joe Primeau**, and Jackson were a young forward **line** of the Maple Leafs, **nicknamed** the "Kid Line." Jackson got the **nickname** "Busher" from Toronto's trainer, Tim Daly. Daly called him "a fresh busher," which was a term to describe a player called up from the **minor league**. Jackson was known for his energetic **skating** and lethal **backhand**. In 1932, he was the NHL's leading **scorer**, with 53 **points**. At 21 years and 3 months of age, he was the youngest player to hold that scoring title, until **Wayne Gretzky** set a new record at 20 years and 3 months of age (1980–1981). Also in 1932, Jackson helped Toronto defeat the **New York Rangers**, 3–0, to win the **Stanley Cup**. On 20 November 1934, in a 5–2 win over the **St. Louis Eagles**, Jackson became the first NHL player to score four **goals** in a single period. **Max Bentley** and **Clint Smith** became the first two players to tie his record. In his final season with Boston, Jackson occasionally filled in as a **defenseman**. In his 636 regular-season career games, he scored 241 goals. Jackson battled alcoholism until his death in 1966. He was inducted into the **Hockey Hall of Fame** in 1971, which directly led to **Conn Smythe** resigning as the hall's president. Smythe believed Jackson did not warrant admission to his character.

JÁGR, JAROMÍR. B. 15 February 1972, Kladno, Czechoslovakia. Jaromír Jágr is a current **right wing** in the **National Hockey League (NHL)** with the **Philadelphia Flyers**. Jágr also played with the **Pittsburgh Penguins** (1990–2001), **Washington Capitals** (2001–2004), and **New York Rangers** (2003–2004, 2005–2008), and he was the captain of the Penguins and Rangers. He also played for three seasons (2008–2011) in the Kontinental Hockey League, with Avangard Omsk, before joining the Flyers for the 2011–2012 season. Jágr was the first Czechoslovakian player to be drafted by the NHL without first having to defect. When the Penguins won back-to-back **Stanley Cups** in 1991 and 1992, Jágr was one of the youngest players in NHL history, at 20 years of age, to **score** a **goal** in the Stanley Cup Finals.

Known for his expert stickhandling skills, Jágr led the NHL in scoring five times and was rewarded with the **Art Ross Trophy** (1995, 1998, 1999, 2000, 2001). He also won the **Hart Memorial Trophy** (1999) and Lester B. Pearson Award (1999, 2000, 2006). Jágr had a **superstition** about eating cookies and drinking milk the night before games, believing that it would settle him down. In his career to date, he has played in 1,346 regular-season NHL games and recorded 665 goals, 988 **assists**, 1,653 **points**, and 937 **penalty minutes**. In his 180 **Stanley Cup Playoff** games, he has had 78 goals and 111 assists, for a total of 189 points. Jágr is one of a small group of hockey players to have won the **Stanley Cup** (1991, 1992), **World Ice Hockey Championships** (2005, 2010), and **Olympic** gold medal in **ice** hockey (1998). Known as the "**Triple Gold Club**," Jágr is one of only two Czech players (the other being Jiří Šlégr) to accomplish this. Jágr represented Czechoslovakia in the 1990 World Ice Hockey Championships and won a bronze medal. Playing for the **Czech Republic**, he also won bronze medals at the **World Cup of Hockey** (2004) and Winter Olympics (2006). Jágr will surely be inducted into the **Hockey Hall of Fame** when he becomes eligible.

JAMAICA. The **National Hockey League (NHL)** has only had one Jamaican-born player to date. Graeme Townshend moved to **Canada** as a small child but was born in Kingston, Jamaica. He played **right wing** in the NHL for the **Boston Bruins** (1989–1991), **New York Islanders** (1991–1993), and **Ottawa Senators** (1993–1994). Twenty years later, spectators of the 2014 **Olympic Games** in **Russia** may see the first-ever Jamaican **ice** hockey team. The Jamaican Olympic Ice Hockey Team (JOIHT), a nonprofit organization based in Colorado, received the endorsement of the Jamaica Olympic Association (JOA). The team will be composed of highly skilled players of Jamaican heritage who currently play across the world. Inspired in part by the Jamaican bobsled team, the JOIHT is planning what they have described as an unprecedented undertaking to bring much needed diversity to a sport dominated by other cultures. The JOIHT was cofounded by 22-year-old level-four **coach** (a step below the NHL stage) Edmond R. Phillips and G. Webster Smith, the first-ever African American to become a master-rated coach by the Professional Skaters Association. **Willie O'Ree**, the NHL's director of youth development and ambassador for NHL Diversity, has added his support to the JOIHT in seeking the endorsement of the JOA.

JAMES, ANGELA. B. 22 December 1964, Toronto, Ontario. Angela James attended Seneca College in Toronto, where she won numerous titles in **ice** hockey and softball. Due to her great talent, she was once **nicknamed** "The **Wayne Gretzky** of Women's Hockey." She was a forward who won four **World Ice Hockey Championships** gold medals (1990, 1992, 1994, 1997) and was the leading **scorer** for Team **Canada** in 1992. James scored 34 **points** in 20 games during four women's World Ice Hockey Championships, including 11 **goals** in five games in the inaugural **International Ice Hockey Federation** World Women's Championships, held in Ottawa, in 1990. James was also a **roller hockey** gold medalist (1992) and silver medalist (1994) for Team Canada, but she was excluded by Shannon Miller from the 1998 **Canadian Women's Olympic Ice Hockey Team**. In 2008, James, **Cammi Granato**, and Geraldine Heaney were the first women inducted into the **International Ice Hockey Federation Hall of Fame**. That same year, the Angela James Bowl trophy was created for the Canadian Women's Hockey League's top scorer. In 2009, James was inducted into **Canada's Sports Hall of Fame**. In 2010, James and Granato became the first women inducted into the **Hockey Hall of Fame**. James currently works in the athletic department at Seneca College, and she has also worked as a **referee**. *See also* WOMEN'S ICE HOCKEY.

JAMES NORRIS MEMORIAL TROPHY. The James Norris Memorial Trophy is the **National Hockey League (NHL)** award given annually to the best all-around **defenseman** in the league. It is named after the former owner of the **Detroit Red Wings**. James Norris and his family owned the Red Wings from 1932–1982. In 1954, the first recipient of the trophy was **Red Kelly**. **Bobby Orr** won the award for a record eight consecutive seasons (1968–1975). **Doug Harvey** of the **Montreal Canadiens** and **New York Rangers** won the award seven times. **Ray Bourque** of the **Boston Bruins** won it five times. In 2011, the Detroit Red Wings' **Nicklas Lidström** won the James Norris Memorial Trophy for the seventh time. In 2012, Erik Karlsson of the **Ottawa Senators** was the recipient of this award.

JARVIS, DOUGLAS M. "DOUG". B. 24 March 1955, Brantford, Ontario. Doug Jarvis was a **center** in the **National Hockey League (NHL)** with the **Montreal Canadiens** (1975–1982), **Washington Capitals** (1982–1985), and Hartford Whalers (1985–1988). He was known as a great **penalty killer**. Jarvis set a NHL record by playing in 964 consecutive games in the regular season (between 8 October 1975 and 10 October 1987), beating **Garry Unger**'s record of 914 games. Jarvis won both the **Frank J. Selke Trophy** (1984) and **Bill Masterton Memorial Trophy** (1987). He helped the Canadiens win the **Stanley Cup** in 1976, 1977, 1978, and 1979. In 1999, Jarvis also won the Stanley Cup as an assistant **coach** with the **Dallas Stars**. He also coached the **minor league** Binghamton Whalers (1987–1988) and Hamilton Bulldogs (2003–2005). He is currently an assistant coach for the **Boston Bruins** of the NHL. In 964 regular-season NHL games, Jarvis recorded 139 **goals**, 264 **assists**, 403 **points**, and 263 **penalty minutes**.

JERSEY. A jersey is the large shirt worn by hockey players. It is also known as a sweater, because in the early days of hockey, players would wear patterned turtleneck sweaters from a men's clothing store and add a number on the back. By the late 1930s, most jerseys were made of solid colors. Dating to the 1940s, the captain of a team displayed a "C" on the front of his jersey, and the alternate captain displayed an "A." From 1942–1967, jerseys were colored red, blue, black, gold, or white. After the **National Hockey League (NHL)** expansion, team jerseys had logos on them and came in many colors, including orange and green. In the 1970s, names on the backs of the jerseys made a comeback. The **New York Americans** experimented with them in 1926, but the idea didn't catch on. The **New York Rangers** were one of the first teams to reintroduce them in the NHL, and this time they were accepted. Until 1977, home teams could wear names at their discretion, and road teams could wear them by permission of the home team. In the 1977–1978 season, names straight across the jersey back became mandatory. In 1982, the **De-**

troit Red Wings became the first team to use vertically arched names. Hockey players have rituals, and some of them involve their jerseys. When **Wayne Gretzky** started playing hockey, he was the youngest player on his team, and the jerseys were much too large for his small frame. As a result, he tucked one side of it into his pants, so that it would not interfere with his shooting. The "tuck" became part of Gretzky's signature, just like his **jersey number, 99.**

JERSEY NUMBER. The **National Hockey Association (NHA)** first displayed **jersey** numbers on the back of each hockey player in 1912. This made it easier for the **referees** to identify the players when calling **penalties.** The number originally corresponded with the player's position. The **goaltender** was number 1, **defensemen** 2 and 3, **center** 4, and the **wings** 5 and 6. Replacement players were assigned 7, 8, 9, and the backup goalie wore 30. This changed as time went on, but players generally wore low numbers, from 2 to 29. Well-known goalie **Ron Hextall** wore nontraditional number 27, and 72 when that was unavailable. Evgeni Nabokov and **Ed Belfour** both wore jersey number 20 in honor of their mentor **Russian** goalie, **Vladislav Tretiak.** Tretiak wore number 20, because in the Soviet Union it was a tradition that the starting goalie wore number 1, all the **skaters** wore numbers 2 to 19, and the backup goalie wore the biggest number, 20.

Other players have chosen their numbers for reasons important to them. **Jaromír Jágr** has worn number 68 in honor of the year of his grandfather's death. Alexander Mogilny wore number 89 to honor the year he defected to the **United States** from the Soviet Union. **Sidney Crosby** wears number 87 because his birth date is 7 August 1987. **Patrick Kane** wears number 88 for his birth year, 1988. **Jordin Tootoo** wears number 22, as a play on his last name. **Wayne Gretzky's** hero, **Gordie Howe,** wore number 9, but on his **junior** team it was already taken, so Gretzky doubled it and wore **99.** To honor great players, teams will often retire their players' numbers when they retire. In the **National Hockey League (NHL),** the number 9 is the most frequently retired number by individual teams. Due to his incredible contribution to hockey, Gretzky's 99 is the only number retired by the entire NHL.

JIŘÍK, JAROSLAV. B. 10 December 1939, Vojnův Městec, Bohemia-Moravia. D. 11 July 2011, Brno, **Czech Republic.** Jiřík was the first player that an Eastern Bloc country released to play in the **National Hockey League (NHL).** He played **right wing** for the Kansas City Blues, a **minor-league** team, but he also appeared in three games with the **St. Louis Blues** during the 1969–1970 season. Even though he was scoreless in those three games, he was asked to stay for the next season but decided to return home. Previously, while playing for Czechoslovakia, he won a bronze medal at the

1964 Innsbruck **Olympic Games** and a silver medal at the 1968 Winter Olympics in Grenoble. In his 450 career games in the Czech League, he **scored** 300 **goals**. Jiřík opened the doors to the NHL for other Czech players, including **Petr Nedvěd**, **Dominik Hašek**, and **Jaromír Jágr**. In July 2011, despite being an experienced pilot, he died in plane crash at the age of 71.

JOHNSON, IVAN WILFRED "CHING," "IVAN THE TERRIBLE". B. 7 December 1898, Winnipeg, Manitoba. D. 16 June 1979, Silver Spring, Maryland. Ching Johnson was a tough **defenseman** who played in the **National Hockey League (NHL)** with the **New York Rangers** (1926–1937) and **New York Americans** (1937–1938). Some say that he earned the **nickname** "Ching," from his talents as a cook, while others say it was from his wide grin and crinkled eyes. Johnson's other nickname, "Ivan the Terrible," came from his hard body shots on the **ice**. Teammate Taffy Abel said that Johnson loved body contact. Johnson helped the Rangers win the **Stanley Cup** in 1928 and 1933. He led the Rangers in **penalty minutes** in eight of his 11 seasons with them. He also led the NHL in **Stanley Cup Playoff** penalty minutes in 1928 (46) and 1932 (24). After retiring as a player, Johnson became a **referee** in the **minor leagues**. In one memorable game that he was officiating, Johnson body **checked** a player. He later said, "The old habit was too deep within me. I forgot where I was and what I was doing." He was inducted into the **Hockey Hall of Fame** in 1958.

JOHNSON, MARK "MAGIC". B. 22 September 1957, Minneapolis, Minnesota. Mark Johnson played **college hockey** for the University of Wisconsin, with his father, **Bob Johnson**, as **coach**. In 1977, Mark helped the Badgers win the **National Collegiate Athletic Association** national championship, and he went on to become the school's second all-time **scorer**. Internationally, Johnson joined the U.S. national team as an 18 year old in 1976. He played in 11 training games for the 1976 **U.S. Men's Olympic Ice Hockey Team**, also coached by his father. In total, Mark represented the United States in 13 international tournaments, which included the 1978, 1979, 1981, 1982, 1985, 1986, 1987, and 1990 **World Ice Hockey Championships**, and the 1981, 1984, and 1987 **Canada Cups**. Johnson may be best-known for scoring two of the four **goals** in the 4–3 **"Miracle on Ice"** win during the 1980 Winter Olympics against the **Soviet Union Men's Olympic Ice Hockey Team**. Johnson scored the final goal against **Finland** in the 4–2 gold medal **match**. He had a total of 11 **points** in the tournament. After the Olympics, Johnson played in 669 games in the **National Hockey League (NHL)** from 1980–1990, with the **Pittsburgh Penguins**, Minnesota North Stars, Hartford Whalers, **St. Louis Blues**, and **New Jersey Devils**. He was an assistant coach for the Wisconsin Badgers men's hockey team from

1996–2002. He then became the coach of the University of Wisconsin **women's ice hockey** team, a position he continues to hold. In 2010, Johnson was the coach of the **U.S. Women's Olympic Ice Hockey Team**, which won a silver medal in the Vancouver games. In 2011, he received the **Lester Patrick Trophy** for outstanding service to hockey in the United States. Following in his footsteps, Mark's son, Patrick Johnson, played on the University of Wisconsin hockey team.

JOHNSON, ROBERT NORMAN "BOB," "BADGER BOB". B. 4 March 1931, Minneapolis, Minnesota. D. 26 November 1991, Colorado Springs, Colorado. Bob Johnson played **college hockey** at the University of Minnesota. After returning from the Korean War, he taught high school and used a **hockey stick** to point to the blackboard. Then he began a successful **coaching** career. He started out as the men's hockey coach for Colorado College from 1963–1966. He received the **nickname** "Badger Bob" when he coached the University of Wisconsin Badgers (1966–1982) and won three national titles (1973, 1977, 1981). He also coached the 1976 **U.S. Men's Olympic Ice Hockey Team**; the 1981, 1984, and 1987 U.S. teams in the **Canada Cup** tournament; and the 1973, 1974, 1975, and 1981 U.S. national teams. Johnson was known for his enthusiasm and saying the phrase, "It's a great day for hockey." He joined the **National Hockey League (NHL)** as a coach in 1982. Johnson took the **Calgary Flames** to the **Stanley Cup** Finals in 1986. In 1988, he received the **Lester Patrick Trophy** for his contributions to the sport. He became only the second American-born coach to win the Stanley Cup when his **Pittsburgh Penguins** defeated the Minnesota North Stars in 1991. Sadly, later that year, at 60 years of age, Johnson passed away from brain cancer. As a sign of respect, the Penguins had his named engraved on the Stanley Cup they won in 1992. His son, **Mark Johnson**, won the 1980 Olympic gold medal. Bob was inducted as a **builder** into both the **Hockey Hall of Fame (1991)** and **U.S. Hockey Hall of Fame** (1991). He won 234 of the 480 NHL games that he coached.

JOHNSON, THOMAS CHRISTIAN "TOM, "TOMCAT". B. 18 February 1928, Baldur, Manitoba. D. 21 November 2007, Falmouth, Massachusetts. Tom Johnson was a **defenseman** who played hockey in the **National Hockey League (NHL)** for 16 seasons. He played with the **Montreal Canadiens** (1947–1948, 1950–1963) and **Boston Bruins** (1963–1965). Johnson earned the **nickname** "Tomcat" because he was always on the prowl on the **ice**. He had a talent for stripping the **puck** from the opponents without body contact. Johnson was also an effective **penalty killer**. He helped the Canadiens win the **Stanley Cup** in 1953, and then again in five consecutive years (1956–1960). Johnson won the **James Norris Memorial Trophy**

(1958–1959). During the early 1960s, he formed an effective partnership with **Jacques Laperriere**. During the 1962–1963 season, Johnson suffered a serious facial **injury** that damaged his eye muscles; however, he continued to play hockey until 28 February 1965, when he suffered a **career-ending injury** in a game against the **Chicago Black Hawks**. The nerves in his leg were severed by another player's **skate**. In 978 regular-season games, Johnson had 51 **goals**, 213 **assists**, 264 **points**, and 960 **penalty minutes**. He was inducted into the **Hockey Hall of Fame** in 1970. Johnson **coached** the Bruins from 1971–1973, and he led them to a Stanley Cup championship in 1972. He continued to work for the Bruins as an executive from 1973–1999.

JOLIAT, AURÈLE (AUREL) ÉMILE "LITTLE GIANT," "MIGHTY ATOM". B. 29 August 1901, Ottawa, Ontario. D. 2 June 1986, Ottawa, Ontario. As a youth, Aurèle Joliat was a star kicker in football, but after breaking his leg, he turned to a career in hockey. He was a tiny but tough **left wing** in the **National Hockey League (NHL)** with the **Montreal Canadiens** (1922–1938). He compensated for his 135-pound frame by expertly **skating** around his opponents and using his great stickhandling skills to **score**. Joliat was paired with **Howie Morenz** in the 1923–1924 season, but when Morenz had his shoulder broken in the **Stanley Cup Playoffs**, Joliat shined. He scored a **goal** against the Calgary Tigers, and Montreal went on to win the 1924 **Stanley Cup**. Joliat also helped them win the Stanley Cup again in 1930 and 1931. In 1934, he won the Hart Trophy.

Joliat always wore a black baseball cap while he played hockey. It covered his bald spot, and his opponents would try to swipe it off his head during the game, setting off his temper. Joliat was also one of hockey's early **agitators**, and he tried to taunt the other team. Once after having his shoulder dislocated by **Eddie Shore**, Joliat jumped over the **boards** and tackled him before finally leaving the **ice**. Joliat also had an ongoing feud with **Hooley Smith** of the **Montreal Maroons**. During one incident, he chased Smith along the boards until the local police chief grabbed him. The two scuffled on the ice, and Joliat later said that it was the only **fight** he ever won. Even in his 70s, Joliat was ready to fight. At a hockey reunion of old-timers, he threw punches at his former rival, **Harry Broadbent**. NHL president **Clarence Campbell** had to intervene and make the two men call a truce.

During his 16-season NHL career, Joliat played in 655 regular-season games, with 270 goals, 190 **assists**, 460 **points**, and 771 **penalty minutes**. He was the **referee** for **Maurice Richard**'s NHL debut in 1942. Joliat was inducted into to the **Hockey Hall of Fame** in 1947. In 1982, at the age of 80, he played in a benefit **All-Star** Game and scored a **hat trick**. Sixty years after he played in the opening game at the **Montreal Forum**, Joliat was invited back as an honorary member of the Canadiens' "dream team." He delighted fans with a display of skating and stickhandling. When he fell due to the red carpet laid on the ice, Joliat said, "The ghost of Eddie Shore must have put that damn rug in front of me."

JUNIORS. *See* YOUNG PLAYERS.

K

KANE, PATRICK TIMOTHY, JR. B. 19 November 1988, Buffalo, New York. Patrick Kane is an American who currently plays **right wing** for the **Chicago Blackhawks**. He wears the **jersey number** 88 for the year he was born. For good luck, he writes his area code (716) on the bottom of his **hockey sticks**. Kane is known for his style of **dekeing**, also known as dangling the **puck**. He **scored** 72 **points** his **rookie** year, which earned him the **Calder Memorial Trophy** in 2008. In the 2008–2009 season, Kane helped his team make the **Stanley Cup Playoffs**. He accumulated 70 points in the regular season and then scored his first career **hat trick** in the 2009 playoffs against the **Vancouver Canucks** in the second round on 11 May 2009. The Blackhawks won the game, 7–5, which secured their spot in the **Western Conference** Final for the first time since 1995. In the sixth game of the 2010 **Stanley Cup** Finals, Kane scored the **overtime goal**, which won the Blackhawks the Stanley Cup. This ended a 49-year Stanley Cup drought for the team. That shot made Kane the youngest player in **National Hockey League (NHL)** history to score a Stanley Cup–winning goal in overtime, breaking the previous record set by **Bobby Orr** in 1970. He was selected to represent the **United States** in the 2010 **Olympic Games** in Vancouver, where he and the team won the silver medal. He scored three goals and two **assists** in six games. As a **young player**, Kane has a long hockey career in the NHL ahead of him.

KELLY, LEONARD PATRICK "RED". B. 9 July 1927, Simcoe, Ontario. Red Kelly was a **defenseman** and **center** who played hockey in the **National Hockey League (NHL)** for the **Detroit Red Wings** (1947–1960) and **Toronto Maple Leafs** (1960–1967). In 1967, Kelly was traded to the **Los Angeles Kings** with the condition that he would not play, but **coach** them instead. He coached the Kings (1967–1969), then the **Pittsburgh Penguins** (1969–1973), and finally the Maple Leafs (1973–1977). His regular-season coaching record was 261-311-128. As a player, Kelly won the **Stanley Cup** in 1950, 1952, 1954, 1955, 1962, 1963, 1964, and 1967. When Kelly broke his ankle in 1959, the Red Wings kept the **injury** a secret. He played through the pain, but Detroit missed the **Stanley Cup Playoffs** for the first time in 21 years. A year later, when a reporter asked Kelly why he hadn't been playing well, Kelly replied, "Don't know. Might have been the ankle." When general manager **Jack Adams** heard that Kelly spilled the secret, he wanted to trade him to the **New York Rangers**. Kelly said that he would rather retire than go to New York. Then the Maple Leafs' coach, **Punch Imlach**, convinced Kelly to play for them. Kelly became a center when he joined the Maple Leafs. He won four Stanley Cups as a defenseman and four as a forward. Kelly played on more Stanley Cup–winning teams (8) than any player without being part of the **Montreal Canadiens**. He was also the only player to be part of two of the nine dynasties in NHL history.

In 1951, Kelly became the first defenseman in NHL history to win the **Lady Byng Memorial Trophy**. Kelly also won it again in 1953, 1954, and 1961, and he is the only player in NHL history to win it as both a defenseman and forward. He once said, "**Joe Primeau** taught me you don't win games in the **penalty box**. You've got to stay on the **ice**. Players would try to get you off the ice sometimes, but you're more valuable to a team when you're on the ice." Although he was mild-mannered and did not smoke or swear and rarely drank alcohol, Kelly was actually a light heavyweight boxing champion in **Canada** before he began his hockey career. In 1954, Kelly was the first recipient of the **James Norris Memorial Trophy**. In 1,316 regular-season NHL games, Kelly **scored** 281 **goals** and 542 **assists**, for 823 **points**. In 164 playoff games, he scored 33 goals and 59 assists, for 92 points. He was also interested in politics and won a seat in the Canadian House of Commons representing the York West district (1962–1965). Kelly was inducted into the **Hockey Hall of Fame** in 1969. After retiring, he owned a bowling alley in his hometown of Simcoe.

KENNEDY, THEODORE SAMUEL "TED," "TEEDER". B. 12 December 1925, Humberstone, Ontario. D. 14 August 2009, Port Colbourne, Ontario. Ted Kennedy was a **center** in the **National Hockey League (NHL)** for 14 seasons. He spent his entire NHL career with the **Toronto Maple Leafs** (1942–1955, 1956–1957). His NHL debut came when he was 17 years old, and he **scored** 26 **goals** during his first full season (1943–1944). Kennedy won his first **Stanley Cup** at the age of 19 (1945), and he then won four more (1947, 1948, 1949, and 1951). In the fourth game of the 1945 Stanley Cup Finals against the **Detroit Red Wings**, he scored a **hat trick**. Although Kennedy was a poor at **skater**, he was good at **checking** and leading his team. After **Syl Apps** retired, Kennedy served as captain of the Maple Leafs (1948–1955). He scored the Stanley Cup–winning goal in Toronto's 2–1 win over the **Montreal Canadiens** on 19 April 1947. He led the NHL in **assists**, with 42 (1950–1951).

Early in the 1950 **Stanley Cup Playoffs** against Detroit, a questionable incident occurred between Kennedy and **Gordie Howe**. Kennedy had the **puck** and was being pursued by **Jack Stewart** and Howe. As Kennedy dodged away from Howe's check, Howe slammed headfirst into the **boards**. He suffered a concussion and lacerated eye, which required surgery. Some believed that Kennedy intentionally **tripped** Howe with his **hockey stick**, but NHL president **Clarence Campbell** and Howe himself said that it was an accident. Determined to "win the series for Gordie," Detroit won the Stanley Cup that year.

In 1955, Kennedy won the Hart Trophy. On 16 March 1957, he had four assists in Toronto's huge 14–1 win over the **New York Rangers**. Leafs' fan John Arnott would yell "C'mon Teeder" to encourage the team during home games at **Maple Leaf Gardens**. In 696 regular-season NHL games, Kennedy recorded 231 goals, 329 assists, 560 **points**, and 432 **penalty minutes**. After retiring from playing, he became a **coach** for the Peterborough Petes (1957–1958). Kennedy was inducted into the **Hockey Hall of Fame** in 1966.

KENORA THISTLES. The Kenora Thistles were an early amateur men's **ice** hockey team based in Kenora, Ontario, **Canada**. They were formed in 1885, as a senior team, by a group of Lake of the Woods lumbermen. The club is mainly known for winning the **Stanley Cup** as an amateur team in 1907, by defeating the **Montreal Wanderers**. **Joe Hall, Si Griffis**, and **Tom Hooper** were members of the winning team. Having only 4,000 people at the time, Kenora is the least-populated town to have ever won the Stanley Cup. Two months later, the Thistles were challenged by the Wanderers once again. Even with the addition of future **Hockey Hall of Famers** Alf Smith, **Harry Westwick**, and Fred Whitcroft, the team lost the Stanley Cup. Most of the team's players moved on to other teams or retired. The Thistles folded during the 1907–1908 Manitoba Professional Hockey League season. Since then, the **nickname** "Thistles" has been used to denote **minor league, junior**, and senior league men's hockey teams in Kenora.

KEON, DAVID MICHAEL "DAVE," "MR. PERPETUAL MOTION". B. 22 March 1940, Noranda, Quebec. Dave Keon was a **center** for 22 seasons with the **National Hockey League (NHL)** and the **World Hockey Association**. He played with the **Toronto Maple Leafs** (1960–1975), **New England Whalers** (1977–1979), and **Hartford Whalers** (1979–1982). Hockey announcer **Foster Hewitt nicknamed** him "Mister Perpetual Motion." Keon was known as a great **penalty killer** and for his **checking** skills. He led the NHL in shorthanded **goals**, with six (1968–1969) and eight (1970–1971). He **scored** the majority of his goals with the **backhand**. Keon won the **Stanley Cup** with Toronto in 1962, 1963, 1964, and 1967. He won the **Calder Memorial Trophy** in 1961 and the **Lady Byng Memorial Trophy** in 1962 and 1963. In 1967, Keon won the **Conn Smythe Trophy** as the Most Valuable Player in the **Stanley Cup Playoffs**. He also served as the captain of the Maple Leafs (1969–1975) and Whalers (1981–1982). In 1986, Keon was inducted into the **Hockey Hall of Fame**. His granddaughter, Kaitlyn Keon, plays **college hockey** on Brown University's **women's ice hockey** team.

KHARLAMOV, VALERI BORISOVICH. B. 14 January 1948, Moscow, Union of Soviet Socialist Republics. D. 27 August 1981, Moscow, Union of Soviet Socialist Republics. Valeri Kharlamov was a talented **Russian** hockey player who died in a tragic car accident at the age of 33. He was a **left wing** known for his stickhandling and **scoring** abilities. Kharlamov played in 436 regular-season games and recorded 293 **goals** and 214 **assists** with CSKA Moscow. He also competed in 11 **World Ice Hockey Championships** from 1969–1979, and he won eight gold medals, two silver medals, and one bronze medal. He helped his team win gold medals at the 1972 and 1976 **Olympic Games**. Kharlamov and his teammate **Vladislav Tretiak** gained international recognition during the 1972 **Summit Series**. In the first game of the eight-game series, Kharlamov impressed **Canadian** hockey fans with his speed, agility, and scoring talent. He **scored** two **goals** and led his team to an upset victory over the professional Canadian players. In the sixth game, **Bobby Clarke** slashed Kharlamov's ankle and fractured it. Following the tournament, scouts from the **National Hockey League (NHL)** wanted to recruit Kharlamov, but it was at a time in history when Russian players weren't allowed to leave their country. He was a member of the **Soviet Union Men's Olympic Ice Hockey Team** that lost to the **U.S. Men's Olympic Ice Hockey Team** in the classic **"Miracle on Ice"** game at the 1980 Winter Olympics in **Lake Placid**. Kharlamov was inducted into both the **International Ice Hockey Federation Hall of Fame** (1998) and **Hockey Hall of Fame** (2005). Kharlamov and Tretiak are the only two European-born and trained players without NHL experience to be inducted into the Hockey Hall of Fame. In honor of Kharlamov, Russian-born **Pittsburgh Penguins'** player **Evgeni Malkin** wears the **jersey number** 71 as a reverse of his 17.

KING CLANCY MEMORIAL TROPHY. The King Clancy Memorial Trophy is the **National Hockey League (NHL)** award given annually to the player who demonstrates leadership both on and off the **ice** and contributes significantly to his community. It was created in 1988, in honor of the late **Francis M. "King" Clancy**. In addition to playing 16 seasons for the **Ottawa Senators** and **Toronto Maple Leafs,** Clancy was also a **coach, referee,**

and executive in NHL. He was also known for being a humanitarian. The first recipient was **Lanny MacDonald** of the **Calgary Flames**. Other winners from the Flames include **Joe Nieuwendyk** (1994–1995) and **Jarome Iginla** (2003–2004). **Boston Bruins** players **Ray Bourque** (1991–1992) and Dave Poulin (1992–1993) won the trophy consecutively. Doug Weight of the **New York Islanders** won the trophy in 2011, and Daniel Alfredsson of the Ottawa Senators won it in 2012. To date, there have not been any multiple winners of the King Clancy Memorial Trophy.

KISZKAN, JOHN. *See* BOWER, JOHN WILLIAM "JOHNNY," "THE CHINA WALL".

KONSTANTINOV, VLADIMIR NIKOLAEVICH "VLADINATOR," "BAD VLAD," "VLAD THE IMPALER". B. 19 March 1967, Murmansk, Union of Soviet Socialist Republics. Vladimir Konstantinov played **ice** hockey internationally in Moscow from 1984–1991. He represented the Union of Soviet Socialist Republics in the 1989 and 1990 **World Ice Hockey Championships** and won two gold medals. Konstantinov was a **defenseman** in the **National Hockey League (NHL)** with the **Detroit Red Wings** (1991–1997). He was known for his hard hits, both on the open ice and along the **boards**, and his frequent use of his **hockey stick** earned him several **nicknames**, including "Vlad the Impaler." Konstantinov was an expert at making his opponents receive **penalties**. He would hit them and then wait for the **referee** to catch them retaliating. He was part of the unit known as "The Russian Five," which consisted of him and fellow defensemen **Viacheslav Fetisov**, and forwards **Igor Larionov**, Sergei Fedorov, and Vyacheslav Kozlov. Konstantinov helped his team win the **Stanley Cup** in 1997, against the **Philadelphia Flyers**. Tragically, his hockey career ended after he suffered a severe **head injury** as a passenger in a car accident on 13 June 1997. The next season, the Red Wings received special permission from the NHL to inscribe his name on the Stanley Cup after they won again in 1998. During his 446 regular-season NHL **matches**, Konstantinov had 47 **goals**, 128 **assists**, 175 **points**, and 838 **penalty minutes**.

KOPITAR, ANŽE. B. 24 August 1987, Jesenice, Slovenia, Yugoslavia. In 2006, Anže Kopitar became the first Slovenian to play in the **National Hockey League (NHL)**. He plays **center** and **left wing** for the **Los Angeles Kings**. As one of the top-**scoring** players in the NHL, he has led the Kings in scoring for four consecutive seasons. Kopitar recorded his first career **hat trick** on 22 October 2009, against the **Dallas Stars**, and he helped the Kings win, 5–4, in **overtime**. On 15 March 2011, Kopitar played his 325th consecutive NHL game and set a new record for the Kings, passing **Marcel Dionne**.

His streak ended at 300 games when he broke his ankle. He also represented Slovenia at the **International Ice Hockey Federation World Ice Hockey Championships**. In his career to date, Kopitar has played in 475 regular-season NHL games and recorded 163 **goals** and 271 **assists**, for a total of 434 **points**. In his 26 **Stanley Cup Playoff** games, Kopitar had 10 goals and 15 assists, for a total of 25 points. On 11 June 2012, when the Los Angeles Kings defeated the **New Jersey Devils** (4–2), he became the first Slovenian player to win the **Stanley Cup**. Kopitar helped his team win the Stanley Cup by scoring the winning overtime goal in the first game. He and teammate Dustin Brown were a strong scoring duo for Los Angeles, each scoring eight goals and getting 12 assists during the 2011–2012 playoffs.

KURRI, JARI PEKKA "THE FINNISH FLASH". B. 18 May 1960, Helsinki, **Finland**. Jari Kurri was a **right wing** who played for Finland in the 1980 and 1998 **Olympic Games**. He also competed in the 1982, 1989, 1991, and 1994 **World Ice Hockey Championships**; the 1981, 1987, and 1991 **Canada Cups**; and the 1996 **World Cup of Hockey**. He won a silver medal at the 1994 World Championships and a bronze medal at the 1998 Olympics. Kurri joined the **National Hockey League (NHL)** in 1980, with the **Edmonton Oilers**. While paired with **Wayne Gretzky**, Kurri **assisted** on 196 of Gretzky's **goals**, and Gretzky assisted on 364 of Kurri's goals. Kurri played 17 NHL seasons, from 1980–1990 and 1991–1998. After playing with the Oilers, he spent the 1990–1991 season playing hockey in Italy. He recorded 27 goals and 48 assists in 30 games in the Italian league. He then returned to the NHL and played with the **Los Angeles Kings** (1991–1996), **New York Rangers** (1995–1996), Mighty Ducks of Anaheim (1996–1997), and **Colorado Avalanche** (1997–1998). Kurri was known for being a great two-way player on both defense and offense. The **nickname** "The Finnish Flash" was due to his **skating** speed. Current **Anaheim Ducks'** player **Teemu Selänne** has since received the same nickname. Kurri received the **Lady Byng Memorial Trophy** in 1985. In 1986, he became the first European-born player to lead the NHL in most goals **scored** (68). On 17 October 1992, Kurri became the first European-born and trained NHL player to record 500 career goals in the Kings' 8–6 victory over the **Boston Bruins**.

At the time of his retirement in 1998, Kurri held or shared eight NHL records and was the top European scorer of all time in the NHL, with 1,251 games, 601 goals, 797 assists, and 1,398 **points**. Several of his records have since been broken by **Jaromír Jágr**, **Nicklas Lidström**, and Teemu Selänne. Kurri won the **Stanley Cup** five times with the Oilers (1984, 1985, 1987, 1988, 1990). He was inducted into the Finnish Ice Hockey Hall of Fame (1998), **International Ice Hockey Federation Hall of Fame** (2000), and

Hockey Hall of Fame (2001). He is currently the general manager of the men's hockey team in Finland. Kurri is married to a former Miss Finland, and Wayne Gretzky is the godfather of two of his children.

L

LACH, ELMER JAMES "ELEGANT ELMER," "NOKOMIS FLASH". B. 22 January 1918, Nokomis, Saskatchewan. Elmer Lach was a **center** for 14 seasons in the **National Hockey League (NHL)** entirely with the **Montreal Canadiens** (1940–1954). His two **nicknames**, "Elegant Elmer" and "Nokomis Flash," both referred to his fast **skating** and ability to handle the **puck**. During the regular season, Lach led the NHL in **points** in 1944–1945 (80) and 1947–1948 (61). During the 1944–1945 season, he became the first player to reach 50 **assists** during single a season. He led the NHL in assists in 1944–1945 (54), 1945–1946 (34), and 1951–1952 (50). Lach also led during the **Stanley Cup Playoffs** in assists, with 11 (1943–1944) and 12 (1945–1946). He was part of the famous **line** that packed a punch in terms of scoring. The "Punch Line" consisted of Lach, **left wing Toe Blake,** and **right wing Maurice Richard.** Lach was vital in helping the Canadiens win the **Stanley Cup** in 1944, 1946, and 1953. He even **scored** the Stanley Cup–winning **overtime goal** in Montreal's win over the **Boston Bruins** on 16 April 1953. He won the **Hart Memorial Trophy** in 1945.

During his career, Lach also earned the nickname "Elmer the Unlucky" due to his numerous **injuries**. Lach's second season ended minutes into the first game, when he crashed into the **boards**, breaking his arm in two places. In a game during the 1947 season against the **Detroit Red Wings**, Lach fractured his skull. In addition, after scoring the Stanley Cup–winning goal in 1953, Lach collided with Richard in a memorable celebratory airborne embrace that broke his nose. Overall, Lach missed more than 150 games due to injury, averaging one injury out of every five games. Despite that misfortune, he was the NHL's leading scorer in 1948, and first recipient of the **Art Ross Trophy**. After his playing career ended, Lach **coached** Montreal **juniors** for a few years. In 1966, Lach was inducted into the **Hockey Hall of Fame**. On 4 December 2009, his famous **jersey number** (16) was ceremoniously retired again by the Montreal Canadiens during their 100th anniversary celebration.

LACROSSE. Lacrosse is a contact team sport played using a small rubber ball and long-handled stick, and it is popular in the **United States** and **Canada**. Lacrosse was the national sport of Canada until 1994. **Ice** hockey is extremely popular, but there were objections to changing it to the new national sport. As a result, since 1994, Canada's winter sport is hockey, and the summer sport is lacrosse, even though it is played in the spring. Many players, including **Wayne Gretzky**, were good lacrosse players before joining hockey teams. In 1984, Gary Roberts and **Joe Nieuwendyk** played on the same lacrosse team. In 1904, Ottawa **goaltender** Bouse Hutton won national championships in lacrosse, football, and hockey in the same season. **Lionel Conacher** and **Newsy Lalonde** were players inducted into both the **Hockey Hall of Fame** and Canadian Lacrosse Hall of Fame. Box lacrosse is a version of lacrosse played indoors on a hockey **rink** with a wooden floor instead of the ice. The **goal light** behind each **goal** in hockey is also used in box lacrosse.

LADY BYNG MEMORIAL TROPHY. The Lady Byng Memorial Trophy is the **National Hockey League (NHL)** award given annually to the player who demonstrates good sportsmanship and gentlemanly conduct, in addition to excellent playing skills. It was originally named the **Lady Byng Trophy**, after the wife of **Canada**'s governor general, in 1925. The first recipient of the trophy was **Frank Nighbor** of the **Ottawa Senators**. **Frank Boucher** of the **New York Rangers** won the trophy the most times, with seven wins in eight seasons. As a result, he was given the original trophy to keep. Then, in 1936, Lady Byng donated a second trophy. After her death in 1949, the NHL changed the trophy's name to include the word *memorial*. Other multiple winners include **Wayne Gretzky**, **Red Kelly**, **Pavel Datsyuk**, **Bobby Bauer**, **Alex Delvecchio**, **Mike Bossy**, and **Ron Francis**. Although **defensemen** are not known for their gentlemanly conduct, both Red Kelly and **Bill Quackenbush** won this trophy. In 2009–2010 and 2010–2011, **right wing** Martin St. Louis of the **Tampa Bay Lightning** won the Lady Byng Memorial Trophy consecutively. For the 2011–2012 season, defenseman Brian Campbell of the **Florida Panthers** received this award.

LADY BYNG TROPHY. Prior to Lady Byng's death in 1949, the name of the trophy to honor gentlemanly conduct was the Lady Byng Trophy. *See also* LADY BYNG MEMORIAL TROPHY.

LAFLEUR, GUY DAMIEN "THE FLOWER," "LE DÉMON BLOND". B. 20 September 1951, Thurso, Quebec. Guy Lafleur was a **right wing** for 17 seasons in the **National Hockey League (NHL)** with the **Montreal Canadiens** (1971–1985), **New York Rangers** (1988–1989), and **Quebec Nordiques**

(1989–1991). He had a smooth **skating** style and was a solid **scorer**. Lafleur was popular with the fans, and they chanted "Guy, Guy, Guy!" whenever he touched the **puck**. English-speaking fans called him "The Flower," while French-speaking fans **nicknamed** him "le Démon Blond" ("The Blonde Demon"). In 1979, Lafleur released an album called *Lafleur*, which had him reciting hockey instructions to disco **music**. He and linemate **Steve Shutt** were known for the one-two scoring rhythm they used for the Canadiens. Lafleur helped Montreal win the **Stanley Cup** in 1973, 1976, 1977, 1978, and 1979. Individually, he won the **Art Ross Trophy** (1976, 1977, 1978), Lester B. Pearson Award (1976, 1977, 1978), **Hart Memorial Trophy** (1977, 1978), and **Conn Smythe Trophy** (1977). During the 1978 Stanley Cup Finals, the **Boston Bruins' coach**, **Don Cherry**, ordered his players to put their **hockey sticks** up and hit Lafleur whenever they saw him. At the end of the series, Lafleur's head was covered in bandages from the numerous slashes. The two teams met again during the 1979 Stanley Cup Semifinals. In the seventh game, Cherry sent too many players on the **ice**. Lafleur scored the **power play goal** for the tie, and Montreal's Yvon Lambert scored the game-winning goal in **overtime**. Cherry was then fired.

Lafleur also played for **Canada** in the 1981 **World Ice Hockey Championships** and 1976 and 1981 **Canada Cups**. During the 1980–1981 Montreal Canadiens' season, due to **injuries**, Lafleur appeared in only 51 **matches** and scored 27 goals. It was the first time since the 1973–1974 Montreal Canadiens' season that he failed to score 50 goals or more in a season. During the previous six seasons, Lafleur had reached or exceeded 100 **points** and 50 goals. On 24 March 1981, he almost died when he fell asleep at the wheel of his Cadillac and crashed into a highway fence. A metal post pierced the windshield, just missing his head and tearing off part of his ear. Toward the end of his career, he was overshadowed by **Mike Bossy** and **Wayne Gretzky**. Lafleur was inducted into the **Hockey Hall of Fame** in 1988. During his NHL career, he played in 1,126 regular-season games and had 560 goals, 793 **assists**, 1,353 points, and 399 **penalty minutes**. He came out of retirement to play for the Rangers and Nordiques. **Goaltender** Vincent Riendeau commented on Lafleur's comeback and said, "Is he scary or what? He's 38 and still shoots 600 miles per hour." Lafleur is only one of three players to play in the NHL after being inducted into the Hockey Hall of Fame. **Gordie Howe** and **Mario Lemieux** are the other two.

LAFONTAINE, PATRICK MICHAEL "PAT". B. 22 February 1965, St. Louis, Missouri. Pat LaFontaine was a hockey **center** who played in the **National Hockey League (NHL)** with the **New York Islanders** (1983–1991), **Buffalo Sabres** (1991–1997), and **New York Rangers** (1997–1998). He once joked about playing for all the New York teams, saying. "I got to play for three great organizations in my career and never once had to buy new license plates." On 19 May 1984, he set the NHL record for the fastest two **goals** from the start of a **Stanley Cup Playoff** period (35 seconds) when the Islanders played the **Edmonton Oilers**. LaFontaine **scored** the winning goal for the Islanders in the fourth **overtime** against the **Washington Capitals** in the seventh game of the 1987 Patrick Division semifinals. Sportswriters called this game the "Easter Epic." He also played for the **United States** in the 1984 and 1998 **Winter Olympics**, the 1989 **World Ice Hockey Championships**, and the 1987 and 1991 **Canada Cups**. He won the gold medal during the 1996 **World Cup of Hockey**. In the 1992–1993 season, LaFontaine set the record for most **points** scored by a U.S.-born player in the regular NHL season (148). He missed most of the 1993–1994 season due to a knee **injury**. Although he never won the **Stanley Cup**, he did win the **Bill Masterton Memorial Trophy** (1995) and **Lester Patrick Trophy** (1997). LaFontaine scored his 1000th NHL career point against the **Philadelphia Flyers** on 22 January 1998. Then, on 16 March 1998, LaFontaine suffered a **head injury** in a game against **Ottawa Senators** that ended his career. During his regular-season NHL career, he recorded 468 goals, 545 **assists**, and 1,013 total points. In 2003, LaFontaine was inducted into both the **Hockey Hall of Fame** and **U.S. Hockey Hall of Fame**.

LAKE PLACID. The 1932 Winter Olympics was held in Lake Placid, New York, in the **United States of America**. More recently, it was also the host city for the 1980 Winter Olympics. It is well-known as the site of the "**Miracle on Ice**," where the **U.S. Men's Olympic Ice Hockey Team** upset the **Soviet Union Men's Olympic Ice Hockey Team** by a **score** of 4–3. The U.S. team then went on to win the gold medal by defeating the team from **Finland**.

LALONDE, EDOUARD CHARLES "NEWSY". B. 31 October 1888, Cornwall, Ontario. D. 21 November 1971. As a young man, Newsy Lalonde worked in a newsprint plant, which is where he acquired the **nickname** "Newsy." In addition to being one of the best hockey players of his day, he was also a top **lacrosse** player. Lalonde was a **center** and **rover** for 21 professional seasons from 1906–1927. He played for several leagues, including the **National Hockey Association (NHA)**, **Pacific Coast Hockey Association**, **Western Canada Hockey League**, Western Hockey League, and **National Hockey League (NHL)**. On 5 January 1910, Lalonde **scored** the first **goal** in the **Montreal Canadiens'** history in a 7–6 win over the Cobalt Creamery Kings. He led the NHA in goals, with 28 (1915–1916). He was the NHL scoring leader in 1919 and 1921. On 1 March 1919, Lalonde scored five goals in a single **Stanley Cup Playoff** game and set a NHL record.

Players who have since tied his record include **Maurice Richard** (1944), **Darryl Sittler** (1976), Reggie Leach (1976), and **Mario Lemieux** (1989). Lalonde had several **fights** with **Joe Hall**. He had the reputation of being a generally rough player. On 22 December 1912, Lalonde pounded Odie Cleghorn into the **boards**. Odie's **brother, Sprague Cleghorn**, retaliated by smashing Lalonde with his **hockey stick**. The **injury** required 12 stitches, and Sprague was suspended for four weeks. Lalonde also **coached** the Montreal Canadiens (1915–1922, 1932–1935), **New York Americans** (1926–1927), and **Ottawa Senators** (1929–1931). In 1950, he was inducted into the **Hockey Hall of Fame**.

LANGWAY, ROD CORRY "THE SECRETARY OF DEFENSE". B. 3 May 1957, Maag, Taiwan. Rod Langway was born in Taiwan, while his father was in the service. Langway was raised in Massachusetts, and he played high school football, baseball, and hockey. He also played football and **college hockey** at the University of New Hampshire. Langway then joined the **World Hockey Association (WHA)** as a **defenseman** with the Birmingham Bulls (1977–1978). In 1978, Langway joined the **National Hockey League (NHL)** and spent his career with the **Montreal Canadiens** (1978–1982) and **Washington Capitals** (1982–1993). He is the only NHL player born in Taiwan. In 1979, he helped the Canadiens defeat the **New York Rangers** to win the **Stanley Cup**. He won the **James Norris Memorial Trophy** as the NHL's best defenseman in 1983 and 1984. From 1982–1993, Langway was the captain of the Capitals. Internationally, he played for the United States in the 1981 **World Ice Hockey Championships** and 1981, 1984, and 1987 **Canada Cups**. Fans remember his game-winning **goal** in **overtime** against Mike Richter of the Rangers in the 1990 **Stanley Cup Playoffs**. During his 16 seasons in the WHA and NHL, Langway played in 1,046 regular-season games and recorded 54 goals, 296 **assists**, 350 **points**, and 901 **penalty minutes**. After retiring from playing, Langway stayed active as a **coach** for the Providence Bruins, Richmond Renegades, and San Francisco Spiders. In 2002, he was inducted into the **Hockey Hall of Fame**.

LAPERRIERE, JOSEPH JACQUES HUGHES. B. 22 November 1941, Rouyn, Quebec. Jacques Laperriere played 12 seasons in the **National Hockey League (NHL)** as a **defenseman** with the **Montreal Canadiens** (1962–1974). He was known for his long **hockey stick** reach and low shots. Laperriere won the **Stanley Cup** six times as a player (1965, 1966, 1968, 1969, 1971, 1973) and twice as an assistant **coach** (1986, 1993). In 1964, he won the **Calder Memorial Trophy**. In 1966, Laperriere received the **James Norris Memorial Trophy** for being the NHL's best defenseman. He suffered a **career-ending injury** to his knee in a game against the **Boston Bruins** on 19 January 1974. During his career of 691 regular-season NHL games, he recorded 40 **goals**, 242 **assists**, 282 **points**, and 674 **penalty minutes**. In 1987, Laperriere was inducted into the **Hockey Hall of Fame** as a player. He was also an assistant coach for the Montreal Canadiens (1981–1997), Boston Bruins (1997–2000), **New York Islanders** (2001–2003), and **New Jersey Devils** (2003–2008). His son, Dan Laperriere, played in the NHL from 1993–1996, with the **St. Louis Blues** and **Ottawa Senators**.

LAPOINTE, GUY GERARD "POINTU". B. 18 March 1948, Montreal, Quebec. Guy Lapointe played a total of 16 seasons in the **National Hockey League (NHL)** as a **defenseman** with the **Montreal Canadiens** (1968–1982), **St. Louis Blues** (1981–1983), and **Boston Bruins** (1983–1984). He was known for being a practical joker, and he cut holes in the hats of his Montreal teammates and nailed their shoes to the floor. He also played for **Canada** in the 1972 **Summit Series** and 1976 **Canada Cup**. During the Canada Cup, Lapointe taped **Phil Esposito**'s favorite pair of flip-flops to the floor. Esposito had a **superstition** about wearing them in the shower and after every game. Luckily, Lapointe's joke did not interfere with Canada winning the tournament. When he joined Boston, Lapointe was given **Dit Clapper**'s retired **jersey number** (5), but he switched it to 27 after his family protested. With defensemen **Larry Robinson** and **Serge Savard**, Lapointe was a member of the "Big Three," who made the Canadiens strong. Lapointe won the **Stanley Cup** six times as a player (1971, 1973, 1976, 1977, 1978, 1979). He holds the Canadiens' team records for **goals** by a **rookie** defenseman, with 15 (1970–1971), and regular-season goals by a defenseman, with 28 (1974–1975). Lapointe also shares the team record with Larry Robinson for all-time **Stanley Cup Playoff** goals by a defenseman, with 25. During his NHL career, Lapointe **scored** 59 **power play** goals and 22 game-winning goals. In his 884 regular-season games, he recorded 171 goals, 451 **assists**, 622 **points**, and 893 **penalty minutes**. In 1993, Lapointe was inducted into the **Hockey Hall of Fame**.

LAPRADE, EDGAR LOUIS "BEAVER". B. 10 October 1919, Mine Center, Ontario. Edgar Laprade was **nicknamed** "Beaver" because of his work ethic and defensive abilities. He delayed his hockey career to serve in the **Canadian** Army during World War II. He then played **center** for 10 seasons in the **National Hockey League (NHL)** with the **New York Rangers** (1945–1955). He chose to play for the Rangers instead of the **Montreal Canadiens** because they gave him a $5,000 bonus to pay the mortgage on his house. Laprade was known for his smooth **skating** and poke **checking** skills.

In his **rookie** year, he won the **Calder Memorial Trophy** (1946). His best season was 1949–1950, when he **scored** 22 **goals** and led the Rangers with 44 **points**. Laprade had two or fewer **penalty minutes** in six of his 10 seasons, and, as a result, he won the **Lady Byng Memorial Trophy** in 1950. He once said, "I was taught early on that you can't score from the **penalty box**." He played against the **Detroit Red Wings** in the 1950 **Stanley** Cup Finals, but the Rangers lost in **overtime** in the seventh game. In his 500 regular-season games, Laprade recorded 108 goals, 172 **assists**, 280 points, and only 42 penalty minutes. After retiring, he ran a sporting goods store in Port Arthur, Ontario. In 1993, Laprade was inducted into the **Hockey Hall of Fame**.

LARIONOV, IGOR NIKOLAYEVICH "THE PROFESSOR". B. 3 December 1960, Voskresensk, Union of Soviet Socialist Republics. Igor Larionov was a **Russian ice** hockey player who, along with **Viacheslav Fetisov**, was a pioneer in breaking the barrier that kept Soviet players from joining the **National Hockey League (NHL)**. Larionov played for Khimik Voskresensk (1977–1981), CSKA Moscow (1981–1989), the **Vancouver Canucks** (1989–1992), HC Lugano (1992–1993), the **San Jose Sharks** (1993–1996), the **Detroit Red Wings** (1995–2000, 2001–2003), the **Florida Panthers** (2000–2001), and the **New Jersey Devils** (2003–2004). He earned the **nickname** "The Professor" because he took a scholarly approach to the game. As a **center**, Larionov was one of the best passers of all time. He won three **Stanley Cup** championships with the Detroit Red Wings (1997, 1998, 2002). The Red Wings beat the **Carolina Hurricanes** in 2002 (4–1). On 8 June 2002, game three featured a triple-**overtime match**. Larionov **scored** the winning **goal**, making him the oldest player to score a last-round goal (at 41 years and seven months of age). During his NHL career, he played in 941 regular-season games and recorded 169 goals, 475 **assists**, 644 **points**, and 474 **penalty minutes**. Internationally, Vladimir Krutov, Larionov, and Sergei Makarov teamed up on the famous KLM **line**. Larionov was known as the "Russian **Wayne Gretzky**" in his home country. He was a gold medal winner in the 1994 and 1998 Winter Olympics, and a bronze medal winner in the 2002 **Olympic Games**. At the **World Ice Hockey Championships**, Larionov won four gold medals (1982, 1983, 1986, 1990), one silver medal (1987), and one bronze medal (1985). He is one of only 25 players in the **Triple Gold Club**. He was part of the unit known as "The Russian Five," with Sergei Fedorov and Vyacheslav Kozlov and **defensemen Viacheslav Fetisov** and **Vladimir Konstantinov**. Larionov retired from playing in 2004, and he was inducted into the **Hockey Hall of Fame** in 2008. After retiring from hockey, he became a professional wine merchant with such wine labels as **"Hat Trick**," **"Slapshot**," and "Triple Overtime."

LAVIOLETTE, JEAN-BAPTISTE "JACK," "THE SPEED MER-CHANT". B. 27 July 1879, Belleville, Ontario. D. 1960. Jack Laviolette was **lacrosse** star and automobile racer, in addition to being a memorable **scoring defenseman**. He earned the **nickname** "The Speed Merchant" because he would fly down the **ice** with great speed. Laviolette played 14 professional ice hockey seasons (1904–1918), mainly with the **National Hockey Association (NHA) Montreal Canadiens**. He was also part of a forward **line** with **Didier Pitre** and **Newsy Lalonde**. Laviolette helped the Canadiens win the **Stanley Cup** in 1916. Unfortunately, his career ended suddenly after part of his leg was amputated following an automobile accident on 1 May 1918. Despite losing his foot, he continued to contribute to the sport of hockey as a **referee**. Laviolette is credited with being the true founding organizer of the Canadiens hockey club. He was their first player, **coach**, and general manager in their inaugural 1910 season. With the formation of the NHA in December 1909, league owner Ambrose O'Brien asked Laviolette to put together a team of French **Canadian** players to play as the "Les Canadiens" franchise in Montreal. Laviolette did so in time for the NHA's inaugural season by assembling Newsy Lalonde, Didier Pitre, and **goaltender Georges Vezina**. The Montreal team was nicknamed "The Flying Frenchmen," and the Canadiens became one of the most successful franchises in professional hockey. For his contributions, Laviolette was inducted into the **Hockey Hall of Fame** in 1962 as a player.

LEETCH, BRIAN JOSEPH. B. 3 March 1968, Corpus Christi, Texas. As a **young player** growing up in Connecticut, Brian Leetch practiced his hockey skills at the local **ice rink,** which his father also managed. Professionally, Leetch was a **defenseman** in the **National Hockey League (NHL)** with the **New York Rangers** (1987–2004), **Toronto Maple Leafs** (2003–2004), and **Boston Bruins** (2005–2006). In 1994, he helped the Rangers defeat the **Vancouver Canucks** in seven games to win the **Stanley Cup.** Leetch won the **Calder Memorial Trophy** in 1989, the **Conn Smythe Trophy** in 1994, and the **James Norris Memorial Trophy** in 1992 and 1997. In 1992, he **scored** 102 **points** and had 80 **assists,** making him one of only five NHL defensemen to score 100 points in a season. In May 2007, he announced his retirement. Later that year, he was awarded the **Lester Patrick Trophy.** Internationally, Leetch played for the **United States** in the 1991 **Canada Cup** (silver medal), and he was the team captain at the 1996 **World Cup of Hockey**. He was part of the U.S. team in the 1988, 1998, and 2002 **Olympic Games,** winning a silver medal in 2002. He scored his 1,000th NHL career point on 18 October 2005. He and his Rangers teammate Mike Richter were inducted into the **U.S. Hockey Hall of Fame** in 2008. Leetch was inducted into the **Hockey Hall of Fame** in 2009.

LEFT WING. A player who plays the position of left wing **skates** on the left side of the **center** and passes the **puck** between the **right wing** and the center. The player in this position attempts to move the puck down the **ice** and **score** a **goal**. Wings are also known as forwards. Defensively, they try to prevent the other team's wings from moving forward and scoring. In the **United States**, left-handed shooters typically play left wing, and right-handed shooters usually play right wing, but European players don't fit that pattern. For example, **Alexander Ovechkin**, who is currently a left wing for the **Washington Capitals**, is a right-handed shooter.

LEHMAN, FREDERICK HUGH "HUGHIE," "OLD EAGLE EYES". B. 27 October 1885, Pembroke, Ontario. D. 8 April 1961, Toronto, Ontario. Hugh Lehman was a **goaltender** who played 22 professional hockey seasons (1906–1928), including 12 of them with the **Pacific Coast Hockey Association (PCHA) Vancouver Millionaires**. Lehman was a strong **skater** and good puck handler. He got the **nickname** "Old Eagle Eyes" from being able to spot loose **pucks** and then chase them down and pass them to his forwards. With his help, the Millionaires won the **Stanley Cup** in 1915. Lehman holds the PCHA career records for most games played by a goalie (262), most wins (142), and most **shutouts** (17). He spent the last two years of his playing career (1926–1928) with the **Chicago Black Hawks** of the **National Hockey League (NHL)**, playing a full season and splitting the second as player and head **coach**. He finished the season with a 3-17-1 record during 21 games and was replaced by **Herb Gardiner** the next season. Lehman was inducted into the **Hockey Hall of Fame** in 1958.

LEMAIRE, JACQUES GERARD. B. 7 September 1945, LaSalle, Quebec. Jacques Lemaire was a **center** in the **National Hockey League (NHL)** with the **Montreal Canadiens** (1967–1979). He **scored** at least 20 **goals** in each of his 12 seasons. He was also a **coach** for the Montreal Canadiens (1983–1985), **New Jersey Devils** (1993–1998), and **Minnesota Wild** (2000–2011). Lemaire won the **Stanley Cup** eight times as a player with the Canadiens. He is only one of five players to have scored two Stanley Cup-winning goals. **Jean Béliveau**, **Mike Bossy**, **Jack Darragh**, and **Henri Richard** are the other players with that distinction. Lemaire scored one winning goal during Montreal's 2–1 victory over the **Boston Bruins** on 14 May 1977, and the other in a 4–1 win over the **New York Rangers** on 21 May 1979. He also won the Stanley Cup once as a coach with the Devils (1995). He received the **Jack Adams Award** 1994 and 2003. Lemaire was the first person in NHL history to play in 100 **Stanley Cup Playoff** games and also coach 100 playoff games. He played in 853 regular-season games and had 366 goals, 469 **assists**, and 835 **points**. He also played in 145 playoff games and had 61 goals, 78 assists, and 139 points. In 1984, Lemaire was inducted into the **Hockey Hall of Fame** as a player. Lemaire also served as the assistant general manager of the Canadiens (1985–1993, 1998–2000), and he won two more Stanley Cups with that team (1986, 1993). He was one of the assistant coaches who helped head coach Mike Babcock lead Team **Canada** to a gold medal at the 2010 **Olympic Games**. On 10 February 2011, Lemaire tallied his 600th regular-season coaching win after Ilya Kovalchuk scored in **overtime** to win the game for the Devils against the **Toronto Maple Leafs** (2–1). Only seven other NHL coaches have accomplished this feat. Lemaire's nephew, Manny Fernandez, was a NHL **goaltender** from 1994–2009.

LEMIEUX, CLAUDE PERCY "SUPERPEST". B. 16 July 1965, Buckingham, Quebec. Claude Lemieux was a **right wing** in the **National Hockey League (NHL)** from 1984–2009. He earned the **nickname** "Superpest" for being an **agitator** on the **ice**. He played for the **Montreal Canadiens** (1983–1990), **New Jersey Devils** (1990–1995), **Colorado Avalanche** (1995–2000), **Phoenix Coyotes** (2000–2002), **Dallas Stars** (2002–2003), and **San Jose Sharks** (2008–2009). He won the **Stanley Cup** in 1986, 1995, 1996, and 2000. During the 1986 **Stanley Cup Playoffs** against the **Philadelphia Flyers**, Lemieux hit the **puck** into the Flyers' **net** during the warm-ups. Flyers' **defenseman** Ed Hospodar became upset and attacked him. After a huge **fight** between the two teams, Hospodar was suspended for the rest of the playoffs. Lemieux had a reputation for being a dirty player, and he once bit an opponent's finger during a fight. While with Colorado in 1996, he checked the **Detroit Red Wings'** Kris Draper into the **boards** from behind, causing Draper to get a concussion, as well as a broken jaw, nose, and cheekbone. The NHL only suspended Lemieux for two games, which caused a rivalry to form between the two teams. On 26 March 1997, the famous Red Wings-Avalanche brawl took place. The Wings' **enforcer** Darren McCarty dropped Lemieux with a right hook to the face and then repeatedly punched him while he was down. Their teammates, including the **goaltenders**, fought and left patches of blood on the ice.

Internationally, Lemieux played for **Canada** in the 1987 **Canada Cup** and 1996 **World Cup of Hockey**. On 19 January 2009, he came out of retirement to join the Sharks. On 19 February, in a game against the **Los Angeles Kings**, he recorded the only **point** of his NHL comeback. In 1995, Lemieux won the **Conn Smythe Trophy**. During his NHL career, he played in 1,215 regular-season games and had 379 **goals**, 407 **assists**, 786 points, and 1,777 **penalty minutes**. He played in 234 playoff games, the fourth highest in the NHL. During the playoffs, he **scored** a total of 80 goals and 158 points. Lemieux's younger **brother**, Jocelyn Lemieux, also played right wing in the NHL (1987–1998). They are unrelated to **Mario Lemieux**.

LEMIEUX, MARIO "LE MAGNIFIQUE," SUPER MARIO". B. 5 October 1965, Montreal, Quebec. Mario Lemieux was a 6-foot, 4-inch **center** in the **National Hockey League (NHL)** for 17 seasons with the **Pittsburgh Penguins** (1984–1994, 1995–1997, 2000–2004, 2005–2006). Eighteen-year-old Lemieux agreed to play for Pittsburgh with the condition that the league would install a satellite dish on his parent's home so they could watch all his games. Mario wore the **jersey number** 66 as an inverted 99, which his hero, **Wayne Gretzky**, wore. In French, "le mieux" means "the best," and Mario lived up to his name. During the 1984–1985 season, he **scored** 100 **points** as a **rookie** and won the **Calder Memorial Trophy**. On 25 April 1989, he scored 5 **goals** in a single **Stanley Cup Playoff** game. He shares this NHL record with **Newsy Lalonde** (1919), **Maurice Richard** (1944), **Darryl Sittler** (1976), and Reggie Leach (1976). **Emile Francis** once said, "He can thread the eye of a needle with the **puck**. Mario is one of the best passers I have ever seen."

On 31 December 1988, Lemieux became the only player in NHL history to score a goal in all five possible game situations in the same game (even strength, shorthanded, **penalty** shot, **power play**, and empty **net**). He helped his team win two consecutive Stanley Cups, in 1991 and 1992. In 1994–1995, Mario took the entire season off because of a series of back **injuries** and his battle with cancer. There was a 103-day **lockout** that season, and only 48 games were played by each team. He retired from hockey at the end of the 1996–1997 season and was immediately inducted into the **Hockey Hall of Fame** (1997). After becoming the owner of the Pittsburgh Penguins on 24 June 1999, Lemieux decided to start playing again in December 2000. He played until January 2006. **Gordie Howe** and **Guy Lafleur** are the only other NHL players to return to the **ice** after being inducted into the Hockey Hall of Fame. Lemieux joined **Mike Bossy**, **Wayne Gretzky**, **Brett Hull**, and **Maurice Richard** as players who scored 50 goals in 50 or fewer games. Lemieux played for **Canada** in the 1985 **World Ice Hockey Championships**, 1987 **Canada Cup**, 2002 **Winter Olympics**, and 2004 **World Cup of Hockey**. As captain of the team, he won an Olympic gold medal in 2002. Lemieux also won the **Hart Memorial Trophy** (1988, 1993, 1996), **Art Ross Trophy** (1988, 1989, 1992, 1993, 1996, 1997), **Conn Smythe Trophy** (1991, 1992), Lester B. Pearson Award (1986, 1988, 1993, 1996), and the **Lester Patrick Trophy** (2000).

LESTER B. PEARSON AWARD. *See* TED LINDSAY AWARD.

LESTER PATRICK TROPHY. The Lester Patrick Trophy is an annual award presented for outstanding service to hockey in the **United States**. It has been presented by the **National Hockey League (NHL)** and USA Hockey since 1966, to honor a recipient's contribution to **ice** hockey in the United States. Players, officials, **coaches**, executives, **referees**, and other individuals are eligible, and, as such, it is considered a non-NHL trophy. For example, *Peanuts* creator **Charles Schulz** won it for his contribution to the sport. The trophy is named after **Lester Patrick** (1883–1960), player and longtime coach of the **New York Rangers** and **builder** of the sport. Coach **Jack Adams** was the first recipient. The three teams that have won the award include both the 1960 and 1980 **U.S. Men's Olympic Ice Hockey Teams**, and the 1998 **U.S. Women's Olympic Ice Hockey Team**. No one has won the award twice individually, but people have won with a team and by themselves separately, for example, **Cammi Granato**.

LESUEUR, PERCY "PEERLESS PERCY". B. 21 November 1881, Quebec City, Quebec. D. 27 January 1962, Hamilton, Ontario. Percy LeSueur played 13 elite and amateur professional hockey seasons from 1903–1916. He played **right wing** in Quebec City but then was a **goaltender** with the **Ottawa Senators**, Toronto Shamrocks, and Toronto Blueshirts. LeSueur was **nicknamed** "Peerless Percy" by sportswriter Malcolm Brice. On 2 January 1908, the **Montreal Wanderers** and a team of **All-Star** players from the teams of the Eastern **Canada** Amateur Hockey Association held a game to raise money for the family of Wanderers' player **Hod Stuart**, who had drowned. LeSueur was the goalie on the All-Star Team. He was a member of the **Stanley Cup**–winning Ottawa Senators team that successfully defended the title twice in 1910. During the 1909–1910 season, LeSueur wrote a small booklet for children entitled *How to Play Hockey*. He led the **National Hockey Association (NHA)** in wins, with 13 (1910–1911). Shortly after netminder **Clint Benedict** joined Ottawa, LeSueur went to Toronto. His playing career ended in 1916, when he joined the Canadian Army during World War I. From 1923–1924, LeSueur coached the **Hamilton Tigers**. His entire hockey career spanned 50 years as player, **coach**, manager, columnist, and broadcaster. During his playing days, LeSueur improved the existing hockey **equipment**. He invented the gauntlet-style goaltender **glove**, which protected the forearms, and created and patented the LeSueur **Net**, which was designed to catch high-rising shots. As a journalist, he was the first reporter to include shots on **goal** statistics in game summaries. LeSueur was inducted into the **Hockey Hall of Fame** in 1961 as a player.

LEWIS, HERBERT A. "HERBIE," "THE DUKE OF DULUTH". B. 17 April 1906, Calgary, Alberta. D. 20 January 1991, Indianapolis, Indiana. Herbie Lewis was given the **nickname** "The Duke of Duluth" because he played amateur hockey with the Duluth Hornets (1924–1928). He was known for his fast **skating**. Lewis played 11 seasons in the **National Hockey**

League (NHL) as a left wing with all three Detroit franchises: the Detroit Cougars (1928–1930), Detroit Falcons (1930–1932), and Detroit Red Wings (1932–1939). When he earned an $8,000 salary in 1935, he was the NHL's highest-paid player. Lewis helped the Red Wings win the Stanley Cup in 1936 and 1937. In 483 regular-season NHL games, Lewis recorded 148 goals, 161 assists, 309 points, and 248 penalty minutes. He also played for (1939–1941) and coached (1939–1943) the Indianapolis Capitals of the American Hockey League. Lewis was inducted into the Hockey Hall of Fame in 1989.

LIDSTRÖM, NICKLAS ERIK "MR. PERFECT". B. 28 April 1970, Vasteras, Sweden. Nicklas Lidström was a Swedish defenseman in the National Hockey League (NHL) for 20 seasons (1991–2004, 2005–2012), all with the Detroit Red Wings. He was the captain of the Red Wings from 2006–2012. He earned the nickname "Mr. Perfect" due to his hard work and consistency. Lidström had the ability to anticipate the game. He was also an excellent skater who had a talent for being at the right spot of the ice at the right time. Instead of delivering a big body check, Lidström would steal the puck and create a turnover. Relying on his brains, he was able to avoid serious injuries and have a long and productive career. Lidström was the first European-born player to win both the Conn Smythe Trophy and James Norris Memorial Trophy and the first European-born player to win the Stanley Cup as captain. He was a member of four Stanley Cup–winning teams (1997, 1998, 2002, 2008). Lidström was on a team in the Stanley Cup Playoffs in every season since his rookie year (1991–1992), except for during the lockout.

On 15 December 2010, Lidström became the oldest defenseman and oldest NHL player to record their first career hat trick. After a 5–2 win over the St. Louis Blues, the 40-year-old veteran was asked how it felt. Lidström said, "It feels great, I've never in my life been able to notch three goals in a game." Lidström retired on 31 May 2012, after 20 seasons with Detroit. Former teammate Steve Yzerman described Lidström as "one of the all-time best defensemen to ever play." Lidström set an NHL record by playing 1,564 games with a single team. During his career, he had 264 goals, 1,142 points, and a relatively low 514 penalty minutes for a defenseman. Representing Sweden, he won the World Ice Hockey Championships in 1991. Lidström scored the gold medal-winning goal for Sweden over Finland in the 2006 Winter Olympics. He became the 17th member of the Triple Gold Club by winning those championships and the Stanley Cup. As a four-time Stanley Cup champion and seven-time Norris Trophy winner, Lidström will surely be inducted into the Hockey Hall of Fame when he becomes eligible.

LIGUE INTERNATIONALE DE HOCKEY SUR GLACE. *See* INTERNATIONAL ICE HOCKEY FEDERATION (IIHF).

LINDROS, ERIC BRYAN. B. 28 February 1973, London, Ontario. In 1991, 6-foot, 4-inch, 240-pound Eric Lindros was drafted by the **Quebec Nordiques** but refused to play for them. One reason was that they were the worst team in the **National Hockey League (NHL)** at the time. After he won a silver medal in the 1992 Winter Olympics with **Canada**, Lindros was auctioned off by Quebec to the **Philadelphia Flyers**. The Nordiques gained several key players for Lindros, including **Peter Forsberg**, and went on to become a strong team. Since the trade, Quebec, renamed the **Colorado Avalanche**, has won eight division titles and two **Stanley Cup** championships. Lindros also did well and **scored** more than 40 **goals** in each of his first two seasons. In 1995, he won the **Hart Memorial Trophy** by scoring 29 goals and 41 **assists** in 46 games and leading the Flyers to their first **Stanley Cup Playoff** appearance in six years. He averaged more than one **point** per game during his time with the Flyers (1992–2000). Lindros was known for being a tough competitor, and, as a result, he had many **injuries** that frequently sidelined him. He suffered several concussions and a collapsed lung.

As a powerful forward, Lindros and his Flyers' teammates John LeClair and Mikael Renberg formed a **line** called the "Legion of Doom," as they **skated** down the **ice intimidating** their opponents. Lindros also played with the **New York Rangers** (2001–2004), the **Toronto Maple Leafs** (2005–2006), and **Dallas Stars** (2006–2007). He played in the 1998 and 2002 **Olympic Games** and won a gold medal in 2002. During his NHL career, he played in 760 regular-season games and recorded 362 goals, 493 points, 865 assists, and 1,398 **penalty minutes**. Speaking about Lindros, teammate LeClair said, "He had it all, size, strength, and finesse." Lindros will surely be inducted into the **Hockey Hall of Fame** when he becomes eligible. On 31 December 2011, he played in the **Winter Classic** Alumni Game between the New York Rangers and Philadelphia Flyers. His younger **brother**, Brett Lindros, played briefly in the NHL with the **New York Islanders**. The Lindros family is good friends with **well-known fans** Goldie Hawn and Kurt Russell.

LINDSAY, ROBERT BLAKE THEODORE "TED," "SCARFACE," "TERRIBLE TED". B. 29 July 1925, Renfrew, Ontario. Ted Lindsay's father, Bert Lindsay, was a **goaltender** who invented the collapsible hockey **net**. Ted played **left wing** for 17 seasons in the **National Hockey League (NHL)** with the **Detroit Red Wings** (1944–1957, 1964–1965) and **Chicago Black Hawks** (1957–1960). Lindsay was part of the famous **line** the "Production Line," with Detroit players **Sid Abel** and **Gordie Howe**. In 1950,

Lindsay won the **Art Ross Trophy** after recording 78 **points**. Feared by his opponents, he was a tough player with a bad temper. He received more than 400 stitches in his face during his hockey career. At only 5 feet, 8 inches tall, he called his **hockey stick** the "Great Equalizer." A brutal incident happened on 25 January 1951, when Lindsay attacked **Boston Bruins'** player Bill Ezinicki. When the **fight** was over, Ezinicki had a broken nose, two black eyes, and a missing tooth and needed 19 stitches. Lindsay's hand was severely swollen from all the punches he threw. With his **scoring** talent, Lindsay helped Detroit win four **Stanley Cups** in the 1950s. During the 1956 Stanley Cup Semifinals against the **Toronto Maple Leafs**, Lindsay and Gordie Howe both received death threats. Lindsay **scored** twice during the third game and then angered the Toronto crowd when he held his hockey stick like a rifle and pretended he was shooting them.

But off the **ice**, Lindsay was different. When he read about the boating accident of teammate **Bobby Hull**'s mother, he drove five hours to visit her in the hospital. In 1957, he organized the first National Hockey League Players' Association, and, as a result, he was traded to the last-place team, Chicago. Lindsay first retired in 1960, but he came back four years later and rejoined the Red Wings at the age of 39 (1964–1965). He recorded 173 **penalty minutes** upon his return. Lindsay was inducted into the **Hockey Hall of Fame** in 1966. He went on to become a television announcer for the **New York Rangers**. Lindsey was known for saying, "That's laying the lumber on 'em" when a player got away with a good hit with a stick. He was also the general manager and **coach** for the Red Wings briefly in the late 1970s. During 1,068 regular-season NHL games, he recorded 379 **goals**, 472 **assists**, 851 points, and 1,808 penalty minutes. Lindsay often gave **referee Red Storey** trouble throughout the years. After the "noncall" in the sixth game of the 1952 **Stanley Cup Playoffs**, Lindsay tried to start a fight with him, until James Norris intervened. The two never spoke again, until 1993, when the new Hockey Hall of Fame opened in Toronto. Lindsay walked over to Storey and said, "Come on, Red, this has gone on too long. It's all over." With that, the two buried the hatchet. In 2008, Lindsay received the **Lester Patrick Trophy**. In 2010, the Lester B. Pearson Award was renamed the **Ted Lindsay Award** due to Lindsay's role in establishing the NHL's first players' union.

LINE. The *line* is a term used to describe the three players in the positions of **left wing**, **center**, and **right wing**. Many teams throughout the course of hockey history have had famous lines. In the 1920s, **Bun Cook**, **Frank Boucher**, and Bill Cook of the **New York Rangers** were named the "A Line," after the A Train, which ran under **Madison Square Garden**. Also in the 1920s, **Cooney Weiland**, Dutch Gainor, and **Dit Clapper** of the **Boston Bruins** made up the "Dynamite Line." In the 1930s, the "Kid Line" was made up of **Charlie Conacher, Joe Primeau**, and **Busher Jackson** of the **Toronto Maple Leafs**. The "Bread Line" was a famous line with Alex Shibicky and **brothers** Mac Colville and **Neil Colville**. The line's **nickname** came from sportswriters who said the trio was the New York Rangers' "bread and butter." Known for their speed, in the 1940s, the **Chicago Black Hawks** had the "Pony Line," with **Max Bentley, Doug Bentley**, and **Bill Mosienko**. The "Kraut Line" was composed of Boston Bruins players **Milt Schmidt, Woody Dumart**, and **Bobby Bauer**. Also playing in the 1940s was the "Punch Line," which included **Henri Richard, Toe Blake**, and **Elmer Lach** of the **Montreal Canadiens**. The "Black Aces" of the Quebec Aces had the only line in hockey history with three black players, including **Herb Carnegie**, Ossie Carnegie, and Manny McIntyre. In the 1940s and 1950s, the **Detroit Red Wings** had the "Production Line," with **Ted Lindsay, Gordie Howe**, and **Sid Abel**. The line was named for its **scoring** ability and the production on the assembly lines in the Motor City. In the 1990s, **Mario Lemieux, Jaromír Jágr**, and Kevin Stevens of the **Pittsburgh Penguins** formed the "Sky Line." Also in the 1990s, **Eric Lindros**, John LeClair, and Mikael Renberg of the **Philadelphia Flyers** formed a line called the "Legion of Doom." "The Swedish Five" of the Red Wings in the 2000s included Tomas Holmstrom, Niklas Kronwall, **Nicklas Lidström**, Mikael Samuelsson, and Henrik Zetterberg. All five participated in the 2006 **Olympic Games** in Torino, Italy. Kronwall, Lidström, and Zetterberg **scored** all of the **goals** for **Sweden** against **Finland** in the gold medal game.

LINESMAN. The linesman is the **on-ice official** who is able to call **offside** and **icing** infractions, as well as assess certain **penalties**, including too many men on the **ice**. A linesman is responsible for dropping the **puck** during all **face-offs** not occurring at center ice. He can also notify the **referee** of any fouls observed. In 1939, a rule was made that allowed referees to award a penalty to a player who verbally abused a linesman or referee and send the offending player to the **penalty box**. Games in the **National Hockey League (NHL)** were officiated with one referee and one linesman until the rule was changed on 24 October 1941, when a second linesman was added. In 1945–1946, another rule required neutral linesmen on each **rink**. At one time, it was the job of the home team to provide the linesmen. Notable linesman **Ray Scapinello** set many records for NHL linesmen, with 33 seasons, 2,500 consecutive games, and 426 **Stanley Cup Playoff** games. Scapinello was chosen for the playoffs in only his second season (1972), and he continued every year until he retired in 2004. He also never missed an assignment in his career. Scapinello and John D'Amico were linesmen together, and they both were inducted into the **Hockey Hall of Fame** for their accomplishments.

LOCKOUT. When hockey players and team owners disagree about financial issues, games are cancelled until the issues are resolved. Known as a lockout, there have been two major ones in the history of the **National Hockey League (NHL)**. The 1994–1995 NHL lockout caused the season to be shortened to 48 games. This 104-day lockout stretched from 1 October 1994 to 11 January 1995. A total of 468 games were lost, along with the **All-Star** Game. The NHL owners wanted to implement a salary cap, while the players were opposed to it. The same issue was the cause of the lengthy lockout during the 2004–2005 NHL season. This 310-day lockout lasted from 16 September 2004 to 22 July 2005. It was the first time since 1919 that the **Stanley Cup** was cancelled. *The Lost Season: A Year in Hockey without the NHL* (2005), by Andrew Podnieks, describes how some of the NHL players stayed busy during that year.

LORD STANLEY OF PRESTON, FREDERICK ARTHUR. B. 15 January 1841, London, England. D. 14 June 1908, England. Lord Stanley is best-known to sports fans as the person who donated the 1892 trophy now known as the **Stanley Cup**. He was **Canada**'s sixth governor general; however, Lord Stanley was not Canadian, or even a hockey fan. As the 16th Earl of Derby, he was sent from England to be Canada's head of state, while still representing England. His connection to hockey was through his association with Canadian **P. D. Ross**. Ross truly loved hockey, and he taught the game to Lord Stanley's two sons. While hockey was becoming popular in Canada, Ross encouraged Lord Stanley to provide a trophy to the best team. The Stanley Cup, a bowl with a band of silver below it, was given to honor Canada's best amateur hockey team. Ironically, Lord Stanley returned to England before ever seeing a Stanley Cup game. Today, the Stanley Cup is awarded to the top professional hockey team in the **National Hockey League**. Throughout the years, the Stanley Cup has had additional bands of silver added to display the names of the players from each season's winning team. In 1945, Lord Stanley was inducted into the **Hockey Hall of Fame** as a **builder**.

LOS ANGELES KINGS. The Los Angeles Kings are a professional **ice** hockey team in the **Pacific Division** of the **National Hockey League (NHL) Western Conference**. The Kings joined the league as one of the six new franchises during the NHL expansion in the 1967–1968 season. In its NHL history, the team has made the **Stanley Cup** Finals two times. They lost to the **Montreal Canadiens** in 1993 (4–1). In 1967, **defenseman Red Kelly** was traded to Los Angeles on the condition that he would not play, but **coach** them instead. He coached the Kings from 1967–1969. Their most recent coach was Darryl Sutter, who led them to the Stanley Cup. **Bob Pulford**

played **left wing** for the Kings before becoming their coach (1972–1977). Some of the better-known players for the team include **Paul Coffey, Marcel Dionne, Grant Fuhr, Jari Kurri, Luc Robitaille, Terry Sawchuk, Eddie Shack,** and **Billy Smith**. But the most well-known player for the Kings was **Wayne Gretzky**.

On 9 August 1988, new team owner Bruce McNall acquired Gretzky in a huge trade with the **Edmonton Oilers**. In his first season with the Kings, Gretzky led the team with 168 **points**, with 54 **goals** and 114 **assists**. Not only did he help the Kings make it to the Stanley Cup Finals in 1993, but Gretzky created many new hockey fans in California, including celebrities and **well-known fans**. On 11 September 2001, team scouts Garnet Bailey and Mark Bavis were both killed in the terrorist attack against the **United States**. The Los Angeles Kings won the **Clarence S. Campbell Bowl** twice (1993, 2012). In 44 seasons in the NHL (1967–1968 to 2011–2012), the Kings have compiled a record of 1,428-1,561-424-93 (3,373 points) and made 26 **Stanley Cup Playoff** appearances. In Phoenix, on 22 May 2012, the Kings beat the **Phoenix Coyotes** (4–3) in **overtime** to advance to the Stanley Cup Finals for the first time since 1993. On 11 June 2012, the Kings defeated the **New Jersey Devils** during the 2012 Stanley Cup Finals (4–2) to win their first Stanley Cup in the history of the franchise. Current players for the team include captain Dustin Brown, defenseman Drew Doughty, **center Anže Kopitar,** and **goaltender** Jonathan Quick.

LUCKY LOONIE. The one–dollar, golden-colored **Canadian** coin with a loon on it, **nicknamed** a "loonie," was the basis of the hockey **superstition** about the "lucky loonie." During the 2002 **Olympic Games**, Canadian **ice** resurfacer Trent Evans buried a loonie at center ice. Because the ice at the Salt Lake City **rink** had a large logo instead of the typical circle, the **referee** needed a target for the **puck** during **face-offs**. The buried loonie was visible through the ice and worked well. Both the **Canadian Men's Olympic Ice Hockey Team** and **Canadian Women's Olympic Ice Hockey Team** won gold medals. This started the lucky loonie superstition. After the tournament, **Wayne Gretzky** recovered the coin and gave it to the **Hockey Hall of Fame** to display. A loonie was also used at the **World Ice Hockey Championships** between Canada and **Sweden** on 11 May 2003. This lucky loonie was called the Helsinki Loonie. It was hidden before the gold-medal game, which Canada won, 3–2. The legend is kept alive by the Royal Canadian Mint, which has since issued specially designed "lucky loonies" for each year that the Summer Olympics and Winter Olympics are held. Team **Russia** also made use of the lucky loonie in the 2008 World Ice Hockey Championships in Quebec City. **Alexander Ovechkin** dug out the lucky loonie from center ice after

Russia beat Canada, 5–4, in **overtime**. He gave it to his teammate, Ilya Nikulin, who cut it in half and made two necklaces out of the souvenir. In addition to hockey, the loonie legend is also prevalent in the sport of curling.

LUMLEY, HARRY "APPLE CHEEKS". B. 11 November 1926, Owen Sound, Ontario. D. 13 September 1998, London, Ontario. Harry Lumley was a **goaltender** in the **National Hockey League (NHL)** for 16 seasons. He played for the **Detroit Red Wings** (1943–1944, 1944–1950), **Chicago Black Hawks** (1950–1952), **Toronto Maple Leafs** (1952–1956), and **Boston Bruins** (1957–1960). He also filled in for one game against his own team in a 1943 game against the **New York Rangers**, when the Rangers' goalie, Ken McAuley, could not finish the final 20 minutes of the game due to an **injury**. Without a backup, the Wings agreed to loan their young goalie for the rest of the game. Lumley stepped out of his seat in the audience and onto the **ice**. Lumley's cheeks would get red while he played, hence the **nickname** "Apple Cheeks," but when he didn't play well, the fans called him "Redneck." He was the youngest goalie in NHL history. He was only 17 years old when he joined the Red Wings in 1943. Even though he helped the Red Wings win the **Stanley Cup** in 1950, Lumley was traded to Chicago when **Terry Sawchuk** went to Detroit. On 25 November 1951, when Lumley injured his knee, the team's 46-year-old trainer replaced him. Although Moe Roberts had not played in the NHL for 18 years, he held Detroit scoreless in the third period. Lumley led the league in **shutouts**, with seven (1947–1948), 10 (1953–1954), and 13 (1953–1954). He won the **Vezina Trophy** in 1954. He won 330 games and recorded 71 shutouts during his NHL career playing with five teams of the **"Original Six."** In 1980, Lumley was inducted into the **Hockey Hall of Fame**.

LUNDQVIST, HENRIK "THE KING," "KING HENRIK". B. 2 March 1982, Are, **Sweden**. Henrik Lundqvist and his twin **brother**, Joel Lundqvist, played hockey together in Sweden as **young players**. Their older sister was a talented tennis player. In 2001, Henrik joined the **National Hockey League (NHL)** as a **goaltender** for the **New York Rangers**. Joel joined the NHL in 2006, as a **center** for the **Dallas Stars**. Henrik played against his brother in Dallas, on 14 December 2006, and the Rangers won. It was the first time that a goaltender faced his twin. Henrik uses the butterfly style of goaltending, which originated with **Glenn Hall**. In the days of hockey before goalies wore **face masks**, they were easily **injured** when the **puck** was fired at them. **Gump Worsley** even said, "My face is my mask." But Lundqvist protects his good looks. In April 2006, Lundqvist was named one of *People's* World's 100 Most Beautiful People. Hockey fans enjoy seeing his specially decorated **helmet**-face mask combos each year. He had a strong starting season in the NHL (2001–2002) and became the first **rookie** goaltender to record a **shutout** for the Rangers since 1985.

Lundqvist's most memorable international performance came at the 2006 **Olympic Games** in Turin, Italy, where he led Sweden to the gold medal over their rival, **Finland**. In six Olympic starts, Lundqvist went 5–1 and allowed only 12 **goals**, with a .907 **save** percentage. On 27 February 2012, Lundqvist became the first NHL goalie to win at least 30 games in his first seven seasons in a 2–0 shutout over the **New Jersey Devils** at **Madison Square Garden**. Clearly upset after losing to the Devils in the **Eastern Conference** Finals in May 2012, Lundqvist responded to reporters by saying, "I'm just a goalie."

During his NHL career thus far (2001–2012), Lundqvist has played in 468 regular-season games and had 252 wins, 155 losses, and 43 shutouts. He was nominated for the **Vezina Trophy** four times (2006, 2007, 2008, 2012), as well as both the **Hart Memorial Trophy** (2012) and **Ted Lindsay Award** (2012). He was awarded his first Vezina Trophy in 2012. When he retires from playing, Lundqvist will surely be inducted into the **Hockey Hall of Fame**. In 2012, he launched a clothing line called the "Crown Collection" to benefit the Garden of Dreams Foundation, a hockey charity.

M

MACKAY, DUNCAN MCMILLAN "MICKEY," "THE WEE SCOT".
B. 25 May 1894, Chelsey, Ontario. D. 30 May 1940, Ymir, British Columbia. Mickey MacKay joined the **Canadian** Army at the age of 14, but he was discharged when the officers learned his real age. He then wrote to Frank Patrick, founder of the **Pacific Coast Hockey Association (PCHA)**, and was offered a chance to try out to play hockey. MacKay was successful and became a professional **center** and **rover** in the PCHA and **Western Canada Hockey League** for the **Vancouver Millionaires**, the renamed Vancouver Maroons. He made his professional debut on 8 December 1914, playing on a **line** with **Frank Nighbor** and Ken Mallen, and **scored** a **hat trick** in his first game. MacKay finished the season as the league's scoring leader, with 33 **goals** in just 17 games. He was known as a fast **skater** and top scorer, and he led the PCHA in goals three times and **assists** twice and was the league's all-time leading scorer. He was also a favorite with the fans due to his happy personality and clean playing style. MacKay's **nickname**, "The Wee Scot," was inspired by his small stature, which often led to **injuries** and missed games. **Right wing** Cully Wilson was banned from the PCHA after breaking MacKay's jaw with his **hockey stick**. **Lester Patrick** called MacKay the greatest **center** to ever play in the coast league. MacKay moved to the **National Hockey League (NHL)** after the other leagues folded. He finished his career playing with the **Chicago Black Hawks** (1926–1928), **Pittsburgh Pirates** (1928–1929), and **Boston Bruins** (1928–1930). MacKay won the **Stanley Cup** twice during his career, first with the Millionaires, in 1915, and later with the Bruins, in 1929. He scored four goals and recorded six **points** in the 1915 Stanley Cup victory over the **Ottawa Senators**. MacKay died from a heart attack while he was driving in British Columbia. In 1952, he was posthumously inducted into the **Hockey Hall of Fame**.

MADISON SQUARE GARDEN "THE GARDEN," "MSG". Madison Square Garden was one of the six original **National Hockey League (NHL)** arenas. It was located in New York City, New York, and was home to the **New York Rangers** from 1925–1968. It was actually the third building to use that name. The first one operated from 1879–1890, and had a seating capacity of 10,000 spectators. It was replaced with a new building on the same site, which was used from 1890–1925. The site selected for the third Garden was Eighth Avenue, between 49th and 50th streets. It had three tiers of seats and could seat 18,500 for boxing. The first event was a six-day bicycle race that began on 24 November 1925. On 6 December 1925, the first professional basketball game was played in Madison Square Garden. On 8 December, flyweight champion Jack McDermott was upset by Johnny Erickson in the first boxing match at the new Garden. The official opening of Madison Square Garden (III) was 15 December 1925, when the **Montreal Canadiens** defeated the **New York Americans**, 3–1. The first **goal** ever **scored** in the Garden was by New York American winger **Frank Boucher**. The New York Rangers made their debut by defeating the **Montreal Maroons** (1–0) at Madison Square Garden on 17 November 1926. Between 1928–1940, the Rangers won three **Stanley Cups**. Madison Square Garden was also the home of the New York Knicks basketball team and the site for many boxing matches and other events throughout the years, including the circus. In May 1962, Marilyn Monroe sang to President John F. Kennedy when his birthday party was held there. On 11 February 1968, the Rangers played the last hockey game there against **Gordie Howe** and the **Detroit Red Wings**. **Jean Ratelle** and **Norm Ullman** each scored twice for their teams in a 3–3 tie. *See also* ORIGINAL ARENAS.

MAHOVLICH, FRANCIS WILLIAM "FRANK," "THE BIG M". B. 10 January 1938, Timmins, Ontario. Frank Mahovlich was a Croatian–**Canadian** hockey player in the **National Hockey League (NHL)**. In 1957, the **Toronto Maple Leafs** wanted a look at the young Mahovlich. **Ted Kennedy** said that, "It was time for a new generation to lead the team." Mahovlich had practiced with Kennedy the previous day, and, in expressing regret at never having played in a game with Kennedy, Mahovlich said, "Teeder Kennedy's last practice was my first." Mahovlich was a **left wing** for Toronto from the 1956–1957 season until the 1967–1968 season. He also played with the NHL **Detroit Red Wings** (1967–1971) and **Montreal Canadiens** (1970–1974). Mahovlich then played in the **World Hockey Association (WHA)** with the Toronto Toros (1974–1976) and Birmingham Bulls (1976–1978). In his first WHA game, he **scored** a **hat trick,** and he had 82 **points** that season. He was **nicknamed** "The Big M" because of his long, flowing **skating** style and lanky build.

Mahovlich played on six **Stanley Cup**–winning teams. He also played in both the 1972 and 1974 **Summit Series**. He was known for his powerful **slapshot**, and he finished second in the NHL in **goals**, with 48 (1960–1961), 33 (1961–1962), 32 (1965–1966), and 49 (1968–1969). After scoring 61 goals in his first three years, he put a lot of pressure on himself. Others interpreted his serious nature as moodiness. The Maple Leafs' **coach, Punch Imlach**, was tough on Mahovlich and almost caused him to have a nervous breakdown twice. When he joined Detroit, Mahovlich skated on a **line** with **Gordie Howe** and **Alex Delvecchio**. The line scored 118 goals and broke the existing record of 105 set by the "Punch Line" of **Maurice Richard, Toe Blake**, and **Elmer Lach**. Mahovlich was happy when the Canadiens chose him. He showed his gratitude by helping Montreal win the 1971 Stanley Cup and breaking the **Stanley Cup Playoff** goal-scoring record, with 14. He scored 96 points in 76 games (1971–1972) and 93 points in 78 games (1972–1973).

During his NHL career, Mahovlich played in 1,182 regular-season games and had 533 goals, 570 **assists**, 1,103 points, and 1,056 **penalty minutes**. In 1964, he made a promotional record for Ford Mercury of Canada called *All My Hockey Secrets*, on which he teaches listeners about the basics of hockey. His 1968 Topps hockey card is highly collectible because Mahovlich's head was placed on a different player's body. Mahovlich was inducted into the **Hockey Hall of Fame** in 1981. He once said that, "I have the body of an athlete and the mind of a librarian," and, in 1998, he became the first former NHL player to be appointed to the Canadian Senate. His younger brother, Peter Mahovlich, played in the NHL with Detroit (1965–1969, 1979–1981), Montreal (1969–1977), and the **Pittsburgh Penguins** (1977–1979).

MALKIN, EVGENI VLADIMIROVICH "GENO". B. 31 July 1986, Magnitogorsk, Soviet Union. Evgeni Malkin is a current **center** with the **Pittsburgh Penguins** in the **National Hockey League (NHL)**. After hurting his shoulder during a preseason game, Malkin made his NHL debut on 18 October 2006, against the **New Jersey Devils**. This young talent scored his first NHL **goal** against veteran **goaltender Martin Brodeur**. Malkin also set a modern record as the first player to score at least one goal in each of his first six games. No player had achieved this feat since **Joe Malone** set the record during the 1917–1918 season. Malkin received the **Calder Memorial Trophy** as the **Rookie** of the Year (2007). On 12 June 2009, the Penguins won the **Stanley Cup** by defeating the **Detroit Red Wings** in seven games. Malkin tallied 36 **points** (14 goals, 22 **assists**) to become the first player to lead both the regular season and **Stanley Cup Playoffs** in scoring since **Mario Lemieux** accomplished the feat in 1992. Malkin had the highest playoff total of any player since 1993, when **Wayne Gretzky** recorded 40 points. In 2009, Malkin became the first **Russian** player to win the **Conn Smythe Trophy**.

When he first arrived in the **United States**, Malkin spoke little English, and, as a result, he gave only brief interviews, but with the help of his fellow Russian teammate Sergei Gonchar, his English improved. At the 2012 awards ceremony, he thanked Gonchar for his help and friendship. Malkin has won the **Art Ross Trophy** (which he also won in 2009), **Hart Memorial Trophy**, and **Ted Lindsay Award**. Despite being sidelined by several **injuries**, he has played in 427 regular-season games to date and recorded 208 goals, 319 assists, 527 points, and 426 **penalty minutes**. He was the second-fastest Russian to score 500 NHL points (413 games), trailing only **Alexander Ovechkin** (373 games). Internationally, Malkin represented Russia in the 2010 **Olympic Games**. He also competed in the **World Ice Hockey Championships** and won one gold medal (2012), two silver medals (2007, 2010), and one bronze medal (2005). Malkin became only the second player ever to lead both the NHL and World Ice Hockey Championships in scoring in the same season (2011–2012). Wayne Gretzky accomplished it during the 1981–1982 season.

MALONE, MAURICE JOSEPH "JOE," "PHANTOM JOE". B. 28 February 1890, Quebec City, Quebec. D. 15 May 1969, Montreal, Quebec. Joe Malone was a professional **ice hockey center** who played in the **National Hockey Association** and **National Hockey League (NHL)** from 1909–1924. He was known for his **scoring** feats and clean play. He **scored** the second-most career **goals** of any player in the first half-century. Malone scored nine goals for the **Quebec Bulldogs** in the Bulldogs' 14–3 **Stanley Cup Playoff** win over the Sydney Millionaires on 8 March 1913. During the NHL's first season (1917–1918), he led the league in scoring, with 44 goals in 20 games, and was paid a salary of $1,000. This record stood for 27 years, until **Maurice Richard** broke it with 50 goals (1944–1945). Malone has the distinction of being the only player in the history of the NHL to score seven goals in a single game, which he accomplished on 31 January 1920. He was also the only NHL player to score six or more goals in a single game twice. Malone was also an expert stickhandler. He earned the **nickname** "Phantom Joe" from being able to find openings and weave his way to the **net** almost invisibly. Malone was a member of three **Stanley Cup**–winning teams, the Quebec Bulldogs (1912, 1913) and **Montreal Canadiens** (1924); however, his name was not engraved on the 1924 Stanley Cup because he did not play in the playoffs. His record 49 **points** during regular-season games was broken by **Howie Morenz**, with 59 (1927–1928). Malone was inducted into both the **Hockey Hall of Fame** (1950) and **Canada's Sports Hall of Fame** (1975).

MANTHA, SYLVIO. B. 14 April 1902, Montreal, Quebec. D. 7 August 1974, Montreal, Quebec. Sylvio Mantha played **ice** hockey for 14 seasons in the **National Hockey League (NHL)** as a **defenseman** with the **Montreal Canadiens** (1923–1936) and **Boston Bruins** (1936–1937). He began as a forward for Montreal, but, after **Sprague Cleghorn**, retired Mantha became a dominant two-way defenseman. Mantha was paired with **Herb Gardiner** and his younger **brother**, Georges. Mantha was also part of the Canadiens from 1928–1941. On 20 November 1928, Mantha **scored** the first-ever **goal** in **Boston Garden** in a 1–0 Canadiens triumph over the **Boston Bruins**. He won the **Stanley Cup** in 1924, 1930, and 1931. He was part of the 1924 Stanley Cup team that forgot the trophy by the side of the road after changing a flat tire. In 1936, Mantha was traded to the Bruins, but, after playing four games for Boston, he realized it was time to retire. He then became a **linesman** and **referee** in the **American Hockey League** and the NHL and coached **juniors** for several seasons. In 1960, Mantha was inducted into the **Hockey Hall of Fame**.

MAPLE LEAF GARDENS. Maple Leaf Gardens was one of the six original **National Hockey League (NHL)** arenas. It was located in Toronto, Ontario, and was home to the **Toronto Maple Leafs** from 1931–1999. The arena was built in 1931, at a cost of $1.5 million dollars. The Gardens opened on 12 November 1931, with the Maple Leafs losing, 2–1, to the **Chicago Black Hawks**. Reported attendance on opening night was 13,542. The Leafs won the **Stanley Cup** 11 times from 1932 through their last Stanley Cup win in 1967. In 1934, an **All-Star Team** played a game at the Gardens as a benefit for Leafs' forward **Ace Bailey**, who had suffered a **career-ending injury**. The first annual NHL All-Star Game was also held at Maple Leaf Gardens in 1947. Other sporting events for basketball, boxing, **lacrosse**, and wrestling were also held there. It was one of the few venues outside of the **United States** where Elvis Presley performed (2 April 1957). In 1972, Maple Leaf Gardens hosted Game 2 of the Summit Series, where Team **Canada** defeated the Union of Soviet Socialist Republics Team, 4–1. On 13 February 1999, the Toronto Maple Leafs ended a 67 year tradition when they played their last game at Maple Leaf Gardens. Similar to their first game there, they lost to the **Chicago Blackhawks** (6–2). Former Leaf **Doug Gilmour scored** a fluke **goal** in that game, and tough guy Bob Probert scored the final NHL goal there during the third period. *See also* ORIGINAL ARENAS.

MARSHALL, JOHN CALDER "JACK". B. 14 March 1877, Saint-Vallier, Quebec. D. 7 August 1965, Montreal, Quebec. Jack Marshall was the only nongoaltender to be a member of four different **Stanley Cup** championship teams, including the 1901 Winnipeg Victorias, the 1902 and 1903 Montreal AAA, the 1907 and 1910 **Montreal Wanderers**, and the 1914 Toronto Blueshirts. His teammate, **Hap Holmes**, accomplished this same feat as a **goaltender**. Marshall was also an all-around athlete who excelled in football, baseball, soccer, bowling, and **lacrosse**. On 17 March 1903, he **scored** the Stanley Cup–winning **goal** in the AAA's 2–1 win over the Winnipeg Victorias. Marshall won the Stanley Cup with the Wanderers first as a **center**, and then again as a **defenseman**. In the 1910–911 season, he suffered a serious eye **injury** that kept him off the **ice**. During the 1913–1914 season with the Blueshirts, he was a player and **coach**. After retiring, he became a **referee** in the **National Hockey Association**. Marshall was inducted into the **Hockey Hall of Fame** in 1965.

MASON, RON. B. 14 January 1940, Blyth, Ontario. Ron Mason earned a bachelor of arts degree in physical education from St. Lawrence University in 1964, and a master's degree in physical education from the University of Pittsburgh in 1965. Although he played **college hockey**, Mason spent his career **coaching**. He coached at three different universities, including Lake Superior State University (1967–1973), Bowling Green State University (1974–1979), and Michigan State University (1980–2002). He has the distinction of being the winningest college hockey coach in the **United States**, with 924 career wins. In 36 seasons of coaching, Mason had 33 seasons with a winning record, 30 seasons winning 20 or more games, and 11 seasons winning 30 or more games. He helped his teams advance to the **National Collegiate Athletic Association** tournament 24 times, six times as the number one seed. Active coaches Jerry York of Boston College (911 wins) and Jack Parker of Boston University (853 wins) are chasing his record.

MASTERTON, WILLIAM J. "BILL". B. 13 August 1938, Winnipeg, Manitoba. D. 15 January 1968, Minneapolis, Minnesota. As a student and hockey **center**, Bill Masterton helped the University of Denver win three **National Collegiate Athletic Association (NCAA)** national titles, in 1958, 1960, and again in his senior year, in 1961, when he was named the Most Valuable Player of the entire NCAA tournament. He played in the **minor league** for six years. Then, in 1967, he had his chance to play professionally for a new expansion team, the Minnesota North Stars. Masterton **scored** the first **goal** in North Stars history on 11 October 1967, but tragically, only 38 games into the season, in a game against the Oakland Seals, he was body **checked** and fell unconscious after hitting his head on the **ice**. He died two days later, on 15 January 1968. Masterton was the first player to die as a direct result of an **injury** during a **National Hockey League (NHL)** game. As a result of this incident, **on-ice officials** became stricter on **penalty** enforcement. At the end of the 1967–1968 season, in his honor, the NHL introduced the **Bill Masterton Memorial Trophy**. It is awarded to the player who best exhibits the dedication and sportsmanship that Masterton embodied. His death also resulted in the push for mandatory **helmets**, which were not common in professional hockey at the time. Helmets were made a mandatory piece of **equipment** for incoming professional players before the start of the 1979–1980 season. *See also* CAREER-ENDING INJURIES.

MATCH. Unlike the sport of tennis, where the terms *game* and *match* have different meanings, they are synonymous in **ice** hockey. When two teams compete against one another, it is called a match or a game. A regulation **National Hockey League (NHL)** game consists of three 20-minute periods, with two 10-minute intermissions between the first and second periods. One of the more severe **penalties** in hockey, which results from intentional **injury** to an opponent, is called a match penalty. Instead of going to the **penalty box** for a few minutes, the player is suspended for the rest of the game.

MAURICE "ROCKET" RICHARD TROPHY. The newest trophy in the **National Hockey League (NHL)** was established by the **Montreal Canadiens** in 1999, to honor **Maurice Richard**. Richard was the first player to have a 50-**goal** season, and he was the league's top **scorer** five times. This trophy is presented to the NHL's leading goal scorer for the season. The first recipient was **Teemu Selänne**, and **Pavel Bure**, **Jarome Iginla**, **Alexander Ovechkin**, and Steven Stamkos have each won the trophy twice. Recent winners include **Sidney Crosby** of the **Pittsburgh Penguins**, Corey Perry of the **Anaheim Ducks**, and Steve Stamkos of the **Tampa Bay Lightning**.

MCDONALD, LANNY KING. B. 16 February 1953, Hanna, Alberta. Lanny McDonald's father was a big fan of the **Toronto Maple Leafs**, and Lanny was given the middle name King after Maple Leafs' star **King Clancy**. McDonald played in the **National Hockey League (NHL)** as a **right wing** from 1973–1989, and he was captain of the **Calgary Flames** when the team won the **Stanley Cup** in 1989. He also played for the **Toronto Maple Leafs** and **Colorado Rockies** and **scored** 500 career **goals**. It was easy for fans to spot McDonald on the **ice** due to his bushy red mustache. One time, his practical joker teammate, **Nick Fotiu**, put Vaseline in the folds of the dressing room towels, and McDonald got it smeared into his large mustache. One highlight of McDonald's career in Toronto came during the 1978 **Stanley Cup Playoffs**, against the **New York Islanders**. The Maple Leafs were considered the underdogs in the series, while the Islanders were considered one of the best in the league. Toronto overcame a 2–0 series deficit to force a seventh and deciding game. McDonald's wrist and nose were both broken during the series, but he scored the **overtime** winning goal that eliminated the Islanders and allowed the Maple Leafs to advance to the league semifinals for the first time in 11 years. Unfortunately, Toronto was then eliminated by the **Montreal Canadiens**, who swept the series in four games. On 19

March 1988, McDonald recorded his 1,000 career NHL **point** in Calgary's 9–5 win against the **Winnipeg Jets**. His 500th career goal came during the **match** between the Flames and Islanders on 21 March 1989. McDonald won the **Bill Masterton Memorial Trophy** (1983) and King Clancy Memorial Trophy (1988). In 1992, he was inducted into the **Hockey Hall of Fame**. During his 1,111 regular-season NHL games, McDonald had 500 goals, 506 **assists**, 1,006 points, and 1,006 **penalty minutes**.

MCFARLANE, BRIAN. B. 10 August 1931, New Liskeard, Ontario. Brian McFarlane is a **Canadian** television sportscaster and hockey expert. He attended St. Lawrence University on a hockey scholarship, but he is best known for being a commentator on *Hockey Night in Canada* for 25 years. McFarlane also broadcasted **National League Hockey (NHL)** games for the American networks CBS and NBC. His father, Leslie McFarlane, wrote many of the original Hardy Boys books, and Brian has written more than 50 books about hockey. He is often given credit for creating the cartoon character **Peter Puck**, when actually it was NBC executive Donald Carswell's idea. McFarlane purchased the rights to Peter Puck after the network stopped carrying NHL hockey. In 1995, he was inducted into the **Hockey Hall of Fame** under the media honoree distinction. Also in 1995, the Society for International Hockey Research created the Brian McFarlane Award, named for its first honorary president in appreciation of his support and ongoing contributions to the preservation of hockey history.

MCGEE, FRANCIS "FRANK," "ONE-EYED FRANK". B. 4 November 1880, Ottawa, Ontario. D. 16 September 1916, Courcelette, France. Frank McGee played as a **center** and **rover** for seven elite amateur hockey seasons, from 1899–1906. He earned the **nickname** "One-Eyed Frank" after he was struck in his left eye during a game on 21 March 1900. On 16 January 1905, McGee set the **Stanley Cup Playoff** record for most **goals** in a single game (14), including eight in a row, in a 23–2 victory over the Dawson City Nuggets. That same year, while playing with a broken wrist, he **scored** the **Stanley Cup**–winning goal against the Rat Portage Thistles (5–4). He was killed in combat while serving in the **Canadian** Army during World War I. In seven seasons, McGee played in 23 regular-season games and scored 71 goals. Including playoff games, he had a total of 134 goals. McGee was elected to the **Hockey Hall of Fame** in 1945, as one of the 12 original inductees. When describing McGee, hockey **builder** Frank Patrick said, "He had everything . . . speed, stickhandling, **scoring** ability, and was a punishing **checker**."

MCSORLEY, MARTIN JAMES "MARTY". B. 18 May 1963, Hamilton, Ontario. Marty McSorley played in the **National Hockey League (NHL)** from 1983 until 21 February 2000. Although he was able to play both the forward and defense positions, his main contribution was as an **enforcer**. He followed in **Dave Semenko**'s footsteps as **Wayne Gretzky**'s bodyguard on the **ice**. While with the **Los Angeles Kings**, McSorley was caught with an illegal **hockey stick** during Game 2 of the 1993 **Stanley Cup** Finals against the **Montreal Canadiens**. Montreal won the game in **overtime** and went on to win the series, 4–1. McSorley had 10 **points** in the **Stanley Cup Playoffs** and was the only King to **score** during the final game. His hockey career ended suddenly in a game against the **Vancouver Canucks** on 21 February 2000. While playing for the **Boston Bruins**, he swung his stick and hit Donald Brashear in the head with 3 seconds left in the game. Brashear fell backward and hit his head hard on the ice as a result of the stick's contact with his head and **helmet**. As a result, Brashear lost consciousness and suffered a serious concussion. McSorley was charged with assault and suspended by the NHL for the remainder of the 1999–2000 season. On 4 October 2000, a jury found McSorley guilty of assault with a weapon for his attack on Brashear. The trial was the first for an on-ice attack by an NHL player since 1988. During his suspension, McSorley attempted to continue playing hockey in **Great Britain** with the London Knights, where his brother, Chris McSorley, was **coaching**. He was banned from ever playing again in the NHL by the **International Ice Hockey Federation**; however, he did appear as a hockey player in several television shows and **movies**. *See also* INJURIES.

MESSIER, MARK DOUGLAS "THE CAPTAIN," "THE MESSIAH," "THE MOOSE". B. 18 January 1961, Edmonton, Alberta. In 1979, Mark Messier was selected by the **Edmonton Oilers** of the **World Hockey Association (WHA)**, and he remained with them as they transitioned into the **National Hockey League (NHL)**. In his 26 hockey seasons, Messier played with the WHA (1978–1980), Edmonton Oilers (1979–1991), **New York Rangers** (1991–1997, 2000–2004), and **Vancouver Canucks** (1997–2000). He and **Wayne Gretzky** were the two youngest players on the Edmonton Oilers. The 18-year-old phenoms were an important part of the Oilers' dynasty of the 1980s. Messier won the **Stanley Cup** five times with the Edmonton team (1984, 1985, 1987, 1988, 1990). He was known for his strength, fast **skating**, and aggressive style of play on the **ice**. As a power forward, he played **left wing** and sometimes **center**. In the 1989–1990 season, Messier had an excellent year, recording 129 **points** and finishing second to Gretzky. Messier's career awards include the **Conn Smythe Trophy** (1984), **Hart Memorial Trophy** (1990, 1992), and Lester B. Pearson Award (1990, 1992). Early in his career, Messier had a wild side off the ice. As he matured, he stepped into a leadership role for both his teammates and fans. This leadership was evident when he led the New York Rangers to the 1994 Stanley Cup over the Vancouver Canucks in seven games. This ended a 54-year Stanley Cup drought for the Rangers and earned Messier the **nickname** "The Messiah." He was the first NHL player to captain two different teams to the championships.

In addition to his six Stanley Cups, Messier also played hockey for **Canada** at the **Canada Cup** (1984, 1987, 1991), **World Ice Hockey Championships** (1989), the **World Cup of Hockey** (1996). In October 1998, Messier **scored** his 600th career **goal** in a win over the **Florida Panthers**. He and two of his former Oilers teammates, Gretzky and **Jari Kurri**, were three of only 10 players to ever top that mark. Messier is second on the all-time career lists for regular-season points (1,887), **Stanley Cup Playoff** points (295), and regular-season games played (1,756). His 1,193 NHL career **assists** are the third highest in history. In 2007, Messier was inducted into the **Hockey Hall of Fame**. In 2009, he received the **Lester Patrick Trophy** and returned to the Rangers' organization in a management position. On 11 September 2001, Messier and the Rangers were supposed to be near the World Trade Center for training, but by chance they changed locations. Thankful for their good fortune, Messier and his teammates volunteered at Ground Zero. On 6 November 2011, Messier ran in the New York City Marathon to raise money for the New York Police and Fire Widows' and Children's Benefit Fund.

MIAMI SCREAMING EAGLES. The Miami Screaming Eagles were the best-known hockey team that never played. In 1972, Herb Martin bought a franchise in the newly created **World Hockey Association**. The Eagles recruited **National Hockey League (NHL)** players **Bernie Parent** from the **Toronto Maple Leafs** and Derek Sanderson from the **Boston Bruins**. Unfortunately, the team could not find an acceptable arena in Miami, so it moved to Philadelphia and became the Philadelphia Blazers. After one season, the franchise was moved to Vancouver, and then to Calgary in 1975, before folding in 1977. **Ice** hockey eventually returned to Miami in 1993, when the NHL **Florida Panthers** franchise was established.

MICHAELS, ALAN RICHARD "AL". B. 12 November 1944, Brooklyn, New York. Al Michaels is a well-known television sportscaster for various sports. He joined ABC as the backup announcer on *Monday Night Baseball* in 1977. During the next three decades, Michaels covered a wide variety of sports for ABC, including Major League Baseball, college football, college basketball, **ice** hockey, track and field events, horse racing, golf, boxing, figure skating, road cycling, and many events of the **Olympic Games**; however, even nonsports enthusiasts are likely to know him from the famous line he uttered during the 1980 Olympic hockey **match** between the underdog U.S. team and the champion Soviet Union team. As the clock was winding down and the U.S. team was about to **score** an upset, Michaels yelled, "Do you believe in miracles? . . YES!" Michaels's name will forever be associated with the **"Miracle on Ice."**

MIDGETS. *See* YOUNG PLAYERS.

MIGHTY DUCKS OF ANAHEIM. *See* ANAHEIM DUCKS.

MIKITA, STANISLAV "STAN," "MOUSE". B. 20 May 1940, Sokplce, Czechoslovakia. Stanislav Guoth changed his name from Guoth to Mikita when he was adopted by his aunt and uncle who lived in Ontario. Stan Mikita was a **center** and **right wing** in the **National Hockey League (NHL)** for 22 seasons. He was a member of the **Chicago Black Hawks** from 1959–1980, making him one of only a small group of players to have **skated** in the NHL for four decades. He helped his team defeat the **Detroit Red Wings** to win the **Stanley Cup** in 1961. During the 1960s, Mikita played on the "MPH line," with Jim Pappin and **Bobby Hull**. The name of the line referred to their speed, as well as the initials of their last names. His one **superstition** was that he would have one cigarette before each game to help him relax. Mikita smoked it going up the stairs to the **ice** at the **Chicago Stadium**, and he would then toss the butt over his left shoulder. Mikita was an aggressive agitator who accumulated 154 **penalty minutes** in one season (1964–1965). Mikita once said, "There are rough players and there are dirty players. I'm rough and dirty." But then he changed his game around, kept his mouth shut, and became a composed **scorer**. During the 1966–1967 season, Mikita only recorded 12 penalty minutes. He was also one of the few players to use a curved **hockey stick** known as a "banana blade." He scored 541 **goals** during his career. Mikita was the first NHL player to win the **Hart Memorial Trophy**, **Art Ross Trophy**, and **Lady Byng Memorial Trophy** all in the same season, which he did consecutively in the 1966–1967 and 1967–1968 seasons. He earned the **nickname** "Mouse" because whenever he made a good play, the Chicago fans would chant, "M-I-K-I-T-A M-O-U-S-E." In 1976, he received the **Lester Patrick Trophy**. Mikita is one of only four NHL players to play at least 20 seasons with one organization **Alex Delvecchio**, **Mike Modano**, and **Steve Yzerman** are the other three. Mikita holds the Chicago team records for most seasons (22), most games (1,394), most **assists** (926), and most career **points** (1,467). In 1983, he was inducted into the **Hockey Hall of Fame**. An ice **rink** in Ruzomberok, Slovakia, is named after him.

MINNESOTA NORTH STARS. *See* DALLAS STARS.

MINNESOTA WILD. The Minnesota Wild are a professional **ice** hockey team in the **Northwest Division** of the **National Hockey League (NHL) Western Conference**. After the Minnesota North Stars relocated to Dallas and were renamed the Dallas Stars, the state of Minnesota was without an NHL team for seven seasons. The Minnesota Wild franchise was founded in 2000, with **Hockey Hall of Famer Jacques Lemaire** as their **coach** (2000–2009). **Marián Gáborík** joined the team and **scored** the first-ever **goal** for the Wild in their franchise debut on 6 October 2000, at Anaheim. In 11 seasons in the NHL, from 2000–2001 to 2011–2012, the Minnesota Wild have compiled a record of 405-362-55-80 (945 **points**) and made three **Stanley Cup Playoff** appearances. In 2003, the team advanced to the Western Conference Finals but were swept, 4–0, by the Mighty Ducks of Anaheim. In 2007, the renamed **Anaheim Ducks** eliminated them again in the playoffs. During the 2007–2008 season, Gáborík set a franchise record of 42 goals and 83 points. On 3 April 2008, Lemaire recorded his 500th career coaching win, and the Wild clinched their first Northwest Division title in a 3–1 victory over the **Calgary Flames**. In their third playoff appearance, they were defeated in six games in the quarterfinals by the **Colorado Avalanche**. Their current coach is Mike Yeo. To date, the young franchise has not won a **Stanley Cup**.

MINOR LEAGUE. Similar to baseball players, hockey players often start in the minor league, or "minors," while they improve their skills. If their talents are noticed, they will move up and play for a **National Hockey League (NHL)** team. Sometimes a player who is already in the NHL will go back to the minors to work through a slump and improve his skills. The **American Hockey League (AHL)** is the minor league division below the NHL. Each AHL team is connected to a NHL team. The AHL teams are also called "farm teams." Other minor professional leagues include the **East Coast Hockey League**, Central Hockey League (CHL), Southern Professional Hockey League, Ligue Nord-Américaine de Hockey, Federal Hockey League, and Northern Professional Hockey League. The majority of these teams play in the **United States**. One reason for the large number of U.S.-based teams is that minor league franchises often move from city to city, and even between leagues. While NHL players compete for the **Stanley Cup** each season, AHL players try to win the **Calder Cup**, which was named after the first president of the NHL, **Frank Calder**.

"MIRACLE ON ICE". "Miracle on Ice" refers to the upset victory by the **U.S. Men's Olympic Ice Hockey Team** over the **Soviet Union Men's Olympic Ice Hockey Team** at the 1980 **Olympic Games** at **Lake Placid**, New York. The team from the Soviet Union was heavily favored to win the gold medal due to their talent, as well as the fact that they had been playing together for eight years. They had previously won gold medals in 1972 and 1976. Conversely, the young U.S. team mainly consisted of **college hockey** players, including **goaltender Jim Craig, Mike Eruzione,** and **Mark Johnson,** recruited by **coach Herb Brooks.** A few days prior to the Olympics, the Russian team beat the U.S. team in an exhibition match by a **score** of 10–3. As underdogs, the U.S. team was not even expected to win a bronze medal, let alone a gold one. As the clock was winding down with a score of 4–3, sportscaster **Al Michaels** yelled that it was a miracle, and the name went down in history. The United States then defeated **Finland** in the finals to win the gold medal. The only other gold medal they had won in hockey was at the 1960 Olympics. *See also* MOVIES.

MISCONDUCT. A misconduct **penalty** in **ice** hockey results in a player being in the **penalty box** for 10 minutes; however, his or her team doesn't have to play shorthanded. Examples of misconduct include extended **fighting,** verbal or physical abuse of officials, or failure to go to the penalty bench or box. A penalized **goaltender** has another player serve his penalty time. To signal misconduct, the **on-ice official** places both hands on his hips and motions to the player. Misconduct was defined in the 1937–1938 **National Hockey League (NHL)** rule book. It originated during Game 2 of quarterfinal series between the **Toronto Maple Leafs** and **Boston Bruins,** on 26 March 1936. Toronto's **King Clancy** egged on Boston's short-tempered **Eddie Shore** to question a call made by **referee** Odie Cleghorn. After yelling at Cleghorn, Shore tossed a **puck** at his backside, which earned him a 10-minute misconduct penalty. While Shore was in the penalty box, the Leafs **scored** four **goals** to win the game. For behavior more severe than misconduct, the NHL can fine or suspend a player as punishment for their actions.

MITES. *See* YOUNG PLAYERS.

MODANO, MICHAEL THOMAS "MIKE". B. 7 June 1970, Livonia, Minnesota. Mike Modano was a **center** for 21 seasons in the **National Hockey League (NHL).** He played with the Minnesota North Stars (1989–1993), **Dallas Stars** (1993–2010), and **Detroit Red Wings** (2010–2011). His highest-scoring seasons were in 1992–1993 and 1993–1994, when he **scored** 93 points each time. Modano won the **Stanley Cup** in 1999 with the Dallas Stars and had consecutive seasons of more than 20 **Stanley Cup Playoff**

points in 1999 and 2000. Internationally, he played for the **United States** in the 1990 and 1993 **World Ice Hockey Championships** and 1991 **Canada Cup**. He won a gold medal at the 1996 **World Cup of Hockey**. He also competed in the 1998, 2002, and 2006 Winter Olympics, winning silver in 2002. On 13 March 2007, Modano scored his 500th career NHL **goal**. Although the Minnesota team was renamed and relocated, it's considered one franchise. Modano is one of only four NHL players to play at least 20 seasons with only one organization. **Alex Delvecchio**, **Stan Mikita**, and **Steve Yzerman** are the other three. In his NHL career, Modano played more games (1,499), has more points (1,374), and scored more goals (561) than any other American-born player. He made a brief cameo appearance in the 1992 **movie** *The Mighty Ducks*. Modano will likely be inducted into the **U.S. Hockey Hall of Fame** when he becomes eligible.

MONTREAL CANADIENS. The Montreal Canadiens are a professional **ice** hockey team in the **Northeast Division** of the **National Hockey League (NHL) Eastern Conference**. Founded in 1909, the Canadiens are the longest continuously operating professional ice hockey team and the only existing NHL club to predate the creation of the NHL. From 1909–1917, the team was part of the **National Hockey Association (NHA)**. The team won its first **Stanley Cup** championship in 1916. In 1917, with four other NHA teams, the Canadiens formed the NHL, and they won their first NHL Stanley Cup during the 1924 season. They were also one of the **"Original Six"** teams, a term used to describe the teams that made up the NHL from 1942 until the 1967 expansion. They are nicknamed the "Habs" based on the French word for "habitant." On 5 January 1909, in their first-ever professional hockey game, the Montreal Canadiens played the Cobalt Silver Kings. The Canadiens won, 7–6. In its NHL history, the team has made the Stanley Cup Finals more than any other team, 34 times. They have a 70 percent winning rate, with 24 wins, 9 losses, and one undecided in 1919. They made the Stanley Cup Finals each year from 1951–1960.

Sixty-one individuals associated with the Canadiens have been inducted into the **Hockey Hall of Fame**. Thirty-six of these players were from three separate dynasties: 12 from 1955–1960, 11 from 1964–1969 and 13 from 1975–1979. **Howie Morenz** and **Georges Vezina** were the first Canadiens inducted in 1945, and **Doug Gilmour** was the most recent player inducted, in 2011. Some of the best players for the Canadiens include Hockey Hall of Famers **Jean Béliveau**, **Toe Blake**, **Bernie Geoffrion**, **Guy Lafleur**, **Jacques Plante**, **Henri Richard**, and **Maurice Richard**. The NHL franchise has had many notable head **coaches**, namely **Newsy Lalonde**, **Cecil Hart**, Toe Blake, **Dick Irvin**, and **Scotty Bowman**. In 1963, Montreal was the first team to draft a player. Although only a total of 21 players were drafted at that time, that number has grown to more than 250 players each year. With **Ken**

Dryden, Jacques Lemaire, and several other key players retiring after the conclusion of the 1979 season, the Canadiens' final dynasty came to an end, and they lost in the second round of the 1980 **Stanley Cup Playoffs** to the Minnesota North Stars in seven games. Since 1980, they have only made the Stanley Cup Finals three times. In 94 seasons in the NHL, from 1917–1918 to 2011–2012, the Montreal Canadiens have compiled a record of 3,135-2,052-837-96 (7,203 **points**) and made 79 playoff appearances.

MONTREAL FORUM. The Montreal Forum was one of the six original **National Hockey League (NHL)** arenas. It was located in Montreal, Quebec, and was home to the **Montreal Maroons** from 1924–1938, and the **Montreal Canadiens** from 1926–1996. The Forum opened on 29 November 1924, and the Maroons defeated the Toronto St. Patricks, 7–1. Montreal also won the **Stanley Cup** in 1926 and 1935. On 28 January 1937, in a game between the Montreal Canadiens and **Chicago Black Hawks** at the Montreal Forum, **Howie Morenz** broke his leg. The incident was a **career-ending injury**, and Morenz later died from complications. On 8 September 1964, the Beatles held a concert at the Forum. It was also the site of five events in the 1976 Summer Olympics: gymnastics, handball, basketball, volleyball, and boxing. The gymnastics event included Nadia Comaneci's famous perfect 10, the first one ever in **Olympic** history. On 11 March 1996, the Montreal Canadiens played their last game at the Montreal Forum, beating the **Dallas Stars**, 4–1. Although it was specifically built for the Maroons, the Forum became the most famous hockey arena, mainly because of the Canadiens and their 22 Stanley Cup wins. *See also* ORIGINAL ARENAS.

MONTREAL MAROONS. After the Montreal Arena burned down on 2 January 1918, the **Montreal Wanderers** disbanded. In 1924, the Montreal Maroons **ice** hockey team was created to take their place in the **National Hockey League (NHL)**. The Maroons won the **Stanley Cup** in 1926 and 1935. They were a competitive team with many great players, including **Nels Stewart, Lionel Conacher, goaltender Clint Benedict, George Boucher**, forward **Punch Broadbent**, and **Toe Blake**. The **Stanley Cup Playoffs** of the 1935–1936 season are famous for the longest NHL playoff game of all time, when, on 24–25 March 1936, the Maroons lost, 1–0, to the **Detroit Red Wings** in 176:30 of play (16:30 of the sixth **overtime** period). Following a losing season and financial troubles, the Montreal Maroons folded in 1938.

MONTREAL WANDERERS. The Montreal Wanderers were an **ice** hockey team that won the **Stanley Cup** four times (1906, 1907, 1908, 1910). They belonged to the Federal Amateur Hockey League (1904–1905), Eastern Canada Amateur Hockey Association (1906–1908), Eastern Canada Hockey

Association (1909), and **National Hockey Association (NHA)** (1910–1917). The Wanderers defeated the **Kenora Thistles** on 23–25 March 1907, to win their second Stanley Cup. One of their **defensemen**, **Hod Stuart**, tragically died three months later in a diving accident. On 2 January 1908, a benefit game was played between Montreal and an **All-Star Team** from the NHA. The Wanderers won that game, 10–7; however, they were not winning in their regular seasons, so they acquired **goaltender Hap Holmes** to turn their luck around. They joined the **National Hockey League (NHL)** in 1917–1918, but they only played four games in the NHL's inaugural season before their home **rink**, the Montreal Arena, burned down on 2 January 1918. After the fire, the team soon disbanded. In 1924, a new team, the **Montreal Maroons**, was established to take the place of the Wanderers. Although they won the Stanley Cup in 1926 and 1935, the Maroons folded in 1938.

MOORE, RICHARD WINSTON "DICKIE". B. 6 January 1931, Montreal, Quebec. Dickie Moore played **left wing** for three **National Hockey League (NHL)** teams, including the **Montreal Canadiens** (1951–1963), **Toronto Maple Leafs** (1964–1965), and **St. Louis Blues** (1967–1968). Even though Moore was hit by a car when he was 12, and he came from a family of 12, Moore's famous **jersey number** (12) was the only number available at the time. He also happened to play 12 seasons in Montreal. Moore was part of the successful Montreal **line** that included **brothers Henri Richard** at **center** and **Maurice Richard** at **right wing**. Moore **scored** the winning championship **goal** in Montreal's 5–1 victory over the **Boston Bruins** on 16 April 1957. For being the league's leading scorer, he won the **Art Ross Trophy** in 1958 and 1959. He earned the 1959 title even while playing part of the season with a broken wrist. During his 719 regular-game hockey career, he scored 261 goals, 347 **assists**, and a total of 608 **points**. Moore won six **Stanley Cups** (1953, 1956–1960), and his name is spelled differently on the trophy five times (D. Moore, Richard Moore, R. Moore, Dickie Moore, Rich Moore). Moore and **Detroit Red Wings'** player **Ted Lindsay** had a known rivalry and kept facing each other during the Stanley Cup Finals. Moore's family was athletic as well. His sister, Dolly Moore, was a track and field star who almost qualified for an **Olympic** team. In 1974, Dickie was inducted into the **Hockey Hall of Fame**.

MORAN, PATRICK JOSEPH "PADDY". B. 11 March 1877, Quebec City, Quebec. D. 24 January 1966, Quebec City, Quebec. Paddy Moran was a **goaltender** for the **Quebec Bulldogs** (1905–1909, 1910–1917) of the **National Hockey Association (NHA)** during the days of stand-up goaltending. He was known as a clutch goalie who would win difficult **matches**. Moran played prior to the **crease**, but he created his own and kept players away from the **goal** with his **hockey stick**. He is also remembered for wearing a baggy sweater that he said kept him warm in the drafty, old arenas. With the sweater unbuttoned, he would catch shots in it. Moran helped the Bulldogs win the **Stanley Cup** in 1912 and 1913, and he led the **Stanley Cup Playoffs** in wins (2) during the 1911–1912 season. He also led the NHA in **shutouts**, with one each season (1912–1914). He retired one year prior to the formation of the **National Hockey League**. Moran built his house entirely from his hockey earnings at a cost of about $4,000. After retiring as a player, he was a faithful follower of the Quebec Aces Hockey Club. Moran was inducted into the **Hockey Hall of Fame** in 1958.

MORENZ, HOWARD WILLIAM "HOWIE," "STRATFORD STREAK". B. 21 September 1902, Mitchell, Ontario. D. 8 March 1937, Montreal, Quebec. Howie Morenz was a **Canadian** professional **ice** hockey player with several **nicknames**. Due to his speed and **puck** skills, he was called "Stratford Streak," "Canadiens Comet," and "Mitchell Meteor." Morenz played **center** for 14 seasons in the **National Hockey League (NHL)** with the **Montreal Canadiens** (1923–1934), **Chicago Black Hawks** (1934–1936, 1936–1937), and **New York Rangers** (1935–1936). He was one of the early stars of the NHL, and he a led the Canadiens in both **goals scored** and **points** for seven straight seasons. During his NHL career, Morenz won three **Stanley Cups** (1924, 1930, 1931) and scored the Stanley Cup winning goal in Montreal's 3–0 win over the Calgary Tigers on 25 March 1924.

Morenz was the first player in NHL history to die as a direct result of an on-ice incident during a **match**. On 28 January 1937, his Montreal Canadiens faced the Chicago Black Hawks at the **Montreal Forum**. In the game, Morenz was cleanly **checked** into the **boards** by Chicago player **Earl Seibert**, but when his leg hit the wooden boards it shattered in five separate sections above the ankle. He was carried off the ice and remained in the hospital for more than a month. Morenz died on 8 March 1937, from a heart attack, but his teammate, **Aurèle Joliat**, said it was from a "broken heart." Seibert felt very guilty.

While Morenz was in the hospital, plans for a benefit game for him were in progress, but the game was not as financially successful as **Ace Bailey**'s benefit game. The match included two **All-Star Teams**; The first was a team of stars from the Canadiens and **Montreal Maroons**, and the second was made up of players from the other teams, with the latter team winning, 6–5. Morenz became the first player to have his **jersey number** (7) retired by the Canadiens. He was inducted into the **Hockey Hall of Fame** in 1945, as one of the 12 original inductees. In 1950, the Canadian Press named him the best ice hockey player of the first half of the 20th century. During his NHL career,

Morenz played in 550 regular-season games and recorded 271 goals, 201 **assists**, and 472 points. His daughter, Marlene Morenz, married hockey player **Bernie Geoffrion**. Their son, Danny Morenz, and grandson, Blake, both played in the NHL, making a **family** with four generations of NHL hockey players. *See also* CAREER-ENDING INJURIES.

MOSIENKO, WILLIAM "BILL". B. 2 November 1921, Winnipeg, Manitoba. D. 9 July 1994, Winnipeg, Manitoba. Bill Mosienko played **right wing** for 14 seasons in the **National Hockey League (NHL)**, all with the **Chicago Black Hawks** (1941–1955). On 8 February 1942, he **scored** his first two NHL **goals** in 21 seconds in Chicago's 4–3 loss against the **New York Rangers**. From 1945–1948, Chicago had a quick, young **line** called the "Pony Line," with Bill and **brothers Doug Bentley** and **Max Bentley**. Mosienko finished among the top five in NHL goals (28) and **points** (54) in 1944–1945. He won the **Lady Byng Trophy** in 1945, due to his **penalty**-free season. Mosienko also played the entire 1947–1948 season without a penalty. He was one of the fastest **skaters** of his time. Mosienko became famous for scoring the fastest **hat trick** ever. With Gus Bodnar **assisting**, Mosienko scored three goals in 21 seconds in a single game in a 7–6 win against the Rangers on 23 March 1952. Although he was never part of a **Stanley Cup** championship team, he played in 711 regular-season NHL games and recorded 258 goals, 282 assists, and 540 points. After retiring from playing hockey, Mosienko **coached** the Winnipeg Warriors (1959–1961) of the World Hockey League. He was inducted into the **Hockey Hall of Fame** in 1965.

MOVIES. Sports like football, baseball, and boxing have had numerous movies made about them, but **ice** hockey movies are scarce. Seven worth mentioning include the lesser-known 1937 film *Idol of the Crowds*, with John Wayne, about a hockey player who retires to a chicken farm in Maine and then makes a comeback. Of the 147 movies Wayne made during his career, this was one of his worst, but hockey fans do have the opportunity to see a Hollywood legend **skate** around on the insides of his ankles and try to shoot the **puck**. The 1977 cult classic *Slap Shot*, with Paul Newman, has stood the test of time, as evidenced by fans who have the ability to recite it line by line. Newman plays Reggie Dunlop as the **coach** and player of the **minor league** Charlestown Chiefs during their final season in the Federal League. Newman once said that, "This is the raunchiest film I have ever done." Other memorable features of *Slap Shot* include the **Hanson Brothers**, the **fight** scenes, the well-done skating, and the mention of actual hockey players **Eddie Shore** and **Dit Clapper**. Rob Lowe and Patrick Swayze star in the 1986 hockey film *Youngblood*. Lowe plays a teenager from upstate New

York who is invited to try out for a **junior** team in Ontario. The hockey scenes are not convincing, but, due to the limited number of hockey movies, it is worth watching.

The 1992 *The Mighty Ducks* is a good family movie, and its success inspired The Walt Disney Company to form a new **National Hockey League** team, the **Mighty Ducks of Anaheim**, in 1993. Another family movie made was *MVP: Most Valuable Primate*, in 2000. After escaping from a research lab, Jack the chimpanzee plays hockey with a group of teenagers. Although it is a movie that features hockey, it is not worth watching. On the other hand, the 2004 film *Miracle* is worth watching more than once. Starring Kurt Russell as coach **Herb Brooks**, it depicts the victory by the **U.S. Men's Olympic Ice Hockey Team** over the **Soviet Union Men's Olympic Ice Hockey Team** at the 1980 **Olympic Games**. In *The Ultimate Book of Sports Movies* (2009), by Ray Didinger and Glen Macnow, *Miracle* is rated the 16th greatest sports movie of all time, and the motion picture had the best hockey scenes ever filmed. The 2005 movie *Rocket: The Legend of Maurice Richard* transports the viewer back into the classic hockey of the 1950s. Although it is a long film, it is worth taking the time to view due to the quality ice scenes and its depiction of how heroic Richard was to the French Canadiens. *See also* MUSIC.

MR. HOCKEY. *See* HOWE, GORDON "GORDIE," "MR. HOCKEY".

MULDOON, PETE. B. 1881, Ontario. D. 6 March 1929, Tacoma, Washington. Because the pursuit of a professional sports career was looked down upon at that time in Ontario, Pete Muldoon changed his given name of Linton Muldoon Treacy to Pete Muldoon. In the 1900s, he played **ice** hockey for the Ontario Hockey Association. A well rounded athlete, Muldoon won Pacific Coast regional titles in boxing in both the middleweight and light heavyweight divisions. He also played professional **lacrosse** in Vancouver in 1911. In 1914, he took over as the **coach** and manager of the Portland Rosebuds. He led them to the **Pacific Coast Hockey Association (PCHA)** championship, making Portland the first team from the **United States** to compete for the **Stanley Cup**. For the 1915–1916 season, Muldoon changed teams and went to Seattle to manage a new team in the PCHA, the Metropolitans. He spent eight seasons coaching in Seattle, and amassed a record of 115 wins, 105 losses, and four ties. With Muldoon, the Metropolitans played for the Stanley Cup three times and won it in 1917, when he was only 30 years old. But Muldoon is probably best known for putting a **curse** on the **National Hockey League (NHL) Chicago Black Hawks**. After coaching the Chicago team to third place during the 1926–1927 season, Muldoon was fired by owner Frederic McLaughlin. He was upset after being fired after only one season and was reported to have placed an Irish curse on the Hawks that would keep them out of first place forever. Whether it was true, or just a story created by sportswriter Jim Coleman, the Chicago Black Hawks endured a 41-year drought. At the time, finishing in first place was considered to be as much of an achievement as winning the Stanley Cup. Chicago did win the Stanley Cup in 1934, 1938, and 1961, but they did so without finishing in first place either in a multidivision or a single-league format. In 1967–1968, the last season of the six-team NHL, Chicago finished first, breaking the supposed Curse of Muldoon.

MULLEN, JOSEPH PATRICK "JOE," "SLIPPERY ROCK JOE". B. 26 February 1957, New York, New York. As a **young player**, Joe Mullen played **roller hockey** in his neighborhood streets, and he went on to play **college hockey** at Boston College. Professionally, he played **ice** hockey for 17 seasons in the **National Hockey League (NHL)** as a **right wing** with the **St. Louis Blues** (1980–1986), **Calgary Flames** (1986–1990), **Pittsburgh Penguins** (1990–1995, 1996–1997), and **Boston Bruins** (1995–1996). Mullen led the **Stanley Cup Playoffs** in **goals** in 1985–1986 (12) and 1988–1989 (16). He won three **Stanley Cups**, in 1989 with Calgary, and in 1991 and 1992 with Pittsburgh. Mullen was the first American-born and trained player to record 500 goals and 1,000 **points**. The **nickname** "Slippery Rock Joe" was in reference to his agility and toughness on the ice. Internationally, Mullen played for the **United States** in the 1979 and 1999 **World Ice Hockey Championships**, as well as the 1984, 1987, and 1991 **Canada Cups**. His **brother**, Brian Mullen, also played in the NHL, and his son, Patrick Mullen, signed with the **Los Angeles Kings**. Joe received the **Lady Byng Trophy** in 1987 and 1989, and the **Lester Patrick Trophy** in 1995. In 2000, he was inducted into the **Hockey Hall of Fame**.

MURPHY, LAWRENCE THOMAS "LARRY". B. 8 March 1961, Scarborough, Ontario. Larry Murphy played **ice** hockey for 21 seasons in the **National Hockey League (NHL)** as a **defenseman** with the **Los Angeles Kings** (1980–1983), **Washington Capitals** (1983–1989), Minnesota North Stars (1989–1990), **Pittsburgh Penguins** (1990–1995), **Toronto Maple Leafs** (1995–1997), and **Detroit Red Wings** (1997–2001). He won four **Stanley Cups**, in 1991 and 1992 with Pittsburgh, and in 1997 and 1998 with Detroit. While with the Penguins, Murphy would often dump the **puck** down the ice by lifting it high over the opposing team so that it eventually stopped before the opposing **goal line**. Not only would it clear the zone safely, but **icing** was not called. Broadcasters called it the "Murphy Dump." Murphy was also a powerful ice partner with Ulf Samuelsson in Pittsburgh and **Nicklas Lidström** in Detroit. Murphy holds the NHL record for most **points** by a

rookie defenseman, with 76 (1980–1981), and the record for most **assists** by a defenseman in the Stanley Cup Finals, with 9 (1990–1991). His NHL career totals include 287 goals and 929 assists for 1,216 points through 1,615 regular-season games. In 215 **Stanley Cup Playoff** games, he added 37 goals and 115 assists for 152 points. Internationally, Murphy played for **Canada** in the 1985, 1987, and 2000 **World Ice Hockey Championships** and the 1987 and 1991 **Canada Cups**. In 2004, he was inducted into the **Hockey Hall of Fame**. Murphy is currently a commentator for the Detroit Red Wings.

MURŠAK, JAN. B. 20 January 1988, Maribor, Yugoslavia. Jan Muršak is a current forward with the **Detroit Red Wings**. In 2007, he signed a contract with the Wings but did not make his **National Hockey League (NHL)** debut until 28 December 2010, in a game against the **Colorado Avalanche**. Muršak became the second Slovenian, after **Anže Kopitar** of the **Los Angeles Kings**, to play in the NHL. He **scored** his first NHL **goal** on 10 January 2011, also in a game against the Avalanche against Peter Budaj. In February 2011, Muršak signed a new two-year contract with Detroit. To date, he has played in 44 games and recorded two goals, two **assists**, and four **points**.

MUSIC. Many teams have favorite music for their practices or warm-ups, but there are also a few songs written specifically about hockey. The theme song of *Hockey Night in Canada* from 1968–2008 was "The Hockey Theme," which some people have called the second national anthem of Canada. In 2008, CBC lost their rights to the song, and it was replaced by the contest-winning "Canadian Gold." In 1963, Big Bob and The Dollars recorded "**Gordie Howe** Is the Greatest of Them All." In 1964, **Frank Mahovlich** made a promotional record for Ford Mercury of Canada called *All My Hockey Secrets*, in which he teaches listeners about the basics of hockey. During the 1966–1967 season, **Eddie Shack scored** his career-high 26 **goals** on the **Toronto Maple Leafs'** line, with Ron Ellis and **Bob Pulford**, and his popularity inspired a novelty song called "Clear the Track, Here Comes Shack," written in his honor and played by Douglas Rankine with the Secrets. It lasted three months on the Canadian pop charts and even hit number one. **Dave Schultz** sang a local Philadelphia hit song called "The **Penalty Box**" in the mid-1970s. In 1979, **Guy Lafleur** released an album called *Lafleur*. The album consisted of Lafleur reciting hockey instructions, accompanied by disco music. A country song, "The **Darryl Sittler** Song," commemorating Sittler's 60th birthday, was written by Vancouver songwriters Dan Swinimer and Jeff Johnson. The song "Double Vision," by Foreigner, was inspired by **goaltender John Davidson** of the **New York Rangers** after he was shaken up when a **puck** hit his goalie mask. *See also* MOVIES.

MYSHKIN, VLADIMIR SEMENOVICH. B. 19 June 1955, Kirovo-Che-petsk, Soviet Union. Vladimir Myshkin was a **Russian ice** hockey **goaltender** who was a back-up to **Vladislav Tretiak**. He replaced Tretiak after the first period in the famous **"Miracle on Ice"** game versus the **United States** in the medal round of the 1980 **Olympic Games**. Myshkin faced and stopped both shots in the second period, but he gave up two **goals** in the third period. Americans **Mark Johnson** and **Mike Eruzione** each **scored** a goal and helped the United States win the game, 4–3. In 1981, Myshkin was a member of the Soviet team that won the **Canada Cup**. In 1984, he acted as back-up for Tretiak for the final time and won an Olympic gold medal. After Tretiak retired, Myshkin was the starting goalie for the 1984 Canada Cup, and he led the Soviets to a perfect 5–0 record in the round robin but was defeated by **Canada**, 3–2, in **overtime** in the semifinals. Although the Soviets lost, Myshkin played well, and was named player of the game for his team. At the **World Ice Hockey Championships**, he helped his team win a bronze medal (1985) and gold medal (1986). Myshkin had a successful final season, in which he won the Soviet League championship for the only time in his career. After watching his team's first nine **matches**, he was also given the start in the last game at the 1990 World Ice Hockey Championships. Myshkin finished his career by shutting out Czechoslovakia, 5–0, and winning the gold medal.

N

NANNE, LOUIS VINCENT "LOU". B. 2 June 1941, Sault Ste. Marie, Ontario. Lou Nanne played hockey with **brothers Phil Espositio** and **Tony Esposito** in Ontario. Then, in 1960, he played at the University of Minnesota while studying business. While there, he was **coached** by John Mariucci, and Nanne became one of the biggest stars in U.S. **college hockey** during the 1960s. In 1967, he became a U.S. citizen, which allowed him to play for and captain the 1968 **U.S. Men's Olympic Ice Hockey Team**, alongside future **"Miracle on Ice"** coach **Herb Brooks**. Nanne went on to become a **defenseman** and **right wing** in the **National Hockey League (NHL)**, where he played 635 games for the Minnesota North Stars (1968–1978). He was known for being a good **penalty killer** and playmaker. Of his 225 career **points**, 157 were **assists**. He often partnered with Murray Oliver and **Dean Prentice**. In 1970–1971, Nanne scored nine points in 12 games as the North Stars extended the eventual **Stanley Cup** champion **Montreal Canadiens** to six games in the semifinals. He was a member of the team that finished fourth at the 1976 **World Ice Hockey Championships**, and, a few months later, he played on Team USA at the inaugural **Canada Cup**. Nanne also played in the 1977 World Ice Hockey Championships and suited up for 26 games during the 1977–1978 NHL season before retiring as a player.

After his retiring, Nanne became the general manager and coach of the North Stars, as well as the Canada Cup entries for the **United States**. He rebuilt the North Stars and led them to the Stanley Cup Finals in 1981 and the semifinals in 1984. He led the team to the Stanley Cup **Playoffs** seven consecutive seasons (1979–1980, 1985–1986). This winning run saw the North Stars average more than 35 wins per season and encompassed the team's sole 40-win season and six of the organization's 10 seasons of 35-plus wins. As coach, Nanne had **superstitions**, which included wearing the same clothes to keep a winning streak going and moving his seat from the press box to find a new seat if the team was losing a game. He was also the general manager of the U.S. team in the 1981 and 1984 Canada Cup tournaments. In 1988,

Nanne resigned from the North Stars. In 1989, he received the **Lester Patrick Trophy**. He was inducted into the **U.S. Hockey Hall of Fame** (1998) and **International Ice Hockey Federation Hall of Fame** (2004) as a player.

NASHVILLE PREDATORS. The Nashville Predators are a professional **ice** hockey team in the **Central Division** of the **National Hockey League (NHL) Western Conference**. Based in Nashville, Tennessee, they made their NHL debut during the 1998–1999 season. A highlight of the 2001–2002 season for the Predators was recording their 100th victory as a franchise, on 6 December 2001. With that win, Nashville became the second-fastest expansion team of the 1990s to reach the 100-win plateau. In 2002–2003, **Coach Barry Trotz** broke the record for most games coached (392) by the original coach of an expansion team. He is their current coach. When Blake Geoffrion made his debut with the Predators (2010–2011), he became the NHL's first fourth-generation player. His paternal grandmother's father was **Hall of Famer Howie Morenz**, and his paternal grandfather was **Bernie Geoffrion**. Blake's father, Dan Geoffrion, played three NHL seasons with the **Montreal Canadiens** and **Winnipeg Jets**. Some of the top **scorers** for the Nashville Predators include Jason Arnott, Patric Hornqvist, Paul Kariya, and Steve Sullivan. **Jordin Tootoo** is a current Nashville **right wing**. Nashville fans have modified the **octopus** tradition of the **Detroit Red Wings** and throw catfish onto the ice to show their support. Although they have not won a **Stanley Cup**, the Predators did make it to the semifinals in 2011. In 13 seasons in the NHL, from 1998–1999 to 2011–2012, the Nashville Predators have compiled a record of 503-424-60-79 (1,145 **points**), including 7 **Stanley Cup Playoff** appearances. They were defeated in 2012 by the **Phoenix Coyotes**, 4–1, in the Western Conference Semifinals.

NATIONAL COLLEGIATE ATHLETIC ASSOCIATION (NCAA). The National Collegiate Athletic Association (NCAA) is an association of more than 1,000 institutions, conferences, organizations, and individuals responsible for organizing the athletic programs of many colleges and universities in the **United States** and **Canada**. Since 1973, the colleges have been divided into Division I, Division II, and Division III schools, generally based on size. Division I and Division II schools can offer scholarships to athletes for playing a sport, while Division III schools may not. The NCAA sponsors both the National Collegiate Men's Ice Hockey Championship and National Collegiate Women's Ice Hockey Championship. The semifinals and finals of the Division I championship are called the "Frozen Four," similar to basketball's "Final Four." The most championships by state include Michigan, Massachusetts, Colorado, North Dakota, and Minnesota (for men's **ice** hockey), and Minnesota and Wisconsin (for **women's ice hockey**).

NATIONAL HOCKEY ASSOCIATION (NHA). The National Hockey Association (NHA) was formed in 1909, and a few years later the association became rivals with the **Pacific Coast Hockey Association**. **Frank Calder** was the league's first secretary. Early teams included the Cobalt Silver Kings, Haileybury Comets, **Montreal Canadiens**, Montreal Shamrocks, **Montreal Wanderers**, **Ottawa Senators**, and Renfrew Creamery Kings. The Montreal Wanderers won the 1910 **Stanley Cup**. The **Quebec Bulldogs** and Toronto Blueshirts also joined the NHA. The league changed the sport from seven-man teams to six-man teams by eliminating the **rover** position. In 1912, the NHA put **jersey numbers** on their players. The **goaltender** was number 1, the **defensemen** were 2 and 3, the **center** was 4, and the **wings** were 5 and 6. Replacement players were assigned 7, 8, and 9. This made it easier for the **referees** to identify players when calling fouls. World War I disrupted the entire hockey establishment, and the NHA folded in 1917. This hockey organization was the precursor to the **National Hockey League**.

NATIONAL HOCKEY LEAGUE (NHL). After the **National Hockey Association** folded in 1917, it was replaced with the National Hockey League (NHL). **Frank Calder** was the league's first president. The NHL has the distinction of being the oldest professional major hockey league in existence. The league began with four teams, the **Montreal Canadiens; Montreal Wanderers; Ottawa Senators**; and former Toronto Blueshirts, renamed the Toronto Arenas. During the 1919–1920 season, the Arenas were renamed the Toronto St. Patricks. In 1927–1928, the team chose their final name, the **Toronto Maple Leafs**. The Canadiens and Maple Leafs are the two oldest NHL teams currently playing. In 1924, the league added the **Boston Bruins** as their first American team. Several teams were short-lived, like the **Hamilton Tigers**, and others had several name changes or location changes, for example, the California Seals. Six teams have consistently played in the NHL over the years. The **"Original Six"** include the Boston Bruins, **Chicago Black Hawks**, **Detroit Red Wings**, the Montreal Canadiens, **New York Rangers**, and Toronto Maple Leafs. These teams continue to play in the NHL today. The history of the NHL is usually described according to the following four eras: the Founding Era (1917–1942), "Original Six" Era (1942–1967), Expansion Era (1967–1992), and Modern Era (1992–present). There are currently 30 NHL franchises, seven in **Canada** and 23 in the **United States**. **Gary Bettman** is the current NHL commissioner. *See also* APPENDIX A for the NHL franchise movement.

NATIONAL HOCKEY LEAGUE OFFICIAL RULES. The **National Hockey League (NHL)** outlines the rules of **ice** hockey in their annual publication, *NHL Official Rules*. These rules address the **equipment** allowed,

rink dimensions, various **penalties**, and any new rules added. It also includes a list of current **on-ice officials** and the season's team schedules. Since the start of the NHL in 1917, the rules have evolved as the game has changed. For example, a bylaw was added stating that players who are blind in one or both eyes are ineligible to play. This rule was named for Frank Trushinski, a **minor-league** hockey player who lost his sight in one eye in a game in 1921, but was allowed to continue playing. In a later game, he suffered a **head injury** that cost him most of the sight in his other eye.

NEDVĚD, PETR. B. 9 December 1971, Liberec, Czechoslovakia. Petr Nedvěd defected to **Canada** and played one hockey season (1989–1990) for the Seattle Thunderbirds of the Western Hockey League before joining the **National Hockey League (NHL)**. He was a forward for a total of 15 NHL seasons, from 1990–2007. He played with the **Vancouver Canucks, St. Louis Blues, New York Rangers, Pittsburgh Penguins, Edmonton Oilers, Phoenix Coyotes**, and **Philadelphia Flyers**. Several contract disputes were responsible for his numerous trades. Nedvěd had his best season with Pittsburgh, when he recorded 45 **goals** and 99 **points**. He helped the Penguins reach the **Eastern Conference** Finals by scoring 20 points in the **Stanley Cup Playoffs**. One highlight was his goal against the **Washington Capitals** in a quadruple-**overtime match**. Nedvěd **scored** the winning goal at 79:15 of overtime in the longest NHL game in 60 years. In 2000–2001, with the Rangers, he had his second-best season and scored 32 goals and 78 points. Nedvěd played with Jan Hlaváč and Radek Dvořák, and the media **nicknamed** them the "Czech Mates." Internationally, Nedvěd played for **Canada** and won a silver medal at the 1994 **Olympic Games**. He played for the **Czech Republic** in the 1996 **World Cup of Hockey**. At the age of 40, he joined the Czech Republic national team at the 2012 **World Ice Hockey Championships**, hosted by **Finland** and **Sweden**. On 10 May 2012, Nedvěd scored the game-winning goal against Latvia, making him the oldest Czech Republic player to accomplish that feat. He was 40 years, six months, and one day old.

NEELY, CAMERON MICHAEL "CAM," "BAM-BAM-CAM". B. 6 June 1965, Comox, British Columbia. Cam Neely was a **right wing** in the **National Hockey League (NHL)** with the **Vancouver Canucks** (1983–1986) and **Boston Bruins** (1986–1996). He **scored** 72 **points** in his first season with Boston. Neely played a physical game and was a good fit for the Bruins. He was equally effective at body **checking** and **scoring**. As a power forward, he earned the **nickname** "Bam-Bam Cam." Neely's career was cut short due to numerous **injuries** and a medical condition where muscle turns to bone. He played only 22 games during two seasons, from

1991–1993. With intensive rehabilitation, he came back and scored 50 **goals** in the 1993–1994 season. In recognition for his determination, Neely won the **Bill Masterton Memorial Trophy** in 1994. During his 13-season NHL career, he played in 726 regular-season games and recorded 395 goals, 299 **assists**, 694 points, and 1,241 **penalty minutes**. In 2005, Neely was inducted into the **Hockey Hall of Fame**. He was the vice president of the Boston Bruins in 2007, and then president in 2010. In 2010, he received the **Lester Patrick Trophy**. In 2011, his Bruins beat the **Vancouver Canucks**, 4–0, to win the sixth **Stanley Cup** in franchise history and Neely's first. Neely has appeared as a hockey-playing fireman in the television show *Rescue Me*, with his friend, Denis Leary.

NET. In hockey, a nylon mesh net hangs over the back of the **goal**, and a canvas strap is attached around the bottom of the net to protect it from being cut by **skate** blades. Rubber pegs connect the bottom front corners of the goal net to the **ice**. If the net pops out of the peg holders, the **referee** blows his whistle and the play is stopped. Standard regulation size for **National Hockey League** nets is 6 feet wide by 4 feet tall. The **goaltender** is responsible for protecting his net and not allowing the **puck** to enter it.

NETMINDER. *See* GOALTENDER.

NEW ENGLAND WHALERS. *See* CAROLINA HURRICANES.

NEW JERSEY DEVILS. The New Jersey Devils are a professional **ice** hockey team in the **Atlantic Division** of the **National Hockey League (NHL) Eastern Conference**. The team began in 1974, as an expansion team named the Kansas City Scouts (1974–1976). The Scouts were renamed the **Colorado Rockies** and relocated to Denver, Colorado (1976–1982). In 1982, the franchise moved to East Rutherford, New Jersey, and renamed the New Jersey Devils. In its NHL history, the team has made the **Stanley Cup** Finals 5 times. They lost to the **Colorado Avalanche** in 2001 (4–3), and the **Los Angeles Kings** in 2012 (4–2). The Devils won the Stanley Cup in 1995, by defeating the **Detroit Red Wings** (4–0); in 2000, by defeating the **Dallas Stars** (4–0); and, in 2003, by defeating the Mighty Ducks of Anaheim (4–3). Among the best players for the Devils have been **Hockey Hall of Famers Viacheslav Fetisov, Doug Gilmour, Igor Larionov, Joe Nieuwendyk, Peter Stastny**, and Scott Stevens. **Coaches** for the New Jersey franchise include **Herb Brooks** (1992–1993), **Jacques Lemaire** (1993–1998, 2009–2010, 2011), **Larry Robinson** (2000–2002, 2005), and Brent Sutter (2007–2009). In 37 seasons in the NHL (1974–1975 to 2011–2012), the Devils have compiled a record of 1,260-1,313-328-67 (2,915 **points**) and made 22 **Stanley Cup Playoff** appearances. In his first year as coach of the Devils, Peter DeBoer helped them have a successful season. Although they rallied after losing the first three games, the Devils were defeated by the Los Angeles Kings during the 2012 Stanley Cup Finals (4–2). Current players for the team include Steve Bernier, **goaltender Martin Brodeur**, Ryan Carter, Stephen Gionata, Adam Henrique, Ilya Kovalchuk, captain Zach Parise, and **center** Travis Zajac.

NEW YORK AMERICANS. In 1925, **Bill Dwyer** bought the **Hamilton Tigers** (formerly the **Quebec Bulldogs**) and brought them to New York. They were **nicknamed** the "Star Spangled Skaters" and made their debut at the newly created **Madison Square Garden**, on 15 December 1925. **Shorty Green scored** the first **goal**, but the **Montreal Canadiens** won, 3–1. **Roy Worters** was the **goaltender** for the Americans from 1928–1937. They changed their team name to the Brooklyn Americans in 1942, but the new name didn't help, and the team folded after the 1941–1942 season. They never won the **Stanley Cup**. In 17 seasons in the NHL (1925–1942), the Americans compiled a record of 255-402-127-0 (637 **points**) and made five **Stanley Cup Playoff** appearances.

NEW YORK ISLANDERS. The New York Islanders are a professional **ice** hockey team in the **Atlantic Division** of the **National Hockey League (NHL) Eastern Conference**. When the franchise joined the NHL in 1972, New York fans had a new team to cheer for, in addition to their **New York Rangers**. During their first season, the inexperienced team posted one of the worst records in NHL history (12-60-6). With **goaltender Billy Smith**, **Clark Gillies**, and **Denis Potvin**, the Islanders started improving. During the 1975–1976 season, the four-year-old team had its first of four consecutive seasons with 100 **points**. With Bill Torrey as their general manager, the team had 14 consecutive winning seasons (1974–1975 to 1987–1988). Although they had winning seasons, the Islanders played poorly during the **Stanley Cup Playoffs**. **Coach Al Arbour** changed his strategy and had the players focus on the postseason. This was successful. With a **line** of **Mike Bossy**, **Bryan Trottier**, and Clark Gillies, the New York Islanders dominated the early 1980s.

The Islanders became the first franchise based in the **United States** to win four consecutive **Stanley Cups** (1980–1983). They defeated the **Philadelphia Flyers** (4–2), Minnesota North Stars (4–1), **Vancouver Canucks** (4–0), and **Edmonton Oilers** (4–0). The Islanders' Stanley Cup streak ended in 1984, when they lost to the next hockey dynasty, the Edmonton Oilers. Unfortunately, the Islanders have not made a strong comeback, although they have tried. Their strongest recent showing was when they advanced to the

2007 Eastern Conference Quarterfinals, but they lost to the **Buffalo Sabres**. In 39 seasons (1972–1973 to 2011–2012), the New York Islanders had a career record of 1,347-1,345-347-85 (3,126 points), with 21 playoff appearances and four Stanley Cups. The hockey **superstition** about growing playoff beards was started in the 1980s by the Islanders.

NEW YORK RANGERS. The New York Rangers are a professional **ice** hockey team in the **Atlantic Division** of the **National Hockey League (NIIL) Eastern Conference**. The Rangers are one of the oldest teams in the NHL, having joined in 1926, as an expansion franchise. Home games are played at the famous **Madison Square Garden**. They were one of the **"Original Six"** teams, a term used to describe the teams that made up the NHL from 1942 until the 1967 expansion. Unlike other long-standing franchises, this New York team has not been part of a dynasty. The Rangers have won four **Stanley Cups** in a sporadic manner (1928, 1933, 1940, 1994). Their most recent win in 1994 was accomplished after they defeated the **Vancouver Canucks** in seven games. Some **coaches** for the New York Rangers have included **Frank Boucher, Herb Brooks, Lester Patrick,** and **Fred Shero**. Earlier Rangers' players who have been inducted into the **Hockey Hall of Fame** include **Andy Bathgate, Doug Bentley, Max Bentley, Frank Boucher, Johnny Bower, Bill Cook, Bun Cook, Bernie Geoffrion, Eddie Giacomin, Ching Johnson,** and **Gump Worsley. Phil Esposito, Wayne Gretzky, Jari Kurri, Guy Lafleur, Mark Messier,** and **Luc Robitaille** played more recently for this organization. The Rangers won the **Presidents' Trophy** twice (1992, 1994) and the **Prince of Wales Trophy** three times (1932, 1942, 1994). In 85 seasons in the NIIL (1926–1927 to 2011–2012), the Rangers have compiled a record of 2,535-2,464-808-87 (5,965 **points**) and made 54 **Stanley Cup Playoff** appearances. They were defeated by the **New Jersey Devils** in the 2012 Eastern Conference Finals. John Tortella is the franchise's current coach. Several current players with the New York Rangers are Ryan Callahan, **Marián Gáborík**, Dan Giradi, **goaltender Henrik Lundqvist,** and Brad Richards. **Sean Avery** recently retired from the Rangers.

NICKNAMES. Throughout the years, many hockey players have been known by their nicknames. Some have been called animal names: "Camile the Eel" (Camille Henry), "Eddie the Eagle" (**Ed Belfour**), "Jake the Snake" (**Jacques Plante**), "Mouse" (**Stan Mikita**), "Rat" (**Harry Westwick**), "Shrimp" (**Roy Worters**), and "Turk" (**Walter Broda**). Other nicknames have described playing styles: "Boom Boom" (**Bernie Geoffrion**), "The China Wall" (**Johnny Bower**), "The Golden Jet" (**Bobby Hull**), "The Great One" (**Wayne Gretzky**), "Mr. Hockey" (**Gordie Howe**), "Mr. Zero" (**Frank**

Brimsek), "Old Lamplighter" (**Hector Blake**), "Old Poison" (**Nels Stewart**), "Pocket Rocket" (**Henri Richard**), "The Rocket" (**Maurice Richard**), and "The Russian Rocket" (**Pavel Bure**). Hector Blake was also nicknamed "Toe" by a family member. Other interesting player names include **Sid "Old Bootnose" Abel, Aubrey "Dit" Clapper, Clarence "Happy" Day, George "Punch" Imlach, Ivan "Ching" Johnson, Harry "Apple Cheeks" Lumley,** Edwin "The Tourist" McGregor, **Georges "The Chicoutimi Cucumber" Vezina,** and **Lorne "Gump" Worsley.**

NIEDERMAYER, SCOTT. B. 31 August 1973, Edmonton, Alberta. From 1989–1992, Scott Niedermayer was a **defenseman** with the Kamloops Blazers of the Western Hockey League. He then played a total of 18 seasons in the **National Hockey League (NHL)** with the **New Jersey Devils** (1991–2004), Mighty Ducks of Anaheim (2005–2006), and **Anaheim Ducks** (2006–2010). He won both the **James Norris Memorial Trophy** (2004) and the **Conn Smythe Trophy** (2007). In 2003–2004, he had his second 50-**point** season, with 14 **goals** and 40 **assists.** Niedermayer played with the Devils against his younger **brother,** Rob Niedermayer, of Anaheim, in the 2003 **Stanley Cup** Finals. He then joined the Ducks, and the two men played together in the 2007 finals. Together they helped Anaheim defeat the **Ottawa Senators** (4–1) to win the team's first and only Stanley Cup. During his NHL career, Scott played in 1,263 regular-season games and recorded 172 goals, 568 assists, 740 points, and 784 **penalty minutes.** He is the only hockey player to win every major North American and international championship in his career. He won the World Junior Championship (1991), Memorial Cup (1992), **World Ice Hockey Championships** (2004), two Winter Olympic gold medals (2002, 2010), four Stanley Cups (1995, 2000, 2003, 2007), and the **World Cup of Hockey** (2004).

NIEUWENDYK, JOSEPH "JOE". B. 10 September 1966, Oshawa, Ontario. Joe Nieuwendyk led the Whitby Warriors to the 1984 Minto Cup national junior championship in box **lacrosse.** He went on to play **college hockey** at Cornell University. In 81 **matches** with Cornell, Nieuwendyk **scored** 73 **goals** and 151 **points**, both among the highest totals in the school's history. His **jersey number** (25) was retired by Cornell, just like **Ken Dryden**'s number 1. Nieuwendyk was a **center** in the **National Hockey League (NHL)** with the **Calgary Flames** (1986–1995), **Dallas Stars** (1995–2002), **New Jersey Devils** (2001–2003), **Toronto Maple Leafs** (2003–2004), and **Florida Panthers** (2005–2007). During his NHL **rookie** season, he scored 51 goals, including 31 **power play** goals and eight game-winning goals. Maybe his **superstition** of eating two pieces of peanut butter toast before each game helped him. Nieuwendyk was known for his aggressive style of play and great passing skills. Besides three **Stanley Cup** championships (1989, 1999, 2003), he won the **Calder Memorial Trophy** (1988), **King Clancy Memorial Trophy** (1995), and **Conn Smythe Trophy** (1999). Internationally, he represented **Canada** at the 1990 **World Ice Hockey Championships** and 1998 and 2002 **Olympic Games**. The Canadian team won the gold medal in 2002. During his career, Nieuwendyk tallied 564 goals, 562 **assists**, 1,126 points, and 677 **penalty minutes** in 1,257 regular-season games. In the **Stanley Cup Playoffs**, he added 66 goals and 50 assists for 116 points in 158 games. Nieuwendyk retired from playing during the 2006–2007 season, due to chronic back pain. He then worked in management with the Florida Panthers, Toronto Maple Leafs, and Dallas Stars. Nieuwendyk was inducted into the **Hockey Hall of Fame** in 2011.

NIGHBOR, JULIUS FRANCIS "FRANK," "DUTCH," "THE PEMBROKE PEACH". B. 1893, Pembroke, Ontario. D. 13 April 1966, Pembroke, Ontario. Frank Nighbor was a **center** for 18 professional hockey seasons from 1912–1930. He started with the Toronto Blueshirts (1912–1913) of the **National Hockey Association (NHA)** and then joined the **Vancouver Millionaires** (1913–1915) of the **Pacific Coast Hockey Association**. It was with Vancouver that Nighbor won his first **Stanley Cup** (1915). He joined the **Ottawa Senators** in 1915, where he remained until 1930. Nighbor helped the Senators win the Stanley Cup in 1920, 1921, 1923, and 1927. He led the NHA in **goals** (41) and **points** (51) in 1916–1917, and in **assists** in 1919–1920 (15) and 1925–1926 (13). The **nickname** "The Pembroke Peach" came from his sweet and smooth style of play, and "Dutch" was short for "The Flying Dutchman." He was known for popularizing the sweep **check** (also known as the poke check), as well as for his stickhandling skills and excellent all-around playing.

In 1924, Nighbor was the Most Valuable Player in the **National Hockey League (NHL)**, and he received the first **Hart Trophy**. He was also known as a gentleman and was the first recipient of the **Lady Byng Trophy** in 1925, which he also won in 1926. Unfortunately, not everyone was a clean player, and Frank suffered a broken arm in a 1922 **match** with **Sprague Cleghorn**. During that same game, Cleghorn gave **Eddie Gerard** a **head injury** and damaged **Cy Denneny**'s leg. He finished his career playing one season with the NHL **Toronto Maple Leafs** (1929–1930). During a career of 438 regular-season games, he had 257 goals, 125 assists, and a total of 382 points. In 1947, Nighbor was inducted into the **Hockey Hall of Fame**.

NINETY-NINE, 99. This number ninety-nine (99) was the **jersey number** worn by **Wayne Gretzky** and, as a sign of respect and in tribute to him, it can no longer be worn by any other player in the **National Hockey League**

(NHL). Gretzky chose 99 in honor of his favorite player, **Gordie Howie**, who wore number 9. The number 9 is the number most often retired by individual teams, but 99 is the only number retired by the entire NHL. The number is synonymous with Gretzky, but other NHL players who wore 99 include Leo Bourgault, Rick Dudley, Joe Lamb, Wilf Paiement, and Des Roche.

NOBLE, EDWARD REGINALD "REG". B. 23 June 1896, Collingwood, Ontario. D. 19 January 1962, Alliston, Ontario. During his 17 professional hockey seasons (1916–1933), Reg Noble was a **left wing, center**, and **defenseman**. He was a tough player and great stickhandler. He played for all three teams in the history of the Detroit franchise: the Detroit Cougars (1927–1930), Detroit Falcons (1930–1932), and **Detroit Red Wings** (1932–1933). Noble led the **National Hockey League (NHL)** in **assists** in 1917–1918 (10), and he was in the top five for 1922–1923 (11) and 1925–1926 (9). Noble was the NHL leader in **penalty minutes**, with 79 (1923–1924). He won the **Stanley Cup** with the Toronto Arenas (1918), Toronto St. Patricks (1922) and **Montreal Maroons** (1926). During a **match** with the **Ottawa Senators** during the 1925–1926 season, Noble suffered a fractured skull after **Hooley Smith** clipped him with his **hockey stick**. Noble only missed four games after the **injury**. After retiring, he worked as an NHL **referee** (1937–1939). Noble was inducted into the **Hockey Hall of Fame** in 1962. His niece, Gayle Noble, was a college soccer star at McGill University.

NORTHEAST DIVISION. In 1993, the **National Hockey League (NHL)** renamed the conferences and divisions to reflect their geographic locations. In the NHL, the Northeast Division is one of the three sections of the **Eastern Conference**. The **Atlantic Division** and **Southeast Division** are the other two.

NORTHWEST DIVISION. In 1993, the **National Hockey League (NHL)** renamed the conferences and divisions to reflect their geographic locations. In the NHL, the Northwest Division is one of the three sections of the **Western Conference**. The **Central Division** and **Pacific Division** are the other two.

NORWAY. In 1935, Norway became a member of the **International Ice Hockey Federation (IIHF)**. At the 1951 **World Ice Hockey Championships**, Norway defeated the **United States** and **Great Britain** to finish fourth overall, their best finish since. Norway then competed in its first **Olympic** tournament, as the host nation of the 1952 Olympic Games. In 1953, Norway also became the first Western nation to play the Soviet Union. They have had sporadic participation at the Olympics (1952, 1964–1972, 1980–1994, 2010). Their highest finish was in 1972, with eighth place. The men's team currently has a ninth-place ranking by the IIHF, and the women's team has a 12th-place ranking. There have been seven **National Hockey League** players born in Norway. Two recent players include **Colorado Avalanche defenseman** Jonas Holos and **New York Rangers right wing** Mats Zuccarello.

O

O'CONNOR, HERBERT WILLIAM "BUDDY". B. 21 June 1916, Montreal, Quebec. D. 24 August 1977, Montreal, Quebec. Buddy O'Connor was a **center** for 10 seasons in the **National Hockey League (NHL)** with the **Montreal Canadiens** (1941–1947) and **New York Rangers** (1947–1951). He was part of the Montreal Royals' **line**, with Pete Morin and Gerry Heffernan, who then all joined the Canadiens. They were **nicknamed** the "Razzle Dazzle Line" because of their great speed and passing plays, which often rendered opponents lost in confusion. Their first season with the Canadiens, they combined for 67 **points** in just 48 games. O'Connor won the **Stanley Cup** in 1944 and 1946. He was the first player to win both the Hart Trophy and **Lady Byng Trophy** in the same year (1948). During his NHL career, O'Connor played in 509 games and **scored** 140 **goals**, 257 **assists**, and 397 total points. In 1988, he was inducted into the **Hockey Hall of Fame.**

O'REE, WILLIAM ELDON "WILLIE". B. 15 October 1935, Fredericton, New Brunswick. Despite an **injury** as a **junior** that left him blind in one eye, O'Ree had an **ice** hockey career that spanned three decades (1951–1979). He began with the Fredericton Merchants and ended with the San Diego Hawks. Then, on 18 January 1958, O'Ree became the first black player to play in the **National Hockey League (NHL)** when he played **right wing** for the **Boston Bruins** in a 3–0 win over the **Montreal Canadiens**. He only played two games that season before returning to the **minor league**. The Bruins gave him another chance during the 1960–1961 season, and the fast-skating O'Ree played in 43 more games. He had four **goals**, 10 **assists**, and 26 **penalty minutes**. He faced a lot of discrimination, and players taunted him, but since O'Ree didn't back down, he spent time in the **penalty box** for **fighting**. After breaking the color barrier, he was often referred to as the "Jackie Robinson of Hockey." After O'Ree, there were no other black players in the NHL until 1974, when **Canadian** player Mike Marson was drafted by the **Washington Capitals**. In 2000, O'Ree published *The Autobiography of Willie O'Ree: Hockey's Black Pioneer*. In 2003, for his hockey contributions, he received the **Lester Patrick Trophy**. As the NHL's director of youth development and ambassador for NHL Diversity, O'Ree is currently working on developing a **Jamaican** ice hockey team to participate in the 2014 Winter Olympics.

OAKLAND SEALS. *See* MINNESOTA WILD.

OATES, ADAM. B. 27 August 1962, Weston, Ontario. While pursuing his degree in management at Rensselaer Polytechnic Institute, Adam Oates was the leading **scorer** for the schools' 1985 **National Collegiate Athletic Association** Division I championship team. He also played professional **lacrosse** but retired to pursue his professional **ice** hockey career. Oates holds the distinction of having most career **points** of any collegian (216) to go on to play in the **National Hockey League (NHL)**. He holds the sixth-place record for NHL career **assists**, with 1,079, when he was with the **Washington Capitals**. At the age of 39, he was the oldest player to lead the NHL in assists in a single season (64) in 2001–2002. Oates was a clean player, and, as a result, he was a finalist for the **Lady Byng Trophy** six times. His NHL career spanned from 1984–2004, with two losing trips to the **Stanley Cup** Finals. In 2002–2003, his team, the Mighty Ducks of Anaheim, were beaten by the **New Jersey Devils** in seven games. Ironically, Oates is currently an assistant **coach** with the Devils. He was inducted into the **Hockey Hall of Fame** in 2012.

OCTOPUS. Fans of the **Detroit Red Wings** have an odd way of celebrating **goals**. The tradition of tossing an octopus on the **ice** began in the 1950s, when there were only two rounds of **Stanley Cup Playoffs**. A team that won back-to-back series, a total of eight games, won the **Stanley Cup**. During the playoffs, on 15 April 1952, **brothers** and market owners, Pete and Jerry Cusimano tossed an octopus into the **rink**. Detroit then swept the **Toronto Maple Leafs** and **Montreal Canadiens** to win the championship and two of the next three championships.The eight-armed octopus became a good luck charm for the Red Wings. Today, even though it takes more than eight games to win the Stanley Cup, and it is against the **National Hockey League** rules to toss anything on the ice, Detroit fans continue this tradition. Fans from other teams have imitated this practice with other objects. During the 2011 Stanley Cup Playoffs, **Vancouver Canucks** fans threw salmon on the ice because British Columbia is renowned for its salmon fishing.

OFF-ICE OFFICIALS. The term *off-ice officials* is given to the individuals in hockey who primarily serve administrative and advisory roles. It does not include the **referees** and **linesmen** who officiate. The off-ice officials are comprised of the game timekeeper, the official **scorer** or statistician, two goal judges, and a video goal judge. The video goal judge is the only off-ice official who can affect the outcome of the match. On 28 April 1992, the Detroit Red Wings defeated the Minnesota North Stars in overtime of Game 6 of the division semifinals after the referee consulted with the video goal judge. Sergei Federov's shot appeared to have bounced off the net, but it was reviewed and credited as a goal.

OFFSIDES. Prior to the introduction of the blue line, the offside rule stated that a hockey player could not touch or play the puck if he was ahead of it, no matter where he was on the ice. This created a game that had no forward passing and highlighted stickhandling skills. To open up the game and increase scoring, the National Hockey League made passing in all three zones legal in 1929, but then too many goals were scored, with an average of 6.91 goals in the first 66 games. The current offside rules were developed prior to the 1943–1944 season. Essentially, an offside penalty is called if any player on the offensive team is too far ahead of the puck. To avoid an offside penalty, players must always stay between the puck and their team's goal. After offsides has been called by the on-ice official, a face-off down the rink restarts the play.

OLIVER, HAROLD "HARRY," "PEE WEE". B. 26 October 1898, Selkirk, Manitoba. D. 16 June 1985, Winnipeg, Manitoba. Harry Oliver grew up playing pond hockey. He went on to play ice hockey for 16 professional seasons, which included 11 Stanley Cup Playoffs and one Stanley Cup championship (1929). The nickname "Pee Wee" described his height (he was 5 feet, 8 inches tall). As a right wing, he played for the Western Canada Hockey League (WCHL) Calgary Tigers (1921–1926), as well as the National Hockey League (NHL) Boston Bruins (1926–1934) and New York Americans (1934–1937). He led the WCHL in assists (13) and points (33) in 1924–1925. In Boston, he played on a line with Frank Fredrickson and Perk Galbraith. On 26 March 1929, Oliver scored the opening goal and set up the Stanley Cup-winning goal in Boston's 2–1 victory over the New York Rangers. Oliver was known for both his gentlemanly conduct on the ice and his impeccable attire off of it. He was inducted into the Hockey Hall of Fame in 1967.

OLMSTEAD, MURRAY ALBERT "BERT," "DIRTY BERTIE". B. 4 September 1926, Sceptre, Saskatchewan. Bert Olmstead was a left wing in the National Hockey League (NHL) for the Chicago Black Hawks (1948–1951), Montreal Canadiens (1951–1958), and Toronto Maple Leafs (1958–1962). He was known as a power forward with hard body checks. Olmstead earned the nickname "Dirty Bertie" from provoking other players to **fight** him. He had a long and vicious feud with Lou Fontinato. During a 1959 **match** against the **New York Rangers**, Olmstead started an altercation by **high-sticking** Fontinato, which led to Fontinato giving Olmstead a black eye and cracking his **hockey stick** over his head. Not only did the fight continue after they each served time in the **penalty box**, but it spilled over into future games. Olmstead won the **Stanley Cup** four times with the Canadiens (1953, 1956–1958) and once with the Maple Leafs (1962). His 14 seasons with the NHL resulted in 848 regular-season games played and 181 **goals**, 421 **assists**, and 884 **penalty minutes**. After retiring in 1962, he was a **coach** for a few seasons. Olmstead was inducted into the **Hockey Hall of Fame** in 1985.

OLYMPIA STADIUM. Olympia Stadium was one of the six original **National Hockey League (NHL)** arenas. It was **nicknamed** "The Old Red Barn" and sometimes called the Detroit Olympia. It was located in Detroit, Michigan, and was home to the **Detroit Red Wings** from 1927–1979. On 26 October 1927, the first event at the Olympia was a rodeo. Eleven days later, a crowd of 16,000 people watched a heavyweight boxing **match** between Tom Heeney and Johnny Risko. The Detroit Cougars played their first hockey game at the Olympia on 22 November 1927, and Detroit's Johnny Sheppard **scored** the first **goal** at the new arena; however, the visiting **Ottawa Senators** defeated the Cougars, 2–1. After the Olympia went bankrupt, James Norris bought the place for $5 million in 1933, and he renamed the Cougars the **Detroit Red Wings**. Hockey became popular in the late 1940s and early 1950s. Led first by **Sid Abel** and then **Ted Lindsay** and **Gordie Howe**, the Red Wings won seven straight league championships and eight in nine years, and they won four **Stanley Cups**. In the 1960s, the Beatles held concerts at the Olympia. Throughout the years, the Olympia also featured such well-known boxers as Thomas Hearns, Jake LaMotta, Joe Louis, and Sugar Ray Robinson. On 15 December 1979, the Red Wings played their final home game at the Olympia, a 4–4 tie against the **Quebec Nordiques**. More than 15,000 fans attended that game. *See* ORIGINAL ARENAS.

OLYMPIC GAMES. The sport of men's **ice** hockey made its debut at the 1920 Summer Olympics in Belgium. Four years later, it became a permanent sport at the 1924 Winter Olympics in France. Between 1920–1968, the Olympic hockey tournament also counted as the **World Ice Hockey Championships** for that year. The Olympics were originally intended for amateur athletes only, but after other countries sent professionals to compete, the **United States** did too, starting in 1998. **Canada** was the most successful team of the first three decades, and the Canadians won six of seven gold medals. Czechoslovakia, **Sweden**, and the United States were also competitive during this period and won several medals. When the **Soviet Union Men's Olympic Ice Hockey Team** first participated in 1956, they replaced Canada as the dominant international team, winning seven of the nine tournaments in which they participated. The United States won gold medals in 1960 and 1980, which included their **"Miracle on Ice"** upset of the Soviet Union. Canada went 50 years without another gold medal, until 2002 and 2010. Erich Kühnhackl was part of the West Germany bronze medal-winning team in 1976. It was one of only two Olympic ice hockey medals for **Germany**. At the 1992 Olympics, Armenia, Belarus, Kazakhstan, **Russia**, Ukraine, and Uzbekistan competed as one entity, known as the Unified Team. In the final, the Unified Team defeated Canada to win gold, while Czechoslovakia won the bronze. Other nations to win gold medals include **Great Britain** in 1936, Sweden in 1994 and 2006, and the **Czech Republic** in 1998. Other medal-winning nations include **Switzerland**, **Finland**, and Russia.

The sport of **women's ice hockey** made its debut at the 1998 Winter Olympics in Nagano, Japan. Six countries competed for the gold medal. The **U.S. Women's Olympic Ice Hockey Team** won gold, the **Canadian Women's Olympic Ice Hockey Team** won silver, and the Finnish Women's Olympic Ice Hockey Team won bronze. China, Sweden, and Japan also participated. The U.S. women's team won silver medals during the 2002 and 2010 Olympics and a bronze medal during the 2006 competition. *See also* PARALYMPIC GAMES; APPENDIX H for a list of Olympic champions.

ON-ICE OFFICIALS. The term *on-ice officials* is given to one category of inductees into the **Hockey Hall of Fame**. It includes the **referees** and **linesmen** who officiate at hockey games. Inducted members include **Neil Armstrong**, John Ashley, **Bill Chadwick**, Chaucer Elliott, Bobby Hewitson, Mickey Ion, Mike Rodden, **Ray Scapinello**, Cooper Smeaton, **Red Storey**, and Frank Udvari. *See also* APPENDIX E for a list of Hockey Hall of Fame on-ice official inductees.

ORIGINAL ARENAS. The six original **National Hockey League (NHL)** arenas include **Boston Garden** (1928–1995), **Chicago Stadium** (1929–1994), Detroit Olympia (1927–1979), **Madison Square Garden** (1925–1968), **Maple Leaf Gardens** (1931–1999), and the **Montreal Forum** (1924–1996). The **"Original Six"** NHL teams that played there were the **Boston Bruins**, **Chicago Black Hawks**, **Detroit Red Wings**, **New York Rangers**, **Toronto Maple Leafs**, and **Montreal Canadiens**.

"ORIGINAL SIX". The history of the **National Hockey League (NHL)** can be divided into different eras. These include the Founding Era (1917–1942), "Original Six" Era (1942–1967), Expansion Era (1967–1992), and Modern Era (1992–present). The "Original Six" Era refers to a time when there were only six NHL teams that competed against one another. These six teams were the **Boston Bruins, Chicago Black Hawks, Detroit Red Wings, Montreal Canadiens, New York Rangers**, and **Toronto Maple Leafs**. These six franchises all currently play in the NHL.

ORR, ROBERT GORDON "BOBBY". B. 20 March 1948, Parry Sound, Ontario. Bobby Orr was a **defenseman** who played his first **National Hockey League (NHL)** game on 19 October 1966, with the **Boston Bruins**. He remained with the Bruins until 1976. He then joined the **Chicago Black Hawks** for two seasons. Orr's last NHL game was on 1 November 1978, with Chicago. He had 11 major knee surgeries during his playing days, which led to the end of his career at 31 years of age. Orr had two additional operations after retiring. He was the first and only defenseman to **score** nine career **hat tricks** and the first defenseman to score more than 100 **points** in a single season (1969–1970). Orr was the leading scorer in the NHL during the 1969–1970 season (120 points) and 1974–1975 season (135 points). He was the first NHL player in history to win the **Conn Smythe Trophy** twice (1970, 1972). Orr also won the **Calder Memorial Trophy** (1967), **Hart Memorial Trophy** (1970, 1971, 1972), **Art Ross Trophy** (1970, 1975), Lester B. Pearson Award (1975), and **Lester Patrick Trophy** (1979). He was the first player to win eight consecutive trophies when he won the **James Norris Memorial Trophy** consecutively from 1967–1978, while playing with the Bruins. After Orr scored seven **goals** in a six-game **Stanley Cup Playoff** series against the **New York Rangers, Rod Gilbert** said, "Hockey is a team game. One man is not supposed to beat a whole team." Orr won two **Stanley Cups** (1970, 1972).

Internationally, Orr played for **Canada** in the 1976 **Canada Cup**. He was unable to play in the 1972 **Summit Series** due to his knee **injuries**. During his 12-season NHL career, Orr played in 657 regular-season games and recorded 270 goals, 645 **assists**, 915 points, and 953 **penalty minutes**. The only players in NHL history who averaged more points per game than Orr are **Wayne Gretzky, Mario Lemieux**, and **Mike Bossy**, and they were forwards, not defensemen. Because he was such a vital player, the mandatory three-year waiting period for induction into the **Hockey Hall of Fame** was waived, and Orr was inducted into the Hockey Hall of Fame in 1979.

OTTAWA SENATORS. The Ottawa Senators are a professional **ice** hockey team in the **Northeast Division** of the **National Hockey League (NHL) Eastern Conference**. The team is the second NHL franchise to use the Ottawa Senators name. The original Ottawa Senators team was founded in 1883, and the group was also called the Silver Seven. One of their top

scorers was **Cyclone Taylor**. The Senators won 11 **Stanley Cups**, including four while they were part of the NHL (1917–1934). Their NHL Stanley Cup wins were in 1920, 1921, 1923, and 1927. **King Clancy** was one of their stars during that time. But, in 1934, the Senators faced financial difficulties. The franchise moved to St. Louis and became known as the **St. Louis Eagles**. After only one year, the team folded. In 16 seasons in the NHL (1917–1918 to 1933–1934), the original Ottawa Senators compiled a record of 258-221-63-0 (579 **points**) and made nine **Stanley Cup Playoff** appearances. During the 1967 expansion, the **St. Louis Blues** franchise brought hockey back to Missouri.

In 1992, businessman Bruce Firestone brought hockey back to Ottawa with a new franchise, but he kept the old name. Although the new Ottawa Senators have never won the Stanley Cup, they came close in the 2006–2007 season. They met the **Anaheim Ducks** in the finals but were defeated in five games. The Ottawa fans started a tradition of walking downtown in the "Sens Mile," which is similar to the "Red Mile" of the **Calgary Flames**' fans. The Senators have won the **Presidents' Trophy** (2003) and **Prince of Wales Trophy** (2007). The Binghamton Senators are their **American Hockey League** affiliate. The Senators' **coach**, Roger Neilson, was inducted into the **Hockey Hall of Fame** as a **builder** in 2002. In 19 seasons in the NHL (1992–1993 to 2011–2012), the Ottawa Senators have compiled a record of 679-651-115-83 (1,556 points) and made 13 playoff appearances. Several of the top scorers in the team's history include Daniel Alfredsson, Dany Heatley, Chris Phillips, and Jason Spezza.

OVECHKIN, ALEXANDER MIKHAYLOVICH "ALEX". B. 17 September 1985, Moscow, **Russia**. Alexander Ovechkin comes from an athletic family. His father, Mikhail Ovechkin, was a professional soccer player, and his mother, Tatyana Ovechkina, was a member of the Soviet women's basketball team and won gold medals at the 1976 and 1980 **Olympic Games**. Alexander was a star as a **young player**. Russian **coach Viktor Tikhonov** noticed his talent and selected him to play in a EuroTour tournament. At the age of 17, Ovechkin became both the youngest **skater** ever to play or **score** for the Russian national team. He then played hockey with the Dynamo Moscow team (2001–2005), before joining the **National Hockey League (NHL)**. In 2005, Ovechkin became a **left wing** for the **Washington Capitals**, and he is still with them today. He was named the NHL's top **rookie** for the 2005–2006 season, after scoring 52 **goals** and 54 **assists** for 106 **points**. As a result, he received the **Calder Memorial Trophy**. Ovechkin then scored 46 goals during the 2006–2007 season. On 15 December 2006, in a **match** against the **Atlanta Thrashers**, he tied the NHL record with Mats Sundin and David Legwand for the fastest **overtime** goal (6 seconds). Ovechkin is known for his stickhandling expertise.

In 2008, Ovechkin became the first player to win the **Art Ross Trophy**, **Maurice "Rocket" Richard Trophy**, Lester B. Pearson Award, and **Hart Memorial Trophy**, as well as the only player to win all four in a single season. He is the third youngest player to win consecutive Hart Trophies, behind **Wayne Gretzky** and **Bobby Orr**. On 5 February 2009, Ovechkin scored his 200th goal against the **Los Angeles Kings** and became only the fourth player in NHL history to reach that milestone in four seasons, joining Wayne Gretzky, **Mike Bossy**, and **Mario Lemieux**. In 2010, he won the Lester B. Pearson Award once again, now renamed the **Ted Lindsay Award**. In his seven NHL seasons to date, Ovechkin has played in 553 regular-season games and recorded 339 goals, 340 assists, 679 points, and 372 **penalty minutes**. In his 51 **Stanley Cup Playoff** games, he has recorded 30 goals, 29 assists, 59 points, and 26 penalty minutes. Ovechkin also represented Russia at the **World Ice Hockey Championships**, and he won two gold medals (2008, 2012), one silver medal (2010), and two bronze medals (2005, 2007). He was named an ambassador for the 2014 Winter Olympics in Sochi, Russia. Ovechkin will surely be inducted into the **Hockey Hall of Fame** when he becomes eligible.

OVERTIME. When **ice** hockey teams have a tied **score** after regulation play, overtime is used to determine a winner. The two main methods are the extra overtime period and the shootout. A shootout is when teams take a series of **penalty** shots to determine the winner. The overtime period during **National Hockey League (NHL)** regular-season games is limited to five minutes, but it is unlimited during the **Stanley Cup Playoffs**. International **matches** vary the length of overtime depending on the medal round. The longest **Stanley Cup** Playoff game ever took place on 24 March 1936, in Montreal. Mud Bruneteau of the **Detroit Red Wings** scored the winning **goal** (1–0) against the **Montreal Maroons** at 16:30 in the sixth overtime period. The game, with 116:30 of overtime, was almost the same as playing three full hockey games in a row.

P

PACIFIC COAST HOCKEY ASSOCIATION (PCHA). The Pacific Coast Hockey Association (PCHA) was an early hockey organization that included the **Vancouver Millionaires**, who played in the first professional **Stanley Cup** championship. Hugh Lehman of Vancouver holds the PCHA career record for games played by a **goaltender** (262), with 142 wins, 118 losses, and 17 **shutouts**. The PCHA folded, and, in 1926, the 10 teams of the **National Hockey League** were divided into two **divisions**.

PACIFIC DIVISION. In 1993, the **National Hockey League (NHL)** renamed the conferences and divisions to reflect their geographic locations. The Pacific Division is one of the three sections of the **Western Conference** in the NHL. The **Central Division** and **Northwest Division** are the other two.

PARALYMPIC GAMES. The Paralympic Games are an international sporting event where athletes with a physical disability compete. Just like the seasonal **Olympic Games**, there are Winter Paralympic Games and Summer Paralympic Games. The Paralympics began in 1948, with a group of British World War II veterans. The first Winter Paralympic Games were held in 1976, in Örnsköldsvik, **Sweden**. A form of hockey incorporating sleds instead of **skates** and called **ice** sledge hockey became one of the five events of the 1994 Winter Games. The Winter Games were held every four years with the summer ones, just as the Olympics were. This tradition was practiced until the 1992 Games in Albertville, France. Then, beginning with the 1994 Games, the Winter Paralympics and Winter Olympics have been held in even-numbered years separate from the Summer Games. During the 2010 games in Vancouver, **Canada**, women were allowed to be part of the men's teams for the first time at the Paralympics. Eleven countries participated in the 2010 ice sledge hockey event. Since 1994, only five countries have won medals for the sport: Canada, Japan, **Norway**, Sweden, and the **United States**.

PARENT, BERNARD MARCEL "BERNIE". B. 3 April 1945, Montreal, Quebec. As a **young player**, Bernie Parent's hockey hero was **goaltender Jacques Plante**. Parent became a professional goalie who played for the **Boston Bruins**, **Philadelphia Flyers**, and **Toronto Maple Leafs** during his career in the **National Hockey League (NHL)**. In 1972, the **Miami Screaming Eagles** of the **World Hockey Association (WHA)** recruited him from the Maple Leafs, but they never played a game. He played one season with the WHA team the Philadelphia Blazers (1972–1973), before joining the Flyers. Parent helped his team win the **Stanley Cup** in 1974 and 1975. During the 1973–1974 season, he played in 73 out of 78 regular-season games, winning 47 of them. He also had a great 1.89 **goals** against average. Parent once said, "You don't have to be crazy to be a goalie, but it helps." He had a **superstition** about showing his face. From the dressing room to the **ice** and back to the dressing room, he kept his mask on at all times. He believed that his phantom of the **crease** character psyched out his opponents. He won the **Conn Smythe Trophy** in 1974 and 1975. Parent also won the **Vezina Trophy** in 1974 (tied with **Tony Esposito**) and 1975.

Parent was a stand-up goalie, just like Plante, who became his mentor. At one point, Parent was playing poorly and considering retirement. Plante watched him practice and then told Bernie what he was doing wrong, which included sitting back on his heels, backing into his crease, and losing concentration. Parent followed Plante's advice and returned to form. On 17 February 1979, Parent suffered a **career-ending injury** when he was hit in the eye through his **face mask** by a **hockey stick** during a game against the **New York Rangers**. In 1984, he was inducted into the **Hockey Hall of Fame**.

PARK, DOUGLAS BRADFORD "BRAD". B. 6 July 1948, Toronto, Ontario. Brad Park was a **defenseman** for 17 seasons in the **National Hockey League (NHL)** with the **New York Rangers** (1968–1976), **Boston Bruins** (1975–1983), and **Detroit Red Wings** (1983–1985). He was a tough but clean player known for his hard body **checking**. Park was involved in some **fights** with **Gordie Howe** and **Dave Schultz**, but he was a good sport when their teams won. He once said, "I decided that if I have to maim somebody to win the **Stanley Cup**, I don't want to win it." Park never won the Stanley Cup, but he was selected for nine **All-Star Teams**. On 12 December 1971, against the **Pittsburgh Penguins**, he became the first defenseman in New York Rangers history to record a **hat trick**. He also finished as runner-up to **Bobby Orr** in the **James Norris Memorial Trophy** voting six times. When he joined the Red Wings, the team's owner, Mike Ilitch, gave him two Little Caesars franchises, which he also owned. After retiring due to knee problems, Park tried **coaching** (1985–1986), but he led Detroit to a losing season of 9-34-2. In 1984, he won the **Bill Masterton Memorial Trophy**. Park was inducted into the **Hockey Hall of Fame** in 1988.

PATRICK, CRAIG. B. 20 May 1946, Detroit, Michigan. Craig Patrick is the grandson of **builder Lester Patrick** and the son of **Lynn Patrick**. Craig was a **right wing** who played **college hockey** at the University of Denver, and he helped his team win the **National Collegiate Athletic Association** championships in 1968 and 1969. He also competed in the 1970 and 1971 **World Ice Hockey Championships**. From 1971–1979, Patrick played in the **National Hockey League (NHL)** with the California Golden Seals, **St. Louis Blues**, Kansas City Scouts, and **Washington Capitals**. He recorded 72 **goals**, 91 **assists**, and 163 **points** in 401 NHL games during his playing career. Patrick also competed in the 1976 **Canada Cup** and 1979 World Ice Hockey Championships before retiring from playing. He was the assistant general manager and assistant **coach** with **Herb Brooks** at the 1980 Winter Olympics, when the U.S. team defeated the **Russian** team in the "**Miracle on Ice.**" He also managed the 2002 **Olympic** team and won the silver medal.

In the NHL, Patrick coached the **New York Rangers** (1980–1981, 1984–1985) and **Pittsburgh Penguins** (1989–1990, 1996–1997). He then became the general manager of the Pittsburgh Penguins (1989–2006) and won the **Stanley Cup** with them in 1991 and 1992. He was responsible for obtaining hockey stars **Sidney Crosby**, Marc-André Fleury, and **Evgeni Malkin** for the Penguins. Patrick is the third generation of his family to have his name inscribed on the Stanley Cup and the third generation to be enshrined in the **Hockey Hall of Fame**. He was inducted into the **U.S. Hockey Hall of Fame** in 1996. In 2000, for his service to hockey, he received the **Lester Patrick Trophy**, named after his grandfather.

PATRICK, CURTIS LESTER "THE SILVER FOX". B. 30 December 1883, Drummondville, Quebec. D. 1 June 1960, Victoria, British Columbia. Lester Patrick was a **defenseman** in the early 1900s, but he also played as a **rover** and occasionally filled in for the **goaltender**. He played a total of 22 elite amateur and professional hockey seasons (1903–1922, 1925–1927, 1927–1928). Patrick was a member of the Brandon Hockey Club when they unsuccessfully challenged the **Ottawa Senators** for the **Stanley Cup** in March 1904. In March 1906, Patrick **scored** two crucial **goals** for the **Montreal Wanderers** when they defeated Ottawa to win the Stanley Cup. Patrick played with **Newsy Lalonde**, **Cyclone Taylor**, and Fred Whitcroft of the Renfrew Millionaires in the **National Hockey Association**. Lester's **nickname**, "The Silver Fox," was due to his shock of gray hair. With his brother, Frank Patrick, he built the first artificial **rinks** in **Canada** and formed the **Pacific Coast Hockey Association**. In addition to being a player, Lester was a **coach** and general manager of several teams. He won the **Stanley Cup** with the Victoria Cougars as president, manager, and coach (1925), and the **New York Rangers** as manager and coach (1928, 1933, 1940).

The **Lester Patrick Trophy**, named after him, is an annual award presented for outstanding service to hockey in the **United States**. It has been presented by the **National Hockey League (NHL)** and USA Hockey since 1966, to honor a recipient's contribution to **ice** hockey in the United States. Patrick was inducted into the **Hockey Hall of Fame** in 1947 as a player. The Patrick **family** has been called "Hockey's Royal Family." Lester was the father of **Lynn Patrick** and the grandfather of **Craig Patrick**, both of whom are Hall of Famers. Another son, Muzz Patrick, was a star player who became the coach and general manager of the Rangers. In the 1970s, Lester's grandson, Glenn Patrick, also played in the NHL. Another grandson, Dick Patrick, has been president of the **Washington Capitals** since 1982.

PATRICK, JOSEPH LYNN. B. 3 February 1912, Victoria, British Columbia. D. 26 January 1980, St. Louis, Missouri. Lynn Patrick's entire **family** was involved with **ice** hockey. He was the son of **Lester Patrick**, the nephew of Frank Patrick, the **brother** of Muzz Patrick, and the father of Lester Lee Patrick and **Craig Patrick**. Lynn was a forward in the **National Hockey League (NHL)** with the **New York Rangers** (1934–1943, 1945–1946). He played both **left wing** and **center** during his NHL career. In 455 regular-season games, Lynn **scored** 145 **goals** and 190 **assists** for a total of 335 **points**. As a child, he and his brother etched their names into the **Stanley Cup** that their father brought home, but, in 1940, Lynn had his name legitimately added after the Rangers defeated the **Toronto Maple Leafs** in the series, 4–2. He led the NHL in goals, with 32 for the 1941–1942 season. In 1943, Patrick left hockey to serve in the armed forces, but returned in 1945 to play one more year. After retiring from playing, he began his **coaching** career. He coached the New York Rangers (1948–1950), **Boston Bruins** (1950–1955), and **St. Louis Blues** (1967–1968, 1974–1976). Patrick is credited with introducing **Scotty Bowman** to coaching. He was inducted into the **Hockey Hall of Fame** in 1980 as a player. In 1989, Patrick was awarded the **Lester Patrick Trophy** posthumously.

PEEWEES. *See* YOUNG PLAYERS.

PENALTY. When the **on-ice official** removes a player for breaking a rule on the **ice**, it is called a penalty. The player then leaves the ice and spends the allotted time in the **penalty box**. Minor penalties include cross-**checking**, **hooking**, and **tripping** and equal two minutes in the penalty box. A major penalty like **fighting** equals five minutes in the box. A player who receives a misconduct penalty can get 10 minutes in the box or be thrown out of the game. Fines and suspension can also be added. Early hockey teams were shorthanded for the entire length of a minor penalty. The **National Hockey**

League changed this rule following the 1955–1956 season after the **Montreal Canadiens** frequently **scored** multiple **goals** on one **power play**. In a famous game on 5 November 1955, **Jean Béliveau** scored three goals in 44 seconds, all on the same power play, in a 4–2 victory over the **Boston Bruins**. Today, if the team with the advantage scores a goal while the other team is shorthanded, the penalty is over, unless it was a major penalty or **match** penalty. *See also* PENALTY KILLER; PENALTY MINUTES.

PENALTY BOX "SIN BIN". When hockey players break the rules, they have to leave the **ice** and spend time in the penalty box as punishment. In the **National Hockey League (NHL)**, the penalty box is a small area with a bench surrounded by walls on all four sides. The side facing the ice has the access door, and each team has their own penalty box. Originally, players from both teams would share one bench. A league representative or local policeman was responsible for keeping the peace. **Madison Square Garden** had the players sit on chairs in an aisle behind the **New York Rangers'** bench. During a game on 17 December 1944, Bob Dill and **Maurice Richard** had a fight on the ice, but it continued after they were put side-by-side in the sin bin. Another famous incident occurred at a **Toronto Maple Leafs** and **Montreal Canadiens** game on 30 October 1963, between **Bob Pulford** and Terry Harper. Their continued fighting in the box led to a lengthy game delay. On 8 November 1963, separate box doors were installed at **Maple Leaf Gardens** with the humorous labels "Les Canadiens - Good Guys," and "Visiteurs - Bad Guys." During the 1965–1966 season, the NHL passed a rule requiring separate penalty boxes with separate entrances. Although **goaltenders** can be assessed **penalty minutes**, they never go to the penalty box. Their time is served by a teammate. During 1987–1988 season, with the **Philadelphia Flyers, Ron Hextall** set a single-season record for penalty minutes by a goaltender, with 113. **Dave Williams** spent 3,966 minutes in the sin bin, while **Detroit Red Wing** Val Fonteyne only spent 28 minutes there during 820 NHL games throughout the course of 13 years.

PENALTY KILLER. When a player is in the **penalty box**, his or her team plays shorthanded. When a team is shorthanded, it is killing a **penalty**. They try to prevent the other team from **scoring** on the **power play**. Stalling for time by **icing** the **puck** is allowed when a team is shorthanded. Other strategies used to kill a penalty include being able to anticipate where the puck will go and good stickhandling skills to prevent and break up passes. **Coach Bob Johnson** once said that, "You don't need great skill to be a good penalty killer. You just need hard work. There's no reason why every team shouldn't have a good penalty kill." Some of the great penalty killers include **Zdeno Chára**, **Bob Gainey**, **Doug Jarvis**, Craig MacTavish, Derek Sanderson, and **Esa Tikkanen**.

PENALTY MINUTES. A **penalty** is called when a hockey player breaks a rule and has to leave the **ice** for a short time as punishment. The amount of time spent in the **penalty box** is determined by the seriousness of the infraction. A minor penalty is assessed two penalty minutes, while a major penalty is five minutes. More serious violations can result in 10 minutes in the box or removal from the game. On 11 March 1979, in the **National Hockey League (NHL)**, Randy Holt of the **Los Angeles Kings** set the record for the most penalty minutes one game (67). The record for the most accrued during the regular season is held by **Dave Schultz**, with 472, during the 1974–1975 season. **Dave Williams** holds the career record for penalty minutes, with 3,966.

PERREAULT, GILBERT "GIL". B. 13 November 1950, Victoriaville, Quebec. Gilbert Perreault was a **center** in the **National League Hockey (NHL)** with the **Buffalo Sabres** from 1970–1987. In his **rookie** season, he **scored** 38 **goals** and won the **Calder Memorial Trophy**. Perreault also received the **Lady Byng Memorial Trophy** in 1973. His best season was 1975–1976, when he scored 44 goals and 113 **points**. He holds the Buffalo team records for career games (1,191), goals (512), **assists** (814), and points (1,326). During the 1976–1977 season, he led the NHL in game-winning goals, with nine. Perreault was on the Buffalo **line** known as the "French Connection Line," with Rick Martin and Rene Robert. In 1976, **Canada** hosted the first **Canada Cup** series. Perreault played on a team with **Marcel Dionne**, **Bobby Hull**, **Guy Lafleur**, **Bobby Orr**, and **Darryl Sittler**. Canada won after beating Czechoslovakia in a best-of-three series. Perreault later played in the 1981 Canada Cup on a line with **Wayne Gretzky** and Guy Lafleur. Unfortunately, Perreault never played on a **Stanley Cup** championship team. After retiring from playing, he coached **juniors**. In 1990, he was elected into the **Hockey Hall of Fame**.

PETER PUCK. Peter Puck, a hockey **puck**-shaped cartoon character that appeared on both NBC's *Hockey Game of the Week* and CBC's *Hockey Night in Canada* during the 1970s, was the creation of NBC executive Donald Carswell. **Brian McFarlane** is often incorrectly cited as the creator of Peter Puck. After the network stopped carrying **National League Hockey matches**, McFarlane purchased the rights to Peter Puck from NBC's production partner, Hanna-Barbera.

PHILADELPHIA FLYERS. The Philadelphia Flyers are a professional **ice** hockey team in the **Atlantic Division** of the **National Hockey League (NHL) Eastern Conference**. The Flyers joined the league as one of the six new franchises during the NHL expansion in the 1967–1968 season. The Flyers adopted the orange and black colors used by the **Philadelphia Quakers** in 1930–1931. Keith Allen was hired as the first head **coach** of the team, with his former coach and teammate Bud Poile as general manager. In their first season, the Flyers finished first in their division with the best record among the six new teams. They fell to third place in their division during the 1968–1969 NHL season, and Allen then became the Flyers' general manager. He helped to build the famous "Broad Street Bullies" and led the Flyers to consecutive **Stanley Cups** in 1974 and 1975. The team also made the Stanley Cup Finals six additional times, but they were defeated by the **Montreal Canadiens** in 1976 (4–0), the **New York Islanders** in 1980 (4–2), the **Edmonton Oilers** in 1985 (4–1) and 1987 (4–3), the **Detroit Red Wings** in 1997 (4–0), and the **Chicago Blackhawks** in 2010 (4–2).

Since the 1970s, the Flyers' main rival has been the **New York Rangers**; however, Philadelphia has also developed more recent rivalries with the **New Jersey Devils** and **Pittsburgh Penguins**. Among the best players for Philadelphia have been **Hockey Hall of Famers Bill Barber, Bobby Clarke, Paul Coffey, Dale Hawerchuk, Mark Howe, Bernie Parent, Darryl Sittler**, and **Allan Stanley**. **Dave Schultz** also played for the Philadelphia Flyers. In 1991, after being drafted by the **Quebec Nordiques**, **Eric Lindros** refused to play for them. The Flyers acquired Lindros by trading forwards **Peter Forsberg** and Mike Ricci, **goaltender Ron Hextall**, and **defensemen** Steve Duchesne and Kerry Huffman. As a powerful forward, Lindros and teammates John LeClair and Mikael Renberg formed a **line** called the "Legion of Doom," and they **skated** down the ice **intimidating** their opponents. Mike Keenan (1984–1988) and **Fred Shero** (1971–1978) were both coaches for the Flyers, and Peter Laviolette is the current coach. In 44 seasons in the NHL (1967–1968 to 2011–2012), the Philadelphia Flyers have compiled a record of 1,756-1,202-457-91 (4,060 **points**) and made 36 **Stanley Cup Playoff** appearances. The Flyers' all-time point percentage of .579 (as of the end of the 2011–2012 season) is the second best in the NHL, behind the **Montreal Canadiens'** .588 point percentage. Current players for the team include goaltender Sergei Bobrovsky, **center** Danny Briere, **right wing Jaromír Jágr**, and captain Chris Pronger.

PHILADELPHIA QUAKERS. When the **National Hockey League (NHL)** team the **Pittsburgh Pirates** moved to Philadelphia, Pennsylvania, for the 1930–1931 season, they were renamed the **Philadelphia Quakers**. The Quakers were a terrible team and finished their only season with a 4-36-4 record. Their .136 winning percentage was the lowest in NHL history. This record stood for 45 years, until the **Washington Capitals** finished with a .131 winning percentage in 1974–1975. At the end of their only season (1930–1931), the Quakers, along with the **Ottawa Senators**, announced that they would not field a team for the 1931–1932 NHL season. This left Philadelphia without an NHL team until the **Philadelphia Flyers** began in 1967. **Center Syd Howe** was the only player inducted to the **Hockey Hall of Fame** who also played for the Philadelphia Quakers.

PHILLIPS, THOMAS NEIL "TOMMY," "NIBS". B. 22 May 1883, Rat Portage, Ontario. D. 30 November 1923, Toronto, Ontario. As a **young player**, Tommy Phillips played hockey with **Si Griffis**, Tom Hooper, and Billy McGimsie. He attended McGill University and also played elite and amateur hockey as a **left wing** and **rover** for the Montreal AAA (1902–1903), Toronto Marlboros (1903–1904), **Kenora Thistles** (1905–1907), **Ottawa Senators** (1907–1908), and **Vancouver Millionaires** (1911–1912). Phillips helped his team win the **Stanley Cup** in 1903 and 1907. He captained the Stanley Cup–winning Kenora team and **scored** four **goals** in their 4–2 victory over the **Montreal Wanderers** in the **Stanley Cup Playoffs** on 17 January 1907, and three goals in the next game. Phillips was known for his **skating** speed, passing skills, and stickhandling abilities. **Lester Patrick** considered him to be one of the greatest players of his era. Phillips had a gap in his career due to a broken ankle. After retiring from hockey, he ran his own lumber company. In 1923, after his tooth was pulled, he died of blood poisoning at the age of 40. Phillips was inducted into the **Hockey Hall of Fame** in 1945, as one of the 12 original inductees.

PHOENIX COYOTES. The Phoenix Coyotes are a professional **ice** hockey team in the **Pacific Division** of the **National Hockey League (NHL) Western Conference**. In 1996, the **Winnipeg Jets** moved to Phoenix, Arizona, and created a new identity as the Phoenix Coyotes for the 1996–1997 season. From 2005–2009, **Wayne Gretzky** was their **coach. Hockey Hall of Famers Mike Gartner** and **Brett Hull** both played for the team. Their current coach, Dave Tippett, has been helping the Coyotes improve their season. In their combined 32 seasons (1979–1980 to 2011–2012), the Jets/Coyotes franchise record stands as 1,063-1,158-266-81 (2,473 **points**), with 19 **Stanley Cup Playoff** appearances, but no **Stanley Cups**. In 2012, they defeated the **Nashville Predators**, 4–1, in the Western Conference Semifinals. They were then defeated by the **Los Angeles Kings**, 4–1, in the conference finals.

PILOTE, JOSEPH PIERRE ALBERT PAUL. B 11 December 1931, Kenogami, Quebec. Pierre Pilote was an **ice** hockey **defenseman**. During his 890-game career in the **National Hockey League (NHL)**, he **scored** 80 goals and 418 **assists** for 498 **points** with the **Chicago Black Hawks** (1955–1968) and **Toronto Maple Leafs** (1968–1969). Pilote was known as an iron man who played in 376 consecutive games. He and **Elmer Vasko** were a strong defensive pair on the Chicago team. As a tough player, Pilote led the NHL with 165 **penalty minutes** (1960–1961). He often carried the **puck** up the ice. He was a fixture on the Chicago **power play** on the point due to his ability to handle the puck. During the 1960–1961 season, he led the NHL in assists (12) and points (15). He learned some of his skills from watching his hero, **Doug Harvey**. In 1961, Pilote won the **Stanley Cup** with Chicago. He also won the **James Norris Memorial Trophy** in 1963, 1964, and 1965. Pilote was inducted into the **Hockey Hall of Fame** in 1975.

PITRE, DIDIER "PIT," "CANNONBALL," "BULLET SHOT," "OLD FOLKS". B. 1 September 1883, Valleyfield, Quebec. D. 29 July 1934, Sault Ste. Marie, Ontario. In 1909, Didier Pitre was the first player signed by the new **Montreal Canadiens** franchise of the **National Hockey Association (NHA)**. He earned the **nickname** "Cannonball" from firing the **puck** like a cannon. In 1914, chicken wire was installed at the ends of Victoria's **rink** to protect the fans from his shots. Pitre was also known by other names, including "Bullet Shot" and "Old Folks." He **scored** 30 **goals** during the 1914–1915 season with the Canadiens. This was half of the total goals scored by the entire team. In the best-of-five series against the Portland Rosebuds, Pitre scored four goals, including a **hat trick**, to help the Canadiens win their first **Stanley Cup** (1916). Pitre was also a professional **lacrosse** player for 12 seasons with the Montreal Nationals. Known as a fast-**skating**, flashy player, he often drank champagne during periods. In 1962, Pitre was inducted into the **Hockey Hall of Fame**.

PITTSBURGH PENGUINS. The Pittsburgh Penguins are a professional **ice** hockey team in the **Atlantic Division** of the **National Hockey League (NHL) Eastern Conference**. The Penguins joined the league as one of the six new franchises during the NHL expansion in the 1967–1968 season. On 21 October 1967, they became the first team from the expansion class to beat an **"Original Six"** team as they defeated the **Chicago Black Hawks**, 4–2. But the Penguins finished their season with the third worst record in the league, 27 34 13. George Sullivan was the first **coach** for the club's first two seasons, but he was replaced by **Hockey Hall of Famer Red Kelly**. Michel Briere joined the team in November 1969, and he finished as the top **rookie scorer** in the NHL, with 44 **points**. Tragically, on 15 May 1970, Briere was in a car crash in Quebec, and he died a year later.

During the 1970s and 1980s, the franchise faced bankruptcy and didn't do well in the **Stanley Cup Playoffs**. After six seasons of failing to qualifying for the postseason, Pittsburgh was finally successful in the 1988–1989 season. **Mario Lemieux** led the league in **goals**, **assists**, and points. In its NHL history, the team has made the **Stanley Cup** Finals four times. They beat the Minnesota North Stars in 1991 (4–2) and the Chicago Blackhawks in 1992 (4–0). In the 2008 Stanley Cup Finals, Pittsburgh was defeated by the **Detroit Red Wings** (4–2), but the roles were reversed in 2009, when the Penguins beat the Red Wings (4–3). Some of the best players for Pittsburgh include **Paul Coffey**, **Sidney Crosby**, **Jaromír Jágr**, Mario Lemieux, **Evgeni Malkin**, and **Bryan Trottier**. Among the Pittsburgh coaches have been **Scotty Bowman**, **Herb Brooks**, **Bob Johnson**, and **Craig Patrick**. The Pittsburgh Penguins won the **Presidents' Trophy** in 1993. In 44 seasons in the NHL, from 1967–1968 to 2011–2012, the Penguins have compiled a record of 1,507-1,530-383-86 (3,483 points) and made 27 playoff appearances. In the 2011–2012 playoffs, they were defeated, 4–2, by the **Philadelphia Flyers** in the Eastern Conference Quarterfinals. Mario Lemieux is the current owner of the Pittsburgh Penguins.

PITTSBURGH PIRATES. The Pittsburgh Pirates were a professional **ice** hockey team in the **National Hockey League (NHL)** from 1925–1926 to 1929–1930, owned by **Bill Dwyer**. Their name comes from the baseball team also based in the city. In their first game, on 26 November 1925, against the **Boston Bruins, defenseman** and captain **Lionel Conacher scored** Pittsburgh's first NHL **goal. Goaltender Roy Worters** stopped 26 of 27 shots to record the first win in franchise history. Their first season was their best, but they lost to the **Montreal Maroons** in the **Stanley Cup Playoffs**. After the Great Depression, the franchise faced financial difficulties, and the team moved to Philadelphia, Pennsylvania. They played one season (1930–1931) as the **Philadelphia Quakers** before folding. The city of Pittsburgh was without an ice hockey team until the **Pittsburgh Penguins** were formed in 1967.

PLANTE, JOSEPH JACQUES OMER "JAKE THE SNAKE". B. 17 January 1929, Shawinigan Falls, Quebec. D. 27 February 1986, Geneva, **Switzerland**. Jacques Plante was one of the top **goaltenders** of the **National Hockey League (NHL)**. His hockey career spanned four decades (1947–1975) and included 19 NHL and **World Hockey Association** seasons. As a child, Plante played **pond hockey** in the freezing Quebec winters. His mother taught him how to knit his own caps to protect him from the cold. Plante continued knitting and embroidering throughout his life. He had a **superstition** that wearing underwear that he had knit himself would make him play better hockey. Plante played for the **Montreal Canadiens** (1952–1963), **New York Rangers** (1963–1965), **St. Louis Blues** (1968–1970), **Toronto Maple Leafs** (1970–1973), **Boston Bruins** (1972–1973), and **Edmonton Oilers** (1974–1975). He retired three times but kept returning to the **ice**. He was 44 years old when he played his last game, and he won seven of his last eight games. The **nickname** "Jake the Snake" described the way he frequently snaked away from the **crease** to grab the **puck** and pass it off to a teammate. During his time with the Canadiens, the team won the **Stanley Cup** six times, including five consecutive wins (1953, 1956–1960). Plante had 82 career **shutouts** and played in 868 regular-season games, winning 434 of them. He led the NHL in **goals** against average nine times between 1956–1971. Plante won the **Hart Memorial Trophy** in 1962, and he holds the record for winning the **Vezina Trophy** the most times (7).

Clint Benedict was the first goalie to ever wear a **face mask**, but Plante was the first NHL goaltender to wear a mask in regulation play on a regular basis. He first wore it on 1 November 1959, to protect a recent **injury**, and then went on an 18-game unbeaten streak. The face mask he designed was the prototype for the goalie masks worn today. In 1972, Plante wrote the book *Goaltending,* which outlines a program of development that includes off-ice exercises, choice of **equipment**, styles of play, and game-day preparation. He also advised on the best **coaching** methods for goaltenders. His book remained popular with coaches and players and was reprinted in both French and English in 1997. In 1978, Plante was inducted into the **Hockey Hall of Fame**.

PLAYOFFS. *See* STANLEY CUP PLAYOFFS.

POINTS. The game of hockey gives points to players, as well as to the whole team. A player gets one point for **scoring** a **goal** and one point for an **assist**. The record for the most consecutive games with at least one point **scored** is 51, by **Wayne Gretzky,** during his 1983–1984 season with the **Edmonton Oilers**. He also holds many more records having to do with points. A team gets two points for winning a game and zero points for losing, unless they lose in **overtime**, and then they get one point. The **Montreal Canadiens** hold the record for the most points during the regular season with 132 during the 1976–1977 season.

POND HOCKEY. Many **National Hockey League (NHL)** stars began as **young players** who played hockey with their friends on frozen ponds in their backyards or on a local creek or in a park. They cleared the **ice** with shovels and played in the freezing weather. To relive those happy childhood experiences, Fred Haberman created a pond hockey tournament for adults. In 2006, the first U.S. Pond Hockey Championships attracted nearly 120 teams of pond hockey players from across the country to Minneapolis, Minnesota, to play on 25 **rinks**. The winners of the different divisions were presented with a trophy called the Golden Shovel. It has become an annual event with a portion of the proceeds going to youth charities. The **Winter Classic** is the NHL version of a pond hockey game. It is an annual event held outdoors on or around New Year's Day since 2008.

POTVIN, DENIS CHARLES. B. 29 October 1953, Ottawa, Ontario. Denis Potvin was a **defenseman** in the **National Hockey League (NHL)** for 15 seasons with the **New York Islanders** (1973–1988). He served as the team captain from 1979–1987. Potvin was known for his **checking** skills, as well as his passing talents. He **scored** 30 **goals** in the 1977–1978 season and accumulated 100 **points** during the 1978–1979 season. On 4 April 1987, he became the first NHL defenseman to score 1,000 career points. Potvin helped the Islanders win four **Stanley Cups** in a row from 1980–1983. Internationally, he played for **Canada** in the 1976 and 1981 **Canada Cups** and 1986 **World Ice Hockey Championships**. In 1974, he won the **Calder Memorial Trophy**. Potvin also won the **James Norris Memorial Trophy** three times (1976, 1978, 1979). Denis's **brother**, Jean Potvin, played in the NHL from 1970–1981 and was part of the 1980 and 1981 Stanley Cup–winning Islanders with Denis. Their cousin, Marc Potvin, was a **right wing** in the NHL. After retiring from his playing career, Denis became a hockey commentator for the **Florida Panthers** from 1993–2009. He is currently an analyst for the **Ottawa Senators**. In 1991, Potvin was inducted into the **Hockey Hall of Fame**.

POWER PLAY. A power play is when a team has more players on the **ice** than the opposition due to one or more **penalties** against the opposing team. The **icing** rule does not apply when a team is shorthanded. The shorthanded team tries to kill time to prevent a power play **goal**. During the 1985–1986 season, Tim Kerr of the **Philadelphia Flyers scored** a record 34 power play goals in one season. **Left wing** Dave Andreychuk holds the record for career power play goals at 274. Following him are **Hockey Hall of Famers Brett Hull** (265) and **Phil Esposito** (249) and **Anaheim Ducks'** current player **Teemu Selänne** (248).

PRATT, WALTER "BABE". B. 7 January 1916, Stony Mountain, Manitoba. D. 16 December 1988, Vancouver, British Columbia. Babe Pratt was a **defenseman** in the **National Hockey League (NHL)** for a total of 12 seasons with the **New York Rangers** (1935–1943), **Toronto Maple Leafs** (1943–1946), and **Boston Bruins** (1946–1947). In addition to hockey, he loved baseball and was **nicknamed** "Babe" after Babe Ruth. Pratt had a good sense of humor and was outspoken on the frugality of his Rangers coach, **Lester Patrick**. Pratt won the **Stanley Cup** in 1940, with New York. In September 1940, Patrick fined Pratt $1,000 for drinking, but he said he would refund the money if Pratt gave up alcohol. He did, but then the Rangers had a long losing streak. Patrick and the players asked him to take an occasional drink, but he refused. The Rangers wound up in fourth place that year. During the 1942–1943 season, he was traded to Toronto and received more money, which inspired him to play better. On 22 April 1945, Pratt **scored** Toronto's Stanley Cup–winning **goal** against the **Detroit Red Wings**. In 1944, he was the NHL's Most Valuable Player and received the Hart Trophy, but, in 1946, he was suspended for nine games for betting on hockey games. In the early 1950s, Pratt **coached** the New Westminster Royals hockey team. After retiring from coaching, he became a spokesman for the **Vancouver Canucks**. Pratt was inducted into the **Hockey Hall of Fame** in 1966 as a player.

PRENTICE, DEAN SUTHERLAND. B. 5 October 5 1932, Schumacher, Ontario. Dean Prentice was an **ice** hockey forward who played in the **National Hockey League (NHL)** for 22 seasons (1952–1974). He was a **left wing** with the **New York Rangers** (1952–1963), **Boston Bruins** (1962–1966), **Detroit Red Wings** (1965–1969), **Pittsburgh Penguins** (1969–1971), and Minnesota North Stars (1971–1974). Prentice played a total of 1,378 regular-season NHL games and recorded 391 **goals** and 469 **assists** for 860 **points**. He was one of the greatest players for the Rangers. His best season with New York came in 1959–1960, when he **scored** 32 goals to earn a place on the NHL's second **All-Star Team** and won the Rangers Most Valuable Player award. That was the first of three straight seasons with 20 or more goals for the **left wing**, who finished his career with the Rangers scoring close to 200 goals. But his long hockey career never included a **Stanley Cup** win. At 41 years of age, Prentice retired from the NHL. His **brother**, Eric Prentice, played five games for the **Toronto Maple Leafs** during the 1943–1944 NHL season and was the youngest Leafs' player in history.

PRESIDENTS' TROPHY. The Presidents' Trophy is one of only four team awards given out by the **National Hockey League (NHL)**. The other three include the most famous one, the **Stanley Cup**, as well as the **Clarence S. Campbell Bowl** and **Prince of Wales Trophy**. The Presidents' Trophy is awarded annually to the team with the most **points** in the regular season. If two teams tie for the most points, then the trophy goes to the team with the most wins. The **Edmonton Oilers** were the first winner, after the 1985–1986 season. The **Detroit Red Wings** have won this trophy the most often (6 times). In 2010–2011, the **Vancouver Canucks** won the trophy. But having a great season doesn't guarantee a great postseason. Of the 25 winners of the Presidents' Trophy, only six teams went on to win the Stanley Cup.

PRESTON RIVULETTES. The Preston Rivulettes were a **Canadian** women's baseball team that played hockey during the winter months. In the 1930s, this all-female hockey team competed with other female teams from Toronto, Kitchener, Stratford, London, Hamilton, Guelph, and Port Dover. The Rivulettes dominated the sport, and, between 1930–1940, they lost only two of 350 **matches** they played. At one match in Edmonton, the Rivulettes traveled with a shorthanded team, as many players were suffering from the flu. "In Edmonton," said star player **Hilda Ranscombe**, "the atmosphere was so different, and we went with nine players and three were sick. All I did on the **ice** was cough. The girls played good hockey, but we only had one spare."

They lost 2–1 to Edmonton, and the **referee** of that game was the future **National Hockey League (NHL)** president, **Clarence Campbell**. As the most successful Canadian team in **women's ice hockey** history, the Preston Rivulettes won 10 Ontario titles, 10 Eastern Canadian Championships, and six Dominion Championships. The team was supposed to play in Europe but never got the chance. When World War II broke out, it folded. Players in addition to Hilda Ranscombe included her sister, Nellie Ranscombe, as **goaltender**; Ruth Dargyl (Collins); the Dykeman sisters; Marg Gabitas; Norma Hipel; Pat Marriot; Myrtle Parr; Gladys Pitcher; Helen Sault; sisters Helen and Marm Schmuck; and Toddy Webb. This legendary team was **coached** by Herb Fach. The Preston Rivulettes hockey team was inducted into the Cambridge Sports Hall of Fame in 1997.

PRIMEAU, ALFRED JOSEPH FRANCIS "JOE," "GENTLEMAN JOE". B. 29 January 1906, Lindsay, Ontario. D. 14 May 1989, Toronto, Ontario. Joe Primeau was a **center** in the **National Hockey League (NHL)** with the **Toronto Maple Leafs** from 1927–1936. His **nickname**, "Gentleman Joe," was based on his calm and classy presence on the **ice,** and he was awarded the **Lady Byng Trophy** in 1932, disrupting **Frank Boucher**'s winning streak. Primeau was part of a young forward **line** of the Maple Leafs known as the "Kid Line," with **Charlie Conacher** and **Busher Jackson**. During a 1931 Christmas Eve **match** against the **Montreal Canadiens**, the teams were tied, 1–1, after **overtime**. The siren sounded accidentally, and the **referee** called the players back for 10 final seconds of play. Montreal's **Howie Morenz** was anxious to go home to his family and told Primeau to just let the clock run down and not touch the **puck** after it was dropped on the ice, but, instead, Primeau passed it to Busher Jackson, who **scored** the winning **goal**. This made Morenz furious, and he got his revenge by scoring the winning overtime goal when the teams played again two days later. The "Kid Line" also worked together to help Toronto win the **Stanley Cup** in 1932. Primeau retired from playing at the age of 30 to operate a successful concrete business. He had played in 310 regular-season NHL games and recorded 66 goals and 177 **assists** for a total of 243 **points**. He returned to hockey as a **coach** and won the **Allan Cup** in 1950 with the Toronto Marlboros. Primeau won the Stanley Cup in his first year as head coach of the Toronto Maple Leafs, in 1950–1951. In 1963, he was inducted into the **Hockey Hall of Fame**.

PRINCE OF WALES TROPHY. The Prince of Wales Trophy is one of only four team awards given out by the **National Hockey League (NHL)**. The other three include the most famous one, the **Stanley Cup**, as well as the **Clarence S. Campbell Bowl** and **Presidents' Trophy**. The Prince of Wales Trophy, also known as the **Wales Trophy**, was donated by the Prince of Wales in 1924. Throughout history, the trophy has been awarded for several different accomplishments, including: the NHL regular-season champions (1924–1927), the American Division regular-season champions (1927–1938), the East Division season champions (1938–1967), the Wales Conference regular-season champions (1974–1981), and the Wales Conference playoff champions (1981–1993). Since 1993–1994, the Wales Trophy has been given to the playoff champion of the **Eastern Conference**. The **Montreal Canadiens** were the first winner, after the 1923–1924 season. The Canadiens have also won this trophy the most often (25 times). In 2010–2011, the **Boston Bruins** won the trophy for the sixteenth time.

PRONOVOST, JOSEPH RENE MARCEL. B. 15 June 1930, Lac-a-la-Tortue, Quebec. As one of 12 children, Marcel Pronovost grew up playing hockey with his nine brothers. Two of his brothers also played in the **National Hockey League (NHL)**. Claude Pronovost was a **goaltender** (1955–1959), and Jean Pronovost was a **right wing** (1968–1992). Marcel was a **defenseman** who played for the **Detroit Red Wings** (1950–1965) and **Toronto Maple Leafs** (1965–1970). He helped the Red Wings win four **Stanley Cups**, in 1950, 1952, 1954, and 1955. Pronovost won a fifth Stanley Cup with the 1967 Maple Leaf team. In 1952, the **octopus** tradition began, and Pronovost carried the first one thrown onto the **ice** with him to the **penalty box**. As a fearless player, he became the most **injured** ice hockey player in history. He was also one of only two players in NHL history to **score** a reverse **hat trick**. Pronovost once scored three **goals** in one game against his own goaltender, **Terry Sawchuk**. During his career, he played in 1,206 regular-season games and had 88 goals, 257 **assists**, 345 **points**, and

851 **penalty minutes**. Pronovost was inducted into the **Hockey Hall of Fame** in 1978. After retiring from playing, he served as a scout for the **New Jersey Devils** (1989–2009). In 2003, he won the Stanley Cup as part of the Red Wings executive team. This set a record for the longest period of time between someone winning their first Stanley Cup (1950) and last Stanley Cup (2003), a 53-year span.

PUCK. Hockey pucks were originally made of wood and then pieces of rubber. Rubber pucks were first made by slicing a rubber ball and then trimming the disk into a square. The Victoria Hockey Club of Montreal is credited with making and using the first round pucks in the 1880s. Children often played street hockey with frozen horse droppings that they found from the horse-drawn wagons. They called them horse apples, horse buns, or horse puckies. A popular slang term for puck is *biscuit*. A **National Hockey League (NHL)** regulation **ice** hockey puck has to weigh between five and a half and six ounces (156 to 170 grams). It is made of vulcanized rubber and is one inch (2.54 centimeters) thick and three inches (7.62 centimeters) in diameter. To minimize bouncing, it is frozen for several hours before a game. Some players regularly shoot the puck at speeds of 90 to 100 miles per hour. In 1900, **Fred C. Waghorne refereed** a game where a puck split in two. Only half of the puck ended up in the **goal,** and, after much deliberation, he ruled it as "no goal," because the official definition of a puck included specific dimensions, and since the piece of rubber in the goal did not meet these specifications, it could not be a puck. He then instituted the rule that the entire puck must cross the goal line for a goal to be **scored**. In the 1995–1996 season, a customized, glowing "FoxTrax" puck was tried. With a tracking device, it was supposed to be easier to see on television; however, it was not successful and is no longer used. *See also* "RAG THE PUCK".

PULFORD, HARVEY. B. 22 April 1875, Toronto, Ontario. D. 31 October 1940, Ottawa, Ontario. Harvey Pulford was a well-rounded athlete who not only participated in football, **lacrosse**, boxing, paddling, and rowing, but also won championships. He was the heavyweight boxing champion in Eastern **Canada**, a member of Ottawa's championship football and lacrosse teams, and a world-class rower. He was also an **ice** hockey player with the Ottawa Silver Seven. As a **defenseman**, he helped his team win the **Stanley Cup** in 1903, 1904, 1905, and 1906. He led the **Stanley Cup Playoffs** in **penalty minutes,** with 24 (1905–1906). During the 1907–1908 season with the **Ottawa Senators**, Pulford was paired up with **Cyclone Taylor**. Pulford was a solid defender who rarely **scored**, and Taylor earned the **nickname** "Cyclone" because of his scoring rushes. Pulford was known for his **checking** and stickhandling abilities. He had a talent for carrying the **puck** out of danger when it was near his team's **goal**. After retiring from playing, Pulford became an **on-ice official** in the **National Hockey Association** (1912–1917) and **National Hockey League** (1917–1918). He was elected to the **Hockey Hall of Fame** in 1945, as one of the 12 original inductees.

PULFORD, ROBERT JESSE "BOB," "MUTE ROCKNE". B. 31 March 1936, Newton Robinson, Ontario. Bob Pulford played 16 seasons in the **National Hockey League (NHL)** as a **left wing** with the **Toronto Maple Leafs** (1956–1970) and **Los Angeles Kings** (1970–1972). He won the **Stanley Cup** in 1962, 1963, 1964, and 1967. Pulford led the NHL in shorthanded **goals**, with four (1963–1964), and in **assists** in the **Stanley Cup Playoffs**, with 10 (1966–1967). On 23 April 1964, he was awarded the assist on Bobby Baun's game-winning **overtime** goal against the **Detroit Red Wings** in Game 6, even though Pulford wasn't on the **ice** at the time. From 1967–1972, Pulford served as president of the National Hockey League Players' Association. He was the captain (1971–1973) and **coach** (1972–1977) of the Los Angeles Kings and won the **Jack Adams Award** (1975). For 30 years (1977–2007), he was a coach and executive for the **Chicago Black Hawks (Chicago Blackhawks)**. Pulford's coaching record was 365-347-139. Since he was a quiet man, he was **nicknamed** "Mute Rockne." Pulford was inducted into the **Hockey Hall of Fame** in 1991 as a player. In 2011, he received the **Lester Patrick Trophy** for his contributions to hockey.

Q

QUACKENBUSH, HUBERT GEORGE "BILL". B. 2 March 1922, Toronto, Ontario. D. 12 September 1999, Newtown, Pennsylvania. Bill Quackenbush, who was given the **nickname** "Bill" by an aunt who disliked his given name, was a **National Hockey League (NHL) defenseman** for the **Detroit Red Wings** (1943–1949) and **Boston Bruins** (1949–1956). He was known for his offensive playing style, including skillful poke **checking**. After playing the entire 1948–1949 season for Detroit without recording a **penalty**, Quackenbush became the first defenseman to win the **Lady Byng Memorial Trophy**. General manager **Jack Adams** did not believe that hockey players should behave like gentlemen, and he quickly traded Quackenbush to Boston. Quackenbush was named to the NHL **All-Star Team** five times and played in eight NHL All Star games. During his career, he accumulated only **95 penalty minutes** in 774 games, averaging out to seven seconds a game, one of the lowest in NHL player history. After retiring from the NHL in 1956, Quackenbush began a successful new career as Princeton University's head **coach** of the men's golf team and both the men's **ice hockey and women's ice hockey** teams that lasted 18 years. In 1976, he was inducted into the **Hockey Hall of Fame**.

QUEBEC BULLDOGS. The Quebec Bulldogs were one of the teams in the original **National Hockey Association** (1910–1917). Their official name was the Quebec Athletics, but due to their tough playing style the fans called them the Quebec Bulldogs. They won the **Stanley Cup** in 1912 and 1913, with star player **Joe Malone**. In 1920, the franchise moved and was renamed the **Hamilton Tigers** (1920–1925). In 1925, the players were bought out by the **New York Americans** franchise. Quebec City did not have a professional **ice** hockey team until the **Quebec Nordiques** were founded in 1972.

QUEBEC NORDIQUES. The Quebec Nordiques played in the **World Hockey Association (WHA)** (1972–1979) and **National Hockey League (NHL)** (1979–1995). **Maurice Richard** (1972–1973) and **Jacques Plante** (1973–1974) were two of the early **coaches** for the Nordiques. **Guy Lefleur**,

Joe Sakic, and **Peter Stastny** all played for the NHL franchise. The Nordiques were never a top team, and they had only two strong seasons, 1976–1977 (WHA) and 1985–1986 (NHL). After being drafted by the team in 1991, **Eric Lindros** refused to play for them. After a long dispute and arbitration, the Nordiques sent Lindros to the **Philadelphia Flyers** in exchange for forwards **Peter Forsberg** and Mike Ricci, **goaltender Ron Hextall**, and **defensemen** Steve Duchesne and Kerry Huffman. In 1995, the franchise relocated to Denver, Colorado, and was renamed the **Colorado Avalanche**.

QUINN, JOHN BRIAN PATRICK "PAT," "THE BIG IRISHMAN". B. 29 January 1943, Hamilton, Ontario. Pat Quinn made his **National Hockey League (NHL)** debut as a **defenseman** for the **Toronto Maple Leafs** in 1968. As a player, he is remembered for an open-**ice** body **check** on **Bobby Orr** in the 1969 **Stanley Cup Playoffs** against the **Boston Bruins** that left Orr unconscious and started a brawl. During his nine NHL seasons, Quinn also played for the **Vancouver Canucks** and Atlanta Flames; however, his major hockey contribution was as a NHL head **coach** (1978–2010) for the **Philadelphia Flyers**, **Los Angeles Kings**, **Vancouver Canucks**, Toronto Maple Leafs, and **Edmonton Oilers**. Quinn reached the **Stanley Cup** Finals twice, with the Flyers in 1980 and the Canucks in 1994. For his coaching, Quinn won the **Jack Adams Award** twice (1979–1980, 1991–1992). Internationally, he has coached Team **Canada** to gold medals at the 2002 **Olympic Games**, 2008 **International Ice Hockey Federation** World U18 Championships, and 2009 World Junior Championship, as well as **World Cup of Hockey** championship in 2004.

R

RADULOV, ALEXANDER VALERIEVICH. B. 5 July 1986, Nizhny Tagil, **Russia**. Alexander Radulov is a Russian professional **ice** hockey forward currently with the **Nashville Predators** of the **National Hockey League (NHL)**. He is the all-time leading **scorer** of the Kontinental Hockey League (KHL), with 254 **points**. He also holds the records for most career **assists** (163) and points (80) in a single KHL season. Radulov joined the NHL Nashville Predators during the 2006–2007 season. During the 2007 NHL **Stanley Cup Playoffs**, he was suspended for one game for hitting Steve Bernier of the **San Jose Sharks**. Bernier was hit from behind and sent into the **boards** headfirst and lay motionless on the ice for three minutes. Luckily, Bernier did not suffer any permanent **injuries**. In 2008, Radulov announced that he wanted to return to Russia to play hockey. Immediately after that, the Predators, NHL, and **International Ice Hockey Federation** all released statements emphasizing that Radulov's contract obligated him to the Predators through the 2008–2009 season. After Radulov missed a 1 September 2008 deadline to return to Nashville, the Predators suspended him without pay for the 2008–2009 season. He returned to Nashville late in the 2011–2012 season and played nine games. His older **brother**, Igor Radulov, was a **left wing** with the **Chicago Blackhawks** from 2002–2004.

"RAG THE PUCK". The term *rag the puck* is used to describe when a player **skates** with the **puck** only trying to maintain control of it. It is done to use up time, as a **penalty killer**, or toward the end of a game.

RANSCOMBE, HILDA. B. 11 September 1913, Preston, Ontario. D. 25 August 1998, Cambridge, Ontario. Hilda Ranscombe was an all-round athlete who excelled in softball and tennis and captured several titles in each; however, her name is synonymous with **women's ice hockey**. She was one of the best hockey players of all time. Some writers have called Ranscombe the **Wayne Gretzky** of women's hockey; others have said that she was the **Aurèle Joliat** or **Gordie Howe** of her era. She was an outstanding stickhandler and **scorer**. Unfortunately, accurate statistics weren't kept to chronicle

263

her scoring feats. When asked about her hockey abilities, Ranscombe said, "The whole team was the Most Valuable Player." Ranscombe and the **Preston Rivulettes** dominated the 1930s. When World War II began, the team disbanded and ended this remarkable era of women's hockey. Ranscombe devoted her life to hockey, and she became a **coach** after retiring as a player. Before her death in 1998, she donated all of her **equipment** to the **Hockey Hall of Fame**. The Preston Rivulettes hockey team was inducted into the Cambridge Sports Hall of Fame in 1997, and Ranscombe was also inducted individually.

RATELLE, JOSEPH GILBERT YVON "JEAN," "GENTLEMAN JEAN". B. 3 October 1940, Lac Saint-Jean, Quebec. Jean Ratelle was a **center** in the **National Hockey League (NHL)** for a total of 21 seasons with the **New York Rangers** (1960–1976) and **Boston Bruins** (1975–1981). Ratelle was part of the GAG (**goal**-a-game) **line**, with Vic Hadfield and **Rod Gilbert**. In 1972, they had a combined total of 138 goals. Ratelle won the **Bill Masterton Memorial Trophy** in 1971. On 27 February 1972, he became the first Ranger in history to **score** 100 **points** in a single season. Less than a week later, a **puck** fractured his ankle and he was out for the rest of the season. That same year, he won the Lester B. Pearson Award. Sometimes called by the **nickname** "Gentleman Jean," Ratelle was known for his sportsmanship, and he won the **Lady Byng Memorial Trophy** twice (1971, 1976). During his career, Ratelle scored 491 goals and played in the **Stanley Cup** Finals with the Rangers in 1972 and the Bruins in 1977 and 1978. Unfortunately, his teams never won the Stanley Cup. In 1985, Ratelle was inducted into the **Hockey Hall of Fame**.

RAYNER, CLAUDE EARL "CHUCK," "BONNIE PRINCE CHARLI". B. 11 August 1920, Sutherland, Saskatchewan. D. 6 October 2002, Langley, British Columbia. Chuck Rayner was a professional **goaltender** with the Springfield Indians of the **American Hockey League (AHL)** in 1940–1941, and he led the AHL in **shutouts** (6) that season. He was then called up to the **National Hockey League (NHL)** and played in 36 games for the newly formed Brooklyn Americans. Rayner interrupted his hockey career to enlist in the Royal **Canadian** Navy during World War II. In 1945, he returned to the NHL as a member of the **New York Rangers**. During the 1945–1946 season, he formed the first two-goalie partnership in NHL history with Jim Henry. **Coach Frank Boucher** played them in alternate games, in alternate periods, and on a few occasions he even changed them from shift to shift, just as he changed **defensemen**. Rayner led the NHL in shutouts (5) during the 1946–1947 season. In 1950, he was awarded the Hart Trophy as Most Valuable Player, and he is one of only five goalies to have earned that recognition. Rayner was known as one of the first wandering goalies. On more than one occasion, he made a **save** and **skated** up the **ice** with the **puck** before returning to protect his **net**. Two times he came right in on the opposing goalie and almost **scored**. Unfortunately, Rayner never played on a **Stanley Cup** championship team. Due to his numerous **injuries**, he retired in 1953, and was replaced by **Gump Worsley**. In 1973, Rayner was inducted into the **Hockey Hall of Fame**.

REARDON, KENNETH JOSEPH "KENNY," "BEANS," "HORSE-FACE," "BIG OX," "BUTCHER". B. 1 April 1921, Winnipeg, Manitoba. D. 15 March 2008, Saint-Sauveur, Quebec. Kenny Reardon was a **defenseman** for the **Montreal Canadiens** (1940 1942, 1945–1950). His teammates **nicknamed** him "Beans" because he was full of it on the **ice**. He was also called "Horseface," "Big Ox," and "Butcher." Reardon was known as a tough player who continued to play while **injured**. He left hockey when he enlisted in the **Canadian** Army in 1942. He was awarded the Field Marshall Montgomery Certificate for his bravery in battle. After World War II, Reardon returned to the Canadiens and won the **Stanley Cup** in 1946. He and **Butch Bouchard** were a tough pair on the Montreal team. Reardon and Cal Gardner of the **New York Rangers** had an ongoing feud. In a 1946 game, Gardner knocked out six of Reardon's teeth. Then, on 31 December 1949, Reardon got even by breaking Gardner's jaw. In 1950, Reardon retired from playing due to the numerous injuries he had sustained, but he continued his career off the ice as a hockey executive, mainly with the Canadiens. After scouting and managing farm teams to many **minor-league** championships, he became the vice president of the Canadiens. As part of the Montreal management, the team won five Stanley Cup titles. In 1966, Reardon was inducted into the **Hockey Hall of Fame** as a player. **Don Cherry** said that Reardon was his childhood hero.

RED LINE. The red line, or center line, has existed in **ice** hockey since 1943. It is 12 inches wide and runs across the entire width of the **rink**. It runs parallel to the **goal lines** and divides the rink into two halves. Its main purpose is to serve as a reference point for the **referees** for calling **icing** and **offsides**. In addition, the **center face-off** circle is in the middle of the red line. Play starts at the center face-off circle at the beginning of each period and after a goal has been **scored**.

REFEREE. The referee is the **on-ice official** who has the final word on infractions and rule interpretations during a hockey game. The referee is also responsible for dropping the **puck** during all **face-offs** occurring at **center ice**. In the early days of hockey, only one referee and an occasional assistant were on the ice. Former players often became referees, including **King Clancy**, **Clarence Day**, **Cecil Dye**, and Frank Foyston. In 1937, the first referee training camp was opened, with Bill Stewart instructing. The three-official system uses one referee and two **linesmen**. This is the most common officiating system, and it is currently used by the **American Hockey League**. The **National Hockey League (NHL)** previously used this system, until changing to the four-official system in the late 1990s. Today, each NHL game is officiated by two referees and two linesmen. The referee has a designated spot on the ice at the **penalty box** area, called the referee's **crease**, which is off-limits to the players during disputes or **penalty** assessments. Several referees have been inducted into the **Hockey Hall of Fame**, including **Neil Armstrong**, John D'Amico, **Ray Scapinello**, **Red Storey**, and Frank Udvari. On 30 December 1979, Udvari made NHL history when he came out of retirement to officiate a game after the referee was injured. Udvari was 55 years old, and he became the first Hockey Hall of Famer to participate in a game after being inducted. *See also* APPENDIX E for a list of Hockey Hall of Fame on-ice official inductees.

RHÉAUME, MANON "THE FIRST WOMAN OF HOCKEY". B. 24 February 1972, Lac-Beauport, Quebec. Manon Rhéaume was a female hockey **goaltender**. **Nicknamed** "The First Woman of Hockey," she achieved a number of historic firsts during her career. In 1992, Rhéaume tried out for the **Tampa Bay Lightning** of the **National Hockey League (NHL)** and was signed as a free agent. This was the first time a woman tried out for an NHL team or signed a professional hockey contract. She played one period in an exhibition game against the **St. Louis Blues** on 23 September 1992, and allowed two **goals**. She played in another exhibition game against the **Boston Bruins** in 1993. Manon's younger **brother**, Pascal Rhéaume, was a **center** for the NHL's **New Jersey Devils**. Rhéaume spent five years in the professional **minor leagues**, playing for a total of seven teams and appearing in 24 games. She also played on the **women's ice hockey** team for **Canada** and won gold medals at the Women's **World Ice Hockey Championships** in 1992 and 1994. As a member of the **Canadian Women's Olympic Ice Hockey Team**, Rhéaume helped her team win the silver medal at the 1998 Winter Olympics in Nagano, Japan. She also played professional **roller hockey** during the summers. Rhéaume wrote her autobiography, *Manon: Alone in Front of the Net*, in 1994. She retired from professional hockey in 2000, but continued to be a pioneer. She focused on designing hockey **equipment** better suited for girls.

RICHARD, JOSEPH HENRI "POCKET ROCKET". B. 29 February 1936, Montreal, Quebec. Henri Richard is **Maurice Richard**'s younger **brother** and was a talented hockey player in his own right. Because he was 15 years younger and three inches shorter than Maurice, he was given the **nickname** "Pocket Rocket." He played 20 seasons in the **National Hockey League (NHL)** with the **Montreal Canadiens** (1955–1975). Henri served as team captain from 1971–1975. He played **center** and led the NHL in **assists**, with 52 (1957–1958) and 50 (1962–1963). Richard was a fast **skater** with great stickhandling skills, and he was also known for his **checking** abilities. On 5 May 1966, he **scored** the **Stanley Cup**–winning **overtime goal** in Montreal's 3–2 win over the **Detroit Red Wings**. Richard also scored the Stanley Cup–winning goal against the **Chicago Black Hawks** on 18 May 1971. With his name engraved on the Stanley Cup eleven times, Richard played on more Stanley Cup champions than any other player. He is followed by **Jean Béliveau** of the Canadiens, with 10 championships.

Henri and Maurice played together for Montreal from 1955 until Maurice retired in 1960. Henri was known for being very quiet in the locker room. When **Coach Toe Blake** was asked if Henri spoke English, he said, "Hell, I don't even know if he speaks French." During his career, Henri played in 1,256 regular-season games and recorded 358 goals, 688 assists, 1,046 **points**, and 928 **penalty minutes**. He also played in 180 **Stanley Cup Playoff** games, with 49 goals, 80 assists, 129 points, and 181 penalty minutes. Henri was always being compared to Maurice, but they had very different styles. Henri once said that, "I am me, not my brother. Maurice is the best hockey player of all time." Although Maurice scored more goals (544 compared to Henri's 358), Henri played two more seasons and recorded more points than his brother (1,046 to Maurice's 965). In 1979, Henri was inducted into the **Hockey Hall of Fame**.

RICHARD, MAURICE "THE ROCKET". B. 4 August 1921, Montreal, Quebec. D. 27 May 2000, Montreal, Quebec. Maurice Richard was the oldest of eight children, and his brother, **Henri Richard**, was also a professional hockey player. Maurice played 18 seasons in the **National Hockey League (NHL)** with the **Montreal Canadiens** (1942–1960). He was the captain of his team from 1956–1960. Maurice played **right wing** and set several NHL records. On 19 October 1957, he became the first player in NHL history to record 500 career **goals**. Maurice had a talent for scoring spectacular goals, which he did 544 times during his career. He was an important member of the Montreal franchise during their **Stanley Cup** dynasty (1955–1956 to 1959–1960). Maurice **scored** three **overtime** goals in a single Stanley Cup series, a record he shares with Mel Hill. He got the **nickname** "The Rocket" from the fire and fury he used to **skate** down the **ice**. Maurice's passion sometimes led to **fighting**. **Sid Abel** earned the nickname "Old Bootnose" after Richard punched him and broke his nose in two places. On 17 March 1955, Maurice was suspended for the remainder of the season and the **Stanley Cup Playoffs** after punching a **linesman** during a fight. The suspension sparked the "Richard Riot" in Montreal. Conversely, Maurice was very shy off the ice. Some people have also called him the "Babe Ruth of Hockey." He received the **Hart Memorial Trophy** in 1947.

Maurice was inducted into the **Hockey Hall of Fame** in 1961, without the customary waiting period. In 1996, at the closing of the **Montreal Forum**, he received the longest standing ovation in the Montreal's history. Fans chanted his nickname over and over again. The shy Richard waved and mouthed "thank you" while he choked back tears. The newest trophy in the NHL was established by the Montreal Canadiens in 1999, to honor Maurice Richard. He was the first player to have a 50-goal season (1944–1945), and he was the league's top scorer five times. The **Maurice "Rocket" Richard Trophy** is presented to the NHL's leading goal scorer for the season. The first recipient was **Teemu Selänne**. During his 18 seasons in the NHL, Maurice played in 978 regular-season games and recorded 544 goals, 421 **assists**, 985 **points**, and 1,285 **penalty minutes**. His career playoff record includes 133 games, during which he recorded 82 goals, 44 assists, 126 points, and 188 penalty minutes. In 2005, the French version of the **movie** *Maurice Richard* was released. A year later, the English-subtitled version entitled *The Rocket: The Maurice Richard Story* was released.

RIGHT WING. A player who plays the position of right wing **skates** on the right side of the **center** and passes the **puck** between the **left wing** and the center. The player in this position attempts to move the puck down the **ice** and **score** a **goal**. Wings are also known as forwards. Defensively, they try to prevent the other team's wings from moving forward and scoring. Left-handed shooters typically play left wing, and right-handed shooters usually play right wing. One great player who was an exception to this rule was **Maurice Richard**, who played right wing but was a left-handed shooter.

RILEY, JOHN P. "JACK," JR. B. 15 June 1920, Medford, Massachusetts. Jack Riley was a great **college hockey** player at Dartmouth College (1940–1942, 1946–1947). He left to serve as a U.S. naval aviator during World War II. Riley returned to college in 1946, and he captained the team that tied the University of Toronto for the North American hockey title. Riley was also a member of the fourth-place U.S. team at the 1948 **Olympic Games** in **Switzerland**. He joined the U.S. Military Academy in 1950, where he was head **coach** until 1986. His son, Rob Riley, later took over. Jack was twice named Coach of the Year by the **National Collegiate Athletic Association (NCAA)**. He had only six losing seasons in his 36 years at

West Point, and, at the time of his retirement, his 541 career wins were second only to Michigan Tech's John McInnes in the history of NCAA hockey. One highlight of his career was when he coached the **U.S. Men's Olympic Ice Hockey Team** in 1960, and won the country's first gold medal in hockey. They defeated the strong **Russian** team, 3–2, and came from behind to defeat the team from Czechoslovakia with a **score** of 9–4. Riley received the **Lester Patrick Trophy** in 1986, and again in 2002, as part of the 1960 U.S. Olympic team.

RINK. The word *rink* is a Scottish word meaning "course," and it was used as the name of the area used for the sport of curling. A hockey rink is the sheet of **ice** used for **skating**. Before 1929, ice hockey rink dimensions could range from 112 feet by 58 feet to 250 feet by 116 feet. During the 1929–1930 season, the **National Hockey League (NHL)** included specific rink dimensions in the rule book, and they remain in place to this day. The official size of a NHL rink is 200 feet long by 85 feet wide, with the corners rounded in the arc of a circle with a radius of 28 feet. Because the **Boston Bruins'** and **Chicago Blackhawks'** arenas were built prior to or during the 1929–1930 season, their rinks have been grandfathered into the rules. The Bruins play on a rink that is 191 feet by 88 feet, and the Blackhawks' rink is 188 feet by 85 feet. When the **Buffalo Sabres** entered the NHL, they were granted permission to use the War Memorial Auditorium rink (which is 193 feet by 84 feet) if they increased the seating capacity from 10,000 to 15,000, which they did. The rink is also surrounded by a wooden or fiberglass wall known as the "boards." The term *boarding* describes a player being aggressively slammed into the side of the rink. This illegal **checking** results in a **penalty**. Ice hockey rinks used for international events, like the **Olympic Games**, follow the **International Ice Hockey Federation** specifications, which is 61 meters (200 feet) by 30 meters (98 feet), with a corner radius of 4.2 meters (14 feet).

ROBERTS, GORDON WILLIAM "GORDIE," "DOC". B. 5 September 1891, Ottawa, Ontario. D. 2 September 1966, Ottawa, Ontario. Although Gordie Roberts was never on a team that won the **Stanley Cup**, he was a memorable hockey player. He was a **left wing** for the **Ottawa Senators** (1909–1910), **Montreal Wanderers** (1910–1916), Seattle Metropolitans (1917–1918), and **Vancouver Millionaires** (1916–1917, 1919–1920). During the 1916–1917 season, he set a **Pacific Coast Hockey Association** record by **scoring** 43 **goals** in 23 games. Roberts was known as a good shooter with a curved shot. In 1918, he helped lead Seattle to the **Stanley Cup Playoffs**, but they were defeated by Vancouver. Roberts was a gentleman player, before the **Lady Byng Trophy** was created. He would help players up if they fell and apologize to them after knocking them down on the **ice**. He earned the **nickname** "Doc" after receiving his medical degree from McGill University in 1916. Roberts practiced medicine during the off-season before he retired as a player in 1918. By 1919, he was practicing medicine in Howe Sound, British Columbia, and he then moved to New York in 1922 to do postgraduate work. He moved west and taught at Stanford University and then practiced medicine in Oakland, California. Roberts had the chance to make a comeback with the Ottawa Senators in 1922, but he decided against it. During his 10-year hockey career, he **scored** 204 goals in 167 games. Roberts was inducted into the **Hockey Hall of Fame** in 1971.

ROBINSON, LARRY CLARK "BIG BIRD". B. 2 June 1951, Winchester, Ontario. Larry Robinson was a **defenseman** for 20 seasons in the **National Hockey League (NHL)** with the **Montreal Canadiens** (1972–1989) and **Los Angeles Kings** (1989–1992). The **nickname** "Big Bird" came from his height (he stood at 6 feet, 4 inches tall), and because some people thought he moved like the character from *Sesame Street.* Robinson was part of six **Stanley Cup** championship teams (1973, 1976, 1977, 1978, 1979, 1986). He holds the NHL record for most consecutive years appearing in the **Stanley Cup Playoffs** (20). He also shares the Canadiens' team record with **Guy Lapointe** for all-time playoff **goals** by a defenseman, with 25. Robinson **scored** 85 **points** during the 1976–1977 season. He won the **James Norris Memorial Trophy** in 1977 and 1980, and the **Conn Smythe Trophy** in 1978. Montreal defenders Robinson, **Serge Savard**, and Guy Lapointe were known as "Les Trois Gros," or "The Big Three." Internationally, Robinson played for **Canada** in the 1981 **World Ice Hockey Championships** and the 1976, 1981, and 1984 **Canada Cups**. After retiring from playing, he became an assistant to **Coach Jacques Lemaire** of the **New Jersey Devils** (1993–1994). Robinson then coached the **Los Angeles Kings** (1995–1999) and New Jersey Devils (1999–2006). He won the Stanley Cup in 2000 as the Devils' coach. When asked to describe his biggest thrill in hockey, Robinson once said, "That's like eating a can of beans and asking which one gives you gas. Honestly, I couldn't even pick." During his career, he played in 1,384 regular-season games and had 208 goals, 750 **assists**, 958 points, and 793 **penalty minutes**. Robinson grew up on a farm in Ontario and loved horses. With teammate **Steve Shutt** and a local veterinarian, he founded the Montreal Polo Club in Quebec. In 1995, Robinson was inducted into the **Hockey Hall of Fame** as a player.

ROBITAILLE, LUC "LUCKY LUC". B. 17 February 1966, Montreal, Quebec. Luc Robitaille played **left wing** in the **National Hockey League (NHL)** with the **Los Angeles Kings** (1986–1994, 1997–2001, 2003–2004, 2005–2006), **Pittsburgh Penguins** (1994–1995), **New York Rangers**

(1995–1997), and **Detroit Red Wings** (2001–2003). During his **rookie** year, he **scored** 84 **points** and won the **Calder Memorial Trophy** (1987). Internationally, Robitaille played for **Canada** in the 1991 **Canada Cup** and 1994 **World Ice Hockey Championships**. During the 1992–1993 season, he set season records for left wings with 63 **goals** and 125 points. On 29 January 1998, he earned his 1000th career point in a Los Angeles **match** against the **Calgary Flames**. Close to a year later, on 7 January 1999, Robitaille scored his 500th career goal in a 4–2 victory over the **Buffalo Sabres**. On 18 January 2002, he scored his 611th goal, breaking **Bobby Hull**'s record for left wings. Robitaille helped the Red Wings defeat the **Carolina Hurricanes** to win the **Stanley Cup** in 2002. When he retired in 2006, he had recorded 668 goals and 1,394 points in 1,431 regular-season games, making him the highest-scoring left wing in NHL history. He also ranks fourth in NHL career **power play** goals, with 247.

During his hockey career, Robitaille had two unique **superstitions**. One day, his Kings' roommate, Tomas Sandstrom, checked out of the hotel for both of them, and Robitaille had a great game that night. After that, Sandstrom always checked out for them. Robitaille also had a specific routine regarding the tape on his **hockey stick**. Once as a **young player**, his team ran out of white tape, so he used black tape for the second period. Because he played well in that one game, the superstition began. After that, Robitaille always used white tape for his stick in periods one and three, and black tape in period two. In 2009, he was inducted into the **Hockey Hall of Fame**.

ROLLER HOCKEY. Roller hockey is a form of hockey played on a dry surface, with players on **skates** with wheels. In 1863, J. L. Plimpton invented the roller skate in the **United States**. Then, in 1870, the first games of roller hockey were played in Europe. Other than the obvious footwear difference, a main difference between **ice** hockey and roller hockey is the rule about **checking**. Body checking is prominent in the sport of ice hockey, while in roller hockey, body checking is forbidden. Roller hockey also does not have **offsides** and **icing** rules, like ice hockey. In 1999, the Pan-American Games included roller hockey as an event for the first time. In Barcelona, Spain at the 1992 Summer Olympics, roller hockey was an exhibition sport; however, it has not become an official **Olympic** sport like ice hockey. **National Hockey League** players **Chris Chelios**, **Marty McSorley**, and Joe Sakic all have **brothers** who played in the Roller Hockey International. Some famous roller hockey players include brothers Brian and Joey Mullen, female player **Manon Rhéaume**, and Tony Szabo.

ROOKIE. A player is considered a rookie during his first year playing in the **National Hockey League (NHL)**. The Rookie of the Year is honored with the **Calder Memorial Trophy**. **Teemu Selänne** holds the records for the most **goals** (76) and most **points** (132) by a rookie in one season. **Peter Stastny** and Joe Juneau both recorded 70 **assists** in a single season for a high record. Dino Ciccarelli and Ville Leino share the NHL record for most points by a rookie in a single **Stanley Cup Playoff** year, with 21. **Wayne Gretzky** had 137 points and 86 assists (1979–1980), but he was not considered a rookie because he had previously played a season in the **World Hockey Association**.

ROSS, ARTHUR HOWEY "ART". B. 13 January 1886, Naughton, Ontario. D. 5 August 1964, Boston, Massachusetts. Art Ross played football and hockey as a youth. He was a **defenseman** who was loaned to the **Kenora Thistles** and became a member of their **Stanley Cup**–winning team in January 1907. In 1908, with the **Montreal Wanderers**, he won the Stanley Cup once again. Ross's playing career ended when the Wanderers withdrew from the league during the 1917–1918 season. He played in a total of 183 regular-season games during his 14-year career and recorded 100 **goals**, 19 **assists**, 119 **points**, and 492 **penalty minutes**. He went on to **coach** the **Hamilton Tigers** (1922–1923) and **Boston Bruins** (1924–1928, 1929–1934, 1936–1939, 1941–1945). Ross also served as the general manager of the Bruins from 1924–1954. He built up the Boston team by adding **Frank Brimsek**, **Dit Clapper**, and **Eddie Shore**.

For many years, Ross had an ongoing feud with **Conn Smythe**, owner of the **Toronto Maple Leafs**. They gave each other grief, and sometimes **Frank Calder**, the president of the **National Hockey League (NHL)**, had to intervene. After World War II, they patched up their disagreement. According to Smythe, "His two sons served overseas and had excellent records. I figured anybody who could rear two boys like that must be all right." Ross was also a hockey innovator who created a type of **puck** that is still used today. Previous pucks had sharp edges and were not beveled. He also improved the style of the goal **nets**. Pucks frequently bounced out the back of the old nets, while his improved version kept the pucks contained. Ross was elected to the **Hockey Hall of Fame** in 1945, as one of the 12 original inductees. He donated the **Art Ross Trophy**, which has been given to the NHL's leading **scorer** each year since 1948. In 1984, he was awarded the **Lester Patrick Trophy** posthumously.

ROSS, PHILIP DANSKEN "P. D". B 1 January 1858, Montreal, Quebec. D. 5 July 1949, Montreal, Quebec. P. D. Ross studied at McGill University and Queen's University, and he was on the football, **lacrosse**, and rowing teams. In 1886, Ross became coowner of the almost bankrupt *Ottawa Evening Journal* newspaper, and he made it into a highly successful and respected paper. He was also known as an **ice** hockey **builder**. Ross was involved in the early days with the Ontario Hockey Association, playing on the Ottawa senior team that later became the **Ottawa Senators**. He then befriended the sons of **Lord Stanley of Preston**, the governor general of **Canada**. Ross loved hockey and taught the game to Lord Stanley's two sons. Lord Stanley is known to sports fans as the person who donated the trophy now known as the **Stanley Cup**; however, Ross is the true father of the trophy. While hockey was becoming popular in Canada, Ross convinced Lord Stanley to provide a trophy to honor Canada's top amateur hockey team. In 1892, Lord Stanley appointed him to be a trustee for the championship ice hockey trophy. Ross served that role for 56 years, until his death in 1949. He also served as trustee for the Minto Cup of lacrosse. He turned down the trusteeship for the Grey Cup of Canadian football. Ross was inducted into **Canada's Sports Hall of Fame** in 1974 and the **Hockey Hall of Fame** in 1976 as a builder.

ROUGHING. A two-minute **penalty** is given to a player who engages in excessive physical play. Descriptions of roughing include one player throwing a punch, two players each throwing one punch, and pushing and shoving after the **referee** blows his whistle. When players "**drop the gloves**" and have a full-blown fight, they each get a five-minute penalty for **fighting**.

ROVER. In the days of seven-man hockey, a player who roamed the entire **rink** was known as a rover. The rover was positioned behind the front **line** and became either an extra attacker or an extra defensive player. Rover Tom Hooper **scored** three **goals** for the **Kenora Thistles** in their **Stanley Cup** win over the **Montreal Wanderers**. **Hobey Baker**, **Cy Denneny**, **Si Griffis**, **Newsy Lalonde**, **Frank McGee**, Ernie Russell, and **Cyclone Taylor** were some other notable rovers. Former rover Frank Rankin coached the 1924 **Canadian Men's Olympic Ice Hockey Team** to a gold medal finish.

ROY, PATRICK EDWARD ARMAND "ST. PATRICK". B. 5 October 1965, Quebec City, Quebec. Patrick Roy was a **goaltender** for 19 seasons in the **National Hockey League (NHL)** for the **Montreal Canadiens** (1984–1996) and **Colorado Avalanche** (1996–2003). On 2 December 1995, in a game against the **Detroit Red Wings**, Montreal played its worst home game in franchise history, losing 12–1. Roy was then traded to Colorado. This may be the reason why the Avalanche and Red Wings had such a rivalry. Roy once fought Detroit's goalie, Mike Vernon, and another time he fought another Red Wings goalie, Chris Osgood. The Avalanche and Red

Wings met in the **Stanley Cup Playoffs** four times after 1996, with both teams winning two series. Roy popularized the butterfly style of goaltending. He won four **Stanley Cups**, two with the Canadiens (1986, 1993) and two with the Avalanche (1996, 2001). He also won the **Calder Cup** (1985), **Conn Smythe Trophy** (1986, 1993, 2001), and **Vezina Trophy** (1989, 1990, 1992), as well as the **William M. Jennings Trophy** three times in a row with Brian Hayward (1987–1989). Roy is the only player to have won the Conn Smythe Trophy three times.

Roy earned the **nickname** "St. Patrick" after his heroic play during the 1986 Stanley Cup Playoffs. He also played for **Canada** in the 1998 **Olympic Games**. He led the NHL in **shutouts** in 1991–1992 (5), 1993–1994 (7), and 2001–2002 (9). On 26 December 2001, against the **Dallas Stars**, Roy became the first NHL goaltender to win 500 games. He holds the NHL record for the most playoff games played by a goalie (247), most playoff wins (151), and most combined regular-season and playoff wins (704). He ranks second in career games played by a goaltender, with 1,029. Roy retired with the most wins by a goaltender in NHL history, with 551, although he has since been passed by **Martin Brodeur** of the **New Jersey Devils**. Roy had 23 career playoff shutouts, and Brodeur has had 24 to date.

Roy was known for being very **superstitious**. He refused to step on the **blue lines** or the **red line** and would skip over them, even during the pregame **skate**. He was often seen talking to the goalposts, and during intermissions Roy would bounce and juggle a **puck** and then hide it from his teammates. He wrote the names of his children on his **hockey stick** and wound tape around the knob exactly 60 times, one for each minute of play. Roy was inducted into the **Hockey Hall of Fame** in 2006. His younger **brother**, Stephane Roy, was a hockey **center** who briefly played in the NHL with the Minnesota North Stars during the 1987–1988 season.

RUGGIERO, ANGELA MARIE. B. 3 January 1980, Simi Valley, California. Angela Ruggiero played **women's ice hockey** as a **defenseman**. While still a high school senior, she played on the gold medal–winning 1998 **U.S. Women's Olympic Ice Hockey Team** in Nagano, Japan. She then played **college hockey** at Harvard University while studying for a degree in government. Ruggiero was also a member of the silver medal–winning 2002 U.S. **Olympic** team in Salt Lake City, Utah; the bronze medal–winning 2006 U.S. Olympic team in Torino, Italy; and the silver medal–winning 2010 U.S. Olympic team in Vancouver, **Canada**. She made history on 28 January 2005, when she played for the Tulsa Oilers in a Central Hockey League game against the Rio Grande Valley Killer Bees. She was the first woman to actively play in a regular-season professional hockey game in the **United States** at a position other than goalie. And, since her **brother**, Bill Ruggiero, also played for the Oilers, they were the first brother and sister combination to play professionally at the same time. Angela also won silver medals in the Women's **World Ice Hockey Championships** in 1997, 1999, 2000, and 2001. In addition, she is credited with the game-winning **goal** in the shootout that won the 2005 Women's World Ice Hockey Championships for the United States against the Canadian national women's hockey team, winning the first-ever gold medal for the United States at the World Ice Hockey Championships. Ruggiero's memoir, *Breaking the Ice: My Journey to Olympic Hockey, the Ivy League, and Beyond*, was published in 2005. She recently retired from playing and is pursuing a master's degree in sports management at the University of Minnesota.

RUSSIA. When hockey fans yell "Chaïbou!" it means "**Score** a goal!" in Russian. In 1952, the Soviet Union became a member of the **International Ice Hockey Federation (IIHF)**. They competed in a total of nine **Olympic Games** (1956–1988). The **Soviet Union Men's Olympic Ice Hockey Team** dominated the Olympics, winning seven gold medals, one silver, and one bronze. The **United States** defeated the Soviet team twice (1960, 1980), and these upsets were considered miracles. The team also won nearly every **World Ice Hockey Championships** between 1954–1991. The amateur status of the Soviet players was questionable, but they were strong competitors in both amateur and professional tournaments. In 1972, the first **Summit Series**, consisting of professional players, was held between the Soviet team and the **Canadian** team. A second Summit Series was held in 1974. The countries won one tournament each. Goalie **Vladislav Tretiak, defenseman Viacheslav Fetisov**, and forwards **Valeri Kharlamov** and Sergei Makarov, who all played for the Soviet teams in the 1970s and the 1980s, were all excellent hockey players.

Anatoli Tarasov was their legendary and successful **coach**. After 1991, the Soviet team competed as the Unified Team at the 1992 Winter Olympics, and as the Commonwealth of Independent States at the 1992 World Ice Hockey Championships. In 1993, it was replaced by national teams for Belarus, Estonia, Kazakhstan, Latvia, Lithuania, Russia, and Ukraine. The IIHF recognized the Ice Hockey Federation of Russia as the successor to the Soviet Union Ice Hockey Federation and passed its ranking on to Russia. The other national hockey teams were considered new and sent to compete in other divisions. Russia is currently a member of the "Big Six," which is a term for the six strongest men's **ice** hockey nations. The other five teams include Canada, the **Czech Republic**, **Finland**, **Sweden**, and the United States. The men's team currently has a first-place ranking by the IIHF, and the women's team has a fifth-place ranking. In the mid-1990s, the **Detroit Red Wings** of the **National Hockey League** had the "Russian Five," consisting of forwards Sergei Fedorov, Slava Kozlov, and **Igor Larionov**, and defensemen **Vladimir Konstantinov** and Slava Fetisov. Recent NHL star players from Russia include **Pavel Datsyuk**, Ilya Kovalchuk, **Evgeni Malkin**, and **Alexander Ovechkin**.

S

SALMING, ANDERS BÖRJE. B. 17 April 1951, Kiruna, **Sweden**. Börje Salming was **defenseman** from Sweden who played in the **National Hockey League (NHL)** with the **Toronto Maple Leafs** (1973–1990). In his **rookie** season (1973–1974), he accumulated 39 **points** and was able to handle the rough play of the NHL, unlike his predecessor, **Ulf Sterner**. Salming combined excellent **puck**-handling skills with solid defensive play to become one of Toronto's most popular players. In 1976, he joined the first of three consecutive NHL **All-Star Teams**. When an eye **injury** stopped him in the 1978 **Stanley Cup Playoffs**, thousands of international fans sent him get-well wishes. He recovered and registered 73 points the next season. On 4 January 1988, Salming became the first European-born player to appear in 1,000 NHL games. He spent his final NHL season with the **Detroit Red Wings** (1989–1990) and then played in Sweden until 1993. Salming helped open the door of the NHL to players born and trained in Europe. In 1,148 NHL regular-season games during 17 seasons, Salming recorded 150 **goals** and 787 points. He also had 12 goals and 49 points in 81 **Stanley Cup** Playoff games. He represented Sweden at the 1976, 1981, and 1991 **Canada Cups**; the 1972, 1973, and 1989 **World Ice Hockey Championships**, and the 1992 **Olympic Games**. In 1973, Salming's goal in the medal-round **match** versus **Finland** gave Sweden the victory it needed to clinch the silver medal at the World Ice Hockey Championships. He was inducted into both the **Hockey Hall of Fame** (1996) and **International Ice Hockey Federation Hall of Fame** (1998).

SAN JOSE SHARKS. The San Jose Sharks are a professional **ice** hockey team in the **Pacific Division** of the **National Hockey League (NHL) Western Conference**, based in San Jose, California. Since their first season in 1991–1992, the team has not made it to the **Stanley Cup** Finals. During their third season, the Sharks pulled off the biggest turnaround in NHL history, finishing with a 33-35-16 record and making the **Stanley Cup Playoffs** with 82 **points**, a 58-point jump from the previous season. They were seeded eighth in the Western Conference Playoffs and faced the **Detroit Red**

Wings, one of the favorites to win the Stanley Cup. In one of the biggest upsets in Stanley Cup Playoff history, the underdog Sharks shocked the Red Wings in seven games. In the last game, Jamie Baker **scored** the game-winning **goal** in the third period after goalie Chris Osgood was out of position, and the Sharks won, 3–2. In the second round, the Sharks had a 3–2 series lead over the **Toronto Maple Leafs**, but the team lost the final two games in Toronto, including one in **overtime**. At the beginning of each home game, the lights go down, a 17-foot-long shark mouth is lowered from the rafters, and the players **skate** through the mouth onto the ice. The *Jaws* theme song is played when the Sharks go on the **power play**. Among the best players for the Sharks have been **Hockey Hall of Famers Ed Belfour** and **Igor Larionov**. There have been eight head **coaches** for the franchise. The first head coach was George Kingston, who coached the team for two seasons. Darryl Sutter coached the most games of any San Jose head coach, with 434 games. Their current coach is Todd McLellan. San Jose won the **Presidents' Trophy** in 2009. On 31 March 2011, the Sharks clinched their 13th (and seventh consecutive) playoff slot in franchise history with a 6–0 victory over the **Dallas Stars**. Five days later, they clinched their sixth Pacific Division championship. In 20 seasons in the NHL (1991–1992 to 2011–1912), the Sharks have compiled a record of 721-672-121-94 (1,657 points) and made 15 playoff appearances. In 2012, the San Jose lost (4–1) to the **St. Louis Blues** in the Western Conference Quarterfinals.

SATHER, GLEN CAMERON "SLATS," "TOMATO FACE". B. 2 September 1943, High River, Alberta. Glen Sather was a **left wing** in the **National Hockey League (NHL)** for the **Boston Bruins** (1966–1969), **Pittsburgh Penguins** (1969–1971), **New York Rangers** (1970–1974), **St. Louis Blues** (1973–1974), **Montreal Canadiens** (1974–1975), and Minnesota North Stars (1975–1976). He also played for the **Edmonton Oilers** (1976–1977) when they were part of the **World Hockey Association (WHA)**. While he was a player, Sather was **nicknamed** "Tomato Face" because his face got red during **matches**. During his NHL career, he played in 688 regular-season games and recorded 80 **goals**, 113 **assists**, 193 **points**, and 724 **penalty minutes**. His WHA career record included 81 games, 19 goals, 34 assists, 53 points, and 77 penalty minutes. Sather was better known for his **coaching** abilities. He coached the Oilers (1979–1989, 1993–1994) and was responsible for drafting **Mark Messier**. He won the **Stanley Cup** as a coach in 1984, 1985, 1987, and 1988. In 1986, he received the **Jack Adams Award**. In 1990, he won his fifth Stanley Cup with the Oilers, this time as their general manager. Sather also coached the **Canadian** team in the **World Ice Hockey Championships**, the **Canada Cup**, and the 1996 **World Cup of Hockey**. From 2002–2004, he coached the **New York Rangers**. Sather was inducted into the **Hockey Hall of Fame** in 1997, in the **builder** category.

Since 2000, he has been the president and general manager of the Rangers. His team made it to the 2012 **Eastern Conference** Finals before being defeated by the **New Jersey Devils** in six games.

SAVARD, DENIS JOSEPH. B. 4 February 1961, Pointe Gatineau, Quebec. Denis Savard recorded 455 **points** as a hockey player on his hometown **junior** team. He was known for his end-to-end rushes and playing on the effective "Trois Denis" **line**, with Denis Cyr and Denis Tremblay. All three men were born on the exact same day of the same year and were all drafted by the **National Hockey League (NHL)**. Savard played **center** for 17 NHL seasons with the **Chicago Black Hawks (Chicago Blackhawks)** (1980–1990, 1995–1997), **Montreal Canadiens** (1990–1993), and **Tampa Bay Lightning** (1993–1995). He recorded three **assists** in his first NHL game and 75 points his **rookie** year. Savard was known for his stickhandling expertise and fast **skating**. He also copied **Serge Savard** by performing the "Savardian Spin-o-rama," by quickly spinning around with the **puck** to avoid being **checked**. Internationally, Denis played for **Canada** in the 1984 **Canada Cup**. His highest **goal** total (47) came during the 1985–1986 season, and his highest **point** total (131) came during the 1987–1988 campaign.

On 12 January 1986, in the third period against the Hartford Whalers, Savard tied Claude Provost's record for the fastest goal **scored** from the start of a period (four seconds). In 1990, he was traded to Montreal for **Chris Chelios**. On 11 March 1990, against the **St. Louis Blues**, Savard scored his 1,000th NHL career point. In 1993, he won the **Stanley Cup** when the Canadiens defeated the **Los Angeles Kings** in five games. In 1,196 regular-season NHL games, Savard scored 473 goals and made 865 assists, totaling 1,338 points. He ranks third, after **Bobby Hull** and **Stan Mikita**, for total points in Chicago's history. Five times during his career, Savard scored at least 100 points, and for seven straight years he had at least 30 goals per season. In 169 **Stanley Cup Playoff** games, he scored 66 goals and 109 assists for a total of 175 points. After retiring from playing, Savard was Chicago's assistant **coach** (1997–2006) and then head coach (2006–2008). He was inducted into the **Hockey Hall of Fame** in 2000.

SAVARD, SERGE AUBREY "THE SENATOR," "MINISTER OF DEFENSE". B. 22 January 1946, Montreal, Quebec. Serge Savard was a **defenseman** who played for **Canada** in the 1972 **Summit Series**. The team won every game that Savard played in. He also played in the 1976 **Canada Cup**. During his **National Hockey League (NHL)** career, Savard was a member of the **Montreal Canadiens** (1966–1981) and **Winnipeg Jets** (1981–1983). In 1969, he became the first defenseman to win the **Conn Smythe Trophy**. Savard, **Guy Lapointe**, and **Larry Robinson** made up the

"Big Three" defensive unit for the Canadiens. To avoid being checked, Savard created a move known as the "Savardian Spin-o-rama," where he would quickly spin around with the **puck**. He won seven **Stanley Cups** from 1968–1979. Although the Canadiens also won the Stanley Cup in 1971, Savard missed most of the season due to a leg **injury**. He won the **Bill Masterton Memorial Trophy** in 1979. Savard played in 1,040 regular-season games and had 106 **goals**, 333 **assists**, 439 **points**, and 592 **penalty minutes**. In 1983, he became Montreal's general manager and led them to Stanley Cups in 1986 and 1993. Savard was inducted into the **Hockey Hall of Fame** in 1986. He was made an Officer of the Order of Canada (1994) and a Knight of the National Order of Quebec (2004). He was also a successful businessman in Montreal.

SAVE. In sports like **ice** hockey and **lacrosse**, the **goaltender** is credited with a save when they prevent the **puck** or ball from entering the **net**. A statistic to measure the goalie's abilities is the save percentage, which is the percentage of shots stopped divided by shots on **goal**. After beating **Dominik Hašek**'s record of .937, Tim Thomas of the **Boston Bruins** set the record for the highest save percentage in a regular season, at .938 (2010–2011). That same season, he also made the most saves during a **Stanley Cup Playoff** run (798) and the most saves in a **Stanley Cup** Finals series (238). The goaltender who made the most saves in one regular-season game (80) is **Chicago Black Hawks'** Sam LoPresti, on 4 March 1941. In 2003–2004, Roberto Luongo of the **Florida Panthers** made the most saves in one season (2,303).

SAWCHUK, TERRANCE GORDON "TERRY," "UKEY". B. 28 December 1929, Winnipeg, Manitoba. D. 31 May 1970, New York, New York. Terry Sawchuk was a **goaltender** in the **National Hockey League (NHL)** for 21 seasons. His NHL hockey career was spent with the **Detroit Red Wings** (1949–1955, 1957–1964, 1968–1969), **Boston Bruins** (1955–1957), **Toronto Maple Leafs** (1964–1967), **Los Angeles Kings** (1967–1968), and **New York Rangers** (1969–1970). He was the only player to be named **Rookie** of the Year in three different professional hockey leagues. He won with the Omaha Knights of the United States Hockey League (1947–1948), the Indianapolis Capitols of the **American Hockey League** (1948–1949), and the Detroit Red Wings of the NHL (1950–1951). His teammates called him "Ukey" after his Ukrainian heritage. Sawchuk hurt his arm playing rugby as a child and it never properly healed, but he continued to play hockey. Throughout the years, Sawchuk had many **injuries**, including a severed wrist tendon, a damaged elbow, a collapsed lung, ruptured discs in his back, and more than 400 stitches in his face, but through it all, he still played hockey. He was also quirky and kept the bone spurs from his elbow, the teeth that had been knocked out, and his removed appendix. Despite his injuries, Sawchuk won 447 regular-season NHL games. He also led the NHL in **shutouts**, with 11 (1950–1951), 12 (1951–1952), and 12 (1954–1955). Between 1951–1955, he allowed less than two **goals** per game for five consecutive years. He helped Detroit win the **Stanley Cup** in 1952, 1954, and 1955. While Sawchuk enjoyed playing for Detroit, he said that the highlight of his career was Toronto's 1967 Stanley Cup underdog victory over the **Montreal Canadiens**. He won the **Vezina Trophy** in 1952, 1953, 1955, and 1965 (with **Johnny Bower**). Sawchuk ranks third in NHL career games played by a goalie (971) and second in NHL career shutouts (103).

On 29 April 1970, Sawchuk and his Rangers' teammate, Ron Stewart, got into an alcohol-related scuffle on his front lawn. Sawchuk suffered a lacerated liver, and clots had to be surgically removed. After two operations, Sawchuk died of heart failure on 31 May 1970, at the age of 40. An investigation into possible involuntary manslaughter was conducted, but Stewart was cleared of any wrongdoing. In 1971, Sawchuk was inducted into the **Hockey Hall of Fame** and awarded the **Lester Patrick Trophy** posthumously.

SCAPINELLO, RAYMOND ANGELO JOSEPH "RAY," "SCAMPY". B. 5 November 1946, Guelph, Ontario. Ray Scapinello has been called the **"Wayne Gretzky** of officiating" because he set so many records for **linesmen** in the **National Hockey League (NHL)**. He had the longest on-ice career of anyone in the history of the NHL. At the beginning of his hockey career, he worked full-time during the week and officiated **American Hockey League** games on the weekends. He was then hired as an NHL official for the start of the 1971–1972 season. Scapinello's first NHL game was in upstate New York, on 17 October 1971, with the **Buffalo Sabres** playing the Minnesota North Stars. On 2 April 2004, he officiated his 2,500th and final NHL **match**, also in Buffalo, with the visiting **Toronto Maple Leafs** playing the hometown Sabres. Scapinello joined the NHL before **helmets** were made mandatory for officials. Through 33 years as an NHL **on-ice official**, Scapinello never missed an assignment, and, on 20 occasions, he was selected as the best linesman in the business. He was chosen for the **Stanley Cup Playoffs** in his second season (1972), and he continued officiating playoff games every year until he retired in 2004, for a total of 426 games. Scapinello was also a linesman in three NHL **All-Star** Games, and he was one of the officials selected to work at the 1998 Winter Olympics in Nagano, Japan. Growing up, he earned the **nickname** "Scampy" due to his small size and excellent **skating** ability. He stayed fit during training camp by juggling and riding a unicycle. He was well-respected and liked by his peers. Since his retirement, Scapinello has been a supervisor for Central Hockey League, and he also wrote *Between the Lines: Not-So-Tall Tales from Ray "Scampy" Scapinello's Four Decades in the NHL* (2006), a book about his lengthy career. Scapinello was inducted into the **Hockey Hall of Fame** in 2008.

SCHMIDT, MILTON CONRAD "MILT," "THE COUNT OF SAUER-KRAUT". B. 5 March 1918, Kitchener, Ontario. Milt Schmidt was a **National Hockey League (NHL) center** for 16 seasons with the **Boston Bruins** (1936–1942, 1945–1955). He earned the **nickname** "The Count of Sauerkraut" because he was part of the famous **line** known as the "Kraut Line," with **Bobby Bauer** and **Woody Dumart**. During the 1939–1940 season, the entire line finished first, second, and third in **scoring**, the first time for such an occurence in hockey history. Schmidt was the leading **scorer** that season. He won the **Stanley Cup** in 1939 and 1941, and he led the **Stanley Cup Playoffs** in **points** (11) in 1940–1941. Due to World War II, Schmidt, Bauer and Dumart missed three NHL seasons. In his first year back, Schmidt scored a personal high of 27 **goals** and 62 points. In 1951, he won the Hart Trophy. Schmidt was known for his stickhandling skills and for playing a clean but tough game. The 1952 playoff series between the Bruins and **Montreal Canadiens** was particularly brutal. **Maurice Richard** returned to the seventh game after receiving six stitches as a result of being hit with a **hockey stick**. The Canadiens' **coach, Dick Irvin**, even needed stitches after a **puck** shot off the **boards** by Schmidt hit him in the nose.

Schmidt served as captain of the Bruins (1951–1954), then coach (1954–1961, 1962–1966), and then general manager (1967–1972). He then became general manager of the newly formed **Washington Capitals** (1974–1976). Washington set a record for the worst NHL record ever of 8-67-5 (1974–1975). Their three coaches that season were Jim Anderson, Red Sullivan, and Schmidt. Schmidt finished his playing career with 229 goals and 346 **assists** for 575 points in 776 regular-season NHL games. He was inducted into the **Hockey Hall of Fame** in 1961. In 1996, he received the **Lester Patrick Trophy**. Still a fan of hockey in his 90s, Schmidt once reminisced about playing during the helmetless, mouth guard free–era and joked, "Maybe we had concussions and didn't know it."

SCHRINER, DAVID "SWEENEY". B. 30 November 1911, Saratov, Russian Federation. D. 4 July 1990, Calgary, Alberta. David Schriner earned the **nickname** "Sweeny" due to his fondness of baseball player Bill Sweeney. Schriner played 11 seasons in the **National Hockey League (NHL)** as a **left wing** with the **New York Americans** (1934–1939) and **Toronto Maple Leafs** (1939–1943, 1944–1946). In 1935, he won the Calder Trophy as **Rookie** of the Year. He led the NHL in **scoring** in 1936 and 1937, with 45 and 46 **points**, respectively. Trailing three games to zero, Sweeney helped the Maple

Leafs come back to defeat the **Detroit Red Wings** in seven games during the 1942 **Stanley Cup** Finals. In the final game, Schriner **scored** to tie the game, 1–1, and then Pete Langelle scored for Toronto. Schriner scored the final **goal** to make the score 3–1. He won the Stanley Cup again in 1945, against the Wings, also in seven games. A year later, he retired from playing hockey in the NHL. Schriner played 484 regular-season NHL games and had 201 goals and 204 **assists** for 405 points. He coached **minor-league** teams from 1946–1952. Schriner was inducted into the **Hockey Hall of Fame** in 1962.

SCHULTZ, DAVID WILLIAM "DAVE," "THE HAMMER". B. 14 October 1949, Waldheim, Saskatchewan. Dave Schultz was a **left wing** in the **National Hockey League (NHL)** with the **Philadelphia Flyers** (1971–1976), **Los Angeles Kings** (1976–1978), **Pittsburgh Penguins** (1977–1979), and **Buffalo Sabres** (1978–1980). He earned the **nickname** "The Hammer" as a physical, hardworking **enforcer**, and he was one of the reasons why the Flyers were called "Broad Street Bullies." Schultz **scored** the series-clinching **goal** in **overtime** in the first round of the 1974 **Stanley Cup Playoffs** against the Atlanta Flames, and he helped the Flyers win the Stanley Cup in 1974 and 1975. He played in 535 regular-season NHL games and recorded 79 goals, 121 **assists**, 200 **points**, and 2,294 **penalty minutes**. Schultz set a NHL single-season record of 472 penalty minutes in 1974–1975. By comparison, **Alex Delvecchio** accumulated a total of only 383 penalty minutes during 24 NHL seasons. Schultz met his equal during the 1975 playoffs, when **rookie Clark Gillies** of the **New York Islanders** beat him up. Once, after **injuring** his hand in a **fight**, Schultz wore boxing wraps to protect his hands. Other NHL enforcers also started wearing them to prevent injuries during conflicts. The NHL went on to pass the "Schultz Rule," which prohibits hockey players from wearing hand wraps. When speaking about stick-swinging, Schultz once said, "Dennis Hextall, one of the worst offenders, gave me great respect for the injury potential of wood when he nearly put the blade of his stick through my neck." After retiring from playing in 1980, Schultz coached a few **minor-league** teams. He sang a local Philadelphia hit song called "The Penalty Box" in the mid-1970s. In 1983, Schultz wrote his autobiography, *The Hammer: Confessions of a Hockey Enforcer*, with the help of **Stan Fischler**.

SCHULZ, CHARLES MONROE "SPARKY". B. 26 November 1922, Minneapolis, Minnesota. D. 21 February 2000, Santa Rosa, California. Charles Schulz was most famous for his career in cartooning; however, he was also an avid hockey fan and often incorporated **ice** hockey and figure **skating** into his comic strip, *Peanuts*. He sometimes drew Snoopy driving a **Zamboni**. Schulz was the owner of the Redwood Empire Ice Arena, in Santa

Rosa, which opened in 1969, and featured a snack bar called "The Warm Puppy." In 1975, at his Redwood Empire Ice Arena, he formed Snoopy's Senior World Hockey Tournament, which had age divisions, starting at 40 years old but with no maximum age restriction. Schulz played in all of his annual tournaments, and, as he reached an age milestone, he created another division. The divisions, named after his comic strip characters, include the Charlie Brown Division, Lucy Division, Peppermint Patty Division, Marcie Division, Linus Division, Rerun Division, Spike Division, and Woodstock Division. In 1998, Schulz hosted the first Over 75 Hockey Tournament. On 12 February 2000, while battling cancer, he suffered a fatal heart attack. The last original *Peanuts* strip was published the next day, on Sunday, 13 February 2000, just hours after his death. In 2001, Saint Paul renamed the Highland Park Ice Arena the Charles M. Schulz Highland Arena in his honor. In 1981, he received the **Lester Patrick Trophy** for his outstanding contribution to the sport of hockey in the **United States**. Schulz was inducted into both the **U.S. Hockey Hall of Fame** (1993) and the U.S. Figure Skating Hall of Fame (2007).

SCORE. In hockey the word *score* means to put the **puck** in the **net**. Like many other sports, it also measures which team won, for example, "What was the final score of the game?" Since the **National Hockey League** was formed in 1917, the official scorer has been one of the **off-ice officials**. They are responsible for keeping the statistics, including crediting players with **goals** and **assists**. **Joe Malone** scored the most goals in one regular-season game (7) on 31 January 1920. When a team doesn't score any goals, it is called a **shutout**. The highest-scoring game ever played was on 3 March 1920, when the **Montreal Canadiens** defeated the **Quebec Bulldogs**, 16–3.

SEIBERT, EARL WALTER. B. 7 December 1911, Berlin, Ontario. D. 20 May 1990, Agawam, Massachusetts. Earl Siebert was the son of hockey player Oliver Siebert. They have the distinction of being the first father and son team to be inducted into the **Hockey Hall of Fame** in the player category. Earl was a **defenseman** in the **National Hockey League (NHL)** who played 15 seasons for the **New York Rangers** (1931–1936), **Chicago Black Hawks** (1935–1945), and **Detroit Red Wings** (1944–1946). He won the **Stanley Cup** with New York in 1933, and Chicago in 1938. Seibert was known for his rugged physical play, and even tough guys **Eddie Shore** and **Red Horner** avoided him. Unfortunately, it was Siebert who caused **Howie Morenz** of the **Montreal Canadiens** to slide into the **boards** during a 28 January 1937 game. Morenz broke his leg in several places and subsequently died in the hospital. Seibert felt guilty, even saying that he had killed Morenz. After his NHL retirement, Seibert was a **coach** for Eddie Shore's Springfield Indians from 1946–1951. His Hockey Hall of Fame induction was in 1963, two years after his father's.

SELÄNNE, TEEMU ILMARI "THE FINNISH FLASH". B. 3 July 1970, Helsinki, **Finland.** Teemu Selänne grew up playing hockey with his twin **brother,** Paavo Selänne, who played goalie. Paavo remained in Finland and became a teacher, while Teemu left his country to join the **National Hockey League (NHL)** in 1992 as a **right wing.** During his **rookie** year with the **Winnipeg Jets,** Teemu broke **Mike Bossy**'s previous NHL rookie 53-**goal** record. Selänne **scored** 76 goals and 132 **points** and received the **Calder Memorial Trophy** (1993). In 1999, Selänne was the first recipient of the newest NHL trophy, the **Maurice "Rocket" Richard Trophy**, presented to the NHL's leading goal scorer for the season. Selänne has 248 career **power play** goals. **Left wing** Dave Andreychuk holds the record, with 274. Selänne's **skating** speed and talent earned him the **nickname** "The Finnish Flash." **Jari Kurri** of the **Edmonton Oilers** also had the same nickname. After overcoming major knee surgery and scoring 90 points (40 goals and 50 **assists),** Selänne was awarded the **Bill Masterton Memorial Trophy** (2006). He won the **Stanley Cup** in 2007. On 28 March 2011, he collected three goals and two assists against the **Colorado Avalanche.** He was the first 40-year-old player to earn five points with a **hat trick** in one game. One of Selänne's goals was scored on a **penalty** shot, which also made him the oldest NHL player in history to have a penalty shot goal. Aside from the Jets, teams he's played with include the Mighty Ducks of Anaheim, **San Jose Sharks,** and **Colorado Avalanche.**

At the end of the 2011–2012 season, he had played in 1,341 regular-season NHL games and recorded 663 goals, 743 assists, and 1,406 points. Despite rumors that he plans to retire, Selänne currently plays for the **Anaheim Ducks.** Internationally, he played for **Finland** in the 1999 **World Ice Hockey Championships.** At the **Olympic Games,** he won a silver medal (2006) and two bronze medals (1998, 2010). He is also the all-time point leader in men's Olympic **ice** hockey. Selänne won the Best Hockey Player of Finland Trophy five times. Off the ice, he can be found signing autographs for his fans, playing golf, or watching auto racing. Selänne will surely be inducted into the **Hockey Hall of Fame** when he becomes eligible.

SEMENKO, DAVID JOHN "DAVE," "SAMMY," "CEMENTHEAD". B. 12 July 1957, Winnipeg, Manitoba. Dave Semenko played in the **National Hockey League (NHL)** from 1977–1988 in the **left wing** position. He played for the **Edmonton Oilers** (1977–1987), Hartford Whalers, and **Toronto Maple Leafs.** When the Oilers were part of the **World Hockey Asso-**

ciation (WHA), Semenko **scored** the last **goal** in WHA history on 20 May 1979, in a 7–3 loss to the **Winnipeg Jets**. During his career, he made a name for himself as **Wayne Gretzky**'s on-**ice** bodyguard and **enforcer**. Semenko was a tough player who offered protection to his other teammates, allowing the Edmonton's stars, **Jari Kurri**, **Mark Messier**, and **Paul Coffey** more freedom to score. Semenko helped the Oilers win **Stanley Cups** in 1984 and 1985. He also fought boxing legend Muhammad Ali in an exhibition fight on 12 June 1983. After playing briefly with the Hartford Whalers and Toronto Maple Leafs, he retired after the 1987–1988 season. Semenko finished his 575 regular-season NHL games with 65 goals, 88 **assists**, and 1,175 **penalty minutes**. After retiring, he became a commentator on the Oilers' radio broadcasts and then an assistant **coach** with the Oilers in 1996, before joining the scouting staff.

SHACK, EDWARD STEVEN PHILLIP "EDDIE". B. 11 February 1937, Sudbury, Ontario. Eddie Shack was a **left wing** in the **National Hockey League (NHL)** from 1958–1973. He played for numerous teams, including the **New York Rangers**, **Toronto Maple Leafs**, **Boston Bruins**, **Los Angeles Kings**, **Buffalo Sabres**, and **Pittsburgh Penguins**. He earned the **nickname** "Eddie the Entertainer" from his legendary mad dashes up and down the **rink,** and for putting on a show for the fans. During the 1966–1967 season, Shack broke out, scoring his career-high 26 **goals** on the Toronto **line** with Ron Ellis and **Bob Pulford**, and his popularity inspired a novelty song called "Clear the Track, Here Comes Shack," written in his honor and played by the group Douglas Rankine with the Secrets. It lasted three months on the **Canadian** pop charts and even hit number one. Shack also used to sing the chorus of the song "**Gordie Howe** Is the Greatest of Them All" when young **Mark Howe** entered the opponents' dressing room. When describing Shack's unique hockey style, **Coach Punch Imlach** said, "Shackie can play all three forward positions, but his trouble is that he tries to do it all at the same time." Recognized by his large nose and classic mustache, Shack was known for his powerful body **checks**, hard shot, and great sense of humor. After "coco-bonking" **Henri Richard** with his head, **Maurice Richard** told Eddie, "Thank God you never hit my brother with your nose, or you would have split him in two."

Shack played for **Stanley Cup**–winning teams in 1962, 1963, 1964, and 1967. He **scored** the Stanley Cup–winning goal in 1963, claiming that he had scored the goal off of his backside and was only trying to get out of the way. In 1968, while playing for the Bruins, Shack was involved in a major **hockey stick** incident with the **Philadelphia Flyers' Larry Zeidel**.

Shack was the son of Ukrainian immigrants. He disliked school and was illiterate for most of his life, but, as an adult, he became an advocate for literacy programs in Ontario. He also entertains school children with his hockey stories and tells them to focus on their education. Shack may never be inducted into the **Hockey Hall of Fame**, but his combination of toughness, leadership, character, and showmanship made a mark in the history of hockey.

SHERO, FREDERICK ALEXANDER "FRED," "THE FOG". B. 23 October 1925, Winnipeg, Manitoba. D. 24 November 1990, Camden, New Jersey. As a child, Fred Shero began boxing and became a **Canadian** bantamweight champion at 13 years of age, but he chose to pursue a career in hockey instead. He was a **defenseman** from 1947–1958 in the **National Hockey League (NHL)**. On 16 October 1947, he made his NHL debut with the **New York Rangers** against the **Montreal Canadiens** at the **Montreal Forum**. While Shero was a loner and often seemed to be lost in thought, his **nickname**, "The Fog," had a different origin. On night during a 1948 game in St. Paul, Minnesota, the high humidity resulted in heavy fog on the indoor **rink**. Shero was the only player who said he could see the **puck**, and his teammates started calling him "Freddy the Fog." In 1971, he was named head **coach** of the **Philadelphia Flyers**. In the seven seasons Shero served as the team's coach, he guided them to four consecutive seasons with a .700 or better winning percentage. He often wrote motivational sayings on a blackboard to inspire his players. One classic phrase he is known for came before Game 6 of the 1974 **Stanley Cup** Finals. Shero wrote his now famous quote, "Win today and we walk together forever." He led the Flyers to the Stanley Cup championship in 1974 and 1975. In 1974, he became the first coach to win the **Jack Adams Award**. After the 1978–1979 season, he retired from Philadelphia and joined the New York Rangers as their coach and general manager. In his first year with New York, he led them to the Stanley Cup Finals, but they lost to the Montreal Canadiens. In 1980, he received the **Lester Patrick Trophy**. Shero left the Rangers during the 1980–1981 season. Between 1971–1981, his teams had a record of 390-225-119. He was the first coach to hire a full-time assistant coach, have his players use strength training, study films, and utilize a morning **skating** session. He briefly coached in Holland (1987–1988) and then worked as a radio analyst for the **New Jersey Devils**. Commenting on Shero's preoccupied nature, **Scotty Bowman** once said, "Sometimes I don't think he knows the difference between Tuesday and Wednesday. And sometimes I think he's a genius who has us all fooled." His son, Ray Shero, also played hockey and is the current general manager of the **Pittsburgh Penguins**.

SHORE, EDWARD WILLIAM "EDDIE," "THE EDMONTON EX-PRESS". B. 25 November 1902, Fort Qu'Appelle, Saskatchewan. D. 16 March 1985, Springfield, Massachusetts. Eddie Shore was a tough **defenseman** who played 16 professional hockey seasons from 1924–1940. He played one season for the Regina Capitals (1924–1925) of the **Western Canada Hockey League** and one season for the Edmonton Eskimos (1925–1926) of the renamed Western Hockey League. He and **Bun Cook** were the league's star players. After the league folded in 1926, Shore joined the **Boston Bruins** of the **National Hockey League (NHL)**, where he remained until he retired from the NHL in 1940. He helped the Bruins win the **Stanley Cup** in 1929 and 1939. Individually, Shore won the Hart Trophy in 1933, 1935, 1936, and 1938. Due to his rough and sometimes dirty play, many fans disliked him. Sportswriter Ring Lardner once called him, "The only man in hockey generally known to people who dislike hockey." His own teammate, Billy Coutu, nearly severed Shore's ear during a **fight** at training camp in 1926.

One of the most brutal fights in hockey history involved Shore. In a 1929 **match** against the **Montreal Maroons**, Shore was **checked** throughout the game. Near the end, **Babe Siebert high-sticked** him and knocked Shore unconscious. Even though it was an obvious foul, Siebert wasn't given a **penalty**. Shore once left the hospital and played against the **Montreal Canadiens, scoring** two **goals** and one **assist,** all while nursing three broken ribs. During a game in the 1930s, he was given a beating by Murray Patrick, who had been the heavyweight boxing champion of the **Canadian** armed forces. During the course of Shore's career, he broke his nose 19 times and his jaw five times; had 978 stitches in his face; and fractured his hip, back, and collarbone.

In 1933, Shore was the first hockey player to wear a **helmet** because he feared retaliation from players and fans after severely **injuring Ace Bailey** in a game on 12 December 1933. Shore had several **superstitions**, including wearing only blue shirts on game days; needing a towel on his dressing room chair; and requiring that he was undressed by his trainer, "Hammy" Moore. In 1940, he purchased the Springfield Indians of the **American Hockey League**, managed them until 1967, and owned them until 1978. He was a player, **coach**, manager, and popcorn seller. As a coach, he was known for his frugal and eccentric style. He once traded a player for a hockey **net** and had his other players pass out programs. His reputation was well-known, and some NHL players specifically had their contracts say that they couldn't be sent to the Indians. His players went on strike in December 1966, to protest the suspensions of four Springfield players. The strike was settled with the help of Alan Eagleson, who later helped form the NHL union. Shore was inducted into the **Hockey Hall of Fame** in 1947. In 1970, he received the **Lester Patrick Trophy.**

SHUTOUT. A game in which a **goaltender** does not allow a single **goal** is called a shutout. The term *cob* is slang for a shutout; for example, "We won the game three-cob." The record for the most shutouts in one season is 22, by **George Hainsworth** (1928–1929). **Martin Brodeur** and **Patrick Roy** hold the record for the most career shutouts in the **Stanley Cup Playoffs**, with 23. Brodeur also holds the record for most career shutouts, with 116. In the 2003–2004 season, Brian Boucher of the **Phoenix Coyotes** recorded five consecutive shutouts, which broke the previous record of four set by the **Montreal Canadiens'** **Bill Durnan** (1948–1949). More recently, goalie Ilya Bryzgalov of the **Philadelphia Flyers** had three consecutive shutouts in March 2012.

SHUTT, STEPHEN JOHN "STEVE," "BULLET," "GARBAGE MAN". B. 1 July 1952, Toronto, Ontario. Steve Shutt was a forward in the **National Hockey League (NHL)** with the **Montreal Canadiens** (1972–1984) and **Los Angeles Kings** (1984–1985). He was given the **nickname** "Bullet" because of his powerful shot. Some people also called him the "Garbage Man" because he netted so many garbage **goals** on rebound shots. He and linemate **Guy Lafleur** were known for the one-two scoring rhythm they used. Shutt was an important part of the Montreal team that won five **Stanley Cups** in 1973, 1976, 1977, 1978, and 1979. In 1976–1977, Shutt led the NHL in total goals (60), even-strength goals (52), and game-winning goals (9). He also holds Montreal's team record for career goals (408) and **points** (776) by a **left wing**. Internationally, Shutt played for **Canada** in the 1976 **Canada Cup**. In 1993, he was inducted into the **Hockey Hall of Fame**. As an avid polo player and lover of horses, he founded the Montreal Polo Club in Quebec with **Larry Robinson** and a local veterinarian.

SIEBERT, ALBERT CHARLES "BABE". B. 14 January 1904, Plattsville, Ontario. D. 25 August 1939, Zurich, Ontario. Babe Siebert began his hockey career as a **rover** during the era of seven-man hockey. He then played 14 seasons in the **National Hockey League (NHL)** as both a **left wing** and **defenseman.** Siebert played with the **Montreal Maroons** (1925–1932), **New York Rangers** (1932–1934), **Boston Bruins** (1933–1936), and **Montreal Canadiens** (1936–1939). While playing for the Maroons, he was part of a **line** known as the "S line," with **Hooley Smith** and **Nels Stewart**. Siebert won the **Stanley Cup** in 1926 and 1933. After **Eddie Shore** was suspended for **injuring Ace Bailey**, Bruins **coach Art Ross** switched Siebert from left wing to defense. When Shore returned to the game, he and Siebert made a strong defensive team; however, they had once been violent opponents and never became friends as teammates. Siebert won the Hart Trophy in 1937. On the **ice**, he was a physical player and **fighter**, but off the ice he was a soft-spoken family man. Babe's wife, Bernice, became a paraplegic due to child-birth complications. Fans at the **Montreal Forum** often saw him carry her to the seats before every home game, and then carry her off at the end. Shortly after retiring, on 25 August 1939, while swimming with his family on Lake Huron, Siebert drowned. The Canadiens and Maroons organized a benefit game on 29 October 1939, at the Montreal Forum, between the Canadiens and the "NHL **All-Stars**." Although the Canadiens lost the game, 5–2, a large amount of money was raised for Siebert's family. In 1964, Siebert was posthumously inducted into the **Hockey Hall of Fame**.

SILVER SEVEN. *See* OTTAWA SENATORS.

SIMPSON, HAROLD EDWARD JOSEPH "JOE," "BULLET JOE". B. 13 August 1893, Selkirk, Manitoba. D. 25 December 1973, Coral Gables, Florida. Joe Simpson was a **defenseman** for the Edmonton Eskimos of the **Western Canada Hockey League (WCHL)** from 1921–1925. He set WCHL records for **goals** (21) and **points** (33) by a defenseman (1921–1922), and for **assists** (14) (1922–1923). Simpson went on to play in the **National Hockey League** with the **New York Americans** (1925–1931), including three years as their **coach**. As a great **skater** who made end-to-end rushes on the **rink**, he earned the **nickname** "Bullet Joe." It was also in reference to the wounds he suffered during World War I, which earned him the Military Medal for Valor. Simpson was inducted into the **Hockey Hall of Fame** in 1962. In 1975, he was inducted into **Canada's Sports Hall of Fame**. In 1994, the Marine Museum of Manitoba in Selkirk restored a 1963 flat-bottomed freighter and renamed it the *Harold Bullet Joe Simpson*.

SIN BIN. *See* PENALTY BOX "SIN BIN".

SITTLER, DARRYL GLEN. B. 18 September 1950, Kitchener, Ontario. Darryl Sittler was a **center** for 15 seasons in the **National Hockey League (NHL)** with the **Toronto Maple Leafs** (1970–1982), **Philadelphia Flyers** (1981–1984), and **Detroit Red Wings** (1984–1985). He was the captain of the Maple Leafs from 1975–1981. On 7 February 1976, Sittler set a NHL record by **scoring** 10 **points** in an 11–4 win against the **Boston Bruins**. It was the last NHL game played by Boston **goaltender** Dave Reece, who was **nicknamed** the "Human Sieve." The owner of the Maple Leafs, Harold Ballard, gave Sittler a silver tea service in honor of his six **goals** and four **assists** in the one game; however, Sittler and Ballard had multiple disputes throughout the years. On 22 April 1976, in an 8–5 victory over the Philadelphia Flyers, Sittler **scored** 5 goals in a single **Stanley Cup Playoff** game. He shares this NHL record with **Newsy Lalonde** (1919), **Maurice Richard**

(1944), Reggie Leach (1976), and **Mario Lemieux** (1989). While with the Flyers, Sittler expected to be named the team captain, but **Bobby Clarke** traded him to Detroit instead. Sittler said that was a big disappointment, and he retired after only one season with Detroit. Internationally, Sittler played for **Canada** in the 1976 **Canada Cup** and scored the winning **overtime** goal in Canada's 5–4 win over Czechoslovakia. At the 1982 and 1983 **World Ice Hockey Championships**, he helped Canada win bronze medals. In Philadelphia's 5–2 victory over the **Calgary Flames** on 20 January 1983, Sittler recorded his 1,000th NHL career point. Although he played with three teams and scored 484 career goals, he never won the **Stanley Cup**. During his NHL career, he played 1,096 regular-season games and recorded 637 assists, 1,121 points, and 948 **penalty minutes**. Sittler was inducted into the **Hockey Hall of Fame** in 1989. In 1991, he wrote his autobiography, *Sittler*, with Chris Goyens.

SKATE. Skates are the bladed footwear that helps hockey players glide across the **ice**. Hockey **equipment** has been modified throughout the years to reduce **injuries**. Early skates had a sharp heel blade, but then steel guards were developed to cover them. On 13 November 1958, **Maurice Richard** and Marc Réaume tangled their skates during a game, and Richard's Achilles tendon was severed, causing him to miss 42 games that season. In the 1960s, a plastic "safety heel" was created. Long-reaching skates have been prohibited by the **National Hockey League (NHL)**, and most players wore tube skates until the 1970s. Lighter skates were then introduced and are currently worn by players in the NHL. The skates used by **goaltenders** are cut lower in the ankle than a regular hockey skate, and the boot sits closer to the ice for a lower center of gravity. Unlike regular hockey skates, goalie skates are usually protected by a synthetic material covering the toe of the skate to prevent foot injuries from the **puck**. Some hockey players have had **superstitions** about the order in which they would skate onto the ice. **Ray Bourque**'s skate routine included changing the skate laces during each intermission and throwing them all out at the end of every game.

SLAPSHOT. When a hockey player uses a full windup and takes a hard shot at the **puck**, it is called a slapshot. Alex Shibicky is credited with being the first player to use a slapshot. Shibicky once said, "I learned it from **Bun Cook**, but he only used it in practice. I was the first to use it in a game." Shibicky and Cook were teammates on the **New York Rangers** during the 1935–1936 season. **Zdeno Chára** of the **Boston Bruins** holds the record for the fastest slapshot, at 108.8 miles per hour, during the 2012 **All-Star** Game, which broke his previous record. *Slap Shot*, starring Paul Newman, was the title of a **movie** that parodied the violence of hockey in the 1970s.

SLASHING. When a player swings a **hockey stick** at an opponent's body or stick, a slashing **penalty** is called. The **referee** signals it by using a chopping motion against his arm. He has the discretion of calling a minor or major penalty that decides the amount of time the offending player spends in the **penalty box**. A notable slashing incident happened on 5 May 1992, between the **New York Rangers** and **Pittsburgh Penguins**. Pittsburgh's scoring star, **Mario Lemieux**, was slashed on the wrist by Adam Graves. Graves only got a two-minute penalty, and, with Lemieux out of the game, the Penguins lost, 4–2. After discovering that Mario's wrist was broken, the **National Hockey League** suspended Graves for four games. *See also* HIGH-STICKING; HOOKING; TRIPPING.

SLOT. The term *slot* refers to the area on the **ice** hockey **rink** directly ahead of the **goaltender** between the **face-off** circles on each side. Defensive players guard offensive players in the slot. **Left wings** and **right wings** often hover in the deep slot waiting to move toward the **net** and **score**.

SLOVAKIA. In 1993, Slovakia became a member of the **International Ice Hockey Federation (IIHF)**. Since 1994, they have competed in five Winter Olympics. Their highest finish was in 2010, with fourth place. The men's national **ice** hockey team of Slovakia is one of the most successful national ice hockey teams in the world. In 2004, the IIHF ranked them as the third-strongest national team in the world. Since 1994, Slovakia has competed 17 times and won three medals at the **World Ice Hockey Championships**. They earned a silver medal in **Russia** (2000), a gold medal in **Sweden** (2002), and a bronze medal in **Finland** (2003). In the **Olympics**, Slovakia's highest achievement was fourth place in Vancouver in 2010. In the tournament, they won against favorites Russia and Sweden and lost against **Canada** in the semifinals and Finland in the bronze-medal game. The men's team currently has a 10th-place ranking by the IIHF, and the women's team has an eighth-place ranking. There have been more than 50 **National Hockey League (NHL)** players born in Slovakia. **Hockey Hall of Famer Stan Mikita** was born in Slovakia, but he moved to Canada as a child and never represented Slovakia in international tournaments. Current NHL players Peter Budaj, **Zdeno Chára**, **Marián Gáborík**, and Marián Hossa play for Slovakia internationally.

SMITH, CLINTON JAMES "CLINT," "SNUFFY". B. 12 December 1913, Assiniboia, Saskatchewan. D. 19 May 2009, Vancouver, British Columbia. Clint Smith was a **center** in the **National Hockey League (NHL)** who played for the **New York Rangers** (1936–1943) and **Chicago Black Hawks** (1943–1947). He was **nicknamed** "Snuffy" after the 1930s comic strip character Snuffy Smith from *Barney Google*. Smith wore tube **skates**, which added extra ankle and toe protection on the **ice**. He led the Rangers in **scoring** in his second full NHL season, in 1938–1939, with 41 **points**. Smith once said, "I really looked up to **Frank Boucher**. I enjoyed the way he played and wanted to fashion my game after him." Smith did imitate the gentlemanly player when he played 85 consecutive games without being called for a **penalty**. He was awarded his first **Lady Byng Trophy**, in 1939, and a second, in 1944. On 11 November 1943, Smith **scored** the first empty **net goal** in NHL history in Chicago's 6–4 win over the **Boston Bruins**. He helped lead the Rangers to the 1940 **Stanley Cup** championship by defeating the **Toronto Maple Leafs** in six games. That was the last time the Rangers would win the Stanley Cup for 54 years. When he was traded to Chicago, Smith played on a **line** with **Doug Bentley** and **Bill Mosienko**. During the 1943–1944 season, Smith led the NHL in **assists**, with 49. On 4 March 1945, in a game against the **Montreal Canadiens**, he scored four goals in one period to tie a record with **Max Bentley**, and originally set by **Busher Jackson**. After retiring from playing, he was a **coach** for the Cincinnati Mohawks of the **American Hockey League**. Smith was inducted into the **Hockey Hall of Fame** in 1991, and he continued to attend their ceremonies throughout his 90s.

SMITH, REGINALD JOSEPH "HOOLEY". B. 7 January 1903, Toronto, Ontario. D. 24 August 1963, Montreal, Quebec. Hooley Smith was **nicknamed** "Hooley" by his father after the comic strip character Happy Hooligan. He was a skilled oarsman, rugby player, and boxer, but he chose to play **ice** hockey. Smith won the **Allan Cup** in 1922 and 1923. Internationally, he played for **Canada** in the 1924 **Olympics**, where he won a gold medal. Smith was a **defenseman** and **right wing** for a total of 17 seasons in the **National Hockey League (NHL)**, with the **Ottawa Senators** (1924–1927), **Montreal Maroons** (1927–1936), **Boston Bruins** (1936–1937), and **New York Americans** (1937–1941). He was known for his **scoring** abilities and **checking** skills. Smith sometimes lost his temper, and NHL president **Frank Calder** suspended him for one month in 1927, after he attacked **Boston Bruins** player **Harry Oliver**. Smith had an ongoing feud with **Aurèle Joliat** of the **Montreal Canadiens**, and also with **Coach Red Dutton**. While playing for the Maroons, Smith was part of the **line** known as the "S line," with **Babe Siebert** and **Nels Stewart**. Smith won the **Stanley Cup** in 1927 and 1935. He was the captain of the Maroons when they won their second and last Stanley Cup in 1934–1935. The following year, he **scored** 19 **goals** and 19 **assists**. On 24–25 March 1936, Smith's Maroons lost the longest game in NHL history, a **match** against the **Detroit Red Wings** that went to a sixth **overtime** period. When he retired in 1941, Smith was one of the few players to reach the 200-goal mark. During his NHL career, he played in 769 regular-season games and had 211 goals, 223 assists, 434 **points**, and 1,013 **penalty minutes**. Smith was posthumously inducted into the **Hockey Hall of Fame** in 1972.

SMITH, WILLIAM JOHN "BILLY," "BATTLIN' BILLY," "HATCH-ET MAN". B. 12 December 1950, Perth, Ontario. Billy Smith won a **Calder Cup** in 1971 as part of the Springfield Kings of the **American Hockey League**. He went on to become a **goaltender** for 18 seasons in the **National Hockey League (NHL)**. After one season with the **Los Angeles Kings** (1971–1972), Smith spent the rest of his career with the **New York Islanders** (1972–1989). He became the first goalie to be credited with **scoring** a goal. On 28 November 1979, in a game between the Islanders and **Colorado Rockies**, the Rockies' goaltender left the **ice** for an extra attacker. The **puck** was deflected off Smith's chest protector. Then Colorado **rookie** Rob Ramage accidentally made a blind pass from the corner **boards** in the opposing zone to the **blue line**. No one was there to receive the pass, and the puck flew down the length of the ice into the Colorado **net**. Smith had been the last Islander to touch the puck and was credited with the goal. Smith helped the Islanders win the **Stanley Cup** four consecutive times, in 1980, 1981, 1982, and 1983. In 1981, he led the NHL in wins (32). He won the **Vezina Trophy** (1982) and **Conn Smythe Trophy** (1983). In 1983, he also shared the **William M. Jennings Trophy** with Roland Melanson.

Smith earned the **nicknames** "Battlin' Billy" and "Hatchet Man" because of his temper and the way he used his **hockey stick** on players who came near his **crease**. He slashed **Wayne Gretzky**'s ankle in 1981. When his own teammate, **Mike Bossy**, fired a shot at him in practice, Smith objected and charged after him with his stick. He was tackled by some teammates before he attacked Bossy. Smith also refused to shake hands at the end of a **Stanley Cup Playoff** series because he didn't want to feel any worse than he already did. He was also known for faking **injuries**, which often resulted in **penalties** against his opponents. In 1982, **Dave Williams** was suspended for seven games after he retaliated by choking Smith.

During his NHL career, Smith played in 680 regular-season games, with 305 wins, 233 losses, 105 ties, 22 **shutouts**, and 489 **penalty minutes**. Internationally, he played for **Canada** in the 1981 **Canada Cup**. After retiring from playing, Smith was the assistant **coach** for the Islanders (1989–1993) and **Florida Panthers** (1993–2001). He was inducted into the **Hockey Hall of Fame** in 1993. Smith's **brother**, Gord Smith, was a NHL **defenseman** with the **Washington Capitals** (1974–1979) and **Winnipeg Jets** (1979–1980).

SMYTHE, CONSTANTINE FALKLAND CARY "CONN". B. 1 February 1895, Toronto, Ontario. D. 18 November 1980, Toronto, Ontario. At the University of Toronto, Conn Smythe played **college hockey** as a **center**. He captained the Varsity Blues men's **ice** hockey team to the finals of the 1914 Ontario Hockey Association (OHA) junior championships. They won the 1915 OHA junior championship. Frank J. Selke, who later worked for Smythe at **Maple Leaf Gardens**, was the **coach** of the losing team. Smythe was the coach, general manager, and owner of the **Toronto Maple Leafs** of the **National Hockey League (NHL)** from 1927–1961. He was also responsible for having Maple Leaf Gardens built. As the Leafs' owner, Smythe won the **Stanley Cup** eight times (1932, 1942, 1945, 1947, 1948, 1949, 1951, 1962). He served in both World War I and World War II and was in a prisoner of war camp for 14 months during World War I. For many years, Smythe had an ongoing feud with **Art Ross**, general manager of the **Boston Bruins**. They gave each other trouble, and sometimes **Frank Calder**, the president of the NHL, had to intercede. After World War II, they patched up their feud. According to Smythe, "[Ross's] two sons served overseas and had excellent records. I figured anybody who could rear two boys like that must be all right." After returning from World War II, Smythe became involved in several charities and gave back to the community for the rest of his life.

Smythe was inducted into the **Hockey Hall of Fame** in 1958 as a **builder**. In 1961, he supervised the construction of the Hockey Hall of Fame building in Toronto. He also served as the hall's chairman for several years, but he resigned in June 1971, when **Busher Jackson** was posthumously elected as a member. Smythe disapproved of Jackson's off-ice lifestyle of drinking and broken marriages. The **Conn Smythe Trophy** is the NHL award given annually to the Most Valuable Player during the **Stanley Cup Playoffs**. In addition to hockey, Smythe loved horse racing. His own horses won 145 stakes races during his lifetime. His autobiography, *Conn Smythe: If You Can't Beat 'Em in the Alley*, written with Scott Young, was published posthumously in 1981.

SOUTHEAST DIVISION. In 1993, the **National Hockey League (NHL)** renamed the conferences and divisions to reflect their geographic locations. In the NHL, the Southeast Division is one of the three sections of the **Eastern Conference**. The **Atlantic Division** and **Northeast Division** are the other two.

SOVIET UNION MEN'S OLYMPIC ICE HOCKEY TEAM. The Soviet Union Men's Olympic Ice Hockey Team has represented the Soviet Union in the **Olympic Games** since 1956. Historically, the Soviets were the most dominant hockey team in international play. They won nearly every world championship and Olympic tournament held by the **International Ice Hockey Federation (IIHF)** between 1954–1991. Due to the questionable nature of the amateur status of the Soviet players, their participation in the Olympics was heavily debated. This controversy was one reason that the **Summit Series** was created. In this series, professional hockey players from **Canada** competed against the Soviet players. After 1991, the Soviet team competed as the Unified Team at the 1992 Winter Olympics, and as the Commonwealth of Independent States at the 1992 **World Ice Hockey Championships**. In 1993, it was replaced by national teams for Belarus, Estonia, Kazakhstan, Latvia, Lithuania, **Russia**, and Ukraine. The IIHF recognized the Ice Hockey Federation of Russia as the successor to the Soviet Union Ice Hockey Federation and passed its ranking on to Russia. The other national hockey teams became new teams in a different division. The U.S. team defeated the Canadian and Soviet teams to win its first gold medal in the 1960 Olympics. Then, in 1980, the **"Miracle on Ice"** took place. At **Lake Placid**, New York, with **Jim Craig** as their **goaltender**, the young **U.S. Men's Olympic Ice Hockey Team** upset the veteran Soviet Union Men's Olympic Ice Hockey Team by a **score** of 4–3. At the time, it was the most-watched hockey game in the **United States**. Four of the country's most well-known players include **defenseman Viacheslav Fetisov**, forwards **Valeri Kharlamov** and Sergei Makarov, and goaltender **Vladislav Tretiak**. Anatoli **Tarasov** and **Viktor Tikhonov** were two very successful **coaches** for the team.

SQUIRTS. *See* YOUNG PLAYERS.

ST. LOUIS BLUES. The St. Louis Blues are a professional **ice** hockey team in the **Central Division** of the **National Hockey League (NHL) Western Conference**. The Blues joined the league as one of the six new franchises during the NHL expansion in the 1967–1968 season. In its NHL history, the team has made the **Stanley Cup** Finals three times but has never won. The Blues lost in four straight games, twice to the **Montreal Canadiens** (1968, 1969), and once to the **Boston Bruins** (1970). Among the best players for St. Louis have been **Hockey Hall of Famers Bernie Federko, Grant Fuhr, Doug Gilmour, Wayne Gretzky, Glenn Hall, Doug Harvey, Dale Hawerchuk, Brett Hull, Dickie Moore, Jacques Plante,** and **Peter Stastny**. The franchise's first head **coach** was **Scotty Bowman**, who coached the team for three seasons. **Al Arbour** and **Emile Francis** also coached the Blues in the 1970s. The Blues won the **Clarence S. Campbell Bowl** in 1969 and 1970, and the **Presidents' Trophy** in 2000. In 44 seasons in the NHL (1967–1968 to 2011–2012), the St. Louis Blues have compiled a record of 1,544-1,429-

432-101 (3,621 **points**) and made 36 **Stanley Cup Playoff** appearances. They advanced to the 2012 playoffs but were eliminated in the Western Conference Semifinals, 4–0, by the **Los Angeles Kings**.

ST. LOUIS EAGLES. The St. Louis Eagles were a professional **ice** hockey team in the **National Hockey League (NHL)** based in St. Louis, Missouri. They only existed for one season (1934–1935). Following their last-place finish, the **Ottawa Senators** moved their NHL franchise to St. Louis, where it was nicknamed the Eagles, but due to financial troubles, the team was disbanded. Notable players who were on the team included **goaltender** Bill Beveridge and **center Bill Cowley**. During the 1967 expansion, the **St. Louis Blues** franchise brought hockey back to Missouri.

STANLEY, ALLAN HERBERT "SNOWSHOES". B. 1 March 1926, Timmins, Ontario. Allan Stanley was the nephew of **Hockey Hall of Fame** inductee **Barney Stanley**. Allan earned the **nickname** "Snowshoes" due to his plodding style of **skating**. He was a **defenseman** for 21 seasons in the **National Hockey League (NHL)** and played for the **New York Rangers** (1948–1955), **Chicago Black Hawks** (1954–1956), **Boston Bruins** (1956–1958), **Toronto Maple Leafs** (1958–1968), and **Philadelphia Flyers** (1968–1969). Boston fans thought that Stanley was too old to play, but he proved them wrong when he joined the Maple Leafs. He led all NHL defensemen in **goals** (10) during the 1959–1960 season. He then helped Toronto win the **Stanley Cup** four times (1962, 1963, 1964, 1967). He was 41 years old when he played on the 1967 Stanley Cup–winning team, and 43 years old when he finished his career with the Flyers. During his hockey career, Stanley often drank tea with honey during periods, believing that it made him play better. In total, he played 1,244 regular-season NHL games and recorded 100 goals, 333 **assists**, 433 **points**, and had 792 **penalty minutes**. In 1981, Stanley was inducted into the Hockey Hall of Fame, just like his uncle.

STANLEY CUP. The Stanley Cup is the most famous of the four team awards given out by the **National Hockey League (NHL)**. The other three include the **Clarence S. Campbell Bowl**, **Presidents' Trophy**, and **Prince of Wales Trophy**. In 1893, the Stanley Cup was given to honor **Canada**'s top amateur team. The Montreal Amateur Athletic Association was the first winner. In 1912, it was opened to professional teams, and the **Quebec Bulldogs** won. In 1917, the Stanley Cup went international, and the Seattle Metropolitans were the first non-Canadians to win the trophy. In 1926, the NHL and its 10 members became the only ones eligible to compete for it. The same is true today; however, the NHL has grown to 30 teams. The **Montreal Canadiens** have won the trophy the most (24 times).

The Stanley Cup is engraved with the names of the winning players, **coaches**, management, and club staff, and additional metal has been added to accommodate this throughout the years. Of the 12 women who have had their names engraved on the trophy, Marguerite Norris was the first, as president of the winning **Detroit Red Wings** in 1954 and 1955. In 1955, Larry Hillman, also of the Red Wings, became the youngest player to win the Stanley Cup, at 18 years, 2 months, and 9 days of age. **Johnny Bower** was the oldest player to win the prize. He was 42 years and 9 months of age and won while playing with the **Toronto Maple Leafs** in 1967.

After winning the Stanley Cup, players traditionally **skate** around the **rink** holding the trophy above their heads. This tradition began in 1950, when **Ted Lindsay** hoisted it over his head to give the fans a better look at it. The winning team's captain is typically the first person to hold the Stanley Cup; however, there have been three exceptions. In 1993, after the Montreal Canadiens defeated the **Los Angeles Kings**, Guy Carbonneau handed the trophy to **Denis Savard**, as Savard had been the player that many fans had urged the Canadiens to draft back in 1980. Then, in 1998, after the Detroit Red Wings had defeated the **Washington Capitals**, **Steve Yzerman** immediately passed the Stanley Cup to **Vladimir Konstantinov**, whose career with the Red Wings ended due to serious **injuries** in an accident the previous year. Konstantinov had to be wheeled on the **ice**. And, in 2001, the **Colorado Avalanche** won the trophy, and when captain Joe Sakic received the trophy, he immediately handed it to **Ray Bourque**. The deciding game of the finals was the last of Bourque's 22-year NHL career, and he had never been on a Stanley Cup–winning team until then.

Many books have been written about hockey's most famous trophy, including the quest for it and the adventures the Stanley Cup has been on once acquired. One book, by Kevin Allen, is entitled *Why Is the Stanley Cup in Mario Lemieux's Swimming Pool?* (2001). It is no surprise that a chaperone has since been appointed to protect the historic Stanley Cup during its travels. *See also* APPENDIX G for a list of Stanley Cup champions.

STANLEY CUP PLAYOFFS. After the regular hockey season, postseason games are played to determine the season champions. Top teams in the divisions or conferences compete with one another. During the series of playoff games, the winning team advances, and the losing team is eliminated. The final two teams play a series of games to determine the winner of the **Stanley Cup**. Two notable series-changing **penalty** calls during the playoffs happened in 1979 and 1993. In the seventh game of the 1979 semifinals, the **Boston Bruins** were leading, 4–3, over the **Montreal Canadiens**, when they received a penalty for too many men on the **ice**. **Guy Lafleur scored** the **power play goal** for the tie, and Montreal's Yvon Lambert scored the game-winning goal in **overtime**. The Bruins' coach, **Don Cherry**, was then fired. While with the **Los Angeles Kings**, **Marty McSorley** was caught with an illegal **hockey stick** during the second game of the 1993 Stanley Cup Finals against the Canadiens. Montreal won the game in overtime and took the series, 4–1. Six current teams have never made it to the Stanley Cup Finals, including the **Columbus Blue Jackets**, **Phoenix Coyotes**, **Winnipeg Jets**, **Nashville Predators**, **San Jose Sharks**, and **Minnesota Wild**. Many players start growing facial hair at the beginning of the playoffs, believing in the **superstition** that having a beard will help them win the Stanley Cup.

STANLEY, FREDERICK ARTHUR. *See* LORD STANLEY OF PRESTON, FREDERICK ARTHUR.

STANLEY, RUSSELL "BARNEY". B. 1 January 1893, Paisley, Ontario. D. 16 May 1971, Edmonton, Alberta. Barney Stanley played 14 elite and professional hockey seasons from 1914–1928. He was a **right wing** who played for the **Vancouver Millionaires** of the **Pacific Coast Hockey Association (PCHA)** from 1915–1919. Stanley helped them win their first **Stanley Cup** in 1915, by **scoring** four **goals** in the third and final game against the **Ottawa Senators**. He led the PCHA in **assists**, with 18 (1916–1917). When he was traded to the Calgary Tigers, Stanley **scored** 26 goals in 24 games. During the 1925–1926 season, he played for the Edmonton Eskimos of the World Hockey League, paired on **defense** with **Eddie Shore**. Stanley played one game in the **National Hockey League (NHL)** with the **Chicago Black Hawks** and then became their **coach** for the 1927–1928 season. After Chicago's captain, **Dick Irvin**, suffered a **head injury** during a game, Stanley designed a hockey **helmet** for protection. Unfortunately, at that time the NHL was not interested in helmets. In 1962, Barney was inducted into the **Hockey Hall of Fame** as a player. His nephew, **Allan Stanley**, was also inducted (1981). Barney's son, Don Stanley, won a gold medal for **Canada** in the 1950 **World Ice Hockey Championships**.

STASTNY, PETER "PETER THE GREAT". B. 18 September 1956, Bratislava, Czechoslovakia. Peter Stastny and his **brothers**, Anton and Marian Stastny, played hockey together in Czechoslovakia. As **juniors**, they won three times in a row. After playing in the 1976 **Canada Cup**, they went to Austria to play in the 1980 European Championships. For better opportunities, Gilles Léger prepared and executed the Stastny brothers' escape from Czechoslovakia to Quebec. Together, the Stastny brothers played on a **line** in the **National Hockey League (NHL)** with the **Quebec Nordiques**. Peter was their **center** (1980–1990), Anton was their **left wing** (1980–1989), and Marian was their **right wing** (1981–1985).

When Peter became the first player in NHL history to record 100 **points** in a **rookie** season (1980–1981), he received the **Calder Memorial Trophy**. He was a favorite with the Quebec fans and learned to speak both French and English. On 19 October 1989, he became the first European-born and trained player in NHL history to register 1,000 points. From 1979–1989, Stastny ranked second in NHL points (986), trailing only **Wayne Gretzky**. Stastny also played for the **New Jersey Devils** (1989–1993) and **St. Louis Blues** (1993–1995). Internationally, he played for Czechoslovakia in the **World Ice Hockey Championships** (1976–1980) and won two gold medals (1976, 1977) and two silver medals (1978, 1979). He then represented **Canada** in the 1984 Canada Cup. The Velvet Revolution allowed Stastny to return to his homeland, and he was the captain of the **Slovakian** hockey team at the 1994 **Olympic Games**. He also played for Slovakia at the 1995 World Ice Hockey Championships.

Despite never playing on a **Stanley Cup** championship team, Stastny was inducted into the **Hockey Hall of Fame** in 1998. In 2000, he was also inducted into the **International Ice Hockey Federation Hall of Fame**. His son, Paul Stastny, played on the 2010 **U.S. Men's Olympic Ice Hockey Team**. His other son, Yan Stastny, made his NHL debut in 2005–2006 with the **Edmonton Oilers** and is currently playing in **Russia**. Born in Quebec City but raised in St. Louis, Yan represented the **United States** in the 2005 and 2006 World Ice Hockey Championships. The Stastnys are the first hockey **family** to have represented four different countries internationally: Czechoslovakia, Canada, Slovakia, and the United States.

STERNER, ULF IVAR ERIK "UFFE". B. 11 February 1941, Forshaga Municipality, **Sweden**. Ulf Sterner made his hockey debut at 15 years of age on a second division club, where his speed and **scoring** abilities were noticed. On 12 November 1959, he made his international debut in a friendly **match** against the Czechoslovakian team. Sterner **scored** his first **goal** in that game and was the team's youngest player of all time. Throughout the late 1950s and early 1960s, he played **left wing** and **center** and was one of Sweden's most popular players. He was also credited with inventing the "stick to **skate** to stick" maneuver. Sterner played in nine **World Ice Hockey Championships** for Sweden. He won a gold medal, five silver medals, and one bronze medal. At the 1963 tournament, he scored a **hat trick** against **Canada** in a 4–1 win. After the game, he and teammate Sven Johansson met King Gustaf VI Adolf. Sterner's first **Olympic Games** were in 1960, in Squaw Valley, and he was also a member of the silver medal-winning team at the 1964 Winter Olympics.

On 27 January 1965, Sterner joined the **New York Rangers** in a game against the **Boston Bruins,** making him the first European to play in the **National Hockey League (NHL).** He had been reluctant to play physically or instigate physical play and only played in four NHL games. In 1969, the **International Ice Hockey Federation** adopted the same body **checking** rules as the NHL, and, four years later, **Börje Salming** joined the **Toronto Maple Leafs** and played 17 years in the NHL.

Growing up, Pia Grengman idolized Sterner. Despite their 13-year age difference, Grengman and Sterner got married. She is mostly known as Mrs. Ulf Sterner, but Grengman has her own hockey accomplishments. In the 1960s, girls playing hockey was almost unheard of in Sweden, and girls playing with boys was strictly prohibited, but Grengman pioneered the movement in Sweden, playing with men in what was then considered to be Division II and Division III clubs in the Gothenburg area, including Chalmers and Göteborgs IK. Around the age of 20, Grengman realized that she was just too small to play hockey with men, and she refocused her love of the game on **coaching.** She moved to Moscow for six months to be tutored by **Anatoli Tarasov.** His influence worked, and she went on to coach both men's and **women's ice hockey** teams in **Germany** and Sweden, as well as a men's team in **Denmark,** in the 1970s. Grengman was also a world champion weightlifter and tug-of-war competitor, and she has a black belt in karate. She participated with males in soccer, bandy, and handball, while pioneering female inclusion in these sports along the way. Today, Grengman and Sterner live on a farm near Deje, Sweden, and raise horses named after hockey players. A horse that broke Sterner's nose was **nicknamed** Alexander Ragulin.

STEWART, JOHN SHERRATT "JACK," "BLACK JACK". B. 6 May 1917, Pilot Mound, Manitoba. D. 26 May 1983, Detroit, Michigan. Jack Stewart was a **defenseman** in the **National Hockey League (NHL)** with the **Detroit Red Wings** (1938–1943, 1945–1950) and **Chicago Black Hawks** (1950–1952). He was known as a tough player who earned the **nickname** "Black Jack" from his bruising body **checking** skills. As a result, Stewart accumulated 50 scars and 220 stitches during his first 10 seasons. He also played an entire season with a broken hand by attaching a device to his **hockey stick** to hold his wrist. He used one of the heaviest hockey sticks in the league. When asked how he could shoot with it, Stewart said, "I don't use it for shooting. I use it for breaking arms." Not surprisingly, he led the NHL in **penalty minutes**, with 73, in 1945–1946. Once while he was with Detroit, Stewart and Chicago's Johnny Mariucci had a **fight** on the **ice**, and the two men continued their disagreement while they were in the **penalty box.** Off the ice, Stewart was quiet, and his teammates called him "Silent Jack." Stewart won the **Stanley Cup** twice, in 1943 and 1950. From 1950–1952, he served as the captain of the Chicago Black Hawks. An avid sportsman, Stewart was an active curler during his playing career, and he played softball in the summer. After retiring from hockey in 1963, he focused on a career in harness racing. In 1964, Stewart was inducted into the **Hockey Hall of Fame**.

STEWART, ROBERT NELSON "NELS," "OLD POISON". B. 29 December 1902, Montreal, Quebec. D. 21 August 1957, Wasaga Beach, Ontario. Nels Stewart was a **center** in the **National Hockey League (NHL)** with the **Montreal Maroons** (1925–1932), **Boston Bruins** (1932–1935, 1936–1937), and **New York Americans** (1935–1940). The **nickname** "Old Poison" was due to his deadly accurate shot. While playing for the Maroons, Stewart was part of the **line** known as the "S line," with **Babe Siebert** and **Hooley Smith**. Stewart helped the Maroons win the **Stanley Cup** in 1926. As a **rookie** in 1926, he was the leading **scorer** and won the Hart Trophy, a feat that he repeated in 1930. Stewart led the 1926 **Stanley Cup Playoffs** in scoring, with six **goals,** three **assists,** and nine **points** in eight games. In 1927, he led the NHL with 133 **penalty minutes.** He had a habit of chewing tobacco and spitting in the **goaltender's** eyes before shooting and scoring. On 3 January 1931, against the Boston Bruins, Stewart set a record for the fastest two goals scored (four seconds apart). Deron Quint of the **Winnipeg Jets** tied this record during the 1995–1996 season. During the benefit for **Ace Bailey** in 1934, Stewart scored a goal and an assist as a member of the **All-Star Team**. He is credited as the only hockey player in history to score a goal against **Lester Patrick**. During his 650 regular-season NHL game career, Stewart had 324 goals, 191 assists, 515 points, and 953 penalty minutes. His 324 NHL career goals was a record until 1952, when **Maurice Richard** surpassed it. In addition, his 515 NHL career points was a record until **Syd Howe** broke it in 1945. In 1962, Stewart was inducted into the **Hockey Hall of Fame**.

STICK. *See* HOCKEY STICK.

STOREY, ROY ALVIN "RED". B. 5 March 1918, Barrie, Ontario. D. 15 March 2006, Montreal, Quebec. **Nicknamed** for his hair color, "Red" Storey played professional football with the Toronto Argonauts (1936–1941). He retired after suffering a knee **injury**. Storey played **lacrosse** in the Ontario Lacrosse Association and was also a solid baseball player. He briefly played hockey, but mainly officiated football, lacrosse, and hockey games in the 1940s. In 1950, Storey became an **on-ice official** in the **National Hockey League (NHL)**. He was a quality **referee** for many years and was popular with the players. **Goaltender Gump Worsley** once said, "When Red Storey was refereeing in the NHL, I used to ask him where he was going to get a beer after the game. He usually told me, too." Unfortunately, Storey's career ended after a controversial game.

On 4 April 1959, Storey was officiating the sixth game of the **Stanley Cup Playoffs** between the **Montreal Canadiens** and **Chicago Black Hawks**. The **penalty** that wasn't called on Montreal's Albert Langlois late in the third period of a 4–4 tie allowed the Canadiens to **score** the series-winning **goal**. The Black Hawks coach, Rudy Pilous, accused Storey of choking. The fans went wild. When one dumped a beer on Storey's head, **Doug Harvey** punched the fan. He protected Storey as they made their way off the **ice** together. NHL president **Clarence Campbell** spoke with his friend and newsman Bill Westwick "off the record" and said that Storey had "frozen" on two calls that should have been penalties against the Canadiens, but Westwick printed the story, and Storey resigned after reading it.

Storey's career included 480 regular-season games and seven consecutive **Stanley Cup** Finals from 1952–1958. He was inducted into both the **Hockey Hall of Fame** (1967) and **Canada's Sports Hall of Fame** (1986). **Left wing Ted Lindsay** and Storey gave one another trouble throughout the years, and after the "noncall" game that ended Storey's career, Lindsay tried to start a **fight** with him until James Norris intervened. The two never spoke again, until 1993, when the new Hockey Hall of Fame opened in Toronto. Lindsay walked over to Storey and said, "Come on, Red, this has gone on too long. It's all over." With that, the two men buried the hatchet.

STUART, BRUCE. B. 30 November 1881, Ottawa, Ontario. D. 28 October 1961, Ottawa, Ontario. Bruce Stuart played 13 elite amateur and professional seasons as a hockey forward from 1898–1911. He played both **center** and **rover**. While he was with the **Montreal Wanderers** (1907–1908) and **Ottawa Senators** (1908–1911), he won the **Stanley Cup** in 1908, 1909, and 1911. In his regular-season career, Stuart **scored** 197 **goals** in 135 games. After retiring from hockey, he ran a successful shoe store in Ottawa, and enjoyed playing golf and curling. Stuart was inducted into the **Hockey Hall of Fame** in 1961. His **brother, Hod Stuart**, also played hockey (1898–1907) and was inducted into the Hockey Hall of Fame in 1945.

STUART, WILLIAM HODGESON "HOD". B. 20 February 1879, Ottawa, Ontario. D. 23 June 1907, Belleville, Ontario. Hod Stuart was a **defenseman** for the **Montreal Wanderers**. His hard body **checks** and long reach frustrated his opponents as much as his offensive rushes dazzled fans. Alf Smith was tried for assault after knocking Stuart out with his **hockey stick** during a 1907 game. Stuart was with the Wanderers in March 1907, when they defeated the **Kenora Thistles** for the **Stanley Cup**. Tragically, three months after winning the Stanley Cup, he died in a diving accident on 23 June 1907. On 2 January 1908, the Montreal Wanderers played a game against an **All-Star Team** composed of players from the teams of the Eastern Canada Amateur Hockey Association. The Wanderers won, 10–7, and the **match** raised money for Stuart's family. Stuart was elected to the **Hockey Hall of Fame** in 1945, as one of the 12 original inductees. In his regular season career, Hod **scored** 66 **goals** in 107 games, and had 161 **penalty minutes.** His **brother, Bruce Stuart**, also played hockey (1898–1911) and joined the Hockey Hall of Fame in 1961.

SUMMIT SERIES. The Summit Series, originally called the "Friendship Series," was the first competition between an **ice** hockey team from the Soviet Union and a team from **Canada**. The Canadian team included professionals from the **National Hockey League (NHL)**. It was an eight-game series of four **matches** in Canada and four matches in Moscow, held in September 1972. Canada won the series, four games to three, with one tie. In French, the Summit Series is known as *La Série du Siècle* (The Series of the Century), and in Russian it is known as *Суперсерия СССР-Канада* (U.S.S.R.–Canada Superseries). The series was played when the **Olympic Games** only allowed amateurs and the two countries were involved in the Cold War. The games showcased the talent of several Russian players, including **Valeri Kharlamov, Vladislav Tretiak,** and Alexander Yakushev. Team Canada's players included top **scorer Phil Esposito** and Gary Bergman. NHL player **Bobby Orr** was unable to play due to a knee **injury.** Thinking that their hotel room in Russia had been "bugged," Esposito and his teammates unscrewed a metal object under the rug, but what they had done was loosen the anchor for the chandelier in the room below theirs.

In the second Summit Series (1974), Canada formed their team with **World Hockey Association (WHA)** players instead of NHL players, as they had done in 1972. The Soviet team won the series, 4-1-3, over Canada. The format also had four games in Canada and four in Moscow. Canada's only victory came at **Maple Leaf Gardens** in Toronto. WHA players had been banned from playing in the 1972 series. The 1974 series gave **Bobby Hull** and 46-year-old **Gordie Howe** a chance to play for Canada against the Soviet team. Playing on both the 1972 and 1974 teams for Canada were Paul Henderson, **Frank Mahovlich,** and Pat Stapleton. **Mark Howe**, who retired in 1995, was the last active player from the series.

SUPERSTITIONS. Hockey players are known for having superstitions about routines that they believe will help them play better. Most fans know that players grow beards during the **Stanley Cup Playoffs** and only shave after winning the **Stanley Cup** or being eliminated. In 1980, Swedish players on the **New York Islanders** began this tradition after copying tennis player Björn Borg, who wouldn't shave until the Wimbledon tournament ended. The Islanders won four straight Stanley Cups, and the playoff beard superstition stuck. The **hockey stick** is a piece of **equipment** that many players have superstitions about. For example, Daniel Brière talks to his, **Joe Nieuwendyk** sprinkled baby powder on his stick blades, **Luc Robitaille** had a routine with wrapping black and white tape on his stick, and **Phil Esposito** and many other players believed that crossed sticks were bad luck. Superstitions about uniforms include getting dressed in a certain order (a belief held by many players, including **Wayne Gretzky**), wearing hand-knitted underwear (**Jacques Plante**), wearing the same unwashed socks during a **scoring** streak (**Bobby Orr**), and changing **skate** laces during periods (**Ray Bourque**).

 Goaltenders are known for being especially quirky. **Glenn Hall** would throw up before each game, and **Bernie Parent** refused to let fans see him without his **face mask**. **Patrick Roy** talked to the goalposts, avoided skating on the **lines**, and wound tape around the knob of his stick 60 times. **Sidney Crosby** is one of the nongoaltenders with multiple superstitions. He walks a specific path to the rink, has routines regarding his sticks, won't talk to his mother on game days, and has to sit next to certain players when he eats. Wayne Gretzky also had multiple routines that he believed helped his game. Before each **match**, he would drink Diet Coke, **ice** water, Gatorade, and a second Diet Coke, in that order. He also refused to get his hair cut during road trips, because the one time he did, his team lost. **Mark Messier** was one of the few hockey players who didn't believe in superstitions. Andrew Podnieks's 2010 book *Hockey Superstitions* covers many players and their unique beliefs in depth. *See also* CURSES.

SUTHERLAND, JAMES THOMAS "FATHER OF HOCKEY". B. 10 October 1870, Kingston, Ontario. D. 30 September 1955, Kingston, Ontario. James Sutherland was a **Canadian ice** hockey player, **coach**, administrator, and developer. He has been **nicknamed** the "Father of Hockey" because he was so passionate about the sport and worked very hard to inspire others to love it as well. Sutherland made his hometown of Kingston a famous ice hockey place during the years before World War I. He coached the Kingston Frontenacs **junior** team to several championships. He served in Europe with the Canadian Army during World War I, reaching the rank of captain. Sutherland first became connected with the Ontario Hockey Association as a district representative, and his drive and interest pushed him through executive ranks until he became president, a post he held from 1915–1918. In 1919, he served as president of the Canadian Amateur Hockey Association. He was instrumental in the founding of the Memorial Cup in 1919; the tournament serves as the championship of the Canadian Hockey League. Sutherland also helped establish the annual exhibition **match** between the

Royal Military College of Canada and West Point in 1923. He was the main force behind the creation of the International Hockey Hall of Fame (IHHF) in 1943. He was also a major influence in the **National Hockey League** and Canadian Amateur Hockey Association selecting Kingston as the IHHF's original home. The IHHF took his honor one step further by naming one of the display halls after him. Sutherland was inducted into the **Hockey Hall of Fame** in 1947 as a **builder.**

SWEATER. *See* JERSEY.

SWEDEN. In 1912, Sweden became a member of the **International Ice Hockey Federation (IIHF).** The Swedish team competed in 20 **Olympic Games,** beginning in 1920. Their highest finishes include two gold medals (1994, 2006), two silver medals (1928, 1964), and four bronze medals (1952, 1980, 1984, 1988). Sweden is a member of the "Big Six," which is a term for the six strongest men's **ice** hockey nations. The other five teams are **Russia,** the **United States,** the **Czech Republic, Finland,** and **Canada.** In addition to being voted best forward at the 1957 and 1962 **World Ice Hockey Championships** and being top **scorer** at the 1964 Winter Olympics, Sven Johansson also played on the Swedish national team in soccer and golf. There have been more than 200 **National Hockey League (NHL)** players born in Sweden, including Anders Hedberg, **Henrik Lundqvist,** Ulf Nilsson, and **Ulf Sterner** of the **New York Rangers; Börje Salming** of the **Toronto Maple Leafs;** and **Nicklas Lidström** of the **Detroit Red Wings. Peter Forsberg** and Mats Sundin were also NHL players from Sweden. Niklas Bäckström from Finland is a goalie for the **Minnesota Wild,** while Nicklas Bäckström from Sweden is a **center** for the **Washington Capitals.**

Bob Nystrom was born in Sweden but raised in Canada. His Swedish teammates on the **New York Islanders,** Stefan Persson and Anders Kallur, started a hockey tradition. In 1980, they imitated Swedish tennis player Björn Borg, who wouldn't shave his beard until the Wimbledon tournament ended. The Islanders won four straight **Stanley Cups,** and the **Stanley Cup Playoff** beard **superstition** took hold. At the 2006 Winter Olympics, the men's team from Sweden won the gold medal after an exciting 3–2 final against Finland. Then, at the 2006 World Ice Hockey Championships, Sweden won the final against the Czech Republic and became the first hockey team ever to win both the Winter Olympics and World Championships in the same year. The Swedish men's team currently has a third-place ranking by the IIHF, and the **women's ice hockey** team has a fourth-place ranking. *See also* APPENDIX F for a list of IIHF Hall of Fame inductees.

SWITZERLAND. In 1908, in Paris, France, the federation known as the Ligue Internationale de Hockey sur Glace was created, with representatives from Belgium, France, **Great Britain**, Switzerland, and Bohemia (now the **Czech Republic**). Although Switzerland was a founding member of the organization also known as the **International Ice Hockey Federation (IIHF)**, the Swiss men's national **ice** hockey team has not won a medal at a major senior ice hockey tournament since taking a bronze medal at the 1953 **World Ice Hockey Championships**. In 1998, Switzerland hosted the World Ice Hockey Championships, and the Swiss national team finished in fourth place; however, the team **scored** two historic upsets at the 2006 Winter Olympics in Turin, Italy. They defeated the Czech Republic, 3–2, and two days later they **shutout Canada**, 2–0. Unfortunately, they fell to **Sweden** in the quarterfinals. At the 2010 Winter Olympics in Vancouver, the Swiss team almost stunned Canada again, taking the heavily favored Canadians to a shootout, which they Switzerland, 1–0, for a narrow 3–2 loss. The Swiss men's team currently has a seventh-place ranking by the IIHF, and the **women's ice hockey** team has a sixth-place ranking. There have been 17 **National Hockey League** players born in Switzerland, including Jonas Hiller, Mark Streit, and Yannick Weber. *See also* APPENDIX F for a list of IIHF Hall of Fame inductees.

T

TAMPA BAY LIGHTNING. The Tampa Bay Lightning are a professional **ice** hockey team in the **Southeast Division** of the **National Hockey League (NHL) Eastern Conference**. During the 1992–1993 season, **Hockey Hall of Famers Phil Esposito** and **Tony Esposito** were awarded the franchise in the NHL expansion. Phil became the president and general manager, his **brother** was the chief scout, and Terry Crisp was the first **coach**. The team was named the Lightning because Tampa is known as the "Lightning Capital of North America." They are **nicknamed** the "Bolts" because of the emblem on their **jerseys**. Their best season was 2003–2004, when they defeated the **Calgary Flames** in seven games and became the southernmost franchise to ever win the **Stanley Cup**. The next year brought the NHL **lockout**. Since then, Tampa Bay has struggled as a team. Their worst season was 2007–2008, when their record was 31-42-9 (71 **points**), and they only won 11 games on the road. The franchise was sold during the 2009–2010 season and has slowly been improving. **Steve Yzerman** was hired as the general manager, and Guy Boucher became the new coach. Tampa Bay made it to the 2011 Eastern Conference Finals but lost to the **Boston Bruins** in seven games. Among the best players for Tampa Bay were Dino Ciccarelli and **Denis Savard**. The Lightning won the **Prince of Wales Trophy** in 2004. In 19 seasons (1992–1993 to 2011–2012), their career record was 588-732-112-96 (1,384 points), with six **Stanley Cup Playoff** appearances and one Stanley Cup (2004).

TARASOV, ANATOLY VLADIMIROVITCH. B. 10 December 1918, Moscow, Soviet Union. D. 23 June 1995, Moscow, **Russia**. Anatoli Tarasov was a successful bandy player in the 1930s, and he later developed an interest in **coaching**. After World War II, Anatoli and his **brother**, Yuri, began playing **ice** hockey, which was popularized in **Canada** but new to his country. As an on-ice coach of the Soviet Army team, he won 100 games and **scored** 106 **goals**. He played until 1953, and then focused solely on coaching. Tarasov was an outstanding Russian coach, and he is often called the "Father of Russian Ice Hockey." His innovative methods of coaching estab-

309

lished the Soviet Union as the dominant force in international competitions. Tarasov was known for his ruthless training methods and tough discipline among his players. He insisted that his trainees continue their education. "It's easier to work with educated people," he said. He also required his players to participate in an off-ice training program that included long-distance running, soccer, swimming, and weightlifting. Star players **Valeri Kharlamov** and **Vladislav Tretiak** were both trained by Tarasov. He coached the Russian team from 1958–1972. Tarasov led the Soviets to nine straight **World Ice Hockey Championships** (1963–1971) and three gold medals in the **Olympic Games** (1964, 1968, 1972). Due to his strict coaching, he was fired shortly before the 1972 **Summit Series**. Tarasov became **Lou Vairo's** mentor. Tarasov was inducted into both the **Hockey Hall of Fame** (1974) and **International Ice Hockey Federation Hall of Fame** (1997) as a **builder**. His daughter, Tatiana Tarasova, became a figure skating coach.

TAYLOR, FREDERICK WELLINGTON "CYCLONE". B. 23 June 1884, Tara, Ontario. D. 9 June 1979, Vancouver, British Columbia. Cyclone Taylor was a **defenseman** and **rover** who played hockey for 17 professional seasons (1905–1921, 1922–1923). He was part of the **Ottawa Senators** and **Vancouver Millionaires**, later renamed the Vancouver Maroons. Taylor earned the **nickname** "Cyclone" from his fast **skating** and rushes on the **ice**. As one of the top **scorers** of his era, he helped his teams win the **Stanley Cup** in 1909 and 1915. During the 1913–1914 season, Taylor tied **Tommy Dunderdale** for the most **goals** scored (24) in the **Pacific Coast Hockey Association (PCHA)**. On 1 February 1916, Taylor set a PCHA record by scoring six goals in one game. During his PCHA career, he recorded 16 **hat tricks** and seven four-goal games. He was awarded the Order of the British Empire by King George VI for his services during World War II. Taylor was president of the Pacific Coast Hockey League from 1936–1940. He was inducted into the **Hockey Hall of Fame** in 1947. After retiring from hockey, he became the commissioner of immigration for British Columbia and the Yukon. In 1970, Taylor dropped the **puck** in the ceremonial **face-off** for the **Vancouver Canucks'** first home game when the expansion team joined the **National Hockey League (NHL)**. He often attended Vancouver Canucks' games. In 1977, Eric Whitehead wrote the biography *Cyclone Taylor: A Hockey Legend*. Taylor was nearly 95 years old when he passed away in 1979. Prior to the first game of the 1979–1980 season, the Vancouver Canucks renamed their team award for Most Valuable Player as the Cyclone Taylor Award. His grandson, Mark Taylor, was an NHL **center** with the **Philadelphia Flyers**, **Pittsburgh Penguins**, and **Washington Capitals** (1981–1986).

TED LINDSAY AWARD. The Ted Lindsay Award is given for the year's best **National Hockey League (NHL)** player, as voted by members of the National Hockey League Players' Association. The prize was known as the Lester B. Pearson Award from its inception in 1971 until 2010. Pearson was an outstanding sportsman in a variety of sports, as well as a football and **ice hockey coach** at the University of Toronto. When he turned to politics, he won the Nobel Peace Prize in 1957, and, in 1963, he became the 14th prime minister of **Canada**. The award was first handed out at the conclusion of the 1971–1972 NHL season. In 2010, the award's name was changed to the Ted Lindsay Award to honor one of the union's pioneers. **Hockey Hall of Famer Ted Lindsay**, was not only known for his hockey skills, but also for his leadership role. The award's first recipient was **Phil Esposito** of the **Boston Bruins. Wayne Gretzky** won the trophy the most times (5). Players from the **Pittsburgh Penguins** have won the award the most often (7).

THOMPSON, CECIL R. "TINY". B. 31 May 1905, Sandon, British Columbia. D. 9 February 1981, Calgary, Alberta. Tiny Thompson was a **goaltender** who played in the **National** Hockey **League (NHL)** for the **Boston Bruins** (1928–1939) and **Detroit Red Wings** (1938–1940). He earned the **nickname** "Tiny" due to his small **goals** against average (GAA), not his physical size. During his **rookie** season, he had a low 1.15 GAA. In his first NHL game, on 15 November 1928, Thompson recorded a 1–0 **shutout** over the **Pittsburgh Pirates**. He had a **superstition** where he always allowed teammate **Cooney Weiland** to **score** at the end of the pregame **skate**. If Thompson touched the **puck** on its way to the **net**, he thought he'd have a bad game. In 1929, Thompson helped the Bruins win the **Stanley Cup** in a best-of-three series against the **New York Rangers**. He led the NHL in wins for five seasons and was the first goalie to win the **Vezina Trophy** four times (1930, 1933, 1936, 1938). During the 1935–1936 season, he became the first goalie to record an **assist** when he passed the **puck** to his teammate, **Babe Siebert**, who skated down the **ice** and scored a goal. After **Frank Brimsek** joined the Boston team, Thompson went to play for Detroit. Thompson ranks sixth in all-time NHL career shutouts (81). After his playing career, he became a scout for the **Chicago Black Hawks**. In 1959, Thompson was inducted into the **Hockey Hall of Fame**.

TIKHONOV, VIKTOR VASILYEVICH. B. 4 June 1930, Soviet Union. Viktor Tikhonov was a legendary **Russian ice** hockey **coach**. As a player, he **scored** 35 **goals** in 296 games in the Soviet elite hockey league from 1949–1963. He also won four gold medals at the Soviet National Championships. In 1964, Tikhonov started a coaching career with a dictatorial style. His teams practiced 10 months a year and were confined to barracks during that time. He often cut players when he thought they might defect. In 1991, he cut **Pavel Bure**, Evgeny Davydov, **Vladimir Konstantinov**, and Valeri Zelepukin just before the 1991 **Canada Cup**. After the dissolution of the Soviet Union, Tikhonov relaxed his coaching style. As coach, he won 13 straight Soviet titles (1978–1989); **World Ice Hockey Championships** gold in 1978–1979, 1981–1983, 1986, 1989, and 1990; the **Canada Cup** in 1981, and **Olympic Games** gold in 1984, 1988, and 1992. In 1998, Tikhonov was inducted into the **International Ice Hockey Federation Hall of Fame** as a **builder**. His son, Vasily Tikhonov, became a professional ice hockey coach in **Finland** and Russia. His grandson, also named Viktor Tikhonov, played **right wing** in the Kontinental Hockey League and spent one season in the **National Hockey League** with the **Phoenix Coyotes** (2008–2009). On 10 August 2011, the Coyotes resigned the younger Tikhonov to a one-year deal.

TIKKANEN, ESA "THE GRATE ONE". B. 25 January 1965, Helsinki, **Finland**. Esa Tikkanen was a hockey player in Finland before he joined the **National Hockey League (NHL)** in 1985. He made his NHL debut with the **Edmonton Oilers** during the second round of the 1985 **Stanley Cup Playoffs**. Tikkanen played one game in the Stanley Cup Finals and had his name engraved on the Stanley Cup even before playing his first regular-season game in the NHL. He was a forward on a **line** with **Wayne Gretzky** and **Jari Kurri**. While Gretzky and Kurri **scored goals**, Tikkanen was the line's defensive player. Not only was he a great two-way player and a good **penalty killer**, he was considered one of the best **agitators** in the NHL. Tikkanen had the ability to distract and confuse his opponents by using a bizarre combination of his native Finnish and English. His teammates called it "Tikkanese" or "Tiki-Talk." The **nickname** "The Grate One" was a play on Gretzky's "The Great One" and his ability to grate on other players' nerves.

Tikkanen helped Edmonton win the Stanley Cup again in 1987, 1988, and 1990. Between 1986–1990, he scored 30 or more goals three times. He won a bronze medal for Finland at the 1998 Winter Olympics. He also represented Finland at the **World Ice Hockey Championships** (1985, 1989, 1993, 1996, 2000) and **Canada Cup** (1987, 1991). Tikkanen won the Best Hockey Player of Finland Trophy in 1991. He also played with the **New York Rangers, St. Louis Blues, New Jersey Devils, Vancouver Canucks, Florida Panthers,** and **Washington Capitals**. Tikkanen won another Stanley Cup in 1994 with the Rangers. He retired from the NHL in 1999, after playing in 877 regular-season games and recording 244 goals, 386 **assists**, 630 **points**, and 1,077 **penalty minutes**. In 186 Stanley Cup Playoff games, he scored 72 goals and 60 assists for 132 points, with 275 penalty minutes. Tikkanen played in Finland, **Germany**, and Korea for several years before returning to Finland to **coach** hockey.

TKACZUK, WALTER ROBERT "WALT". B. 29 September 1947, Emsdetten, **Germany**. As a child, Walt Tkaczuk moved to Northern Ontario, where his father worked in the mines. He played briefly in the **American Hockey League** before joining the **New York Rangers** in 1968 as a **center**. This made him the first German-born player to play in a **National Hockey League (NHL)** game. Tkaczuk, who was an effective **penalty killer**, was part of a **line** with Bill Fairbairn and Dave Balon (who was later replaced by Steve Vickers) called the "Bulldog Line." On the **ice**, Tkaczuk was a strong physical presence, but he only accumulated 556 **penalty minutes** during 14 seasons. In 1970, the Ranger fans voted Tkaczuk the most popular player both on and off the ice, but hockey management disagreed. They suspended him in September of that year for participating in contract rebellion with other players. He played a key role in the 1972 **Stanley Cup Playoffs**, as the Rangers defeated the defending champion **Montreal Canadiens** and previous season's finalists, the **Chicago Black Hawks**, to reach the **Stanley Cup Finals**. They lost to the **Boston Bruins** in six games, but Tkaczuk earned respect for holding the Bruins' **Phil Esposito** without a **goal** in the series. At the age of 33, Tkaczuk's hockey career came to an abrupt end after he became partially blind in one eye after being hit by a deflected **puck** shot by Larry Murphy in a game against the **Los Angeles Kings** on 2 February 1981. Tkaczuk played in 945 career NHL games, scoring 227 goals and 451 **assists** for 678 **points**.

TOOTOO, JORDIN JOHN KUDLUK "THUNDER". B. 2 February 1983, Churchill, Manitoba. Jordin Tootoo is a current **right wing** with the **Nashville Predators** of the **National Hockey League (NHL)**. On 29 May 2001, he became the first person of Inuit descent to be drafted by the NHL. On 9 October 2003, at the age of 20, he became both the first Inuk player and the first player who grew up in Nunavut to play in a NHL game. Tootoo wears the **jersey number** 22 as a play on his name. In 2002, the suicide of his older **brother**, Terence Tootoo, who was bound for the NHL, devastated Jordin. While working through his grief, he often engaged in hockey **fights**. On 10 January 2004, and 8 December 2007, Jordin earned two **Gordie Howe hat tricks** when he **scored** a **goal** and an **assist** and had a fight in each game. On 19 March 2007, the NHL suspended Tootoo for five games after he hit **defenseman** Stéphane Robidas of the **Dallas Stars** with his **glove** during a game two days before. Robidas suffered a concussion and was rendered unconscious. The NHL issued a five-game suspension without pay, and accusations of "dirty" play were leveled at Tootoo. These accusations reemerged after an incident on 11 October 2007, in which Tootoo hit Daniel Winnik of the **Phoenix Coyotes** on the head with his shoulder. In December 2011,

Tootoo became the first player to be punished under the NHL's crackdown on contact involving **goaltenders** after he crashed into Ryan Miller of the **Buffalo Sabres**.

TORONTO MAPLE LEAFS. The Toronto Maple Leafs are a professional **ice** hockey team in the **Northeast Division** of the **National Hockey League (NHL) Eastern Conference**. The Toronto Maple Leafs joined the NHL during its inaugural season in 1917, as the Toronto Arenas. The Arenas won the NHL's first-ever **Stanley Cup** when they defeated the Pacific Coast Hockey League champions, the **Vancouver Millionaires**. In 1919–1920, and for the next eight seasons, the Toronto franchise was called the Toronto St. Patricks. When **Conn Smythe** became the new owner, he changed the team's name a final time to the Maple Leafs in 1927. In 1922, they took home their second Stanley Cup, by beating the Millionaires once again. **Cecil Dye** scored a record nine **goals** in the five games and was awarded the very first **penalty** shot. **Maple Leaf Gardens** was one of the six original NHL arenas. Located in Toronto, Ontario, it was where the Toronto Maple Leafs played their home **matches** (1931–1999). Even during their losing seasons, tickets to home games consistently sold out from 1946–1999. Their current arena is the Air Canada Centre, which seats close to 19,000 fans. The Leafs were one of the **"Original Six"** teams, a term used to describe the teams that made up the NHL from 1942 until the 1967 expansion. **Clarence Day** and **Red Kelly** each **coached** the team. Including individuals who have taken multiple turns behind the bench, for example, **King Clancy** and **Punch Imlach**, the team has had more than 30 coaches.

In its NHL history, the Toronto team has won the Stanley Cup 13 times, which is second only to their rivals, the **Montreal Canadiens**, who have won the trophy 24 times. The team's dominant years were from 1946–1947 to 1950–1951, and again from 1961–1962 to 1966–1967. Toronto won its last Stanley Cup in 1967, and the team has had a 45-year drought since then. Among the best players for the Maple Leafs have been **Hockey Hall of Famers Syl Apps, George Armstrong, Max Bentley, Turk Broda**, Clarence Day, **Fernie Flaman, Tim Horton, Ted Kennedy**, Frank Mathers, Bud Poile, **Joe Primeau, Conn Smythe**, and **Harry Watson**. In 94 seasons in the NHL (1917–1918 to 2011–2012), the Maple Leafs have compiled a record of 2,671-2,570-783-96 (6,221 **points**) and made 64 **Stanley Cup Playoff** appearances.

TORONTO ST. PATRICKS. *See* TORONTO MAPLE LEAFS.

TRAGEDIES. Tragic events have affected athletes from many sports, including hockey. In 1907, **Hod Stuart** died in a diving accident. **Joe Hall** died from the Spanish influenza outbreak in 1919. **Georges Vezina** died from tuberculosis in 1926. In 1937, **Howie Morenz** died from complications after suffering a leg **injury**. In 1968, **Bill Masterton** died from an on-**ice head injury. Terry Sawchuk** died in 1970, from injuries resulting from horseplay with a teammate. Four players from the World Hockey League Swift Current Broncos died in a team bus accident on 30 December 1986. Car accidents claimed the lives of **Tim Horton** (1974), **Valeri Kharlamov** (1981), Pelle Lindbergh (1985), and Dan Snyder (2003). In 1997, **Vladmir Konstantinov** was paralyzed in a car accident six days after winning the **Stanley Cup.** Plane crashes claimed the lives of **Hobey Baker** (1918), **Bill Barilko** (1951), and Garnet Bailey (2001). Eleven members of the Soviet hockey team died in a plane crash on 5 January 1950. Forty-three people died in the 7 September 2011 plane crash carrying the Yaroslavl Lokomotiv team in **Russia**'s Kontinental Hockey League. The individuals had played for national teams from Belarus, the **Czech Republic, Germany**, Latvia, Russia, **Slovakia, Sweden**, and the Ukraine. *See also* CAREER-ENDING INJURIES.

TREACY, LINTON MULDOON. *See* MULDOON, PETE.

TRETIAK, VLADISLAV ALEKSANDROVICH. B. 25 April 1952, Dmitrov, Union of Soviet Socialist Republics (USSR). Vladislav Tretiak was an amazing **Russian goaltender** (1969–1984) who was **coached** by the legendary **Anatoli Tarasov.** Tretiak won 13 major international titles, an accomplishment matched only by former Soviet **defenseman** Alexander Ragulin. Tretiak wore the **jersey number** 20, because in the Soviet Union it was a tradition that the starting goalie wore the number 1, all the **skaters** wore numbers 2 through 19, and the backup goalie wore the biggest number, 20. **Ed Belfour** also wore number 20 in honor of Tretiak, his childhood hero. Tretiak played for the USSR in 13 **World Ice Hockey Championships** (1970–1984), winning 10 gold medals and two silver medals. He also competed in the Winter Olympics and is the only athlete in **Olympic** hockey history to win three gold medals (1972, 1976, 1984) and one silver medal (1980). He was on the losing team when the **United States** won during the **"Miracle on Ice,"** but he wasn't the goalie to give up the winning **goal.** His team was winning, 2–1, when the United States **scored** to tie the game. Then, **Coach Viktor Tikhonov** replaced Tretiak with backup goaltender Vladimir Myshkin immediately after **Mark Johnson's** tying goal. Tikhonov later called it the "biggest mistake of my career." The Russian team lost, 4–3, but they won the silver medal. Tretiak also played in the 1972 and 1974 **Summit Series** against **Canada.**

Tretiak was drafted by the **Montreal Canadiens** in 1983, and general manager **Serge Savard** tried to obtain permission from the Soviet Union to allow Tretiak to leave Russia and play in the **National Hockey League**, but he was refused. Tretiak once said, "I would have loved to play in the **Montreal Forum** . . . I regret not having the chance." In 1988, he wrote his autobiography, *Tretiak: The Legend.* After he retired from playing, he worked as goalkeeping coach with the **Chicago Blackhawks**. Tretiak was inducted into both the **Hockey Hall of Fame** (1989) and **International Ice Hockey Federation Hall of Fame** (1997).

TRIPLE GOLD CLUB. The Triple Gold Club describes **ice** hockey players and **coaches** who have won the three most important hockey championships: an **Olympic Games** gold medal, a **World Ice Hockey Championships** gold medal, and the **National Hockey League Stanley Cup**. Tomas Jonsson, Mats Näslund, and Håkan Loob became the first members on 27 February 1994, when **Sweden** won the gold medal at the 1994 Winter Olympics. The 25 members of the Triple Gold Club represent the following countries in this manner: Sweden (9), **Canada** (8), **Russia** (6), and the **Czech Republic** (2). Ten of the players are **defensemen**, and 15 players are forwards. No **goaltenders** have won all three championships. Jonathan Toews was the youngest player to accomplish the feat when he won the Stanley Cup at the age of 22 years and 42 days. **Viacheslav Fetisov** became the oldest player to join the Triple Gold Club when he won the Stanley Cup at 39 years and 48 days of age. Fetisov, **Igor Larionov**, and **Peter Forsberg** are the only players to have won each of the three championships more than once. On 28 February 2010, Mike Babcock became the first coach to win all three championships when he led Canada to a gold medal at the 2010 Winter Olympics. He won the World Championship in 2004 and coached the **Detroit Red Wings** to a Stanley Cup win in 2008.

TRIPPING. When a player uses a **hockey stick**, arm, or leg to cause an opponent to fall, a tripping **penalty** is called. The player then spends two minutes in the **penalty box**. If the player was tripped on a **breakaway**, a tripping call may result in a penalty shot for the tripped player. *See also* HIGH-STICKING; HOOKING; SLASHING.

TROTTIER, BRYAN JOHN "TROTS". B. 17 July 1956, Val Marie, Saskatchewan. As a **young player**, Bryan Trottier played **pond hockey** and had his pet border collie retrieve **pucks** for him. Professionally, he was a **center** in the **National Hockey League (NHL)** for 18 seasons. He played for the **New York Islanders** (1975–1990) and **Pittsburgh Penguins** (1990–1992, 1993–1994). Trottier holds the NHL record for **points** in a single period, with 6 (4 **goals**, 2 **assists**), in the second period against the **New York Rangers** on 23 December 1978. He and **right wing Mike Bossy** helped the Islanders win the **Stanley Cup** in 1980, 1981, 1982, and 1983. Trottier also won two more with Pittsburgh in 1991 and 1992, and one as an assistant **coach** in 2001. He played more games (1,123) with the New York Islanders than any other player in the franchise's history. In addition to his **scoring** talents, he also had solid body **checking** skills. Trottier won the **Calder Memorial Trophy** (1976), **Hart Memorial Trophy** (1979), **Conn Smythe Trophy** (1980), **Art Ross Trophy** (1979), and **King Clancy Memorial Trophy** (1989). He was inducted into the **Hockey Hall of Fame** in 1997. Because he had dual citizenship due to his status as a North American Indian, Trottier played for **Canada** in the 1981 **Canada Cup**, and then for the **United States** in the 1984 tournament. During his NHL career, he played in 1,279 regular-season games and recorded 524 goals, 901 assists, 1,425 points, and 912 **penalty minutes**. After retiring from playing, Trottier played **roller hockey** in 1994, with the Pittsburgh Phantoms of the Roller Hockey International League. He then became an assistant hockey coach for the Islanders (1992–1993), Penguins (1994–1997), **Colorado Avalanche** (1998–1999), and Rangers (2002–2003). His younger **brother**, Rocky Trottier, played one season in the NHL with the **New Jersey Devils**.

TSUJIMOTO, TARO. Taro Tsujimoto was an invented **ice** hockey player who was legally drafted by the **Buffalo Sabres** 183rd overall in the 11th round of the 1974 **National Hockey League (NHL)** Entry Draft. The Sabres' general manager, **Punch Imlach**, got annoyed with the slow telephone drafting process, which was intended to keep draft picks secret from the rival **World Hockey Association**. Imlach planned a prank at the expense of the league and president of 28 years, **Clarence Campbell**, and found a common Japanese name in a Buffalo phone book. Then, during the 11th round, Imlach chose to select star **center** Taro Tsujimoto of the Japanese Hockey League's Tokyo Katanas. In Japanese, the word *katanas* means "swords" or "sabres." The NHL made the pick official, and it was reported by all major media outlets, including *Hockey News*. Imlach admitted to the fake draft pick at the start of training camp that year, but Campbell was not amused, because Tsujimoto's name had appeared in several NHL publications. The NHL eventually changed the pick to an "invalid claim" for its official record-keeping purposes. Tsujimoto is still listed among Sabres' draft picks in the Buffalo media guide. He became an inside joke for Sabres' fans, and, years later, during one-sided games, fans would chant "We Want Taro." Unlike the 1940s football hoax of Johnny Chung, Tsujimoto has his own sports card in Panini America's *2010–11 Score Rookies and Traded* box set.

U

ULLMAN, NORMAN VICTOR ALEXANDER "NORM". B. 26 December 1935, Provost, Alberta. In 1952–1953, Norm Ullman led the West Coast Junior Hockey League in **scoring**, with 76 **points**. The next year, he **scored** an amazing 101 points. Speaking about his early days, Ullman said, "I played on the same **line** as Johnny Bucyk in midget and **junior**." Professionally, Ullman was a **center** for the **Detroit Red Wings** (1955–1967) and **Toronto Maple Leafs** (1967–1975). He played on a Detroit **line** with **Gordie Howe** and **Ted Lindsay**. Ullman was known for being a productive two-way player with great stickhandling skills. He led the **National Hockey League (NHL)** in **goals** in 1965, with 42. After 13 seasons with the Red Wings, Ullman was part of one of hockey's biggest trades when the Toronto Maple Leafs acquired Ullman, Paul Henderson, and Floyd Smith in exchange for **Frank Mahovlich**, Pete Stemkowski, **Garry Unger**, and Carl Brewer. Even though the Toronto air quality affected his health, Ullman remained a solid player for the Leafs for eight seasons. Despite playing for 20 years, he never got the chance to play on a **Stanley Cup** championship team. He finished his career with two years in the **World Hockey Association** with the **Edmonton Oilers**. Ullman was one of the NHL's quietest yet most prolific goal scorers. He scored at least 20 goals 16 times in 20 years and had a total of 490 goals and 739 **assists** for 1,229 career points. In 1982, Ullman was inducted into the **Hockey Hall of Fame**.

UNGER, GARRY DOUGLAS "IRON MAN". B. 7 December 1947, Edmonton, Alberta. Garry Unger was a forward in the **National Hockey League (NHL)** from 1967–1983. He earned the **nickname** "Iron Man" from rarely missing a game. In fact, Unger set an NHL record by playing 914 consecutive games in the regular season between 24 February 1968 and 21 December 1979, doing so with four teams, the **Toronto Maple Leafs**, **Detroit Red Wings**, **St. Louis Blues**, and Atlanta Flames. His record has since been surpassed by **Doug Jarvis**, who played 964 consecutive games. Also known for his good looks and playboy lifestyle, Unger dated Miss America in 1970. When Unger refused to cut his shoulder-length blonde hair, Detroit's **coach**, Ned Harkness, traded him to St. Louis in February 1971. This was a mistake, as Unger led the Blues in **scoring** (1971–1972) with 36 **goals** and 34 **assists** for 70 **points**. He played in 1,105 games and scored 413 goals and had 391 assists for a total of 804 points. Unger retired from the NHL in 1983. In 1985, he came out of retirement to play hockey in **Great Britain**. In his later years, Unger became spiritual and spent time giving back as a coach at hockey schools.

UNION OF SOVIET SOCIALIST REPUBLICS (U.S.S.R.). *See* RUSSIA.

UNITED STATES OF AMERICA. In 1920, the United States became a member of the **International Ice Hockey Federation (IIHF)**. The United States won silver medals at the 2002 and 2010 Winter Olympics and the gold medal at the 1996 **World Cup of Hockey**. At the 2004 World Cup of Hockey, the U.S. team was unable to defend its title and lost to **Finland** in the semifinals. The team's most recent medal at the **World Ice Hockey Championships** was a bronze in 2004, and they won the tournament in 1933 and 1960 (from 1920–1968, the **Olympic** gold medalist was also crowned the world champion for that year). The United States is a member of the "Big Six," which is a term for the six strongest men's **ice** hockey nations. The other five teams are **Russia**, **Sweden**, the **Czech Republic**, **Finland**, and **Canada**. The U.S. men's team currently has a sixth-place ranking by the IIHF, and the **women's ice hockey** team has a first-place ranking. Many players and **builders** from the United States have been inducted into the **International Ice Hockey Federation Hall of Fame**.

The majority of hockey players in the **National Hockey League (NHL)** are from Canada and the United States. The original six teams of the NHL include four located in the United States, the **Boston Bruins**, **Chicago Black Hawks (Chicago Blackhawks)**, **Detroit Red Wings**, and **New York Rangers**. Many universities in the United States have Division I ice hockey teams to prepare young athletes for a future in the sport. They are regulated by the **National Collegiate Athletic Association**. Strong **college hockey** programs can be found at Boston College, Boston University, Bowling Green State University, Colorado College, Cornell University, Harvard University, Lake Superior State University, Michigan State University, Michigan Tech, Northern Michigan University, Rensselaer Polytechnic Institute, University of Denver, University of Maine, University of Michigan, University of Minnesota, University of Minnesota Duluth, University of North Dakota, and University of Wisconsin.

Although of Canadian descent, **Wayne Gretzky** was very influential in promoting hockey on the West Coast when he was traded to the **Los Angeles Kings**. In addition, NHL commissioner **Gary Bettman** has expanded the league to cities all across the country. Under his direction, the **Nashville Predators** (1998), **Atlanta Thrashers** (1999), **Minnesota Wild** (2000), and **Columbus Blue Jackets** (2000) franchises were added, bringing the NHL to 30 teams. During the 1990s, he also relocated four teams, including the Minnesota North Stars to Dallas (1993), the **Quebec Nordiques** to Denver (1995), the **Winnipeg Jets** to Phoenix (1996), and the Hartford Whalers to North Carolina (1997). While the popularity of ice hockey in the United States cannot compare to the sport's popularity in Canada, it continues to flourish as one of the favorite sports for American fans. *See also* "MIRACLE ON ICE"; U.S. HOCKEY HALL OF FAME; U.S. MEN'S OLYMPIC ICE HOCKEY TEAM; U.S. WOMEN'S OLYMPIC ICE HOCKEY TEAM.

U.S. HOCKEY HALL OF FAME. Not to be confused with Toronto's original **Hockey Hall of Fame** established in 1943, the U.S. Hockey Hall of Fame, established on 21 June 1973, is located in Eveleth, Minnesota. Its purpose is to honor the sport of **ice** hockey in the United States by preserving American legends of the game. New members are inducted annually and must have made extraordinary contributions to hockey in the United States during the course of their careers. There are currently 153 members, consisting of 96 players, 26 **coaches**, 23 administrators, two dual players/administrators, one **referee**, one physician, one media member, and three teams. The only referee inducted was **Bill Chadwick**, in 1974. The teams include the 1960 and 1980 gold medal **U.S. Men's Olympic Ice Hockey Teams**, as well as the 1998 gold medal **U.S. Women's Olympic Ice Hockey Team**. **Frank Zamboni** was inducted in 2009 for his invention. Several player members include Taffy Abel, **Hobey Baker, Frank Brimsek, Moose Goheen, Cammi Granato, Mark Howe, Brett Hull**, and **Brian Leetch**. Recent inductees include **Chris Chelios, Mike Emrick**, Ed Snider, Gary Suter, and Keith Tkachuk. *See also* CANADA'S SPORTS HALL OF FAME.

U.S. MEN'S OLYMPIC ICE HOCKEY TEAM. The U.S. Men's Olympic Ice Hockey Team has represented the **United States** in the **Olympic Games** since 1920. They lost to **Canada** in the finals six times (1920, 1924, 1932, 1952, 2002, 2010), and to the **Soviet Union** twice (1956, 1972). In total, the U.S. team won eight silver medals. In **Germany**, in 1936, **Great Britain** won the gold, Canada won the silver, and the United States won its first and only bronze medal. The U.S. team defeated the Canadian and Soviet teams to win its first gold medal in the 1960 Olympics. This is often referred to as the "Forgotten Miracle," because the 1980 **"Miracle on Ice"** is much more famous. At **Lake Placid**, New York, with **Jim Craig** as their **goaltender**, the young U.S. team upset the veteran **Soviet Union Men's Olympic Ice Hockey Team** by a **score** of 4–3. The United States then defeated **Finland** in the finals to win the second gold medal in U.S. hockey history. At the time, this was the most-watched hockey game in America. As a result, the team was awarded the **Lester Patrick Trophy** for their outstanding contribution to hockey. In 2010, the U.S. team beat Finland, 6–1, to advance to the finals against Canada. This gold-medal game between Canada and the United States became the most-watched hockey game in America, with an estimated 27.6 million U.S. households watching Canada win in **overtime**, 3–2. **Herb Brooks**, **Jack Riley**, and Ron Wilson have been some of the team's **coaches**. Notable players who have played on the Olympic team include **Chris Chelios**, **Patrick Kane**, **Pat LaFontaine**, **Mike Modano**, and Paul Stastny.

U.S. WOMEN'S OLYMPIC ICE HOCKEY TEAM. The U.S. Women's Olympic Ice Hockey Team has represented the **United States** in the **Olympic Games** since 1998. Women's hockey was played in the Winter Olympics for the first time ever in Nagano, Japan, from 7–22 February 1998. Six countries competed for the gold medal, which the United States won. **Canada** won the silver medal, and **Finland** won the bronze. China, **Sweden**, and Japan also participated. The U.S. women's team won silver medals during the 2002 and 2010 Olympics and a bronze medal during the 2006 competition. In 1998, the team was awarded the **Lester Patrick Trophy** for their outstanding contribution to hockey. The team's **coaches** have included **Mark Johnson**, Julie Sasner, and Ben Smith. Notable players who have played on the Olympic team include Kacey Bellamy, Julie Chu, Natalie Darwitz, **Cammi Granato**, Jenny Potter, and **Angela Ruggiero**.

V

VAIRO, LOU. B. 25 February 1945, Brooklyn, New York. Lou Vairo was an American **ice** hockey **coach** often referred to as "The Godfather of American Hockey" because of his strong New York accent. At the start of his career in the 1970s, he contacted **Anatoli Tarasov**, the **Russian** hockey coach, for advice. After their meeting, Tarasov became Vairo's mentor. While coaching **junior** hockey in Minnesota, Vairo implemented a style of hockey that was influenced by his experience in the Soviet Union. His team focused on controlling the **puck, passing**, and pursuing **scoring** chances through a transition game. At the time, the University of Minnesota coach, **Herb Brooks**, befriended Vairo. Brooks went on to coach the 1980 **U.S. Men's Olympic Ice Hockey Team**, and Vairo then coached the 1984 team. Vairo had such a young team that his forwards, **Pat LaFontaine**, David A. Jensen, and Ed Olczyk were called the "Diaper Line." The 1984 men's Olympic team also featured future **National Hockey League** star **Chris Chelios**. Unfortunately, the team was eliminated in the early rounds. Vairo then became the assistant coach for the **New Jersey Devils** for two seasons. He also coached in the **Netherlands** and **Italy**, before returning to the **United States**. In 1992, Vairo became the director of special projects for USA Hockey. He led the 2000 U.S. National Team to a 4-1-2 overall record and a fifth-place finish at the **International Ice Hockey Federation World Ice Hockey Championships**, in St. Petersburg, Russia. In 2000, Vairo received the **Lester Patrick Trophy** for his contributions to hockey. In 2002, Herb Brooks asked him to be the assistant coach on the men's Olympic team. Together they helped the team win the silver medal in Salt Lake City, Utah.

VANCOUVER CANUCKS. The Vancouver Canucks are a professional **ice** hockey team in the **Northwest Division** of the **National Hockey League (NHL) Western Conference**. After the **Vancouver Millionaires** disbanded following the 1925–1926 season, Vancouver was home to only **minor-league** teams for many years. The current Canucks had a minor-league predecessor, with the same name, that played from 1945–1970 in the **Pacific Coast Hockey Association** and **Western Canada Hockey League**. The

NHL Canucks joined the league in the 1970–1971 season as an expansion team, along with the **Buffalo Sabres**. In its NHL history, the team has made the **Stanley Cup** Finals three times but never won. They lost to the **New York Islanders** in 1982 (4–0), the **New York Rangers** in 1994 (4–3), and the **Boston Bruins** in 2011 (4–3). During the 1982 Western Conference Finals, against the **Chicago Black Hawks**, in response to questionable calls, **Coach** Roger Neilson placed a white towel on the end of a **hockey stick** and held it up, faking a surrender. The Vancouver players and fans copied him, starting the Canuck fan tradition known as "Towel Power." The Canucks won the series and made it to the **Stanley Cup** Finals for the first time in team history. Among the best players for the Canucks have been **Hockey Hall of Famers Igor Larionov, Mark Messier**, and **Cam Neely**. There have been 16 head coaches for the Canucks. The franchise's first head coach was Hal Laycoe, who coached them for two seasons. Marc Crawford coached the most games of any Canucks head coach, with 529 games, and he has the most **points**, with 586. Before he became a coach, **Pat Quinn** was a **defenseman** for the Canucks. The Canucks recently won the **Presidents' Trophy** as the team with the league's best regular-season record in 2010–2011. In 41 seasons in the NHL (1970–1971 to 2011–2012), the Vancouver Canucks have compiled a record of 1,353-1,454-391-82 (3,179 points) and made 25 **Stanley Cup Playoff** appearances. In 2012, the Canucks were eliminated by the **Los Angeles Kings** in the Western Conference Quarterfinals, 4–1.

VANCOUVER MAROONS. *See* VANCOUVER MILLIONAIRES.

VANCOUVER MILLIONAIRES. The Vancouver Millionaires were a professional **ice** hockey team that competed in the **Pacific Coast Hockey Association** and **Western Canada Hockey League** between 1911–1926. Frank Patrick **coached**, managed, and played for the team. He set a record as a **defenseman** by scoring six **goals** in one game in March 1912. Also in 1912, the Millionaires acquired star player **Cyclone Taylor**, who played for Vancouver for the next 10 seasons until he retired. He accumulated 263 **points** in 131 games. Other **Hockey Hall of Fame** players include **Mickey Mackay** and **Frank Nighbor**. In its history, the team made the **Stanley Cup** Finals four times. They defeated the **Ottawa Senators** in 1915, to earn their first and only Stanley Cup championship. In a best-of-five series, the Millionaires swept Ottawa by **scores** of 6–2, 8–3, and 12–3. Taylor led the team with 6 goals. The Millionaires then lost to the Toronto Arenas in 1918. In 1921, they were defeated by the Senators, and by the Toronto St. Patricks the following year. They changed the team name to the Vancouver Maroons in 1922. The team eventually folded in 1926. In 2010, the **Vancouver Canucks** purchased the rights to the maroon **jerseys** with the white "V" logo and other trademarks of the Vancouver Millionaires.

VARIATIONS. There are currently four variations in hockey that get a lot of attention. They may seem strange, but each has an official nationalized competition attached to it. Ringette and bandy are basically hockey with different rules, types of **hockey sticks**, and **pucks**. **Ice** sledge hockey, which began in **Norway** in 1967, is hockey adapted for the disabled with sleds instead of **skates**. Sledge hockey is played at the **Paralympic Games**. Octopush, or underwater ice hockey, is a new weird sport that uses a snorkel mask and the bottom of a swimming pool. Although it is relatively new, there are championships being played all around the world. *See also* ROLLER HOCKEY.

VASKO, ELMER "MOOSE". B. 11 December 1935, Duparquet, Quebec. D. 30 October 1998, Maywood, Illinois. Elmer Vasko was a 6-foot, 3-inch, 210-pound **defenseman** who earned the **nickname** "Moose" from his large presence on the **ice**. He played for the **Chicago Black Hawks** from 1956–1966. During those years, Chicago was not a winning team. Because of an **injury**, Vasko wore a special shoulder harness to play a shift. After his shoulder surgery in 1959, his play greatly improved, and so did the Black Hawks. Partnered with **Pierre Pilote**, they were one of the toughest defensive duos in the league. The result was a **Stanley Cup** victory in 1961. Vasko retired five years later but then returned to play for the expansion team the Minnesota North Stars from 1967–1970. In 1970, he retired for good. He played in 786 NHL games in his career and had 34 **goals** and 166 **assists** for a total of 200 **points**. After retiring, Vasko opened a fast-food business called the Dog Patch, serving hot dogs in the Hillside, Minnesota, shopping mall, with his wife, Claudette. The couple ran the business for 17 years. Vasko was proud that he never lost any teeth during the days of hockey before mouth guards and **helmets** were used. His son, Rick Vasko, played briefly for the **Detroit Red Wings**.

VEZINA, JOSEPH GEORGES GONZAGUE "CHICOUTIMI CU-CUMBER". B. 21 January 1887, Chicoutimi, Quebec. D. 27 March 1926, Chicoutimi, Quebec. Georges Vezina was a **goaltender** for the **Montreal Canadiens**, both in the **National Hockey Association** (1911–1917) and **National Hockey League** (1918–1925). He is famous for perfecting the stand-up style of goaltending, when goalies were not allowed to drop to the **ice** to make a **save**. He was able to pick off more shots with his **hockey stick** than with his **glove**. Vezina was also known for his cool, quiet nature, which is how he earned the **nickname** "The Chicoutimi Cucumber." In the off-season, he operated a tannery. He and his wife raised two sons. Some historians say that he had 22 children who died in infancy, while others agree that it was a rumor started by the Canadiens' manager, Leo Dandurand. Vezina played all 16 games for the Canadiens in the 1910–1911 season, finishing with a record of eight wins and eight losses, while allowing the fewest **goals** in the league. He recorded his first career **shutout** during the 1912–1913 season, defeating the **Ottawa Senators**, 6–0, on 18 January 1913, for one of his nine wins in the season. He led the Canadiens to five **Stanley Cup** Finals, where they won the title twice. Seven times in his career, Vezina had the lowest goals against average in the league, and he had the second-best average another five times.

From the time when he joined the Canadiens in 1910, until he was forced to retire in 1925, Vezina never missed a game or allowed a substitute, playing in 328 consecutive regular-season games and an additional 39 **Stanley Cup Playoff** games. When he returned for training camp for the 1925–1926 season, he was noticeably sick but said nothing about it. During Montreal's first game on 28 November against the **Pittsburgh Pirates**, he played with a high fever but completed the first period without allowing a goal. Vezina began vomiting blood in the intermission, and, at start of the second period, he collapsed in his goal area. Several months later, at the age of 39, he died from tuberculosis. Although he only played part of one game, his wife was given his entire year's salary. As another sign of respect, the best goaltender award, the **Vezina Trophy**, was named for him. When the **Hockey Hall of Fame** opened in 1945, Vezina was one of the original 12 inductees.

VEZINA TROPHY. The Vezina Trophy is the **National Hockey League (NHL)** award given to **goaltenders**. During the 1926–1927 season, the former owners of the **Montreal Canadiens** donated the trophy in memory of their goaltender, **Georges Vezina**. It was originally awarded to the goalkeeper of the team that allowed the fewest number of **goals** during the regular season. The first recipient was **George Hainsworth**. With the original criteria, **Jacques Plante** won this trophy the most times, with seven wins. During the 1981–1982 season, the definition of the award changed. The NHL's general managers voted on the league's best goalkeeper overall. After the award was redefined, the first recipient was **Billy Smith**. With the new definition, **Dominik Hašek** has won the Vezina Trophy the most times (6).

VILLEMURE, GILLES. B. 30 May 1940, Trois Rivieres, Quebec. During **goaltender** Gilles Villemure's **minor-league** career, he led his league in **goals** against average (GAA) three times and **shutouts** five times. He was hoping to move up to the **National Hockey League (NHL)**, but each of the six NHL franchises already had their one goaltender. He patiently stayed in the minor league for 10 years, only filling in for the **New York Rangers** when their goalie was **injured**. In the off-seasons, he was a professional harness racing driver. Villemure's big NHL break came during the 1970–1971 season, when the Rangers implemented a two-goalie system to take pressure off of their starter, **Eddie Giacomin**. Villemure and Giacomin rotated their way through the season effectively, and, as a result, they both won the **Vezina Trophy** as the league's top goalies. Villemure was one of just eight goalies to win the Vezina catching the puck right-handed. Some others include **Charlie Gardiner**, **Tony Esposito**, Tom Barrasso, and **Grant Fuhr**. Villemure used a cool, stand-up style and played the angles confidently for five seasons with the Rangers before injuries affected his performance. In 1975, he was traded to the **Chicago Black Hawks**, who already had Tony Esposito as a star goalie. As a result, Villemure was a backup who didn't play often. At the end of the 1976–1977 season, he retired. During his career, he appeared in 205 NHL games and had 100 wins, 13 shutouts, and a 2.81 career GAA. Villemure shares the same birthplace as **Hockey Hall of Famer Jean Béliveau**.

W

WAGHORNE, FRED C., SR. "OLD WAG". B. 1866, Tunbridge Wells, Kent, England. D. 1956. Fred Waghorne was one of hockey's first **on-ice officials** and a true hockey pioneer. He was a **referee** for more than 50 years and officiated 2,400 hockey **matches** in his career, all during the pre-**National Hockey League** era. Waghorne also introduced several innovations that have remained in the modern game. The modern **face-off** style and the use of the whistle were his ideas. In 1900, he had a situation where a **puck** split in two, and only one half ended up in the **goal**. After much deliberation, Waghorne ruled it as "no goal" because the official definition of a puck included specific dimensions, and since the piece of rubber in the goal did not meet these specifications, it could not be a puck. He then instituted the rule that the entire puck must cross the **line** for a goal to count. Waghorne was inducted into the **Hockey Hall of Fame** in 1961 as a **builder**. After refereeing 1,500 lacrosse matches and founding the Toronto Lacrosse Hockey League, he was inducted into the Canadian Lacrosse Hall of Fame in 1965 as a builder of the sport.

"WAIKIKI HOCKEY". "Waikiki Hockey" is the name of the classic **Wayne Gretzky** sketch on *Saturday Night Live (SNL)*, which aired on 13 May 1989 (season 14, episode 19). Gretzky only agreed to host *SNL* to please his actress wife, Janet Jones. His discomfort with acting, combined with the poorly written script, make it humorous. The sketch was a parody of an Elvis movie, and it also starred Jon Lovitz, Kevin Nealon, Phil Hartman, Jan Hooks, and Dana Carvey. Gretzky's character, Chad, was a busboy who joins the Coconut Kings hockey team. After they beat the Flying Yachtsmen, the cast broke into song, with such lyrics as, "Mona luckahiki means hockey." The six-minute sketch is worth watching and can be found in the *SNL* archives.

WALES TROPHY. *See* PRINCE OF WALES TROPHY.

WASHINGTON CAPITALS. The Washington Capitals are a professional **ice** hockey team in the **Southeast Division** of the **National Hockey League (NHL) Eastern Conference**. The 1974–1975 Washington Capitals were the first team to wear white pants. They wore white pants with red jerseys for the first month of their inaugural season for the road games. The Capitals finished with a .131 winning percentage in 1974–1975, which broke the 45-year-old record held by the **Philadelphia Quakers** for the lowest winning percentage in NHL history (.136). In 37 seasons in the NHL (1974–1975 to 2011–2012), the Capitals have compiled a record of 1,305-1,269-303-91 (3,004 **points**), and, despite making 23 **Stanley Cup Playoff** appearances, they have yet to win a **Stanley Cup**. Bruce Boudreau is their current **coach**. Top players for the team include **center** Nicklas Backstrom, **rookie goaltender** Braden Holtby, **left wing Alexander Ovechkin**, and **right wing** Joel Ward. In the 2011–2012 playoffs, Washington defeated the reigning Stanley Cup holders, the **Boston Bruins**, in seven games to get one step closer to the trophy, but they were then defeated, 4–3, by the **New York Rangers** in the Eastern Conference Semifinals.

WATSON, HARRY E. "MOOSE". B. 14 July 1898, St. John's, Newfoundland. D. 11 September 1957, Toronto, Ontario. Harry E. Watson was a **left wing** who played amateur hockey and was known for his **scoring** talents. After serving as a pilot in World War I, he helped the Toronto Granite Club win the **Allan Cup** in 1922 and 1923. He led the 1923 **Stanley Cup Playoffs** in **goals** (11) and **points** (15). The team also represented **Canada** at the 1924 **Olympic Games**. Watson **scored** 36 goals in five games, and Canada crushed their opponents to win the gold medal. Some of the scores in the preliminary round were 30–0 against Czechoslovakia, 22–0 against **Sweden**, and 33–0 against **Switzerland**. Watson scored 13 times in the **match** against Switzerland. The **Montreal Maroons** offered him a contract for $30,000, which at the time would have made him the highest-paid player in the **National Hockey League (NHL)**, but Watson turned down their bid. He continued to play hockey as an amateur until retiring in 1932. Watson was inducted into the **Hockey Hall of Fame** in 1962.

WATSON, HARRY PERCIVAL "WHIPPER". B. 6 May 1923, Saskatoon, Saskatchewan. D. 19 November 2002, Toronto, Ontario. Harry Watson was **nicknamed** "Whipper" after a famous wrestler, Billy "Whipper" Watson, due to the resemblance. He was a **left wing** for the Brooklyn Americans (1941–1942), **Detroit Red Wings** (1942–1943, 1945–1946), **Toronto Maple Leafs** (1946–1954), and **Chicago Black Hawks** (1954–1957). Watson also joined the Royal **Canadian** Air Force during World War II. While with Toronto, he played on a strong **line**, with **Syl Apps** and Bill Ezinicki. Watson was a powerful **skater** with a hard shot. Although he had solid body **checking** skills, he became a candidate for the **Lady Byng Trophy** for his good sportsmanship. He played the entire 1948–1949 season without a single **penalty minute** and only had 150 penalty minutes during his 809 regular-season NHL career games. Watson won the **Stanley Cup** in 1943, 1947, 1948, 1949, and 1951. He **scored** the Stanley Cup–winning **goal** in Toronto's victory over the **Detroit Red Wings** on 14 April 1948. Watson also **assisted** on **Bill Barilko**'s Stanley Cup–winning goal on 2 April 1951, against the **Montreal Canadiens**. After retiring, he became a **minor-league** coach. Watson was inducted into the **Hockey Hall of Fame** in 1994.

WEILAND, RALPH "COONEY". B. 5 November 1904, Edmondville, Ontario. D. 3 July 1985, Boston, Massachusetts. Cooney Weiland was a **center** for 11 seasons in the **National Hockey League (NHL)** for the **Boston Bruins** (1928–1932, 1935–1939), **Ottawa Senators** (1932–1933), and **Detroit Red Wings** (1933–1935). He was a member of the famous Boston **line** known as the "Dynamite Line," with **Dit Clapper** and Dutch Gainor. Weiland won the **Stanley Cup** in 1929 and 1939. In 1930, not only did Weiland lead the league in **goal scoring**, but he also won the **points** title, with 73, shattering **Howie Morenz**'s single-season record of 51 points. In addition to excelling at scoring, Weiland was known as a great **penalty killer**. He also **coached** the Bruins (1939–1941) and led them to win the 1941 Stanley Cup. In 1950, he began his longest coaching stint at Harvard University, where he compiled a record of 316-172-17, before retiring in 1971. Four of Weiland's **college hockey** players helped the 1960 **U.S. Men's Olympic Ice Hockey Team** win the gold medal in Squaw Valley, California. Among that group was the legendary **Bill Cleary**, who went on to assist Weiland and succeed him as head coach. Cleary served in that role for 19 seasons, and as athletic director for 11. Weiland was inducted into the **Hockey Hall of Fame** in 1971 as a player. In 1972, he received the **Lester Patrick Trophy** for his multiple contributions to hockey.

WELL-KNOWN FANS. Many celebrities enjoy hockey as much, or more, than less-famous individuals. Several famous fans include the late John Candy, Michael J. Fox, Goldie Hawn, Anne Murray, Mike Myers, Matthew Perry, Kurt Russell, Susan Sarandon, and Cheryl Tiegs. The 2005 American Idol winner, Carrie Underwood, married **Nashville Predators center** Mike Fisher. Legendary baseball player Honus Wagner attended hockey **matches** in the early 1900s. *Peanuts* creator **Charles Schulz** was such an avid **ice** hockey fan that he often drew Snoopy driving a **Zamboni**. Schulz even received the **Lester Patrick Trophy** in 1981, for his contributions to the sport.

WESTERN CANADA HOCKEY LEAGUE (WCHL). The Western Canada Hockey League (WCHL) was founded in 1921 as a professional **ice** hockey league originally based in the prairies of **Canada**. They played six-man hockey, without the **rover** position. The WCHL had star player **Bun Cook** and **rookie Eddie Shore**. The league was renamed the Western Hockey League in 1925. The Victoria Cougars team, coached by **Lester Patrick**, won the league championship and went on to face the **Montreal Canadiens** for the **Stanley Cup**. Victoria beat Montreal, three games to one, outscoring them 16–8. Since the **National Hockey League (NHL)** was formed in 1917, no non-NHL team had won the Stanley Cup until the Cougars did in 1925–1926. Due to financial issues, the WCHL folded in 1926. Detroit bought the Victoria team and renamed them the Detroit Cougars, which later became the **Detroit Red Wings**. In 1970, a top-level professional hockey team returned to western Canada, when the **Vancouver Canucks** joined the NHL.

WESTERN CONFERENCE. In 1993, the **National Hockey League (NHL)** renamed the conferences and divisions to reflect their geographic locations. The Western Conference is one of two conferences in the NHL used to divide the teams. Its counterpart is the **Eastern Conference**. The Western Conference is currently comprised of 15 teams in three divisions: the **Central Division**, **Northwest Division**, and **Pacific Division**.

WESTWICK, HARRY "RAT". B. 22 April 1876, Ottawa, Ontario. D. 3 April 1957, Ottawa, Ontario. Harry Westwick was **nicknamed** "Rat" due to his small size. He was a **goaltender** before becoming a star **rover** and a member of many **Stanley Cup**–winning teams, and he played for the Ottawa "Silver Seven." Westwick helped Ottawa win the Stanley Cup for three straight seasons (1902–1903 to 1904–1905) and defend it successfully in two challenges during the 1905–1906 season. He joined the **Kenora Thistles** (1906–1907) but was unable to help them defend their Stanley Cup title. Westwick often played hurt and was forced to leave the **ice** three times during games due to his **injuries**. He only retired after breaking a bone in his ankle. He **scored** 92 **goals** in 91 regular-season games. After the 1908–1909 season, Westwick became a **referee** in the **National Hockey Association**. He was also a **lacrosse** player and member of the World Lacrosse champion Ottawa Capitals in 1900. Westwick was posthumously inducted into the **Hockey Hall of Fame** in 1962.

WICKENHEISER, HAYLEY. B. 12 August 1978, Shaunavon, Saskatchewan. As a **young player**, Hayley Wickenheiser played hockey on outdoor **rinks** mainly with boys. In 1994, she was named to the **Canadian** women's national **ice** hockey team and has remained a member ever since. Wickenheiser became the first woman to play professional hockey full time in a position other than goalie. As a forward with a great **slapshot**, she has represented Canada at the Winter Olympics four times, winning three gold medals and one silver medal. She also competed at the 2000 Summer Olympics on Canada's softball team. In 2003, Wickenheiser became the first woman to **score** a **goal** playing in a men's professional league in **Finland**. During the course of the season, she played 23 games, scoring 2 goals and adding 10 **assists**. She has played on Canada's national team since she was 15 and has played more games in international competition and has more goals, assists, and **penalties** than any other woman in the game. She currently plays for the University of Calgary women's ice hockey team.

WILLIAM M. JENNINGS TROPHY. The William M. Jennings Trophy is the **National Hockey League (NHL)** award given to **goaltenders**. It is named for **William M. Jennings**, who was the owner of the **New York Rangers**. As a **builder**, he was inducted into the **Hockey Hall of Fame** in 1975, and the **U.S. Hockey Hall of Fame** in 1981. After the definition of the **Vezina Trophy** was changed during the 1981–1982 season, the William M. Jennings Trophy was introduced. It is awarded to the goalkeeper of the team that allowed the fewest number of **goals** during the regular season. During a typical season, the goalie must have played in at least 25 games. It is often presented to both goalkeepers on the team. The first recipients were **Montreal Canadiens** Rick Wamsley and Denis Herron. **Patrick Roy** and **Martin Brodeur** have each won the trophy five times, the most of any goalkeeper. Several players have won both the Jennings and Vezina trophies in the same season, including **Ed Belfour** (1990–1991, 1992–1993) and **Dominik Hašek** (1993–1994, 2000–2001). The only time that there has been a tie between players from different teams was during the 2002–2003 season. The trophy was awarded to Martin Brodeur of the **New Jersey Devils** and Robert Esche and Roman Cechmanek of the **Philadelphia Flyers**. In 2010–2011, Roberto Luongo and Cory Schneider of the **Vancouver Canucks** won the William M. Jennings Trophy by allowing only 180 team goals against them. In 2012, the trophy was awarded to Brian Elliott and Jaroslav Halak of the **St. Louis Blues**.

WILLIAMS, DAVE JAMES "TIGER". B. 3 February 1954, Weyburn, Saskatchewan. Dave Williams was **nicknamed** "Tiger" by his hockey **coach** when he was five years old. He was a forward in the **National Hockey League (NHL)** from 1974–1988, and best known as an **enforcer**. Williams played for the **Toronto Maple Leafs** (1974–1980), **Vancouver Canucks** (1980–1984), **Detroit Red Wings** (1984–1985), **Los Angeles Kings**

(1985–1988), and Hartford Whalers (1987–1988). He holds the NHL career record for **penalties** in minutes, at 3,966, from 1974–1988, during the regular season, and 4,421, including the **Stanley Cup Playoffs**. Although Williams spent much of his time in the **penalty box**, when he was on the **ice**, he **scored** 241 **goals** and had 272 **assists** for 513 **points** during his NHL career. Unfortunately, he was never a member of a **Stanley Cup**–winning team. Williams will never be inducted into the **Hockey Hall of Fame** due to the way he terrorized his opponents. In 1976, he hit **Pittsburgh Penguins' defenseman** Dennis Owchar with his **hockey stick**. Owchar needed 46 stitches to close the wound. He also hit the **coach** of the **Buffalo Sabres**, **Scotty Bowman**, with his stick. He even left teeth marks in **Dave Schultz** when he bit him. Williams was suspended in 1982, after he hit **goaltender Billy Smith** of the **New York Islanders** in the head and then tried to choke him. In 1993, Williams briefly became a **roller hockey** player for the Vancouver Voodoo team and appeared in one game and scored two points.

WINGER. The slang term *winger* is used to describe a hockey player who plays the offensive position of **left wing** or **right wing**.

WINNIPEG JETS. The Winnipeg Jets were a professional **ice** hockey team in the **World Hockey Association (WHA)** (1972–1979), and they were one of four the franchises absorbed into the **National Hockey League (NHL)** when the WHA folded in 1979. In total, the Jets played for seven seasons, from 1972–1979, and had six **Stanley Cup Playoff** appearances. In the last WHA game in history, on 20 May 1979, the Jets defeated the **Edmonton Oilers** by a **score** of 7–3. In 1996, the NHL Jets relocated to Arizona, and became the **Phoenix Coyotes**. Their 11-season record (1999–2000) was 378-471-45-87 (888 **points**), with no **Stanley Cup** wins. In May 2011, the **Atlanta Thrashers** were sold, and the franchise moved to Winnipeg, Manitoba. This marked a second life for the Winnipeg Jets. During the new season of the Jets (2011–2012), they won 36 of the 79 games they played and finished in third place in the **Eastern Conference Southeast Division**.

WINTER CLASSIC. The Winter Classic is the **National Hockey League (NHL)** version of a **pond hockey** game. It is an annual event held outdoors on or around New Year's Day. The first Winter Classic was held 1 January 2008, between the **Buffalo Sabres** and **Pittsburgh Penguins**, at Ralph Wilson Stadium, in Orchard Park, New York. The game had a record crowd of 71,217 fans in attendance. Pittsburgh won, 2–1, in a shootout. The success of the 2008 NHL Winter Classic led to a second one in 2009. It was held at Wrigley Field in Chicago, on 1 January 2009, and matched the **Detroit Red Wings** against the **Chicago Blackhawks**. That game had the highest U.S.

television ratings of any **ice** hockey game in 33 years. Since then, the NHL Winter Classic has become an annual event. In 2010, the **Philadelphia Flyers** beat the **Boston Bruins**, 2–1, in **overtime**, at Fenway Park. In 2011, the **Washington Capitals** beat the Pittsburgh Penguins, 3–1, in Pittsburgh. In 2012, the **New York Rangers** beat the Philadelphia Flyers, 3–2. The 2013 Winter Classic will include the first **Canadian** team. The **Toronto Maple Leafs** are scheduled to play the Detroit Red Wings.

WINTER OLYMPICS. *See* OLYMPIC GAMES.

WIRTZ, ARTHUR MICHAEL. B. 23 January 1901, Chicago, Illinois. D. 21 July 1983, Chicago, Illinois. After graduating from the University of Michigan in 1923, Arthur Wirtz became a real estate businessman. In 1929, he formed a partnership with businessman James E. Norris. Three years later, they teamed up to buy the Detroit Falcons hockey franchise and renamed them the **Detroit Red Wings**. Detroit then went on to win the **Stanley Cup** four times (1936, 1937, 1943, 1950). In 1936, they made more money by starting the Hollywood Ice Revue with **Olympic** figure skater Sonja Heine. Together with James D. Norris, Wirtz purchased the **Chicago Black Hawks** in 1946 and turned them from a failing franchise into one of the strongest teams of the early 1960s. Chicago won the Stanley Cup in 1961. In 1949, Wirtz and Norris formed the International Boxing Club, which later promoted 47 of the 51 championship **matches** held in the **United States** between 1955 and 1959. Norris and Wirtz also owned **Chicago Stadium**, the Bismarck Hotel in Chicago, the Chicago Bulls, the St. Louis Arena, and most of the stock in New York's **Madison Square Garden**. Wirtz was a major factor in the growth of the **National Hockey League**, and he was inducted into the **Hockey Hall of Fame** in 1971 as a **builder**. His son, Bill Wirtz, was the president of the Chicago Black Hawks from 1966–2007, and his grandson, Rocky Wirtz, is the current owner of the Chicago franchise.

WOMEN'S ICE HOCKEY. In 1895, women's **ice** hockey gained popularity at universities, mainly at the University of Toronto and Queen's University in Kingston, Ontario. In the 1920s, Bobbie Rosenfeld and Myrtle Cook, former track stars and hockey players, became **Canada**'s first female sports reporters, and the two women specialized in hockey during the winter. Elizabeth Graham was a **goaltender** in Kingston, Ontario, for the Queen's University women's hockey team. In 1927, she appeared in a game wearing a fencing mask. She may have been the first goalie to ever wear a **face mask** in an organized hockey game. The **Preston Rivulettes**, with star player **Hilda Ranscombe**, dominated women's ice hockey during the 1930s. World War II in the 1940s halted the development of women's ice hockey, but then, in

1956, Abby Hoffman challenged hockey's gender barrier by disguising herself as a male and playing in a boys' league. Women's ice hockey eventually made a strong comeback in the early 1970s, with Shirley Cameron as the first star of the modern era.

The "no intentional body **checking** rule" differentiates women's ice hockey from men's ice hockey. In 1987, the first Women's **World Ice Hockey Championships** were held in Toronto; however, the event was not recognized as an official tournament by the **International Ice Hockey Federation (IIHF)**. In 1990, the first official and IIHF-sanctioned Women's World Ice Hockey Championships were held in Ottawa. Women's hockey became a full medal sport at the 1998 Winter Olympics for the first time, and the U.S. team won a gold medal. The **Canadian Women's Olympic Ice Hockey Team** won the next three **Olympic Games** (2002, 2006, 2010). Due to the international growth of the sport, the women's division at the World Championships expanded to two pools, A and B, in 1999. Since 1990, the IIHF has held 13 World Ice Hockey Championships for women. Canada has won nine gold medals, and the **United States** has won the remaining four. The two strong teams have met in all 13 of the final games. **Finland** has won 10 bronze medals. **Sweden** won two, and **Russia** earned one. In 1994 and 1997, China was competitive on the world scene with fourth-place finishes. **Switzerland** was fourth in 2008. No other teams have even reached the final four. In 2005, the United States ended Canada's streak of eight straight (nine unofficial) world titles in a shootout. Sweden became the first non-North American team to earn a silver medal at the 2006 Winter Olympic Games, after beating the United States in the semifinals. In 2010, Canada won its third straight Olympic gold medal by defeating the rival Americans in a tough 2–0 final.

American **Cammi Granato** and Canadians **Angela James** and **Manon Rhéaume** were pioneers in the sport of women's hockey. Several other top Canadian players include Jennifer Botterill, **Cassie Campbell**, Danielle Goyette, Geraldine Heaney, Jayna Hefford, Caroline Ouellette, Cherie Piper, and **Hayley Wickenheiser**. Star American players include Karyn Bye, Julie Chu, Natalie Darwitz, Katie King, Jenny Potter, **Angela Ruggiero**, and Krissy Wendell. Riikka Nieminen played for Finland, and Maria Rooth played for Sweden. In 2010, Cammi Granato and Angela James became first women inducted into the **Hockey Hall of Fame**. *See also* STERNER, ULF IVAR ERIK "UFFE".

WORLD CUP OF HOCKEY. The World Cup of Hockey is an international **ice** hockey tournament. It began in 1996, as the successor to the previous **Canada Cup** (1976–1991). The tournament has occurred twice, with the **United States** defeating **Canada** in 1996, and Canada defeating **Finland** in 2004. **U.S. Hockey Hall of Fame** members Gary Suter and Keith Tkachuk helped the United States capture the first World Cup of Hockey crown in 1996. The World Cup of Hockey occurs outside of the hockey season, which allows for the best players in the world to be available to compete, unlike the **World Ice Hockey Championships**, which overlaps with the **Stanley Cup Playoffs**. Because the World Cup of Hockey is organized by the **National Hockey League (NHL)**, games are played under NHL rules and not those of the **International Ice Hockey Federation**.

WORLD HOCKEY ASSOCIATION (WHA). From 1972–1979, the World Hockey Association (WHA) was a North American professional **ice** hockey league that was a successful competitor of the **National Hockey League (NHL)**. Sixty-seven players jumped from the NHL to the WHA in the first year, including star forward **Bobby Hull**. The WHA also signed European players previously thought to be unsuited to the North American style of play. Due to many legal battles with the NHL, franchises in the WHA often relocated or folded. In 1979, the WHA ceased operations, and their teams merged with the NHL teams. On 20 May 1979, the last WHA game was played, and the **Winnipeg Jets** defeated the **Edmonton Oilers**, 7–3. **Wayne Gretzky** played in that game, and because he played for the WHA Oilers before they joined the NHL, he never had a **rookie** year with the NHL. The four teams that still exist from the WHA are the Hartford Whalers (now the **Carolina Hurricanes**), Edmonton Oilers, **Quebec Nordiques** (now the **Colorado Avalanche**), and Winnipeg Jets (now the **Phoenix Coyotes**).

WORLD ICE HOCKEY CHAMPIONSHIPS. The annual World Ice Hockey Championships is an event sanctioned by the **International Ice Hockey Federation**. Because the World Ice Hockey Championships overlaps with the **Stanley Cup Playoffs**, some of the better **National Hockey League** players are unable to participate. **Canada** was the tournament's first dominant team, winning the event 12 times between 1930–1952. The **United States**, Czechoslovakia, **Sweden**, **Great Britain**, and **Switzerland** were also competitive during this period. The Soviet Union first participated in 1954, and soon became rivals with Canada. From 1963 until the nation's breakup in 1991, the Soviet Union was the dominant team, winning an amazing 20 championships. During that period, only three other nations won medals: Canada, Czechoslovakia, and Sweden. **Russia** first participated in 1992, and the **Czech Republic** and **Slovakia** began competing in 1993. During the 2000s, the countries became more evenly matched. At the 75th World Ice Hockey Championships in Slovakia, **Finland** defeated Sweden in the final to win their second championship. In 2012, Italy and Kazakhstan joined the competition. The 76th championship was held from 4–20 May 2012, in Helsinki, Finland, and Stockholm, Sweden. Russia defeated Slovakia in the finals. *See also* APPENDIX I for a list of World Ice Hockey champions.

WORSLEY, LORNE JOHN "GUMP," "THE GUMPER". B. 14 May 1929, Montreal, Quebec. D. 26 January 2007, St. Hyacinthe, Quebec. Gump Worsley got the **nickname** "The Gumper" because he resembled the comic strip character Andy Gump. He was a **goaltender** in the **National Hockey League (NHL)** with the **New York Rangers** (1952–1953, 1954–1963), **Vancouver Canucks** (1953–1954), **Montreal Canadiens** (1963–1970), and Minnesota North Stars (1970–1974). Worsley helped his team win the **Stanley Cup** in 1965, 1966, 1968, and 1969. In 1953, he won the **Calder Memorial Trophy**. During the 1967–1968 season, he led the NHL in **goals** against average (1.98) and finished second in NHL **shutouts**, with six that season. He won the **Vezina Trophy** twice, in 1966, with Charlie Hodge, and in 1968, with Rogatien Vachon. Worsley was a colorful goalie who was very quotable. He remarked that most goalies were crazy to do what they did and said, "The only job worse is a javelin catcher at a track and field meet." When he was asked why he never wore a **face mask**, he explained that his face was his mask, and that the fans wanted to see his beautiful face. When his **coach** commented on his beer belly, Worsley said, "He should know better than that. He knows I only drink Scotch." Although he enjoyed alcohol, Worsley won 335 career games. He had a fear of flying but managed the NHL travel schedule for 21 seasons. Worsley was inducted into the **Hockey Hall of Fame** in 1980. He was the last Hockey Hall of Fame goaltender to play in the NHL without a face mask.

WORTERS, ROY "SHRIMP". B. 19 October 1900, Toronto, Ontario. D. 7 November 1957, Toronto, Ontario. Roy Worters joined the **Pittsburgh Pirates** in 1925, as a **goaltender**, and remained with them until 1928. At 5 feet, 3 inches, he was the shortest goalie ever to play in the **National Hockey League (NHL)**. Worters was known for his toughness, and he once played seven games with a hernia. On 26 December 1926, he stopped 70 shots on **goal** (SOG) for the Pirates against the **New York Americans**. The Pirates and Americans combined for 141 SOG, which is still an NHL record. After a contract dispute, Worters left Pittsburgh for New York. He instantly helped the Americans become a strong team, recording a second-place overall record of 16-12-10, which was a huge improvement over the last-place finish the season before. That set up a memorable **Stanley Cup Playoff** showing with the **New York Rangers**, but the Rangers won. For his efforts, Worters became the first goalie to win the **Hart Memorial Trophy** as the league's Most Valuable Player in 1929. He joined the **Montreal Canadiens** for one season (1929–1930) but returned to the Americans to finish out his career (1928–1929, 1930–1937). He won the **Vezina Trophy** in 1931, but never won the **Stanley Cup**. His 171-229-83 career won-loss record reflects the weak teams he played for, but his 67 career **shutouts** shows how good he really was. Worters was also a hockey innovator, because he was the first goalie to really use the blocker as a tactic. In those days, the blocker was just a heavily padded **glove**, but he was the first to use that hand to deflect shots into the corner as opposed to trying to catch them. More than a decade after passing away from throat cancer in 1957, Worters was inducted into the **Hockey Hall of Fame** in 1969.

Xs AND Os. The letters X and O are the basic symbols used to represent players on play diagrams used by **coaches**.

Y

YASHIN, ALEXEI VALERYEVICH. B. 5 November 1973, Sverdlovsk, **Russia**. Alexei Yashin was a Russian **center** who was drafted by the **Ottawa Senators** in 1992, and played for them from 1993–2001. He **scored** 79 **points** in his **rookie** season. In 1998, he scored a key **overtime goal** against the **New Jersey Devils** that helped the Senators win their first ever **Stanley Cup Playoff** series. On 10 November 1999, after several contract disputes, Yashin refused to play, and the Senators suspended him for the rest of the 1999–2000 season. The **National Hockey League (NHL)** supported this decision. Yashin attempted to sign with a team in **Switzerland**, but the **International Ice Hockey Federation** suspended him from playing internationally until the dispute was resolved. Yashin played with the Senators for the 2000–2001 season, but he was then traded to the **New York Islanders** (2001 2007). In 2006, a knee **injury** shortened his NHL career. Internationally, Yashin represented Russia in the 1996 and 2004 **World Cup of Hockey** and the 1998, 2002, and 2006 **Olympic Games**. He won Olympic silver (1998) and bronze (2002) medals. In the 2011–2012 season, Yashin played for an **ice** hockey team in Moscow, Russia.

YOUNG PLAYERS. Children of all ages enjoy playing **ice** hockey. When grouped by ages, they are referred to by the following names: mites: ages seven and eight; squirts: ages nine and 10; bantams: ages 11 and 12; peewees: ages 13 and 14; midgets: ages 15 and 16; and juniors: over 16 years of age. Professional players often start out playing in these leagues. For example, **Bobby Orr** progressed through the various leagues in Parry Sound before he signed his Junior A card with the **Boston Bruins**. Retired players sometimes stay connected to the sport by **coaching** or assisting children. **Wayne Gretzky** was known for inspiring the young players through training camps. **Builder** Ed Snider was inducted into both the **Hockey Hall of Fame** and **U.S. Hockey Hall of Fame** for his contribution to youth hockey. In 2005, he founded the Ed Snider Youth Hockey Foundation to provide unprivileged children in the Philadelphia area with an opportunity to learn to play hockey at local **rinks**. In 2008, the organization rescued five inner-city ice skating rinks in Philadelphia that had been targeted for closure.

YUGOSLAVIA. In 1939, Yugoslavia became a member of the **International Ice Hockey Federation (IIHF)**. They competed in five **Olympic Games** (1964–1976, 1984). Their highest finish was in 1968, with ninth place. In 1984, Yugoslavia was the host country for the Olympics. In 1992, Yugoslavia was broken up into five republics: Bosnia and Herzegovina, Croatia, the Republic of Macedonia (sometimes referred to as the Former Yugoslav Republic of Macedonia, or FYROM), Slovenia, and the Federal Republic of Yugoslavia. The latter country was renamed Serbia and Montenegro in 2003, and, in 2006, Serbia and Montenegro each became two separate, independent nations. Of the six new nations, only Slovenia has produced any players who have played in the **National Hockey League**, namely **Anže Kopitar** and **Jan Muršak**. In 1992, Croatia and Slovenia each became members of the IIHF, and both Bosnia and Herzegovina and FYROM joined in 2001. Serbia's IIHF membership is considered to be an extension of the original Yugoslavia and dates back to 1939, and the newest country, Montenegro, has yet to join the IIHF.

YZERMAN, STEPHEN GREGORY "STEVE," "STEVIE Y". B. 9 May 1965, Cranbrook, British Columbia. Steve Yzerman played for Peterborough and was drafted fourth overall by the **Detroit Red Wings** in 1983. He played **center** for the Red Wings for 22 seasons (1983–2004, 2005–2006). Yzerman is one of only four **National Hockey League (NHL)** players to play at least 20 seasons with only one organization. **Alex Delvecchio, Stan Mikita**, and **Mike Modano** are the other three. He holds more single-season Detroit Red Wings **scoring** records than even **Gordie Howe**. Yzerman scored a career-high 155 **points**, 65 **goals**, and 90 **assists** during the 1988–1989 season. This record has only been beaten by **Wayne Gretzky** and **Mario Lemieux**. Yzerman was the captain of the Red Wings when they defeated the **Philadelphia Flyers** in 1997 for the **Stanley Cup**. He won the **Conn Smythe Trophy** in 1998, the **Frank J. Selke Trophy** in 2000, and the **Bill Masterton Memorial Trophy** in 2003. In 2006, he received the **Lester Patrick Trophy**. Later that year, Yzerman retired, finishing his career ranked as the sixth all-time leading scorer in NHL history. He was inducted into the **Hockey Hall of Fame** in 2009. In 2010, Yzerman became the general manager and vice president of the **Tampa Bay Lightning**. Also in 2010, Yzerman was the executive director for Team **Canada** at the Vancouver **Olympic Games**. He recently agreed to fill that same position for the 2014 Olympics in Sochi, **Russia**.

Z

ZALAPSKI, ZARLEY BENNETT "ZZ". B. 22 April 1968, Edmonton, Alberta. Zarley Zalapski is a former **National Hockey League (NHL)** left-handed **defenseman**. He is also the only player in NHL history with the initials Z. Z., which became his **nickname**. His career included playing for the **Pittsburgh Penguins** (1987–1990), Hartford Whalers (1990–1994), **Calgary Flames** (1994–1998), **Montreal Canadiens** (1997–1998), and **Philadelphia Flyers** (1999–2000). In 2006, he became a citizen of **Switzerland** after his marriage and played for the Lausanne Class B Swiss team.

ZAMBONI. In 1949, the "Model A Zamboni Ice Resurfacer" became patented (#2,642,679) by **Frank J. Zamboni Jr.** Simply known as a Zamboni, this is the four-wheel-drive machine that resurfaces the **ice** between periods of a hockey game. Zambonis are used in **rinks** all across the world. In 1950, **Olympic skater** Sonja Henie saw a Zamboni in action while practicing at a California skating rink and was impressed. She immediately ordered one for her national tour and later took one to Europe. Today, in addition to hockey games, Zambonis are used at the Ice Capades and Olympics.

ZAMBONI, FRANK JOSEPH, JR. B. 16 January 1901, Eureka, Utah. D. 27 July 1988, Paramount, California. Frank Zamboni is the Californian inventor who literally changed the face (surface) of **ice** hockey with his four-wheel-drive vehicle that scrapes, cleans, and floods the surface of a hockey **rink**. His rough prototype in 1949 transformed the job of resurfacing an ice rink from a three-man, 90-minute task to a one-man, 10-minute job, and it was first used for amateur matches. A more refined **Zamboni** made its **National Hockey League (NHL)** debut on 10 March 1955, in Montreal, at a **Montreal Canadiens'** game. Frank J. Zamboni & Co. has sold more than 8,500 Zamboni Ice Resurfacers. Zamboni passed away in 1988, from lung cancer, but the company remains family owned and operated by Frank's son and grandson. For his significant contribution to hockey, Zamboni was posthumously elected into the **U.S. Hockey Hall of Fame** in 2009. The Iceland Skating Rink, a 20,000 square-foot rink in Paramount, California, which Frank built in 1939, with his brother and cousin, is still open today.

ZEIDEL, LAZARUS "LARRY," "ROCK". B. 1 June 1928, Montreal, Ontario. Larry Zeidel was a **defenseman** with the Hershey Bears of the **American Hockey League** for nine seasons. He played for the **Detroit Red Wings** and **Chicago Black Hawks** in the early 1950s. Zeidel won a **Stanley Cup** in 1952 with the Red Wings. He spent 13 seasons in the **minor league**. In 1967, Zeidel promoted himself to all the expansion franchises, and, as a result, the **Philadelphia Flyers** signed him to a contract at the age of 39. At the time, he was the only Jewish player in the **National Hockey League (NHL)**. He received the title of "fastest stick in the Midwest" because he often used his **hockey stick** as a spear. No other NHL player was involved in more stick-swinging incidents than Zeidel. In 1968, while playing for the Flyers, Zeidel was involved in a major stick **fight** with **Eddie Shack** of the **Boston Bruins**. Photos of their bloodied faces were widely published in the newspapers. But off the **ice**, Zeidel was described as mild mannered. During the 1967–1968 season, he helped lead the Flyers to a first-place finish. Early in the 1968–1969 season, he ended his career nearing the age of 41.

ZIEGLER, JOHN A., JR. B. 9 February 1934, Grosse Pointe, Michigan. In 1977, John Ziegler became the fourth president of the **National Hockey League (NHL)**, succeeding **Clarence Campbell**. In August 1979, Ziegler announced that protective **helmets** would become mandatory in the NHL. "The introduction of the helmet rule will be an additional safety factor," he said. Veterans who signed professional contracts prior to 1 June 1979 were able to choose whether they wanted to wear helmets. In 1984, he received the **Lester Patrick Trophy**. In 1987, he was inducted into the **Hockey Hall of Fame** as a **builder**. In 1992, Ziegler was forced out of office by a settlement that resolved the 10-day pension strike.

Appendix A: National Hockey League Franchise Movement

Note: Italic indicates that teams are active in 2011–2012 season.

1917–1918 TO 1966–1967

Montreal Canadiens

1917–1918 founded

Montreal Wanderers

1917–1918 founded

1917–1918 folded after season

Ottawa Senators

1934–1935 folded after season

1993–1994 reborn as *Ottawa Senators*

Toronto Maple Leafs

Founded as Toronto Arenas

1919–1920 renamed Toronto St. Patricks

1927–1928 renamed *Toronto Maple Leafs*

Quebec Bulldogs

1919–1920 founded

1919–1920 folded after season

Hamilton Tigers

1920–1921 founded

347

1924–1925 folded after season

Boston Bruins

1924–1925 founded

Montreal Maroons

1924–1925 founded

1937–1938 folded after season

New York Americans

1925–1926 founded

1941–1942 renamed Brooklyn Americans

1941–1942 folded after season

Pittsburgh Pirates

1926–1927 founded

1929–1930 folded after season

Chicago Blackhawks

1926–1927 founded as Chicago Black Hawks

1986–1987 renamed *Chicago Blackhawks*

Detroit Red Wings

1926–1927 founded as Detroit Cougars

1930–1931 renamed Detroit Falcons

1932–1933 renamed *Detroit Red Wings*

New York Rangers

1926–1927 founded

Philadelphia Quakers

1930–1931 founded

1930–1931 folded after season

St. Louis Eagles

1934–1935 founded

1934–1935 folded after season

No other changes until league expansion in 1967–1968

1967–1968 TO 2011–2012

Los Angeles Kings

1967–1968 founded

Minnesota North Stars

1967–1968 founded

1993–1994 relocated as *Dallas Stars*

California Seals

1967–1968 founded

1967–1968 renamed Oakland Seals midway through season

1970–1971 renamed California Golden Seals

1976–1977 relocated as Cleveland Barons

1977–1978 folded after season

Philadelphia Flyers

1967–1968 founded

Pittsburgh Penguins

1967–1968 founded

St. Louis Blues

1967–1968 founded

Buffalo Sabres

1970–1971 founded

Vancouver Canucks

1970–1971 founded

Calgary Flames

1972–1973 founded as Atlanta Flames

1980–1981 relocated as *Calgary Flames*

New York Islanders

1972–1973 founded

New Jersey Devils

1974–1975 founded Kansas City Scouts

1976–1977 relocated as Colorado Rockies

1982–1983 relocated as *New Jersey Devils*

Washington Capitals

1974–1975 founded

Phoenix Coyotes

1979–1980 as Winnipeg Jets, joined NHL from WHA

1996–1997 relocated as *Phoenix Coyotes*

Edmonton Oilers

1979–1980 joined NHL from WHA

Carolina Hurricanes

1979–1980 as Hartford Whalers, joined NHL from WHA

1997–1998 relocated as *Carolina Hurricanes*

Colorado Avalanche

1979–1980 as Quebec Nordiques, joined NHL from WHA

1995–1996 relocated as *Colorado Avalanche*

San Jose Sharks

1991–1992 founded

Tampa Bay Lightning

1992–1993 founded

Florida Panthers

1993–1994 founded

Anaheim Ducks

1993–1994 founded as Mighty Ducks of Anaheim

2006–2007 renamed *Anaheim Ducks*

Nashville Predators

1998–1999 founded

Winnipeg Jets

1999–2000 founded as Atlanta Thrashers

2011–2012 relocated as *Winnipeg Jets*

Columbus Blue Jackets

2000–2001 founded

Minnesota Wild

2000–2001 founded

Appendix B: World Hockey Association Franchise Movement

Note: Italic indicates that teams were active in 1978–1979 season.

Edmonton Oilers

1972–1973 founded as Alberta Oilers

1973–1974 renamed *Edmonton Oilers*

Chicago Cougars

1972–1973 founded

1975–1976 folded after season

Cleveland Crusaders

1972–1973 founded

1976–1977 relocated as Minnesota Fighting Saints

1976–1977 folded midseason

Houston Aeros

1972–1973

1978–1979 folded after season

Los Angeles Sharks

1972–1973 founded

1974–1975 relocated as Michigan Stags

1974–1975 relocated as Baltimore Blades

1975–1976 folded midseason

Minnesota Fighting Saints

1972–1973

1976–1977 folded

New England Whalers

1972–1973 founded

New York Raiders

1972–1973 founded

1973–1974 renamed New York Golden Blades

1973–1974 relocated as New Jersey Knights during season

1974–1975 relocated as San Diego Mariners

1977–1978 folded after season

Birmingham Bulls

1972–1973 founded as Ottawa Nationals

1973–1974 relocated as Toronto Toros

1976–1977 relocated as *Birmingham Bulls*

Philadelphia Blazers

1972–1973 founded

1973–1974 relocated as Vancouver Blazers

1975–1976 relocated as Calgary Cowboys

1977–1978 folded after season

Quebec Nordiques

1972–1973 founded

Winnipeg Jets

1972–1973 founded

Indianapolis Racers

1974–1975 founded

1978–1979 folded midseason

Phoenix Roadrunners

1974–1975 founded

1977–1978 folded

Cincinnati Stingers

1975–1976 founded

Denver Spurs

1975–1976

1975–1976 relocated as Ottawa Civics

1975–1976 folded midseason

Czechoslovakian All-Stars

1977–1978 played limited schedule

Soviet All-Stars

1977–1978 played limited schedule

Finnish National Team

1978–1979 played one game

Appendix C: Current NHL Teams and Their Arenas and Cities

Anaheim Ducks	Honda Center	Anaheim, CA
Boston Bruins	TD Garden	Boston, MA
Buffalo Sabres	First Niagara Center	Buffalo, NY
Calgary Flames	Scotiabank Saddledome	Calgary, AB
Carolina Hurricanes	PNC Arena	Raleigh, NC
Chicago Blackhawks	United Center	Chicago, IL
Colorado Avalanche	Pepsi Center	Denver, CO
Columbus Blue Jackets	Nationwide Arena	Columbus, OH
Dallas Stars	American Airlines Center	Dallas, TX
Detroit Red Wings	Joe Louis Arena	Detroit, MI
Edmonton Oilers	Rexall Place	Edmonton, AB
Florida Panthers	Bank Atlantic Center	Sunrise, FL
Los Angeles Kings	Staples Center	Los Angeles, CA
Minnesota Wild	XCel Energy Center	St. Paul, MN
Montreal Canadiens	Bell Centre	Montreal, QC
Nashville Predators	Bridgestone Arena	Nashville, TN
New Jersey Devils	Prudential Center	Newark, NJ
New York Islanders	Nassau Veterans Memorial Coliseum	Uniondale, NY
New York Rangers	Madison Square Garden (IV)	New York, NY
Ottawa Senators	Scotiabank Place	Ottawa, ON
Philadelphia Flyers	Wells Fargo Center	Philadelphia, PA
Phoenix Coyotes	Jobing.com Arena	Glendale, AZ
Pittsburgh Penguins	Consol Energy Center	Pittsburgh, PA
San Jose Sharks	HP Pavilion	San Jose, CA
St. Louis Blues	Scottrade Center	St. Louis, MO

Tampa Bay Lightning	Thunderdome	St. Petersburg, FL
Toronto Maple Leafs	Air Canada Centre	Toronto, ON
Vancouver Canucks	Rogers Arena	Vancouver, BC
Washington Capitals	Verizon Center	Washington, D.C.
Winnipeg Jets	MTS Centre	Winnipeg, MB

Appendix D: Hockey Hall of Fame Player Inductees

*Note: * indicates no one inducted that year.*

1945

Donald Henderson

"Dan" Bain

Hobart Amery Hare "Hobey" Baker

Russell G. "Dubbie" Bowie

Charles Robert "Chuck" Gardiner

Edward George "Eddie" Gerard

Francis "Frank" McGee

Howard William "Howie" Morenz

Thomas Neil "Tommy" Phillips

Harvey Pulford

Arthur Howey "Art" Ross

William Hodgeson "Hod" Stuart

Georges Vezina

1946*

1947

Aubrey Victor "Dit" Clapper

Aurèle Émile Joliat

Frank Nighbor

Lester Patrick

Edward William "Eddie" Shore

Frederick "Cyclone" Taylor

1948–1949*

1950

Allan McLean "Scotty" Davidson

Charles Graham Drinkwater

Michael "Mike" Grant

Silas Seth "Si" Griffis

Edouard "Newsy" Lalonde

Maurice Joseph "Joe" Malone

George Richardson

Henry Judah "Harry" Trihey

1951*

1952

Richard Robinson "Dickie" Boon

William "Bill" Cook

Francis Xavier "Moose" Goheen

Ernest "Moose" Johnson

Duncan McMillan "Mickey" MacKay

1953–1957*

1958

François-Xavier "Frank" Boucher

Francis Michael "King" Clancy

Henry William Sprague Cleghorn

Alex Connell

Norman "Mervyn" "Red" Dutton

Frank C. Foyston

Frank Fredrickson

Herbert Martin "Herb" Gardiner

William George Hay

James Dickinson "Dick" Irvin

Ivan Wilfred "Ching" Johnson

Gordon Blanchard "Duke" Keats

Frederick Hugh "Hughie" Lehman

George McNamara

Patrick Joseph "Paddy" Moran

1959

John James "Jack" Adams

Cyril Joseph "Cy" Denneny

Cecil R. "Tiny" Thompson

1960

John George "Buck" Boucher

Sylvio Mantha

John Phillip "Jack" Walker

1961

Charles Joseph Sylvanus "Syl" Apps

Charles William "Charlie" Conacher

Clarence "Happy" Day

George Hainsworth

Joseph Henry "Joe" Hall

Percy LeSueur

Frank Rankin

Maurice "The Rocket" Richard

Milton Conrad "Milt" Schmidt

Oliver Levi Seibert

Bruce Stuart

1962

Harry L. "Punch" Broadbent

Harold Hugh "Harry" Cameron

Samuel Russell "Rusty" Crawford

John Proctor "Jack" Darragh

James Henry "Jimmy" Gardner

Hamilton Livingstone "Billy" Gilmour

Wilfred Thomas "Shorty" Green

William Milton "Riley" Hern

Charles Thomas "Tom" Hooper

John Bower "Bouse" Hutton

Harrold Macarius "Harry" Hyland

Jean-Baptiste "Jack" Laviolette

Fred G. "Steamer" Maxwell

William George "Billy" McGimsie

Edward Reginald "Reg" Noble

Didier "Pit" Pitre

J. D. "Jack" Ruttan

David "Sweeney" Schriner

Harold Joseph "Bullet Joe" Simpson

Alfred Edward "Alf" Smith

Russell "Barney" Stanley

Robert Nelson "Old Poison" Stewart

Martin "Marty" Walsh

Harry E. "Moose" Watson

Harry "Rat" Westwick

Frederick Whitcroft

Gordon Allan "Phat" Wilson

1963

Ebenezer Ralston "Ebbie" Goodfellow

Alfred Joseph "Joe" Primeau

Earl Walter Seiber

1964

Douglas Wagner "Doug" Bentley

William Ronald "Bill" Durnan

Albert Charles "Babe" Siebert

John Sherratt "Black Jack" Stewart

1965

Martin J. "Marty" Barry

Clinton Stevenson "Clint" Benedict

Arthur F. Farrell

George Reginald "Red" Horner

Sydney Harris "Syd" Howe

John Calder "Jack" Marshall

William "Bill" Mosienko

Blair Russel

Ernest "Ernie" Russell

Fredrick R. "Fred" Scanlan

1966

Maxwell Herbert Lloyd "Max" Bentley

Hector "Toe" Blake

Emile "Butch" Bouchard

Francis Charles "Frank" Brimsek

Theodre Samuel "Ted" Kennedy

Elmer James Lach

Robert Blake Theodore "Ted" Lindsay

Walter "Babe" Pratt

Kenneth Joseph "Kenny" Reardon

1967

Walter Edward "Turk" Broda

Neil McNeil Colville

Harold "Harry" Oliver

1968

William Malles "Bill" Cowley

1969

Sidney Gerald "Sid" Abel

Bryan Aldwyn Hextall

Leonard Patrick "Red" Kelly

Roy "Shrimp" Worters

1970

Cecil Henry "Babe" Dye

William Alexander "Bill" Gadsby

Thomas Christian "Tom" Johnson

1971

Harvey "Busher" Jackson

Gordon William "Gordie" Roberts

Terrance Gordon "Terry" Sawchuk

Ralph "Cooney" Weiland

1972

Jean Arthur Béliveau

Joseph Andre Bernard "Bernie" Geoffrion

Harry "Hap" Holmes

Gordon "Gordie" Howe

Reginald "Hooley" Smith

1973

Douglas Norman "Doug" Harvey

Claude Earl "Chuck" Rayner

Thomas J. Smith

1974

Harry William "Billy" Burch

Arthur Edmund "Art" Coulter

Thomas "Tommy" Dunderdale

Richard Winston "Dickie" Moore

1975

George Edward "Chief" Armstrong

Irvine Wallace "Ace" Bailey

Gordon Arthur "Gordie" Drillon

Glenn Henry Hall

Pierre Paul Pilote

1976

John William "Johnny" Bower

Hubert George "Bill" Quackenbush

1977

Alexander Peter "Alex" Delvecchio

Miles Gilbert "Tim" Horton

1978

Andrew James "Andy" Bathgate

Joseph Jacques "Jake the Snake" Plante

Joseph Rene Marcel Pronovost

1979

Henry Vernon "Harry" Howell

Robert Gordon "Bobby" Orr

Joseph Henri "Pocket Rocket" Richard

1980

Harry "Apple Cheeks" Lumley

Jospeph Lynn Patrick

Lorne John "Gump" Worsley

1981

John Paul "Johnny" Bucyk

Francis William "Frank" Mahovlich

Allan Herbert Stanley

1982

Yvan Serge "Roadrunner" Cournoyer

Rodrigue Gabriel "Rod" Gilbert

Norman Victor Alexander "Norm" Ullman

1983

Kenneth Wayne "Ken" Dryden

Robert Marvin "Bobby" Hull

Stanislav "Stan" Mikita

1984

Philip Anthony "Phil" Esposito

Jacques Gerard Lemaire

Bernard Marcel "Bernie" Parent

1985

Gerald Michael "Gerry" Cheevers
Murray Bert Olmstead
Joseph Gilbert Yvon "Jean" Ratelle

1986

Leo Joseph Boivin
David Michael "Dave" Keon
Serge Aubrey Savard

1987

Robert Earle "Bobby" Clarke
Edward "Eddie" Giacomin
Joseph Jacques Hughes Laperriere

1988

Anthony James "Tony" Esposito
Guy Damien Lafleur
Herbert William "Buddy" O'Connor
Douglas Bradford "Brad" Park

1989

Herbert A. "Herbie" Lewis
Darryl Glen Sittler
Vladislav Aleksandrovich Tretiak

1990

William Charles "Bill" Barber
Ferdinand Charles "Fernie" Flaman
Gilbert "Gil" Perreault

1991

Michael Dean "Mike" Bossy
Denis Charles Potvin
Robert Jesse "Bob" Pulford
Clinton James "Clint" Smith

1992

Marcel Elphege Dionne

Woodrow Clarence "Woody" Dumart

Robert Michael "Bob" Gainey

Lanny King McDonald

1993

Guy Gerard Lapointe

Edgar Louis Laprade

Stephen John Shutt

William "Bill" John Smith

1994

Lionel Pretoria Conacher

Harry Percival Watson

1995

Frederick Joseph "Bun" Cook

Larry Clark Robinson

1996

Robert Theodore "Bobby" Bauer

Anders Börje Salming

1997

Mario Lemieux

Bryan John Trottier

1998

Roy Gordon Conacher

Michel Goulet

Peter Stastny

1999

Wayne Douglas Gretzky

2000

Joseph Patrick Mullen

Denis Joseph Savard

2001

Viacheslav Alexandrovich Fetisov

Michael Alfred Gartner

Dale Hawerchuk

Jari Pekka Kurri

2002

Bernard Allan "Bernie" Federko

Clark "Jethro" Gillies

Rod Corry Langway

2003

Grant Scott Fuhr

Patrick Michael "Pat" LaFontaine

2004

Raymond Jean "Ray" Bourque

Paul Douglas Coffey

Lawrence Thomas "Larry" Murphy

2005

Valeri Borisovich Kharlamov

Cameron Michael "Cam" Neely

2006

Terrance Richard "Dick" Duff

Patrick Edward Roy

2007

Ronald Michael "Ron" Francis Jr.

Al MacInnis

Mark Douglas Messier

Ronald Scott Stevens

2008
Glenn Christopher "Andy" Anderson
Igor Nikolayevich Larionov

2009
Brett Andrew Hull
Brian Joseph Leetch
Luc Robitaille
Stephen Gregory Yzerman

2010
Dino Ciccarelli
Catherine "Cammi" Granato
Angela James

2011
Edward John "Ed" Belfour
Douglas Robert "Doug" Gilmour
Mark Steven Howe
Joseph "Joe" Nieuwendyk

2012
Pavel Vladimirovich Bure
Adam Oates
Joe Sakic
Mats Johan Sundin

Appendix E: Hockey Hall of Fame Builder and On-Ice Official Inductees

*Note: * indicates on-ice official.*

1945

H. Montagu Allan

Frederick Stanley, 16th Earl of Derby

1947

Frank Calder

W. A. Hewitt

Francis Nelson

William Northey

John Ross Robertson

Claude C. Robinson

James Sutherland

1950

Frank Patrick

1958

George Dudley

James E. Norris

Allan Pickard

Donat Raymond

Conn Smythe

Lloyd Turner

1960

Charles Adams

John Kilpatrick

Frank J. Selke

1961

George V. Brown

Paul Loicq

Fred Waghorne

Chaucer Elliott*

Mickey Ion*

Cooper Smeaton*

1962

Frank Ahearn

Walter A. Brown

Frederick Hume

James D. Norris

Ambrose O'Brien

Frank Smith

Mike Rodden*

1963

Leo Dandurand

Tommy Gorman

Frederic McLaughlin

Bobby Hewitson*

1964

Angus Daniel Campbell

Frank Dilio

Bill Chadwick*

1965

Foster Hewitt

Tommy Lockhart

1966

Clarence Campbell

1967

Red Storey*

1968
James Dunn
Jim Hendy

1969
Al Leader
Bruce Norris

1970
Robert Lebel

1971
Arthur Wirtz

1972
Weston Adams

1973
Hartland Molson
Frank Udvari*

1974
Charles Hay
Tommy Ivan
Anatoli Tarasov
Carl Voss

1975
Frank Buckland
William M. Jennings

1976
Jack Gibson
Philip Dansken Ross

Bill Wirtz

1977
Bunny Ahearne
Harold Ballard
Joseph Cattarinich

1978
Jack Bickell
Sam Pollock
William Thayer Tutt

1979
Gordon Juckes

1980
Jack Butterfield

1981
John Ashley*

1982
Emile Francis

1983
Harry Sinden

1984
Punch Imlach
Jake Milford

1985
John Mariucci
Rudy Pilous

1986

Bill Hanley

1987
John Ziegler
Matt Pavelich*

1988
Ed Snider
George Hayes*

1989
Father David Bauer

1990
Bud Poile

1991
Scotty Bowman
Neil Armstrong*

1992
Keith Allen
Bob Johnson
Frank Mathers

1993
Frank Griffiths
Seymour Knox
Fred Page
John D'Amico*

1994
Brian O'Neill

1995
Gunther Sabetzki

Bill Torrey

1996
Al Arbour

1997
Glen Sather

1998
Athol Murray

1999
Scotty Morrison
Andy Van Hellemond*

2000
Walter Bush

2001
Craig Patrick

2002
Roger Neilson

2003
Mike Ilitch
Brian Kilrea

2004
Cliff Fletcher

2005
Murray Costello

2006
Harley Hotchkiss

Herb Brooks

2007

Jim Gregory

2008

Ed Chynoweth

Ray Scapinello*

2009

Lou Lamoriello

2010

Jim Devellano

Daryl "Doc" Seaman

Appendix F: International Ice Hockey Federation Hall of Fame Inductees

Austria

Hans Dobida	2007	builder
Josef Puschnig	1999	player
Walter Wasservogel	1997	builder

Belgium

Paul Loicq	1997	builder

Canada

Father David Bauer	1997	builder
Roger Bourbonnais	1999	player
Mike Buckna	2004	builder
Wayne Gretzky	2000	player
Geraldine Heaney	2008	player
William Hewitt	1998	builder
Derek Holmes	1999	builder
Fran Huck	1999	player
Angela James	2008	player
Marshall Johnston	1998	player
Gordon Juckes	1997	builder
Dave King	2001	builder
Bob LeBel	1997	builder
Mario Lemieux	2008	player
Vic Lindquist	1997	player
Barry MacKenzie	1999	player
Seth Martin	1997	player
Jack McLeod	1999	player
Andy Murray	2012	builder
Terry O'Malley	1998	player
Gordon Renwick	2002	builder
Harry Sinden	1997	player

Harry E. Watson	1998	player

Czech Republic

Quido Adamec	2005	referee
Vladimir Bouzek	2007	player
Vlastimil Bubnik	1997	player
Ludek Bukac	2007	builder
Josef Cerny	2007	player
Jaroslav Drobny	1997	player
Karel Gut	1998	player
Ivan Hlinka	2002	player
Jiri Holecek	1998	player
Jiri Holik	1999	player
Vladimir Kostka	1997	builder
Oldrich Machac	1999	player
Josef Malecek	2003	player
Vladimir Martinec	2001	player
Bohumil Modry	2011	player
Vaclav Nedomansky	1997	player
Milan Novy	2012	player
Frantisek Pospisil	1999	player
Miroslav Subrt	2004	builder
Jan Suchy	2009	player
Frantisek Tikal	2004	player
Vladimir Zabrodsky	1997	player

Denmark

Jorgen Hviid	2005	builder

Finland

Raimo Helminen	2012	player
Timo Jutila	2003	player
Matti Keinonen	2002	player
Jari Kurri	2000	player
Harry Lindblad	1999	builder
Pekka Marjamaki	1998	player
Riikka Nieminen-Välilä	2010	player
Kalevi Numminen	2011	builder

Lasse Oksanen	1999	player
Esa Peltonen	2007	player
Goran Stubb	2000	builder
Jorma Valtonen	1999	player
Juhani Wahlsten	2006	player
Unto Wiitala	2003	referee
Urpo Ylonen	1997	player

France

Philippe Bozon	2008	player
Jacques Lacarriere	1998	player
Louis Magnus	1997	builder

Germany

Rudi Ball	2004	player
Dieter Hegen	2010	player
Heinz Henschel	2003	builder
Gustav Jaenecke	1998	player
Udo Kiessling	2000	player
Josef Kompalla	2003	referee
Erich Kuhnhackl	1997	player
Hans Rampf	2001	player
Dr. Gunther Sabetzki	1997	builder
Alois Schloder	2005	player
Xaver Unsinn	1998	builder
Joachim Ziesche	1999	player

Great Britain

Bunny Ahearne	1997	builder
Carl Erhardt	1998	player
Peter Patton	2002	builder

Hungary

Gyorgy Pasztor	2001	builder
Laszlo Schell	2009	referee

Italy

Enrico Calcaterra	1999	builder

Japan

Tsutomu Kawabuchi	2004	builder
Shoichi Tomita	2006	builder
Yoshiaki Tsutsumi	1999	builder

Latvia

Helmuts Balderis	1998	player
Arturs Irbe	2010	player

Norway

Tore Johannessen	1999	builder

Poland

Henryk Gruth	2006	player

Romania

Eduard Pana	1998	player
Doru Tureanu	2011	player

Russia

Veniamin Alexandrov	2007	player
Vsevolod Bobrov	1997	player
Pavel Bure	2012	player
Arkady Chernyshev	1999	builder
Vitaly Davydov	2004	player
Igor Dmitriev	2007	builder
Vyacheslav Fetisov	2005	player
Anatoli Firsov	1998	player
Yuri Karandin	2004	referee
Alexei Kasatonov	2009	player
Valeri Kharlamov	1998	player
Viktor Konovalenko	2007	player
Vladimir Krutov	2010	player
Viktor Kuzkin	2005	player
Igor Larionov	2008	player
Konstantin Loktev	2007	player
Sergei Makarov	2001	player
Alexander Maltsev	1999	player

Boris Mayorov	1999	player
Boris Mikhailov	2000	player
Vladimir Petrov	2006	player
Alexander Ragulin	1997	player
Nikolai Sologubov	2004	player
Andrei Starovoitov	1997	builder
Vyacheslav Starshinov	2007	player
Anatoli Tarasov	1997	builder
Viktor Tikhonov	1998	builder
Vladislav Tretyak	1997	player
Valeri Vasiliev	1998	player
Alexander Yakushev	2003	player
Vladimir Yurzinov	2002	builder

Slovakia

Vladimir Dzurilla	1998	player
Josef Golonka	1998	player
Ladislav Horsky	2004	builder
Jan Starsi	1999	builder
Peter Stastny	2000	player
Ladislav Trojak	2011	player

Slovenia

Ernest Aljancic Sr.	2002	player
Rudi Hiti	2009	player

Sweden

Curt Berglund	2003	builder
Sven Bergqvist	1999	player
Lars Bjorn	1998	player
Ove Dahlberg	2004	referee
Rudolf Eklow	1999	builder
Rickard Fagerlund	2010	builder
Arne Grunander	1997	builder
Bengt-Ake Gustafsson	2003	player
Anders Hedberg	1997	player
Leif Holmqvist	1999	player
Sven "Tumba" Johansson	1997	player

Tomas Jonsson	2000	player
Hakan Loob	1998	player
Tord Lundstrom	2011	player
Mats Naslund	2005	player
Kent Nilsson	2006	player
Nils "Nisse" Nilsson	2002	player
Ronald Pettersson	2004	player
Thomas Rundqvist	2007	player
Börje Salming	1998	player
Ulf Sterner	2001	player
Roland Stoltz	1999	player
Arne Stromberg	1998	builder

Switzerland

Ferdinand "Pic" Cattini	1998	player
Hans Cattini	1998	player
Jakob Kolliker	2007	player
Cesar Luthi	1998	builder
Richard "Bibi" Torriani	1997	player

Ukraine

Anatoli Khorozov	2006	builder

United States

Art Berglund	2008	builder
Herb Brooks	1999	Builder
Walter Brown	1997	builder
Walter Bush Jr.	2009	builder
Karyn Bye (-Dietz)	2011	player
Bill Christian	1998	player
Bill Cleary	1997	player
Gerry Cosby	1997	player
Jim Craig	1999	player
Mike Curran	1999	player
Cammi Granato	2008	player
Phil Housley	2012	player
Mark Johnson	1999	player
John Mayasich	1997	player

Jack McCartan	1998	player
Lou Nanne	2004	player
Bob Ridder	1998	builder
Jack Riley	1998	builder
Hal Trumble	1999	builder
Thayer Tutt	2002	builder

Appendix G: Stanley Cup Champions

EARLY CHALLENGE CUP ERA

During these years there was a series of challenges.

Year	Winner	Challenger
1893	Montreal	AAA
1894	Montreal	AAA
1895	Montreal	Victorias
December 1895	Montreal	Victorias
February 1896	Winnipeg	Victorias
1897	Montreal	Victorias
1898	Montreal	Victorias
1899	Montreal	Shamrocks
1900	Montreal	Shamrocks
1901	Winnipeg	Victorias
January 1902	Winnipeg	Victorias
March 1902	Montreal	AAA
February 1903	Montreal	AAA
March 1903	Ottawa	Senators
1904	Ottawa	Senators
1905	Ottawa	Senators
February 1906	Ottawa	Senators
March 1906	Montreal	Wanderers
January 1907	Kenora	Thistles
March 1907	Montreal	Wanderers
1908	Montreal	Wanderers
1909	Ottawa	Senators

NHA CHALLENGE CUP ERA

Year	Winner	Challenger	Result
1910	Montreal Wanderers	Berlin Professionals	1 game, 7–3

1911	Ottawa Senators	Galt Professionals	1 game, 7–4
1912	Quebec Bulldogs	Moncton Victorias	best-of-3, 2–0
1913	Quebec Bulldogs	Sydney Miners	best-of-3, 2–0
1914	Toronto Blueshirts	Montreal Canadiens	2 games, total goals 6–2
1915	Vancouver Millionaires	Ottawa Senators	best-of-5, 3–0
1916	Montreal Canadiens	Portland Rosebuds	best-of-5, 3–2
1917	Seattle Metropolitans	Montreal Canadiens	best-of-5, 3–1

NHL, PCHA, WCHL CHALLENGE CUP ERA

Year	Winner	Challenger	Result
1918	Toronto Arenas	Vancouver Millionaires	3–2
1919*	no decision (cancelled due to Spanish influenza)		
1920	Ottawa Senators	Seattle Metropolitians	3–2
1921	Ottawa Senators	Vancouver Millionaires	3–2
1922	Toronto St. Patricks	Vancouver Millionaires	3–2
1923	Ottawa Senators	Vancouver Maroons	3–1
1924	Montreal Canadiens	Vancouver Maroons	2–0
1925	Victoria Cougars	Montreal Canadiens	3–1
1926	Montreal Maroons	Victoria Cougars	3–1

BEST-OF-5 GAME SERIES

Year	Winner	Challenger	Result
1927	Ottawa Senators	Boston Bruins	2–0–2
1928	New York Rangers	Montreal Maroons	3–2
1929	Boston Bruins	New York Rangers	2–1 (best-of-3)
1930	Montreal Canadiens	Boston Bruins	2–0 (best-of-3)
1931	Montreal Canadiens	Chicago Black Hawks	3–2

1932	Toronto Maple Leafs	New York Rangers	3–0
1933	New York Rangers	Toronto Maple Leafs	3–1
1934	Chicago Black Hawks	Detroit Red Wings	3–1
1935	Montreal Maroons	Toronto Maple Leafs	3–0
1936	Detroit Red Wings	Toronto Maple Leafs	3–1
1937	Detroit Red Wings	New York Rangers	3–2
1938	Chicago Black Hawks	Toronto Maple Leafs	3–1

BEST-OF-7 GAME SERIES

Year	Winner	Challenger	Result
1939	Boston Bruins	Toronto Maple Leafs	4–1
1940	New York Rangers	Toronto Maple Leafs	4–2
1941	Boston Bruins	Detroit Red Wings	4–0
1942	Toronto Maple Leafs	Detroit Red Wings	4–3
1943	Detroit Red Wings	Boston Bruins	4–0
1944	Montreal Canadiens	Chicago Black Hawks	4–0
1945	Toronto Maple Leafs	Detroit Red Wings	4–3
1946	Montreal Canadiens	Boston Bruins	4–1
1947	Toronto Maple Leafs	Montreal Canadiens	4–2
1948	Toronto Maple Leafs	Detroit Red Wings	4–0
1949	Toronto Maple Leafs	Detroit Red Wings	4–0
1950	Detroit Red Wings	New York Rangers	4–3
1951	Toronto Maple Leafs	Montreal Canadiens	4–1
1952	Detroit Red Wings	Montreal Canadiens	4–0
1953	Montreal Canadiens	Boston Bruins	4–1
1954	Detroit Red Wings	Montreal Canadiens	4–3
1955	Detroit Red Wings	Montreal Canadiens	4–3
1956	Montreal Canadiens	Detroit Red Wings	4–1
1957	Montreal Canadiens	Boston Bruins	4–1
1958	Montreal Canadiens	Boston Bruins	4–2
1959	Montreal Canadiens	Toronto Maple Leafs	4–1
1960	Montreal Canadiens	Toronto Maple Leafs	4–0

1961	Chicago Black Hawks	Detroit Red Wings	4–2
1962	Toronto Maple Leafs	Chicago Black Hawks	4–2
1963	Toronto Maple Leafs	Detroit Red Wings	4–1
1964	Toronto Maple Leafs	Detroit Red Wings	4–3
1965	Montreal Canadiens	Chicago Black Hawks	4–3
1966	Montreal Canadiens	Detroit Red Wings	4–2
1967	Toronto Maple Leafs	Montreal Canadiens	4–2
1968	Montreal Canadiens	St. Louis Blues	4–0
1969	Montreal Canadiens	St. Louis Blues	4–0
1970	Boston Bruins	St. Louis Blues	4–0
1971	Montreal Canadiens	Chicago Black Hawks	4–3
1972	Boston Bruins	New York Rangers	4–2
1973	Montreal Canadiens	Chicago Black Hawks	4–2
1974	Philadelphia Flyers	Boston Bruins	4–2
1975	Philadelphia Flyers	Buffalo Sabres	4–2
1976	Montreal Canadiens	Philadelphia Flyers	4–0
1977	Montreal Canadiens	Boston Bruins	4–0
1978	Montreal Canadiens	Boston Bruins	4–2
1979	Montreal Canadiens	New York Rangers	4–1
1980	New York Islanders	Philadelphia Flyers	4–2
1981	New York Islanders	Minnesota North Stars	4–1
1982	New York Islanders	Vancouver Canucks	4–0
1983	New York Islanders	Edmonton Oilers	4–0
1984	Edmonton Oilers	New York Islanders	4–1
1985	Edmonton Oilers	Philadelphia Flyers	4–1
1986	Montreal Canadiens	Calgary Flames	4–1
1987	Edmonton Oilers	Philadelphia Flyers	4–3
1988	Edmonton Oilers	Boston Bruins	4–0
1989	Calgary Flames	Montreal Canadiens	4–2
1990	Edmonton Oilers	Boston Bruins	4–1
1991	Pittsburgh Penguins	Minnesota North Stars	4–2

1992	Pittsburgh Penguins	Chicago Black Hawks	4–0
1993	Montreal Canadiens	Los Angeles Kings	4–1
1994	New York Rangers	Vancouver Canucks	4–3
1995	New Jersey Devils	Detroit Red Wings	4–0
1996	Colorado Avalanche	Florida Panthers	4–0
1997	Detroit Red Wings	Philadelphia Flyers	4–0
1998	Detroit Red Wings	Washington Capitals	4–0
1999	Dallas Stars	Buffalo Sabres	4–2
2000	New Jersey Devils	Dallas Stars	4–2
2001	Colorado Avalanche	New Jersey Devils	4–3
2002	Detroit Red Wings	Carolina Hurricanes	4–1
2003	New Jersey Devils	Mighty Ducks of Anaheim	4–3
2004	Tampa Bay Lightning	Calgary Flames	4–3
2005	not played due to lockout		
2006	Carolina Hurricanes	Edmonton Oilers	4–3
2007	Anaheim Ducks	Ottawa Senators	4–1
2008	Detroit Red Wings	Pittsburgh Penguins	4–2
2009	Pittsburgh Penguins	Detroit Red Wings	4–3
2010	Chicago Blackhawks	Philadelphia Flyers	4–2
2011	Boston Bruins	Vancouver Canucks	4–3
2012	Los Angeles Kings	New Jersey Devils	4–2

The 1919 Stanley Cup series was contested by the Seattle Metropolitans and the Montreal Canadiens. After five games had been played, each team had won two, lost two, and tied one. Health officials cancelled the deciding game of the series due to an influenza outbreak.

Appendix H: Olympic Champions

Note: Women's ice hockey appears in italic.

Year	Gold	Silver	Bronze	Host Country
1920	Canada	United States	Czechoslovakia	Belgium
1924	Canada	United States	Great Britain	France
1928	Canada	Sweden	Switzerland	Switzerland
1932	Canada	United States	Germany	United States
1936	Great Britain	Canada	United States	Germany
1948	Canada	Czechoslovakia	Switzerland	Switzerland
1952	Canada	United States	Sweden	Norway
1956	Soviet Union	United States	Canada	Italy
1960	United States	Canada	Soviet Union	United States
1964	Soviet Union	Sweden	Czechoslovakia	Austria
1968	Soviet Union	Czechoslovakia	Canada	France
1972	Soviet Union	United States	Czechoslovakia	Japan
1976	Soviet Union	Czechoslovakia	W. Germany	Austria
1980	United States	Soviet Union	Sweden	United States
1984	Soviet Union	Czechoslovakia	Sweden	Yugoslavia
1988	Soviet Union	Finland	Sweden	Canada
1992	Unified Team	Canada	Czechoslovakia	France
1994	Sweden	Canada	Finland	Norway
1998	Czechoslovakia	Russia	Finland	Japan
1998	*United States*	*Canada*	*Finland*	*Japan*
2002	Canada	United States	Russia	United States
2002	*Canada*	*United States*	*Sweden*	*United States*
2006	Sweden	Finland	Czechoslovakia	Italy
2006	*Canada*	*Sweden*	*United States*	*Italy*
2010	Canada	United States	Finland	Canada
2010	*Canada*	*United States*	*Finland*	*Canada*

Appendix I: World Ice Hockey Champions

Note: Women's ice hockey appears in italic.

Year	Gold	Silver	Bronze	Host Country
1920	Canada	United States	Czechoslovakia	Belgium
1924	Canada	United States	Great Britain	France
1928	Canada	Sweden	Switzerland	Switzerland
1930	Canada	Germany	Switzerland	France/Germany/ Austria
1931	Canada	United States	Austria	Poland
1932	Canada	United States	Germany	United States
1933	United States	Canada	Czechoslovakia	Czechoslovakia
1934	Canada	United States	Germany	Italy
1935	Canada	Switzerland	Great Britain	Switzerland
1936	Great Britain	Canada	United States	Germany
1937	Canada	Great Britain	Switzerland	Great Britain
1938	Canada	Great Britain	Czechoslovakia	Czechoslovakia
1939	Canada	United States	Switzerland	Switzerland
1947	Czechoslovakia	Sweden	Austria	Czechoslovakia
1948	Canada	Czechoslovakia	Switzerland	Switzerland
1949	Czechoslovakia	Canada	United States	Sweden
1950	Canada	United States	Switzerland	Great Britain
1951	Canada	Sweden	Switzerland	France
1952	Canada	United States	Sweden	Norway
1953	Sweden	W. Germany	Switzerland	Switzerland
1954	Soviet Union	Canada	Sweden	Sweden
1955	Canada	Soviet Union	Czechoslovakia	W. Germany
1956	Soviet Union	United States	Canada	Italy
1957	Sweden	Soviet Union	Czechoslovakia	Soviet Union
1958	Canada	Soviet Union	Sweden	Norway
1959	Canada	Soviet Union	Czechoslovakia	Czechoslovakia
1960	United States	Canada	Soviet Union	United States
1961	Canada	Czechoslovakia	Soviet Union	Switzerland
1962	Sweden	Canada	United States	United States

1963	Soviet Union	Sweden	Czechoslovakia	Sweden
1964	Soviet Union	Sweden	Czechoslovakia	Austria
1965	Soviet Union	Czechoslovakia	Sweden	Finland
1966	Soviet Union	Czechoslovakia	Canada	Yugoslavia
1967	Soviet Union	Sweden	Canada	Austria
1968	Soviet Union	Czechoslovakia	Canada	France
1969	Soviet Union	Sweden	Czechoslovakia	Sweden
1970	Soviet Union	Sweden	Czechoslovakia	Sweden
1971	Soviet Union	Czechoslovakia	Sweden	Switzerland
1972	Czechoslovakia	Soviet Union	Sweden	Czechoslovakia
1973	Soviet Union	Sweden	Czechoslovakia	Soviet Union
1974	Soviet Union	Czechoslovakia	Sweden	Finland
1975	Soviet Union	Czechoslovakia	Sweden	W. Germany
1976	Czechoslovakia	Soviet Union	Sweden	Poland
1977	Czechoslovakia	Sweden	Soviet Union	Austria
1978	Soviet Union	Czechoslovakia	Canada	Czechoslovakia
1979	Soviet Union	Czechoslovakia	Sweden	Soviet Union
1981	Soviet Union	Sweden	Czechoslovakia	Sweden
1982	Soviet Union	Czechoslovakia	Canada	Finland
1983	Soviet Union	Czechoslovakia	Canada	W. Germany
1985	Czechoslovakia	Canada	Soviet Union	Czechoslovakia
1986	Soviet Union	Sweden	Canada	Soviet Union
1987	Sweden	Soviet Union	Czechoslovakia	Austria
1989	Soviet Union	Canada	Czechoslovakia	Sweden
1990	Soviet Union	Sweden	Czechoslovakia	Switzerland
1990	*Canada*	*United States*	*Finland*	*Canada*
1991	Sweden	Canada	Soviet Union	Finland
1992	Sweden	Finland	Czechoslovakia	Czechoslovakia
1992	*Canada*	*United States*	*Finland*	*Finland*
1993	Russia	Sweden	Czechoslovakia	Germany
1994	Canada	Finland	Sweden	Italy
1994	*Canada*	*United States*	*Finland*	*United States*
1995	Finland	Sweden	Canada	Sweden
1996	Czechoslovakia	Canada	United States	Austria
1997	Canada	Sweden	Czechoslovakia	Finland
1997	*Canada*	*United States*	*Finland*	*Canada*
1998	Sweden	Finland	Czechoslovakia	Switzerland

1999	Czechoslovakia	Finland	Sweden	Norway
1999	*Canada*	*United States*	*Finland*	*Finland*
2000	Czechoslovakia	Slovakia	Finland	Russia
2000	*Canada*	*United States*	*Finland*	*Canada*
2001	Czechoslovakia	Finland	Sweden	Germany
2001	*Canada*	*United States*	*Russia*	*United States*
2002	Slovakia	Russia	Sweden	Sweden
2003	Canada	Sweden	Slovakia	Finland
2003	*cancelled due to outbreak of SARS*		*China*	
2004	Canada	Sweden	United States	Czechoslovakia
2004	*Canada*	*United States*	*Finland*	*Canada*
2005	Czechoslovakia	Canada	Russia	Austria
2005	*United States*	*Canada*	*Sweden*	*Sweden*
2006	Sweden	Czechoslovakia	Finland	Latvia
2007	Canada	Finland	Russia	Russia
2007	*Canada*	*United States*	*Sweden*	*Canada*
2008	Russia	Canada	Finland	Canada
2008	*United States*	*Canada*	*Finland*	*China*
2009	Russia	Canada	Sweden	Switzerland
2009	*United States*	*Canada*	*Finland*	*Finland*
2010	Czechoslovakia	Russia	Sweden	Germany
2011	Finland	Sweden	Czechoslovakia	Slovakia
2011	*United States*	*Canada*	*Finland*	*Finland*
2012	Russia	Slovakia	Czechoslovakia	Finland/Sweden
2012	*Canada*	*United States*	*Switzerland*	*United States*

Bibliography

CONTENTS

I. INTRODUCTION

There is a wealth of information about the sport of ice hockey. Readers of any age can find books written on the subject. These include juvenile picture books, young reader's chapter books, instructional guides, biographies, team books, photographic essays, behind-the-scenes accounts by referees, encyclopedias, women's ice hockey books, and international books. There are also books with quotes by players and trivia books for complete sports fans; however, the autobiographies are the most interesting for most, partly because the details of games are given, but also because some previously untold stories are recounted. In some ways, there is nothing more fascinating than a hockey player or referee detailing anecdotes that fans would have never heard anywhere else. Speaking of autobiographies and biographies, Wayne Gretzky not only shattered numerous records on the ice, but he also became the subject of hundreds of books. Sportswriter Stan Fischler has written numerous books that contain interviews he has conducted with players. He has also helped some players write their own stories.

Well-written books about famous hockey families include *Gretzky: From Backyard Rink to the Stanley Cup*, written by Wayne's father, Walter Gretzky, with Jim Taylor; *My Three Hockey Players*, by Colleen Howe; and *The Patricks: Hockey's Royal Family*, by Eric Whitehead.

Fans who enjoy the behind-the-scenes fight stories will enjoy Dave Schultz's *The Hammer: Confessions of a Hockey Enforcer* (written with Stan Fischler). Also of interest may be Lloyd Freeberg's *In the Bin: Reckless and Rude Stories from the Penalty Boxes of the NHL*, Trent Frayne's *The Mad Men of Hockey*, and Frank Orr's *Tough Guys of Pro Hockey*. *The Code: The Unwritten Rules of Fighting and Retaliation in the NIIL*, written by Ross Berenstein, gives an insightful description of why hockey players start fights.

For readers interested in old-time hockey, S. Kip Farrington Jr.'s *Skates, Sticks, and Men: The Story of Amateur Hockey in the United States* and Stan Fischler's *Those Were the Days: The Lore of Hockey by the Legends of the Game* are worth reading. Other positive hockey stories such Olympic accounts as Wayne Coffey's *The Boys of Winter: The Untold Story of a Coach, a Dream, and the 1980 U.S. Olympic Hockey Team* and Tim Wendel's *Going for the Gold: How the U.S. Won at Lake Placid*. For one who needs strictly statistics, Andrew Podnieks's *World of Hockey: Celebrating a Century of the IIHF* and David Wallechinsky's *The Complete Book of the Olympics* should be useful. And James Duplacey combines facts with stories in *The Official Rules of Hockey.* For example, in addition to providing the National Hockey League (NHL) rule about how curved a hockey stick can be, he explains the story about Marty McSorley's illegal stick during the 1993 Stanley Cup Playoffs.

Many hockey books have been written about the coveted Stanley Cup, but one of the more humorous ones is Kevin Allen's *Why Is the Stanley Cup in Mario Lemieux's Swimming Pool?: How Winners Celebrate with the World's Most Famous Cup.* Another lighthearted one is Andrew Podnieks's *Hockey Superstitions: From Playoff Beards to Crossed Sticks and Lucky Socks.*

Books have been written about the NHL expansion and how some people think that greedy players and owners were ruining the sport and the fans' experience. Books in this category include Jeff Z. Klein and Karl-Eric Reif's *The Death of Hockey* and former president of the NHL Gil Stein's *Power Plays: An Inside Look at the Big Business of the National Hockey League.* There were even books written about the lockouts, and one interesting one is Andrew Podnieks's *The Lost Season: A Year in Hockey without the NHL.* It details how many of the players joined leagues in Europe so that they could play the sport they loved and others who raised money by playing for charities.

In addition to hockey books, there are several magazines listed in this bibliography. Young fans may appreciate a subscription or two for their birthday. They are also an excellent way to encourage students who are not avid readers. The glossy photographs catch their attention, and the articles are short enough to maintain their attention. When their reading skills improve, they can progress to chapter books. Matt Christopher is a prolific sportswriter for children. Roy MacGregor has also written hockey books for young fans. Young girls may enjoy Tami Johnson's *Girls' Ice Hockey: Dominating the Rink*, Stacy Wilson's *The Hockey Book for Girls*, and Barbara Stewart's *She Shoots . . . She Scores!*

The works in the bibliography are divided into sections for the reader's ease. Several of the most current websites have been added, including the recently created foreign-language websites of the NHL. While every effort has been made to create a well-rounded hockey bibliography, there is an excellent source for anyone interested. The Resource Centre at the Hockey Hall of Fame in Toronto, Ontario, contains an extensive amount of hockey-related material from various leagues and international tournaments. Their collection, dating back to the turn of the 20th century, is preserved and catalogued. One can contact them for an appointment for any researching needs.

II. REFERENCE

A. Encyclopedias

Blevins, Dave. *The Sports Hall of Fame Encyclopedia: Baseball, Basketball, Football, Hockey, Soccer*. Lanham, Md.: Scarecrow Press, 2011.

Diamond, Dan, ed. *Total Hockey: The Official Encyclopedia of the National Hockey League*. New York: Total Sports, 1998.

Duplacey, James, and Eric Zweig. *Official Guide to the Players of the Hockey Hall of Fame*. Toronto: Firefly Books, 2010.

Edginton, K., Thomas Erskine, and James M. Welsh. *Encyclopedia of Sports Films*. Lanham, Md.: Scarecrow Press, 2010.

Fischler, Stan, and Shirley Fischler. *Fischler's Ice Hockey Encyclopedia*, Rev. ed. New York: Thomas Y. Crowell, 1979.

Hollander, Zander. *The Complete Encyclopedia of Ice Hockey*. Detroit, Mich.: Invisible Ink Press, 1992.

Podnieks, Andrew, ed. *IIHF Guide and Record Book, 2012*. Toronto: McClelland & Stewart, 2011.

Wukovits, John. *The Encyclopedia of the Winter Olympics*. New York: Franklin Watts, 2001.

B. Annuals and Yearbooks

Hockey Hall of Fame. *Hockey's Heritage*, 6th ed. Toronto: Hockey Hall of Fame, 1978.

C. Bibliography

Malherbe, W. A. *Chronological Bibliography of Hockey: Revised to 1964*. Johannesburg, South Africa: Johannesburg Public Library, 1965.

Thom, Douglas J. *The Hockey Bibliography: Ice Hockey Worldwide*. Ontario: Ontario Institute for Studies in Education, 1978.

D. Other

Beckett Hockey Card Price Guide and Alphabetical Checklist, 18th ed. Dallas, Tex.: Beckett Media, 2009.

Hammond, Tim. *Sports*. New York: Random House, 1988.

Podnieks, Andrew, ed. *The Complete Hockey Dictionary*. Bolton, Ontario: Fenn Publishing, 2007.

Webster's Sports Dictionary. Springfield, Mass.: Merriam-Webster, 1976.

III. HISTORY

A. General

Beddoes, Richard, Stan Fischler, and Ira Gitler. *Hockey: The Story of the World's Fastest Sport*. New York: Macmillan, 1971.

Davidson, John, with John Steinbreder. *Hockey for Dummies*, 2nd ed. Indianapolis, Ind.: Wiley, 2001.

Dryden, Ken, with Mark Mulvoy. *Face-Off at the Summit*. Boston: Little Brown, 1973.

Duplacey, James. *The Annotated Rules of Hockey*. New York: Lyons & Burford, 1996.

Eskenazi, Gerald. *Hockey*. Chicago, Ill.: Follett Publishing, 1969.

Farrington, S. Kip, Jr. *Skates, Sticks, and Men: The Story of Amateur Hockey in the United States*. New York: David McKay, 1972.

Fischler, Stan. *Those Were the Days: The Lore of Hockey by the Legends of the Game*. New York: Dodd, Mead, 1976.

Italia, Bob. *100 Unforgettable Moments in Pro Hockey*. Minneapolis, Minn.: Abdo and Daughters, 1996.

McFarlane, Brian. *Everything You've Always Wanted to Know about Hockey: Histories of the National Hockey League and Stanley Cup*, Rev. ed. New York: Charles Scribner's Sons, 1973.

Orr, Frank. *The Story of Hockey*. New York: Random House, 1971.

Podnieks, Andrew. *The Lost Season: A Year in Hockey without the NHL*. Bolton, Ontario: Fenn Publishing, 2005.

Young, Scott. *The Boys of Saturday Night*. Toronto: Macmillan, 1990.

B. Stanley Cup

Allen, Kevin. *Why Is the Stanley Cup in Mario Lemieux's Swimming Pool?: How Winners Celebrate with the World's Most Famous Cup*. Chicago: Triumph Books, 2001.

Coleman, Charles L. *The Trail of the Stanley Cup, Vol. 1, 1893–1926*. Sherbrooke, Quebec: Sherbrooke Daily Record Company, NHL, 1964.

———. *The Trail of the Stanley Cup, Vol. 2, 1927–1946*. Sherbrooke, Quebec: Sherbrooke Daily Record Company, NHL, 1966.

———. *The Trail of the Stanley Cup, Vol. 3, 1947–1967*. Sherbrooke, Quebec: Sherbrooke Daily Record Company, NHL, 1969.

Diamond, Dan, James Duplacey, and Eric Zweig. *The Ultimate Prize: The Stanley Cup*. Kansas City, Mo.: Andrews McMeel Publishing, 2003.

Liss, Howard. *Goal! Hockey's Stanley Cup Playoffs*. New York: Delacorte Press, 1970.

McGuire, William. *The Stanley Cup*. Mankato, Minn.: Creative Education, 1990.

Shea, Kevin. *Lord Stanley: The Man behind the Cup*. Toronto: Key Porter Books, 2007.

Wiseman, Blaine. *Stanley Cup*. New York: Weigel Publishers, 2011.

C. Olympic Games

Coffey, Wayne. *The Boys of Winter: The Untold Story of a Coach, a Dream, and the 1980 U.S. Olympic Hockey Team*. New York: Crown Publishers, 2005.

Harris, Jack C. *The Winter Olympics*. Mankato, Minn.: Creative Education, 1990.

Podnieks, Andrew. *World of Hockey: Celebrating a Century of the IIHF*. Toronto: Key Porter Books, 2008.

Wallechinsky, David. *The Complete Book of the Olympics*. New York: Penguin Books, 1988.

Wendel, Tim. *Going for the Gold: How the U.S. Won at Lake Placid*. Westport, Conn.: Lawrence Hill, 1980.

Zweig, Eric. *Long Shot: How the Winnipeg Falcons Won the First Olympic Hockey Gold*. Toronto: James Lorimer, 2007.

D. Black Players

Carnegie, Herb. *A Fly in a Pail of Milk: The Herb Carnegie Story*. Oakville, Ontario: Mosaic Press, 2010.

Harris, Cecil. *Breaking the Ice: The Black Experience in Professional Hockey*. Toronto: Insomniac Press, 2003.

Mortillaro, Nicole. *Jarome Iginla: How the NHL's First Black Captain Gives Back*. Toronto: James Lorimer & Company, 2011.

O'Ree, Willie, with Michael McKinley. *The Autobiography of Willie O'Ree: Hockey's Black Pioneer*. New York: Somerville House, 2000.

E. Minor League

Kane, Mike. *Minor in Name Only: The History of the Adirondack Red Wings*. Champaign, Ill.: Sagamore Publishing, 1994.

Mancuso, Jim. *20 Years of the ECHL, 1988–2008: Building Tradition*. Utica, N.Y.: Mancuso Publishing, 2007.

———. *American Hockey League Legends: 75 Seasons, 1936–2011*. Utica, N.Y.: Mancuso Publishing, 2010.

———. *Hockey Night in Utica: Featuring the Comets, the Mohawks, and the Stars*. Utica, N.Y.: Mancuso Publishing, 2010.

Mancuso, Jim, and Fred Zalatan. *The Clinton Comets: An EHL Dynasty*. Utica, N.Y.: Mancuso Publishing, 2004.

IV. BIOGRAPHY

A. Collections

Bliss, Jonathan. *The Legends*. Vero Beach, Fla.: Rourke Book Company, 1994.

Conner, Floyd. *Hockey's Most Wanted: The Top 10 Book of Wicked Slapshots, Bruising Goons, and Ice Oddities*. Washington, D.C.: Potomac Books, 2002.

Doeden, Matt. *The Greatest Hockey Records*. Mankato, Minn.: Capstone Press, 2009.

Fischler, Stan. *Hockey Stars of 1972*. New York: Pyramid Books, 1971.

———. *Hockey Stars Speak*. Toronto: Warwick Publishing, 1996.

———. *Kings of the Rink*. New York: Dodd, Mead, 1978.

———. *Strange but True Hockey Stories*. New York: Cowles, 1970.

Fischler, Stan, and Shirley Fischler. *Up from the Minor Leagues*. New York: Cowles, 1971.

Frayne, Trent. *The Mad Men of Hockey*. Toronto: McClelland & Stewart, 1978.

Frederick, Shane. *The Best of Everything Hockey Book*. Mankato, Minn.: Capstone Press, 2011.

Hockey Hall of Fame. *Legends of Hockey*. Toronto: Hockey Hall of Fame, 1996.

Howe, Colleen. *My Three Hockey Players*. New York: Hawthorn Books, 1975.

Italia, Bob. *Hockey Legends*. Minneapolis, Minn.: Abdo and Daughters, 1990.

Kariher, Harry C. *Who's Who in Hockey*. New Rochelle, N.Y.: Arlington House, 1973.

Libby, Bill. *Pro Hockey Heroes of Today*. New York: Random House, 1974.

McDonnell, Chris. *Hockey's Greatest Stars: Legends and Young Lions*. Buffalo, N.Y.: Firefly Books, 1999.

McFarlane, Brian. *Real Stories from the Rink*. Toronto: Tundra Books, 2002.

Orr, Frank. *Tough Guys of Pro Hockey*. New York: Random House, 1974.

Roche, Bill. *The Hockey Book: The Favourite Hockey Stories of All Time Told by the Men Who Know the Game Best*. Toronto: McClelland & Stewart, 1953.

Weir, Glenn, Jeff Chapman, and Travis Weir. *Ultimate Hockey*. Toronto: Stoddart Publishing, 1999.

Whitehead, Eric. *The Patricks: Hockey's Royal Family*. New York: Doubleday, 1980.

B. Single Individuals

Banks, Kerry. *Pavel Bure: The Riddle of the Russian Rocket*. Vancouver, B.C.: Greystone Books, 1999.

Béliveau, Jean, with Chrys Goyens and Allan Turowetz. *Jean Béliveau: My Life in Hockey*. Vancouver, B.C.: Greystone Books, 2005.

Berenstein, Ross. *The Code: The Unwritten Rules of Fighting and Retaliation in the NHL*. Chicago: Triumph Books, 2006.

Boucher, Frank, with Trent Frayne. *When the Rangers Were Young*. New York: Dodd, Mead, 1973.

Bower, Johnny, with Bob Duff. *The China Wall: The Timeless Legend of Johnny Bower*. Bolton, Ontario: Fenn Publishing, 2009.

Brown, William. *Doug: The Doug Harvey Story*. Montreal: Vehicule Press, 2002.

Cheevers, Gerry, with Harry Sinden. *Unmasked: The Autobiography of Gerry Cheevers*. Boston: Sports Improper Publications, 2012.

Christopher, Matt. *On the Ice with . . . Wayne Gretzky*. Boston: Little, Brown, 1997.

Cox, Damien, and Gare Joyce. *The Ovechkin Project: A Behind-the-Scenes Look at Hockey's Most Dangerous Player*. Indianapolis, Ind.: Wiley, 2010.

Denault, Todd. *Jacques Plante: The Man Who Changed the Face of Hockey*. Toronto: McClelland & Stewart, 2010.

Dryden, Ken. *The Game: A Thoughtful and Provocative Look at a Life in Hockey*. New York: Times Books, 1983.

Dryden, Ken, with Roy MacGregor. *Home Game: Hockey and Life in Canada*. Toronto: McClelland & Stewart, 2006.

Dupuis, David. *Sawchuk: The Troubles and Triumphs of the World's Greatest Goalie*. Toronto: Stoddart Publishing, 1998.

Esposito, Phil, with Gerald Eskenazi. *Hockey Is My Life*. New York: Dodd, Mead, 1972.

Fischler, Stan. *Stan Mikita: The Turbulent Career of a Hockey Superstar*. New York: Cowles, 1969.

Fleury, Theo, and Kirstie McLellan Day. *Playing with Fire: The Theo Fleury Story*. Chicago: Triumph Books, 2009.

Florence, Melanie. *Jordin Tootoo: The Highs and Lows in the Journey of the First Inuit to Play in the NHL*. Toronto: James Lorimer, 2011.

Freeberg, Lloyd. *In the Bin: Reckless and Rude Stories from the Penalty Boxes of the NHL*. Chicago: Triumph Books, 1998.

Gilbert, John. *Herb Brooks: The Inside Story of a Hockey Mastermind*. Minneapolis, Minn.: MVP Books, 2008.

Gretzky, Walter, and Jim Taylor. *Gretzky: From the Backyard Rink to the Stanley Cup*. New York: Avon Books, 1984.

Gretzky, Wayne, with Rick Reilly. *Gretzky: An Autobiography*. New York: Harper Paperbacks, 1990.

Hunter, Douglas. *Open Ice: The Tim Horton Story*. Toronto: Viking, 1994.

Jágr, Jaromír, and Jan Šmid. *Jágr: An Autobiography*. Pittsburgh: 68 Productions, 1997.

Joyce, Gare. *Sidney Crosby: Taking the Game by Storm*. Markham, Ontario: Fitzhenry and Whiteside, 2005.

Kendall, Brian. *Shutout: The Legend of Terry Sawchuk*. Toronto: Penguin Books Canada, 1997.

Klein, Jeff Z. *Messier*. Chicago: Triumph Books, 2003.

Knapp, Ron. *Sports Great Mario Lemieux*. Springfield, N.J.: Enslow Publishers, 1995.

O'Reilly, Don. *Mr. Hockey: The World of Gordie Howe*. Chicago, Ill.: Henry Regnery, 1975.

Orr, Bobby, with Dick Grace. *Orr on Ice*. Englewood Cliffs, N.J.: Prentice-Hall, 1970.

Orr, Bobby, with Mark Mulvoy. *Bobby Orr: My Game*. Boston: Little, Brown, 1974.

Parent, Bernie, Bill Fleischman, and Sonny Schwartz. *Bernie! Bernie! Bernie!* Englewood Cliffs, N.J.: Prentice-Hall, 1975.

Potvin, Denis, with Stan Fischler. *Power on Ice*. New York: Harper & Row, 1977.

Rappoport, Ken. *Sports Great Wayne Gretzky*. Springfield, N.J.: Enslow Publishers, 1996.

Richard, Maurice "Rocket," with Stan Fischler. *The Flying Frenchmen: Hockey's Greatest Dynasty*. New York: Hawthorn Books, 1971.

Roy, Travis, with E. M. Swift. *Eleven Seconds: A Story of Tragedy, Triumph, and Courage*. New York: Warner Books, 2005.

Sanderson, Derek, with Stan Fischler. *I've Got to Be Me*. New York: Dodd, Mead, 1970.

Santella, Andrew. *Wayne Gretzky: The Great One*. New York: Franklin Watts, 1998.

Schultz, Dave, with Stan Fischler. *The Hammer: Confessions of a Hockey Enforcer*. New York: Berkley Books, 1983.

Semenko, Dave, with Larry Tucker. *Looking Out for Number One*. Toronto: Stoddart Publishing, 1989.

Shea, Kevin. *Barilko: Without a Trace*. Toronto: Key Porter Books, 2010.

Sittler, Darryl, with Chris Goyens. *Sittler*. Toronto: Macmillan Canada, 1991.

Smythe, Conn, with Scott Young. *Conn Smythe: If You Can't Beat 'em in the Alley*. Toronto: McClelland & Stewart, 1981.

Stewart, Mark. *Eric Lindros: Power Player*. New York: Children's Press, 1997.

Tarasov, Anatoly. *Tarasov: The Father of Russian Hockey*. Trans. by Svetlana Kokhanovskaya. Spokane, Wash.: Griffin Publishing, 1997.

Taylor, Jim. *Gretzky: The Authorized Pictorial History*. Buffalo, N.Y.: Firefly Books, 1994.

Tretiak, Vladislav. *Tretiak: The Legend*. Toronto: Penguin Books Canada, 1988.

Whitehead, Eric. *Cyclone Taylor: A Hockey Legend*. Toronto: Doubleday Canada, 1977.

Williams, Dave, with Mike Lawton. *Tiger: A Hockey Story*. New York: HarperCollins, 1984.

Worsley, Lorne, with Tim Moriarty. *They Call Me Gump*. New York: Dodd, Mead, 1975.

C. Teams

Brown, Frank. *New York Rangers: Broadway Blues*. Champaign, Ill.: Sagamore Publishing, 1993.

Conte, Andrew. *Breakaway: The Inside Story of the Pittsburgh Penguins' Rebirth*. Indianapolis, Ind.: Blue River Press, 2011.

Danakas, John, and Richard Brignall. *Small-Town Glory: The Story of the Kenora Thistles' Remarkable Quest for the Stanley Cup*. Toronto: James Lorimer, 2007.

DeCock, Luke. *Great Teams in Hockey History*. Chicago, Ill.: Heinemann-Raintree, 2005.

Duplacey, James, and Joseph Romain. *Toronto Maple Leafs: Images of Glory*. Toronto: McGraw-Hill Ryerson, 1990.

Fischler, Stan. *The Champion Bruins: Stanley Cup Winners*. Englewood Cliffs, N.J.: Prentice-Hall, 1972.

———. *Motor City Muscle: Gordie Howe, Terry Sawchuk, and the Championship Detroit Red Wings*. Toronto: Warwick Publishing, 1995.

Halligan, John. *Game of My Life: New York Rangers*. New York: Sports Publishing, 2006.

Halligan, John, with Russ Cohen and Adam Raider. *100 Ranger Greats*. New York: John Wiley and Sons, 2009.

Hunter, Douglas. *Champions: The Illustrated History of Hockey's Greatest Dynasties*. Chicago: Penguin Group, 1999.

Kurtzberg, Brad. *Shorthanded: The Untold Story of the Seals, Hockey's Most Colorful Team*. Bloomington, Ind.: AuthorHouse, 2006.

Meisel, Barry. *Losing the Edge: The Rise and Fall of the Stanley Cup Champion New York Rangers*. New York: Simon & Schuster, 1995.

Podnieks, Andrew. *Hockey's Greatest Teams: Teams, Players, and Plays That Changed the Game*. Toronto: Penguin Studio, 2000.

Rennie, Ross. *New York Islanders*. Mankato, Minn.: Creative Education, 1990.

———. *New York Rangers*. Mankato, Minn.: Creative Education, 1990.

Tedesco, Theresa. *Offside: The Battle for Control of Maple Leaf Gardens*. Toronto: Penguin Books, 1998.

D. Photographic Essays

Cameron, Steve, and Matthew Manor. *Hockey Hall-of-Fame Treasures*. Toronto: Firefly Books, 2011.

Gretzky, Wayne, with John Davidson. *99: My Life in Pictures*. Toronto: Total Sports Canada, 1999.

Pincus, Arthur, David Rosner, Len Hochberg, and Chris Malcolm. *The Official Illustrated NHL History: The Official Story of the Coolest Game on Earth*. London: Carlton Books, 2010.

Romain, Joseph. *Pictorial History of Hockey*. New York: Smithmark, 1995.

Simpson, Rob, and Steve Babineau. *Black and Gold: Four Decades of the Boston Bruins in Photographs*. Mississauga, Ontario: John Wiley and Sons Canada, 2008.

V. WOMEN'S HOCKEY

A. History

Adams, Carly. *Queens of the Ice: They Were Fast, They Were Fierce, They Were Teenage Girls*. Toronto: James Lorimer, 2011.

McFarlane, Brian. *Proud Past, Bright Future: One Hundred Years of Canadian Women's Hockey*. Stoddart Publishing, 1995.

Nicholson, Lorna Schultz. *Pink Power: The First Women's World Hockey Champions*. Toronto: James Lorimer, 2008.

Stewart, Barbara. *She Shoots . . . She Scores!* Toronto: Doubleday Canada, 1993.

Theberge, Nancy. *Higher Goals: Women's Ice Hockey and the Politics of Gender (Sport, Culture, and Social Relations)*. New York: SUNY Press, 2000.

Turco, Mary. *Crashing the Net: The U.S. Women's Olympic Ice Hockey Team and the Road to Gold*. New York: HarperCollins, 1999.

B. Single Individuals

Rhéaume, Manon, with Chantal Gilbert. *Alone: In Front of the Net*. Toronto: HarperCollins Canada, 1994.

Ruggiero, Angela. *Breaking the Ice: My Journey to Olympic Hockey, the Ivy League, and Beyond*. Plymouth, Mass.: Drummond Publishing Group, 2005.

Wickenheiser, Hayley. *Gold Medal Diary: Inside the World's Greatest Sports Event*. Vancouver, B.C.: Greystone Books, 2010.

C. Instructional

Johnson, Tami. *Girls' Ice Hockey: Dominating the Rink*. Mankato, Minn.: Capstone Press, 2008.

Wilson, Stacy. *The Hockey Book for Girls*. Toronto: Kids Can Press, 2000.

VI. INSTRUCTIONAL

A. Rules and Officiating

Duplacey, James. *The Annotated Rules of Hockey*. New York: Lyons & Burford, 1996.

———. *The Official Rules of Hockey*. New York, Lyons Press, 2001.

Garlett, Kyle, and Patrick O'Neal. *The Worst Call Ever!: The Most Infamous Calls Ever Blown by Referees, Umpires, and Other Blind Officials*. New York: HarperCollins, 2007.

Triumph Books, ed. *2011 Official Rules of the NHL*. Chicago: Triumph Books, 2011.

B. Coaching

Driver, Bruce, and Clare Wharton. *The Baffled Parent's Guide to Coaching Youth Hockey*. Camden, Maine: International Marine/Ragged Mountain Press, 2004.

Kilrea, Brian, and James Duthie. *They Call Me Killer: Tales from Junior Hockey's Legendary Hall-of-Fame Coach*. Indianapolis, Ind.: Wiley, 2011.

MacAdam, Don, and Gail Reynolds. *Coaching Hockey for Dummies*. Indianapolis, Ind.: Wiley, 2006.

Pecknold, Rand, and Aaron Foeste. *Hard Core Hockey: Essential Skills, Strategies, and Systems from the Sport's Top Coaches*. New York: McGraw-Hill, 2009.

Smith, Michael A. *The Hockey Play Book: Teaching Hockey Systems*. Buffalo, N.Y.: Firefly Books, 2008.

Walford, Gerald. *Coaching Hockey*. New York: McGraw Hill, 1993.

C. Playing

Allaire, François. *The Hockey Goalie's Complete Guide*. Buffalo, N.Y.: Firefly Books, 2010.

Francis, Emile (Cat), with Tim Moriarty. *The Secrets of Winning Hockey*. New York: Doubleday, 1972.

Gilbert, Rod, and Brad Park. *Playing Hockey the Professional Way*. New York: Harper & Row, 1972.

Jensen, Julie. *Beginning Hockey*. Minneapolis, Minn.: Lerner Publications, 1996.

Kelley, Jack, and Milt Schmidt, with Al Hirshberg. *Hockey. Bantam to Pro*. Boston: Allyn & Bacon, 1974.

MacDonald, James. *Hockey Skills: How to Play Like a Pro*. Berkeley Heights, N.J.: Enslow Elementary, 2009.

Miller, Saul L. *The Complete Player: The Psychology of Winning Hockey*. Toronto: Stoddart Publishing, 2001.

Percival, Lloyd. *The Hockey Handbook*. Toronto: Copp Clark, 1951.

———. *The Hockey Handbook*. Rev. by Wayne Major and Robert Thom. Toronto: McClelland & Stewart, 1992.

Plante, Jacques. *Step By Step Hockey Goaltending: The Complete Illustrated Guide*. Plattsburgh, N.Y.: Studio 9 Books, 1997.

Rossiter, Sean, and Paul Carson. *Power Plays and Penalty Killing*. Vancouver, B.C.: Greystone Books, 2000.

Savage, Jeff. *Top 25 Hockey Skills, Tips, and Tricks*. Berkeley Heights, N.J.: Enslow Publishers, 2012.

Stewart, Mark, and Mike Kennedy. *Score!: The Action and Artistry of Hockey's Magnificent Moment*. Minneapolis, Minn.: Millbrook Press, 2011.

Thomas, Keltie. *How Hockey Works*. Toronto: Maple Tree Press, 2006.

Walsh, Kevin. *Hockey for Beginners*. New York: Four Winds Press, 1976.

D. Books by Referees

Buffy, Vern. *Black and White and Never Right*. Toronto: John Wiley and Sons, 1983.

Chadwick, Bill, with Hal Bock. *The Big Whistle: The Courageous Lifetime on Ice of Bill Chadwick, Player, Referee, Broadcaster*. New York: Hawthorn Books, 1974.

Finn, Ron, with David Boyd. *On the Lines: The Adventures of a Linesman in the NHL*. Oakville, Ontario: Rubicon Publishing, 2002.

Fraser, Kerry. *The Final Call: Hockey Stories from a Legend in Stripes*. Bolton, Ontario: Fenn Publishing, 2010.

Hood, Bruce. *Calling the Shots: Memoirs of a NHL Referee*. Toronto: Stoddart Publishing, 1988.

Irvin, Dick. *Tough Calls: NHL Referees and Linesmen Tell Their Story*. Toronto: McClelland & Stewart, 1997.

Scapinello, Roy, and Rob Simpson. *Between the Lines: Not-So-Tall Tales from Ray "Scampy" Scapinello's Four Decades in the NHL*. Mississauga, Ontario: John Wiley and Sons, 2006.

VII. OTHER BOOKS

A. Anthology

Falla, Jack. *Open Ice: Reflections and Confessions of a Hockey Lifer*. Indianapolis, Ind.: Wiley Publishing, 2008.

Gowdey, David, ed. *Riding on the Roar of the Crowd: A Hockey Anthology*. Toronto: Macmillan Canada, 1989.

Kennedy, Michael P. J. *Going Top Shelf: An Anthology of Canadian Hockey Poetry*. Victoria, B.C.: Heritage House, 2005.

LaSalle, Peter. *Hockey Sur Glace: Stories*. New York: Breakaway Books, 1998.

Milks, James. *Pucklore: The Hockey Research Anthology (Society for International Hockey Research, Volume 1)*. Kingston, Ontario: Quarry Heritage Press, 2010.

Urstadt, Bryant. *The Greatest Hockey Stories Ever Told: The Finest Writers on Ice*. Guilford, Conn.: Lyons Press, 2006.

Wimmer, Dick. *The Fastest Game: An Anthology of Hockey Writings*. Indianapolis, Ind.: Masters Press, 1997.

B. Fiction

MacGregor, Roy. *The Last Season*. Toronto: Penguin Books Canada, 1985.
Scalise, Frank. *All That Counts: A Novel*. Spokane, Wash.: Gray Dog Press, 2010.

C. Juvenile Fiction

Baker, Eugene. *I Want to Be a Hockey Player*. Chicago: Children's Press, 1973.
Bourgeois, Paulette, and Brenda Clark. *Franklin Plays Hockey*. Toronto: Kids Can Press, 2002.
Carrier, Roch, Sheldon Cohen, and Sheila Fischman. *The Hockey Sweater*. Montreal: Tundra Books, 1985.
Christopher, Matt. *Face-Off*. Boston: Little, Brown, 1972.
———. *The Hockey Machine*. Boston: Little, Brown, 1986.
———. *Ice Magic*. Boston: Little, Brown, 1973.
Christopher, Matt, with text by Paul Mantell. *Cool as Ice*. Boston: Little, Brown, 2001.
Christopher, Matt, with text by Robert Hirschfeld. *Body Check*. Boston: Little, Brown, 2003.
MacGregor, Roy. *The Complete Screech Owls, Volume 1*. Toronto: McClelland & Stewart, 2005.
———. *The Complete Screech Owls, Volume 2*. Toronto: McClelland & Stewart, 2006.
———. *The Complete Screech Owls, Volume 3*. Toronto: McClelland & Stewart, 2006.
Napier, Matt. *Z Is for Zamboni*. Chelsea, Mich.: Sleeping Bear Press, 2002.
Nicholson, Lorna Schultz. *Too Many Men*. Toronto: James Lorimer and Company, 2006.
Schulz, Charles M. *Your Dog Plays Hockey?* New York: HarperFestival, 1996.
Shapiro, Howard. *Hockey Player for Life*. Pittsburgh, Pa.: Supersonic Storybook Productions, 2008.
Slote, Alfred. *The Hotshot*. New York: Dell Publishing, 1977.
Stevenson, James. *Sam the Zamboni Man*. New York: Greenwillow Books, 1998.
Woolgar, Jack. *Hot on Ice*. Chicago: Albert Whitman, 1965.

D. Quotes

Liebman, Glenn. *Hockey Shorts: 1,001 of the Game's Funniest One-Liners.* Chicago: Contemporary Books, 1996.
McDonnell, Chris. *Shooting from the Lip: Hockey's Best Quotes and Quips.* Buffalo, N.Y.: Firefly Books, 2004.

E. Field Hockey and Roller Hockey

Anders, Elizabeth, and Susan Myers. *Field Hockey: Steps to Success*, 2nd ed. Champaign, Ill.: Human Kinetics, 2008.
Barth, Katrin, and Lutz Nordmann. *Learning Field Hockey.* Aachen, Germany: Meyer and Meyer Sport Publishing, 2007.
Egan, Tracie, and Helen Connolly. *Field Hockey: Rules, Tips, Strategy, and Safety.* New York: Rosen Publishing Group, 2005.
Kennedy, Mike. *Roller Hockey.* New York: Franklin Watts, 2001.
Siller, Greg. *Roller Hockey.* New York: McGraw-Hill, 1998.
Wein, Horst. *The Science of Hockey.* Trans. from German by David Belchamber. London: Pelham Books, 1973.

F. Miscellaneous

Bidini, Dave. *Tropic of Hockey: My Search for the Game in Unlikely Places.* Toronto: McClelland & Stewart, 2000.
Didinger, Ray, and Glen Macnow. *The Ultimate Book of Sports Movies.* Philadelphia, Pa.: Running Press, 2009.
Eskenazi, Gerald. *A Thinking Man's Guide to Pro Hockey.* New York: E. P. Dutton and Co., 1972.
Fischler, Stan. *Slapshot!* New York: Grosset & Dunlap, 1973.
Fox, Larry. *Little Men in Sports.* New York: W. W. Norton, 1968.
Klein, Jeff Z., and Karl-Eric Reif. *The Death of Hockey.* Toronto: Macmillan Canada, 1998.
Ludwig, Jack. *The Great Hockey Thaw, or the Russians Are Here!* Garden City, N.Y.: Doubleday, 1974.
Plimpton, George. *Open Net.* New York: W. W. Norton, 1985.
Podnieks, Andrew. *Hockey Superstitions: From Playoff Beards to Crossed Sticks and Lucky Socks.* Toronto: McClelland & Stewart, 2010.
Richards, David Adams. *Hockey Dreams: Memories of a Man Who Couldn't Play.* Toronto: Doubleday Canada, 1996.
Scanlan, Lawrence. *Grace under Fire: The State of Our Sweet and Savage Game.* Toronto: Penguin Canada, 2002.

Stein, Gil. *Power Plays: An Inside Look at the Big Business of the National Hockey League*. Secaucus, N.J.: Carol Publishing Group, 1997.

Swados, Robert O. *Counsel in the Crease: A Big-League Player in the Hockey Wars*. New York: Prometheus Books, 2006.

Weekes, Don. *Crease-Crashing Hockey Trivia*. Vancouver, B.C.: Greystone Books, 2007.

Williams, David Tiger, with Kasey Wilson. *Done Like Dinner: Tiger in the Kitchen*. Vancouver, B.C.: Douglas and MacIntyre, Ltd., 1987.

G. Foreign Language

1. Czechoslovakian

Gut, Karel, and Gustav Vlk. *Světový Hokej*. Prague: Olympia Praha, 1990.

Knap, Karel. *Dominik Hašek: Národni Hrdina*. Czechoslovakia: Eurotel, 1999.

Koliš, Jiři, and Dominik Hašek. *Příběhy z Hokejové Branky*. Czechoslovakia: Eurotel, 2002.

Loněk, Pavel. *Jaromír Jágr: Hledáni Nebe*. Prague: Fighters Publications, 2007.

2. French

Boulonne, Gerard, Jacques Caron, and Christian Pelchat. *L'offensive rouge: Les secrets de la tactique soviétique au hockey*. Montreal: Editions du Jour, 1976.

Carrier, Roch, and Sheldon Cohen. *Le chandail de hockey*. Toronto: Livres Toundra, 1985.

Duquennoy, Jacques. *Camille fait du hockey*. Paris: Albin Michel Jeunesse, 2005.

Léger, Gilles, and Robert Laflamme. *La saga des Stastny: Le coup de génie de Gilles Léger*. Quebec City: Hurtubise, 2012.

McKinley, Michael. *Temps de glace: L'histoire du hockey*. Toronto: Livres Toundra, 2006.

3. German

Biedermann, Hannes. *Das Hockey Yearbook 2011*. Stoughton, Wis.: Books on Demand, 2012.

Disney, Walt. *Donald Spielt Eishockey*. Leipzig, Germany: Rowohlt Verlag, 1951.

4. Polish

Zieleskiewicz, Wladyslaw. *Historia polskiego hokeja.* Krynica-Zdrój, Poland: Sport I Turystyka, 2006.

5. Russian

Boivin-Chouinard, Mathieu. *Chaïbou!: Histoire du hockey russe.* Moscow: Kéruss: 2011.
Tarasov, A. V. *Ice Hockey of the Future.* Moscow: Fizkultura i sport, 1971.

6. Spanish

Feldman, Heather, with Wayne Gretzky and Joy Paige. *Wayne Gretzky, estrella del hockey: Hockey Star (Superstars of Sports).* New York: Rosen Publishing Group, 2002.
Suen, Anastasia. *La historia del hockey.* New York: Buenas Letras, 2003.

7. Other

Absolon, Jakub, with Diana Husakova, Martin Kovac, Olga Petrova, Katarina Absolnova, and Eva Pehanicova, eds. *English-German-Russian-Slovak-Czech Ice-Hockey Glossary.* Kindle Edition, eBook.sk, 2010.

VIII. PERIODICALS

American Hockey Magazine, Colorado Springs, Colo.
Hockey Digest, Evanston, Ill.
Hockey Illustrated, New York.
Hockey News, Toronto, Ontario.
Let's Play Hockey, Minneapolis, Minn.
Sporting News
Sports Illustrated
Sports Illustrated for Kids
USA Hockey In-Line Magazine, Colorado Springs, Colo.

IX. WEBSITES

A to Z Encyclopedia of Ice Hockey www.azhockey.com
Bertagna Goalie Schools www.bertagnagoaltending.com
Canadian Hockey Association www.canadianhockey.ca
Hockey Canada www.hockeycanada.ca
Hockey Hall of Fame www.hhof.com
Hockey Hall of Fame On-Line Course http://fcet.senecac.on.ca/fcet/
    fcet_hockey/can699#
Hockey in Print (Bibliography) www.hip.english.dal.ca/index.php
Ice Sledge Hockey www.ipc-icesledgehockey.org
International Ice Hockey Federation www.iihf.com
NHL Kids www.nhl.com/kids/index.html
Science of Hockey www.exploratorium.edu/hockey/
Society for International Hockey Research www.sihrhockey.org/main.cfm
Statistics Database www.hockeydb.com/
Statistics and History www.hockey-reference.com/
USA Hockey www.usahockey.com/
U.S. Hockey Hall of Fame www.usahockeyhall.com/

A. NHL Websites in Other Languages

Czech www.nhl.com/cz/
Finnish www.nhl.com/fi/
French www.nhl.com/fr/index.html
German www.nhl.com/de/
Russian www.nhl.com/ru/
Slovak www.nhl.com/sk/
Swedish www.nhl.com/se/

About the Author

Laurel Ann Grasso Zeisler has had a lifelong love of a variety of sports based on the influence of her father, John Grasso. He is the author of *Historical Dictionary of Basketball* (2011) and *Historical Dictionary of Tennis* (2011). A strong tennis player herself, she also played field hockey for the first time while in South Africa as a Rotary Youth Exchange student. She attended both the 1984 and 1988 Summer Olympics, in Los Angeles and Seoul, respectively, and is looking forward to watching hockey at her first Winter Olympics. Zeisler's educational background includes a B.A. in journalism from Binghamton University, a M.A. in speech language pathology from Kean University, and a Ph.D. in health sciences from Seton Hall University. She has applied her research training to this historical dictionary. Zeisler is a current member of the Society for International Hockey Research and International Society of Olympic Historians. Also an avid collector of books, her hockey collection has multiplied considerably during this endeavor. In addition, she has created new hockey fans by bringing her daughters to the Binghamton and Albany American Hockey League games. She teaches public-speaking classes at State College of New York at Dehli. Zeisler's other research interests include decisional procrastination and stress, Prader-Willi syndrome, and fourth-place Olympians.